W9-BJO-544

Bedouin

dara
e
a

Nuer

Nandi

Nayar

Toda

Truk Islanders

Gilbert Islanders

Manu

Trobriand Islanders

Balinese

Alorese

Keraki

Kung Bushmen

INTRODUCTION TO

Anthropology

Elmer S. Miller

Temple University

Charles A. Weitz

Temple University

INTRODUCTION TO
Anthropology

Prentice-Hall, Inc.
Englewood Cliffs, New Jersey

Library of Congress Cataloging in Publication Data

Miller, Elmer S., 1931–
  Introduction to anthropology.

  Comprises: Miller, E. S. Introduction to
cultural anthropology. Weitz, C. A. Introduction
to physical anthropology and archaeology.
  Bibliography
  Includes indexes.
  1. Anthropology. I. Weitz, Charles A., joint
author. II. Miller, Elmer S., 1931–
Introduction to cultural anthropology. 1979.
III. Weitz, Charles A. Introduction to physical
anthropology and archaeology. 1979. IV. Title.
GN316.M48   301.2   78-31962
ISBN 0-13-478008-6

Cover photo of Guatemalan mother and child by Luis Villota

Part-opening photo credits: Part One: David Brill, National Geographic Society Pho-
tograph; Part Two: George Holton, Photo Researchers, Inc.; Part Three: George
Rodger, Magnum; Part Four: Josef Koudelka, Magnum; Part Five: Marylin Yee,
The New York Times.

Chapter-opening photo credits: Chapter 1: Jacques Jangoux, Peter Arnold Photo Ar-
chives; Chapter 2: Miguel Castro, Photo Researchers, Inc; Chapter 3: Pro Pix,
Monkmeyer Press Photo Service; Chapter 4: Brian Brake, Photo Researchers, Inc.;
Chapter 5: Nancy Nicolson, Anthro-Photo; Chapter 6: Jen and Des Bartlett, Photo
Researchers, Inc.; Chapter 7: George Tames, *The New York Times*; Chapter 8: Cour-
tesy of the American Museum of Natural History; Chapter 10: Courtesy of the
American Museum of Natural History; Chapter 11: Paul Mangelsdorf and R. S.
MacNeish; Chapter 12: George Gerster, Photo Researchers, Inc.; Chapter 13: Stan
Washburn, Anthro Photo; Chapter 14: Marc and Evelyne Bernheim, Woodfin
Camp; Chapter 15: Laima Druskis, Photo Researchers, Inc.; Chapter 16: Ken
Heyman; Chapter 17: Fred A. Anderson, Photo Researchers, Inc.; Chapter 18:
Katrina Thomas, Photo Researchers, Inc.; Chapter 19: David Strickler, Monkmeyer;
Chapter 20: Paul Conklin, Monkmeyer; Chapter 21: Jen and Des Bartlett, Photo
Researchers, Inc.; Chapter 22: Marc and Evelyne Bernheim, Woodfin Camp; Chap-
ter 23: Jason Lauré, Woodfin Camp; Chapter 24: Homer Sykes, Woodfin Camp;
Chapter 25: Y. Jeanmougin/Viva, Woodfin Camp; Chapter 26: Georg Gerster,
Rapho/Photo Researchers, Inc.; Chapter 27: Georg Gerster, Rapho/Photo Re-
searchers, Inc.; Chapter 28: Jim Cron, Monkmeyer.

Prentice-Hall International, Inc., London
Prentice-Hall of Australia Pty. Ltd., Sydney
Prentice-Hall of Canada, Ltd., Toronto
Prentice-Hall of India Private Limited, New Delhi
Prentice-Hall of Japan, Inc., Tokyo
Prentice-Hall of Southeast Asia, Pte. Ltd., Singapore
Whitehall Books Limited, Wellington, New Zealand

Outline

v

vi

Contents

Preface

STUDENTS often sign up for introductory anthropology courses in order to learn more about human groups that they see as fundamentally different from them. But further acquaintance with the discipline leads to the discovery that some of the most fascinating problems center on the attempt to define what human beings everywhere have in common. Documenting human differences, whether biological or cultural, was at one time a major concern of anthropology. Explaining these differences, along with those conditions that humans share in common, is another matter. The major efforts in anthropology today are addressed to explanation, and it is this concern that informs our text. Although ample descriptive material is provided to give students a clear understanding of the information with which anthropologists deal, this text stresses the processes of interaction and change, not only among different human social groups but also between these groups and the ecosystems in which they live.

Many introductory texts approach anthropology from a particular viewpoint. Descriptive materials from each of the four subdisciplines are then organized to reinforce this perspective. We have chosen an alternative and, we feel, more useful strategy. Rather than present a single perspective, we have decided to inform students of the different theories and approaches that have been used to organize the same or similar data. We have tried to balance our own views to give students a clearer understanding of the theoretical diversity that vitalizes anthropology.

General Plan and Organization

The first part of this text concerns human biological and cultural origins and separates the discussion of physical anthropology from that of archaeology. Although it is clearly recognized that the distinction between human biology and culture is arbitrary, it helps introductory students to see how concepts, research data, and theory unique to each field are linked together.

The book begins with a chapter designed to present anthropology and its subfields. The second chapter, an introduction to physical anthropology, considers the many different ways in which human biological diversity has been studied, as well as the neo-Darwinian framework by which it is now explained. Chapter 3, a presentation of the principles of ecology, serves as a foundation for discussions of change in later chapters. Descriptions of primate anatomy and behavior are presented next in order to provide students with the information necessary to understand many of the current explanations of the fossil record. The next three chapters discuss the fossil evidence for primate and hominid evolution. A final physical anthropology chapter is concerned with explaining genetics and modern human variation. Genetics is introduced here, primarily because it is more relevant to understanding the biological nature of living human populations than to interpreting fossils.

Following the introductory archaeology chapter, three chapters deal separately with the early stone age, the invention and spread of agriculture, and the emergence of complex societies. In this text the traditional lithic terminology is used, simply because of its general familiarity. The problems some archaeologists have attributed to this typology are presented clearly in the text, although most are avoided by defining precisely each lithic term in both geographical and temporal terms.

The chapters covering agriculture and the emergence of complex societies stress the hypothesis-testing approach to archaeology. In both chapters major theoretical statements are presented first. Then, the theories are assessed in terms of the archaeological data from different parts of the world. This is designed to provide students with clear examples of the dynamic features of archaeological model building.

The second half of this volume is concerned with human cultural and social life. It is divided into three parts. Part Three (chapters 13 and 14) presents an overview of cultural anthropology together with general statements about methodology and theory. Here a broad perspective on the concept of culture is provided in order to prepare the student for arguments presented later in the book. The concept of culture is shown to be an analytic construct that enables researchers to make sense of their observations and to systematize their inferences and interpretations. Part Four (chapters 15 to 27) treats the major topics generally covered in an introductory cultural anthropology course. In addition to the standard topics of kinship and marriage, political organization and economic life, and religion and the arts, separate chapters address such important topics as social control, social stratification, ecology, and the performing and expressive arts. All of these topics are presented in such a manner as to demonstrate those conceptual approaches that have contributed most significantly to the matters under consideration. The social and cultural institutions discussed are shown to possess a dynamic character, such that the topic of culture change is approached in nearly every chapter. Part Five (chapter 28) is concerned with regional systems. It deals with the issue of change in a more direct manner and in a way that incorporates some of the most recent research in the discipline.

Learning Aids Within the Text

Illustrations

In the preparation of this text we have included numerous photographs and illustrations so that readers can better visualize what is being discussed in the text. Because this need is especially strong in the chapters on the primates and primate and human evolution, these chapters are lavishly illustrated. In all, the book contains over 100 charts, graphs, and drawings and over 160 photographs.

Chapter Summaries

Rehearsal is an important part of long-term learning. With this fact in mind, we have concluded each chapter with a summary of the major points that should be remembered from it.

Glossary and Bibliography

As each new important term is introduced in the text it is defined. A glossary at the end of the book redefines each term for the student, and a bibliography contains references to all of the material cited within each chapter.

Supplements to the Text

The text is supplemented by a study guide and workbook for the student and an instructor's manual and a test bank for the teacher.

The study guide is divided into four parts: a study outline, a list of key terms and concepts, a pretest consisting primarily of multiple-choice questions on the most important points covered in the chapter, and a study outline, consisting of questions of varied sorts that ensure that the reader has learned the material covered in the chapter at a greater depth. Immediate feedback is provided by having the answers to all questions provided in the margin of the workbook directly next to the question and by keying them to the page of the text on which the material appears, so that a reader who misses a question knows immediately where to look to rehearse the material.

The test item file consists of some 750 multiple choice questions. It is available, as is the instructor's manual, free upon adoption. The instructor's manual consists of an overview of each chapter, a group of resources for classroom discussion, a list of paper topics, and a film list keyed to appropriate sections of each chapter.

Acknowledgments

The aim of this text is to present simply, clearly, and completely theory, method, and data in physical anthropology, archaeology, and cultural anthropology. These are ambitious goals in fields of such complexity and rapid change. The strategy adopted in the preparation of this text was to bring together a number of experts in the various stages of publication. A large number of people worked cooperatively to produce an easy-to-read, current product. While our name appears on the title page, all of these people deserve recognition for their contributions.

We wish to thank Stephen Graff and Robert Fredericks, who assisted in the pursuit of relevant literature and who provided the much appreciated legwork necessary to assemble the data that form the basis of this book. We wish to thank the writers, who took the data, along with our notes and outlines, and produced first drafts. In addition, we would like to acknowledge the following, who are experts in their respective fields: physical anthropology and archaeology—John E. Blank, Cleveland State University; Robert B. Eckhardt, The Pennsylvania State University; Leonard Greenfield, Temple University; R. L. Jantz, University of Tennessee; Ellis R. Kerley, University of Maryland; Gery Moreno-Black, University of Oregon; Frank Orlosky, Northern Illinois University; Anthony Zavaleta, Texas Southmost College. Cultural anthropology—Ira Abrams, University of Southern California; Anne Buddenhagen, University of Massachusetts; Thomas Greaves, University of Texas at San Antonio; Robert B. Moorman, Miami Dade Jr. College; Richard W. Stoffle, University of Wisconsin at Parkside; Max W. Witkind, San Antonio College. Our thanks also are due to Cecil H. Brown, Northern Illinois University, and Kenneth M. Kensinger, Bennington College. Stan Wakefield, who handled the book's review process and marketing, has been extremely helpful and also deserves our thanks.

The contributions of technical experts must also include those of Cheryl Mannes, editorial assistant; Nancy Perkus, permissions editor; Alan Forman, photo researcher; Florence Silverman, art director; Susanna Lesan and Marcia Schonzeit, copy editors; and Nancy Myers, manufacturing buyer. Patricia Quinn, production editor, deserves special notice for her expertise, which proved invaluable at crucial points. Ruth Kugelman provided the research base upon which the book was begun. To each of these individuals we express our sincere thanks.

In large measure, however, the creation of this book must be credited to our development editors, David Crook and Ann Torbert. They tirelessly edited the initial versions of each chapter and then re-edited each of our rewrites. Through long stretches of the past year their quick grasp of anthropological concepts, their eye for good style, and their ability to persevere made the book what it is. We are grateful indeed for their comments, guidance, and hard work.

Charles Weitz would like to thank his wife, Velma, for her patience during those frequent episodes when the book took precedence over family life.

ELMER S. MILLER
CHARLES WEITZ

Introduction to Anthropology

PEOPLE have long been curious about the origins and nature of the human species. Many societies have developed beliefs about the creation of humans and their place in relation to the rest of the natural—and perhaps supernatural—world. The organized study of human beings—*anthropology*—has existed as a distinct field of inquiry for over 100 years. Only within the past few decades, however, has anthropology graduated from being a quaint subject that studied the "strange" artifacts and customs of little-known or remote peoples to a systematic attempt to explain human cultural and biological variability.

Modern communications and a world war that carried Westerners to far corners of the earth brought Western technology to isolated people and at the same time made Westerners aware that people once thought to be exotic are very much a part of the real world. As anthropology turned to questions of more direct significance to modern industrial life and adopted a more systematic, scientific approach to human social life everywhere, it acquired an established place among American academic disciplines that it had not had previously.

The Anthropological Approach

Anthropology is somewhat like sociology, history, human biology, and many other disciplines as well. What sets it apart from these ways of looking at humanity is its attempts at holism and relativistic comparison. It is an attempt to understand the origin, evolution, and present diversity of human biology and culture.

1

Holism

Anthropology is an immense subject. It is the most inclusive of any academic discipline, for it seeks to encompass not only all that is known about human beings around the world but also the history of their gradual evolution from small mammals that lived almost 70 million years ago. It covers all that is known of culture—the learned ideas and beliefs that characterize human groups as distinct from other primate groups—and of human biology as well. This takes anthropology through time and space into fields as diverse as paleontology (the study of fossils), anatomy, primatology, economics, archaeology, linguistics, genetics, religion, art, and political science, to name a few.

Anthropology tries to pull all this information together and organize it in some systematic fashion. For instance, anthropology makes inferences about the earliest humans by studying isolated living populations. It also compares the way of life of remote aborigines with that of urban city dwellers, and the behaviors of monkeys and other nonhuman primates with those of humans. It is this all-inclusive scope—called *holism*—that gives anthropology its unique character. Holism is an attempt to incorporate all of this knowledge into a meaningful understanding of humanity.

This claim of holism is more a goal than a reality, however. There is no overall framework—for example, no single theory of how culture works—that all anthropologists would happily use for explaining their data. Different kinds of anthropologists see things from very different points of view. Furthermore, increasingly specialized training has produced a generation of anthropologists who communicate primarily with those in their own subdisciplines. Still, the concept of culture ties together all anthropologists, whether they are interested in social relationships,

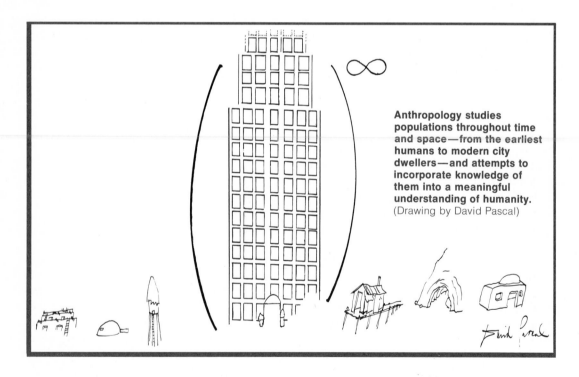

Anthropology studies populations throughout time and space—from the earliest humans to modern city dwellers—and attempts to incorporate knowledge of them into a meaningful understanding of humanity.
(Drawing by David Pascal)

linguistics, archaeology, or physical anthropology.

Traditionally, there was a continuum in anthropology, ranging from those who emphasized biology to those who emphasized culture. At one extreme were those who tended to view humans basically as biological organisms whose behaviors are largely determined by genetic and environmental factors. They analyzed human groups in the same terms by which other organisms are studied: inherited traits, local food supplies, climatic changes, and other features that affect biological survival. At the other extreme were those who saw humans as unique creatures who have asserted their independence from most biological factors by their genius for cultural solutions—houses to modify the effects of climate, tools for manipulating the environment, and political organizations to maintain social control. Today this division is not as important as it once was, since both physical and cultural anthropologists are using more of the same concepts and approaches. As we will see, the main subfields of anthropology continue to be informed by work done in the others, and attempts to integrate the whole field continue to appear.

Relativistic Comparison

In addition to holism, there is another unique aspect of the way anthropology looks at the human condition. This is *cultural relativism:* the attempt to understand and evaluate each cultural system in terms of its own internally consistent logic. Before the need for relativism was recognized, visitors to cannibalistic tribes, for instance, were appalled at their "immoral" practices. They were judging cannibals by their own society's moral code, by which it is unthinkable to eat human flesh. But later anthropologists made an effort to be less culturally subjective in their observations. They tried, for instance, to accept the fact that some cultures consider cannibalism acceptable behavior. Instead of condemning it, they tried to determine what functions cannibalism serves for the groups that practice it. *Ethnocentrism*—the tendency to judge other cultures by the standards of one's own culture—became the devil to be exorcised in every introductory anthropology course.

By the middle of this century, however, it became apparent that anthropologists could not completely free themselves from ethnocentrism. No matter how much they tried to immerse themselves in other cultures in order to understand them better, they were inevitably influenced to some extent by their own society's ways of looking at things. A certain amount of ethnocentrism seemed to be essential to the functioning of any social system, including their own. And in trying to explain their experiences to those back home, they found that they were obliged to translate them into terms which had significance in their own culture. Having to do so destroys the efforts to treat cultural systems in their own terms. Thus, anthropologists continually search for the most appropriate method of translating what they know about a culture into concepts that are meaningful in their own. Only by doing so are they able to offer insights into the operation of our own cultural system.

Another difficulty, which is potentially very serious, is that by attempting to explain objectively the function of practices which seem inhumane to us, anthropologists may seem to be approving them. Infanticide, for instance, can be explained in terms of its biological and social functions. To condemn the practice would require the kind of value judgment that anthropologists have long avoided. However, some anthropologists feel that they must make it clear where they stand on such matters. The question of how to do so without

4 sacrificing relativism is a critical dilemma which anthropology has not yet resolved.

Anthropology and Other Disciplines

Anthropology occupies a central position in any liberal arts curriculum because it serves to link the humanities, natural sciences, and social sciences.

The *humanities* include art, languages, music, philosophy, and history. Anthropological research and interpretation extends into all these areas, often taking them into sectors of time and space that would not otherwise be described. In art, for instance, anthropology has contributed a great amount of information about the folk art of cultures outside Western traditions, as well as data on the role that art plays in society and culture. And in history, archaeology (a branch of anthropology) has pushed our understanding of extinct peoples back into the shadows of prehistoric times, before written records were kept.

The *natural sciences* upon which anthropology draws for some of its explanations include biology, ecology, chemistry, and geology. Chemical analysis, for instance, helps anthropologists figure out how old fossils and artifacts are. Geology contributes knowledge of the environments within which humans evolved. Ecology—the study of the relationships between living things and their environment—clarifies how human populations and the rest of nature influence each other. And biology is a rich source of concepts and information about human anatomy, physiology, variation, evolution, and behavior. The exchange is not just a one-way process, however. To these sciences, anthropology brings knowledge of how human activities have changed human biology. It also provides its special humanistic viewpoint—a fundamental concern for understanding and explaining human cultural differences.

Anthropology is most commonly listed as one of the *social sciences.* It deals with topics covered in a number of other social sciences—economics, psychology, sociology, political science, statistics, law, geography. Anthropology overlaps with geography, for instance, when it studies the links between culture and environment. It coincides with psychology—the study of individual behavior—when it looks at the relationship between culture and individual personalities and actions. And over and over again, anthropologists have pointed out that law, economics, and politics are parts of integrated cultural systems and cannot be fully understood unless the rest of these systems are described and explained.

Sociology cuts across some of the same territory as anthropology. But its subject matter is more limited, and its methods different. Traditionally, sociology has been concerned with Western societies, whereas anthropology studies societies and cultures everywhere in the world. Sociologists tend to isolate only certain influences on group behaviors—such as age, sex, income level, social status, and educational background. By contrast, anthropologists try to look at everything that may affect how people in a certain culture behave. This includes not only the factors listed above, but also the environmental setting, the group's survival strategies, its religious beliefs, its history and political organization, and so on. Sociologists run surveys with questionnaires and statistical samplings that reveal the relationships between certain variables (such as divorce, income, and educational level). By contrast, anthropologists try to figure out how a whole culture works by making in-depth studies. They may also compare features of one culture with those of others to see if there are any regularities in the ways humans tend to approach various facets of social life—sex, incest, adolescence, and so on (Fried, 1972). *Cross-cultural comparison* is one of the hallmarks of anthropology.

Subdisciplines

Anthropology is commonly divided into four subdisciplines: physical anthropology, archaeology, linguistics, and cultural or social anthropology. The major distinction traditionally has been between the first—the study of humans as biological animals—and the last—the study of humans as creatures who are unique because of culture. This is no longer necessarily the case, as we have seen. Archaeology is closely tied to cultural anthropology in its attempt to reconstruct life ways prior to written records. But it also works with fossil remains and biological concepts in reconstructing history. Linguistics is perhaps the most independent of the four subdisciplines because its body of data has distinct boundaries. As you will see, all of these branches are in a state of flux, revising their traditional methods to help them get at the heart of the questions that people are interested in today.

Physical Anthropology

Physical anthropology, the study of the biological aspects of human existence, was once a rather static science. Its nineteenth-century practitioners spent much of their time measuring people in the effort to group humans into races according to head shape and various other traits. The initial concern was to describe the variation of a few features in modern and ancient populations. Today, however, physical anthropology not only describes the variation of hundreds of features—from blood protein composition to limb length —but also encompasses the entire history and nature of human biological change. This new anthropology represents an enormous expansion in scope.

We can begin to make sense of the diversity of the field by thinking of physical anthropology as the study of the events and processes of human evolution. An event can be described as the appearance in the fossil record of any of the traits that characterize a species in different stages of its evolution. These events take place within a geological time frame and occur much more slowly than the events we read about in the papers. By placing thousands of fossils together in the correct time sequence, physical anthropologists have begun to reconstruct the history of our evolution.

An ideal picture of how we evolved would be complete in every detail, including a vivid

Physical anthropologist Donald Johanson uses an air scribe to clean sandstone from around the fossil skull of a child that lived 3 million years ago in East Africa. (David Brill © The National Geographic Society)

description of the climates, plants, and animals comprising ancient environments. The actual picture is far from ideal. Crucial periods early in the history of our evolution are almost completely unrepresented by fossils. For instance, during the period from 14 to 5 million years ago, our humanlike ancestors began to walk upright on their hind limbs. But we have no fossil leg bones or pelvises from this time. In fact, the known primate remains from this period are a single tooth. We do, however, have a fairly complete record of the human evolution during the past 3 million years. Geologists and a host of other specialists have developed techniques for determining prehistoric precipitation, geography, flora, and fauna. But for a complete understanding of how these features affected past human evolution, much more data must be collected.

The present is also a valuable source of clues to the past. By studying the anatomy and behavior of the other primates, physical anthropologists can reconstruct how fossil species (including the earliest humanlike creatures) probably moved and, to some degree, how they may have behaved together in social groups.

Physical anthropologists want to know more than what happened; they are also curious about *why* evolutionary events occurred as they did. They are interested in what evolutionary processes have been responsible for the events. The most important source of this knowledge is living human populations. Analysis of how the frequency of various physical traits in human groups is shifting in response to changing environments and cultural practices can provide analogies to evolution in prehistoric groups.

Physical anthropologists who study modern human variation face the problem of distinguishing environmental action on an individual during his or her lifetime—such as the effects on the body of growing up in a cold or a high-altitude setting—from those that are truly the result of inherited factors. Research-

ers must also separate the cultural influences on human biology from those of the natural environment. Cultural beliefs and values can shape the process of reproduction and therefore influence the course of evolution. Physical anthropologists have come to understand human variation as the consequence of enormously complex interactions with both the environment and culture.

The study of the interaction of biological and cultural factors has led to some unique contributions. For instance, Carleton Gajdusek, of the National Institute for Neurological Diseases and Stroke, won a Nobel Prize in 1976 for applying physical anthropological and epidemiological methods to the study of a progressive neuromuscular disease called kuru. The disease occurs among a group of New Guinea highlanders called the Fore. He found that kuru has a cultural component—the eating of uncooked diseased brains in the course of ritual cannibalism. The virus is then transmitted to those who eat the brains. Gajdusek discovered a genetic factor as well. Although cannibalism is a common practice among highland New Guinea peoples, the disease occurs only among the Fore highland groups. This fact suggested a genetic susceptibility to the disease. Gajdusek's discoveries are important because some progressive muscular disorders found in the West—such as multiple sclerosis—may also be studied in terms of the cultural and genetic factors involved.

Archaeology

Archaeology overlaps both physical and cultural anthropology. But it exists as a distinct discipline with its own subject matter and methods. It can be defined as the study of the history, life styles, and processes of change in prehistoric human cultures. For the most part, archaeologists examine what happened in human societies before they began to keep written records. Recreating what life was once

Archaeology students make a site survey at the Pyramid of the Sun, part of the monumental architecture of Teotihuacán, a city state that dominated much of Mesoamerica from about A.D. 200 to 500. Excavations at this site have added a great deal to our knowledge of the rise of cities and states.
(Marilu Pease/Monkmeyer)

like in the dim past and understanding how it changed is like trying to put together an intricate jigsaw puzzle in which most of the pieces and the picture of the completed puzzle on the box cover are missing.

Generally working without written records, archaeologists use the most durable scraps of human activities as clues. Occasionally these are well-preserved buildings and implements. But more often, evidence consists of such objects as bits of broken pottery, flakes from ancient stone tool making, charred animal bones around an ancient hearth, and slight changes in vegetation or soil patterns caused by prehistoric farming. Archaeologists try to relate these material remains to the behaviors of the humans who left them behind. To do so, they systematically survey, dig up, date, classify, and then interpret the remains.

Interpretation of what went on in the past was once just a matter of organizing bones and artifacts into historical sequences. Long-inhabited sites with many layers built up over the years often reveal, for instance, that one kind of pottery was gradually replaced by another kind and then still another. Archaeologists were at first content merely to catalog these sequences. But in the "new archaeology," scientists analyze a variety of data as clues to the actual activities of the humans who left these traces. In following the spread of early human tribes, for instance, archaeologists analyze tools, indications of environmental conditions, and the remains of animal prey for information on the changing role of hunting.

Among other surprises, archaeologists have found that the appearance of tool-using humans in North America seems to have coincided with the disappearance of many large game animals. One hundred species of mammals—including mammoths, giant beavers, and giant ground sloths—suddenly became extinct about 10,000 years ago. In evolutionary terms, this was not long after the first humans seemingly made their way to the continent from the Far East, probably by way of a land bridge at the site of the Bering Strait. Were humans responsible for these mass extinctions? Had they developed hunting techniques—such as surrounding herds with fire or running them off cliffs—so wasteful that they wiped out their prey? Or was it something else—a major climatic change, perhaps—that killed so many so fast? We are not yet sure. The "Pleistocene overkill" theory is still under investigation, as are many other theories about how our ancestors lived from day to day and changed over the centuries.

To analyze and interpret their finds, today's archaeologists call on a battery of specialists. Analysts range from zoologists who examine deer antlers to determine what times of year a site was occupied to scientists who can tell from minute grains of pollen how old a site is, what kinds of plants once grew there, and what the climate was like. Interpretive models may also draw on the work of economists, ecologists, statisticians, geographers, cultural anthropologists studying modern primitive populations, and even physicists. Growing numbers of archaeologists are unearthing vast quantities of materials at sites around the globe, guided by a desire to find and record as much data as possible before the evidence is destroyed by advancing industrial civilization. The result is a dynamic field undergoing explosive growth. We now know far more about how humans once lived than we did even a few years ago.

Linguistics

Thanks to the work of linguists, scientists who study language, our understanding of this central aspect of social life is also increasing. Anthropological research into language is expanding in many directions at once.

Some anthropological linguists are busy recording languages that will soon become extinct because they are spoken in vanishing cultures. Others are trying to find ways in which all languages are similar. These findings may suggest something about humans' basic capacity for using vocal symbols to communicate with each other, as well as the fundamental structure of the human mind. Other linguists focus on differences, rather than universals, in languages. These, they think, reveal fundamental differences in the ways people of various cultures perceive life. Some languages, for instance, have no way of expressing neat divisions of time into past, present, and future, as ours does. Our vocabulary and grammar reflect a linear view of time—and perhaps an obsession with it—that is by no means universal. People of other cultures are obsessed with other kinds of details. Indians* of northern Canada, for instance, have not 1 word for

*In this text we will use the term *Indian* to identify aboriginal peoples in the New World—in North, Central, and South America. We do, however, recognize the fact that some people prefer various other terms—especially *native American*. We choose *Indian* from among the list of possibilities as the one term that applies everywhere in the New World.

cultures work. For anyone patient enough to record and analyze its intricacies, language is a rich source of information about everything from the patterning of kinship relations to how other domains of culture are perceived (Fried, 1972).

Cultural Anthropology

The fourth subdiscipline, cultural anthropology, is the most familiar of the branches, the one which people usually think of when the word "anthropology" is mentioned. But, given its diversity, it is also the hardest of the four to define.

Cultural anthropologists themselves do not all agree on what it is they are studying. Culture—one of their principal subject matters—is variously defined as a worldwide striving toward "civilization" through the accumulation of practices and beliefs; a unique pattern of beliefs that shapes personalities in each society; a local system of ideas and practices that are functionally integrated; an unconscious structure that generates ideas and behavior; a system of shared symbols that come into play in social interactions; and a system by which people adapt to their environment. Cultural anthropologists work with the concepts culture and society. Those who focus on the interaction of individuals, and the institutions such interaction creates, sometimes stress their particular focus by referring to themselves as social anthropologists. In this text, the emphasis is on culture as an idea system, but the concept of society is absolutely essential to all of the chapters dealing with social organization, such as kinship and marriage, non-kin groupings, and politics and leadership.

Underlying most definitions of culture is the basic assumption that groups of people—Samoans, Americans, members of an Eskimo tribe—come to share a set of understandings about how their society works and how one should behave in it. These un-

Anthropological linguists study the form and use of spoken language, as well as nonverbal systems of communication that are characteristic of various social groups. (Klaus D. Francke, Peter Arnold Photo Archives)

"ice," as we do, but at least 13. Since it is important to them to know whether a stretch of frozen water will support a foot traveler or a dog sled, they are careful to categorize these kinds of ice in their verbal communications (Basso, 1973).

However linguists approach it, language is a key element in the study of culture. Fieldworkers obviously need to know a people's language before they can learn much about them. Models developed for the study of language can also be used to study how whole

Cultural anthropologists study people's understandings about how their particular society works and how to behave in it. Here, the men of a Hoti Indian family in Venezuela inspect the bamboo used to make blowguns with which they will hunt monkeys and birds, and boys of the Ibo of Nigeria dance around a masked figure at their New Year festival.
(Jacques Jangoux, Peter Arnold Photo Archives; Peter Buckley, Photo Researchers)

derstandings in turn affect the ways in which people behave—how they choose marriage partners, build houses, organize politically, procure food, communicate, worship, divide labor, maintain social control, express themselves in art, and so on. Since these beliefs and behaviors may be quite different from one group to another, anthropologists usually see them as products of the local culture rather than as basic aspects of human nature. In each society, though, members tend to accept their own way of looking at things as the norm. In the United States, for example, we "know" that older people need to be retired (and thereby lose the opportunity to contribute their knowledge and skills to society). But in some other societies, the aged are respected for the knowledge and wisdom they have developed over the years.

Collecting information about "strange" practices was the central concern of an-

thropologists during the early years of the discipline. This concern frequently appeared to be separated from any understanding of one's own culture. The information they gathered fascinated and amused the folks back home. But today a crisis of sorts is facing the field: there are very few "unknown tribes" left to describe. The cultures of many peoples are rapidly becoming extinct. In some cases, contact with Westerners has introduced diseases for which their bodies have no built-up immunity. Measles, tuberculosis, smallpox, mumps, and other introduced diseases have decimated many primitive* tribes. And as more technologically advanced peoples have pushed into the environments that once sus-

---

*We use the term *primitive* here to indicate, in general, nonliterate peoples who live without permanent dwellings and by means of simple technology—hunting and gathering of food.

tained them, hunting-and-gathering tribes have been relegated to the most barren settings or resettled in communities that are inadequate for their needs and desires. This disruption of their traditional life style and food supplies has created severe vitamin and mineral deficiencies and, in some cases, destroyed their social structure. As a result of such pressures, the aboriginal population of Australia, for instance, plummeted from 250,000 at the turn of the century to no more than 40,000 today (Lévi-Strauss, 1967).

Elsewhere, though, formerly primitive populations are reproducing rapidly and becoming part of a growing and restless third world. In Latin America, Asia, and Africa, people are increasingly aware of the more technologically advanced nations and of their own lack of power and material wealth. They resent being the objects of anthropological studies, and they express ambivalent feelings about Western technology and ideologies.

To deal with the first crisis—that of extinction of primitive peoples—cultural anthropologists are speeding up their attempts to gather information while they may. Data on how the remaining primitive tribes live provide invaluable clues to the primitive life ways of ancient humans. Observation techniques are therefore being sharpened and made more systematic in the urgency of capturing this information before it is lost forever. At the same time, however, many anthropologists are turning to the study of the far more numerous urban cultures.

The second crisis has serious implications for world harmony. Third world cultures feel that anthropologists from technologically advanced nations are more interested in maintaining the status quo than in helping them develop and join the rest of the political and economic world. This feeling is due to the fact that the study of colonial peoples by anthropologists often stresses traditional systems rather than situations of change and unrest resulting from colonial administration. In the face of this distrust—and of the extinction of their other subjects—many Western anthropologists are turning to a study of their own culture instead. When they do so, they find it hard to maintain anthropology's traditional distinction between the anthropologist and the group being studied. Instead of the perspective of a culturally alien observer trying to be a participant, studies of Western culture have the peculiarly self-reflective point of view of participants who are trying to be observers.

French anthropologist Claude Lévi-Strauss (1967) suggests another alternative: invite third world anthropologists to come study us. This solution might reveal things about our own "strange" customs that are hard for those of us who have grown up with them to see. It might revise anthropology's established use of alien peoples as subjects and permit a more meaningful interaction with the third world.

The fact that there are so few isolated peoples also requires another change in cultural anthropology as it was practiced in the past. Traditionally, in-depth studies described a single social group, in and of itself. But such isolated pictures no longer reflect the whole situation. In Brazil, for example, even the most remote Indian tribes in the Amazon jungle have been affected by the new trans-Amazonian highway and by the policies of government agencies appointed to deal with Indian societies. They also are influenced by the influx of commercial enterprises that have begun to exploit the natural resources of the region. When anthropologists describe village life in these remote areas, they can no longer ignore the effect of these regional influences. This methodological problem is even more acute in the developing countries. There, the lives of people whose parents or grandparents were members of more isolated cultures are now touched more directly, not only by regional economic and political developments but by world events as well. As a result, it is increasingly important that analyses of cul-

The telephone booth in the marketplace in Jedda, Saudi Arabia, is a relatively new addition, one that is indicative of the modern communication systems that are becoming regular features of developing nations all over the world. (Kent Reno, Jeroboam)

tural systems take into account the wider social systems in which they are encapsulated.

Although the days of describing remote tribes are coming to an end, anthropology is needed now more than ever before. All over the world, modern communication systems are bringing a flood of information about other cultures to mass audiences. Anthropologists' perspective and knowledge of these cultures can help to interpret the information and build understanding between peoples. There is also hope that in coming to understand other people better, we will learn something about ourselves—perhaps that our behaviors are to some extent the result of local choices rather than inevitabilities of human nature or of the "right" way of doing things.

In addition to serving the public, anthropologists are also in demand by international organizations. As the third and fourth worlds begin to organize and assert themselves, the major powers need to learn more about these people's life ways, heritages, and points of view. Cultural anthropologists' new studies of urban cultures may also contribute to programs of development and planning.

Instead of being simply a science *of* humanity, anthropology is becoming a science *for* humanity. In all its branches, anthropology is being drawn into the serious questions of the day—the effects of unequal distribution of wealth, of genetic engineering, of loss of cultural identity, of technological impact on the environment, of racial strife, of sex-role stereotyping. Instead of simply observing and describing interesting details of the human scene from afar, anthropologists are becoming aware of the serious implications of their research for people's lives. Sensitive topics are now being handled with greater care than they once were. The American Anthropological Association, for instance, is very concerned about information collected by anthropologists and how it is disseminated to the public. The result may be a science that is at the same time more systematic and more humane.

Summary

1. Anthropology is the study of everything human—from our biological origins to how our cultural systems influence our behaviors.

2. Anthropology cuts across the entire liberal arts curriculum, taking other disciplines into sectors of time and space that might otherwise be neglected; it studies people from all times and in all places. It also distinguishes itself from the subjects it overlaps by its *holism* (all-inclusiveness) and its *relativism* (considering people in terms of their own cultures). But some of its own branches and points of view do not mesh well with each other. And in some serious matters, anthropologists feel that they must reveal their value judgments.

3. There are four main branches of anthropology: physical anthropology, archaeology, linguistics, and cultural anthropology.

4. Physical anthropologists traditionally studied a limited range of biological variations in living human populations. But now they study as well the events and processes by which humans have evolved.

5. Archaeologists study extinct human cultures. Using durable fragments of human activities as clues, they devise theories about how people behaved and changed before they began to keep written records.

6. Linguistics—the study of languages—has been adopted by some anthropologists as a way of understanding how cultures work. The language that a people uses may reveal many features of their social life.

7. Cultural anthropologists generally study the understandings about human life and the external world that people in every human group learn from those around them. This understanding—that is, culture—tends to shape everything they do, as well as their beliefs and attitudes. Cultural anthropologists have traditionally studied the "strange" (to us) ways of "exotic" peoples. But today the cultures of these remote and primitive peoples are vanishing as they are touched by the industrial world. The focus of anthropology is, therefore, shifting to urban cultures elsewhere and at home.

PART ONE

Human Biological Evolution

An Introduction to Physical Anthropology

PHYSICAL anthropology presently focuses on three central questions: (1) Through what stages has the human species developed to the form that we know today? (2) What is the mechanism that has caused these changes to occur? and (3) What is the nature of ongoing change in living human populations? The organizing principle of physical anthropology is *evolution*—biological change over time.

Because we are human, living within our own limited time span, it is often hard to appreciate the enormous amounts of time involved in evolution. Humans have existed in approximately their present form for the last 40,000 years. Although this may seem like an incomprehensibly long period of time, 40,000 years is but an instant in the millions of years that humans have been evolving and in the billions of years that life on earth has been evolving.

Within this vast time span, nothing has been static. The number and variety of life forms have been changing all the time. This change has not occurred randomly; it has followed a pattern. But it was not until the nineteenth century that the major mechanism of evolution was recognized by naturalists. And Charles Darwin, more than any other, brought to light the nature of this mechanism.

The History of the Theory of Evolution

Early Views of Nature

Theories of evolution were not new when Darwin published *On the Origin of Species* in 1859. In fact, the idea of evolution itself had evolved for over 2,500 years before Darwin's time. Aristotle (384–322 B.C.) believed that new forms of life could arise from old forms. Some kind of intelligent design, he felt, was directing these transformations toward an ideal form. Everything in nature could be arranged in a scale according to how close it came to the ideal. Humans were closest to the ideal, and inorganic matter was farthest from it.

Early commentators of the biblical history of creation were strongly influenced by Aristotle's ideas. Their readings of the Book of Genesis allowed room for the possibility that new species could arise from those first placed on earth by God. But in the seventeenth century a more literal reading of Genesis became accepted not only in the church but also among scientists and lay people in general.

According to the new church doctrine, every form of life now on earth had been shaped during the original creation and had stayed unchanged into the present. The extinction of a species was inconceivable. As in Aristotle's theory, however, all nature was arranged in a scale of perfection. This hierarchy was called the *Scala Naturae,* or the Great Chain of Being. Humans, because of their ability to reason, were placed at the top of the Chain, closest to the divine. Monkeys and apes were placed just below humans, but above simpler animals, plants, and inorganic matter.

The concept of slow change from one form of life to another was not part of this world view, not only because species were thought to be permanent, but also because the world was believed to be only a few thousand years old. In the seventeenth century, James Ussher, archbishop of Armagh, set 4004 B.C. as the date of creation. His date and the *Scala Naturae* were generally accepted until the nineteenth century, although they did not go completely unchallenged.

During the Middle Ages, there was little interest in firsthand observation of nature.

Scientific writers were content to base their writings on classical authorities. But in the seventeenth and eighteenth centuries there was a renewed interest in observation. This interest was sparked to some extent by the insistence of the English philosopher Francis Bacon in his book *Novum Organum,* published in 1620, that the *inductive method* be followed in scientific inquiry. This method was a system of reasoning from the facts of observation to generalizations based on those facts. These generalizations, or *hypotheses,* were to be tested by experiment and gradually refined into natural laws.

The inductive method became popular among scientists and gave tremendous impulse to research. First among the observers who followed Bacon was the great Swedish naturalist, Carolus Linnaeus (1707–1778). Linnaeus was intrigued by the steady flow of unknown plants and animals into Europe, a result of greater global exploration. His research led him to develop a *taxonomy,* a system of naming plants and animals and placing them in a series of categories each more inclusive than the one below it. This taxonomy was set forth in the classic *Systema Naturae,* published when Linnaeus was only 28.

Linnaeus's work shows a remarkable blend of traditional belief and brilliant insight. He was the first to classify human beings with monkeys and chimpanzees, showing his awareness of the close physical similarity among them. He did not, however, speculate about a common ancestry. At first Linnaeus accepted the idea that the species were fixed in form. Later, however, he felt that new forms could arise. But it was his earlier view that was well known, and it reinforced the traditional religious notions about natural history. In the long run, however, his taxonomy helped those who followed to see the relationships among different life forms and organize the evidence of evolution.

During the eighteenth century, this evidence was being gathered rapidly in the fields of geology, paleontology (the study of fossilized remains), and comparative anatomy. In speculations that foreshadowed Darwin's theory to a remarkable degree, the Comte de Buffon (1707–1788) drew on this new knowledge. He believed (1) that variations within a species occurred, (2) that the best-adapted individuals would survive in the fight for survival, and (3) that species had evolved from one another. Natural history, he asserted further, must have unfolded over a much longer time span than was generally thought. But because Buffon changed his mind on some of these issues several times, his views were not influential at the time.

Jean-Baptiste de Lamarck (1744–1829) also believed that species evolved from one another. He, however, carefully supported the notion with a comprehensive roadmap of evolution—a sequence of organisms arranged from the least to the most complex. In this scheme a simple common ancestor had gradually given rise to higher forms, until the present diversity of life was reached.

Lamarck is chiefly remembered today not for this bold evolutionary idea, but for his discredited theory that acquired traits could be inherited. He believed that organisms in the course of their life acquired certain characteristics that better adapted them to their surroundings. These traits were then passed on to the next generation. In this way, the characteristics of a species were altered slowly. Lamarck's theory now has few supporters because no one has been able to prove that acquired traits can be passed on.

During the later eighteenth and early nineteenth centuries, geologists were digging up vast numbers of fossils. They found that few living species existed in the fossil record in their present form. To reconcile this evidence of evolution with church doctrine, Georges Cuvier (1769–1832) proposed a theory called *catastrophism.* According to the theory, the earth periodically had been swept by violent upheavals such as floods and vol-

canoes. These catastrophes killed all existing species, trapping and preserving their remains as fossils. Divine creation then populated the earth with an entirely new set of species, the remains of which were preserved in the next catastrophe.

The English geologist Sir Charles Lyell (1797–1875) was not convinced by catastrophism. His studies of rock layers and the geological processes responsible for them convinced him that there had been no supernatural interventions, and that if any catastrophes had occurred, they were local. In his *Principles of Geology,* published in 1830, he set forth the theory of *uniformitarianism.* According to this theory, the earth always had been shaped and still was being shaped by geological forces such as volcanic action and erosion. These forces acted slowly over long periods of time. This theory directly conflicted with the idea that special divine acts had from time to time radically altered the makeup of the earth.

Because geological forces act so slowly, Lyell reasoned that the earth and the fossils preserved in it must be millions of years old. Although some thinkers before him had felt that the earth was actually older, there had been no way of proving it until now. Lyell's study did much to convince other scientists of the earth's great age and provided the time frame that would be needed for Darwin's theory of evolution by natural selection.

Charles Darwin's Theories

Linnaeus, Buffon, Lamarck, Lyell, and many others contributed important parts of the theory of evolution. But it remained for Charles Darwin (1809–1882), the brilliant observer and generalizer, to put the pieces together in one theory. Darwin not only presented a forceful case that evolution had occurred, he also presented a theory, natural selection, to explain and account for evolutionary change.

Two of the Galápagos islands. Darwin was puzzled by the diversity of life forms in the uniform climate here. (Miguel Castro, Photo Researchers)

Darwin's work was distinguished not only by his ability to generalize but also by the quantity and quality of the evidence with which he supported his hypotheses. Most of his observations were made during his five-year voyage around the world aboard H.M.S. *Beagle.*

We can now see two stages in Darwin's solution to the question of the origin of species. First, he had to show that evolution had taken place—that species evolved from previously existing species. Second, he had to describe the mechanism that caused this transformation of species. On his voyage he managed to solve only the first part of the problem, though the observations he made served as a base for the solution of the second part (Eiseley, 1961).

When the *Beagle* reached South America, Darwin made many long trips into the interior. He noticed as he traveled south from Brazil that certain animal species were replaced by forms only slightly different from those further north. To him, these animals seemed to be local variants of the same species, not the products of separate and independent acts of creation. In Argentina, Darwin found the fossils of huge creatures that shared many features with armadillos living in the area at the time. From this and other evidence, he concluded that new species must emerge from older species that are very similar in form. Lyell's uniformitarianism also seemed correct. Because the fossil forms shared so many traits with the living forms, Darwin discounted the conventional view that episodes of creation had from time to time repopulated the earth with wholly new species.

Although Darwin did not work out the mechanism of evolutionary change on his journey, he found baffling clues in the Galápagos archipelago, a group of volcanic islands in the Pacific, 600 miles west of Ecuador. Darwin had hoped to continue his study of fossils there, but the islands turned out to be cinder heaps newly risen from the ocean floor. So instead of digging for fossils he set to work collecting specimens of animals, plants, insects, and reptiles. Just before Darwin had to leave the islands the vice-governor of the islands pointed out to him that certain animals showed only a slight variation in form from one island to the next. Darwin had not noticed this fact himself, but in the few days before his ship sailed he confirmed it.

The finches, in particular, interested Darwin. They differed greatly in the structure of their beaks. Some had small beaks, like those of warblers. Others had stout, straight beaks, like those of woodpeckers. In all there were 14 distinct species, none of which existed elsewhere in the world.

Darwin had seen this kind of slight variation in form earlier in South America. As he had approached the Galápagos, he had concluded that different climates and natural surroundings somehow molded organisms into different appropriate forms. But here in the Galápagos there was no variation in climate: One island was exactly like another. Yet variation in form persisted (Eiseley, 1961). What, then, had caused the original finch ancestors to diversify in a uniform climate?

Natural Selection. Darwin was to ponder this problem for 20 years after his return from the voyage. His first set of clues came from studying the breeding of domesticated plants and animals, some of which, he observed, bore little resemblance to their ancestors. In order to focus on what caused this change, Darwin turned his attention to domestic pigeons.

He found that when pigeon breeders developed a new strain, they bred only those pigeons with the traits they desired. The breeders followed the same procedure with each following generation—mating those who had features closest to the desired type and eliminating those who did not have features close to the desired form. The products of several generations of this human-directed, artificial selection differed considerably from their ancestors.

Darwin observed that individual variation occurred in natural populations as well as in domesticated ones, and he reasoned that some sort of *natural selection* must cause evolutionary change. He used the term *natural* to mean that the selective process does not occur by human choice, as is the case with the artificial selection process used by breeders. Some force in nature allowed certain members of a species to reproduce and discouraged others.

Darwin continued to look into the available literature on the subject of variation. He happened to be reading Thomas Malthus (1766–1834) when he found the insight he needed. In his "Essay on Population," Malthus, an economist, foresaw a "struggle for existence" among future humans. He projected a vision of future generations of humans racked by problems caused by an ever-increasing population with a limited food supply. Darwin immediately applied this idea to nonhuman populations. In nature, he observed, populations tend to increase their numbers. If every breeding pair produced two young to replace it, population size would remain constant. However, most organisms known to Darwin produced many more than two offspring. Some of these died quickly because they were born with fatal defects. Others were killed by predators. Still other members of the population died before they could reproduce because they lost out in the competition for limited resources such as food and water.

In each generation, he concluded, a slightly higher percentage of the well-adapted individuals survived. And as the characteristics favoring survival are passed on gradually from generation to generation, they become more common. The unfavorable traits become less common because the individuals that have them are less likely to survive. Over many generations, these slow alterations would produce major evolutionary changes.

In 1859 Darwin published these theories in his classic work, *On the Origin of Species.* He was spurred to publish his findings when Alfred Wallace (1823–1913), another English naturalist, reached many of the same conclusions on his own and communicated them to Darwin in a letter. Darwin's concept of natural selection can be broken down into five major points:

1. Organisms produce more offspring than can survive to reproduce.
2. Since the number of individuals in a species is more or less constant, there must be a high deathrate.
3. Individuals vary in their characteristics; they are not identical.
4. Variations that make individuals more suited to the environment will ensure their survival. Those organisms that survive will pass on their characteristics to future generations.
5. Future generations will possess and continue to modify the adaptations that came

about by gradual changes in their ancestors.

The Descent of Humans. Darwin stopped short of applying the concept of natural selection to human beings. He realized that humans had evolved from more primitive forms and that these same forms probably also gave rise to the apes. But, preferring solitude and peace, he let others defend evolution in the enormous controversy with the church and conservative scientists.

Twelve years after publication of the *Origin,* Darwin finally set forth in *The Descent of Man* (1871) his position on the question of human ancestry. Drawing on comparative anatomy, Darwin described the probable common ancestor of humans and apes as a "hairy, tailed quadruped, probably arboreal in its habits." Ultimately, he said, humans descended from minute organisms living in the dim obscurity of the past (Darwin, 1871).

Darwin based his conclusions on three arguments. First, he believed that nature forms a continuum from simple to complex forms, with human beings as the most complex. Second, he gathered evidence from comparative anatomy to prove that structural similarities linked human beings closely to some animals and more distantly to others. And third, he believed that the mental, emotional, and even moral qualities of human beings also exist in animals, though to a lesser degree.

In time, new evidence modified but did not disprove Darwin's theories. When he first published his theories, however, his concept of evolution and its application to humans were weakened by two flaws. First there was very little fossil evidence of forms that were ancestors of humans to show that humans had evolved. And second, nothing was known about how traits are passed on from one generation to the next. Since Darwin's time, research into genetics has given insights into inheritance. And excavation carried on by physical anthropologists and others has brought to light more and more fossilized

The Rise of Physical Anthropology

The ability to describe the human body precisely was developing rapidly while Darwin was piecing together his theory of evolution. When the *Origin* generated a desire to find fossil evidence of our ancestors, *anthropometry,* the study of the measurements of the human body, proved basic. In order to place one fossil in relation to others, exact comparisons were necessary.

Physical anthropology emerged from anthropometry in the eighteenth century. Its purpose was to find certain physical characteristics by which all living humans could be grouped into races. Linnaeus had established four basic groups on the basis of skin color and geographic origin. But because skin color was shown to fall into an infinite number of intermediate shades, it was not a useful criterion of race. In the early nineteenth century, Johann Friedrich Blumenbach (1752–1840) stressed the shape of the skull in addition to skin color, hair, and body build. He began the science of *craniometry,* the descriptive analysis of skulls. Later anthropometrists refined the science by taking into fuller account certain facial angles and skull contours.

By the end of the nineteenth century, dependence on measures of the skull came under strong attack. Several scientists pointed out that certain head shapes were common to many widely separated groups of people, as were many other physical features. Brown skin, small size, and narrow heads, for instance, typified not only Iberians, but also Berbers, Sicilians, and southern Greeks (Voget, 1975).

In this country, physical anthropologists have developed better methods of measurement, and, as we shall see, they began to develop ways to study previously unexplored aspects of anatomy. The effort to define racial groups did not make much progress. There were almost as many different ways to group humans as there were physical anthropologists. By the end of the nineteenth century, however, the skills of anthropometry were proving valuable in another area.

Fossil Evidence for Human Evolution

A major weakness of Darwin's theory, as you will recall, was the lack of fossil data. The first well-publicized find of fossil humanlike remains was a skeleton found in 1856 in a cave in the Neander Valley of Germany. This so-called Neandertal skeleton presented a striking contrast to modern humans, and for a time status as an ancestor of humans was denied. The volume of the skull, or cranial capacity, was small, and enormous brow ridges made it seem more animal than human. Proof that humans had evolved from primitive forms would have to wait for something more convincing than this.

Excitement was great in 1891 when *Pithecanthropus,* commonly called Java Man, was discovered. The cranial capacity of this skull, placed at 900 cc, was 300 cc greater than the highest recorded for the gorilla and not far below the minimum for modern human skulls. These and many other measurements led, after much debate, to the conclusion that *Pithecanthropus* fell somewhere between all known apes and the Neandertals, the remains of which had been turning up in greater numbers at various sites in Europe.

During the twentieth century, as we shall see in Chapters 7 and 8, thousands of human and humanlike fossils have been uncovered. The task of describing and comparing this material often fell to anthropometrically-trained physical anthropologists. Today more and more physical anthropologists specialize in interpreting the human fossil record. This material has strongly confirmed Darwin's belief that we have evolved from an apelike creature.

The Contribution of Genetics

The second major weakness of Darwin's theory was his inability to explain how traits are inherited. Unfortunately, he was unaware that an Austrian monk, Gregor Mendel (1822–1884), had solved the problem in 1865. But Darwin was not alone in passing over Mendel's work. Mendel's findings gathered dust in a few libraries until 1900.

The early geneticists, building on Mendel's work, tended to explain all variations in nature in terms of large-scale mutations—sudden changes in genes, the factors that Mendel suggested controlled physical traits. These scientists paid little notice to any role for natural selection in evolution. Instead, they believed that some unknown force directed a series of mutations to bring about rapid change in a species.

Population Genetics and the Synthetic Theory of Evolution. By the 1920s Darwinian evolution and Mendelian genetics seemed to be in direct conflict. Darwin had identified the whole population as his unit of study. Mendelian geneticists, on the other hand, focused on individuals. The study of *population genetics,* however, began to resolve this impasse in the early 1930s. Biologists took a new interest in Darwin and applied modern statistical and experimental methods to the level at which evolutionary processes work—the *population.* A population is an interbreeding group of relatively similar individuals that share the same environment. It was therefore recognized that the pool of genes held by the population as a whole was the right thing to study in order to understand evolutionary change.

Population geneticists explain evolution as change in gene frequencies over time in the gene pool of a population. Natural selection increases the frequency of those genes that help the organism survive to reproduce. In addition to change shaped by environmental factors, two other models of how changes in gene frequency can occur were constructed by population geneticists: *gene flow* and *genetic drift.* Both are random processes of evolution that do not necessarily adapt the organism to its environment. We will discuss these processes in more detail in later chapters.

How do today's scientists explain evolution? Surprisingly, there is general agreement on a theory of evolution that combines, or synthesizes, the theories we have just discussed (natural selection, Mendelian genetics, mutation theory, and population genetics. This combination is called the *synthetic,* or NeoDarwinian, *theory of evolution.*

The New Physical Anthropology

Up until the 1950s, physical anthropology was mainly descriptive in nature. For over a century it had been refining ways of measuring and thereby describing the human body. At the end of the nineteenth century it had begun to apply this expertise to the description of our fossil ancestors. Today, the traditional descriptive work continues, though it is a much smaller part of the field. Bones and teeth have been of continuing interest to physical anthropologists, but new techniques have expanded the traditional descriptive range. X-rays, for example, have made analysis of the internal structures of teeth and bones possible. Physical anthropologists also study body composition and build as well as human growth. Much of their descriptive work continues to be of value to designers who need to know the range of human variability for human engineering projects such as public transportation.

Despite physical anthropology's limited, descriptive scope in the early years and the fact that relatively few persons have specialized in the field, it has become highly diversified in its approach to human biology.

The synthetic theory has been a major force behind much of this change. Before this theory, physical anthropologists could compare in great detail the bones of every known human ancestor with one another and with those of modern humans. But they had little idea of how to study the evolutionary processes involved in changing from one form to the next. The synthetic theory provided the chance to apply a refined knowledge of how evolution works to the study of humans. As you will see, physical anthropologists have begun to study mutation, genetic drift, gene flow, and natural selection in modern-day human populations. They presently use the mathematical models of population genetics to analyze patterns of variation in traits such as blood type. They are also studying the anatomy and behavior of monkeys and apes for clues to our own evolution. And, finally, physical anthropologists, seeing fossils through the eyes of population geneticists, now regard them as the remains of members of ancient populations and apply insights gotten from studying modern populations.

Today the work of physical anthropologists can be divided into three basic categories: paleoanthropology, primatology, and the study of modern human variation.

Paleoanthropology

Paleoanthropology, or human paleontology, is the study of fossils relevant to the evolution of humans. Fossils supply the only direct evidence of what our ancestors looked like and how they walked and ate. Only fossils could have told us that the rate of human evolution has not been constant. Bursts of change have followed periods of relative stability. And only fossils could have indicated the general sequence of our bodily evolution. Fossils have shown, for instance, that our legs took their present shape long before our heads did.

The search for fossils can be quite difficult. In recent years workers combing the Afar Desert of Ethiopia, one of the world's most desolate areas, have had to endure constant 120° temperatures. Excavators sometimes have to deal also with volatile political situations, almost inaccessible sites, and a shortage of funds needed to carry on their work.

As they interpret the fossil record, paleoanthropologists try to identify the forces that have effected the evolution of humans. In doing so, they look for both biological factors (interaction with the physical environment) and cultural factors (interaction with the social environment), both of which have influenced the changes in the human body.

Any attempts to explain the course of biological evolution must take into account the development of tools, hunting, fire, and the construction of shelter, all of which, in effect, created a new environment. When humans began to change their environment, they profoundly affected their own biological evolution. Moreover, certain biological changes were probably so closely linked with the development of culture that elements of both evolved at the same time. Early increases in brain size and complexity probably resulted from the selective advantage of toolmaking. Yet more complex tools would have been impossible without the intellectual power to design and make them. Because the interaction between culture and biology can be so important, excavators must look carefully for both kinds of evidence as they dig.

Once a fossil has been uncovered, paleoanthropologists must try to place it chronologically in relation to other fossils. Only then can they make further inferences about the sequence of change through which our ancestors have gone. Establishing the correct sequence can be tricky. On what basis, for example, can we say that a given fossil is closer than another to modern humans? Scientists have tried to answer this question by defining features common to all members of our *lineage,* the line of our descent from the earliest humanlike animals. But lists of such features are always controversial, as is their application to actual fossil remains.

Aside from defining humanness, two kinds of problems hinder the interpretation of fossils: (1) The fossil record may be incomplete, and (2) dating may be inaccurate or impossible.

Though large gaps remain in the fossil record, evidence is being gathered more quickly than ever before. Fifteen years ago the known remains of *Ramapithecus,* possibly a transitional form from apelike creatures to those more closely resembling humans, consisted of about a dozen fossils. Now there are close to 40 fossils (Simons, 1977). Despite the recent deluge of new data, however, fossils of humanlike forms dating from between about 4 to 8 million years are limited to a few teeth. This period is especially crucial because it is possible that during this time the human lineage was diverging from that of the apes. Fossils from this span would be extremely welcome and could very well be uncovered in the near future.

Incomplete fossils add to the problem because guesswork is necessary in reconstructing them. Bones that have been deformed by geological processes or are fragmentary invite misleading interpretations of both their relation to other fossils and their function in the animal.

Before the development of modern dating methods, paleoanthropologists had no way of determining the absolute age of a given fossil. If two fossils were found in different layers of the earth, scientists could only say that one was relatively older than the other. As we will

discuss in Chapter 6, modern techniques can now determine the age of a rock with a margin of error of only a few percent, making possible an accurate time scale for the evolution of all life from its beginnings. Other methods such as flourine and nitrogen dating allow scientists to pinpoint whether two fossils found near each other are of the same age. Each of these latter methods can, however, be used only to date materials from limited time ranges, and only under certain geologic conditions. To compensate, new methods are continually being developed.

The enthusiasm generated by paleoanthropologists such as Louis Leakey and his son Richard has led to the excavation of a great many humanlike fossils. There has been a particularly substantial increase in information for the period between 2 to 4 million years ago. Quite often, new pieces of evidence require changes in our theories about how humans evolved. This makes paleoanthropology one of the most dynamic and intriguing subfields in anthropology.

The Study of Primatology

Primatology is the study of our closest nonhuman relatives—the great apes, monkeys, and primitive animals called prosimians. It is the only possible source of certain kinds of information about our ancestors. *Comparative anatomy,* the systematic comparison of bodily structures, provides the knowledge necessary to reconstruct entire animals from fossil fragments. It also supplies a basis for inferences about the nature of the creatures living in periods unrepresented by fossils. By observing how the other primates eat and move, we can better interpret from fossils how our more apelike ancestors performed these functions. Finally, by looking closely at what other primates do, we can identify not only those behaviors that all members of the order share, but also those that are unique to humans. By isolating what makes us different from the

Beatrice Gardner, a primatologist, teaches symbols to Washoe, a chimp who showed many of the elements of linguistic communication.
(Photo courtesy of R. A. and B. T. Gardner)

other members of the primate order, we can make progress toward a definition of what it means to be human.

Comparative Anatomy. The history of human evolution is the history of cumulative change. Thus, the physical traits that we call human are really modifications of an already elaborate primate inheritance. To get a sense of our origins, we must be able to separate primate characteristics from the traits that are unique to our lineage. We can begin to do this by comparing our anatomy with that of the nonhuman primates. Dissection, for example, has supplied detailed information on the anatomy of gorillas and chimpanzees. Anatomists also have exact knowledge of the bodies of modern humans. This anatomical knowledge is essential to understanding whether a given fossil leg bone, for example, belongs to a human ancestor, an ape ancestor, or a common ancestor.

Anthropologists and comparative anatomists often try to reconstruct the appearance of extinct animals from incomplete fossils. This kind of reconstruction can be done only by anthropologists who know enough about anatomy to be familiar with the muscles and soft tissues of living animals.

Comparative anatomy gives us one picture of how the various members of the primate order emerged. In the 1960s a new approach to understanding evolutionary relationships between living primates was developed. Researchers began to compare the structure of hemoglobins and serum proteins in different primates. By assuming that the changes in these molecules have occurred at a constant rate through time, some researchers feel that they can estimate how long it has been since the primates last shared a common ancestor. The *phylogeny,* or history of the evolution of a group of genetically-related organisms, constructed by Vincent Sarich and Allan Wilson in the 1960s agrees in most respects with that put together on the basis of the fossil record. They have found, for instance, that human blood molecules are most similar to those of apes, confirming their status as our closest relatives.

The Significance of Primate Behavior. If we were to encounter one of our early ancestors on the street we would judge its humanity more by the way it acted than by the way it looked. We would want to know, for example, whether the creature could speak or had a primate communication system of sounds, postures, and facial expressions. Behavior, in effect, has become just as important as anatomy as a criterion of classification. By understanding the relationships between anatomical structure and behavior, paleoanthropologists can make inferences about the locomotion and feeding habits of a fossil animal. Unfortunately, the important aspects of social behavior do not fossilize. For these behaviors, we must rely entirely on our knowledge of living primates. If today's nonhuman primates share certain behaviors with humans, the inference can be made that our humanlike ancestors also possessed them.

AN INTRODUCTION TO PHYSICAL ANTHROPOLOGY

When relating modern primate behavior to animals that are no longer living, anthropologists have always recognized the need for caution. It might be attractive to suggest that the animals we call *Ramapithecus* behaved exactly like chimpanzees. But we must realize that these are two different animal forms, each with its unique biological and behavioral characteristics. Therefore, living primate behavior can only be used as a broad model for what might have been.

Today, anthropology's knowledge of primates comes from two kinds of studies: field and laboratory. In the field, observers record what animals do—when, where, and for how long. They also note how animals behave in groups and how individuals and groups respond to one another as well as to changes in their environment. Back in the laboratory, workers ideally can refine these observations under controlled conditions. Manipulation of environmental conditions, impossible in the wild, is the basis of laboratory work.

Sociobiologists are pursuing another line of research into primate behavior. These scientists assume that any persistent behavior in a population must increase the chances that its members will survive. Behavior, like physical features, will survive only if it increases the organism's chances of survival. Sociobiologists therefore study the behavior of primates with an eye toward its adaptive value.

Primatology and a Definition of Humanness. In the course of observing nonhuman primate anatomy and behavior, a central goal has been to define what makes us different from them. The intense study of primates in recent years has shown that many attributes once thought to be unique to humans are widespread among the primates. In the past, humans were often distinguished on the basis of their ability to use tools and communicate with symbols. This definition had to be modified, however, when researchers observed that chimpanzees also use tools and communicate with symbols. Jane Goodall saw chimpanzees using twigs to get termites out of mounds. Recently chimpanzees and gorillas have been taught American Sign Language, a type of symbolic system. They have learned the meanings of these symbols, used them to convey meanings outside the context in which the symbols were first learned, learned some grammatical rules, and expressed new meanings by putting the symbols together in new combinations. We have therefore come to understand that our uniqueness lies more in the way we rely on certain basic primate behaviors than it does in having unique characteristics.

The Study of Human Variation

The study of how contemporary populations differ from one another is the third major area of physical anthropology. Research in this area has sought to understand the processes of evolution in human populations.

Much of the early work in physical anthropology consisted of descriptive studies, not only of the ancestors of humans but also of living groups. Variations in body build and tooth and skull shape were described in populations around the world. The motivation behind a great deal of this work was to define races by discovering the physical traits shared by the members of each race. Though this concept of race is now discounted by most experts, descriptive studies have made, and continue to make, significant contributions to our knowledge of human variation. Today, in fact, researchers often test theories about the process of evolution in particular cases by drawing on data from the descriptive studies.

Humans vary physically from each other in an almost infinite number of ways. Some human characteristics are controlled by a small number of genes (*simple genetic traits*). Many more are controlled by a large number of genes (*complex genetic traits*).

The structure of certain proteins is the result of simple genetic control. Only a few genes control the making of the amino acids that combine to form proteins such as hemoglobin. One or more of these genes may exist in an alternative form that produces a protein with a variant structure. Chemical analysis of the blood reveals which form is present. Because simple genetic traits are either present or absent, it is easy to map their frequency. By charting such traits, human biologists are able to study the action of mutation, genetic drift, gene flow, and natural selection in human populations.

Complex genetic traits, such as height or skin color, are controlled by the interaction of a large number of genes. The study of these traits is complicated further by the fact that the environment often strongly affects how these traits are expressed. Poor nutrition, for example, may hinder growth. Good nutrition might allow an organism to grow to the upper limit of its genetic potential. The genes, in effect, set limits in complex traits, within which environmental change can occur.

The most basic problem in the studies of complex traits (sometimes called human adaptability studies) is to sort out the effects of genetic control from those of the environment. Take, for example, traits among populations exposed to high altitudes over the course of thousands of years. Anthropologists have found that high-altitude dwellers tend to have larger chests, greater lung capacity, and slower skeletal growth than is typical of sea-level populations (Lasker, 1969). Recent research has shown that these traits are related to long-term developmental adjustments to the low-oxygen content of the air in the mountains. They probably are not caused by genetic factors.

Osteological Studies. Anthropologists can also, to a limited extent, study variations among prehistoric human populations by analyzing their bones. This study is called *os-teology*. Like the rest of physical anthropology, this kind of human variation study has been influenced deeply by the interest in population genetics and the mechanism of evolutionary change.

For decades before the mid-1950s, osteology was a mainstay of physical anthropology. The anthropometrists of the nineteenth and early twentieth centuries, using their calipers and measuring tapes, generated a huge mass of data. They were interested not only in making racial classifications but also in tracing the evolution of racial groups through time.

Modern osteologists have begun to apply the synthetic theory, and population genetics in particular, to their studies. New models are making it possible to describe ancient populations in statistical terms. Because sex and age usually can be determined from bones, it is possible to calculate sex ratios, average life span, and birth and death rates for prehistoric populations.

Patterns of disease, which often leave traces in the bones, also are being studied. Variations in height and robustness, resemblance between parents and offspring, and differing forms of soft tissue can be inferred from bones as well.

Bones also carry a surprising amount of genetic information. Some dental characteristics, such as shovel-shaped incisors, are thought to be simple genetic traits. Blood type, another simple trait, may be learned by close analysis of pieces of bone. Because these traits are much more easily studied than complex traits, osteologists can use them to begin to reconstruct certain aspects of ancient gene pools. As in modern populations, the effects of gene flow, mutation, and genetic drift can be identified, though to a much lesser degree. Since only a portion of a population's original characteristics remains in its bones, evidence for any conclusions is limited.

The study of the skeletal hallmarks of age, sex, and other characteristics also have application in forensic (legal) medicine. Physical anthropologists who specialize in osteology are frequently called upon to make identifications in medical-legal cases.

The Present Evolution of Human Beings

For millions of years, nature molded the genetic makeup of human beings. But when our ancestors began to develop culture, they began to organize the environment to suit their needs. By modifying the effect of the environment, human beings began to exert control over the direction of their own evolution. In fact, some people argue that culture in the twentieth century has completely neutralized natural selection. Although this is an extreme position, most scientists agree that modern technology has a great impact on human biology.

The link between biology and culture has never been more apparent than in modern, industrialized societies. Our technology helps implement important social values. Our desire to ensure a healthy life to everyone, for instance, has stimulated the growth of medical technology. Phenylketonuria, a disease that causes severe mental retardation, is now known to be controlled by a single mutant gene that prevents the body from processing protein normally. All children presently born in America are screened for this disease. If they have it, it is easily corrected by diet. The possessors of the gene that controls the disease suffer no disadvantage in the environment our culture has created for them. They survive and reproduce as well as anyone else.

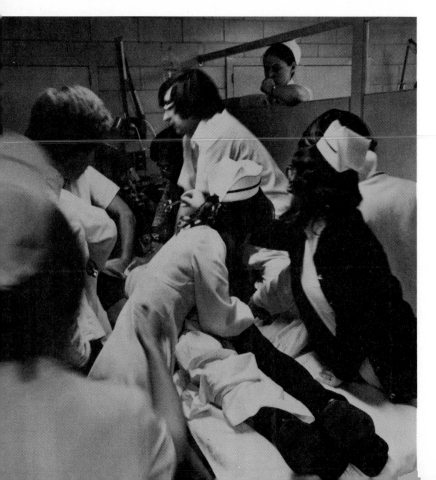

To an increasing degree, culture is replacing nature as a selective agent. Here medical technology allows a victim of a cardiac arrest to survive. (Dan Budnik, Woodfin Camp)

The biological result of our ability to treat the disease is an increase in the frequency of the gene within the population.

Most people are aware of the great advantages of petrochemicals such as pesticides. By allowing us to control insects, they help produce the abundant food supply upon which Americans have come to depend. Yet it is also true that many pesticides can cause mutations or cancer. Many scientists feel that the potential effect of these chemicals on human biology will be significant unless they are controlled. The petrochemical industry argues that by controlling use one runs the risk of limiting food production.

This is the kind of dilemma that will confront us more and more as we gain fuller control over nature. As we reduce nature's impact, it becomes increasingly possible to direct our own evolution. But in so doing, we assume a tremendous responsibility in applying values to decisions concerning survival. Resolving the problems posed by the use of pesticides in agriculture is but one of the biologically significant dilemmas of modern society.

Summary

1. *Physical anthropology* is the study of the events and processes of human *evolution,* the change of human biology over a period of time.

2. The idea that one form of life can evolve from another dates back to early Greek thinkers. Church doctrine of the seventeenth century, however, arranged nature in a hierarchy of unchanging species, called the *Scala Naturae.* In the eighteenth and nineteenth centuries, Linnaeus, Buffon, Lamarck, Lyell, and many others worked out parts of the modern theory of evolution.

3. Darwin, however, first put the pieces together in a single work *(The Origin of Species),* demonstrating that evolution had taken place and describing the mechanism responsible for this change.

4. *Natural selection* is the mechanism of change Darwin described. Individuals compete for survival. Those with certain characteristics survive to breed while those with other traits are eliminated. As the traits favoring survival are passed on from generation to generation, they gradually become more common, and unfavorable characteristics become less common. Over a long period of time, these gradual changes produce major evolutionary trends.

5. Darwin could not explain how traits are passed from one generation to the next. Nor could he cite fossil evidence that humans had evolved from more primitive forms.

6. Early physical anthropologists became adept at measuring variations in the human body in the unsuccessful attempt to define the characteristics of racial groups. Later they became involved in the search for, and analysis of, fossil evidence of human evolution.

7. Mendel and the early geneticists explained inheritance in terms of processes occurring within the cell nucleus.

8. *Population genetics* applied statistical and experimental methods to the level at which evolutionary processes work—the *population.* Population genetics interpreted evolution as a change over time of *gene frequencies* in the *gene pool.* The combination of two random models of change—*drift* and *flow*—and Darwinian natural selection, Mendelian genetics, and mutation theory is called the *synthetic theory* of evolution.

9. Today, the work of physical anthropologists can be divided into three basic categories: paleoanthropology, primatology, and the study of human variation.

10. *Paleoanthropology,* the study of fossils relevant to human evolution, attempts to place fossils in the correct time sequence and

identify the biological and cultural influences on human evolution.

11. *Primatology,* the study of nonhuman primates, is a unique source of data about how structure relates to function in fossil bones.

12. The *study of human variation* attempts to trace evolutionary processes in modern human populations. Both *simple* and *complex* *genetic traits* are studied. *Osteology* attempts to study the same processes in ancient populations by analyzing bones for genetic and demographic information.

13. Today, culture is replacing nature as the agent of selection, and as nature's control is reduced, it becomes increasingly possible to direct our own evolution.

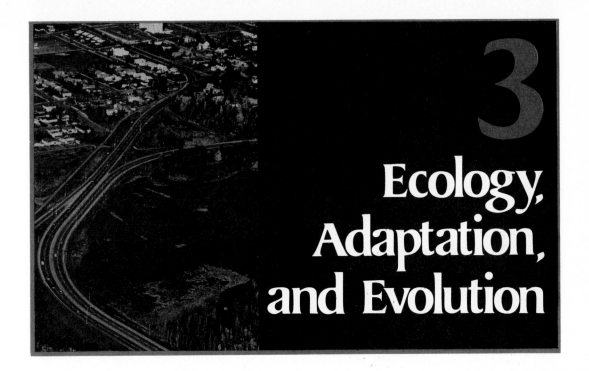

3

Ecology, Adaptation, and Evolution

A s physical anthropologists began to study human evolution, they found it necessary to define precisely the relationships between humans and the environments in which they live. Human biology, they discovered, is influenced not only by nonliving environmental features such as temperature, sunlight, and precipitation, but also by the living features—the organisms with which humans share an area. Microorganisms that depend on human hosts for part or all of their life cycle, for example, often cause serious illness. Certain plants and animals are particularly important because they serve as food: They provide the energy the body needs to move, grow, and reproduce.

Among humans and many other animals, these environmental relationships are complicated by nonbiological, learned behavior. Among humans, this behavior is especially elaborate, and forms a network of values, symbols, and organizations commonly refer-

red to as *culture.* Culture structures perception of the environment, production of the material necessities of life, division of labor, and the procurement and distribution of food. By manipulating the environment through our culture, we can change it radically. Such changes may have great effects on the human body and its evolution. Shelter and clothing can alleviate the stresses of climate. Agricultural technology can reduce forests to grasslands and produce gardens out of deserts. Industrial technology, while making us able to exploit almost all of the world's environments, also produces byproducts that can be devastating to the survival of many life forms, including, possibly, our own.

Any environmentally-oriented study of the human condition, therefore, must see humans as both cultural and biological beings. Often, however, human culture and human biology have been studied separately. Each, in turn, has been further subdivided into many specialized fields. The study of human culture is approached by sociology, economics, history, geography, law, and religion in addition to anthropology. One need only look at a list of social science and humanities departments at a university to see how diversified knowledge of human culture has become. The same tendency occurs in the study of human biology. Genetics, cytology, physiology, epidemiology, and many other specialized approaches have diversified the field considerably.

These specialized studies have produced enormous amounts of information. Unfortunately, this information is not always accessible to others. Each discipline tends to have a special set of assumptions, theories, techniques, and jargon that often makes the communication of knowledge among disciplines difficult. Anthropology is no exception to this tendency, though the special task of explaining human biological and cultural evolution has always led some anthropologists to try to unify many of these subfields in one body of theory. One of the most promising of these unified approaches is ecology. *Ecology* is the study of relationships among all aspects of living and nonliving environments. It provides a theoretical umbrella under which it is possible to bring the environmental sciences, the biological sciences, the social sciences, and evolutionary theory. Because scientists in specialized fields are beginning to use the same principles and concepts, there is a growing body of ecologically-oriented information that can be applied by anthropologists to the understanding of human evolution.

Ecological Definitions of the Environment

Ecologists make a basic distinction between the *abiotic* (or nonliving) part of the environment and the *biotic* (or living) part of the envi-

ronment. The abiotic environment includes features such as temperature, precipitation, humidity, soil types, and solar radiation. The biotic environment includes all living things, from the smallest microorganisms to the tallest trees and the largest animals. Because we are concerned here with humans and human evolution, we will focus on the abiotic and biotic features of *terrestrial* (or land-based) environments, rather than on *marine* (or sea-based) environments.

Abiotic Features

Because ecologists are interested in the relation between the living and nonliving things in an area, they study those abiotic features of an area that affect the biotic features. Not all the abiotic features of an area affect the life that exists in it to the same degree. Some elements of the soil, for instance, may not be used directly by every organism to carry on its life function. Of those abiotic features that do affect life forms, some may be more important than others in determining how well living organisms can survive in an area, and, indeed, whether they can live there at all. Abiotic features, by their scarcity or overabundance, structure the *biotic diversity*—the number of different kinds of life forms in an area. Two basic principles are used to understand the effect of abiotic features on biotic diversity.

The first principle was developed in the 1840s by Baron Justus von Liebig (1830–1873), a German chemist. Basically, it states that the number and diversity of life forms depend on the essential geophysical element that is present in the least quantity. This principle is sometimes referred to as Liebig's Law of the Minimum. This law was modified slightly in the early twentieth century to allow for the fact that the abundance of one factor may offset the scarcity of another. Today, most ecologists study the interaction of factors that limits the diversity of life (Boughey, 1973).

The second principle was developed in 1913 by V. E. Shelford (1877–1968), an American animal ecologist. He studied a whole range of factors that are as harmful to life forms when they are overabundant as when they are too scarce. He theorized that each abiotic factor can be limiting to life in both high and low concentrations. Between these extremes lies a range—sometimes called the limits of tolerance—in which life forms normally exist (Boughey, 1973; Valentine, 1973).

The abiotic features that most commonly affect the diversity of life include temperature, precipitation, soil composition, wind, solar radiation, and, less often, fire.

Temperature. Most organisms, plants included, have fairly narrow temperature ranges within which they are able to carry out vital life processes. Among animals, mammals have the broadest temperature tolerance because of metabolic characteristics that permit them to maintain constant body temperatures in a number of different environments. In humans, death will occur rapidly if internal temperatures fall to 82°F or rise to 106°F. But with protection in the form of clothes and shelter, our range has expanded to include almost every terrestrial ecosystem in the world.

Precipitation. Hail, sleet, rain, and snow comprise another limiting factor. Because all living things are made up of large amounts of water (80 percent of human weight is water), it is essential that access to water be fairly continual (Shepro, Belanarich, & Levy, 1974). In environments with too little water, life forms are scarce. However, abundant water does not necessarily ensure an abundance of life. In cold, wet environments life may be just as scarce as in hot, dry environments. Because both warmth and moisture are so essential for life, the most diverse terrestrial ecosystems are those of the tropical rain forest.

Solar Radiation. Ultimately, the sun provides the energy for all life on earth. Green plants convert solar radiation by means of photosynthesis into carbohydrates, proteins, and lipids, all of which are stored in the leaves. This energy is then consumed by animals, which are incapable of using solar energy directly. In the Arctic and Antarctic, the absence of sunlight for long periods of time restricts the amount of plant life. This in turn limits the diversity of animal life.

Soil. Soils vary in terms of texture (determined by the proportions of silt, sand, clays, etc.), acidity or alkalinity, moisture, air, mineral content, and the amount of organic matter. Because the growth and reproduction of plants depend on these soil characteristics, the diversity of plant life varies from soil to soil. Moisture is a very important feature. In dry areas moisture evaporates quickly, leaving behind minerals in the topsoil. The fertility of these soils can be maintained over long periods. In more humid areas, however, where water filters down to the water table, minerals are drained away from the topsoil, making it less fertile.

Wind. Differences in the frequency and speed of winds can change the effects of both moisture and temperature. In a dry area wind can blow away fertile topsoil. Wind currents can also dry an area so that the effect of precipitation is minimized. Air currents also make the effective temperature colder than the actual temperature. Life forms are therefore scarcer in cold, windy areas than in areas that are just cold.

Fire. Started by lightning and volcanic activity, fire has probably long been a common feature in many environments. Indeed, the biotic features of some environments are structured by the presence of fire. In the chaparrals of the American west coast, the seeds of some cone-bearing trees are not released until the

ECOLOGY, ADAPTATION, AND EVOLUTION

cones have been partly destroyed by fire. The burned areas of the ground then form fertile beds in which the new plants grow well. Naturally, the effects of fire will be made worse by the presence or absence of other abiotic factors, mainly moisture and wind.

It should be obvious in our discussion that single limiting factors are less common than are interactions of factors that limit life. The scarcity of life in the Antarctic and Arctic is due to a combination of cold temperatures, high winds, sometimes low moisture, and the absence of solar radiation for long periods of time. Deserts are created by the lack of moisture, easily leached soils, and, sometimes, drying winds.

Microenvironments

As already pointed out, if humans had no clothes or shelter, they could only live in the tropical and subtropical areas of the world. The fact that humans are biologically best adjusted to these areas may reflect our origins in tropical regions. We can survive in temperate as well as in extremely hot and cold areas only because we can use culture to restructure the environments in which we live. Environments that have been changed in this way are often referred to as *microenvironments*. Interestingly, the microenvironment that we try to create is tropical. The warm reindeer-fur clothing that arctic Laplanders wear in winter gives very effective protection against the cold, even when people remain still for hours in subfreezing temperatures. The human microenvironment inside the fur clothing is such that temperatures next to the skin are the same as they would be in a tropical environment (Schollander et al., 1957).

Humans are not the only animals that create microenvironments. When birds build nests or moles burrow into the ground, they also create microenvironments. Humans, however, have the greatest potential for environmental modification and tend to rely on their microenvironmental adjustments more than on biological adaptability.

The Biotic Hierarchy

Ecologists arrange the biotic environment in a series of categories, each of which includes all the categories below it. (See Figure 1.)

The Individual. At the most basic level the focus is on the individual. The study of the growth and aging of the individual, its interactions with organisms in the same group and with those in other groups, and its functioning in relation to abiotic features is sometimes called *autecology.* These characteristics are used to define an individual's environmental *ecospace*—the biotic and abiotic range within which the individual can live (Valentine, 1973). Although each human has an ecospace, no two ecospaces are totally identical because the genetic factors involved in sexual reproduction give each individual a unique biologi-

Figure 1 The biotic hierarchy.
A group of interbreeding individuals living in the same area make up a population. The populations in a definable area make up a community, which, along with all other communities, is part of the biosphere.

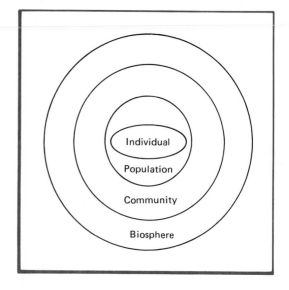

cal nature. Each individual's metabolic activity, immunological system, and bodily proportions (height, weight, muscle mass, amount of body fat, etc.) are unique. In addition, the interaction between heredity and environment that occurs as humans develop gives each individual a unique behavioral profile. Since these factors are part of the definition of *ecospace,* some humans' ecospaces will be better suited to cold environments, others to hot environments, and still others may be poorly structured in both environments. The fact that each individual has a slightly different potential for surviving in different environments is important to evolution. As you have learned, individual differences in survival and reproductive capacity are the basis of biological evolution by natural selection.

The Population. Closely related individuals are studied as a *population*—a group of animals living in the same area and mating almost exclusively with each other. This causes them to be reproductively isolated from other animals in the same environment, although they may mate with members of similar populations nearby.

The makeup of populations is not static. They grow when the birthrate is greater than the deathrate, remain the same when the birth- and deathrates are equal, or decrease when the deathrate is greater than the birthrate. The biological characteristics of their members may change as the result of evolution, and a single population may even give rise to several new ones.

Population ecology studies the interactions of the population as a unit with other populations in the same area, as well as with the important abiotic features of that area. A population can be defined in terms of its *econiche* (*niche* for short). The niche is the sum of all the interactions occurring between a population and its biotic and abiotic environments. The BaMbuti Pygmies, for example, live in the Ituri Forest of Zäire. But their niche is defined on the basis of their interactions with other biotic populations living in the same area. Because the BaMbuti hunt elephants, the interaction between elephants and humans becomes part of the niche definitions of both populations (Turnbull, 1963). Niches are also defined by the population's interaction with abiotic features. The abiotic features of the Ituri rain forest include heat and moisture. The interaction between these abiotic features and the BaMbuti's biology and behavior has produced a number of anatomical, physiological, and cultural traits to cope with these stresses (Austin, 1974). These responses thus also become parts of the BaMbuti's niche structure. The concept of niche is dynamic, in that the niche is defined not only by the presence of biotic populations or abiotic features, but also by the interactions between them.

Often an ecological population is confused with the more familiar term *species*. Unlike the ecological definition of a population, the concept of species is not defined in terms of any particular set of environmental conditions. A species is simply a group of animals whose shared biological background permits individuals to mate with each other and produce fertile offspring. Animals of different species cannot mate to produce fertile offspring.

The makeup of a species, like that of other classification categories, is arbitrary and not without ambiguous boundaries. Two groups of animals that are able to produce offspring are sometimes classified as different species. In some cases, two animals such as horses and donkeys are classified as different species because their offspring (mules) are sterile. In other cases, two groups can be classified as different species because they are geographically isolated from each other or because their behavior normally prevents them from interbreeding, or both. Desert and savannah baboons exist in separate ecosystems, normally do not interbreed, and are distinguishable on the basis of certain physical and behavioral traits. Yet when members of the two species do interbreed, as sometimes happens in zoos, they are completely fertile and produce fertile offspring. Scientists are aware of the ambiguities of the species category, but for the sake of discussion are often forced to make judgments about the limits of the category that are open to question.

In some cases, an ecological population can be the same as the concept of species. This occurs when the term *species* is applied to a group of animals who all live in a certain area and breed only with one another. Koala bears are found only in eucalyptus forests in Australia (Pianka, 1974). Due to its reliance on the fruit of particular eucalyptus trees, the koala has a limited geographical range and occupies a fairly well-defined niche. Because koalas breed only with other koalas, they meet the criterion of reproductive isolation and therefore fit the definition of a *species* as well as an ecological population.

Humans, on the other hand, are located throughout the world in a great many diverse environments. Each local human population has a unique niche structure because its biological and behavioral characteristics are understandable only in terms of the specific biotic and abiotic circumstances that exist in its area. Boundaries between local human populations generally are maintained by cultural, rather than by geographic, mechanisms. Culture often defines the pool of potential mates. The social rules of the BaMbuti pygmies, for example, make it more likely that they will mate with one another than with the neighboring Bantu populations. At the same time, in all human populations there exist circumstances that encourage, or even force, neighboring populations to exchange mates. It is not uncommon for Bantu males to take pygmy females as wives. Thus, while mating among humans tends to be localized within the population, this practice is far from universal. Exchange of mates between local human populations maintains the broad biological unity that is the basis for classifying all humans as the same species. The species category *Homo sapiens* is a biological term that applies to all humans, regardless of the environment in which they live. It does not address itself to the biological diversity that exists within the species. The concepts of niche and population allow us to talk about this diversity in environmental terms.

The Community. As we study populations we come to realize that they do not exist in isolation from one another. Indeed, the same interaction that makes one population a part of the niche definition of another creates a web of life forms, each of which affects the others directly or indirectly. Ecologists call a group of interrelated populations that exist in a definable area a *community*.

The interaction of a biotic community and the physical environment of an area is often referred to as an *ecosystem*. Ecosystems are commonly described in terms of some dominant feature. In marine ecology, coral reefs are usually discussed as an ecosystem and separated from tidal ecosystems or from open-sea ecosystems. In terrestrial ecology, ecosystems are often described by their plant life (forest ecosystems, grassland ecosystems, etc.). Ecologists recognize that these categories are somewhat arbitrary. Grasslands grade imperceptibly into deserts. But the ecosystem concept is useful for describing relationships that exist in areas whose characteristics are familiar to most people.

The Flow of Energy. One way of understanding the organization of an ecosystem is to look at the feeding relationships that exist within it. All energy available to life forms originally comes from the sun. Plants alone can use the radiant energy of the sun by combining simple inorganic compounds (such as water, CO_2, nitrites, sulfates, and phosphates) to form organic compounds. Plant eaters break down the energy compounds in plants into forms they can use—carbohydrates, proteins, and lipids. These broken-down compounds are recombined to form the animal's cell structures. They also provide the energy needed to drive the animal's vital processes. Energy stored in animal cells can, in turn, be broken down to provide the energy needs of other animals.

The simplest way to discuss a community's food relationships is to organize its populations in a *trophic hierarchy*—a series of categories each of which is broadly defined in terms of how its members get their energy. Because plants directly use solar energy they are often referred to as *producers*. Other organisms are called *consumers. Herbivores,* animals that eat only plants, make up the primary consumer trophic level. *Carnivores,* animals that eat only primary consumers, make up the secondary consumer trophic level. Some ecosystems include third and even fourth levels of consumers. Both are sometimes called top carnivores and rely on secondary consumers for their food. Finally, *decomposers* such as bacteria break down the remains of organisms, making basic organic and inorganic compounds available to plants once again. (See Figure 2.)

Not all of the energy that is available at one trophic level is absorbed by the one above it. Only 10 to 20 percent of the food energy that was in the plants eaten by a herbivore is finally stored in its cells. And the energy that is finally stored in the carnivore's cells is only 10 to 20 percent of the energy that was in the cells of the herbivore.

Because so much energy is used at each level to get energy from the one below it, the supportable *biomass,* the total mass of living tissue at a given trophic level, is reduced. Thus, the biomass of the herbivores in an ecosystem is less than the biomass of the plants; the biomass of the carnivores is less than the biomass of the herbivores; and the biomass of the top carnivores is always less than the biomass of lower carnivores. Ecologists estimate the biomass of any one trophic level as roughly 10 percent of the biomass of the level below it.

Although the trophic pyramid is a useful way of remembering basic food energy relationships, it is an ideal representation of what actually exists. In reality, many animals participate at different levels in the trophic pyramid. Consequently, the image of a food

Figure 2 A representation of a trophic pyramid.
Note that the energy at each level is about 10 percent of the level below it.
(After M. A. Little and G. E. Morren, Jr., 1976)

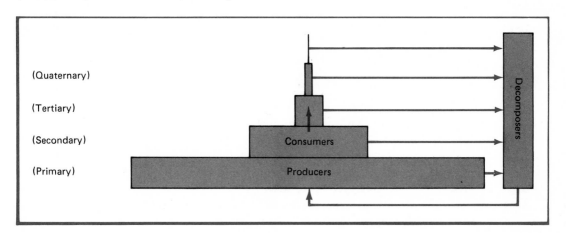

(Quaternary)

(Tertiary)

(Secondary)

(Primary)

Decomposers

Consumers

Producers

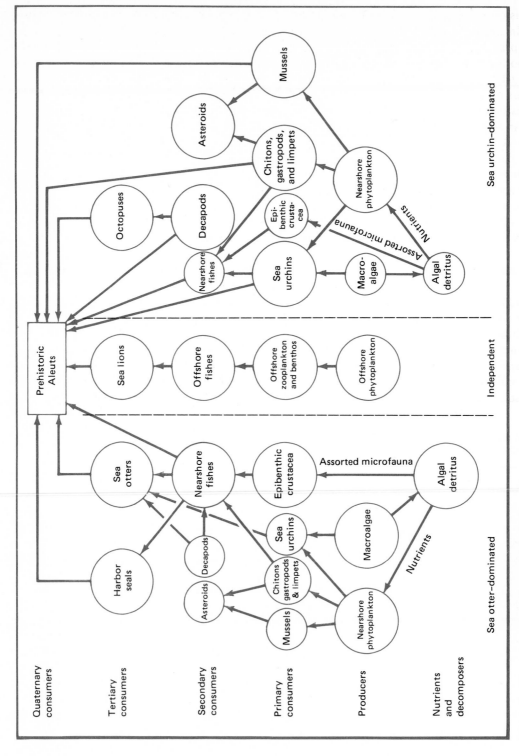

Figure 3 The food web of the prehistoric Aleuts.

web is often used. Humans are a good example. In many environments, they tend to be both primary and secondary consumers. They eat both plants and animals. In some cases, they may be third- and even fourth-level consumers because they also eat other carnivores. Prehistoric Aleuts, for instance, made use of almost all the food chains in their environment. By eating chitons, they were secondary consumers. By eating nearshore fish, which are secondary consumers, they became third-level consumers. Finally, by sometimes eating sea lions, which eat offshore fish, the Aleuts became fourth-level consumers. (See Figure 3.)

The Biosphere. One final level in the biotic hierarchy remains: the *biosphere.* It is the sum total of all the material and energy involved in living systems on the earth (Salthe, 1972). Often, however, it is divided into the world's two major ecological domains—the sea and the land. The marine biosphere includes all the communities that inhabit the sea, and the terrestrial biosphere is made up of all land-

"What do you mean, you're going to work your way up the food chain?" (Bill Maul)

dwelling communities. Except to note in passing that the biosphere concept helps us to understand the interactions between ecosystems, we will not be concerned with what occurs at this level.

Adaptation and Evolution

Evolution is the study of how and why changes occur in life forms. The traditional unit of evolutionary study is the population. Individuals do not evolve, at least in the genetic sense. Even though a person's anatomy and physiology may change during development and aging, the genetic composition remains the same throughout life. The genes we are born with are those that we will pass on to the next generation. However, the individuals that make up a population do not all survive into adulthood. Those that do will not all have the same number of children. As a result, the genetic composition of the population changes from one generation to the next. This process of change, called *adaptation,* allows the population to respond biologically, or *adapt,* to changes in the biotic and abiotic environments.

Because populations are part of ecosystems, any attempt to understand adaptation and evolution must be based on the sort of ecological relationships we discussed in the first part of this chapter. The most important concept here is the niche, the population's position within the interactions that take place in an ecosystem. If ecosystems were stable throughout time, and biotic and abiotic interactions remained the same, the niche of each population within the community would never change. Indeed, the niche structure of some animals has remained constant throughout enormous amounts of time. Seahorses have remained almost unchanged for tens of millions of years. However, such permanence is unusual, because the abiotic features of the earth are continually changing.

The ability of niche structure to respond to changes depends on the specialization of the population. If the population has a very specialized diet and its members show little variation, its ability to adapt to environmental change is limited. The koala bear depends almost entirely on the eucalyptus tree for its food. If a change in the abiotic environment decimated the eucalyptus population, the survival of the koala would be threatened.

Humans, however, occupy an extremely diversified niche. If one food source is eliminated, human populations can switch to a different source. And humans rely on learned behavior for a great part of their interactions with the biotic and abiotic environments. Learning makes human niche structure more flexible than that of other animals. This flexibility has two great advantages. It permits us to exploit diverse ecosystems, and it reduces the number of individuals that die as the population adapts to environmental change. Populations that have depended on biological adaptations (including our early humanlike ancestors) have lost those individuals who could not adjust to environmental change.

Selection

The mechanism by which populations biologically adjust to a changing environment was first suggested by Charles Darwin. Darwin recognized that individuals that make up populations differ in their biological and behavioral characteristics. In ecological terms, their ecospaces (personal interactions with the environment) are different. As the environment changes, the ability of individual ecospaces to adjust to the new circumstances varies. Some individuals possess biological and behavioral characteristics that permit them to survive in the changed environmental conditions. Others do not. Because the characteris-

tics of the survivors will be different from the characteristics of those who do not survive, a new set of biological-behavioral interactions with the changed environmental conditions will emerge, reflecting the attributes of the survivors. The population's niche will have changed, or evolved, as a consequence of changes in the environment.

Darwin thought that selection operated primarily through differences in mortality. That is, individuals unable to adjust to the new environment would not survive to reproduce. However, modern neo-Darwinian biologists see that differences in fertility may also play an important role. An environmental change may not be severe enough to cause the immediate death of unadjusted members of the population. Instead, they may have fewer children than the better-adjusted members. Since (1) the biological and behavioral characteristics of many animals are inherited from their parents and (2) the better-adjusted individuals will contribute more offspring to the composition of later generations, the number of individuals with advantageous traits in the population will gradually increase.

Normally, evolution by natural selection occurs slowly over hundreds of generations. But there are a few cases in which selection has transformed a species almost instantaneously, compared to more usual rates. One of the best-studied cases is the phenomenon of industrial melanism among certain light-colored moths in England. One of these moths, *Biston betularia,* is known to have had a light color in the early 1800s, which permitted it to blend into the pale lichen-covered tree trunks of its environment. In 1848, less than 1 percent existed as dark variants. As industry developed during the course of the century, soot darkened the tree trunks. When this occurred, the birds that ate the moths were able to find the light ones more easily on the darkened trees. Generation by generation, fewer of the light-colored moths were able to survive and reproduce. The dark-colored moths, because they were camouflaged against the dark trees, survived and reproduced in greater numbers. By 1898 about 95 percent of the population consisted of the dark variant. Since the moth produces only one set of offspring a year, only 50 generations were required for the frequency of dark-colored moths to increase 95 times in the population (Kettlewell, 1961).

Two generalizations apply to the process of evolution. The first is that evolution is *opportunistic.* Selection cannot create wholly new anatomy or physiology; it can only operate on the individual variations that already exist in the population. Characteristics that may prove to be useful in new environmental circumstances must be possessed by some individuals in the population before natural selection can operate on them. Black moths could not have become the most common form in industrial England unless some members of the original population possessed the color. In the new environment, made up of sooty trees, the black moths had an advantage that permitted them to survive better and reproduce more than the white-colored moths. If the combination of characteristics necessary for survival in new environmental conditions does not exist in the population, then the population will become extinct.

Evolution is also irreversible. Selection molds a population whose interaction with other niches and with its abiotic environment permits its own survival. After a set of biological and behavioral characteristics has become common among the members of a population, the former set of adaptations will not return, even if environmental conditions revert to the original state. Any single trait can be reversed by selective breeding, but an entire series of traits cannot be recreated.

Random Evolutionary Forces

Selection produces a population whose members are adapted to the environment. The entire process of natural selection occurs in response to, and is therefore oriented toward, changes in the environment.

Two other evolutionary phenomena also produce biological change, but they occur without influence from the environment. They produce changes that may or may not be adaptive. The first of these is called *genetic drift.* In all sexually reproducing populations, particularly small ones, the genetic composition of one generation varies from that of the preceding generation, due to certain random processes. There exists an easily calculable chance that some of each individual's genes will not become part of the germ cells that will create new individuals. The smaller the number of offspring that one has, the greater the chance that this will occur. Thus, in small populations there is a good chance that some genes may be lost from one generation to the next. Although genetic drift does cause changes in the biological makeup of the species, it is thought to be more important in the evolution of small local populations.

The second kind of random evolution is called *gene flow.* When members of a local population exchange mates with a nearby group (as often occurs among humans), genes that control traits that have evolved in one ecosystem may be acquired by members of the other. If the gene continues to spread from one population to the next, the biological nature of the species may also begin to change.

Although both drift and flow give a certain amount of biological variability to the population, the new variants are also subject to natural selection. A trait does not spread by way of gene flow unless it offers an advantage (or at least no disadvantage) in new environments. New gene combinations arising from the action of genetic drift do not persist unless they make survival easier for their possessors. Thus, natural selection in the long run is probably the most important of the evolutionary processes.

Normally, the number of niches in an ecosystem gradually increases. Usually, the creation of new niches is less rapid in harsh environments (those with severely limiting abiotic features) than it is in environments with few abiotic limits. In harsh environments, niches tend to be more broadly defined. More plant and animal species are part of each niche. For example, only a limited number of primary consumers, each depending on a number of different plant resources, can be supported in such areas. Second- and third-level consumers, such as human hunters and gatherers, eat a large number of different foods (as we saw in the Aleuts example) and also have small populations. The low precipitation of deserts and the extreme cold of the Arctic thus reduce diversity and keep the number of possible niches low.

In areas where there are few abiotic limiting factors, however, a variety of plants exists, thereby permitting a great diversity of animal life. Each of the many consumer populations is small and specialized for eating particular plants. Likewise, each member of a large number of small, carnivorous populations feeds on a relatively small number of prey species. Diversification is more rapid in this dense matrix of life because there are more potential niches.

Speciation

As a population evolves in response to changing environmental factors, one of two evolutionary pathways will emerge. The population may persist as a single biological unit through time. The biological characteristics of its membership may change from generation to generation because of individual differences in fertility and mortality, but each generation is directly descended from all earlier ones. This unilinear evolutionary pathway is referred to as *anagenic evolution* (Dobzhansky,

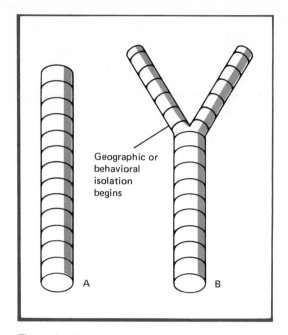

Figure 4 **Anagenic and cladogenic evolution.**
In anagenic evolution (A), the population evolves as a single group. In cladogenic evolution (B), speciation divides the original population into two or more separate populations.

1962). This type of evolution has characterized the human past for at least the last 1 million years. In the other case, the original population may split into two or more distinct biological units. This type of evolutionary pathway, which is responsible for the creation of biological diversity, is called *cladogenic evolution* (Dobzhansky, 1962). Cladogenic evolution is most likely to occur among populations whose interactions with the biotic and abiotic environment have been successful enough to produce an increase in their number and ecological range.

When two or more populations diverge, and new niches are created, the populations may become reproductively isolated from each other. When they are no longer able to reproduce, *speciation* is said to have occurred. There are two basic ways in which speciation can occur. It can begin when part of an expanding population moves to a new area, thereby creating a physical separation between the new and old groups. This is referred to as *allopatric speciation.* It can also begin when parts of an original population no longer interbreed, though they coexist in the same area. This divergence is known as *sympatric speciation.*

Allopatric Speciation. The emergence of two or more distinct econiches, whether due to behavior or to geographic separation, is a necessary condition for speciation. Before allopatric speciation can occur, individuals must migrate into a new area and establish a subpopulation. This subpopulation at first tends to exploit the new ecosystem in the same way that the original population exploited the original area. In doing so it may find itself in direct competition with other populations for the same food resources, or it may find that the new area lacks some or all of the food sources that were in the original area. If the migrant subpopulation is to survive, it will have to establish new relationships with the unique biotic and abiotic features of the new environment; that is, it will have to develop a new niche. Selection will begin to favor those individuals whose characteristics either minimize competition with other species or allow them to overwhelm competing populations in this new ecosystem and establish themselves in their place. The amount of biological divergence between the original and migrant populations depends on how different the two ecosystems are. The greater the difference, the more radical the divergence of the two niches.

Sympatric Speciation. In sympatric speciation, behavioral isolation can produce an effect comparable to geographic isolation. Rather than migrating, a subpopulation modifies its behavior, thereby creating a new niche in the same ecosystem. Using the same food resources at different times of the day is a common way this can occur. Many of the most primitive primate populations have survived because at night they use the same food resources that more advanced primates rely on during the day. Changes in courtship behavior can also lead to niche divergence. Such behavior in many fish, reptiles, and birds is designed to excite females before mating. If environmental forces cause a change in courtship behavior, it may not evoke the proper female response, and reproduction will not occur. The two populations separated in this fashion begin to develop distinct niches that do not overlap.

The Role of Reproductive Isolation. Though two subpopulations may gradually diverge in their differing niches, this process is not enough to cause speciation. *Reproductive isolation,* the absense of interbreeding between two populations, must be maintained over a long period of time for speciation to occur. Humans are distributed throughout the world in numerous subpopulations, yet we remain a single species. In part this is because we rely on culture to reduce the differences between environments, thus reducing differences in selective pressures. It also occurs because human populations are not reproductively isolated from one another. Obviously, a small population of Eskimos in the Arctic is not likely to interbreed with every other human population in the world. However, because they exchange mates with neighboring groups, and because these groups exchange mates with their neighbors, and so on, there is created a web of genetic relationships that binds all human populations together into a single biological entity. Because of this, no human population is reproductively isolated from others long enough to become a separate species.

Thus, the following steps are essential to cause speciation:

1. Behavioral or geographic separation must occur.

2. The niche structure of the two populations must begin to diverge.
3. The two populations must become reproductively isolated.

When members of the two populations are no longer capable of interbreeding, even if contact is restored, speciation has occurred.

Evolutionary Trends

Adaptive Radiation. The fossil record sometimes shows the emergence of a great many species, seemingly at once. This rapid specia-tion is called *adaptive radiation.* It often occurs in environments where there are many potential but unoccupied niches. It can be inferred that the 14 different finch species discovered in the Galápagos islands or nearby are the result of adaptive radiation. A single ancestral population gave rise to subpopulations that exploited various niches in the islands. Today, one of the tree finch species has a parrotlike beak and is basically vegetarian. Another climbs trees to hunt insects in the cracks of bark. Still others have become ground feeders (Boughey, 1973). The behavior and biology of these subpopulations have gradually

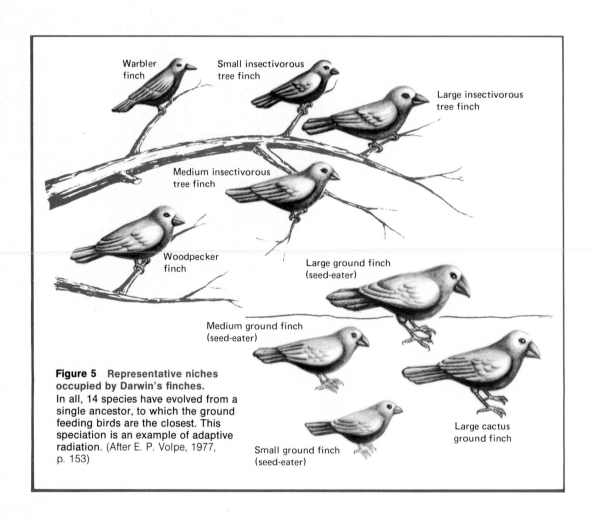

Figure 5 Representative niches occupied by Darwin's finches.
In all, 14 species have evolved from a single ancestor, to which the ground feeding birds are the closest. This speciation is an example of adaptive radiation. (After E. P. Volpe, 1977, p. 153)

Warbler finch
Small insectivorous tree finch
Large insectivorous tree finch
Medium insectivorous tree finch
Woodpecker finch
Large ground finch (seed-eater)
Medium ground finch (seed-eater)
Small ground finch (seed-eater)
Large cactus ground finch

become specialized for particular food resources. These behavioral characteristics eventually caused reproductive isolation and, in this case, a type of sympatric speciation.

A comparable event may have occurred when the earlier primates began to adapt to living in trees. The fossil record shows that in a very short time a large number of anatomically specialized populations developed. This is taken as evidence that a large number of different arboreal niches were exploited, explaining the subsequent emergence of many different arboreal primate species.

Parallelism and Convergence. In widely separated but similar environments throughout the world, certain plants and animals have numerous similarities. The existence of these similarities can be explained as a result of one of two long-term evolutionary trends: parallelism or convergence.

Parallelism occurs when two closely related species or groups of species begin to exploit similar but geographically separate ecosystems in similar ways. Parallelism occurred in the evolution of the primates as the North and South American continental plates drifted away from the European and African continental plates, splitting similar species into two groups. Each one independently began to evolve its own highly efficient arboreal adaptations. Today the biological and behavioral characteristics of the New World monkeys inhabiting the rain forests of Central and South America parallel those of the Old World monkeys, which live in the rain forests of Africa and Asia.

Convergence occurs when two unrelated species or groups of species independently evolve similar biological and behavioral characteristics because of the similarity of their niche structure. Whales, porpoises, seals, and sea lions are mammals that are evolutionarily more closely related to land mammals than they are to fish. Yet, because they occupy a marine niche, their physical and behavioral

characteristics have converged with those of more traditional marine vertebrates such as fish. These similarities are therefore the result of different biologies making similar adaptations to similar environments.

Even though a whale's flippers and the fins of a fish perform similar functions, their structures are different. Such structural similarities, deriving from different evolutionary origins and occurring as a result of convergent evolution, are called *analogies. Homologies,* in contrast, are similar in structure because of common ancestry, regardless of function. The whale's flipper, a bird's wing, and the human arm all share certain similarities. The number of bones in each of these organisms remains the same. However, the structure has been modified in each case to perform a different function.

Coevolution. In some cases, two populations undergo *coevolution:* They become so dependent on each other that any changes in one niche immediately redefine the other. Sometimes the association is so close that the extinction of one causes the extinction of the other. Such a link may have existed between the now extinct dodo bird and the *Calvaria* tree in Mauritius, an island in the western Indian Ocean. The dodo bird ate the seed-bearing fruit of the tree. As it did so, only trees with seeds encased in a thick-walled covering survived. This casing protected the seeds from the dodo's digestive tract. Unfortunately, these casings made germination impossible without the bird's help. As the fruit and its seeds passed through the bird's gizzard, the tough casings were reduced to the point that germination could take place after excretion. When humans exterminated the last dodos in 1681, they removed the only natural means of preparing the *Calvaria* seeds for germination. In 1973, only 13 ancient, dying trees remained. Now, however, the *Calvaria* population may be restored by mechanical preparation of the seeds (Temple, 1977).

Marsupial mouse

House mouse

Flying phalanger

North American flying squirrel

Rabbit bandicoot

Cottontail rabbit

Figure 6 **Adaptive radiation and convergence among the Australian marsupials.**
The marsupials have radiated into a number of species, many of which resemble unrelated animals adapted to similar niches in other parts of the world. (After E. P. Volpe, 1977, p. 176)

The Human Impact on Ecosystem Evolution

In this chapter we have for the most part discussed ecosystem structure and evolution as they occur without the impact of human culture. Some scientists feel that during the long period when humans were hunters and gatherers their impact on ecosystems was minor (Watson & Watson, 1969). But today human agricultural and industrial technology has major effects on many of the ecosystems of the world.

Human exploitation frequently disturbs the tendency of ecosystems to evolve more efficient uses of energy. Energy efficiency increases naturally as ecosystem diversity increases. As more species evolve, the energy captured by the ecosystem increases and is utilized more by the organisms of the ecosystem. An ecosystem exploited extensively by humans, however, tends to have fewer species.

For example, groups that farm in the tropical rain forests of Yucatán burn off dense, highly diversified vegetation and introduce only one or two plant crops. The farmers not only destroy the vegetation but also limit the amount of food available to plant-eating animals. Thus, plant and animal species become less abundant. Furthermore, if animals compete directly with humans, the animals may be systematically exterminated. The natural tendency of agriculturalists to reduce the ecosystem's diversity is directly opposed to the natural tendency of the ecosystem to increase its diversity. In effect, agriculture diverts energy away from an intricate trophic hierarchy and into crops, which permits large numbers of humans to live in areas that would normally support only a few hunter-gatherers.

In less mature temperate and grassland environments, the soil is rich enough to permit continuous agriculture over long periods of time. Unfortunately, not all ecosystems can sustain long-term human exploitation. Very mature ecosystems, such as tropical rain forests, are quite fragile. Soil nutrients are easily leached out of the thin topsoil, and crop productivity can decline dramatically after only a few years. Under these conditions, human populations usually abandon the plot and repeat the same cycle nearby. Given enough time (somewhere between 7 and 15 years), normal plant diversity will be regen-

erated on the abandoned plot. However, as the population in such areas increases, the amount of time a plot is permitted to lie unused is reduced. If such fragile soils become overused, the ecosystem produces less energy than is required by humans, and a population catastrophe can occur. This is often given as an explanation of the collapse of the classic Mayan civilization (Ricketson & Ricketson, 1937).

Industrial societies have an even greater capacity to reduce ecosystem diversity. At the basis of this great potential is a reservoir of fossil fuels, such as oil and coal. Gasoline permits a single farmer to plant and harvest enor-

Figure 7 **The effect of agriculture on the human ecosystem.**
To the left, before agriculture, land areas could support only about 10 million people, primarily hunters and gatherers. Today, agriculture supports 4 billion people on 10 percent of the original land area. Agriculture diverts energy into livestock and crops, forms in which humans can use it efficiently. (Adapted from Brown, 1970)

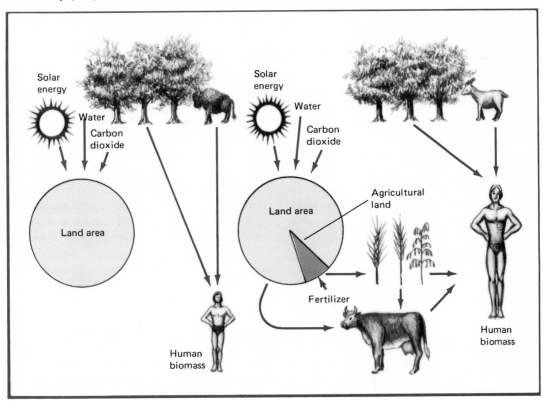

mous quantities of food. The soils of these areas can be continuously rejuvenated by using petrochemical fertilizers. The benefits as well as the drawbacks of industrialized agriculture will be discussed in another chapter.

Summary

1. Human evolution is influenced by the nonliving and living features of the environment. The relationship between humans and the environment is complicated by *culture*—an integrated network of values, symbols, and organizations—because it changes the environment and its effect on our own evolution. *Ecology* provides a theoretical umbrella under which the environmental, biological, and social sciences can be integrated with evolutionary theory.

2. Ecologists divide the environment into *abiotic* and *biotic* features.

3. Abiotic features include temperature, precipitation, solar radiation, soil, wind, and fire. Ecologists study those features that by their scarcity or overabundance influence the *biotic diversity,* the number of different kinds of life forms in an area. Essential abiotic features set limits of tolerance, outside of which life forms cannot exist.

4. Through culture, humans change abiotic conditions to create *microenvironments.* The reindeer-fur clothing of the Lapps, for example, recreates a tropical microenvironment within their cold climate.

5. Ecologists arrange the biotic features of the environment in a series of progressively more inclusive categories: the individual, the population, the community, and the biosphere.

6. The sum of the individual's interactions with other organisms and abiotic features, its *ecospace,* is studied in *autecology.*

7. *Population ecology* centers on the population—a reproductively isolated group of closely related individuals living in the same area. Its interactions with the environment make up the population's *niche.* Both the *population* and the *species* are groups of reproductively isolated individuals. Species, however, is not defined in terms of a set of local environmental conditions.

8. A *community* is a group of interrelated populations that coexist in a definable area. Together their niches make up an *ecosystem.* One way to understand the ecosystem structure is to trace the flow of energy through its *trophic* levels. *Producers,* or plants, store solar energy in their leaves; *herbivores,* or primary *consumers,* get their energy from plants; *carnivores,* or secondary consumers, eat herbivores. Finally, *decomposers* recycle the basic compounds for reuse by plants.

9. The *marine* and *terrestrial biospheres* are made up of all the communities in the sea and on the land.

10. The population is the unit of evolutionary study. As its biological and genetic makeup shifts in response to the pressures of natural selection, it is said to *adapt* to the environment. The more specialized a population's niche, the more limited is its ability to adapt to new environmental conditions.

11. As a population evolves, it follows one of two pathways. It may persist as a single biological unit through time (*anagenic evolution*) or undergo *speciation* and split into two or more distinct units (*cladogenic evolution*).

12. *Allopatric speciation* occurs as a result of expansion into a new area; *sympatric speciation* results in the behavioral isolation of groups living in the same area. Speciation occurs most rapidly in rich environments, which hold many potential niches.

13. Evolutionary trends include *adaptive radiation, parallelism, convergence,* and *coevolution.*

14. Agricultural and industrial technologies often decrease the diversity of ecosystems, increasing their fragility and decreasing the efficiency with which they absorb energy.

4

The Primates

OST people do not give too much thought to our closest animal "relatives," the primates. We tend to think of them in terms of the monkeys or apes we see in zoos. However, *primatologists* (scientists who study the biology and behavior of primates) have shown that this group, which includes the prosimians, monkeys, apes, and humans, is highly diverse and very versatile. As we mentioned in Chapter 2, the work of primatologists has been used to assist in the interpretation of our evolutionary past, as well as to define (both biologically and behaviorally) the uniqueness of humans. Surprisingly, though, scientists began collecting detailed knowledge about the biology of primates only about a century ago. Studies of primate behavior began systematically only after the end of World War II. Even today, however, detailed information on the behavior of many primates is lacking.

This chapter will review the history of our knowledge of, and attitudes toward, primates and describe the different types of primates that are living today. We shall also introduce principles of classification and show how they are used to organize the primates. Along the way, we shall indicate how different groups of primates are distinguished from one another. We shall use this technique to show the traits that humans share with other groups, as well as to isolate those features that are uniquely ours.

The History of the Knowledge of Primates

Humans have always been fascinated by the other primates. Past civilizations were aware of their almost-human qualities long before evolutionists began to suggest that we shared a common ancestry with the apes.

Over the ages, nonhuman primates have been the objects of ridicule as well as worship, superstition as well as scientific observation. That they should provoke emotional reactions in humans is not surprising, for in many ways they remind us very much of ourselves. Today, scientists are probing the physical and social characteristics of primates for clues to our own biological evolution and behavioral background. But present attitudes toward nonhuman primates have emerged from a long and checkered history.

Ancient Conceptions of Primates

Early civilizations in India, Mesopotamia, and Egypt were aware of many types of primates. Langurs and macaques were native to India, and although no primates lived in Egypt, a variety lived in the surrounding areas—Mauretania, Libya, and lands to the south. These primates reached Egypt as objects of trade and as tribute payments before 4000 B.C. (McDermott, 1938). Primates and images of them reached Mesopotamia from Egypt beginning about 3000 B.C., because there was much trade between the two countries. In all three of these cultures monkeys were sacred.

Egyptian tomb painting of Hapi, a guardian spirit of the dead. (Brian Brake, Photo Researchers, Inc.)

Monkey Worship. Religious statues of the hamadryas baboon have been dated as far back as 3500 to 4000 B.C. in Egypt. To the ancient Egyptians the baboon was the symbol and the representative of Thoth, the god of wisdom, learning, and magic. Thoth was also god of the moon. Female baboons were sacred, because their monthly menstrual cycles were thought to be regulated by the moon. The baboon was also associated with time-keeping. This idea was based on the belief that during the two annual equinoxes baboons cry out regularly once an hour (Morris & Morris, 1966).

Some living baboons were considered more sacred than others. Baboons were believed to have taught Thoth the sacred hieroglyphics or sacred writing that he used in his role as a scribe for the gods. So temple priests gave a pen-and-tablet test to baboons to see which ones could write. The animals that in the opinion of the priests passed the test were most sacred. Accordingly, they were housed in the temples and fed the finest wines and roasted meats.

Baboons were believed to play a role in the afterlife. Along with three other guardian spirits, a god named Hapi, depicted with a human body and the head of a baboon, was thought to protect the dead when they appeared for their final judgment before Osiris, god of the dead (Morris & Morris, 1966).

In Mesopotamia monkeys were cult animals sacred to some god, though their exact religious meaning is unclear (McDermott, 1938). Representations of unidentified monkeys suggest that early artists found these exotic animals amusing as well as sacred. A limestone slab found in front of a temple, for instance, shows a monkey sitting at a table and serving drinks from a bowl to the members of an all-animal orchestra.

The hanuman monkey, a larger langur, has been worshiped in India for thousands of years. Originally it was seen as the representative of a god who guarded villages. Every new settlement immediately put up a statue of the monkey god Hanuman to ensure his protection (Morris & Morris, 1966).

Indian reverence for monkeys has been furthered by the epic legends of the noble god Rama, described in the *Ramayana*. Hanuman and his monkey followers performed many heroic feats to help Rama rescue his wife from the king of the demons. Grateful to Hanuman for these and other services, Hindus still protect and worship their primate descendants. The sacred langurs are cared for in temples by priests. Monkeys are graciously tolerated, even when they do great damage to gardens and orchards. And until recently, if any visitor thoughtlessly killed a hanuman monkey, the outraged Hindus considered it their sacred duty to avenge his death by killing the visitor (Morris & Morris, 1966).

Early Scientific Studies of Primates

In contrast to the cultures that viewed primates religiously, the ancient Greeks and Romans made attempts to study monkeys and apes from a scientific point of view. They examined and dissected primate specimens and compared them with one another and with humans in attempts to classify them. Their understanding of primates, however, was always hindered by the tendency to interpret them as if they were some form of humans.

The great Greek philosopher and naturalist Aristotle (384–322 B.C.) was the first to attempt a scientific description of primates. Unlike many other writers, he apparently examined actual specimens. Aristotle's classification scheme was very simple. He divided the primates into apes, baboons, and monkeys. His primate family did not include humans, though Aristotle noted that these three creatures were similar in some ways to humans. He did not suggest that these likenesses had anything to do with a common ancestry.

Although Aristotle's classification scheme left too much out, his description of the Barbary ape in his *Historia Animalium* is fairly accurate. He noted striking likenesses between ape and human facial features (nostrils, ears, teeth, and eyelashes), breasts, distribution of hair, arms, and arm movements. But one aspect of Aristotle's description later caused much confusion. He wrote that dissection of such creatures showed their internal parts were just like those of humans. In fact, they are not. This incorrect assumption was shared by other writers of the time, and the error was not pointed out until the sixteenth century (McDermott, 1938).

It was not until several hundred years later that Galen (A.D. 129–199), a Greek physician at the Roman court, made a significant addition to knowledge about primates. Although Galen was mainly interested in studying how the human body worked, he could not study it directly. Instead, he was forced to rely mostly on dissections and experiments with similar animals—especially monkeys—because dissection of humans was largely forbidden. Although he was aware of five different kinds of primates, he preferred the Barbary ape for his physiological experiments because it had the most upright, human posture. In the course of his dissection, he made up the most complete body of anatomical information since Aristotle. Like Aristotle, however, he wrongly assumed that the internal organs of monkeys matched those of humans. And, like Aristotle, Galen saw likenesses between primates and humans, but did not suggest that there might be any relationship between these two forms of life. Galen did, however, make valuable contributions to the knowledge of anatomy and physiology. He discovered, for instance, that the brain controls the muscles and nerves (Morris & Morris, 1966; McDermott, 1938).

The Middle Ages

During the European Middle Ages scholars retreated from firsthand scientific observation. They considered Galen's works to be authoritative statements to be copied and studied but not improved with new research. As a result, little was learned about primate anatomy and physiology for 1,500 years. Speculation replaced analysis and centered on ape behavior and intelligence, which always were judged by human standards. Apes came to be thought downright evil. Their tendency to remove parasites from one another's fur, a social behavior known as grooming, was cited by one writer as proof that these "monstrous beasts" relished unclean food and would even feast on the vermin they picked off one another's heads. Since captive monkeys were known to bite, scream, and behave aggressively when provoked, they were thought to have evil dispositions (Morris & Morris, 1966).

Despite their revulsion toward monkeys and apes, medieval Europeans nonetheless had to admit some disturbing likenesses between themselves and these hairy creatures. They therefore searched for some distinguishing human trait that would clearly set them above the apes. Christian theologians gave an answer: reason. Reason was believed to be God's gift to humans alone when He created all forms of life. It was believed that monkeys could only mimic or "ape" humans.

Growing Awareness of the Primates

Although ridicule of primates continued well into the nineteenth century, anatomical knowledge of them began to increase somewhat during the late Renaissance. In the sixteenth century, a brilliant Belgian physician, Vesalius (1514–1564), renewed Galen's efforts to base studies of comparative anatomy on observation rather than on reading. He showed that Galen's long-accepted descriptions of human anatomy were inaccurate, because they were based on dissections of monkeys. Although this claim was fiercely attacked, it led to more careful studies of human anatomy. Soon it was impossible for scientists to overlook the differences between primates and humans.

In 1699, Edward Tyson, an English doctor, dissected a chimpanzee for the first time. He found that his specimen resembled humans in 48 ways, and monkeys in only 34 ways. Because it was not exactly like humans or monkeys, Tyson decided that it must be an "intermediate link" between the two.

During the eighteenth century taxonomists tried to classify the primates then being discovered in exotic lands. In 1735 Carolus Linnaeus published his *Systema Naturae*. In this work he made the revolutionary suggestion that humans, monkeys and chimpanzees, and sloths (now not considered primates) could be grouped in the same order—*Anthropomorpha*—on the basis of their physical similarities. He did not mean to imply an evolutionary relationship among these animals. In accordance with beliefs of the time, this grouping mirrored the pattern of the original creation.

During the nineteenth century awareness of the variety of primate types increased greatly. Confusion over how the various primates looked and acted was gradually cleared up as more of the creatures were shipped to Europe for study and classification. Among them was the gorilla, the one great ape not previously examined by Western scientists. At the same time, precise studies of the chimpanzee and orangutan pointed up their physical similarities to each other and to humans.

Darwin used a large amount of primate research in *The Descent of Man,* published in 1871. In this book he stated the theory that he had only hinted at in *The Origin of Species:* Humans are similar to the apes because both have evolved from the same remote ancestor. Darwin held that the physical, mental, and moral differences between humans and their animal relatives are only a matter of degree. A careful observer of the behavior of animals, he noted that they seem to be able to feel a degree of jealousy, devotion, and happiness. He remarked that monkeys used sticks and rocks as tools and that the more complex primates had a sense of curiosity, the ability to do simple reasoning, and a means of communicating with each other.

The Victorians reluctantly began to accept some of Darwin's ideas. The study of primates was therefore changed by two new attitudes. Since primates were now to be considered relatives, Victorians wanted to learn all they could about them. But to avoid disgracing themselves by acknowledging their "poor relations," the Victorians tended to exaggerate the "higher" qualities of the apes (Morris & Morris, 1966).

Studies of Primate Societies. Although anatomical studies of the nonhuman primates have not stopped, twentieth-century primatologists are more and more studying primate societies. A growing number of systematic studies have allowed modern primatologists to gradually do away with the cloud of superstition and emotion that has obscured the nonhuman primates.

Many of the early studies of primate social behavior emphasized their aggressiveness, hostility, and homicidal tendencies. This violent behavior was apparently a result of overcrowding and artificial grouping in the zoos where primates were first studied. The first scientist to try to organize the principles of primate social behavior, Sir Solly Zuckerman, noted that the atypical sex ratio of baboons in the London Zoo was causing them to behave aggressively. Male hamadryas baboons generally collect harems, and in the colony at the London Zoo there were 39 adult males and only 9 adult females (Zuckerman, 1932).

Primatologists quickly gave up studying zoo populations and began to study monkeys in special primate laboratories. In 1930 Robert and Ada Yerkes, for example, began studying chimpanzees at a one-acre compound in Orange Park, Florida. Although the compound was a more natural setting, it was still far from ideal. The pine trees within it, for instance, soon died from all the climbing and branch-breaking that went on.

During the 1930s primatologists finally began taking to the field in order to observe the social behavior of primates in their natural environments. C. R. Carpenter began the trend with his lengthy observations of howler monkeys in Panama, spider monkeys in Central America, and gibbons in Thailand. These were the first really good field studies of primates.

World War II interrupted research, but in the 1950s both laboratory and field studies went on briskly. Harry Harlow and his colleagues at the University of Wisconsin studied the psychology of infant rhesus monkeys in experiments using dummy mothers made of terry cloth and of wire. In the field Irven De Vore and Sherwood Washburn did landmark studies of the organization of baboon troops. Meanwhile, Japanese observation of macaques was yielding new insights into the ability of these primates to adopt learned behavior. Recent studies, such as those of Jane Van Lawick-Goodall (1971), have begun to produce in-depth social studies of single primates.

In many areas our knowledge of the primates is still very scanty. But today there is general agreement among scientists that we humans belong to the biological order Primates.* We share this classification with about 200 other species. We are all thought to have evolved from a common mammal ancestor about 70 million years ago. This ancestor was probably a small insect-eating creature that spent its life in trees. Diverse primate lines, some of which are now extinct, have radiated from this remote ancestor through varying niches in varying ecosystems. But all still show a degree of anatomical, behavioral, and biochemical similarity. In this section we shall look at how the living primates are classified to see where we stand in relationship to the rest of the primate order.

What Is a Primate?

It is not as easy as it might seem to define the characteristics of a primate. Scientists do not agree on the boundaries of this biological grouping. Some experts include in the primate order the tree shrew, a small Southeast Asian creature that looks like a skinny squirrel with a long snout.

Others argue that the animal does not share certain traits common to primates. But when it comes to defining exactly what these shared traits are, taxonomists run into problems. Primates are not like marsupials, for example, which can be identified on the basis of a single characteristic, their pouches. On the whole, living primates are distinctive only for an anatomical and behavioral pattern that has enabled them to live in a

*When capitalized, the word *Primates* (pry-*may*-teez) refers to the order.

variety of environmental settings (Buettner-Janusch, 1973).

Physical Characteristics

Primates can be defined in terms of certain physical traits that they share to some degree. Some of these characteristics are not unique to primates; they are also possessed by members of other orders. The original primate ancestor inherited these *generalized,* or primitive, *characteristics* from its mammal forebears. Features such as the five digits on primate hands and feet are homologous to the basic structure of front and hind paws of other mammals. As they adapted to new environments, the primates evolved certain *specialized characteristics,* such as grasping hands. Primates are, therefore, defined not by a single trait, such as the marsupial's pouch, but by a set of physical traits, or "evolutionary tendencies" (LeGros Clark, 1965). The generalized characteristics of primates are:

1. A primitive limb structure. The generalized skeletal features include a five-finger, five-toe pattern *(pentadactyl).*
2. A simple tooth pattern with grinding molars. This "conservative" pattern contrasts with the very specialized teeth other mammals have developed. The canine teeth of carnivores, for example, are specialized for tearing flesh, and the tusks of elephants are specialized for uprooting.

The specialized characteristics of primates include:

1. *Prehensility* (the ability to grasp) of hands and sometimes feet. This, like most of the other specialized characteristics, evolved as an adaptation to an *arboreal,* or tree-living, existence.
2. A collarbone capable of supporting flexible sideways movements of the arms.
3. Flat nails at the tips of the digits (fingers

and toes) and sensitive touch pads underneath. These features aid in an arboreal habitat by allowing grasping instead of clawing. In some primates, a claw (called a "toilet claw") appears on one of the digits.

4. A thumb that is mobile and can be moved opposite some or all of the other fingers, a trait called *opposability.* This ability allows the more complex primates to manipulate objects with their hands. Other mammals grasp objects with their teeth.

5. Changes in the senses of smell and sight, coupled with a flattening of the face. The olfactory (smell) center of the brain is progressively smaller in higher primates, as they depend more and more on sight. The visual area of the brain and the anatomical structures for seeing are increasingly emphasized, for this sense is most important in exploiting an arboreal niche. The muzzle of early mammals is replaced by a smaller nose with a less protruding mouth. The eyes are shifted toward the front of the face. These changes allow *stereoscopic vision,* in which images from each eye overlap to form a three-dimensional picture. Tree dwellers need this ability in order to judge distances from limb to limb. Many primates can see a broad range of colors as well. The high visual acuity of higher primates contributes to their ability to manipulate objects as well as to better eye-hand coordination.

6. Enlargement of the brain, especially the cerebral cortex, which directs the higher intellectual functions. The brain is large not only in size but also in relationship to the rest of the body.

7. Complex reproductive strategy. This strategy includes a longer gestation period and greater efficiency in getting nutrients to the fetus. A smaller litter size results from these changes. The period of dependence by infants on adult caretakers is also lengthened, adding more opportunities for social learning and intellectual growth.

Although all primates share these physical characteristics, they vary in the degree to which they express them. In general, primates in whom these characteristics are the least developed are called "lower" or "simpler" primates. These characteristics are most developed in the "higher" or more "complex" primates.

Social Characteristics

Defining just how primates behave is even more difficult than defining their physical characteristics. Primates rarely live in isolation. Most are organized into groups in which both sexes and all ages are represented. The interactions between individuals are structured by a *dominance hierarchy* (ranking by social power) that is based on age, sex, and individual differences. Behavior is, to a great extent, learned within the context of the troop; it is not totally instinctive, as in other animals.

There are, however, huge differences among the behaviors of lower primates, monkeys, apes, and humans. A definition of primate behavior that is too general does not distinguish the order from other mammals. A system of communication, cohesive social grouping, and social ties among individuals, for instance, mark the behavior of primates and other mammals as well. More specific definitions, however, may fit certain primates but not others. For instance, to say that all primates learn social roles by living within a social group is to ignore some of the prosimians. Few of them form social groups that are even relatively permanent (Dolhinow, 1972b). We can, however, make the general statement that primates display social behavior that is similar to that of other mammals, but, particularly among the higher primates, it is much more elaborate and sophisticated.

Consider communication, for instance. We now know that animals other than primates can communicate using signals of posture, movement, scent, touch, and vocalization.

The information sent in these signals can be quite complex. A honey bee, for instance, can communicate in its waggle dance complicated directions for finding food. In this dance, all the essentials of a flight to the food are mimicked in miniature. Humans cannot only explain where food is to be found but can also discuss emotions and abstractions through the use of language. Other primates cannot talk, but the higher ones can communicate a wide range of emotions and signals. They use facial expressions and gestures, as well as the methods used by other animals.

Where Are Primates Found?

Because of their culture and technology, humans can survive in all kinds of climates and terrains. The range of nonhuman primates is not nearly as wide, but is still very broad and diverse.

Geographical Distribution. As you can see in Figure 1, all of today's nonhuman primates live fairly close to the equator (within 35 degrees). The only primates living in the western hemisphere are the so-called *New World monkeys,* which inhabit Central and South America. Most primates are found in the eastern hemisphere. The *Old World monkeys* live in Africa and Asia. Various groups of the primitive primates called prosimians are found in these areas too, as are the anthropoid apes. Gibbons and orangutans live in the Far East, and our closest "relatives," chimpanzees and gorillas, live in western and central Africa.

Habitats. As we discussed earlier, most primates have evolved specializations for life in the trees, and most still tend to live in or near trees. A few primates, however, spend some or most of their time on the ground in *terrestrial* habitats. These primates are mainly found in steppes or savannas, where trees are sparse, or in forest clearings.

In South America there are no terrestrial primates. New World monkeys live in tropical rain forests, swamp forests, or lush secondary growth forests, where vegetation is growing back in natural clearings made by humans.

In Africa many primates (including chimpanzees and gorillas) live in the moist, warm, tropical rain forests. Trees there are so big and so dense that they house different species of primates at different levels. Guenons and some other monkeys prefer secondary growth in abandoned clearings in the rain forest. Some chimpanzees and gorillas live in drier mountain forests. Vervets, patas, baboons, and sometimes chimpanzees are found in grassy, semiarid, wooded steppes and in woodland savannas, where grass is tall and trees are 20 to 50 feet high.

In Asia primates live mostly in high forests, though a few live in mangrove swamps. Macaques can tolerate the colder climates of temperate zone woods in China and Japan. Heavily furred Japanese macaques, for instance, get through the winter by eating bark from bare trees. And in India some primates are thriving in human-dominated environments. The sacred hanuman langurs live in the trees surrounding villages; rhesus and bonnet macaques sleep on top of houses, temples, and railroad stations.

Classifying Primates

It would be impossible to study or understand the enormous variety of living things and their evolutionary past without some means of organizing them. Scientists have therefore arranged the primates, like all living things, in hierarchical categories called *taxa.* The organization of taxa, or *taxonomy,* that we use today is based on the system invented in 1758 by Linnaeus. He grouped organisms according to their anatomical features. Organisms that shared most or all of their physical features were placed in the same category. The fewer the number of features any two

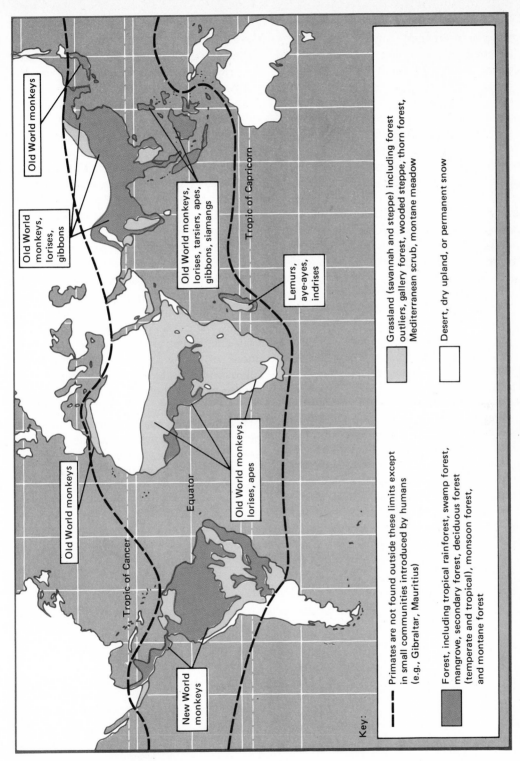

Figure 1 **Distribution of nonhuman primates.** (After Napier & Napier, 1967)

Key:

- - - Primates are not found outside these limits except in small communities introduced by humans (e.g., Gibraltar, Mauritius)

▓ Forest, including tropical rainforest, swamp forest, mangrove, secondary forest, deciduous forest (temperate and tropical), monsoon forest, and montane forest

▒ Grassland (savannah and steppe) including forest outliers, gallery forest, wooded steppe, thorn forest, Mediterranean scrub, montane meadow

☐ Desert, dry upland, or permanent snow

Old World monkeys

Old World monkeys, lorises, gibbons

Old World monkeys, lorises, tarsiers, apes, gibbons, siamangs

Lemurs, aye-ayes, indrises

Tropic of Capricorn

Old World monkeys, lorises, apes

Equator

Old World monkeys

Tropic of Cancer

New World monkeys

species share, the more likely they are to be placed in different categories.

Taxonomy in its modern use also reflects evolutionary relationships. The system takes into account to some degree the *phylogeny,* or evolutionary relationships, of the various species. Orangutans, chimpanzees, gorillas, and humans, for instance, are classified together into a single superfamily, reflecting the present belief that they diverged rather recently from a common ancestor.

Taxonomic Categories. The modern classification system has 21 categories. But for our purposes there are 12 important categories to remember. They range from species to kingdom, as shown in the boxed example. Each category is a subset of the one above it. A *genus,* for example, is a grouping of similar species; a *subfamily* is a grouping of similar genera (the plural of *genus*). There is no subfamily given for humans because there is only one living species and one genus in our line.

The basic unit in this taxonomy is the *species* (though subspecies are often recognized). As you learned in Chapter 3, a species is a group of organisms that can interbreed to produce fertile offspring like themselves. Members of a species are reproductively isolated from members of other species. This modern definition replaces Linnaeus's notion that a

species approximated an ideal established by God.

Species are labeled by two Latin names. According to Linnaeus's system, the first is the genus. It is capitalized. The second is unique to the species and is not capitalized. The familiar chimpanzee, for instance, is called *Pan troglodytes. Pan* is the name of its genus. The term *troglodytes* is used to name the particular species. Some genera, such as *Homo,* contain only one living species *(Homo sapiens).* Others may contain more. *Pan* includes two: *troglodytes* and *paniscus.* Each of these species only breeds within itself. Yet they are anatomically similar, so they are both grouped in the same genus.

Although every effort has been made to bring these classifications in line with real rather than imagined similarities among organisms, the categories are arbitrary and artificial. The taxa we use are imperfect representations of the variety that actually exists. There is no such thing as the primate order in nature—it is simply a category invented by scientists to sort their data. As a result, scientists are always arguing about what the categories are and which animals belong in them. At one time, for example, the family *Pongidae* included gibbons as well as orangutans, chimpanzees, and gorillas. On the basis of recent evidence, however, the gib-

---

The Taxonomic Standing of Humans

Kingdom: Animalia
Phylum: Chordata
Subphylum: Vertebrata
Class: Mammalia
Order: Primates
Suborder: Anthropoidea
Infraorder: Catarrhini
Superfamily: Hominoidea
Family: Hominidae
Subfamily: ———
Genus: Homo
Species: *Homo sapiens*

bon has been taken out of *Pongidae* and placed into a family of its own, the *Hylobatidae*. A set of rules—*The International Code of Zoological Nomenclature*—is used to resolve ambiguities of classification. But since new information about living animals is always being discovered, many categories are constantly being revised.

Other Factors. Anatomy does not always clearly reflect the degree of biological relationship between two species. Sometimes the physical appearance of two animals that are in fact distantly related may be very similar as a result of convergent evolution. In addition, the fossil record may not provide clear evidence of the phylogenetic relationship between two animals. Since the 1950s taxonomists have come to use two other factors to verify apparent relationships: behavioral characteristics and *serological* (or blood serum) characteristics.

Behavioral Evidence. Use of behavioral evidence in classification depends on our ability to link certain behavior with taxonomic status. This has been done successfully with some vertebrates. Song patterns, for example, have been used to classify bird species. And studies show that gestures, vocalizations, and other behavior patterns do not vary much among primate groups of the same species (Dolhinow, 1972a). At the genus level, too, behavioral similarities are being discovered.

As our knowledge of primate social behavior increases, behavior may become a more useful classificatory criterion. However, all primates share the same sort of general behavior pattern. For this reason, it is difficult to distinguish biological relationships on the basis of behavior alone.

Serological Evidence. Compared to behavioral studies, serological data have been of far greater importance in the creation of primate taxonomies. Since the 1960s researchers have been comparing various proteins in the blood to see whether the biochemical charac-

teristics of living primates show the same degree of relationship suggested by anatomical features. It is assumed that primates having similar blood proteins may be relatively closely related. Fewer similarities suggest more distant relationships.

To construct a biochemical taxonomy of the primates, researchers have studied blood serum molecules from a number of primates. The similarity of structure among these molecules is determined in a number of ways. One method uses *antibodies,* proteins formed to protect the body from biochemical structures, such as disease microorganisms, not normally found there. Most commonly, the antibody to a specific blood protein is created by injecting the protein into another animal, often a rabbit or a chicken. The foreign protein differs in shape from that performing the same function in the injected animal. As a result, the animal's immunological system reacts to the invading protein as a foreign substance and creates an antibody to help eliminate it. This antibody is then injected into a number of species related to the animal from which the original protein was extracted. If the intensity of the reaction between the antibody and the protein is similar in any two of these animals, it means that the structure of the protein is also similar. This protein similarity is then taken as evidence of a close biological relationship.

Vincent Sarich (1968) has applied this immunological technique in his study of the blood protein *albumin* among the primates. He isolated human albumin and injected it into rabbits, which then produced an antibody against that protein. The intensity of the reaction to the antibody was naturally greatest when tested with human albumin. Chimpanzee albumin reacted less strongly when tested with the rabbit-developed antibody, macaques still less strongly, and New World capuchin monkeys least strongly of all. This, of course, suggests that the structure of human albumin is more like that of the chimpanzee albumin than it is like those of the macaques and the capuchin monkeys.

Because of the great evolutionary distance between humans and rabbits, however, the antibody produced by the latter does not react differently to proteins that are very similar in structure. It reacts, for example, in the same way when tested with chimpanzee albumin as when tested with gorilla albumin. Thus, it is impossible to determine which of these two species possesses albumin more similar to that of humans. For a finer level of discrimination, the human protein may be injected in a more closely related species, such as macaques. The antibody produced by macaques does react differently to chimpanzee albumin than to gorilla albumin. This result suggests that chimpanzees are most closely related to humans.

A second approach breaks down a protein into its basic amino acid parts. Functionally similar proteins in different species are then compared in terms of the amino acids they contain. It is thought that closely related species have the fewest number of amino acid differences, and more distantly related species have the greatest number of differences. Such studies have been carried out on hemoglobin, the oxygen-carrying protein of the red blood cells. Although this method is more direct than the immunological approach, it provides data that are often difficult to interpret.

Taxonomies developed by the two approaches differ, and the results obtained by either approach also vary if the protein is changed. Analysis of serum albumin generally agrees with the classification scheme based on anatomy. It identifies our nearest "relatives" as the great apes (chimpanzees, gorillas, and orangutans), followed by the Old World monkeys, the New World primates, and then the prosimians.

Comparisons of the amino acid structure of primate hemoglobins also generally support the classification based on anatomy. But it muddles some relationships. The hemoglobins of baboons are as different from human hemoglobins as are those of the prosimians, despite the closer relationship between baboons and humans indicated by anatomical studies (Buettner-Janusch & Hill, 1965).

Despite its limitations, most taxonomists agree that the biomolecular approach, when integrated with anatomical data, can be a valuable aid in the classification of primates. Biomolecular evidence has also led most primate taxonomists to place the gibbons in a separate family. It has also helped to confirm that the African great apes—chimpanzees and gorillas—are more closely "related" to humans than is the Asian great ape, the orangutan.

Distinguishing the Living Primates

Now that we have looked at the basis for taxonomic distinctions, we can begin to sort out the primate taxa. The taxonomy we will use is summarized in Table 1 (see pp. 64–65). It differs in a few ways from others in current use, but there is no single taxonomy that is universally accepted. Note that it does not include the tree shrews in the primate category, as mentioned earlier.

In this overview of the primates we shall progressively isolate the characteristics that define humans. We have already looked at the generalized characteristics that we share with the other primates. Our distinctive human traits will come into focus as we move through increasingly narrow taxonomic categories to *Homo sapiens*. Along the way, the major taxa into which humans fall will be distinguished from those into which they do not fall.

Distinguishing Prosimii
from Anthropoidea

Prosimians are the least complex of the primates. They are distinguishable on the basis of certain primitive characteristics thought to have been possessed by the earliest primates. Some of these traits are also found among nonprimates, especially those in the order Insectivora, which includes shrews, moles, and hedgehogs. In both prosimians and insectivores the sense of smell, for instance, is very well developed. This trait is less emphasized in more complex primates in favor of sight. The eyes of prosimians are placed at the sides of the skull. Because there is a limited overlap in the fields of vision, three-dimensional sight is not fully developed in many species.

In addition to their retention of primitive characteristics, prosimian species also have many specialized characteristics. These characteristics are adaptations that have allowed prosimians to live in new areas and avoid competition with anthropoid populations. Many, for example, have developed specializations for nocturnal, or nighttime, activity. These adaptations (such as huge eyes) have cut down on their competition with diurnal, or day-living, creatures. Varying patterns

of evolution have created prosimians as unalike as the tiny froglike tarsier and the large bearlike indri. The characteristics that distinguish prosimians from the higher primates are:

1. Either of two primitive adaptations to movement in the trees: (a) modifications for clinging to vertical limbs and leaping from tree to tree (as in the tarsiers): long hindlimbs, strong hindlimb muscles, skeletal arrangement to support a vertical posture; (b) modifications for very slow climbing on all fours (as in the slow loris): short limbs, arms almost as long as the legs, mobile hip and ankle joints for hanging, short tail or none at all.
2. Ability of fingers to act in unison; inability to act separately. This arrangement allows powerful grasping, but not manipulation of objects, as in the anthropoids.
3. Claws on some digits instead of nails. These claws are called *toilet claws,* because they are used for cleaning dirt and parasites from fur and skin.
4. Primitive arrangement of the pads on the fingertips and toes. These pads aid in clinging to vertical surfaces. In more complex primates, the pads are smaller and little more than thickened skin.
5. Eyes set apart at a greater angle than in anthropoids.
6. Adaptations by some prosimians to nocturnal life. These include enlarged eyes and loss from the eye structure of retinal cones, which respond to bright light and allow color vision.
7. Large, mobile ears that can scan for sound.
8. Well-developed sense of smell. Some have *olfactory muzzles*—snouts with bare, moist tips, curved nostrils, and a tethered upper lip, attached in such a way as to allow little facial expression. The sense of smell is less emphasized in the anthropoids.

**Figure 2 Distinguishing
Prosimii from Anthropoidea**

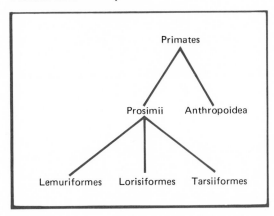

Table 1 Taxonomy of the Primate Order

Suborder	Infraorder	Superfamily	Family	Subfamily	Genus	Common Name
Prosimii (prosimians)	Tarsiiformes				Tarsius	Tarsier
	Lorisiformes	Lorisoidea	Lorisidae	Lorisinae	Loris Nycticebus Perodicticus Arctocebus	(slender lorises) (slow lorises) (pottos) (angwantibos)
				Galaginae	Galago	(galagos)
	Lemuriformes	Lemuroidea	Leumuridae	Lemurinae (true lemurs)	Lemur Hapalemur Lepilemur	(lemurs) (gentle lemurs) (weasel and sportive lemurs)
				Cheirogaleinae (small lemurs)	Cheirogaleus Microcebus Phaner	(dwarf and mouse lemurs) (mouse lemurs) (fork-marked mouse lemurs)
			Indriidae		Indri Lichanotus Propithecus	(indrises) (woolly indrises) (sifakas)
		Daubentonoidea			Daubentonia	(aye-ayes)
		Ceboidea	Cebidae (cebid monkeys)	Cibinae	Cebus Saimiri	(capuchin monkeys) (squirrel monkeys)
				Alouattinae	Alouatta	(howler monkeys)
				Aotinae	Aotus Callicebus	(night monkeys and douroucoulis) (titis)
				Atelinae	Ateles Brachyteles Lagothrix	(spider monkeys) (woolly spider monkeys) (woolly monkeys)

Anthropoidea (anthropoids)						
	Platyrrhini (New World monkeys)		Callithricidae	Callimiconinae	Callimico	(Goeldi's monkey)
				Pitheciinae	Pithecia	(sakis)
					Cacajao	(uakaris)
					Chiropotes	(sakis)
					Callithrix	(marmosets)
					Cebuella	(pygmy marmosets)
					Leontideus	(golden lion tamarins)
					Saguinus	(tamarins)
	Catarrhini (Old World primates)	Cercopithecoidea (Old World monkeys)	Cercopithecidae	Cercopithecinae	Cercopithecus	(guenons, talapoins, vervets)
					Cercocebus	(mangabeys)
					Cynopithecus	(black apes)
					Theropithecus	(gelada baboons)
					Erythrocebus	(patas monkeys)
					Macaca	(macaques)
					Papio	(baboons)
				Colobinae	Colobus	(colobus monkeys and guerezas)
					Nasalis	(the proboscis monkey)
					Presbytis	(leaf monkeys; langurs)
					Pygathrix	(douc langurs)
					Rhinopithecus	(snub-nosed monkeys; Tibetan langurs)
		Hominoidea (hominoids)	Hylobatidae		Hylobates	(gibbons; siamangs)
			Pongidae	(pongids)	Pongo	(orangutans)
					Pan	(chimpanzees)
					Gorilla	(gorillas)
			Hominidae	(hominids)	Homo	(humans)

9. Relatively large olfactory lobes in brain. There is less cortical area than in anthropoids, and ratios of brain size to body weight are smaller.

10. Dental specializations: the upper front teeth, or incisors, are very small, and the canine teeth (pointed teeth between the incisors and the grinding teeth) are large. The lower incisors and canines project forward in many species to form a *dental comb* for grooming the fur. (Adapted from Napier & Napier, 1967; Rosen, 1974; Campbell, 1974)

The Prosimians. There are three major *infraorders* in the prosimian suborder: Tarsiiformes, Lorisiformes, and Lemuriformes.

Tarsiiformes. The tarsier is the only remaining member of the once large *Tarsiiformes* infraorder. These tiny creatures, which live in Borneo and the Philippines, are equipped with a very long tail and hindlimbs for hopping from branch to branch. Their huge eyes and the pads at the ends of their fingers add to their strange froglike appearance. The special pads help them cling to smooth, vertical surfaces. Tarsiers can walk on a vertical sheet of glass. During the day they sleep clinging to a vertical branch. They wake at dusk and spend the evening hopping from tree to tree looking for insects and lizards to eat.

Lorisiformes. Nocturnal primates, *Lorisiformes* are divided into two distinct types— lorises and galagos—according to their locomotor patterns. Lorises are found in subsaharan Africa and in Asia. They are adapted to slow climbing and creeping. This movement is made possible by a very powerful grasp and strong muscles. Lorises can hang by one hindlimb while reaching for food. Insects seem to form the bulk of their diet, but they will eat almost anything from flowers to young birds.

Galagos, by contrast, leap gracefully through the trees, taking long kangaroolike hops with their strong hindlimbs. Their

The slender loris is a slow climber and creeper. This form of locomotion, together with the loris's large eyes, adapt it to a nocturnal, arboreal niche, reducing competition with other animals. (San Diego Zoo Photo)

shorter forelimbs are used to grab hold of branches when they land. They can easily leap from one vertical support to another. Galagos range from the size of large mice to the size of large rabbits. Like the lorises, they are *omnivores,* that is, they eat both plants and animals (Buettner-Janusch, 1966).

Lemuriformes. The *Lemuriformes,* which include lemurs, the indrises, and the aye-ayes, are found primarily on the island of Madagascar, off the southeast coast of Africa. They have developed many variations because of the lack of competition and predators. The members of one genus, the mouse lemurs, are smaller than a mouse; they are the tiniest living primates. The largest members of the infraorder are the indrises, which measure over three feet from head to tail. Most Lemuriformes are active during the day and at dusk, but some are nocturnal. Most are completely arboreal, different species living at different levels in the same trees.

All lemurs are wonderful acrobats. They can leap great distances, sometimes to the smallest of branches, swinging themselves up gracefully at the end of the jump. Their ability to do so is due not only to their musculature but also to unusually well-developed binocular vision. Unlike other prosimians, the lemurs avoid animal foods and seem to be highly social. Among other prosimians, only females and infants live together. But the lemurs live in troops of up to 60 members and sleep huddled in small groups with their tails wrapped around one another (Buettner-Janusch, 1966).

These ring-tailed lemurs are spectacular arboreal acrobats who move almost nonstop throughout the day. Like other Lemuriformes, they have prehensile hands and feet and nails on their digits. (Russ Kinne, Photo Researchers)

The Anthropoids. The anthropoids, too, are a diverse suborder. But they are characterized by their own shared set of specialized adaptations. These adaptations mainly allow a more effective use of arboreal environments. Forward-facing eyes permit stereoscopic vision among the anthropoids, and the visual centers of the brain are complex, allowing integration of large amounts of visual data. Depth perception and quick reaction to visual cues are essential to tree-living. Anthropoids also possess color vision, which aids in depth perception and the sighting of brightly colored fruit in trees. Adaptations for grasping and handling objects are crucial to life in trees, as well. Finally, the characteristically high brain-to-body ratio of anthropoids increases their ability to survive by agility and learning. These qualities are more appropriate in the trees than are the specializations of terrestrial animals for attack and defense, such as large horns, tusks, and claws (LeGros Clark, 1965).

Distinguishing Platyrrhini from Catarrhini

Within the suborder Anthropoidea, there are two infraorders: *Platyrrhini,* the New World monkeys, and *Catarrhini,* the Old World primates. The most important traits that distinguish these two groups are:

1. Distinctive locomotor pattern. New World monkeys usually run along branches on all fours. While feeding at the ends of small branches, they spread their weight between their hands, feet, and tails. Old World primates are more likely to leap from tree to tree, swing by their arms, or walk on the ground.
2. Tails. All New World monkeys have tails, some of which are prehensile. Although some Old World primates have tails, none are prehensile.
3. New World monkeys lack ischial callosities, which are tough pads of skin on the

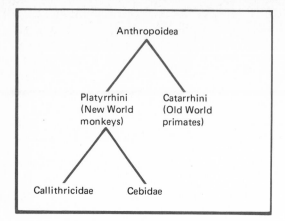

Figure 3 **Distinguishing Platyrrhini from Catarrhini**

rump that allow the animal to sit on tree limbs for long periods of time.

4. New World monkeys have flat noses with round nostrils and a broad fleshy area between them. Old World forms have nostrils that project and point downward.

5. New World monkeys have a $\frac{2.1.3.3.}{2.1.3.3.}$ dental pattern (like that of the prosimians). On each side of the jaw there are two incisors, one canine, three premolars, and three molars. Marmosets, an exception, lack the third molar. Old World forms have one less premolar, top and bottom. (Adapted from Rosen, 1974; Napier & Napier, 1967; Campbell, 1974)

The New World Monkeys. The New World monkeys live throughout the heavily forested regions of Central and South America. They are divided into two families: the Callithricidae, which include the marmosets and tamarins, and the Cebidae, which contain six subfamilies. Most New World monkeys belong to the Cebidae.

Most New World monkeys seem to spend their lives in the trees. The woolly titis, for example, live only in the smallest branches of the highest trees. They do not come down, even for water. Apparently they get enough moisture from the flowers, fruits, and nuts they eat. But the more highly evolved capuchins, which are commonly known as "organ-grinder monkeys," sometimes leave the forests to steal fruit and vegetables from farms. Squirrel monkeys, too, will sometimes come down out of the trees to catch insects.

Locomotor patterns vary among the New World monkeys. Some walk on all fours, both on the ground and on tree limbs. Others, like the spider monkeys, are best at moving in an upright position. They do so by swinging from their arms, which are longer than their legs. Spider monkeys use their strong, prehensile tails to swing and to grasp limbs as they pick fruit. Reportedly, they can jump as far as 30 feet.

We know very little about the social behavior of most New World monkeys because

A strong prehensile tail frees this spider monkey's hands and feet for a variety of uses. Though, like other New World monkeys, its thumbs are not fully opposable, its long limbs and flexible digits adapt it to a largely arboreal life. (D. J. Chivers, Anthro-Photo)

they live in thick jungles, high in the trees, where they cannot be observed easily. They have been seen in troops of up to 30 and in family bands.

Old World Primates. Within the Old World line, there are two superfamilies—*Cercopithecoidea* (or Old World monkeys) and *Hominoidea* (humans, apes, gibbons, orangutans, chimpanzees, and gorillas). The major differences that have evolved between these two groups are:

1. Most species of Old World monkeys have tails; hominoids have no tails.
2. Old World monkeys are generally smaller than hominoids.
3. Old World monkeys have prenatal development of ischial callosities. Most hominoids are not born with these rump pads, although they may grow after birth.
4. Old World monkeys have a shorter life span than the hominoids.
5. Old World monkeys have smaller brain-size to body-weight ratios as well as less complex brains than the hominoids. The cerebral cortex is especially well developed in hominoids. (Adapted from Napier & Napier, 1967; Rosen, 1974)

The distinctions here are somewhat more finely drawn than the others we have made. This is because both superfamilies are included in the same infraorder, a sign of their similarity of anatomy. They are more closely related than, say, members of suborders or infraorders.

The superfamily Cercopithecoidea contains a single family, which can be divided into two subfamilies, the Cercopithecinae and the Colobinae. The most numerous genera in the Cercopithecinae are: (1) the arboreal monkeys of the genus *Cercopithecus;* (2) the mostly arboreal mangabeys, or *Cercocebus;* and (3) the terrestrial macaques and baboons, *Macaca* and *Papio.* Langurs are the most common genus in the Colobinae subfamily.

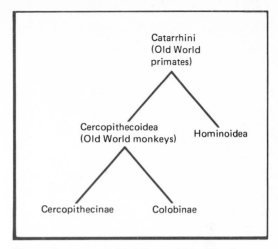

Figure 4 Distinguishing Cercopithecoidea from Hominoidea

Guenons. The cercopithecine monkeys, or guenons, are widely distributed in Africa. Although they live mostly in trees, some species come down to feed on the forest floor, in plantations, in open bush, and in savanna country. They live largely on insects, fruits, and vegetation, but will sometimes eat birds, eggs, and even small mammals. They seem to live in small groups made up of a dominant male and a small harem of females and their children.

Mangabeys. The long-tailed mangabeys, who are sometimes seen with cercopithecines, spend much of their day on the ground. Though they possess some adaptations to life in the trees, they also have some of the traits of terrestrial primates. Their hands, for instance, are more like those of the terrestrial baboon than those of totally arboreal primates. They live mostly in the swampy forests of Africa.

Baboons and Macaques. Though classed as separate genera, baboons and macaques are closely related. If they mate, they can sometimes produce fertile offspring (Buettner-Janusch, 1966). But they inhabit different ranges. The baboons live in Africa and the Arabian peninsula. The macaques range from India east to Japan. They both live mainly on

Savanna baboons. The large canine teeth and mantle of fur around the neck are unique to males and aid in aggressive displays before predators. (Irven De Vore, Anthro-Photo)

the ground, though they sleep in trees. Both have developed finely controlled hands with precision grips that function like ours.

Since terrestrial animals are much easier to watch than those that move in the treetops, the social behaviors of baboons and macaques have been studied fairly well. Baboons live in highly structured troops of 10 to 100 members. Within the troop a clear dominance hierarchy reduces tensions and provides protection from predators. The threat of predators may be the reason for their extreme *sexual dimorphism* (different physical forms for the two genders). Male and female arboreal monkeys, who face few predators and rely on their agility for fleeing, look pretty much the same. But among the ground-living baboons, the males are specialized for defense on the ground. They may be twice as big as the females, and they can put on impressive threat displays with their huge canine teeth and their great ruffs of fur at the neck (Eimerl & DeVore, 1965).

Langurs. Among these slender, long-tailed, Asiatic monkeys, group organization is not

These common langurs are arboreal leaf-eaters. Most Old World monkeys have tails (none of which are prehensile), ischial callosities, and a fully opposable thumb. (Irven De Vore, Anthro-Photo)

as important to defense. They often feed on the ground, but prefer graceful flight into the trees rather than an organized show of force. Langurs sometimes live alone and sometimes in troops. In troops the relationship between males and females is not well defined. The status of females is high when they are paired with a male. But when their infants are born the mothers seem to drop out of the status system altogether. When dominant males are found near temples, they form harems (groups of females) and actually chase away other males (Hrdy, 1977).

Distinguishing Humans from the Apes

The Apes. Finally, we shall look at the differences that divide us from the Hylobatidae (gibbons), and our closest relatives, the Pongidae (chimpanzees, gorillas, and orangutans). A list of the anatomical traits distinguishing these two groups from hominids is as follows:

1. Limited bipedal walking. Although pongids and hylobatids are better than any other nonhumans at walking bipedally in a semierect posture, they do not do so for long periods of time.
2. Short thumbs. As a result, most pongids and hylobatids have a limited precision grip.
3. Ridges of bone directly above the eyes. Pongids lack a forehead.

Figure 5 **Distinguishing humans from the apes.**

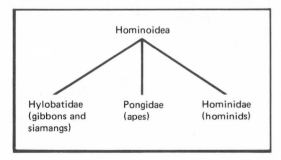

Hominoidea

Hylobatidae (gibbons and siamangs) Pongidae (apes) Hominidae (hominids)

4. Teeth specialized for a diet that includes massive quantities of fruit and vegetation. The canines, used to open fruit and strip plants, are large and projecting. To hold their heavy teeth and support the chewing of such bulky food, pongids have massive jaws that jut forward. A bony *simian shelf* buttresses the inside of the front part of the jaw. Large cheek bones and, in males, a ridge of bone called a *sagittal crest* at the top of the skull, anchor the strong chewing muscles.
5. Lower brain size-to-body weight ratio than among humans, who have the most complex cortical structure of the hominoids.

Gibbons. Brachiation, the hand-over-hand arm-swinging that some monkeys use is developed to the highest degree among the gibbons. In contrast to the highly developed hindquarters of clingers and leapers such as the tarsier, the gibbon's shoulders and long arms are powerfully developed and flexible. Its legs are short and relatively weak. Although the gibbon uses its long fingers as a hook when it swings, tucking its thumb out of the way, the thumb is long enough so that it is able to touch the other fingers. Gibbons spend most of their lives in the trees of southeast Asian rain forests. They do not come down often to drink from springs or to feed in the bushes. Although they rarely move on the ground, they sometimes walk bipedally along branches, standing almost erect and using their long arms for balance (Campbell, 1974).

Gibbons of the same sex do not get along very well. Troops are therefore small, usually made up of a male, a female, and up to four offspring. Sexes are equally dominant in the relationship, and they may take turns grooming each other. The males alone, however, patrol the area. They engage in frequent yelling and chasing confrontations with other gibbons who have moved into their territory (Napier & Napier, 1967).

Orangutans. These red-haired pongids live

71

in the forests of Sumatra and Borneo. Like gibbons, they are largely arboreal. Adapted for brachiation, these animals possess long arms and powerful, mobile shoulders and hands. But because of their larger size, they are not swift and graceful like the gibbon. Instead, they move cautiously, holding onto overhead branches with their hands while trying to find footholds below to spread their weight. On the ground, they walk quadrupedally, with clenched hands and feet Napier & Napier, 1967).

By capturing orangutans for zoos, humans have reduced their numbers in the wild to only a few thousand. Orangs have no other known predators. Quiet and lethargic, they look very much like orange-bearded men, as travelers have described them for centuries. Orangs can oppose their thumb to the other four fingers in order to pick up small objects, feed, and build simple nests.

Very little is known about orangs' behavior in the wild. They seem to live mostly in groups of two to four, though males often live alone. One of the few aggressive behaviors scientists have been able to observe is their habit of dropping or throwing sticks in the direction of people who are watching them.

Gorillas. Despite their intimidating appearance, gorillas are generally peaceful animals. Grown males, in an upright position, measure 6 feet and weigh up to 400 pounds, making them the largest of the primates by far. Gorillas live in a variety of environments in equatorial Africa. Their habitats include low rain forests, woodlands with low trees and lots of undergrowth, bamboo forests, mountain forests, and open mountain slopes up to elevations of 13,500 feet. They are vegetarians, eating a great quantity of stalks, vines, bark, leaves, bamboo shoots, roots, and, in some subspecies, fruit.

This young orangutan displays agility that will disappear during adulthood. Orangs are structurally adapted for brachiation, but large size and weight make cautious climbing a must. (Irven De Vore, Anthro-Photo)

This lowland male gorilla displays its usual form of locomotion—knuckle-walking. The sagittal crest on top of the skull anchors the massive jaw muscles needed to process enormous quantities of vegetation. (San Diego Zoo Photo)

Gorillas look for food on the ground. They walk quadrupedally on the soles of their feet and on their knuckles, which have tough pads to take this punishment. This form of locomotion is called *knuckle walking*. Adults and juveniles have never been seen swinging by their arms through the trees. Tree-climbing is more common among infants and females than among adult males. Though gorillas rarely walk bipedally, they do stand on their hind legs during their chest-beating display. This is part of a ritual sequence of behaviors, including vegetation-uprooting and foot-stamping. The display seems to be an elaborate bluff designed to intimidate an opponent, for an angry gorilla will rarely fight.

Behavior within the troop is peaceful, too. The dominant male acts as leader and protector for a stable group of 5 to 30 gorillas. Since the sex ratio is one male for every two females, many young adult males live alone, occasionally joining existing troops for short periods. At night the troop sleeps in nests made on the ground or in trees. New ones are made each day, perhaps because the gorillas invariably defecate in them during the night (Napier & Napier, 1967; Eimerl & De Vore, 1965).

Chimpanzees. The chimpanzee resembles the gorilla anatomically, but not in size, for a chimp is only a third as big as a gorilla.

Chimpanzees are native to Africa. Like gorillas, they have adapted to a variety of environmental settings: tropical rain forests, savannas, hilly woodlands, forested mountain slopes, and secondary forests. They stay in the trees for 50 to 75 percent of the day and sleep in nests built in trees at least 15 feet above the ground. Though they occasionally eat meat, fish, ants, and termites, their diet is mostly vegetarian: fruits, leaves, nuts, bark, seeds, and stems.

While in the trees, chimpanzees swing by their arms for short distances. They often use their feet, as well, to hold on to limbs. On the ground they move quadrupedally, knuckle

An adult female chimpanzee inspects her hand in the course of leaf grooming. Note that the relatively short thumb allows only a poor precision grip, a trait common to all pongids.
(Richard Wrangham, Anthro-Photo)

walking as gorillas do. Often they stand on their hind legs to see better. But only occasionally do they run or walk bipedally, to carry objects or to put on a display. They have flexible hands and use them to groom themselves, build nests, use crude tools, and, in captivity, even to paint pictures.

Chimpanzees do not form the rigidly hierarchical societies some other primates have developed. They are together only temporarily, in groups of 2 to 48. There is no one pattern that characterizes these groups, nor is there a clearcut dominance structure. Individuals, particularly siblings or mothers and their offspring, do, however, form close and lasting ties to each other (Van Lawick-Goodall, 1971). Social interaction includes juvenile play, adult grooming, noisy group displays, and communication (Napier & Napier, 1967; Eimerl & DeVore, 1965).

Summary

1. People have long been interested in the higher primates. In their likeness to humans, these primates have sometimes been the object of worship, scorn, and amusement.

2. Scientific curiosity about primates began with the Greeks. Aristotle and Galen generated most of the early anatomical information about primates. During the European Middle Ages, interest lay dormant, and there was a tendency to view primates moralistically as evil creatures. By the nineteenth century enough information about primates was available to permit scientists to think of a common ancestry for monkeys, apes, and humans.

3. During the twentieth century, *primatologists* have demonstrated the diversity in behavior and biology of the primates. Studies of primate societies were conducted in laboratories, controlled environments (such as compounds), and natural environments. As a result, there is now general agreement that humans belong to the biological order *Primates* and share certain characteristics with other species in this order. The *generalized characteristics,* the primitive traits possessed by the earliest primates, include a primitive limb structure and a simple tooth pattern. *Specialized characteristics,* adaptations developed in the course of primate evolution, include prehensility; a collarbone that permits flexibility in arm movements; nails instead of claws; touch pads; an opposable thumb, which allows a precision grip; reduction in the number of teeth; emphasis on sight rather than smell; high body-to-brain ratio; and more complex reproductive and caretaking (of the young) strategies. Behaviorally, primates emphasize social learning and may organize into complex troops.

4. Primates have been grouped according to anatomical features into hierarchical categories called *taxa.* The organization of taxa is called *taxonomy* and is based on the system developed by Linnaeus. The basic unit in this taxonomy is the *species.* Today taxonomy also takes into account *phylogeny* and *serological* and behavioral characteristics.

5. The order Primates is divided into two suborders: *Prosimii* and *Anthropoidea.* The former consists of the least complex of the primates and includes the three *infraorders Tarsiiformes, Lorisiformes,* and *Lemuriformes.* The anthropoids are characterized by a shared set of specialized adaptations that allow more effective use of arboreal environments and by a high brain-to-body ratio. The suborder is divided into the infraorders *Platyrrhini* (New World monkeys) and *Catarrhini* (Old World primates).

6. The New World monkeys are divided into two *families:* Callithricidae and Cebidae. They are primarily arboreal, and because they live in dense jungle areas, little is known about their social behavior.

7. Within the Old World line are two *superfamilies: Cercopithecoidea* (Old World monkeys) and Hominoidea (humans, gibbons, orangutans, chimpanzees, and gorillas). The former superfamily consists of one family, which is divided into two subfamilies: Cercopithecinae (guenons, mangabeys, macaques, baboons) and Colobinae (langurs). The superfamily Hominoidea is divided into three families: Hylobatidae (gibbons), Pongidae (chimpanzees, gorillas, orangutans), and Hominidae (humans). The gibbons and orangutans are farthest from the human pattern while chimpanzees and gorillas are considered to be our closer "relatives."

5

Primate Behavior

AFTER painstakingly removing a fossil molar from the rock in which it has been embedded, paleontologists can describe its form in detail and compare it with other fossil molars. But how can they reconstruct the animal's diet and its method of food-getting? A fossil shoulder joint also is found. What can it reveal about how the animal moved? Questions about simple behavior such as eating or moving can only be answered by studying the teeth and limbs of contemporary descendants of the fossil creature and by watching how these animals eat and move.

How did our apelike ancestors forage and live together? In families? In bands? To what extent could they communicate? Complex behaviors like these do not correspond to specific structures in the body—a set of teeth or leg bones, for example. As a result, they leave few if any traces in the fossil record. So for clues as to the complex behavior of our an-

cestors, we must study ourselves and the other living primates. It is particularly revealing to search for basic similarities between the behavior of humans and that of the great apes (chimpanzees, gorillas, and orangutans). These similar behaviors probably did not emerge independently in each evolutionary line. More likely, they were present, in some form, among our common ancestors. During the last 15 to 20 million years, the many evolutionary descendants of this ancestral group probably also have possessed these behaviors, so that they are present in all living great apes and humans.

In this chapter we shall examine two kinds of primate behavior. The first consists of anatomically based activity called *first-order behavior.* Feeding and locomotion, for example, are made up of hundreds of mechanical actions that are structured by the size and shape of different bones. *Second-order behavior* consists of interactions between individuals and between populations—hunting together, communication, and social organization, for example. Although these types of behaviors depend on the movement of muscles, bones, and teeth, they are structured by the function of the brain, and are either learned (as in the case of humans and many primates) or programmed genetically. It is possible to get an idea of the gross brain structure of extinct primates by studying their skulls, but it is impossible to guess at the type of behavior these structures controlled. The relationship between brain structure and behavior is so complicated that we are barely beginning to understand it in living animals.

We do know, however, a great deal about the behavior of living primates. Some primatologists are trying to link behavior with the ecosystems in which different primates live. In this way, it may be possible to associate behaviors of living primates with those of extinct species living in similar ecosystems.

Primate Behavioral Systems

Fieldworkers observing a group of primates see an enormous number of details. To make sense of this information, anthropologists break up what they see into groups of related actions. Sets of activities that have a functional relationship to each other are called *behavioral systems.* Information about a first-order behavioral system is found through dissection of muscles and bones and observations of behavior in the field. In this way function is assigned to structure. Information about second-order behavioral systems involves knowing the age, sex, and relationship of the participants, the environmental setting, and the relation of the behavior to previous and later behavior. Behavioral systems are arbitrary concepts. In real life, first- and second-order behaviors are integrated into the nonstop activity seen by the primatologist. In the next section we shall look at two of the main first-order behaviors: locomotion and feeding.

First-Order Behaviors

Locomotion

Most primates spend some or all of their time in trees. But not all of them use the same pattern of locomotion. Locomotion depends partly on the evolutionary history of the species and partly on the animal's niche. Some primates have adapted to the small top branches of trees, others to the middle parts. Still others live only partly in trees and spend much of their time on the ground. Finally, a few primates spend all of their time on the ground.

Primatologists often distinguish four major locomotion patterns among the primates: *vertical clinging and leaping, quadrupedalism, brachiation,* which are shown in Figure 1, and *bipedalism.* But the distinctions are not hard and fast. Although each kind of primate has a preference for a certain pattern, they all display a great range of locomotory behavior. For instance, all primates are capable of moving about on all fours. And most monkeys and every kind of ape can stand and sometimes walk upright.

Vertical Clinging and Leaping. Some prosimians have developed modifications that allow them to rest clinging to vertical tree trunks and to leap with their hind legs from one tree to another. In these animals the hindlimbs are greatly lengthened and strengthened in comparison to the forelimbs. Elongated heels make the back feet effective levers for spring-

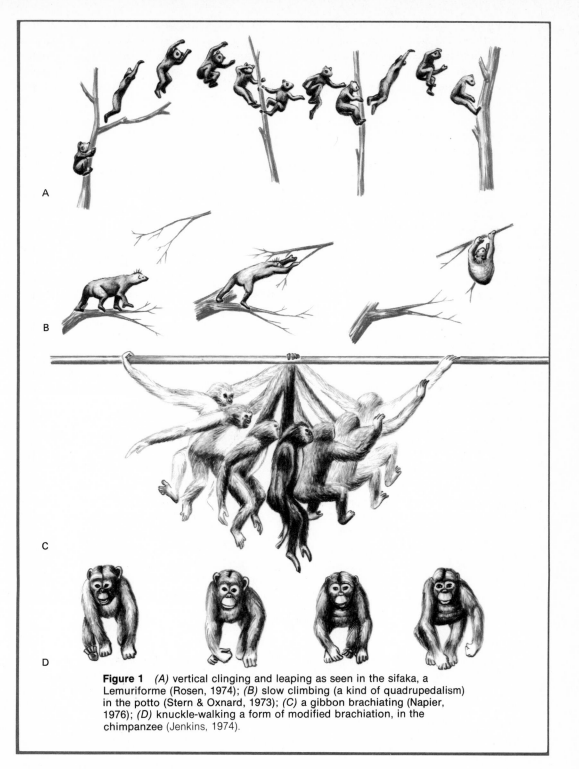

Figure 1 *(A)* vertical clinging and leaping as seen in the sifaka, a Lemuriforme (Rosen, 1974); *(B)* slow climbing (a kind of quadrupedalism) in the potto (Stern & Oxnard, 1973); *(C)* a gibbon brachiating (Napier, 1976); *(D)* knuckle-walking a form of modified brachiation, in the chimpanzee (Jenkins, 1974).

ing. The forelimbs play a part in propelling the body when the prosimians move slowly on the ground, for then they walk quadrupedally. For rapid movement on the ground, they hop using their hindlimbs (Napier & Napier, 1967).

Quadrupedalism. Primates have evolved many ways to use all four limbs in locomotion. In *slow climbing,* the method used by lorises and pottos, at least three of the four limbs are always in contact with branches above.

Some of the Old World monkeys, many New World monkeys, and some lemurs run or walk palms down along the tops of branches. Some terrestrial species, such as macaques, mandrills, vervets, and baboons, walk with only their fingers touching the ground. The fingers are bent back so that the second joints bear the animal's weight.

Semibrachiators use their arms to hang from branches or to swing themselves along. These primates can grasp with their feet, and some of the New World monkeys can also grasp with their prehensile tails. At other times these animals move on all four limbs.

Despite differences in how they use their hands and feet in moving, most quadrupedal primates are very agile. The spinal column between the pelvis and the chest is extremely long and flexible. This is an asset to those species who move rapidly through irregularly spaced branches, as well as to the slow climbers, who wrap themselves around trunks and branches (Eimerl & Devore, 1965; Campbell, 1974).

Brachiation. Bodily flexibility is lessened among the brachiators. Evolutionary emphasis has been placed instead on efficiency of swinging by the arms. In *true brachiation,* the arms alone are used to swing hand-over-hand through the trees and to provide momentum for bridging large gaps from limb to limb. In *modified brachiation,* the arms play the major role in locomotion, but they are sometimes as- sisted by support from the legs. On the ground, many of these animals are knuckle walkers. The chimpanzee, for instance, sup- ports part of its weight on its knuckles, which are equipped for this with tough, callused pads. The gibbon is a true brachiator; gorillas, chimpanzees, and orangutans are modified brachiators. Like the other primates, these animals can move in a variety of ways. Gib- bons, for example, can walk bipedally along branches if arm swinging is not practical (Schultz, 1969).

Evolution of the brachiators has favored overdevelopment of the arms and shoulders in relationship to the legs. This is especially pro- nounced in the gibbon and the orangutan. Emphasis on arm swinging has also decreased flexibility in the trunk, for it is not used much in this type of locomotion. Three of the lum- bar vertebrae, flexible in quadrupeds, are stiff parts of the ribcage in the gibbon.

Bipedalism. Many primates occasionally walk on their hind limbs. But only humans can straighten their hind limbs for a completely upright posture.

Like the great apes, hominids probably never developed the extreme specializations for brachiation that gibbons did. But the fairly inflexible spines and the strong shoulders of the great apes and humans suggest that at some point the hominids may have shared with the gibbon an ancestor with some ability to brachiate. Our closer similarity to the great apes probably means that the common ances- tor of living hominids (humans included) was a modified brachiator. But hominid adaptation to a terrestrial way of life led to structural refinements allowing bipedal locomotion (Buettner-Janusch, 1966).

Unfortunately, no fossils exist that can show the beginning of bipedalism. But skeletal comparisons of living primates with living humans suggest that at least six changes were needed to allow the body to balance and move on two feet.

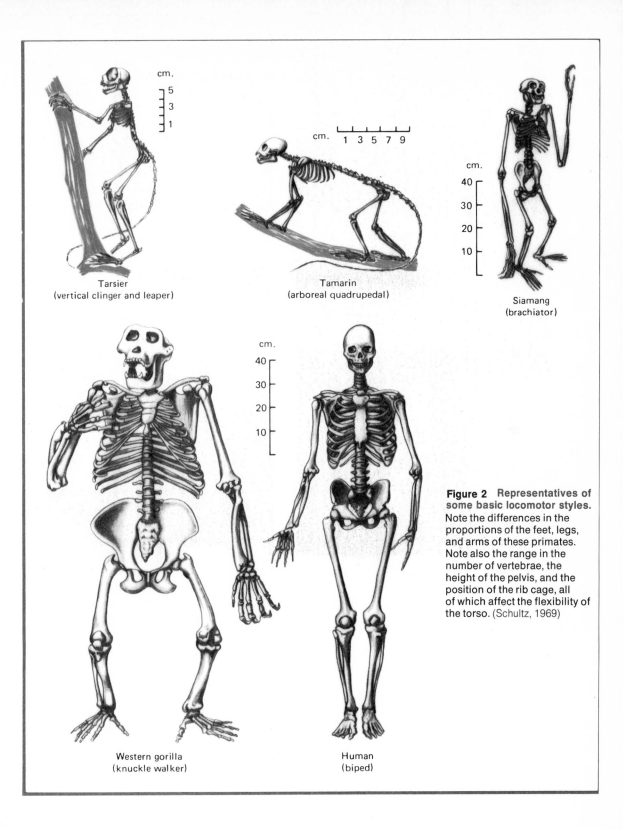

Tarsier
(vertical clinger and leaper)

Tamarin
(arboreal quadrupedal)

Siamang
(brachiator)

Western gorilla
(knuckle walker)

Human
(biped)

Figure 2 **Representatives of some basic locomotor styles.** Note the differences in the proportions of the feet, legs, and arms of these primates. Note also the range in the number of vertebrae, the height of the pelvis, and the position of the rib cage, all of which affect the flexibility of the torso. (Schultz, 1969)

1. The hole in the base of the skull through which the spinal cord passes (called the *foramen magnum*) must have shifted forward to better balance the head's weight. In other primates, the foramen magnum is more toward the rear of the skull.

2. The lumbar vertebrae were reduced in number and lessened the strain on the lower back. An *S*-shaped curve developed in the lower spine so that the torso became positioned directly above the pelvis, instead of in front of it.

3. The human ribcage is flatter than that of the semibrachiators, thus making front-to-back balance easier. As a result, the vertical axis of the body weight is close to the supporting spinal column.

4. The top part of the human pelvis, the ilium, became wider to act as a base for the torso. Among the quadrupeds, the pelvis is a pivotal point for attachment of the leg bones and muscles. The human ilium is also shorter and bends back, bringing the plane at which weight is transferred from the spinal column to the pelvis closer to the plane at which weight is transferred from the pelvis to the upper leg.

5. The bones of the upper and lower leg became larger and thicker to support the weight placed on them.

6. The foot became a strong platform for bearing the weight of the body when the other foot is lifted. In humans, the big toe is shifted up alongside the other toes, where it cannot be opposed to them for grasping, a crucial adaptation for arboreal life.

Feeding

How and what a primate eats are reflected in its hands, teeth, jaws, facial muscles, tongue, and digestive system. But physical anthropologists, who apply their knowledge of living primates to fossil primates, are especially interested in the teeth and jaws because these are most often preserved as fossils. Fossil teeth contain a wealth of information. They can be used as indicators of how close the genetic relationship is between one species and another, because the shape and number of the teeth evolve more slowly than other bodily structures. The teeth also provide information about the extinct animal's size, diet, and ecology. To make inferences of this kind about fossil primates, anthropologists must draw on their observations of how tooth structure and diet are related in the living primates.

Like those of most mammals, primate teeth vary in shape and perform different functions. At the front of the jaw, the *incisors* are used to seize and cut food. Behind the two incisors most primates have a *canine* tooth on both sides of the upper and lower jaws. This is used to grip food and to hold it in the mouth during chewing. As you can see in Figure 3, behind each canine, most prosimians and all New World monkeys have three *premolars,* and the Old World monkeys, apes, and humans have two. Behind the premolars almost all primates have three *molars.* Both premolars and molars have *cusps,* or points, that aid in grinding and cutting food.

Diet affects tooth structure by selecting for those forms that most efficiently process the animal's food. Because small animals require more food energy, their teeth must be able to break down proportionately more food than those of larger animals. The teeth of primates that eat high-energy foods, such as fruit or meat, need to be less efficient and wear-resistant because they process less food than the teeth of leaf-eaters, for instance. Finally, the physical properties of the food itself also affect tooth shape. Tough, hard-to-digest foods such as seeds or nuts require molars with pronounced cusps and a large surface area. Primates adapted for leaf-eating and insect-eating have relatively longer cusps and larger grinding surfaces than fruit-eating primates (Kay, 1975).

Although tooth shape and size are strongly influenced by diet, the selective forces at work are often other than dietary. Gorillas have

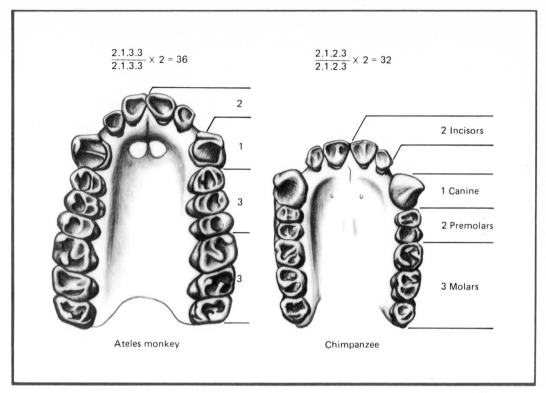

$$\frac{2.1.3.3}{2.1.3.3} \times 2 = 36 \qquad \frac{2.1.2.3}{2.1.2.3} \times 2 = 32$$

2

1

3

3

2 Incisors

1 Canine

2 Premolars

3 Molars

Ateles monkey   Chimpanzee

Figure 3   Reduction of the dental formula in the primates.
The mammals from which primates evolved probably had a total of 44
teeth. But prosimians and New World monkeys, such as the Ateles, whose
lower teeth are shown here, have a total of 36. In Old World primates,
including the chimpanzee (shown here) and humans, among others, the
total is reduced to 32.

large canines, yet never use them for hunting or killing other animals, as they are exclusively vegetarian. Instead, the large canines seem to have evolved as part of threat gesturing. Many prosimians possess forward-projecting incisors that are used not for biting food, but rather for grooming.

The variety of functions for which primate teeth are adapted is best understood in dietary terms. Therefore, in our discussion of dentition, we will speak in terms of major dietary groups. In each case it will be useful to refer to Figure 4 as you read.

Insect-Eaters. These primates must grind their food finely in order to make it digestible.

The incisors are peglike and broadly spaced in the insect-eaters' upper jaw. Below, they are thin and set close together. Both sets of incisors stick out beyond the plane of the face. The crests of the molars are sharp and high, and in many insect-eaters these cusps are connected by ridges that serve as excellent shearing edges.

Leaf-Eaters. In primates that live primarily on bulky vegetable foods such as leaves and stems, both teeth and stomach are adapted for improved digestion of the high-cellulose diet. In general, the incisors are small and the cheek teeth, the premolars and the molars, are large. Leaves are easy to remove from trees,

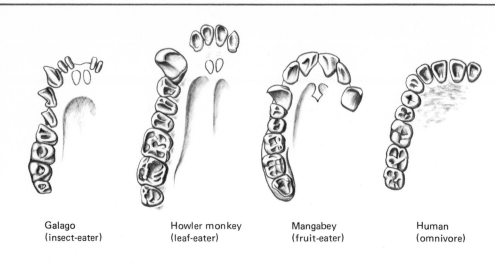

Galago
(insect-eater)

Howler monkey
(leaf-eater)

Mangabey
(fruit-eater)

Human
(omnivore)

Figure 4   Dental pattern of respective primates.
The galago, an insect eater, has peglike incisors and three-cusped molars with high cusps and deep trenches. Like other leaf-eaters, the howler monkey has small incisors and cheek teeth with a large grinding surface and high cusps. Fruit-eaters such as the mangabey have broad incisors, possibly an adaptation to the hard fruit these monkeys crack with their teeth. Their cheek teeth are designed for crushing and have lower cusps than those of leaf-eaters. In humans and other omnivores, the incisors and molars are closer to the same size than in other primates. (Swindler, 1976)

but difficult to chew. Molars are broad, with a large number of extra shearing and grinding surfaces, because leaves must be ground into small bits before the stomach can begin to digest them. The stomach and intestines of a leaf-eater are enormous, for the animal must gorge itself on energy-poor leaves to survive. Langurs and colobus monkeys, both primarily leaf-eaters, have to eat so much that at times their food and digestive tracts make up a fourth of their total weight (Eimerl & De Vore, 1965).

Fruit-Eaters. Fruit can be digested in larger pieces than can insects or leaves, so the shearing molars associated with breaking down food to small particles are reduced in primates whose diet is based on fruit. After it is cut,

fruit is prepared for eating primarily by crushing, but since it is soft, crushing structures, too, are reduced, compared to the molars of leaf- and insect-eaters. Some frugivores (or fruit-eaters), such as the *Cercocebus* monkey, have large chisel-shaped incisors for cracking hard fruits. In general, however, the teeth of fruit-eaters are small in proportion to body size (Kay, 1975).

Omnivores. These animals have few dental specializations. Their incisors, canines, and cheek teeth all perform several different functions, thereby increasing the range of food omnivores can eat. Humans, for example, eat meat by tearing it with their incisors. They also use their incisors to bite fruit. At the same time, vegetable material is ground by molars and premolars. Among humans, many of the more specialized functions of teeth are taken over by tools, so we do not need our teeth to kill other animals. In addition, we often prepare food before eating it, thereby relieving our teeth of the job of breaking down the tough fibrous material in vegetable foods. The use of tools and food preparation has had a significant effect on human dental evolution, as we shall see in Chapter 8.

The Primate Hand. All primates use their hands for both feeding and for locomotion. In addition, hands are the major exploratory organs of the higher primates. In the course of primate evolution, the sense of touch has gradually shifted from the nose, where receptors are still clustered in living prosimians, to the hand. The Anthropoids depend upon their hands for much of their information about objects in the environment.

The use of the hands in locomotion depends, of course, on how the animal moves. Humans rarely rely on their hands for movement, using them instead to handle and explore objects. True brachiators such as the gibbon depend almost entirely upon their hands, which are modified to provide the best grip as they swing through trees.

Primates use one of two types of grips. All primates can use a *power grip,* simply by bending the fingers tightly against the palm to clamp an object there. Counterpressure from the thumb helps hold the object (see Figure 5). Prosimians tend to rely most heavily upon this grasp, both for clinging to branches during locomotion and for seizing food. A *precision grip* depends upon a refined sense of touch in the fingers, and on separate control by the brain over each finger. It allows the greatest accuracy of control, for here the object is pinched between the thumb and fingers (see Figure 6). Precision grips are most highly developed among the Anthropoids, particularly among the Old World monkeys, apes, and humans. In these animals, the thumb is more

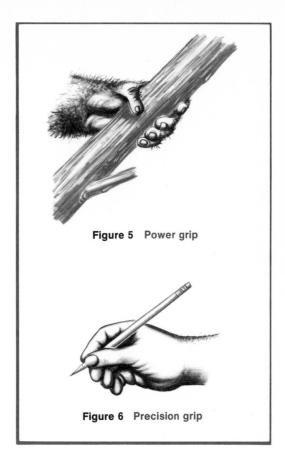

Figure 5   Power grip

Figure 6   Precision grip

truly opposable to the other fingers, allowing greater control over small objects. As you can see in Figure 7, there are many different kinds of primate hands, each one influenced by the locomotor pattern of the animal and its feeding and social patterns.

Second-Order Behaviors

Anthropologists can study form and function fairly directly in the locomotor and feeding systems. They can measure teeth and limbs and observe how the animal uses these structures to eat and move. The ways the animal coordinates its physical actions in differ-

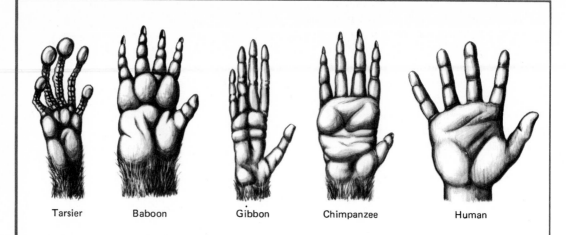

Tarsier   Baboon   Gibbon   Chimpanzee   Human

Figure 7 The tarsier, a vertical clinger and leaper, seldom uses a precision grip because its thumb is not truly opposable. Its thumb cannot rotate in its socket to allow contact with all the fingers. Like the gibbon, however, the tarsier is adept at grasping. The baboon, like almost all Old World monkeys, has and uses an opposable thumb. It can control each finger separately, which makes possible a precision grip able to take the stinger out of a scorpion (Campbell, 1974). The gibbon, chimpanzee, and humans can control each finger separately, but the first two, because of their specializations for brachiation, have a more limited precision grip than baboons or humans. The gibbon's hands are long hooks that grip limbs efficiently. The thumb, a possible hazard in the treetops, has become greatly shortened. Humans have a higher degree of fine control over the fingers than do other primates and greater opposability of the thumb. (Schultz, 1969)

ent situations, its interaction with other animals, its communication, and its learning are far less tangible, and much more difficult to study.

The brain controls these aspects of primate behavior. But assessment of behavior in terms of brain structure among living primates is still at an early stage of development. And what is known can only be applied to fossil species insofar as brain structure can be assessed from the skull. The relative size of gross features such as the part of the brain associated with the sense of smell in primitive primates can be observed by taking *endocranial casts,* or molds, of the inside of the skull. Such molds provide a cast of the external parts of the brain. But it is impossible to trace the evolutionary development of internal structures such as the

secondary association areas, which in the human brain are responsible for integration of experience and greater complexity of thought. The areas of the brain that probably control most of the complex, or second-order, behaviors (actions that are a part of communication and social interaction) are located beneath the surface of the brain and therefore cannot be reproduced in a cast. Because little can be learned about the internal brain structure of fossil primates, anthropologists are forced to infer what they can about second-order behavior by studying it in the living primates. As you will see, these studies have revealed that humans and the higher primates have an unexpected number of behaviors in common. These results in turn have fed speculation about how our earliest ancestors, newly diverged from the ancestors of modern apes, may have communicated and lived together.

Information Processing in the Brain

The primate brain is larger and more complex than that of the other mammals. Primate evolution has been marked by reorganization and continual expansion of the brain, most of which has occurred in the *cerebral cortex*, the outer layer of the brain and seat of the higher functions. These changes have permitted more accurate sensory perception, especially in the senses of touch and sight, better coordination between sensory input and muscular response, and a greater capacity for learned and flexible behavior.

The most primitive primates rely to a great degree on the sense of smell, though many possess excellent vision as well. As a result, the *olfactory lobe*, the most primitive part of the cerebral cortex, is largest in these primates. As primates have evolved, greater emphasis has been placed on the other senses, particularly vision. The olfactory lobe is therefore largest among the prosimians and smallest among the higher primates. In humans and chimpanzees it is only a tiny projection.

The *motor cortex* sends messages to and from nerves in the muscles. This area controls the conscious movement of body parts. The *somatosensory area* receives messages through nerves leading from the skin, muscles, and bodily organs. Large chunks of both cortices are devoted to the hands and mouth, probably in response to the selective advantages of flexible hands and vocal communication. Experiments show that the size of the motor cortical area devoted to the hand in-

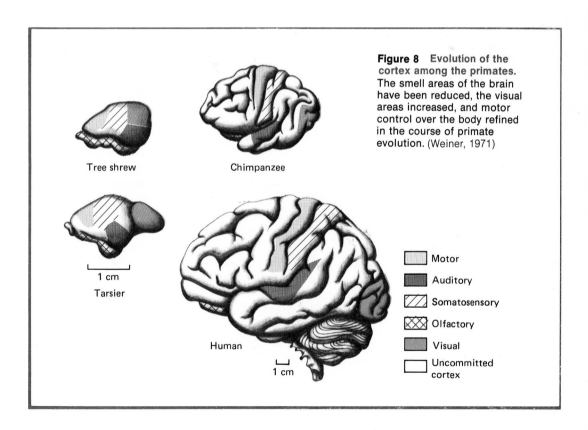

Tree shrew

Chimpanzee

1 cm

Tarsier

Human

1 cm

Figure 8 Evolution of the cortex among the primates. The smell areas of the brain have been reduced, the visual areas increased, and motor control over the body refined in the course of primate evolution. (Weiner, 1971)

Motor
Auditory
Somatosensory
Olfactory
Visual
Uncommitted cortex

85

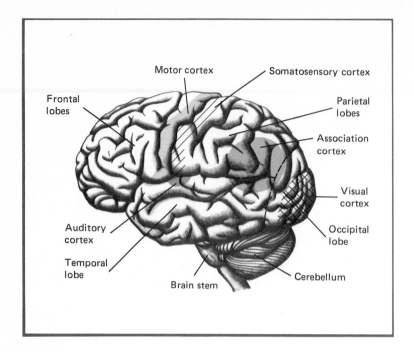

Figure 9 The left side of the human brain, showing the main parts of the cerebral cortex, together with somatosensory and motor cortices.

creases from New World monkeys to Old World monkeys to apes to humans (Campbell, 1974; Napier & Napier, 1967).

Analysis of visual images, especially important in moving quickly through a flurry of tree limbs in the forest canopy, takes place in the *visual cortex* of the *occipital lobe.* It is well developed, even in the lower primates. The tarsier, for example, must analyze large amounts of visual information with precision to succeed in its spectacular leaps from one tree trunk to another. Development of visual acuity probably reached a peak among the early apes and remained high in later apes and humans (Napier & Napier, 1967). The number of connections between the visual cortex and other parts of the brain continued to increase, however. Humans' vision is highly integrated with information from the other senses, as well as with motor activity.

As the primates increasingly became adapted to an arboreal habitat, the ability to integrate sensory information with muscular, or motor, responses became vital for survival.

Integration of auditory, somatic, and visual information from other parts of the brain occurs in the *parietal lobes.* In monkeys and apes the parietal lobes are connected directly to the sensory cortices. But in humans, a highly developed *secondary association area* complicates the nerve pathways and leads to more elaborate integration and interpretation of experiences. Although monkeys and apes have developed very advanced systems for receiving information from the senses and coordinating them with muscular activities, the application of conscious thought to this process is largely a human specialty (Napier & Napier, 1967).

Good coordination is another adaptation to life in the trees. The *cerebellum,* which lies at the base of the brain, is the center of muscular coordination. It is a primitive feature, but highly developed in all primates, for the penalty for clumsiness in the treetops is a long fall. Muscle responses are largely instinctual in the lower primates. But once again there has been a progressive tendency in primate evolution toward conscious control over muscle responses. This trend takes the form of increasing nerve fiber connections between the cerebellum and the cerebral cortex, a trend that is most pronounced in humans (Napier & Napier, 1967).

The ability of areas of the cerebral cortex to direct other areas of the brain extends to some of the most primitive parts of the brain. The *limbic system,* which can be traced back to our reptile ancestors, translates sensory stimuli into states of arousal, perhaps something like emotions. These states of arousal trigger muscle responses through hormone and nerve impulses. These are usually impulses to carry out basic adaptive activities—caring for offspring, finding food, mating, fighting or fleeing from predators, and so on. The limbic system is common to all mammals. But in humans, interconnections with the higher cerebral cortex make it possible to bring these impulses under conscious control and even to inhibit them. We do not mate every time we encounter a willing partner, for instance. Nor do we grab all the food on the table for ourselves. Learning stored in the higher brain can be superimposed on the impulses of the limbic system, giving us greater flexibility in handling them.

The ability to concentrate on a long-term goal, make plans, and suppress conflicting impulses has been traced to the *frontal lobes.* In contrast to nonhuman primates, who usually cannot concentrate on anything for more than 15 to 30 minutes, humans can spend years planning and working toward a goal. Some anthropologists feel that this ability may have developed with the evolution of hunting behavior, for it is found to a degree in carnivores as well. A human hunter who could not follow an animal or lie in wait for a long time would probably come home empty-handed. Ultimately, the ability to concentrate has played a great part in the development of culture, which in turn has allowed specialized behavior to replace physical specialization as a means of adapting to environmental change.

The second-order behaviors controlled by the brain features that we have just discussed are studied by primatologists in three ways: (1) naturalistic studies, in which primates are observed in their natural environments, (2) compound studies, in which primates live in special areas that limit their movement, and (3) laboratory studies, in which researchers observe primate social behavior under controlled conditions. Each approach provides a different kind of information and has its own set of limitations.

Naturalistic Studies. Observation of animals in the wild has several advantages over other methods. First, only in the field can the interaction between behavior and environment be studied effectively. Eating habits, group size, and territorial range, for example, are closely linked to environmental factors. Information about these links in living species is vital to understanding the niche of fossil species. Second, fieldwork can best focus on the social group as a whole, rather than on the individual. To a far greater degree than in other animals, primate behavior is shaped by learning within the group. And finally, naturalistic studies can take into full account the complexity of primate behavior. Although lab studies of patas monkeys, for example, have shown that a son's status ranking is affected by his mother's rank in the troop, field studies reveal that rank is actually the product of a much more complex set of social factors (Hall, 1968).

On the negative side, there is a limit to what field observers can find out, even after years of watching. Nocturnal and arboreal species are especially hard to see and follow. And the behavior that observers do see is the result of learning, rather than the learning process itself. Although we have found out, for instance, that wild chimpanzees sometimes kill other animals for meat and that they use a few crude "tools," we know little about how such behavior has developed (Van Lawick-Goodall, 1971).

Compound Studies. Primate-watching is easier within a compound. Since troop movements are limited by an enclosure or an island setting, many behaviors that would go unobserved in totally naturalistic settings are more easily recorded. But there is one big drawback. Primates are so versatile that they may change their behavior in response to the new environment. The unnaturally boring life and the surplus of males in a two-acre compound in Oregon, for example, probably induced the unusually aggressive behavior noted in one troop of macaques imported from their natural setting in Japan (Alexander & Bowers, 1967).

Laboratory Studies. Scientists can isolate certain important factors in primate social behavior only in the laboratory. Carefully controlled experiments can reveal, for instance, whether physical contact or nursing is more important in the infant's attachment to its mother, the conditions under which certain behaviors are elicited, how behaviors develop as the animal grows, and how behavior is modified. Problems have arisen, however, when experiments have been set up and judged from a human point of view. Experimenters have also tended to overlook the importance of the group and the environment in shaping the individual's behavior.

So far, experimenters and fieldworkers have operated along very different lines. Hypotheses that have come out of field studies are rarely tested in the lab, and vice versa. Although some fieldworkers try simple experiments, such as introducing a new food, a systematic approach and controlled conditions are impossible. Some workers think that lab studies should make more use of the fieldworker's knowledge of the context of behaviors. Experiments might then elicit patterns of behavior instead of a reaction like lever-pressing, which is more typical of the human species (Mason, 1968).

Communication

In field studies, primatologists have learned that primates communicate with each other in a variety of ways, including groups of vocalizations graded according to factors such as volume and duration, facial gestures, and body movements. In laboratories chimpanzees have even been taught to use simplified versions of human symbolic communication, consisting of many, if not all, of the elements of human language.

Primate Communication in Nature. Most primate communications concern the intricacies of group life—domination and subordination, keeping the peace, mating, and caring for infants. Primates communicate not only by vocalizing, but also by signs that can be seen, felt, and sometimes smelled. Although we will consider these modes of communication separately for simplicity's sake, they are often combined into complex clusters that convey subtle variations in meaning.

Olfactory Communication. Scent-marking is rare among monkeys and apes, but prosimians use it to mark their territories. Some rub branches with secretions from special scent glands, and others spread urine or feces. The nocturnal prosimians, who move only within a limited territory, use scent signals because darkness makes visual signals hard to see. Monkeys and apes, however, are diurnal, and their territory is too large and variable to mark with a scent. Among these primates, only the scent of a female in estrus remains as a clear olfactory signal.

Tactile Communication. Although most mammals touch one another with their noses, primates usually use their hands. Grooming is the most common form of communication by touch. Although it does serve to remove de-

Chimp greetings, a form of tactile communication.
(Richard Wrangham, Anthro-Photo)

bris and insects from another's fur, grooming also seems to ease tensions in strongly hierarchical groups. Less dominant animals often soothe a potentially aggressive superior by stroking its fur.

In some species, tactile signals frequently are used in greeting. Chimpanzees, for instance, greet each other by embracing, kissing, nuzzling, and caressing. Much of mother-infant communication is carried on with touch signals. Some primates, however, signal hostility by hitting, pulling fur, and biting.

Visual Signals. Visual signals are an even richer form of communication than tactile signals. Primate visual signaling includes varying postures, tail positions, head movements, changes of coat color, and the swelling of sexual areas. But the most intricate shades of meaning are expressed in the mobile faces of the higher primates. Staring—the so-called direct gaze—is a strong signal of domination designed to make a subordinate give way. A mouth opened with the lips concealing the teeth is meant as a threat. But if the teeth are bared in a grimace, the animal is signaling something more like fear and submission.

Auditory Signals. Primates often use non-vocal sound signals, such as shaking branches, slapping the ground, and beating the chest. But the signals in which anthropologists are most interested are vocalizations, for they could resemble the beginnings of human speech.

Like other animals, primates seem to use about 10 to 15 different sound signals. But in the higher primates, these separate signals can

The yawn and exposed canine teeth of a young male baboon signal a threat. (Timothy Ransom, Woodfin Camp & Associates)

A hanuman langur "grimaces," signaling submission. (San Diego Zoo Photo)

be varied to convey greater subtlety of meaning. Among baboons, for example, "barks" vary in pitch, quality, and timing (Hall & De Vore, 1965).

Vocalizations are not chosen at random. They seem to have a direct relationship to the situation in which they are used. For instance, when juveniles are separated from their mothers or find themselves in danger, they make rapid clicking sounds. These vocalizations cut through other background noises and are very easy to trace to a specific location (Jolly, 1972).

The Nature of Human Language. Humans communicate emotions largely by nonverbal means—a raised eyebrow, a frown, an embrace. These signals are strikingly similar to those used by other primates. But in order to describe things and refine our ideas, we use language, which differs in at least five ways from nonverbal signaling and primate call systems.

Openness. Primate call systems are closed. They are limited to a set of fixed signals. The only way to "say" different things is to stick two signals together or to vary the way they are made (loud or soft; many times, or only once). With language, on the other hand, we can easily say things that we have never said before. Language is always open to new meanings.

Discreteness. Each human language is based on a limited number of discrete, or separate, sounds (*phonemes,* such as the sound *m*) and short meaning-bearing sound combinations (or *morphemes,* such as *man*). This makes it possible for us to listen for known sounds instead of being overwhelmed by an infinite variety of them.

Dual Patterning. Human language is both a system of sounds and a system of meanings. The sound system consists of a limited number of sounds, which lack intrinsic meaning but which can be put together in a structured, or grammatical, form to designate an unlimited number of things and events (Hockett, 1960).

Displacement. Animal calls are directly linked to the immediate situation: food at hand, predator nearby, and so on. But human language can be used in contexts far removed from those to which it refers. While baboons may keep on barking "baboo" an hour after a predator has disappeared, they cannot a week later discuss their narrow escape.

Arbitrariness. A final distinction of human language is its arbitrary nature. The word *apple* bears no relationship whatsoever to the juicy object to which it refers. Instead, it is a symbol that has been arbitrarily linked with that object by members of a human group and must be learned by their children (Jolly, 1972).

Teaching Language to Chimpanzees. Though the chimpanzee brain is smaller than the human brain, there are many structural similarities between the two. This similarity has prompted a number of studies of chimpanzee symbolic communication. In human language, vocal sounds act as symbols, which can be put together to communicate ideas or feelings. But no one has ever had much success in getting chimps to say human words. A chimp named Viki finally learned to say "mama," "papa," and "cup." But she had to force these words out in a strained whisper. The human larynx apparently is better adapted for speech than that of the apes (Lieberman, 1975). Instead of abandoning the attempt altogether, recent experimenters have switched to methods that may be easier for chimpanzees. One method uses gestures as symbols. Another uses plastic symbols instead of spoken words.

Washoe and Sign Language. R. A. and B. T. Gardner have capitalized on the chimpanzee's natural use of gestures to teach American Sign Language, or Ameslan, to a chimp named Washoe. After five years of training, she could use 130 word signs and combine them into simple two- and three-word phrases, such as "gimme tickle" and "more drink please" (Gardner & Gardner, 1969).

But has Washoe learned a communication system that meets the tests for human language? Perhaps so. Ameslan is made of cheremes (distinct hand patterns, actions, and locations) rather than phonemes (sound units). But, like language, it is a system of discrete signal bits. Therefore, Ameslan satisfies the criterion of discreteness. Dual patterning is present, too, for the closed system of meaningless cheremes can be built into an open system of meaningful messages. The ability to learn the names of things shows that chimpanzees are able to learn meanings arbitrarily assigned to symbols. Finally, chimpanzees have been able to create new combinations of gestures to express new meanings. On seeing a swan for the first time, Washoe combined the gestures for water and bird, thus showing the potential for openness. Displacement, however, is more difficult to demonstrate among Ameslan-trained chimpanzees. Knowing the sign for an object and repeating the sign do not satisfy the criterion. To be able to know with certainty whether chimpanzees possess this ability requires being able to communicate in one context information learned in a different context. Research is presently underway to find out whether chimps are capable of displacement.

Refining the Definition of Language. As research on the symbolic abilities of chimps has progressed, there has been a tendency among critics to refine their definitions of human language. Some scientists feel, for instance, that chimps lack *syntax,* the knowledge of how the order of words in sentences affects their meaning (Terrace & Bever, 1976). David Premack has tested the ability of chimps to understand the logic behind sentence structure. He thinks that one chimp named Sarah understands structural rules governing sentences. She placed a banana in a pail and an apple in a dish when given the sentence "Sarah insert banana pail, apple dish" encoded in plastic chips, each of which represented a word. Premack reasons that in order to do this task, Sarah must have understood that *banana* and *pail* go together, as do *apple* and *dish,* and that *insert* applies to both objects.

These studies have not demonstrated to everyone's satisfaction the linguistic ability of chimpanzees. Terrace and Bever (1976) would reserve judgment until chimpanzees use lengthy sentences and are able to refer to themselves symbolically. It is not clear, however, whether these new criteria are meant as a definition of language, or as a means of distinguishing human from nonhuman primate symbolic activities.

In any event, it is certain that humans and the great apes share some symbolic abilities. Differences may result from the fact that chimps have brains that organize experiences differently than human brains. Their abilities seem to be enough like ours, however, that they can communicate on a very simple level, using an approximation of our language, not theirs. These findings suggest that the capacity for language may also have existed in our primate ancestors. Why the early members of our lineage alone began to elaborate is a question we shall begin to answer in the chapters discussing hominid evolution.

Social Organization and the Environment

Symbolic potential is just another example of primate behavioral flexibility. In nature, this flexibility is particularly apparent in group organization. At one extreme there is the simple family group, which consists only of a mated pair and their offspring. Orangutan social structure is of this type. At the other extreme are the rigidly hierarchical baboon troops on the one hand and the chimpanzee "neighborhoods" on the other. Organizational form seems to depend more on the demands of the environment than on the species of the primate. The same forms of social organization are sometimes found in different species living under similar ecological conditions (Dolhinow, 1972). And a single species, such as the anubis baboon, may organize differently, depending on its immediate environment (Wilson, 1975).

Social Classification Systems. Anthropologists have proposed a number of ways of classifying primate social groups. One suggestion is to group primates into two types according to their *attention structure:* (1) groups that pattern their behavior on that of the dominant male, and (2) groups that split up in tense situations, with the males remaining behind to face the danger.

A second set of researchers has sorted primates according to the complexity of their social structure. They suggest five grades, ranging from solitary individuals who meet only for breeding, to large groups headed by a single male, with clearly differentiated social roles.

A third suggestion is that primates can be typed according to how involved the male is in social life. In some primate systems the male is solitary. In others a single dominant male drives away other males. And in still others, males of various ages tolerate one another's presence (Wilson, 1975).

Using Ecological Categories. All these classification systems have their merits—and their limits. None can account fully for all the variations in primate social behavior. But the fact that each can be at least partially supported by observed facts shows the complexity of the influences on social organization.

Taking this intricacy into account, we will use a social classification system based on several ecological factors: the kind of environment, diet, and period of activity—night or day.

This framework allows us to focus on how certain aspects of the biotic and abiotic environments affect a primate's group size and its niche structure. Like any other way of typing primates, ecological categories are somewhat artificial. The adaptations of some animals are highly variable and cannot be fit into a single category. But despite occasional examples of category-defying species, discussing behavior in an ecological context allows us to begin to organize a bewildering array of information in a way that clarifies the adaptive nature of social organization.

Nocturnal Primates *Arboreal Insect-Eaters.* These primates seem to be largely solitary. They feed by themselves, and they escape predators by fleeing. Each has a tiny *home range,* the area within which an adult normally moves. The lepilemur, for instance, rarely ranges farther than 50 meters from its nest in the hole of a tree (Napier & Napier, 1967). In all species studied, individual ranges overlap. Though males and females do not usually live together, they may pass each other in their nightly rounds. And during the day these creatures may huddle together in sleeping groups. Otherwise there is often little contact among individuals during their active periods.

But some species also show what may be the beginnings of primate social grouping. For instance, some bushbabies, tiny clingers and leapers, seem to have much more status than others. According to one observer, there are four different grades of males. The most important have many social contacts with females, while low-status males have none (Jolly, 1972).

Diurnal Primates *Arboreal Leaf-Eaters.* Some Old and New World monkeys—most of them

semibrachiators—tend to live in medium-sized, harmonious troops of 4–30 members that forage for leaves by day. There is little sexual dimorphism, and troop members rarely try to assert dominance over one another. Intruders, however, are loudly warned away with a chorus of howls. The noise serves to divide the forest into a patchwork of defended territories, areas from which intruders are actively excluded. This kind of territoriality is most highly developed among these primates.

Some anthropologists believe that primates whose diet has little nutritive value, such as that of leaf-eaters, or whose locomotion takes a lot of energy, are relatively inactive and live within a small range, which, however, they strongly defend. Their range can be small because food is plentiful (Jolly, 1972).

Arboreal Omnivores. The third kind of social organization appears in the New World capuchins and titis and the Old World mangabeys and guenons. Their diet consists of not only leaves but also more nutritious shoots, nuts, insects, and small birds (Napier & Napier, 1967). This diet seems to promote more activity, and arboreal omnivores are hard to keep track of as they bound through the trees.

Their social organization seems to be more fluid than that of the leaf-eaters, who remain in small groups. Some forage in small bands or alone during the day but form sleeping groups of up to 100 at night. Others forage in large groups during the day, splitting into smaller groups at night. This flexibility may be related partly to their dietary flexibility. When a fig tree, for instance, is covered with ripe figs, it may also be covered with monkeys. At other times they may be better off foraging by themselves or in small groups.

Monkeys in this group do not tend to set up dawn calls to mark their territory. Instead, they may engage in ritualized or actual fighting with other troops, with loud calling and sometimes biting. Within the troops, too, relationships are less harmonious than among the leaf-eaters. Threats and assertions of dominance often are observed.

Semiterrestrial Leaf-Eaters. The primates we have considered so far do their socializing in the treetops. Those who descend to the ground for at least part of the day seem to form larger troops. But group size in this category—which includes only the sacred hanuman langur of India and the gorilla—seems to be held down by their leaf-eating lifestyle.

Despite their great size, gorillas live like other leaf-eaters—in small groups with small home ranges. These sedentary apes consume great quantities of vegetable matter, but they find it within a home range of about $1\frac{1}{2}$ square kilometers. Ranges of the small, male-led gorilla troops overlap considerably. Males may glare at one another and go through their chest-beating rituals when they meet, but troop encounters are generally peaceful.

Relationships within a gorilla troop also are peaceful. Each is headed by a large silver-backed male. The younger black-backed males are next in status. Despite their fierce appearance, these dominant males are rarely aggressive toward their subordinates, who readily yield their sitting places or the right-of-way on narrow trails. Behavioral signals such as glaring or feigned charges reduce actual conflict (Wilson, 1975; Schaller, 1965).

It is hard to fit langurs into this or any other pattern. Their group life varies with the many environments—mountains, swamps, and human villages—to which they are adapted. In the forests langurs usually live in small male-dominated harems that defend their territory as arboreal leaf-eaters do. But in villages, where many langurs live, bachelor bands may take over the small harems, splitting them up or fighting until new leaders are selected (Jolly, 1972).

Semiterrestrial Omnivores. These primates spend some of the day on the ground in areas of partial tree cover. They include one kind of lemur, vervets, mandrills, savanna baboons, and chimpanzees. The first three usually form troops of 4 to 30 males and females; mandrill, macaque, and savanna baboon troops tend to be larger. Social variations within a species are common, differing perhaps with the habitat. The richer the food supply and the less the danger from predators, the smaller and looser the troops tend to be. Tensions within the large troops are held more or less under control, and resistance to predators is made greater by a highly structured dominance hierarchy. And although the wide ranges of different troops often overlap, they tend to avoid one another rather than fight (Napier & Napier, 1967).

The social behavior of chimpanzees, who share this ecological grade, does not really follow this pattern. They seem to live year after year in large, stable communities of 30 to 80 members. But within their overall home range of 5 to 20 square kilometers, they move about in ever-changing smaller groups. The whole community rarely gets together in one place. Though all know one another well from long and intimate association, the only persistent groups seem to consist of a mother and her young or even adolescent offspring. Other small groups—including bunches of companionable males—form and break up after a few hours or days.

One thing that will draw many group members together is the discovery of ripe fruit. Chimpanzees finding a fruiting tree announce it with a *carnival display* that can be heard over a kilometer away. They drum on tree trunks with their hands and run and swing through the trees until a crowd gathers. But before the eating begins, the adult males go through a ritualized greeting ceremony, which includes embracing, kissing, and shaking hands.

Chimpanzees appear to be the only primates, aside from humans, that share their food. If a limited amount of a special delicacy is located, troop members beg for—and sometimes receive—a share of the find.

Cooperation is evident in their hunting behaviors, for chimpanzees sometimes use subtle signals to organize for group attacks on prey such as young baboons and pigs. Sometimes cooperation extends to other troops whose home ranges overlap their own. Though there is no fighting, tensions may be expressed by excited exaggerations of feeding behaviors. The groups may travel together and even trade sexually receptive females. The estrous females' willingness to copulate with a number of males probably helps to minimize aggression among the males (Wilson, 1975).

Terrestrial Arid-Country Primates. A sixth group consists of hamadryas baboons, geladas, and the large patas monkeys. They are the only primates to adapt to a largely terrestrial life in dry environments, where trees are few or even lacking altogether. In order to find grass, bulbs, seeds, and fruit in their harsh habitats, troops must travel up to 18 kilometers a day.

Though the three species in this category are only distantly related, they all have developed a similar social pattern, which is a small harem consisting of one male and up to nine females and their young. Some primatologists think that this grouping may be a way of coping with the limited food resources. Large troops would have to travel even farther in a day to find enough food to go around. Because predators are few in really dry areas, the presence of a number of males to protect the troop may become less important than the need to find food (De Vore and Hall, 1965). In the patas harems, the single male manages to protect his harem by entering new country ahead of them, acting as a lookout and diverting attacks by cheetahs and wild dogs toward himself (Napier & Napier, 1967).

Though hamadryas and gelada harems forage separately during the day, they often join at night to share sleeping cliffs. Since trees are unavailable for safe sleeping spots, ledges on vertical rock faces may serve as a refuge for hundreds of these primates. Though gelada harems usually look for food separately, they join in large groups to forage when the rainy season brings lusher plant growth (Jolly, 1972).

Terrestrial Omnivores (Humans). The social structure of our forerunners also was very much a product of the environment. If, as many anthropologists believe, our ancestors were apelike creatures that had adapted to life in dry, open country, they may have lived in small groups, joining occasionally into larger bands. Primitive hunting and gathering tribes still follow this pattern, using a flexible combination of foraging in small and large groups, according to the availability of food. Their ability to cooperate in hunting is increased by the absence of active territorial defense mechanisms. Among the primates, territorial defense is found mostly in arboreal rather than terrestrial species.

Learning to be a Member of the Troop

The social organization of the various primate groups adapts them for efficient use of the environment, defense against predators, and satisfaction of other basic needs. It does so by structuring behavior for effective responses in different situations. But how do individuals come to adjust their own behavior to fit into group life? The answer lies in social learning, or *socialization*.

Precocial Strategy

Because primates depend so heavily on learned behavior, anything that aids learning is probably adaptive. The reproductive strategy primates have developed is a good example.

Primates follow a *precocial strategy* of reproduction. That is, the gestation period is long, litters are very small (usually only one infant), and offspring are born physically well developed. In humans, the nervous system is well developed, although the rest of the body is relatively immature at birth. Primates nurse for a long time, reach sexual maturity after a long period of development, and then live a long time as adults. Though the length of these life periods varies from group to group, their proportion of the total lifespan is similar. See Figure 10.

Primates probably follow the precocial strategy as a result of early adaptations to limited food supplies. In environments in

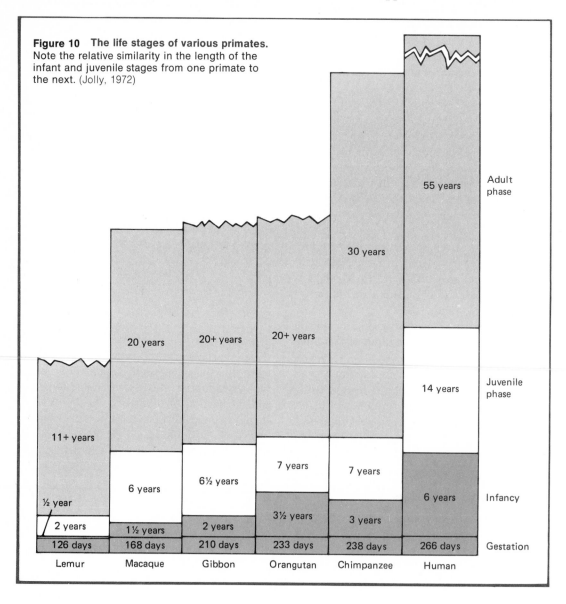

Figure 10 **The life stages of various primates.** Note the relative similarity in the length of the infant and juvenile stages from one primate to the next. (Jolly, 1972)

	Lemur	Macaque	Gibbon	Orangutan	Chimpanzee	Human	
Adult phase	11+ years	20 years	20+ years	20+ years	30 years	55 years	
Juvenile phase		6 years	6½ years	7 years	7 years	14 years	
Infancy	2 years	1½ years	2 years	3½ years	3 years	6 years	
Gestation	½ year / 126 days	168 days	210 days	233 days	238 days	266 days	

which food is plentiful and animals are not crowded, selection will favor those that can raise the largest families and gather the most food. But when animals are competing for a limited food supply and a species population is existing very near the carrying capacity of the environment, natural selection will favor those that have fewer young and therefore consume less food. Large animals—like primates—are more likely to strain the carrying capacity of an environment and are thus under greater pressure to have small litters of young (Martin, 1975).

Small litters and a long period of dependency ensure that each offspring gets a lot of attention from its parents. Not only does this improve their chances of survival, but it also gives them time to absorb a great deal of learned behavior. The environments in which the higher primates in particular have evolved have been characterized by changing feeding relationships and environmental conditions. In such environments, the ability to learn new behavior is an important advantage.

Stages of Development

Socialization occurs mostly in critical sequences of interactions between the mother and the infant and among *age-mates,* or peers. These interactions have been studied carefully in experiments with monkeys and apes that test the importance of such variables as physical contact with the mother. Such experiments may help us to understand early hominid behavior and human development as well.

Infant Stage. The first stage in the young primate's development involves close attachment to its mother. For the first few months of its life the two are in constant contact, because the infant is completely dependent on its mother for food, protection, and transportation.

Infant-Mother Attachment. For the baby, this is a reflex stage. Its behaviors are instinctive responses to specific stimuli, serving mostly to keep the baby in contact with its mother and to help it to feed. When primate young are touched near the mouth, they instinctually turn their head toward the stimulus. Sucking is elicited in the same way. Primate young also are born with the ability to cling to their mother's fur as she moves from place to place.

Experiments run by Harry and Margaret Harlow at the University of Wisconsin show that the cravings for contact and bodily support are even stronger than the food-seeking drive. The Harlows rigged up pairs of surrogate monkey mothers. One was made only of wire but gave out milk through a nipple. The other offered no milk but was covered with terry cloth. Infant rhesus monkeys were separated from their own mothers at birth and placed in cages with both surrogate mothers from which to choose. They invariably spent most of their time clinging to the cloth mother, visiting the wire one only to nurse. Further experiments suggested that infants find this body contact reassuring, especially in new or frightening situations (Harlow & Harlow, 1958).

Mothering. Infant primates are born with reflexes that tie them to their mother. But to what extent is mothering instinctual? Does caring for an infant—suckling, carrying, cleaning, and protecting it, tolerating its clambering and clinging, and gently shaping its behaviors—come naturally? Probably not.

Observations of langurs show that older, more experienced langur mothers are able to keep their infants quiet and contented. Younger mothers, on the other hand, have many more problems. Sometimes they even try to nurse their babies upside down (Jay, 1965). Mothering is apparently learned in part from youthful interaction with a mother and other infants. The Harlows found that rhesus

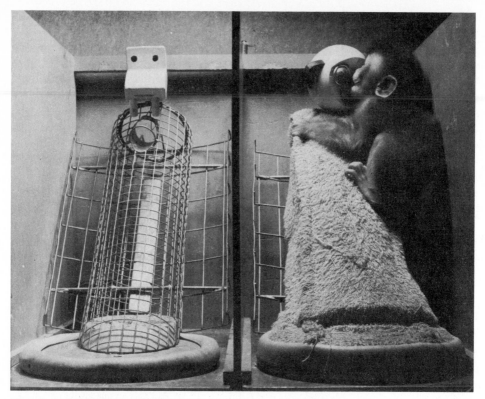

Experiments by Harry and Margaret Harlow show that infant rhesus monkeys have a strong need for the reassurance of bodily contact with their mothers. Here, an infant clings to a surrogate mother made of terry cloth. (Harry F. Harlow, University of Wisconsin Primate Laboratory)

monkeys raised in total social isolation make terrible mothers. When the infants tried to cling, their mothers pushed them away roughly, beat them, and held them to the floor (Harlow, Harlow, & Suomi, 1971).

Fathering. Though the mother is the central figure in the infant's life, sometimes the males also are involved. This varies greatly from troop to troop and species to species. In 3 troops of Japanese macaques that were studied, dominant males took care of the infants when they were about a year old. But in 15 other troops studied, the males rarely or never adopted a parental role. Among baboons, males are protective both of infants and mothers. The dominant males sometimes carry infants around, letting them cling to their belly for up to 20 minutes. Langur males, on the other hand, are indifferent at best. Sometimes they are downright hostile, and are known to kill infants they did not father (Hrdy, 1977).

Late Infant and Juvenile Stage. As the infant grows older, it leaves its mother for longer and longer periods of time and explores its environment. Using the mother as a secure home base, the infant learns to manipulate objects and begins to interact with its age-mates.

Play. Although we humans sometimes regard play as frivolous "monkey business," it serves real adaptive needs for primate young.

For one thing, it seems to aid their physical development. Chimpanzee mothers often play with their babies by hanging them from a branch and giving them pushes so they can swing back and forth. Strength and coordination improve rapidly. Young chimps also spend hours exploring and becoming familiar with the area in which they will spend their lives (Van Lawick-Goodall, 1965).

Play has another important adaptive function: It helps the young learn to interact smoothly with others and thus promotes integration into the troop. Though primatologists long thought that contact with the mother is most critical in socialization, further studies by the Harlows indicate that play with age-mates is equally important (Harlow & Harlow, 1971). Separation from the mother and age-mates can block normal social development in both humans and other primates. But researchers now emphasize that the behavior of both lower primates and humans is rather flexible during their long development period. Individuals can often recover to some extent from early deprivation if they are later exposed to more normal social situations (Clarke & Clarke, 1960).

Dominance Learning. Our best knowledge of dominance relationships comes from the study of terrestrial or semiterrestrial primates. Order within these groups depends largely on recognition of social ranking. Subordinate animals, for instance, usually move away or look away when a dominant animal approaches. In this way, actual fighting and the resulting injuries are avoided. But how do in-

Chimpanzee mother and her 2-year-old son. (Nancy Nicolson, Anthro-Photo)

A juvenile male baboon threatens another, who has sought protection by grooming a dominant adult male. Such interaction probably helps establish dominance relationships in the minds of young primates.
(James Moore, Anthro-Photo)

dividuals learn where they stand in the dominance hierarchy?

Some anthropologists suggest that dominance is learned during play. Wrestling, for instance, makes it clear to young primates who is stronger than whom. If this learning is accompanied by a bit of pain, it will probably be remembered clearly (Dolhinow & Bishop, 1972). It has been found that the social rank of the mother also has a strong influence on the social rank of her offspring. In rhesus monkeys, the offspring's rank seems to rise or fall with changes in its mother's rank (Marsden, 1968). It is also possible that an infant imitates its mother's style of interaction with others, whether assertive or subordinate.

In addition to inhibiting actual fighting, dominance strongly affects the spread of new behaviors through the troop. In a series of experiments to see how new traditions develop among primates, various new foods were set out for wild Japanese macaque troops. In most cases it was the young monkeys who started new behaviors. Some learned to eat candy, and one started to wash sweet potatoes to remove the sand. These new ideas spread first to other young monkeys, then to their mothers, and only gradually to some of the other adults. By contrast, when the leader of one troop introduced the notion of eating wheat, the new behavior was being imitated by the whole troop within four hours. Subordinate animals seem to learn from dominant animals much faster than the other way around (Frisch, 1968).

Adult Stage. In many species, the final stage in the primate life cycle involves complete separation of mother and offspring. At this point the mother instinctually puts distance between herself and her offspring, who finds relations with peers more and more rewarding. Curiosity about the environment also draws young primates away from their mothers. Even after full integration into the larger group, however, separation is not complete in all species. For example, among chimpanzees and macaques mother-offspring relationships continue to be quite strong and may persist for life. Jane Van Lawick-Goodall (1971) saw a chimpanzee mother being rescued by her 13-year-old son from an attack by a low-ranking adult male. And she noted that a socially mature 18-year-old male still spent a good bit of time with his old mother.

Biological Explanations of Social Behavior

To what extent is our social behavior and that of the other primates innate? To what degree are our actions shaped by our genes and therefore the product of thousands or millions of years of evolution? It is easy to see eating and reproduction as primarily instinctual adaptive behaviors that allow the human species to survive. But what about our nobler tendencies, such as altruism? Can these, too, be seen as adaptations to the biological need to survive and reproduce? According to *ethology* (the scientific study of animal behavior) and *sociobiology* (the study of the genetic basis of behavior and its evolution), perhaps so.

Essentially, these schools of thought contend that much behavior is innate. Because it affects the ways in which the organism adapts to its environment, behavior is susceptible to natural selection. Many behaviors, according to these schools, are encoded in the genes. As the organism develops, certain inherited patterns of behavior emerge. To some degree these patterns can be changed or elaborated

by learning. But the basic innate behaviors persist because they offer the species a selective advantage.

In effect, the ethologists and sociobiologists are trying to fit behavior—as well as anatomy and physiology—into the Darwinian theory of evolution. They differ, though, in the emphasis they place on the various aspects of the problem. While ethologists concentrate on the interaction of inheritance and learning in behavior, sociobiologists focus on why certain innate behavior has evolved. Sociobiologists are particularly interested in the adaptive function of behavior. Of the two models, ethology allows more room for the modification of the innate tendencies by learning.

Ethology

Ethologists have identified several kinds of innate behavior. First, there are fixed patterns of action. Red squirrels, for instance, display a highly adaptive behavioral sequence for hiding nuts in the ground. They go through these motions whether they have grown up in the woods or in a wire cage. This instinctual fixed action pattern can be modified by learning, however. With time and practice, wild squirrels learn to make sure that as a result of their movements they have completely buried the nut (Eibl-Eibesfeldt, 1968).

Learning also comes into play in the linking of a series of fixed action patterns. In primates, this learning seems to take place during juvenile play, as the young learn what their bodies can do and what the environment is like. The Harlows' male rhesus monkeys reared in social isolation can make some of the movements required for copulation, for these are instinctive. But linking them into sequences that work requires learning that apparently takes place in juvenile play. Socially deprived male monkeys fail because they do not know just where and how to mount the female (Harlow, Harlow, & Suomi, 1971).

Another kind of inherited behavior is triggered by a particular stimulus in the environment, called a *releaser*. The animal reacts to this stimulus in a set way, even though it has no experience of it. Many primates instinctually launch a blind attack if they hear the distress call of a young one. And sexual responses in male primates may be released by the sight of an estrous female's swollen genitals.

Ethological Explanation of Human Aggression. Ethologists have only recently begun to try to apply these concepts to human behavior. Irenaus Eibl-Eibesfeldt, a German ethologist, found (1968) that expressions and gestures used in greeting, flirting, and praying are similar in many different cultures and may therefore be based on innate behavioral patterns.

Some ethologists suspect that aggression may also be innate, but are unsure of the extent. Ethologists point out that children who are deaf and blind from birth display the same aggressive behavior patterns as people who could have learned these patterns from seeing and hearing them. Even in the most peaceful societies, acts of aggression are common, beginning in childhood. We tend to use the same motor patterns to threaten (glaring and foot-stamping, for instance) and to submit as our primate relatives do. That these patterns are held in common suggests an ancient biological origin. And, as discussed earlier, one area of our brain—the limbic system—seems to be adapted specifically to trigger aggressive responses. Not surprisingly, it is in the most primitive part of the brain.

Eibl-Eibesfeldt thinks that patterns of aggression are handed down genetically because they have adaptive functions. Aggression may promote spacing of individuals so that they do not overburden their environmental resources. Aggression may also establish dominance hierarchies in which the strongest and healthiest individuals emerge as leaders

and protectors. But killing an opponent of the same species is not adaptive in terms of species survival. So along with apparently instinctual predispositions to aggression, animals who could kill each other have evolved inhibitory mechanisms that reduce aggression. In dog fights, the dog that recognizes that it will lose adopts a puppylike posture that seems to melt the other's hostility.

Why then do humans go on killing one another? Ethologists speculate that weapons have made it possible for us to kill before appeasing gestures can inhibit our aggression. But our capacity for modifying innate responses by learning, and the pressure of other humans, tend to keep our potential for aggression in check (Eibl-Eibesfeldt, 1974).

Sociobiology

According to E. O. Wilson, a leading theoretician of sociobiology, one of its goals is to find biological, evolutionary explanations for all of behavior. These ambitions are far-reaching. Sociobiologists predict that their work will bring about a reformulation of the various studies of human behavior—sociology, psychology, economics, and ethnics, for example.

Like the ethologists, sociobiologists do not limit themselves to studying human and nonhuman primate behavior. They have, however, suggested a framework for the sociobiological study of primate behavior. Some of the major social traits of primates are traced through various interacting factors back to ancient mammalian behavioral features that survive relatively unchanged. Aggressive tendencies among the males and a strong mother-infant bond are primitive mammalian traits. Newer trends, such as increasing brain size and adaptation to an arboreal environment, have brought about other behavior. For instance, the ability of higher primates to live in complex societies, in which they must respond differently to many different individuals, can be attributed partly to their increased intelligence. Intelligence in turn is linked in evolution to increasingly skillful manipulation of objects with the hands, larger size (and therefore larger brains), improved vision, and increasingly rich systems of communications (Wilson, 1975).

A Sociobiological Explanation of Altruism. One aspect of sociobiological theory tries to fill an important gap in Darwin's logic: If survival and reproduction are the main evolutionary goals, why would one organism risk its own life for another? Is it possible that such altruism defies biological explanation? The sociobiologists contend that it does not. All persistent behaviors have some biological function. Altruism is adaptive, though sometimes in a roundabout way.

It is easiest to see why individuals might sacrifice themselves for their relatives. In helping each other, blood relatives are improving the chances that the genes they share will be passed on. According to sociobiologists, organisms will unwittingly act as though they understand the mathematics involved. As a British biologist jokingly announced, he would gladly risk his life for two brothers or eight cousins. Altruism within the family can thus be seen as genetic selfishness. It acts to improve the genes' chances of surviving, though not necessarily the individual's chances of enjoying a long life.

The theory of genetic selfishness, however, cannot explain altruistic acts toward nonrelatives. To account for these, sociologists have employed the theory of *reciprocal altruism.* A population that socializes its members to believe that helping one another is good improves its overall genetic fitness. This population also finds it adaptive to promote aggressive morality and guilt in order to punish "cheaters" who do not reciprocate (Wilson, 1975). According to sociobiologists, the existence of many major human institutions— schools, churches, legal systems—can be explained by their contribution to reciprocal altruism.

Like ethological explanations, most of the sociobiologists' arguments are still at a theoretical stage. Ultimately, these scientists hope to be able to predict a population's social characteristics by combining statistical data (such as figures on the growth, age structure, and gene flow of populations) with information about the genetic traits of the population.

Summary

1. The activity of animals can be broken down arbitrarily into *behavioral systems.* In our study of primate behavior, we have discussed *locomotion* and *feeding (first-order behaviors), information processing* (neither first- nor second-order behavior), and *communication* and *social organization,* both *second-order behaviors.*

2. The basic locomotory types among the primates are *vertical clinging and leaping, quadrupedalism, brachiation,* and *bipedalism.*

3. Paleoanthropologists are especially interested in the relation between dentition and ecology among the living primates. *Insect-eaters* and *leaf-eaters* must grind their food into small pieces; their *molars* are relatively large and equipped with many *cusps* and shearing surfaces. In *fruit-eaters'* teeth, which are designed for crushing, these features are reduced. Use of prepared foods has brought about a reduction in canines and size of molars in humans.

4. Primate evolution has been marked by an increase in the size of the *cerebral cortex* and its ability to control the more primitive brain structures.

5. The complex behavior of primates is observed in *naturalistic, compound,* and *laboratory* studies.

6. Primates communicate by means of *olfactory signals* (especially important among the nocturnal prosimians), *tactile signals, visual signals,* and *auditory signals. Call systems* are *closed,* or limited to a set of fixed signals, and linked to environmental stimuli. The highest primates—chimpanzees in particular—have been trained to exhibit some of the abilities needed for human language. They can build a set of discrete symbols into a limited range of meanings *(dual patterning),* understand some logic and causal relationships, and display some self-awareness. Research on their ability to refer to things *displaced* in time and space is proceeding.

7. Because primate social organization is complex, a number of plausible ways of categorizing it have been developed. Group structure is more closely related to the primate's environment than to its taxonomic category. Diet, food supply, and the threat of predators strongly affect group size, structure, *territoriality,* and the size of the *home range.*

8. Primates are born well developed, in small litters: a *precocial reproductive strategy.* During their long period of development they become *socialized,* adjusted for group life. Aspects of this process include increasing separation from the mother, more association with *age-mates,* play, increasing physical development, and dominance learning.

6

Fossils and Primate Evolution

WHEN Darwin wrote *The Descent of Man* (1871), direct evidence of human ancestors was practically nonexistent. So he was forced to rely on what was known of the anatomy and behavior of living primates for his speculations about our beginnings. Today the fossil record of human evolution is much more complete and gives us facts that Darwin never had.

Only the discovery and careful study of fossils will tell us about the sequence of changes leading to modern humans. Without a clear fossil record of our divergence from the apes, we shall never know for sure how *hominids* (humans and their direct ancestors) first distinguished themselves from the evolutionary lineage of the great apes. Only by the study of fossils can we test our theories about what earlier primates looked like; where, when, and how they evolved; and under what environmental pressures.

This search for our origins has intensified in the past few decades and has yielded large numbers of fossil hominids. But fossil evidence is still uneven, so that some parts of our evolutionary past are better known than others.

Fossils and Their Interpretation

A *fossil* consists of the preserved remains of an organism that lived in the past. It may be nothing more than a tooth or a jaw or a footprint. Or it may be a fully preserved body, complete with all its soft parts, such as the woolly mammoths found frozen in the Siberian tundra. Unfortunately, however, most fossils are mere fragments, difficult to find and to interpret.

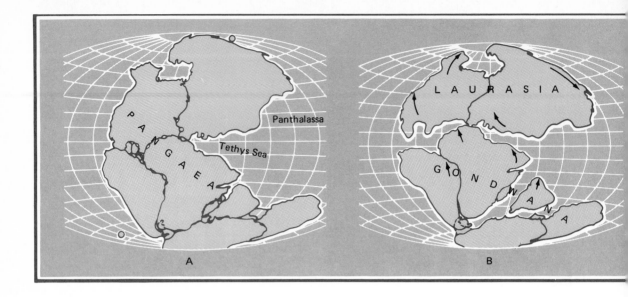

A   B

The Formation of Fossils

When a fossil is found, *paleontologists* (scientists who study fossils) need two kinds of information before they can interpret it. The first of these is an understanding of the processes that shaped the earth in that area; the second is an understanding of the processes that preserved the fossil itself.

The Geological Processes. We tend to think of the earth's surface features—hills, mountains, plains, bodies of water—as permanent fixtures in an otherwise changing world. But they, too, are being changed, though very slowly, by the same forces that have always been at work shaping the earth.

Today, a basic assumption underlying the interpretation of fossils is the concept of *uniformitarianism.* As mentioned earlier, it states that events in the past were subject to the same natural laws that are operating in the present. If we find the petrified remains of a shellfish, for instance, we can guess that the shell was covered by sediments, just as shells are being covered now. We assume that processes such as decomposition and the replacement of the shell with minerals in the sediment operated the same way then as they do now.

Understanding these natural processes first requires some geological knowledge about the earth. On a large scale, the earth's continents are made up of fairly thin crusts of rock and soil gradually being shifted about by the movement of molten material plates beneath them. *Plate tectonics,* the study of the movement of the continental plates of the earth's crust, indicates that all land once formed a huge supercontinent, which has been called Pangaea ("all lands"). Pressures in the underlying rock layer apparently caused it to break into 10 large plates and some smaller ones. As these plates were pulled apart, two supercontinents formed—*Laurasia* in the north and *Gondwana* in the south. Further drifting of the plates gradually split the land masses into the continents we know today. Some of the plates eventually collided again. For example, the plate carrying with it the Indian subcontinent pushed into the Asian mainland, thrusting up the Himalayan Mountains. (See Figure 1.)

Geologists think this process of *continental drift* began about 200 million years ago and

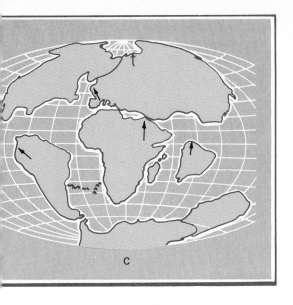

Figure 1 The breakup of Pangaea.
200 million years ago *(A)* all land was part of Pangaea, but by 180 million years B.P. *(B)* Laurasia had split apart from Gondwana, and India had begun its long drift northward. By the end of the Cretaceous period, about 65 million years ago, *(C)* South America had shifted to the west, opening up the South Atlantic, and India had moved far to the north.

continues today at the rate of several centimeters a year. It creates the stresses that now and then cause earthquakes or volcanic eruptions. Knowledge of continental drift is important to our understanding of primate evolution, for areas that are now separated by oceans were once joined in the past. The presence of similar animals or similar fossils in lands that are no longer connected can often be explained by continental drift.

On a smaller scale, all parts of the earth are continually being formed and changed by local geological processes. *Igneous material* is formed when molten mineral matter is brought up from the earth's core (as it does when a volcano erupts) and cools. *Sedimentary material* is the product of the perpetual weathering of the earth's surface. Bits of soil and rock are eroded by wind or water and deposited with organic material in layers in low areas, such as sea bottoms. These deposits may gradually solidify, sometimes preserving traces of plants and animals and patterns such as water ripples or mud cracks. If this sedimentary material becomes buried very deeply by later deposits, the earth's heat or pressure may change it to a third form: *metamorphic material.* Sandstone deposits, for

instance, may be changed to a harder form: quartzite.

Each kind of material bears clues to the circumstances under which it was formed. The material deposited in sediments, for instance, shows no change as long as environmental conditions remain constant. If the environment changes, however, different types of material will be deposited. When the earth's surface can be seen in cross-section—in excavations or on cliffs bordering a river—environmental changes show up as *strata* (or layers), which differ in texture, color, composition, and fossil forms. Younger material is always deposited on top of older material. Reading of the layers is complicated by the fact that a number of strata may be turned sideways or even completely folded over by geological upheavals. Upper layers may not be older than lower ones. As a result, geologists must often compare strata with similar layers in other areas to reconstruct the sequence of deposition.

A paleontologist studying this *stratification* can read the layers as clues to changes in the environment. Deposits laid down during very dry periods, for instance, may consist of sharp-sided particles blown from deserts by

Louis Leakey measures strata at the site in Olduvai Gorge where the first relatively complete East African fossil hominid skull was found in 1959. Part of Olduvai's value as a site is that its datable rock layers extend unbroken to about 2 million years B.P. (Jen and Des Bartlett, Photo Researchers)

the wind. By contrast, sediments deposited when the environment was more favorable to plant and animal life may contain remnants of these organisms and rock particles with edges rounded by river and stream action.

Fossilization. When most organisms die, all traces of their existence soon disappear. Their bodies are soon broken down by mechanical and chemical processes and, as we discussed in Chapter 3, by decomposers. Only those that are protected from these processes may survive as fossils. Rapid burial in silt, resin, peat bogs, tar pits, or volcanic ash prevents decay, but coverage by waterbone sediment is the most common form of protection. Creatures that have no hard parts—such as jellyfish—usually decay before this can happen. But

shells and the hard skeletal remains of vertebrates may resist decay long enough for burial to occur. Since teeth, jaws, and skulls are the hardest, densest parts of the vertebrate skeleton, they are the most common vertebrate fossils.

Once buried, the hard parts may undergo chemical changes. The few that are preserved without chemically changing are known as *subfossils,* or unaltered fossils. The frozen woolly mammoths are an example. Most fossils, however, are altered by chemicals dissolved in water seeping through the sediment. Some chemicals may completely dissolve the organism, perhaps leaving a *mold* of its shape if the sediment around it turns to rock. Sometimes minerals may seep into the spaces left by decayed organic matter in bones, helping to preserve them. This process is called *impregnation. Petrification,* a third possibility, is the gradual replacement of the original mineral matter by harder minerals. Either impregnation or petrification can literally turn the remains into stone. The fossil that results looks much like the original bone or shell. But it is usually heavier and chemically different, and all the fine details that existed in the original may not be reproduced.

Incompleteness of the Fossil Record. The chances that an organism will be preserved as a fossil and then found by a paleontologist are very slim. So far, we have probably discovered only about 1 percent of the kinds of plants and animals that have ever lived (Sawkins et al., 1974). Because producers form the most abundant trophic level, it is natural that more plants than animals are fossilized. And because humans have been only a small percentage of the animal life on the earth, their fossils are rare. In fact, it is quite possible that we have not yet found the earliest hominids.

There are a number of reasons why the fossil record is so incomplete. Conditions in some areas and times have not permitted fossilization. Some soils, for instance, lack the minerals needed for petrification. Sea creatures have the best chances of being preserved, for sedimentation occurs continually at the bottom of the sea. Usually, land creatures have been fossilized only if their remains end up in an environment where sedimentation is taking place, such as a floodplain, a lake, or an area being covered by drifting sands. Since many animals never reach these areas, certain segments of lineages may not be preserved. And even if an organism happens to be sealed in sediment, and fossilization takes place, the sedimentary rock itself may later be altered by metamorphosis or exposed and destroyed by weathering.

As we have seen, only creatures with hard parts are likely to be preserved, and only their hard parts are likely to be fossilized. Often only a fraction of the original skeleton is discovered. Our only evidence of a creature that may have been the first primate is a single tooth. For all these reasons, the fossil record as it presently exists gives an incomplete and distorted view of the flora and fauna living at any given time in the past. Paleontologists must therefore often work with maddeningly incomplete data. They are therefore always looking for new fossils to expand their knowledge of past animals and plants.

Finding and Excavating Fossils

Our knowledge of extinct life is also limited by the difficulty of locating fossils. Millions of years of sedimentation cover them, often in inaccessible spots. But in areas where weathering or cutting into the earth's surface has taken place, layers of fossils may be exposed. Sand or gravel pits, quarries, stream banks, areas of geological upheaval, and caves may contain exposed fossils. These fossils can simply be picked up or dug out, or, if the site is promising, a major excavation may be organized.

In a big excavation, layers of sediment are removed carefully, one at time. Soil and fossil material is excavated in horizontal slices, or *horizons,* which correspond to natural geological layers. As each horizon is exposed, the excavators draw a map showing the position of any fossils found in it. These maps are invaluable in figuring out whether floods or other forces have placed the fossils where they are, or whether the organisms remained in place when they died.

Interpretation of Fossils

Since the primate fossil record is small, the fossils that are found are subjected to minute analysis. Small details take on great importance in interpreting the age, ancestry, characteristics, and evolutionary relationships of extinct animals known only as fossil fragments.

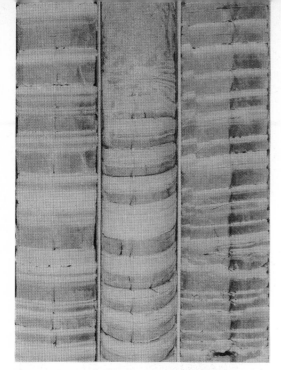

Varves from glacial lakes once located in present-day New Jersey and New York. The light-colored bands were deposited in the summer, the dark-colored ones in the winter.
(Courtesy of the American Museum of Natural History)

Dating Fossils. A crucial part of interpreting fossil evidence is dating it, for only after a fossil is placed in a time sequence with other evidence can its place in evolution be assessed. A sequence of events is very important in reconstructing lines of descent, since, of course, descendants are more recent than ancestors. By dating the remains of animals in a site or in a region, we can also learn whether or not they lived at the same time and were therefore a part of the same ecosystem.

Relative Dating Methods. *Relative dating methods* can tell us the age of a specimen relative to another known specimen or deposit. According to the principle of *superposition,* each geological layer was deposited on top of the one beneath it. Therefore, in deposits that have not been disturbed by geological upheavals, fossils found in upper layers are younger than those in deeper layers. During the nineteenth and twentieth centuries, paleontologists constructed a geological history of the earth by establishing the order in which various strata in different parts of the world were formed. The study of sedimentary rock layers and their sequence is called *stratigraphy.*

The age of any layer was given in relation to the ones above and below it. Traditionally, paleontologists could only estimate the absolute age of a fossil by guessing how long it would have taken geological forces to bury the remains in the layer in which they were found. In the nineteenth and early twentieth centuries, paleontologists' estimates of the age of many fossils were far too low. The lack of an accurate time scale hindered early interpretations of our evolutionary history. As a result, the human-like fossils that were being found in Europe seemed too young geologically to be our ancestors.

Fossils themselves can act as clues to the relative dating of sedimentary deposits found in different areas. According to the principles we discussed in Chapter 3, most species change over time and never return to their earlier forms. Layers from two different sites that contain matching fossils are therefore assumed to be about the same age. Some fossils are so common and widespread that they are used to compare the ages of strata at different sites. These so-called *index fossils* are also used to compare the environmental conditions in different geographical areas.

Stratigraphy is still an essential method of relative dating. To it, paleontologists have added several chemical methods. These more precise methods were necessary partly to date different fossils at separate sites and partly because fossils found at the same level in a single deposit may not have lived at the same time. An *intrusion,* caused by a burial, an earthquake, or some other process, frequently places younger remains in the same layer as older ones. Using chemical methods, paleontologists can analyze the composition of fossils found together to determine whether they are actually the same age. While fossils lie buried, they gradually absorb flourine and uranium and lose nitrogen. Chemical and x-ray analysis can show whether two fossils contain about the same amounts of these elements. If not, the fossils are probably of different ages. Unfortunately, differing environmental conditions affect the rate of absorption or loss of minerals. Consequently, these methods can only be used for relative dating of fossils found at the same site.

Another method of relative dating is *varve analysis*. Varves are layers of silt deposited annually in glacial lakes by the water from melting ice sheets. Sequences have been es-

tablished as far back as 17,000 years for areas that were covered with glaciers for long periods of time, primarily in Scandinavia.

Pollen analysis, or *palynology*, not only provides a sequence by which remains can be dated but also is an invaluable source of data about prehistoric ecologies. Pollen is preserved very well, especially in damp soil. Samples are taken at a site and observed through a microscope. Experts can identify the plants from which the pollen originated and establish regional sequences of vegetational history, some of which stretch back 15,000 years.

Chronometric Dating Methods. Until recently, our ability to date the age of the earth

The excavation of Dragon Bone Hill in Chou-kou-tien, near Peking, China. So-called dragon teeth, which had been sold as medicine in drug stores, led paleontologists to excavate this site in the 1920s and 1930s and find Peking Man, the source of the teeth. (Courtesy of the American Museum of Natural History)

precisely was limited by the lack of any correlation between the way we measure time and the rate at which material is formed into strata. In order to break the continuum of time into measurable chunks, we usually count each revolution of the earth around the sun as a single unit: a calendar year. The problem with trying to measure time in the ancient past is that nothing in the geological record corresponds to our calendar years. Sediments, for instance, are not always laid down in regular yearly bands like tree rings, or at a steady rate measurable in centimeters per year. But scientists have found that certain materials change at a uniform rate through time. In nature, many elements have several forms, each of which is called an *isotope.* Some isotopes are stable, and others are unstable. The stable isotopes do not change over time, but the unstable isotopes, which are said to be *radioactive,* spontaneously change (or decay) into other elements. Decay occurs at a steady rate that can be measured in terms of how long it takes for one-half of the "parent" atoms to decay to atoms of the "daughter" element. The rate is expressed as the *half-life* of the isotope. (See Figure 2.) Unlike chemical changes, these nuclear reactions are not affected by external environmental factors such as heat or pressure. They reflect only the passage of time. These changes can be measured and equated with years to establish the approximate age of fossils. In these absolute, or *chronometric dating* methods, time is often measured backward from the present (set at A.D. 1950 on the Christian time scale). Remains approximately a million years old would be dated one million years before present, or B.P.

Radiometric dating techniques are based on the rate of decay of radioactive isotopes in the rocks surrounding fossil finds. To calculate the age of a rock containing a radioactive isotope, a scientist uses three figures: (1) the initial quantity of the parent isotope in the rock, (2)

the rate of decay of that isotope, and (3) the amount of the isotope now present in the rock. The second figure—the rate of decay—is known for most isotopes. The third is determined by laboratory analysis. And the first is assumed to be the same as similar rocks being formed today. These calculations assume a closed system: None of the "parent" or "daughter" has been lost or added to the rock. In some cases, however, this is not a safe assumption. These radiometric methods do not work for sedimentary rocks, because the mineral grains in sedimentary deposits have been weathered from older rocks. It works best for volcanic igneous materials. When datable igneous rocks are found in association with sedimentary deposits (which may contain fossils), the relative time scale suggested by the stratigraphy can be translated to an absolute one.

To give absolute dates to very ancient material, paleontologists must analyze elements that have an extremely slow rate of decay. Uranium, for instance, has a number of unstable isotopes with very long half-lives. They all decay to stable isotopes of lead. Two isotopes commonly used for dating are ^{235}U and ^{238}U. Their half-lives are 713 million years and 4.5 billion years, respectively. These isotopes are often present in common rocks, such as granite. Since they are frequently found decaying together, though at different rates, the age of the rock can be cross-checked by doing separate calculations for each isotope. If the two dates match, they are probably correct. This method is called *uranium-lead dating* and is used to date the oldest rocks found in the earth.

A second form of radiometric dating uses the decay of unstable potassium isotopes (^{40}K) to argon (^{40}Ar), an inert gas. Potassium is found in many common minerals, and its long half-life (1.3 million years) makes it useful for dating very old material. At Olduvai Gorge in Tanzania, for instance, *potassium-argon dat-*

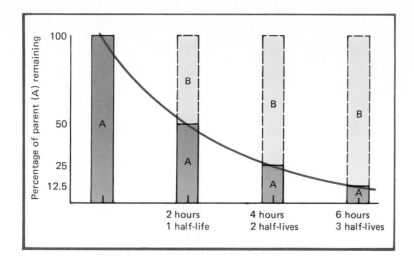

Figure 2 The concept of half-life. One-half of parent isotope *A* remains after one half-life (two hours), and one-quarter is left after two half-lives, the rest having decayed into daughter element *B*. (Sawkins et al., 1974)

ing has been used to date beds of consolidated volcanic ash that buried important early hominid fossils.

Molten rock contains no argon. But as the rock cools, ^{40}K decays at a known rate, and ^{40}Ar is trapped. By determining the ratio of potassium to argon, scientists can measure the time that has passed since the rock was formed. The main problem with this method is that argon sometimes leaks out of the cooled rock, making it impossible to date. Some rocks hold argon gas better than others. Mica, for instance, keeps 80 to 100 percent of its argon; feldspars retain only 40 to 85 percent of theirs (Hole & Heizer, 1973). In addition, not all sites are associated with igneous rock.

A promising method developed in the 1960s—*fission-track dating*—focuses on the short tracks made across a rock by particles of radioactive uranium atoms as they decay. If etched with acid, these tiny trails can be seen under a high-power microscope. To date rock with this method, scientists count the tracks and measure the uranium content of the sample. Because the rate of uranium decay is known, a ratio of the number of tracks to the amount of uranium present yields the age of

the rock. The method seems to be reliable for rocks that are 100,000 to 1,000,000 years old. The dates it gives are used to check the results of potassium-argon dating. The two methods together are very accurate. But heating by fire or by geological processes can erase the tracks, posing a potential for error (Michels, 1973).

Fossils found in association with volcanic rocks can also be dated by the orientation of particles in the rock. This method is called *paleomagnetic dating*. In the 1960s scientists discovered that the earth has regularly reversed its magnetic field. For reasons not yet understood, magnetic north and south have sometimes been where they are now, at other times, they have been reversed. About 20 reversals have occurred during the last four million years. As molten rock cools, metallic particles arrange themselves in accordance with the earth's magnetic field, leaving a record of the field at that time. Samples of ancient volcanic deposits and cores from the seabed have been collected from all over the world. Combining the polarity changes and the potassium-argon dates of the volcanic rocks at different levels has allowed paleontologists to chart an absolute time scale for the reversals, which

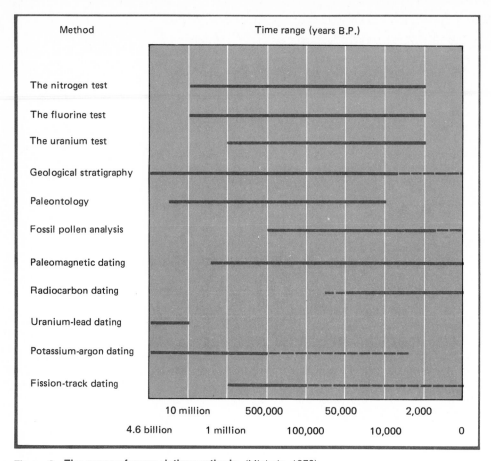

| Method | Time range (years B.P.) |

The nitrogen test

The fluorine test

The uranium test

Geological stratigraphy

Paleontology

Fossil pollen analysis

Paleomagnetic dating

Radiocarbon dating

Uranium-lead dating

Potassium-argon dating

Fission-track dating

10 million   500,000   50,000   2,000

4.6 billion   1 million   100,000   10,000   0

Figure 3 **The range of some dating methods.** (Michels, 1973)

stretch back millions of years. Since the reversals happen very quickly by geological standards, they serve as sharp time markers.

Improvements of chronometric dating have led to continual revision of the geological timescale originally based only on stratigraphy. The new methods make it difficult to fake fossil remains and make it much easier to judge the time relationship of fossils.

See Figure 3 for a summary of the varying time ranges in which the methods we have discussed can be applied. For more recent artifacts and fossils, archaeologists use different methods of dating. *Radiocarbon dating,* for instance, is frequently used to date items up to 50,000 years old. The shortness of the half-life of ^{14}C, the radioactive carbon isotope used, limits its usefulness. We will cover this and other techniques for dating relatively recent remains in a later chapter, where archaeological methods are discussed.

Environmental Reconstructions. In addition to figuring out how old fossils are, paleontologists also try to reconstruct the ancient environment of which the organisms were a part. First it must be determined whether the fossils are *autochthonous* (still surrounded by organisms from their own ecosystem) or *allochthonous* (dumped into a different ecosystem). Predators, scavengers, running water, or wind may have carried the bodies for miles before depositing them in a different habitat. Paleontologists therefore search both the remains and the maps they make of each geological layer for subtle clues to whether the organisms were buried where they had lived. Abrasion marks on bones, for instance, may suggest that they have been transported some distance before being buried by sediment (Behrensmeyer, 1975).

Working from fragments of other flora and fauna and a knowledge of the niche structure of contemporary plants and animals, paleontologists try to reconstruct the ancient ecosystem. For instance, if fossilized palm trees are found, the area was probably tropical to subtropical, for palm trees now grow only in warm regions. Dwarf birches, on the other hand, suggest a very cold climate, for these trees now live only in Arctic or Alpine regions. Vertebrate remains, too, may provide indirect clues to what the region was like. For instance, the presence of animals ancestral to contemporary grazing creatures—such as gazelles—may suggest that the area was once a grassland. Animal clues are not altogether reliable, though, for some animals have adapted to different habitats over time. For example, the ancestors of arctic foxes and polar bears once lived in warm or temperate climates (Thenius, 1973). Nevertheless, environmental reconstructions allow paleontologists to make inferences about the ecological factors that may have influenced the evolution of a species.

Applying Linnaean Taxonomy to Fossils. Because dating methods are becoming more precise, much of the guesswork in paleontology is being eliminated. But figuring out *phylogenies,* theories tracing the evolutionary relationships among a group of organisms, still raises a number of problems. The problem is often further complicated by the scientific names given to fossils. Generally, these taxonomic categories are derived from hypotheses about the relationships between

different fossils. Like any other scientific theories, taxonomic categories and the phylogenic theories from which they are derived are subject to revision in terms of new data. In the evolution of primates, including hominids, we are fairly certain of phylogenic relationships from the present back to about 3 million years B.P. But the record of fossils older than that is more fragmentary, so phylogenies and taxonomies suggested for older periods are more controversial.

A second problem is that the Linnaean system, the basis of modern taxonomy, was designed for living species. Species are now defined as populations that can interbreed successfully. But there is no way to tell directly whether two extinct primates could have interbred or not. We have no way of determining reproductive relationships, other than to judge how different or similar extinct animals were in anatomy. For this reason, many scientists make a distinction between *biospecies,* or reproductively isolated populations of living organisms able to breed successfully with one another, and *paleospecies,* anatomically similar extinct animals.

Paleontology creates a third problem by adding a time perspective that does not exist in the classification of living animals. The fossil record stretches back millions of years. When we try to group these extinct forms into families, genera, and species, how many years can each group encompass? There are as yet no generally accepted rules for this. Part of the problem is that organisms differ in their rates of evolution. The evolution of humans has been especially rapid, so that the physical form of hominids has changed more in a shorter period of time than that of other animals.

Until recently, the time dimension was not much of a problem. When there were huge time gaps between groups of fossils that looked different, it was easy to see them as separate species. But as these gaps are filled by new fossil discoveries, it becomes harder to decide where to divide continually evolving animals into distinct groups. Transitional forms—those having some characteristics of an earlier group and some of a later one—are especially exciting to find. But their discovery is usually accompanied by a storm of controversy over where in the existing phylogeny they should be placed.

Naming fossils has posed a fourth difficulty. Taxonomists have worked out careful rules for naming contemporary species. But the excitement of discovering new fossils has led some researchers to give almost every new find a different name on the basis of slight anatomical variations or geographical distance from other finds. They tend to class variants as separate species. For instance, over 60 taxonomic names have been applied to fossil hominids. Having this many pseudospecies greatly complicates the task of seeing trends and relationships in evolution (Simons, 1972; Harrison & Weiner, 1963).

More recently, some scientists have begun to group together anatomically varied fossils in the same category. They use variations among individuals in a living biospecies as a guide to how much variation there may have been in its ancestral paleospecies. Modern gorillas, for instance, are a single species, but individuals vary greatly in size, skull and tooth shape, color, and skeletal patterns. Age and sex are always important sources of variation among the members of a species. The skeletal differences between mature and immature male and female gorillas and orangutans are quite great. Using this model, some paleontologists feel that the variation seen in early hominids may be explained partially as the difference in shape between the male and female of the species.

Reconstructing Extinct Animals. Researchers' views of phylogeny inevitably influence their ideas of how extinct animals must have looked. We have almost no record of the external features of extinct organisms, for soft parts are rarely preserved. At best, drawings and models of extinct creatures can be based on complete skeletons, if they are found. Anatomists can compare these fossils to the structure of closely related living animals to figure out how the bodies of the extinct animals were filled out with muscles and how they moved. Fur, feathers, manes, and skin texture and color, however, can only be guessed at.

In the case of our own ancestors, reconstruction of soft parts is especially difficult, because relatively complete hominid skeletons are very rare. Illustrations and models of our predecessors therefore tend to reflect the scientist's concept of phylogeny, and even the popular evolutionary notions of the day.

The Record of Primate Evolution

We will devote the rest of this chapter to the earliest creatures thought to be primates and trace the beginnings of the evolutionary path that leads eventually to modern humans. Coverage in this chapter will end with the Miocene Epoch, when the hominid lineage may have split off from the pongid lineage. The earliest hominids and the members of the genus *Homo* will be examined in the next two chapters.

The Geological Time Scale

The history of the earth is divided by geologists into four long *eras:* the *Precambrian,* the *Paleozoic* (ancient life), the *Mesozoic* (middle development of life), and *Cenozoic* (recent life). The Precambrian stretches back to about 4.5 or 4.6 billion years B.P., the current estimate for when the earth was formed.

The other three eras are divided into *periods,* which correspond to changing geological patterns—the building up and wearing down of mountains, temperature changes, glaciation, continental drift, the spreading and shrinking of the seas—and also to distinctive plant and animal forms. The two periods of the most recent era, the Cenozoic, are the Tertiary and the Quaternary. These periods are further subdivided into *epochs,* which provide a more precise correspondence with particular life forms or geological features. Table 1 (pp. 118–119) shows the geological time scale that we shall use in this book.

Anatomical Themes in Evolution

As the earth has evolved, a great variety of plant and animal forms has appeared. But despite their diversity, life forms are variations on a limited number of themes. At the broadest level, these themes of anatomical organization are called *phyla.* Our own line developed from the phylum Chordata, characterized by specialized organs and tissues, bilateral symmetry (most structures on one side are duplicated on the other), and an internal backbone. In some members of the phylum, the backbone is a flexible, supportive rod. The others have jointed vertebrae and first appeared in the Ordovician Period of the Paleozoic Era as primitive fish. Later, amphibians and then reptiles developed successful variations on this basic theme, which allowed them to exploit plant life in terrestrial ecosystems. Mammals, representing our version of the chordate plan, emerged slowly in the Triassic Period of the Mesozoic Era, when reptiles were the dominant form of animal life. But mammals mushroomed in number and variety as the Cretaceous Period ended and the Cenozoic Era (the Age of Mammals) began. It was about this time, 70 million years B.P., that the first primates may have emerged from mammalian stock.

The Cretaceous Period (145–65 million years B.P.)

For most of the long *Cretaceous Period,* Pangaea, the land mass that subsequently formed today's continents, was just beginning to break up. Early mammals were therefore able to spread all over the world. Much of North America and Europe was covered by inland seas and swamps, but the land was rising during cataclysmic mountain-building episodes. Because the land masses were grouped near the equator, the climate of all terrestrial ecosystems was probably subtropical or tropical. Changes in vegetation that occurred during this period were very significant for primate evolution. In contrast to the ferns and conifers dominant in the past, *angiosperms* (flowering plants, shrubs, and trees) were becoming abundant. These plants created a number of new potential econiches, which were rapidly occupied. Insects began to use the rich food supplies offered by flowers and fruits. Birds and mammals fed on both the new vegetation and the insects. All of these forms underwent bursts of adaptive radiation as they took advantage of new environmental opportunities.

Some of the Cretaceous mammals were probably small hedgehoglike creatures that ran about on the ground looking for insects to eat (Cartmill, 1975). These insectivores would have seemed insignificant next to the giant dinosaurs that had long been dominant. But when the dinosaurs died out at the end of the period, one of these tiny mammals probably gave rise to the primate line.

Whether this divergence happened during the Cretaceous Period is uncertain. A single molar screened out of sedimentary rubble in Montana is the only evidence that primates may have appeared during this period. The creature to which it belonged has been named *Purgatorius.* Recent finds of similar teeth, toothbearing lower jaws, and a fragmentary

Table 1 The geological time scale. The time divisions are not drawn to a uniform scale. (Flint & Skinner, 1977)

Uniform Time Scale	Eras	Periods		Epochs	Radiometric dates (millions of years ago)	Outstanding events in the physical history of America	in evolution of living things
0	Cenozoic	Quaternary	Neogene	Recent or Holocene	0		*Homo sapiens*
Phanerozoic				Pleistocene	10,000	Several glacial ages	Later hominids
				Pliocene	2?		Primitive hominids
		Tertiary		Miocene	6	Beginning of Colorado River	Grasses; grazing mammals
			Paleogene	Oligocene	22	Creation of mountain ranges and basins in Nevada	Primitive horses
				Eocene	36	Beginning of volcanic activity at Yellowstone Park	Spreading of mammals
575				Paleocene	58	Beginning of making of Rocky Mountains	Dinosaurs extinct
	Mesozoic	Cretaceous			65	Beginning of lower Mississippi River	Flowering plants / Climax of dinosaurs
		Jurassic			145		Birds
		Triassic			210	Beginning of Atlantic Ocean	Conifers, cycads, primitive mammals / Dinosaurs

Subdivisions based on

Outstanding events

Era	Period		Millions of years ago	Geologic events	Life forms
Paleozoic	Permian		250	Climax of making of Appalachian Mountains	Mammal-like reptiles
	Pennsylvanian (upper carboniferous)	Many	290		Coal forests, insects, amphibians, reptiles
	Mississippian (lower carboniferous)		340		Amphibians
	Devonian		365	Earliest economic coal deposits	Land plants and land animals
	Silurian		415		Primitive fishes
	Ordovician		465	Beginning of making of Appalachian Mountains	Marine animals abundant
	Cambrian		510	Earliest oil and gas fields	Primitive marine animals
			575		Green algae
Precambrian	Precambrian (Mainly igneous and metamorphic rocks; no worldwide subdivisions)		1,000		
			2,000		
			3,000	Oldest dated rocks	Bacteria, blue-green algae
	Birth of planet Earth		~4,650		

upper jaw in the same area have been assigned to the same genus, but dated to the early Paleocene Epoch. The subtle similarity of their features to those of primates seems to substantiate the theory that at least as far back as the early Paleocene, and perhaps even during the late Cretaceous, this group had begun to distinguish itself from other similiar insectivores. It evolved perhaps in response to competition from rodents who were better equipped to exploit a terrestrial, insectivorous niche. *Purgatorious* and its descendants, it is thought, moved into the trees and gradually shifted away from insect-eating to plant-eating. Consequently, the teeth of early primates have increasingly more rounded cusps instead of the long, sharp cusps of teeth specialized for a diet of insects. This traditional theory, however, has been complicated by new evidence, as we shall see.

The Paleocene Epoch (65–58 million years B.P.)

As the *Paleocene Epoch* opened, the world climate was somewhat cooler than it had been. The continents had begun to drift away from the equator. But although no longer tropical, they were at least temperate. Alaska and Canada, for instance, had plants similar to those now found in the southern part of the United States. The northern continental land mass, Laurasia, was still intact. It was in this part of the world that the first primates probably radiated from the primitive insectivores of the Cretaceous Period (Simons, 1972).

Various common Paleocene and early Eocene fossils, found in both Europe and North America, have been interpreted as early primates. Many scientists now agree that these animals fall into at least three families and can be grouped into the superfamily *Plesiadapoidea.* The status of these groupings, however, is still far from settled. For a diagram of primate evolution, see Figure 4.

One of the three families, the *Paromomyidae,* includes *Purgatorius* and other Paleocene and even Eocene representatives. They are the most primitive of all primates, for their snouts are quite long and their brains very small. But they show the beginnings of certain primate evolutionary trends: flat-crowned molars with low, rounded cusps, a distinctive inner ear construction, and skeletal traits that suggest adaptation to arboreal life.

A second family—the *Carpolestidae*—is similar to the paromomyids. But the premolars of these mouse-sized creatures are highly specialized, with long blades on the top teeth fitting into grooves in the large lower teeth. This tooth structure may have been an adaptation that helped them bite through the tough casings of seeds.

Members of the third family—*Plesiadapidae*—are larger, with bodies like heavy squirrels. (See Figure 5.) They are similar in many ways to later primates. They have unspecialized molars, an ear construction like that of primates, and turned-in feet that may have helped them walk along branches. But in some ways they are more like nonprimate mammals of that period: Their olfactory apparatus is large in comparison to their visual equipment, their brains are small and encased in a flat skull, and they have pointed claws instead of nails. In addition, their first incisors project forward, are unusually large, and have three unique, pointed cusps. These strange front teeth, which may have been good for husking seeds and fruits, are separated from the cheek teeth by a large gap (Simons, 1972).

In some respects, the superfamily *Plesiadapoidea* falls midway between the Cretaceous insectivores and the Eocene lemurs and tarsiers, which were undoubtedly primates. It may represent a transition from a terrestrial insect-eating lifestyle to an arboreal, fruit- and vegetation-eating pattern. But the fossil evidence is too incomplete to reveal whether or not these creatures had begun to develop grasping feet. The idea that

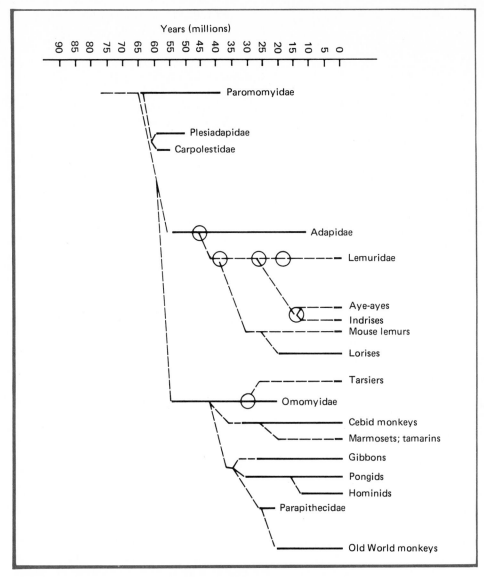

Figure 4 **One theory of the evolutionary relationships of selected primate families.** Solid heavy lines represent known ranges, and broken lines show the probable relationships. (Szalay, 1976)

they were arboreal is still an unproved theory. And what evidence we do have indicates that some of these creatures had developed specialized adaptations of their own. For instance, the dental pattern of the plesiadapids and carpolestids seemed to be evolving away from the unspecialized dental pattern that characterized later primates. They may, therefore, have sprung from the same ancestor but followed evolutionary paths that began to diverge early in the Paleocene Epoch. Perhaps the only group that is primitive enough to

Figure 5 A reconstruction of the Paleocene prosimia *Plesiadapis,* species of which ranged from squirrel- to cat-size. (Simons, 1964)

have been a direct ancestor of the modern primates is the paromomyids (Cartmill, 1975; Szalay, 1973).

The Eocene Epoch
(58–36 million years B.P.)

The primate trends that began during the Paleocene Epoch are clearly expressed in fossils dated to the *Eocene Epoch* (58–36 million years B.P.). The world was again warm and wet. Laurasia was beginning to separate into North America, Greenland, and Europe. But during most of this epoch, some overland connections must have remained, for fossils of mammals found on both sides of the widening Atlantic are still quite similar. All the southern continents, however, were probably separated from the northern ones by oceans (Simons, 1972).

By this time, all the modern orders of mammals had differentiated themselves from the primitive ancestral stock. Although the Paleocene primates died out, three groups of prosimian-like primates appeared, perhaps as descendants of the paromomyids. Their fossilized skulls, teeth, and limbs have been found in both Europe and America. All had distinctly primate characteristics: relatively large braincases, eyes set close together and surrounded by a bony ring, and grasping feet.

One group, the *adapids,* were probably ancestral to modern lemurs. Most of these medium-sized primates were powerfully built, with strong chewing muscles, a possible adaptation to a diet of tough vegetation. Another group, the *tarsiids,* were ancestral to today's tarsiers. Small, with large eyes, they had elongated ankle bones, which suggest the development of a vertical clinging and leaping form of locomotion.

The third group, the *anaptomorphids,* is a hodgepodge of primates that do not fit into any other family. In general, they seem to have been small nocturnal creatures that ate both insects and fruits with their unspecialized teeth, as some prosimians now do. One of the anaptomorphid subfamilies—the somewhat tarsier-like *omomyids*—is of special interest to anthropologists, for it may have been a direct ancestor of the catarrhines, and therefore of the hominids. The remains of this group have been found in both Europe and North America (Szalay, 1973).

Since the Eocene lemur and tarsiers encompassed a great variety of forms, and since the fossil record of earlier times is so fragmented, scientists have varying interpretations of the evidence. For a long time they went by the theory that a change from a terrestrial to an arboreal life-style was taking place in the primate line. But there is still no good fossil evidence for this, and recent finds seem to call for a more complex explanation. Cartmill (1975) suggests that some of the and the *Plesiadapidae*—probably branched off from the line that later led to the higher primates. Those who did not develop specialized dentition advanced in other ways instead. During the Eocene Epoch they evolved grasping feet, larger eyes set close together and facing forward (thus making stereoscopic vision possible), and a larger brain for improved visual perception and eye-hand coordination. These changes may have improved their ability to catch mobile insects and to feed at the slender tips of branches without falling.

The Oligocene Epoch (36–22 million years B.P.)

The most extensive radiation of the ancient prosimians occurred during the Eocene Epoch. During the *Oligocene Epoch* they gave up all but a few specialized niches to their descendants, the monkeys and apes. They disappeared almost entirely from the fossil record in Europe and North America, probably because these northern continents became too cool for them as the world climate cooled. Europe and North America were now temperate regions with cold winters. Primates may have been among the animals that retreated across temporary land bridges to areas that were still warm year-round: Africa and South America. For it is here that we get our next glimpse of primate evolution.

Very little is known about primate evolution in South America. According to current theories of plate tectonics, North and South America were rejoined during the Cretaceous Period, when volcanic activity and crustal uplifting created the Isthmus of Panama (Dietz & Holden, 1970). The same types of generalized prosimian forms (paromomyids or omomyids) that gave rise to Old World catarrhines probably also gave rise to the New World platyrrhines (Szalay, 1973). But in both South America and in Africa the evolution of

Figure 6 A reconstruction of *Smilodectes,* an Eocene prosimian. (Simons, 1964)

primitive insect-eating mammals of the Cretaceous Period began to eat fruit and vegetation as well as insects. During this important adaptive shift, some of the early plesiadapoids, perhaps the paromomyids, may have begun climbing trees in search of fruits, seeds, and leaves, without giving up their taste for insects. They may thus have led dual lives, climbing trees for fruit and vegetation and prowling on the ground for insects. Modern tree shrews still have this mixed life-style and are not specialized for either kind of diet.

The low-cusped molars of the early plesiadapoids were perhaps somewhat better suited for grinding plants than for shearing insects. But they probably managed to crush insect bodies, too, just as small prosimians with similar tooth structure do today. At any rate, it was unlikely that all the plesiadapoids became more specialized for chewing fruit and seeds. Those who did—the *Carpolestidae* arboreal adaptations occurred independently. As we noted in Chapter 3, this represents a classic illustration of parallel evolution.

Because of our interest in human evolution, our focus from the Oligocene Epoch to the present will naturally be on the Old World. We have not yet found any fossil primates in Africa from periods earlier than the Oligocene Epoch. But it is possible that they evolved from advanced paramomyids or omomyids that made their way to Africa from Laurasia during the Paleocene or Eocene Epochs (Dietz & Holden, 1970; Szalay, 1973). At any rate, the primate fossil record in Africa opens in the Oligocene Epoch with a great variety of advanced forms, suggesting that they had been evolving there for some time.

The richest finds from the Oligocene Epoch come from the Fayum Depression at the edge of the Sahara Desert in Egypt. Now an arid wasteland, it was covered 30 million years ago with lush tropical rain forests and slow-moving rivers. Sedimentary beds from these ancient rivers show that the trees there in the Oligocene Epoch must have been over 100 feet tall (Simons, 1972). The Oligocene primates that may have lived in these great trees were probably transitional forms, somewhere between omomyids and later catarrhines, though scientists are not agreed on how to classify them.

Interpretation of their remains has been complicated by the crudity of early paleontological techniques. Fossils found in the Fayum before the 1960s are hard to date, for their collectors merely noted that they were found in beds now known to contain strata ranging from 25 to 45 million years old. And when the lower jaw of a small primate called *Parapithecus* was discovered in the Fayum in 1908, it was improperly reassembled. For instance, the two halves of the jaw were glued directly together in a V-shaped pattern, instead of the U-shape it would have taken if a missing central piece had been reconstructed.

This and other mistakes led to confusing errors in interpretation that persisted until new specimens were found recently. Variously classified in the past as a tarsier-like prosimian, an early ape, or even a possible hominid, *Parapithecus* is now presumed to be an early Old World monkey (Simons, 1972).

The recent finds in the Fayum have led to changes in our interpretation of hominid evolution. Although we once thought that the hominoids (gibbons, apes, and humans) had evolved from monkeys, one current theory holds that the hominoids and the Old World monkeys shared a common catarrhine ancestor (Le Gros Clark, 1965). The Old World monkeys probably diverged from the line by the early Oligocene Epoch, or perhaps earlier, and developed their own specialized adaptations to arboreal life.

In tracing our own ancestors, we shall ignore the monkeys who were developing on both sides of the Atlantic and concentrate on the apes instead. The earliest ape fossil found so far is probably *Oligopithecus,* which dates from about 32 million years B.P. Judging from the size of a fragment of its lower jaw (for this is the only piece of it yet found), it was probably no larger than a squirrel monkey. The pattern of wear on its first premolar suggests that this molar was used as a sharpening edge for a large canine—a feature seen in all Old World monkeys and apes. Its dental formula, 2.1.2.3, also matches that of the higher primates. But its molars are more like those of the omomyids (Simons, 1972).

In the 1960s Elwyn Simons conducted extensive searches of the Fayum site and turned up an almost complete skull of a primitive ape that lived about 28 million years B.P. Called *Aegyptopithecus* ("Egyptian ape"), it was about the size of a fox, and it probably lived high in the forest canopy, eating vegetation and perhaps fruits. Scientists could only guess at how it moved until 1977, when Simons and an associate discovered some of its upper-arm fragments. These indicate that this early ape walked from branch to branch quadrupedally, rather than swinging or leaping through the trees (*Time,* March 6, 1978).

Unlike later hominoids, *Aegyptopithecus* had the relatively long snout and perhaps the tail of its prosimian ancestors. But its eyes are close-set and forward-facing, and its teeth are apelike, with enlarged canines. Its brain, though smaller than that of any living monkey, was nonetheless bigger than that of the earlier prosimians. This combination of primitive and advanced primate characteristics suggests that it is in, or closely related to, the lineage connecting the prosimian creatures of the Eocene Epoch with the pongid line, from which hominids would later diverge. Similarities between *Aegyptopithecus* and *Dryopithecus,* a later Miocene form thought to be a precursor to modern pongids and to humans, underscore the possibility that this early ape may be one of our direct ancestors (Simons, 1972).

Figure 7 **A reconstruction of the Miocene pongid.** *Dryopithecus africanus,* believed by some to have been an ancestor of the chimpanzee. (Napier, 1976)

The Miocene Epoch (22–6 million years B.P.)

Although anthropoids from the Oligocene Epoch have been found only in Africa, during the *Miocene Epoch* they apparently spread throughout parts of Europe and Asia by way of a land bridge created between the land masses about 18 million years ago. Monkeys and apes became less and less like each other as their evolutionary paths continued to diverge.

The geological upheavals that created the land bridge between Africa and Eurasia also caused changes in climate and environment. The most important of these was a gradual drying and cooling trend that changed the previously moist tropical forests of Eurasia into wooded grasslands. During most of the epoch the Miocene pongid *Dryopithecus* lived in an arboreal habitat in which the fruit and leaves it ate were abundant year-round. But toward the middle of the Miocene Epoch the

drier climate made fruit a less dependable food source, and the larger dryopithecines may have found it necessary to forage for nuts and roots at the forest's edge. These animals most likely were the ancestors of the living great apes and of the members of the lineage leading to modern humans.

The Dryopithecines. A number of different forms are included in the genus *Dryopithecus.* Among the many species into which these primates have been classified are the largest, *D. major,* a 150-pound possible ancestor to modern gorillas, and *D. africanus,* a smaller African species, possibly the forerunner of the chimpanzee. (See Figure 7.)

The success of the rather generalized dryopithecine adaptation can be seen in the long span it survived (some 20 million years—from late Oligocene through the

Miocene and into the early Pliocene), as well as in the vast areas of the Old World over which it spread—Europe, Russia, India, China, the Middle East, and Africa.

The tooth structure of *Dryopithecus* shows a combination of pongid and hominid traits. Like modern apes, it had large canines and a space between the lower first premolar and the canine to make way for the upper canine. But, like humans, it lacked such pongid specializations as the simian shelf (a bony ridge that buttresses the inner part of the lower jaws) and enlarged incisors (used to peel fruit). The shape of the *dental arcade,* the curve of the row of teeth in each jaw, is sometimes a clue to phylogenetic relationships. In modern apes, this arcade is U-shaped. In humans, it is a parabola, since the rows of teeth are not parallel to each other. The arcade of *Dryopithecus* is basically U-shaped, but the rows do form a slight angle. Some experts take this as evidence that the U- and the parabolic shapes evolved separately from the dryopithecine original (Simons, 1977). Finally, *Dryopithecus's* molars had a generalized cusp pattern similar to both pongids and humans, but less specialized than that of modern great apes.

Abundant *Dryopithecus africanus* remains from East Africa reveal certain primitive monkeylike traits. These include reduced brow ridges and a small, monkeylike braincase. (See Figure 8.) Controversy exists over dryopithecine locomotion. While some experts argue that the upper limb and wrist of *Dryopithecus africanus* were suited for brachiation, Le Gros Clark (1965) points to its relatively shorter forearm as evidence that it may have favored quadrupedal running and leaping instead.

Descendants of the Dryopithecines. Among the groups thought to have descended from the dryopithecines is *Sivapithecus.* This primate is often grouped with the genus *Dryopithecus,* but a few investigators (Pilbeam et al., 1977) now think that its dentition shares

enough traits with the hominids that it should be placed in a separate genus. Together with *Ramapithecus* it is a possible hominid ancestor.

Gigantopithecus, however, was an evolutionary dead end. An Asian descendant of the dryopithecines, or perhaps of *Sivapithecus,* *Gigantopithecus* inhabited present-day India and China during the Pliocene and Pleistocene Epochs. This creature's enormous size is indicated by molars and jaws so massive that they dwarf those of modern male gorillas. Estimates place *Gigantopithecus* as tall as 9 feet and as heavy as 600 pounds. Currently, *Gigantopithecus* is believed to have been a ground-living herbivorous pongid, resembling a giant gorilla, and perhaps displaying gorillalike sexual dimorphism (Rosen, 1974).

Summary

1. Only fossils can give direct evidence of the structure, habitat, eating habits, locomotory style, and age of extinct animals.

2. *Fossils,* the preserved remnants of organisms from a past geological age, range from a few fully preserved *subfossils* to the more common *molds* and *petrified* remains.

3. Fossil remains do not accurately represent the original environment. Few organisms are preserved as fossils because most decompose before the necessary rapid burial or coverage by sediments. Of the preserved organisms only parts become fossils, very few of which can be found.

4. In a major *excavation* material is removed and mapped in *horizons,* which correspond to geological layers called *strata.*

5. The interpretation of fossils can include dating them, determining the ancient environment, classifying them, and reconstructing them.

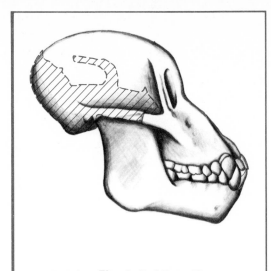

Figure 8 The skull of *Dryopithecus africanus.* Its teeth have a mix of pongid and hominid traits, and the primitive brain case is small and rounded, like that of a monkey. (After Robinson, 1952)

6. There are two kinds of dating techniques: *relative dating* and *chronometric, or absolute,* dating. Relative dating, which can show only whether one deposit is older or younger than another, includes *stratigraphy;* chemical analysis of fluorine, nitrogen, or uranium content; *palynology;* and *varve analysis.* Chronometric methods measure a deposit's distance in time from the present. They include radiometric methods such as *uranium-lead* and *potassium-argon dating* and other techniques such as *fission-track* and *paleomagnetic dating.*

7. *Paleontologists,* scientists who study fossils, can reconstruct the ancient environment by comparing fossil plants and animals to present species and their environments.

8. Geologists divide the earth's history into eras, periods, and epochs. Mammals first appeared during the Triassic Period of the Mesozoic Era, but maintained a low profile until the Cenozoic Era began. Then they rapidly increased in numbers and kinds to exploit the bonanza offered by the new flowering plants and the insects that thrived on them.

9. The earliest possible primate fossil is *Purgatorius,* dated to the late *Cretaceous Period* on the basis of a single tooth. Its family—the paromomyids—is better represented in fossils from the *Paleocene Epoch.*

10. In the *Eocene Epoch,* the paromomyids probably gave rise to three prosimianlike primate groups. One of these—the omomyids—seems to have continued the tendency toward unspecialized tooth structure, grasping feet, better vision, and a larger brain, all of which characterize the higher primates.

11. In the *Oligocene Epoch,* primitive monkeys and apes appear in Africa, where they must have been evolving for some time. The monkeys already show specializations of their own. Fossils of *Aegyptopithecus*—a fox-sized arboreal primate with both primitive and advanced traits—suggest that it is on or near the line leading from the omomyids to modern apes and humans.

12. Hominids and modern pongids emerged from the complex genus *Dryopithecus,* whose members had both some unspecialized, as well as some more specialized apelike traits.

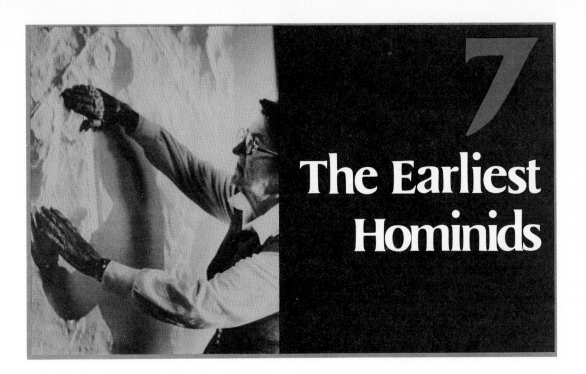

7

The Earliest Hominids

FOR thousands of years, humanity has tried to explain its origins. We have answered in myth such questions as Who were our earliest ancestors? How did they live? What did they look like? Today the answers physical anthropologists give to these same questions are constantly changing and often contradictory. New fossils and new dates often trigger intense debate, which may result in new explanations of certain episodes in our evolution. The exciting discoveries in East Africa during the past 20 years, for example, have made our understanding of human origins much more accurate, if less secure than when they were wrapped in myth.

Because fossils do not come out of the ground with a label, we have to develop some standards by which we can judge if a fossil is or is not an ancestor of living humans. The obvious basis for such standards is *Homo sapiens*. Using ourselves as a model, we can list the following standards for classifying fossils as hominids: a parabolic dental arcade, incisors set vertically in the jaw, thickly enameled molars, large brain size, and changes in the shape of the vertebral column, pelvis, lower limbs, and feet to permit erect posture and bipedal movement. Of course, cultural artifacts, especially stone tools, are extremely important signs of hominid status.

We cannot always assume, however, that the presence of modern human traits in an ancient fossil means that it is ancestral to us. Because fossils are often incomplete—especially the older ones—a part of the skeleton that may be important for judging it to be a hominid could be missing. Also, fossils look less and less human the farther back in time we go. Thus, some of the earliest hominids probably had many pongid features. Because the evolutionary lineages leading to modern humans and to the great apes descended from a common ancestor, it is often hard to distinguish fossils of our ancestors from those of ape ancestors. Finally, there may have been many hominid "experiments"—animals that became extinct because others were better adapted to the same niche. Separating the forms that gave rise to later hominids from those that became extinct adds another difficulty.

Ramapithecus

The middle and late Miocene is a period that produced a number of fossil forms, some of which could have been early hominids. Presently, the form receiving the most attention is called *Ramapithecus*. In 1932, G. Edward Lewis, an American graduate student who was searching Miocene deposits about 100 miles north of New Delhi, India, found an upper jaw that impressed him with its large number of humanlike traits. He named the fossil *Ramapithecus,* or "Rama's ape." Rama is a mythical prince and hero of the Indian epic poem, the *Ramayana.* Lewis placed the primate in the family Hominidae, the only living member of which is *Homo sapiens.*

The Miocene Environment

Today our knowledge of *Ramapithecus* is based on the jaws and teeth of some 40 different individuals who lived between 14 and 8 million years ago. Fossils have been found in Kenya, Spain, Southern Germany, Greece, Turkey, Pakistan, India, and China.

Ramapithecus probably lived in subtropical to warm-temperate forests (Simons, 1977) with abundant water, palm trees, and occasional savannas dotted with trees. In India, *Ramapithecus's* neighbors included warthogs, several kinds of carnivores, ancestors of the modern horse, ancient forms of crocodiles and rhinoceroses, and some dryopithecine apes. In Kenya, *Ramapithecus* shared the same sort of environment with rodents, ancient giraffes, rhinoceroses, cattle, dryopithecine apes, and several other primates (Simons, 1972). Much

"*Must* you hang around with those baboons?"

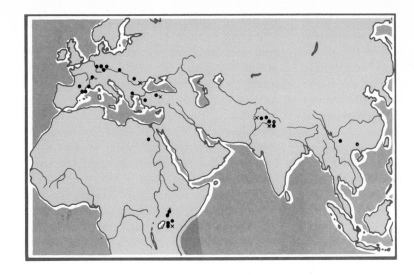

Figure 1 Distribution of *Dryopithecus* (dots), *Gigantopithecus* (circles), and *Ramapithecus* (crosses). Both *Dryopithecus* and *Ramapithecus* lived in subtropical to warm-temperate forests, although the Eurasian and Greek sites show signs that *Ramapithecus* may have lived in a savanna or forest-fringe environment as well. (Simons, 1977)

of Eurasia and Greece, however, was drier than Kenya and India. Only at these sites do *Ramapithecus* fossils seem clearly linked with grassland and wooded savanna environments (Simons, 1977). (See Figure 1.)

The Adaptations of Ramapithecus

A drying trend might have caused some dryopithecine apes to get their food in new ways. Simons (1977) believes that as the climate became drier in Eurasia, fruit, which the dryopithecine apes of the tropical and semi-tropical forests seem to have eaten, became available on a seasonal basis instead of year-round. This may have encouraged some of the Miocene pongids to search for nuts and roots at the forest edge. Indeed, at certain sites in Eurasia, *Ramapithecus* is found in the same deposits as animals that lived in a savanna and steppe environment. The absence of Dryo-pithecines in these deposits suggests that they may not have been able to survive in such an environment. Unfortunately, it is not always possible to clearly link *Ramapithecus* with a savanna environment. In Kenya, Turkey, and Hungary, they are found in areas

with nearby forests. In Kenya, they are found in deposits with forest as well as savanna animals.

Whether *Ramapithecus* lived in the savanna, near the forest fringe, or partly in the savanna and partly in the forest, fossils show the emergence of new dental patterns. The cheek teeth and their enamel covering are larger than those of the Dryopithecines. The teeth also suggest that these animals broke down some of their food by moving their teeth from side to side. *Dryopithecus* probably did not chew this way. Finally, the jaw itself was strong, with internal buttressing in the front.

In a savanna or partly savanna econiche, animals such as *Ramapithecus* with robust jaws and modified molars could have taken advantage of seeds and other small, tough-to-chew foods. Clifford Jolly (1970) has suggested that hominid teeth were, in fact, adaptations to this sort of diet. He has based this "seed-eating" hypothesis on a study of Gelada baboons in Ethiopia. These terrestrial baboons, living in a dry environment, have small incisors and large molars for grinding a diet of seeds, grasses, bulbs, and insects. Their canines are also fairly small to permit effective side-to-side chewing and grinding of seeds. Long canines would hinder this motion. Jolly has suggested that as early hominids moved into more open areas they depended on a diet similar to that of the Geladas. Thus, smaller canines would have made chewing easier. The grinding needed to break down tough vegetation would explain thickly enameled molars and premolars of *Ramapithecus*.

There is some question about the size of ramapithecine canines. Frayer (1974) thinks that they were not really shorter than those of *Dryopithecus*. Simons (1977), however, feels that *Ramapithecus* canines were smaller— about as large as their adjacent teeth. Even if reduction had occurred, however, canines may still have had a function like that of canines in pongids. The pointed form and sharp back edges of some canines may suggest that *Ramapithecus* did not depend totally on tough-to-chew foods. Its incisors retained a cutting edge for tearing food, an edge that the baboons do not have. In fact, some scientists have argued that these slicing incisors point to a carnivorous diet for *Ramapithecus*, but there is too little evidence for any definite conclusions.

Despite the fact that the total fossil evidence for *Ramapithecus* consists of teeth and jaws and does not include brain cases and postcranial remains, scientists have thought about its body and brain size, posture, locomotion, and even social behavior. One worker (Leakey, 1977), judging from the size of the fossils, guesses that *Ramapithecus* was only about 3½ feet tall. Because of its small size and apparent lack of large canines, it could have been easy prey for savanna carnivores. As a result, he suggests, it may have developed a semierect posture, both to see over the tall grass and to permit the aggressive displays that the gorilla and chimpanzee use to frighten off predators. Because an upright posture would have freed the hands, it may also have been promoted by using tools and carrying food from place to place (Leakey, 1977). Clifford Jolly, again drawing on his

studies of the Geladas, thinks that the semierect posture of these animals as they feed may be similar to that of the earliest savanna-foraging hominids. This posture leaves the hands free for feeding. Small object feeding requires another well-developed hominid trait—the precision grip. Finally, greater reliance on social behavior instead of teeth and strength for survival may have begun the hominid trend of larger and more complex brains.

Behavior such as group cooperation and food-sharing may have developed as a defense against predators in an open landscape. Open-country dwellers such as baboons are more tightly organized than are forest dwellers, who can flee to the treetops at the first sign of danger. When *Ramapithecus* began to exploit open country, similar group structure may have taken shape. The move to the savanna may also have caused an elaboration of the meat-eating and meat-sharing behavior known to occur among forest chimpanzees (Leakey, 1977).

How Should We Classify *Ramapithecus*?

There is a great deal of debate as to whether *Ramapithecus* can be considered a hominid. This is natural, seeing the lack of evidence by which to judge. One expert (Simons, 1977) places *Ramapithecus* among the hominids because of its humanlike traits. He argues that the shape of the reconstructed dental arcade is intermediate between that of the Miocene apes and later hominids. (See Figure 2.) The pattern of wear on the molars and the thickness of the bone in the lower jaw, according to him, are more typical of later hominids than of *Dryopithecus* or living apes. Also, the canine teeth and incisors are smaller than those of living apes.

This interpretation is opposed by Frayer (1974), who offers conflicting evidence from certain fossils. He suggests that previous re-

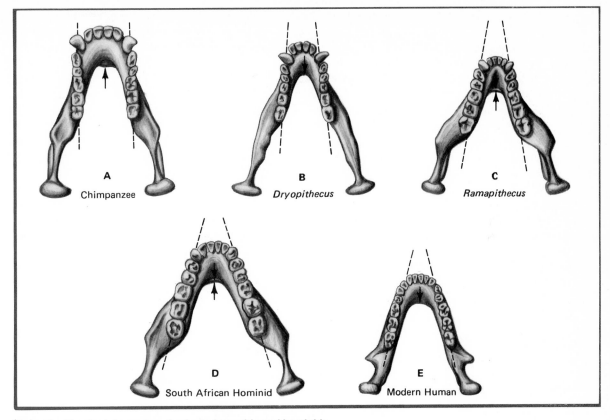

Figure 2   **The dental arcades of selected pongids and hominids.**
Dryopithecus (B) is thought to be the common ancestor of living pongids, represented here by the chimpanzee *(A),* and the hominids, including the gracile South African hominids *(D)* and modern humans *(E).* Those who believe that *Ramapithecus (C)* is a hominid think that: (1) the angle of divergence of its tooth rows is closer to that of *D* and *E* than to that of *B*. As you can see, Elwyn Simons, on whose work this drawing is based, holds this view; (2) the canines are not projecting, like those of *A* and *B* but reduced, like those of *D* and *E*. Although the status of *C* is in doubt, by these two criteria, *D* is clearly a hominid. Note also that *D* has rounded molar cusps, like those of *E*. Note, too, the progressive increase in the size of the back teeth, from *B* to *D,* probably reflecting a growing reliance on a diet of tough vegetable material. (Simons, 1977)

constructions of *Ramapithecus's* dental arcade were faulty and that in fact its shape looks more like the dryopithecine dental arcade. He also finds other apelike features, such as forward-pointing incisors, projecting canines, and a gap between the upper canines and the first premolar. And although the canines may be smaller than those of living apes, they are equal in length to those of at least one female *Dryopithecus*. Frayer concludes that *Ramapithecus* differs from the Miocene apes, but not necessarily in ways that place it in the human lineage (Frayer, 1974).

Other experts have fueled the debate by questioning the practice of defining hominids using modern humans as a model (Pilbeam et al., 1977). The advanced primates dating from this period have a mix of so-called hominid and ape traits. Ape ancestors could well have had a number of hominid characteristics, and hominids could have had ape characteristics. Thus, according to Pilbeam, "Extinct hominoids were not identical with, nor, in some cases, particularly similar to living hominoids, and to interpret extinct hominoids as though they were very 'modern' is potentially misleading." Thus, most experts feel that hominids first diverged from pongids during the Miocene, and that *Ramapithecus* had some hominid features. But they do not agree on how to classify *Ramapithecus*.

The Plio-Pleistocene Hominids

Fossil evidence of advanced primates from the late Miocene and the early *Pliocene* periods, particularly in Africa, is thus far very scanty. The Pliocene began about 6 million years ago and ended at about 1.9 million years ago. The Asian fossil record of the early Pliocene provides the remains of the giant dryopithecine ape called Gigantopithecus, living in India and China from about 9 million to 250,000 years B.P. In Africa, during the transition from early debatable hominid forms such as *Ramapithecus* to the earliest undoubted hominids, there is a gap between about 12 and 4 million years B.P. This is precisely the period during which hominid traits such as erect posture and bipedalism are thought to have evolved. When they are found, fossils from this period will for this reason be of great importance. Presently, only tantalizing pieces of the puzzle are available. Among the most interesting finds to date are parts of a jaw from Lothagam, Kenya, dated at 5 million years B.P. and an upper molar from Ngorora, Kenya,

which has been dated at about 9 million years old. With cusps similar to those of later hominids and a low crown like that of *Ramapithecus,* it may represent a transitional form (Pilbeam, 1972).

Even the most conservative paleontologists agree on the hominid status of the humanlike creatures that lived in southern and eastern Africa about 4 to 1 million years ago. This span of time includes the Pliocene and part of the *Pleistocene Epoch,* which stretches from about 1.9 million to about 10,000 years B.P. It was marked by cool weather and glaciation. The general agreement about the status of the hominids that lived during this time—the Plio-Pleistocene hominids—occurred only after years of debate and discovery.

The Hominids of South Africa

The first Plio-Pleistocene hominid fossil was found in 1924 in the course of mining operations at Taung in the Cape Province of South Africa. The fossil consisted of a remarkably complete child's skull, unlike any hominid fossil previously known, and a brain cast. Eventually it was sent to Raymond Dart, who was a professor of anatomy at Witwatersrand University in Johannesburg. Although the probable brain size was within the range of modern apes, Dart noted that it was larger than expected in a young pongid 5 to 7 years old. And certain other skull features characteristic of apes were smaller in this skull.

Dart interpreted the mix of pongid and human features as belonging to an animal in a family midway between pongids and humans. In 1925, after looking at the skull for only a few weeks, he announced his findings, naming the fossil *Australopithecus africanus,* or "South African ape." Because Dart was young and had not consulted his more experienced colleagues, his conclusions were strongly attacked. Other paleontologists rightly said that a valid classification could only be based on a mature specimen and that a final decision

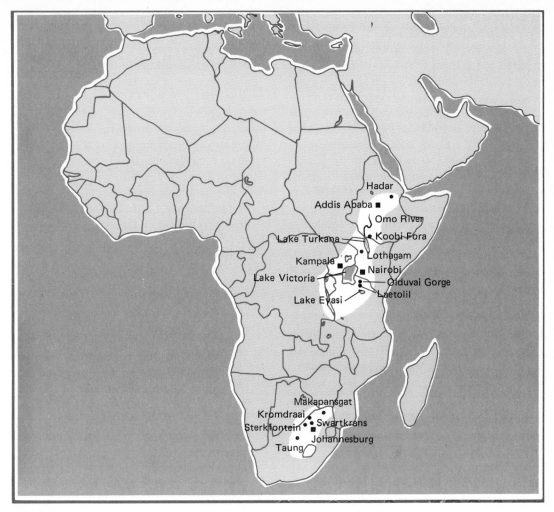

Figure 3 The sites of the major Plio-Pleistocene hominid finds in Africa

would have to await the finding of such a fossil. The Taung child, with its humanlike teeth and apelike cranium, also did not meet the general expectation of what the earliest hominid should look like. Ideas of early human form had been shaped by the fake Piltdown fossil, which had come to light in 1912. This fossil consisted of the jaws and filed teeth of a modern orangutan and the brain case of an Ice-Age human, a fact that was not known until about 25 years after Dart's find.

Robert Broom was the first to find a mature version of the Taung child. An avid amateur paleontologist for most of his life, Broom gave up his medical practice in his sixties to become curator of vertebrate paleontology at Transvaal Museum, Pretoria, South Africa. He had seen the Taung fossil, agreed with Dart's analysis, and begun searching for more evidence. In 1936 miners again made the first find, this time of an adult hominid skull, at Sterkfontein in the Transvaal. Since then, the skulls and some postcranial bones (including a nearly complete pelvis) of several individuals have been found at Sterkfontein.

In the next 15 years Broom and Dart uncovered a rich trove of fossils at several sites. Working in the area near Sterkfontein, Broom found skull fragments and postcranial remains at Kromdraai in 1938, and still other remains at Swartkrans in 1948. In 1947, Dart located more hominid remains at Makapansgat, in the Transvaal, about 150 miles north of Johannesburg. See Figure 3 for the exact locations of these sites, most of which have produced large numbers of fossils since their discovery.

The South African fossils have generally been found in ancient limestone caverns. Limestone, a common rock in the area, is soluble in water. When surface water seeped below the topsoil, it gradually dissolved the limestone, leaving a cavern and a long, narrow shaft that reached from the cavern to the surface. At Swartkrans, the shaft originally opened at the base of a cliff (see Figure 4). Bones lying at the mouth of the opening were washed down the shaft into the cave, where minerals in the limestone allowed fossilization to occur. The resulting material, composed of

jagged pieces of bone stuck together in a cementlike matrix, is called *breccia*. Gradual erosion later washed away the cliff, exposed the breccia, and revealed the fossils.

Dart thought that the hominids actually lived in the cave, but C. K. Brain (1970) has made a convincing case for another explanation. He suggests that the bones of the hominids and other animals are the remains of predators' meals. He thinks that, like today's leopards, those of 3 to 1 million years ago ate their prey in trees next to the mouth of caves. After the bones fell to the ground, they were washed into the cave and preserved. The preserved bones resemble the remains of the meals of modern carnivores.

The Ancient South African Environment

Analysis of the breccia deposits reveals that the South African, Plio-Pleistocene hominids had adapted to a drier and more open environment than that in which *Ramapithecus* had lived. One worker (Brain, 1958) has found that the climate at Makapansgat was desert-like—much drier than the climate in that region today. Sterkfontein and Swartkrans were slightly drier, and Kromdraai was wetter. Today the habitat in these areas is open country, with a few trees and wooded areas located along streams. Slightly less rainfall would not have made the area much different from today. Indeed, the breccias contain the bones of baboons and antelopes, both of which are open country dwellers at the present time.

The Fossils

We shall discuss the early African hominids in two large groups: the graciles and the robusts. Scientists do not agree on how to classify the members of these two groups. But grouping the fossils in this way makes it easier to describe them. Later in the chapter we shall

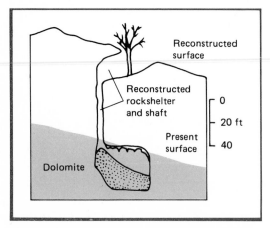

Figure 4   Reconstruction of cavern at Swartkrans. Bones, perhaps of hominids so unlucky as to have become a leopard's dinner, may have collected beneath trees at the mouth of the cave before being washed into the cave eventually to be preserved in breccia. (Reconstruction by C. K. Brain, in Trotter, 1973)

consider various theories of the classification and evolution of these forms.

The South African gracile form has been found possibly at Taung and at Sterkfontein and Makapansgat. Examples of the robust form have come from the sites at Swartkrans and Kromdraai. Dates for these fossils are, unfortunately, highly tentative, because the limestone in which the fossils were formed can be dated only roughly with index fossils. Fossil animals found buried with the hominids are sometimes also found at sites that can be dated with a chronometric method. Present estimates place the gracile form at 3 to 2 million years B.P., slightly older than the robust form, which dates from 2½ to 2 million years ago (Pilbeam, 1972). See Figure 5 for a summary of the dates of these and other African sites.

The Hominid Skull. For the most part, our discussion of the African hominids will center on the remains of their skulls. Teeth and the bones of the head more often are preserved and are the parts of the early hominid body that distinguish it most clearly from that of modern humans. It is therefore necessary to understand some of the mechanical features of the head and face. In hominids, only the lower jaw, or *mandible,* moves. It carries the lower teeth and transfers to them the force of the chewing muscles. These muscles are attached to the skull above. (See Figure 6.) The *temporal muscles,* which run downward along the side of the head, are anchored high up on the skull. In apes and many australopithecines, particularly in the robust forms, these muscles actually join at the top of the head, where they are attached to a bony ridge called a *sagittal crest.* As the hominids evolved, the crest disappeared and the anchoring areas for these muscles moved back down each side of the skull. Another set of muscles, the *masseters,* are attached to the *zygomatic arch,* an extension of the cheekbone, in front of the ear and are joined to the outside of the lower jaw.

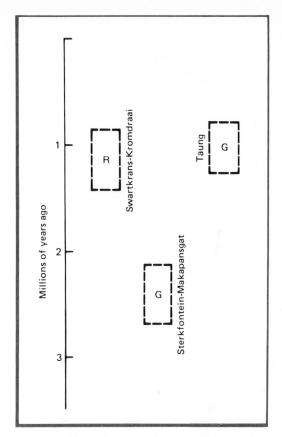

Figure 5 **The age of the early South Africa hominid sites.** Dates are based on relative dating methods, the only techniques applicable to these sites. *G* indicates gracile hominids; *R* indicates robust hominids.

When the food is chewed, two types of forces are used. The first are side-to-side chewing forces. These tend to place great stress on the front of the lower jaw, where the two sides are fused together in early infancy. *Buttresses,* bony structures that strengthen this weak area, are common among early hominid jaws. When a diet of tough foods has required very strong forces, the area has been buttressed with one or two bony swellings running along the inner side of the jaw. When chewing forces lessened, the need for strong internal buttresses diminished, and these were replaced by a weaker external buttress, the chin.

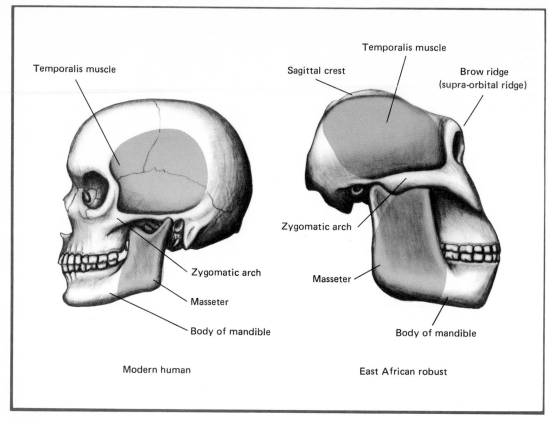

Figure 6 **Two hominid skulls**

The second type of force is vertical. When the lower jaw closes on food (as in biting), a stress is placed on the upper jaw and transmitted to the face. The thick facial bones and heavy browridges of earlier hominids probably developed as a response to these stresses.

The South African Gracile. Several physical features distinguish this creature from the pongids. A well-rounded forehead (compared to the shallow, flatter pongid forehead) and an elevated cranial vault housed a brain about equal in size to that of modern gorillas. (See Figure 7 for a drawing of the gracile skull.) In proportion to body size, however, the brains of the South African graciles were much larger. A full-sized male gorilla weighs from 400 to 500 pounds and has an average cranial capacity of 500 to 550 cc. The South African graciles were only about 4 feet tall and weighed between 40 and 70 pounds. Their brain sizes, however, ranged from 428 to 485 cc. (Holloway, 1970; Tobias, 1975). The brain-size to body-weight ratio of these individuals is thus far above that of the living gorillas, and is, in fact, within the range of modern humans (Holloway, 1974). In addition, the careful study of brain casts has indicated that the frontal and parietal lobes were more developed than in the pongids. These areas are centers of conscious thought and association. Holloway (1974) feels that these brains were basically human in organization.

The teeth of the graciles are clearly those of a hominid. The incisors were set in the jaw vertically, not at an angle, as in the pongids.

Unlike pongid canines, which are large and projecting, the canines of the South African graciles were short and incisorlike. There are no gaps between the upper canines and the first premolars to allow room for large lower canines. Such a gap is typical of dryopithecine and modern apes. Finally, the dental arcade was parabolic (more like that of modern humans), not the U-shape of the pongids and dryopithecines. (See Figure 2.)

The molar teeth were larger than those of *Ramapithecus,* but not as large as those of the robust forms. Still, the form is very similar to ours: The cusps are rounded and coated with a thick layer of enamel. The specimen from Sterkfontein reveals that the thick protective enamel on the cheek teeth had been worn flat—the result of side-to-side and circular chewing motions. This powerful chewing, designed to break down and process vegetable matter and meat, caused the first molars to wear out before the second wore thin. Fortunately for these early hominids, delayed eruption of the second and third molars kept them in enamel—and teeth—during their rather short lives (Pilbeam, 1972).

The chewing and neck muscles of the graciles were smaller than those of the pongids and the robust form. Little or no sagittal crest anchored the temporal muscles, and the cheek bones were small, a sign of small masseter muscles as well. But although the muscles may have been weaker than those of the pongids, they were probably more efficient, because the gracile's face was flatter. Its jaws were tucked in beneath the braincase. In gorillas and other pongids the jaws are located more to the front of the braincase. As a result, the force of the temporal muscles is applied at an angle more perpendicular to the plane of the teeth. This increases the chewing power of the jaws (Pilbeam, 1972). The wear pattern found on the cheek teeth suggests that vegetable matter was a major part of the gracile's diet.

Tooth wear has been studied for informa-tion about the survival rate among the South African graciles. It appears that they, like modern humans, matured slowly, with a long period of dependency on their elders. A prolonged infancy and juvenile stage were followed by a brief adulthood, with only a third surviving 10 or more years beyond reproductive age. The mean age at death was about 20 years, with a maximum age of 40. A mere 15 percent lived to 30 years (Mann, 1968).

Although the gracile form had an upper arm structure suggesting that it was capable of brachiation, it is unlikely that it did so, because it lived in open grassland and was a well-adapted biped. Evidence for bipedalism includes a short pelvis, a curvature in the low part of the spine, and longer legs. A short pelvis lowered the center of gravity in hominids and increased the efficiency of the transfer of weight from the spine to the pelvis and legs. Curvature in the lower back aligned the trunk vertically above the pelvis. Longer legs increased the mass of the lower body, thus lowering the center of gravity.

The South African Robust. Two sites in South Africa's Transvaal have yielded specimens of a much larger, more robust hominid. At Kromdraai, fossil fragments of the skull and postcranial bones of five or six individuals were unearthed between 1938 and 1941. Swartkrans, the other source of robust fossils, was excavated from 1948 to 1952. It contained the largest sample of early Pleistocene hominids. The rich deposits produced pieces of skulls, jaws, teeth, and postcranial bones, as well as some *Homo erectus* remains.

On the basis of a pelvis discovered at Kromdraai, scientists have concluded that the robust South African hominid had a larger body and was probably taller than the gracile form. The robust may have weighed from 80 to 140 pounds. The brain size, too, was larger. An almost complete brain cast of a robust skull from Swartkrans yields a cranial capacity of 530 cc (Holloway, 1970). By contrast, the

139

THE EARLIEST HOMINIDS

mean value for the gracile forms is 442 cc. Most likely, the difference is related to the larger body size of the robust form. If so, the brain of the robusts is somewhat smaller relative to body size than is the gracile brain. A brain cast of this same skull shows that the cerebellum (the brain center that coordinates movement) was relatively larger than in the pongids, perhaps a sign of finer control over hand and limb movements (Pilbeam, 1972).

The teeth of the robust form seem to have suited it to a great deal more chewing than those of the gracile. The incisors and canines are like those of the gracile form, but the molars have a greater surface area, and the premolars look more like molars (Pilbeam, 1972). In some cases, the dental arcade looks more like the U-shaped pongid arcade than the parabolic shape of the human arcade.

These large teeth were designed for crushing and grinding, and needed a system of powerful muscles and rugged bony structures on which to anchor the muscles. The presence of massive jaws and cheekbones and the sagittal crest suggest the heavily developed temporal and masseter muscles that once fleshed out these skulls. (See Figure 7.) And a deeper, flatter face than the graciles gave this system of muscles and bone even greater power (Pilbeam, 1972).

On the basis of a pelvic fragment from Swartkrans, it is clear that the areas where leg muscles were attached were similar to those in modern humans. However, differences in the lower pelvis suggest that the robust form was specialized for greater power and less speed in its bipedal movements than the gracile form (Robinson, 1972). Although mainly bipedal, the robust may also have been good at climbing trees (Robinson, 1972). Robinson feels that the robusts walked upright more clumsily than the graciles did. In both groups, however, the orientation of the hip joint, the small size of the end of the thigh bones, and several other features indicate erect posture (Pilbeam, 1972).

The East African Hominids

The first early hominid fossil discovered in South Africa was found by chance. Fortunately, it was sent to a scientist who could see its importance. The discovery of Plio-Pleistocene hominids in East Africa, in contrast, began as an intentional search to find more evidence of the early history of our evolution. Louis Leakey was convinced that he would find this evidence in Africa, contrary to the accepted opinion of the time. He began his determined search of Olduvai Gorge in 1931. (See Figure 3 for the location of this and the other East African sites.) It was not until 1959 that he and his wife, Mary, made their first hominid find, a skull and a shin bone.

Leakey immediately noticed that the fossil was similar in many ways to the robust form of South Africa. However, because of its much larger size, Leakey originally believed that it was unrelated to the South African robusts.

In the years that followed, new discoveries in East Africa seemed to pour forth, with Olduvai Gorge continuing as one of the richest sites. In 1960 Leakey reported a second find at a slightly lower level than the bed in which the original robust hominid had been excavated. Because of its small teeth and large brain, this new fossil seemed to be a gracile form closer to later stages of human evolution. Leakey distinguished it from all the known African robusts and graciles and singled it out as the form ancestral to later hominids.

Another important East African site is the Omo River basin in Ethiopia, north of Lake Turkana (formerly Lake Rudolf). The area had been explored in 1933 by Camille Arambourg, but the fragments he found were not complete enough for classification. Since 1967, a joint expedition made up of French, Kenyan, and American groups, the latter headed by F. Clark Howell, has been making significant finds. So far, the American and French groups have uncovered about 100 hominid teeth, four jaws, and a partial skull.

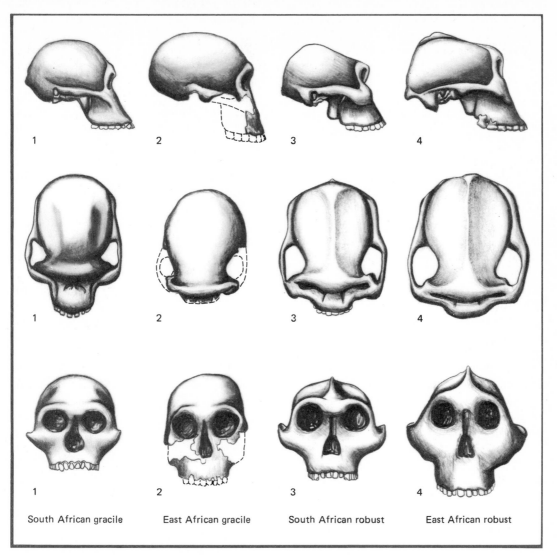

South African gracile   East African gracile   South African robust   East African robust

Figure 7   **Skulls of the South and East African hominids.**   Note the following points of comparison: The gracile skulls are much smaller and lighter than the robust skulls, but have a larger cranial capacity. Number 2 has by far the largest, lightest braincase. The top of the skull (the cranial vault) is rounded in the graciles, flatter in the robusts. The graciles have a rounded forehead; the robusts have practically none. A sagittal crest is absent or reduced in #1, absent in #2, present in #3, and pronounced in #4. Crest size is related to the size and strength of the chewing muscles that were anchored to this ridge. Similarly, brow ridges are most prominent in the robusts, whose massive facial structure anchored strong muscles. The cheekbones are thin in the graciles and massive and flaring in the robusts.

In so doing they have widened the known geographical range of the two hominid forms that had been found at Olduvai.

Several other sites have yielded fossils that extend the known time range of the East African forms. The Laetolil beds at Garusi, in the southern Serengeti Plains, for instance, have produced a fossil bearing a strong resemblance to the East African gracile, but dated between 3.77 and 3.59 million years B.P., twice as old as Leakey's Olduvai gracile (Leakey et al., 1976). These fossils are among the earliest of this type. Similarly, finds made at sites along the east bank of Lake Turkana in Kenya by Richard Leakey, the son of Louis and Mary Leakey, have established the presence of the robust form more than 3 million years ago (Leakey, 1973), although dating of this site is in dispute. In 1974 at Hadar, in the Afar depression of Ethiopia, the party of Maurice Taieb and Donald C. Johanson discovered the most complete skeleton of a single individual older than 100,000 years ever found. Dated at 3 million years B.P., this fossil, nicknamed "Lucy," is believed to be a form similar to, although more primitive than, the South African gracile.

Unlike the South African fossil locations, the East African sites lend themselves to absolute dating. Rather than being preserved in difficult-to-date limestone, the East African fossils were covered with lake or river sediments, which exist today in identifiable rock strata. Fortunately, in Pliocene and Pleistocene times, there was a great deal of volcanic activity. During eruptions, the land surrounding a volcano was covered with a layer of ash. Now these layers are distinct markers that are datable with the K-A and paleomagnetic methods. The age of fossils found between two such layers can be estimated with a great degree of accuracy. Olduvai Gorge is a particularly valuable site because it is the product of river action that laid bare a geological record that runs back into the past almost uninterruptedly for 2 million years.

Ethiopian laborers in the party of Donald Johanson sift gravel in the sun-scorched wastelands of the Afar Desert, looking for fragments of early hominid fossils. The remarkably complete skeleton of Lucy, a primitive South African gracile, was found in this area. (David Brill, National Geographic Society Photograph)

The Ancient East African Environment

Most of the East African hominid sites found so far have been close to ancient rivers, stream beds, lakes, or other sources of water. The Olduvai sites, for instance, were once located on the grassy, lightly forested edge of a lake. The hominids found at Omo lived on the banks of a river that changed its course many times. And the Lake Turkana sites are on the eroded sides of a lake in the floodplain of tributary streams.

Hominids probably preferred to live near such sources of water for a number of reasons. Trees and bushes grew near water and provided shade, shelter, and probably food, such as nuts and berries. Trees may have been a handy escape route when hungry predators approached. There is also some evidence that stream beds with gravel bars were a source of raw materials for making pebble tools (Isaac, 1978). The region was wetter and more lushly vegetated than it is today and than the South African sites were during Plio-Pleistocene times. Fossils show that the hominids shared their tree-dotted grasslands with pigs, hippopotamuses, crabs, turtles, grazing animals, and baboons. The hominids were hunters and gatherers who probably ranged over a large area. It is likely that they only camped at Olduvai seasonally. At other times of the year they may have looked for food in other parts of their range.

The Fossils

The East African fossils also can be grouped into gracile and robust forms, although neither is the same as its South African counterpart. Gracile fossils are not as common in East Africa as the robust forms. In East Africa, however, the two forms are often found side by side at the same site and are of about the same age (unlike the South African forms). Dates for the gracile forms range from 3.77 million years B.P. at Omo to about 1 million years ago for transitional forms at Olduvai. The robusts lived in East Africa as long ago as 3 million years, the age of fossils found at Omo and the eastern shore of Lake Turkana. The latest robust fossils date from about 1 million years ago, the youngest of Richard Leakey's finds at Lake Turkana. (See Figure 8.)

The East African Robust. The robust was a highly specialized vegetarian, and most of its points of difference from earlier and contemporary hominids can be linked to an increase in the size of its cheek teeth, probably an adaptation to chewing many small, tough pieces of vegetable matter (Pilbeam, 1972). Its molars and premolars are broader than those of the South African graciles and robusts. In fact, cheek teeth of the two South African forms are more similar in size than the cheek teeth size of East and South African robusts. The size and mechanical efficiency of the chewing apparatus are much greater than those of the South African robust. The teeth are set in a deep, short, and well-buttressed face designed to anchor more powerful temporal and masseter muscles. The alignment of these two muscles is nearly parallel, and brings to bear greater force on the jaws and teeth. (See Figure 6.) The strength of the masseters is indicated by the size of the area on the cheekbone to which these muscles were attached. And the presence of a sagittal crest at the top of the skull shows that the temporals were larger than in other hominids. Though the robust had large brow ridges, it had almost no forehead. (See Figure 7.)

Like the South African robust from Swartkrans, the East African robust from Olduvai has a cranial capacity of 530 cc (Holloway, 1970). The two Lake Turkana robusts that have been measured have capacities of 506 and 510 cc (Holloway, 1974). Examination of brain casts shows some reorganization of the cerebral cortex and expansion of the parietal lobes, areas of the brain that integrate sensory information. Pilbeam (1972) believes that this evidence is not inconsistent with toolmaking ability, though most workers think that the graciles made the first tools.

In East Africa the robusts were comparable to a short but well-nourished modern human, about 5 feet tall (Pilbeam, 1972). Analysis of some pieces of an upper leg bone seem to show that the robust forms stood erect and

144

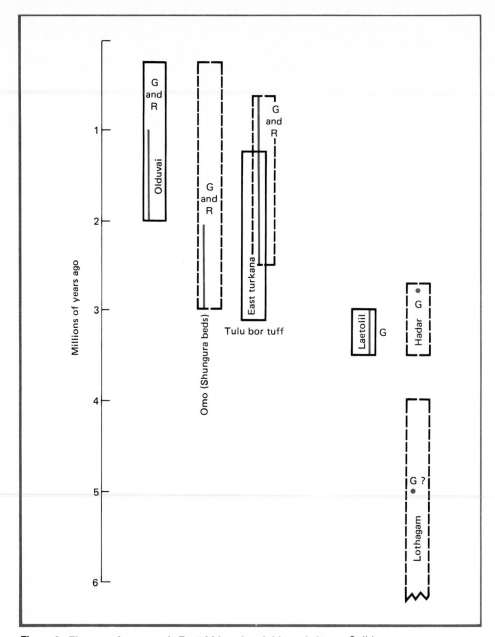

Figure 8 **The age of some early East African hominids and sites.** Solid lines represent dates based on chronometric methods. Broken lines represent relative dating based on index fossils. The color lines show the possible range for the age of the fossils themselves. *G* stands for graciles; *R* for robusts. (Pilbeam, 1972; Leakey, 1978; White & Harris, 1978; Cooke, 1978)

Mary Leakey shows footprints that may have been left by an East African hominid in the bottom of a watering hole 3.5 million years ago in Tanzania. The prints seem to indicate that the animal stood about 4 feet tall and walked slowly, taking steps no longer than its 6-inch long foot. (George Tames, *The New York Times*)

were fully bipedal, though not in the same way that modern humans are bipedal. A major difference may have been that the center of gravity, instead of lying behind the hip joint, as it does in humans, was centered at a point just forward of the hip joint. If this was in fact the case, the East African robusts may have walked with a forward-leaning gait (Day, 1969).

The East African Gracile. In 1964, Louis Leakey and his associates presented their analysis of the first evidence of an East African gracile type. The remains, apparently of a juvenile, consisted of a jaw with teeth, fragments of the skull and hands, and most of a foot and a shoulder blade. The find was exciting because it resembled more modern members of our lineage to a greater degree than any of the other known hominids. The results of dating tests showed that it must have lived

alongside the robust form. Chief among its humanlike traits was an estimated cranial capacity of 650 cc. Though the incompleteness of this skull made such measurement imprecise, later finds of the same form at Olduvai have yielded measures ranging from 593 to 684 cc (Tobias, 1975). And a skull (called by its museum acquisition number, KNM-ER 1470) located in East Turkana in 1972 and dated at 2.9 million years B.P. had a brain of about 800 cc. Unfortunately, the dating of this fossil is widely disputed, and it is possibly less than 2 million years old. But if the older date is correct it would suggest a remarkably large-brained gracile contemporary with the earliest-known robust forms.

In many ways the East African gracile looks like the South African gracile. The jaws and teeth are quite similar to the Sterkfontein gracile, with the incisor teeth set vertically in the jaw and the back teeth large in proportion to the incisors. However, the cheek teeth are somewhat narrower in the East African fossils. Postcranially, the two are also very similar. They were about the same size and weight. Both stood 4 to 4½ feet tall and weighed 40 to 70 pounds. The fossil foot and the clavicle of the first find at Olduvai together suggest that the forelimbs and chest of the gracile were proportionally larger than those of modern humans.

Analysis by Napier (1962) shows that the fingers of the East African gracile were more curved and that the thumb may have been a little shorter than in modern humans. Markings of muscles and ligaments on the bone reveal that the creature had a very strong grip. The thumb, although somewhat shorter than in modern humans, was fully capable of circular motion (Johanson, 1976). Study of the same individual's foot has shown that the ankle was somewhat flexed when the creature was standing. Although undoubtedly bipedal, the East (and probably South) African graciles may have stood or walked with a slightly bent-kneed posture. The arms of the gracile fossil from Afar were longer relative to stature than are those of modern humans. However, as with the South African forms, it is doubtful that this is a sign of brachiation. More likely, it is evidence of descent from a brachiating or semi-brachiating ancestor.

Classifying the Early African Hominids

The large number of late Pliocene and early Pleistocene hominid remains collected over the past 20 years in East Africa has added to, rather than resolved, the debate about how the early African fossils should be classified. Though most scientists now agree that these fossils should be placed with modern humans in the family Hominidae, they disagree sharply on how to group them into genera and species. This is mostly a reflection of differing theories about the phylogeny of these animals. For example, scientists disagree as to which form was the ancestor of the later hominids. The opinion of experts on this issue is reflected in the way they name the various forms. Both Louis and Richard Leakey have believed that East African graciles were ancestral to *Homo erectus* and all later hominids. They have therefore classified these graciles in the genus *Homo*. The Leakeys do not favor ancestral status for the South African graciles, or for the South and East African robusts. They place these fossils in another genus, *Australopithecus*. Other scholars disagree with this phylogeny, and prefer to place the fossils in other species and sometimes other genera. Presently, there are three widely discussed theories: the single-lineage hypothesis, the two-lineage hypothesis, and the multiple-lineage hypothesis. (See Figure 9.)

The Single-Lineage Hypothesis

The *single-lineage hypothesis* is concerned with one of the central problems of classifying fossils—defining the range of variations that should be grouped together in the same species. The extent to which members of the same fossil primate species differ cannot be determined from the fossils themselves. To solve this problem, we often use living primates as models. But, depending on which living primate is selected, the degree of difference within a species may be great or small.

Living apes, for example, vary greatly according to age and sex. Using a modern ape as a model would result in a broadly defined species. Among humans, on the other hand, males and females are much more similar. Using humans as the model for interpreting fossils would result in a narrowly defined species.

The single-lineage hypothesis uses living apes as a model and interprets the differences between the gracile and robust forms as resulting from differences in age, sex, or geographic adaptation. According to this theory, modern humans evolved in a direct line from a single group that included all of the Plio-Pleistocene African hominids. For this reason, all the hominids are placed within a single genus and species.

Age. Differences in form and structure due to age are marked among the living great apes. Juveniles not only lack normal adult features such as brow ridges and projecting canines, but are also much smaller than adults. If we judge by the bones alone, young individuals seem gracile compared to the adults. With this fact in mind, some experts argue that it is impossible to know for sure whether the skulls of immature African hominids would have developed into robust or gracile adults. The Taung fossil child, for instance, could just as likely be an immature robust (Tobias, 1974) as

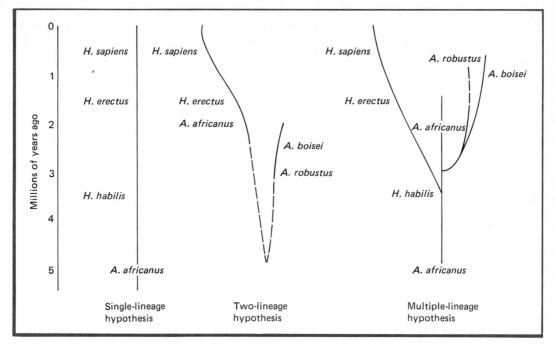

Figure 9 Three theories of early hominid evolution in Africa. Illustrated are: the single-lineage theory (all early hominids are of a single species, varying by age, sex, and geographic location); the two-lineage theory (early hominids are of two groups—the robusts and the graciles, which gave rise to the genus *Homo*); the multiple-lineage theory (the robusts, the South African graciles, and the East African graciles make up at least three separate lineages, of which the last evolved into modern humans).

an immature gracile. For this reason, classification of immature specimens is always guesswork.

Sex. Evidence from the later Pleistocene epoch suggests that as hominids have evolved, males and females have become physically more alike. Thus, the earlier the hominid fossils, the more likely it is that differences in form are sex-related. Consequently, we may unknowingly be using male fossils to draw conclusions about the typical robust, while using female fossils of the same species to stand for the typical gracile. Because of the small sample of Plio-Pleistocene fossils, the

true range of variation among the living animals is not known. It is possible, as anthropologist Loring Brace (1973) suspects, that sexual dimorphism accounts for a large amount of the variation seen among the South African fossils. As an added caution against too readily separating early hominids into two or more lineages, Milford Wolpoff (1975) has plotted the frequency of different gracile and robust dental characteristics, particularly canine size. He believes that the results suggest a type of sexual dimorphism comparable to that of modern pongids. However, the variation appears to be greater than that found among living *H. sapiens*.

Geographic Variation. When these early hominids lived, the environments of both South and East Africa were not completely uniform. Parts of each were wetter than other parts. Because of this variety it is thought that hominids living in both areas could have occupied two different niches. As time passed, the differences between the East and South African graciles and robusts in teeth, jaws, and muscles could have evolved as separate adaptations to different niches. This sort of geographical variation has a rough parallel in the physical variations of living humans.

The single-lineage theory has caused paleoanthropologists to reduce the number of species and genera proposed over the years for these early hominids. But many paleontologists feel that the theory does not take into account the nature of the variations. These workers see one cluster of traits (in the robust) that seems to be a highly specialized adaptation to a diet that requires a large amount of grinding and chewing. These experts feel that the gracile tooth structure and facial structures are a separate pattern, more like that of later hominids. Finally, if the recent dates for *H. erectus* in East Africa and China are valid, they suggest that the East African robusts were a highly specialized form living at the same time as *H. erectus,* clearly a direct ancestor of modern humans. If the two forms lived side by side, the single-lineage hypothesis is not correct. In fact, Brace now believes that the earlier Pliocene hominids made up a single lineage, while the Pleistocene hominids evolved in two lineages (in press).

The Two-Lineage Hypothesis

A second theory sees the graciles and robusts as members of either separate species or separate genera. John Robinson (1972), who has classified the graciles in the genus *Homo* and the robusts in the genus *Paran-*

thropus, attributes the differences in the two forms to a difference in diet. Looking mainly at differences in their teeth, Robinson suggests that the graciles' smaller molars were the result of an omnivorous diet. Robinson also believes that the graciles evolved from the robusts. According to him, the robust kept the more primitive link with wetter environments, while the gracile emerged as the form adapted to a more arid, savanna environment. The robust remained a vegetarian who needed massive teeth to crush and grind its way through a diet of berries and bulbs, roots and shoots, leaves and fibrous wild fruits. The dryness of the graciles' environment, on the other hand, created a scarcity of vegetation and caused it to rely more on animal protein. The gracile was also a toolmaker, who ate meat and perhaps switched some of the work of food preparation from the teeth to tools, according to Robinson.

Extreme wear and scarring on the molars of robust forms lend support to this dietary hypothesis. So does the principle of competitive exclusion, which states that similar creatures can only occupy the same area if they develop mutually exclusive econiches and hence do not compete with one another for the same food supply. Problems with this theory arise, however, when climatological evidence is examined. Soil analysis shows that the gracile sites in South Africa (Sterkfontein and Makapansgat) were indeed drier than one of the robust sites (Kromdraai). But the other South African robust site (Swartkrans) was drier than both gracile sites.

The situation is even more confused when the East African evidence is examined. There, robust and gracile forms seem to have occupied the same sites at roughly the same times. In addition, both groups show considerable variation. The Olduvai robusts were much larger than the South African robusts, and the East and South African graciles differed in ways we discussed earlier. Some experts feel that these differences are the result of specialization in different niches by animals living at the same time. More likely, the differences represent evolution in time. Dates of 2 to 3 million years for the South African sites would place the South African gracile contemporary with the earlier gracile forms from Omo and Lothagam in East Africa. The South African robusts would be older than the Olduvai material and older than the robusts from East Turkana, as well. This being the case, East African graciles and robusts would be later in time than the South African forms.

At one time David Pilbeam (1972) suggested that the apparently older South African graciles and robusts evolved into the younger East African graciles and robusts. He classified the South African graciles as *Australopithecus africanus* (Dart's original classification of Taung), and the later East African graciles as *Australopithecus habilis*. The South African robusts were classified as *Australopithecus robustus*. The later East African robusts were placed in a separate species, *Australopithecus boisei*. Recent redating of the Turkana material to less than 2 million years may stimulate more interest in Pilbeam's hypothesis.

Holders of the two-lineage theory usually think that the gracile gave rise to the robust lineage. They see the robusts as highly specialized herbivores. According to a basic principle of paleontology, generalized forms are ancestral to specialized forms.

The two-lineage theory answers the basic objections to the single-lineage hypothesis. That is, it explains the patterns of variation as evidence of separately evolving lineages. It also explains the presence of the *A. boisei* at the same time as early *H. erectus.* Unfortunately, this theory depends on the acceptance of fairly early dates for the South African material. If (1) the graciles of Sterkfontein are contemporary with the Olduvai fossils, (2) Taung is less than 1 million years old, and (3) the fossils from the Laetolil beds look like *A. habilis* more than *A. africanus,* then three or even four lineages may exist. This possibility is the basis of the multiple-lineage hypothesis.

The Multiple-Lineage Hypothesis

According to this hypothesis, the lineage of East African gracile fossils has many "modern" traits and goes a long way back in time. Louis Leakey is the originator of this theory. Small teeth and jaws, lighter facial bones, and the large brain of the East African gracile are among its advanced features. Louis Leakey felt that it was different enough from the South African gracile to be included in our own genus. He named this form *Homo habilis,* or "handy man."

Most of the *H. habilis* fossils found at Olduvai are relatively late, however. Other paleontologists have therefore suggested that *H. habilis* should be treated as a transitional form of *A. africanus* leading to *H. erectus.* When Richard Leakey excavated an exceptionally large-brained fossil from East Turkana in 1972 and dated it at 2.9 million years B.P., it seemed to document the age of the lineage and to support his father's theory. However, reevaluation of the date suggests that it is probably 1 million years more recent than originally thought. Once again, this seems to leave the proposed "Homo" lineage without time depth, unless Mary Leakey's finds at Laetolil are generally accepted as 3.7 to 3.5 million-year-old representatives of the line. According to the multiple-lineage theory, there are, apart from *H. habilis,* the South African graciles and two robust lineages. The South African graciles would be classified as *A. africanus,* the South African robust as *A. robustus,* and the East African robust as *A. boisei.* Only *H. habilis* was the bearer of culture—the maker of tools and the creator of the oldest archaeological sites in East Africa. The other forms are viewed as more narrowly specialized, without the flexibility of the culture-bearing forms. As *H. habilis* expanded into the niches of the other forms, it gradually

150 won the competition for food and ultimately drove them to extinction.

Presently, the 1470 East Turkana fossil is not firmly dated enough to be used to support the antiquity of *H. habilis*. Evaluation of the Laetolil finds by other scholars is just beginning. The prospect of an early, large-brained, humanlike ancestor is attractive. In the absence of dated early fossils, however, we cannot say with certainty that a separate *Homo* lineage did exist.

Evolutionary Trends in The Early Hominids

All of the early hominids seem to have occupied niches in the same tropical savanna ecosystem. Just how many different niches there were among these hominids is a question of how many lineages one believes existed. Theoretically, each lineage must have been adapted for life in a unique niche.

The earliest hominids shared a set of adaptations that we associate with "humanness." These included large brains essentially human in organization, small canines, and erect bipedal movement. If more than one hominid species is proposed, then we must explain why divergence of the ancestral econiche occurred. Let us assume, correctly or incorrectly, that two lineages existed: a gracile and a robust. We know that niche divergence occurs in one of two ways. A part of the original population either begins to exploit new food resources, or it exploits the same resources in a new way. Because the ranges of the graciles and robusts in South Africa and in East Africa overlapped or were identical, the most likely reason for niche divergence was the exploitation of the same food in slightly different ways. The main difference between the strategy of the robusts and that of the graciles was that the graciles

probably used culture. The use of tools, complex social structure, learning, and food-getting strategies eventually allowed this lineage to adapt culturally, rather than biologically, to their environment.

Many of the features we associate with more advanced hominids—particularly more efficient bipedalism, larger brains, and smaller teeth—are probably related to the growing influence of cultural behavior on hominid biology. Because of the great selective advantage tools would have given their makers, hands shaped and able to move in ways suited for toolmaking would also be an advantage. Thus, genes coding for hands capable of a precision grip and good eye-hand coordination would have become more common in the gracile population. If tools improved the chances of survival, then those qualities of the brain making possible the manufacture of tools would also be selected for. Thus the ability to control the finger, to translate concepts into tools, and to concentrate on a goal would tend to become more common in the population. The enlargement of areas of the brain that permit the integration of a variety of information from the senses and the use of symbolic verbal communication would be an advantage, as well. These abilities would make possible group organization for defense and food getting. The information relevant to group life and survival could be taught and learned through communication as well. Tool use and intelligence probably evolved in a feedback system. Each added to the advantages of having the others. Greater intelligence, for example, made possible the manufacture of better tools, which, together with changes in social organization, fostered the survival of the more intelligent hominids.

As the niche of the graciles was evolving toward that of *H. erectus,* the robust niche was also evolving. But the robusts came to depend on anatomical, rather than cultural, specializations. The relatively large early South African robusts may have given rise to the larger East

HUMAN BIOLOGICAL EVOLUTION

African robusts, whose powerful jaws and large molars and premolars were suited to the vegetable diet that was probably the basis of the animal's existence.

For at least 2 million years these two forms existed together. However, about 1 million years ago the robusts became extinct, as the later graciles were evolving into *H. erectus*. Although we have no direct evidence of how the robusts became extinct, the fact that tools were found with robust fossils at a site in Olduvai suggests to some that robusts were hunted by graciles. A more likely explanation is that the food resources of the robusts were being used more efficiently by the graciles. This could have slowly reduced the fertility of the robusts and finally led to their extinction. Unfortunately, although this theory makes sense ecologically, there is no archaeological evidence to support it. As more fossils are uncovered, however, we shall be able to draw more solid conclusions.

Summary

1. Physical anthropologists use *Homo sapiens* as a model for identifying fossils as hominids in their attempt to outline human evolution. But because the earliest fossils in the line leading to the modern great apes and the earliest hominids shared so many "apelike" and "humanlike" features, it is difficult to identify our earliest ancestors on the basis of our own features.

2. Frequently used criteria for hominid classification are: parabolic dental arcade, incisors set vertically in the jaw, thickly enamelled molars, large brain size, and changes in the shape of the vertebral column, pelvis, lower limbs and feet that permit erect posture and bipedal movement.

3. The hominid skull has features that changed as the stresses associated with strong vertical chewing forces diminished. The *mandible,* or lower jaw, is the only part that moves. The *temporalis muscles* are anchored at the top of the skull and run down the side of the head. The *masseter muscles* extend from the *zygomatic arch* to the lower jaw. The *sagittal crest,* to which the *temporalis muscles* are attached at the top of the head, and the *buttresses* that strengthened the inside of the lower jaw both disappeared as a modern, lighter-boned face evolved.

4. *Ramapithecus* may have been a hominid of the middle Miocene period. It inhabited usually wet environments, from subtropical to warm-temperate forests, but also adapted to the drier grasslands and wooded savannas of Miocene Eurasia and Greece.

5. Since *Dryopithecus* fossils are not found in savanna and steppe deposits, anthropologists think that only *Ramapithecus* made the adaptations necessary to move out into the new econiche at the forest edge as Eurasia became drier.

6. *Ramapithecus* adaptations include robust jaws and thickened tooth enamel for chewing tough foods. The canines may have been shorter than those of *Dryopithecus*. Scientists guess that the animal was $3^{1}/_{2}$ feet tall and had an upright posture for defense, for carrying food, and for using tools. The hominid trend toward larger brains may be the result of greater reliance on the hands and mind than on teeth and brawn.

7. Fossil evidence of advanced primates living in the late Miocene and early Pliocene periods is very scanty. But the earliest African fossils that are definitely hominid have been dated at about 4 million years old.

8. Two groups of Plio-Pleistocene hominids have been found in South African *breccia* deposits—the graciles and the robusts.

9. South African graciles are distinguished from pongids by a larger brain-size to body-weight ratio, well-rounded foreheads,

more developed frontal and parietal lobes, and hominid teeth. The incisors are set vertically in the jaw, the molars are rounded, and the canines are short and incisorlike. The absence of a *sagittal crest* and the small cheekbones indicate smaller temporal and masseter muscles. A shorter pelvis, curved lower spine, and long legs show that the animal was bipedal.

10. South African robusts were much larger than the graciles. Other differences include larger molars, a more U-shaped dental arcade, more massive jaws and cheekbones, and the presence of a sagittal crest. Differences in the lower pelvis indicate that the robusts may have been stronger but slower and more clumsy bipedal walkers than the graciles.

11. East African robusts had larger teeth, broader molars, and a more well-buttressed face than either of the South African hominid forms. The size of the *sagittal crest* and the cheekbone show that the temporal and masseter muscles were also larger and stronger. Pieces of upper-leg bone show that East African robusts were fully bipedal and erect, but may have walked with a forward-leaning gait.

12. East African graciles had several characteristics in common with the South African: body size and weight, vertically set incisors, and shape of jaw. The cheek teeth were narrower, however, and the cranial capacity was largest among the hominids of this time. The thumb was capable of circular motion. Both gracile forms probably walked with a slightly bent knee.

13. There are three current theories as to how the early hominids should be classified. The *single-lineage hypothesis* proposes that humans evolved in a line from a single species that includes all of the Plio-Pleistocene hominids. Using living apes as a model, this hypothesis interprets differences between the graciles and the robusts as variations within one species with respect to age, sex, or geographical adaptation.

14. The *two-lineage hypothesis* classifies the graciles and the robusts in different species or genera. Some experts believe that the East African hominids evolved from the older South African forms. They classify the South African graciles as *Australopithecus africanus* and the East African graciles as *Australopithecus habilis.* The South and East African robusts would be *Australopithecus robustus* and *Australopithecus boisei,* respectively.

15. Leakey's *multiple-lineage hypothesis* suggests that one lineage of fossils, *Homo habilis,* is an ancient member of the human genus with many modern traits. The small teeth and jaw, lighter facial bones, and large brain of the East African gracile characterize *H. habilis. H. habilis* survived, while the *Australopithecus africanus, robustus,* and *boisei* lineages became extinct.

16. The robust hominids became extinct about 1 million years ago. Further evolution of the graciles toward *Homo erectus* was probably aided by the development of culture. Interactions between cultural behavior—use of tools, communication, and intelligence—and hominid biology formed a *feedback system,* in which each element stimulated the evolution of the others.

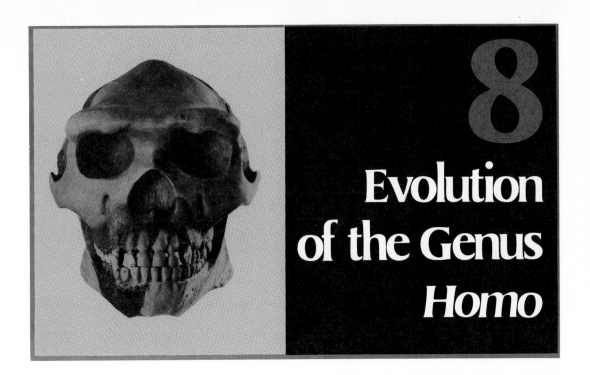

8

Evolution of the Genus *Homo*

ROM the early African hominids, we trace our ancestors into the Pleistocene Epoch, which began about 2 million years B.P. and ended only about 10,000 years ago. During this time, important physical changes occurred in facial form and in head size and shape. Brains became much larger and more complex than those of the earlier hominids. By the end of the epoch, the hominid brain, face, and skull were about the same shape and size as ours are today. The hominids that lived during most of the early and middle Pleistocene are called *Homo erectus,* or "erect man." The more recent, larger-brained forms that appeared in the late middle Pleistocene have been given the same label that we bear: *Homo sapiens,* or "intelligent man."

The hominids of the Pleistocene Epoch probably made up a single lineage, despite their broad geographical range. Cultural artifacts, mostly tools, suggest that the hominid toolmakers of the Pleistocene were the descendants of the early hominids from East Africa. The hunting technology they developed seems to be based on refinements of the crude tools found at sites at Lake Turkana and at Olduvai Gorge. Anatomical characteristics, too, seem to reflect gradual changes from the early East African hominid pattern.

There is, however, some question about the course of human evolution in the Upper Pleistocene Epoch. Some anthropologists claim that the European Neandertals of the late Pleistocene may have represented a separate species that later became extinct. But although some think that these Neandertals are a separate lineage, no one argues that they do not belong in the genus *Homo.* In this chapter we shall trace the gradual evolution of this genus in its biological aspect. Cultural evolution will be covered in detail in a later chapter.

The Pleistocene Time Scale

The time scale for this period is unusually confusing. Whenever possible, we will use absolute dates for fossil groups. But in some cases this is not possible, and we shall have to place fossils within the rather imprecise geological classification system (Lower, Middle, Upper Pleistocene) or within the sequence of glaciers that once covered a third of the earth. The Pleistocene Epoch is characterized by periods of glacial advances and retreats in North America, Europe, and the Himalayan region of Asia. Of these areas, Europe has until recently been the center of fossil and artifact hunting. European finds were traditionally placed according to the European alpine glacial sequence (Günz, Mindel, Riss, and Würm glacial advances, separated by interglacial periods of warmer weather). As fossils have been discovered gradually in other parts of the world, scientists have tended to use the European glacial sequences as a relative dating standard, even though Asian and African environmental events were largely unrelated to events in Europe. In Table 1, a few of the major Pleistocene fossils finds are tentatively placed in a framework that includes all three dating systems: absolute years, geological labels, and European glacial ages.

Major Trends of Hominid Evolution

During the early part of the Pleistocene Epoch, hominids began to live in areas far beyond Africa. Archaeological evidence suggests that they were developing cultural sophistication more rapidly than ever before. Migration and cultural evolution are linked to a growing emphasis on hunting. The earlier hominids probably lived mostly on vegetation, to some extent on small game or meat that they scavenged, and occasionally on large game animals such as mammoths that they killed (Isaacs, 1978). But as the Pliocene ended and the Pleistocene began, meat apparently became more important in the hominids' diet. Hominids probably began following herds of larger mammals into the tropics outside Africa and later into temperate regions. At the same time, they developed systematic hunting methods and rather advanced tools.

Changes in the Teeth and Jaws

The shift from limited meat-eating to big-game hunting and the cultural traits linked with it are also thought to have affected evolution of the human body, particularly the teeth, jaws, and skull. The dietary switch from vegetable to animal matter and the use of stone tools to prepare food, which earlier was done by the teeth, probably caused a gradual decrease in the size of jaws, teeth, and chewing muscles. Strength had been needed in these features for a diet that had consisted only of hard-to-chew raw vegetation (Bilsborough, 1976). The fact that later not as much crushing and grinding was done inside the mouth has often been offered to explain the increasingly smaller chewing apparatus of the Pleistocene hominids. There is not, however, complete agreement as to how to account for this change in size in terms of natural selection. The most likely explanation calls attention to the fact that the bone in which the teeth are set is not under rigid genetic control and is greatly influenced by chewing stresses during growth. The size of the teeth, however, is under fairly direct genetic control. Lightly stressed jaws would not develop the proportions needed to support relatively large teeth, which could result in crowding. Crowding makes it more likely that the person will have tooth or gum disorders, leading to impaction and infection. Such infections can weaken vision and other senses that are needed for hunting, and if the infection reaches the neural pathways leading to the brain, it can be fatal. This would place individuals possessing the genes for larger teeth at a disadvantage, thereby causing a gradual change toward smaller teeth among the population. As cheek teeth were becoming smaller, front teeth were increasing in size, only to decrease again beginning about 150,000 years ago. Possible explanations for this puzzling reversal will be discussed later in the chapter.

The Braincase

The bones of early Pleistocene hominids were much like us below the neck, although some hominids were more robust. But they had massive protruding jaws, thick facial bones, large teeth, and no chin. These features were largely dictated by their powerful chewing apparatus. As *H. erectus* evolved into *H. sapiens,* however, the shape of the hominid skull was determined more and more by the form and size of the brain (Wolpoff, 1975). The bony case protecting the brain of *H. erectus* was generally larger than that of the early African hominids. The average cranial capacity of the South African graciles, for example, was only about 440 cc. The 1470 skull found by Richard Leakey at Lake Turkana is an exception, with a cranial capacity of about 800 cc., larger than that of some early *H. erectus* forms. Nonetheless, the average capacity of *H. erectus,* 950 cc., was larger. A comparable figure for modern *H. sapiens* is 1330 cc. Part of this increase was related to the hominids increased overall size, which naturally produced proportionally larger parts. But the increase in the size of the braincase was relatively greater than the increase in the rest of the body.

Increases in brain size occurred slowly and gradually. The ever-increasing complexity was probably linked to greater cooperative behavior, ingenuity, skill in hunting large game, manual dexterity, and memory. The larger brains made possible a more sophisticated way of life—better tools, a wider range of habitation, more effective hunting techniques, and a more varied diet. Because each of these behaviors had its origin in the African hominids of the Pliocene, it is likely that the new patterns emerged gradually.

As we noted in Chapter 6, the part of the brain associated with vision grew larger early in primate evolution as reliance on the sense of smell declined. The later stages of human evolution were characterized by impressive growth of three other cortical areas—the frontal, temporal, and parietal lobes. Growth of these lobes allowed complex integration of many kinds of information and conscious control over behavior (Campbell, 1974). Large temporal and parietal lobes gave humans an unusually high, rounded skull shape, while the enlarged frontal lobe added a bulging, vertical forehead. The lobes also gave the top of the head its characteristic shape.

Early Homo Erectus

There are considerable structural differences among the fossils of the Pleistocene Epoch. As a means of organizing this varied group of fossils for study, we have divided our discussion of *H. erectus* fossils into those that existed before 700,000 B.P. (early *H. erectus*) and those that are dated to between about 700,000 and 200,000 B.P. (late *H. erectus*).

A variety of early *H. erectus* fossils have been found from Africa to China. Hominids seemed to have spread from East Africa to Indonesia (Java) and China by 1.7 million years

Table 1 The Pleistocene Time Scale

(years)	Geological Age	Climatic Phase	Major Fossil Finds — Africa	Major Fossil Finds — Europe	Major Fossil Finds — Asia	Hominids
10,000	Holocene					Early Modern *Homo sapiens*
40,000	Upper Pleistocene	Würm or Weichsel glaciation	Saldana Bay	Neandertals	Skhul Shanidar	Late Archaic *Homo sapiens*
100,000		Riss/Würm or Eemian inter-glacial	Broken Hill Omo	Krapina Ehringsdorf Petralona	Solo (?) Ma-pa (China)	Early Archaic *Homo sapiens*
		Riss or Saale Glaciation	Rabat Casablanca Temara			
200,000	Middle Pleistocene			Arago Cave Steinheim Swanscomb	Solo (?)	
300,000		Mindel/Riss or Holstein Interglacial				
400,000						

Years	Glaciation / Stratigraphy	Africa	Europe	Asia	Homo erectus
500,000	Mindel or Elster glacial	Swartkrans ?	Vertesszöllös	Chou-kou-tien	Late Homo erectus
600,000	Günz/Mindel or Cromerian interglacial			Lantian	
700,000	Günz Glaciation				
800,000	Donau-Günz or Tiglian interglacial		Ternifine Heidelberg (?)	Sangiran (Trinil)	Early Homo erectus
900,000	Donau glaciation				
1,000,000	Villafranchian				
1,200,000		Hominid 9 (Olduvai)			
1,400,000		East Turkana			
1,600,000				Djetis	
1,800,000 / 2,000,000				Yuanmou	

Lower Pleistocene

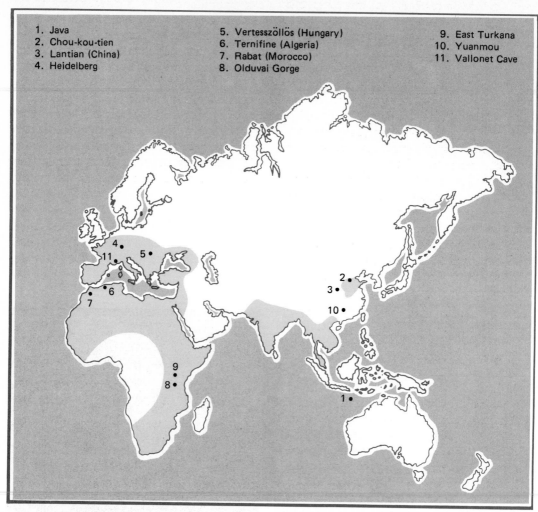

1. Java
2. Chou-kou-tien
3. Lantian (China)
4. Heidelberg

5. Vertesszöllös (Hungary)
6. Ternifine (Algeria)
7. Rabat (Morocco)
8. Olduvai Gorge

9. East Turkana
10. Yuanmou
11. Vallonet Cave

Figure 1 Distribution of *H. erectus* sites.
The colored area indicates the sites of early Paleolithic tool finds.

B.P. Tool finds suggest they appeared in Europe by about 800,000 years B.P.

The Fossils

Some early *H. erectus* fossils from the Lower Pleistocene come from Lake Turkana in Africa. They are dated at 1.6 million years B.P. (See Figure 1.) There, early *H. erectus* populations, represented by a cranium, mandibles, and assorted postcranial fragments, seem to have occupied the same sites as the East African robust hominids discussed in the last chapter. To the south, Olduvai Gorge has also yielded an early *H. erectus* (or erectine) fossil: a faceless skull with an enormous cranial capacity, called Olduvai Hominid 9. It has been dated at 1.2 million years B.P. (Leakey, 1971).

In Java, hominid material found in the Djetis beds is probably about 1.5 million years old, according to potassium-argon dating.

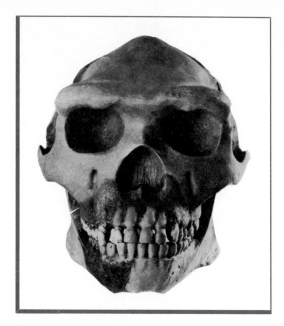

The skull of *H. erectus*. (Courtesy of the American Museum of Natural History)

erectus remains have yet been discovered there among the crude tools and bones of rhinoceroses, horses, elephants, and even whales (Howells, 1974). But early *H. erectus* probably made the pebble and flake tools and killed the animals found at the site.

How did early erectines reach places as farflung as East Africa, Java, and China? One possible explanation is that they followed migrating animal herds. As hominids began to rely more and more on herds of large grazing animals for food, they followed the animals when they migrated. As the animals moved into new areas, so did the hunters. By the end of the Lower Pleistocene, hominids had developed the cultural sophistication—tools, knowledge, clothes, and fire—needed to move from their tropical or subtropical range into a variety of climates, including cooler northerly regions.

The Environment

The earliest Pleistocene hominids lived in tropical or subtropical environments. They seem to have preferred fairly open coastal areas and avoided dense tropical rainforests. They did not venture across the mountains of southern Europe and Asia into regions with extreme seasonal temperatures. The climate of the European sites, lived in much later than the others, was probably warm-temperate: Winters were cooler than summers, but temperatures were still fairly warm.

In Lantian, located in what is now a temperate region of China, hominids shared subtropical forests with saber-toothed tigers, huge deer, and giant macaques and shared grasslands with gazelles, early ruminants, and horses (Ju-kang, 1966).

In Africa, too, the climate was clearly tropical at both Olduvai Gorge and Lake Turkana. At the latter site, early *H. erectus* coexisted with such tropical animals as hippopotamuses, crocodiles, and assorted Old World monkeys (Maglio, 1971).

Another Javanese site, Sangiran, has yielded many fossils, including the back of one individual's skull and some teeth, plus parts of a separate lower jaw. They are probably at least 800,000 years old. Also dated to about 800,000 years B.P. are a mandible and skull cap from the Lantian district in China. Some *H. erectus* teeth found near Yuanmou in the Yunnan Province of China are now dated at 1.7 million years B.P., about a million years before the earliest previously known *H. erectus* fossil in China (*The New York Times,* 2/6/78).

The presence of early *H. erectus* in Europe is less well documented. In 1907, some workers at a German gravel pit near Heidelberg uncovered an ancient lower jaw, complete with all its teeth. Though some paleontologists think it may be as old as 800,000 years (Bilsborough, 1976), others date it at about 500,000 years (Kretzoi & Vértes, 1965). And an early cultural site in Vallonet Cave, in southern France, has been dated to the end of the Lower Pleistocene. No early *H.*

Physical Characteristics

Few postcranial (below the skull) remains of early *H. erectus* have been found. But judging by the shape and position of the foramen magnum, the adjustments to upright posture and bipedalism were just about complete in the early *H. erectus* fossils. These early human ancestors probably stood and walked just about the same way we do. Our ancestors apparently had evolved all the changes necessary for a fully erect modern posture by the Middle Pleistocene (Bilsborough, 1976).

Two major trends distinguish early *H. erectus* fossils from Pliocene hominids: (1) the teeth and jaws became smaller, and (2) there was a dramatic increase in cranial capacity.

The trend toward smaller tooth size started with the molar teeth. The third molars (those farthest to the rear) of early *H. erectus* decreased the most at this time, though there were slight reductions in the second and first molars, too. Premolars did not become much smaller until the Upper Pleistocene. The front teeth were still large as well.

As back teeth began to decrease, the jaw changed, too. The heavily buttressed jaw became thinner and much more parabolic in shape. Although the early erectines were larger than the earlier hominids and had wider faces, their jaws were actually smaller. The part of the lower jaw that holds the teeth, for instance, had become lighter, and the vertical part had thinned out. These decreases in both grinding molars and jaws probably were associated with the gradual switch from unrefined vegetable foods to tool-chopped vegetation and meat (Bilsborough, 1976; Wolpoff, 1975).

The brain case underwent an expansion that nearly doubled its capacity. The relative proportions of different brain lobes also changed. (See Figure 2.) The parietal and occipital lobes became larger, broadening the face and the back of the head. There was also a trend toward greater thickness and strength in

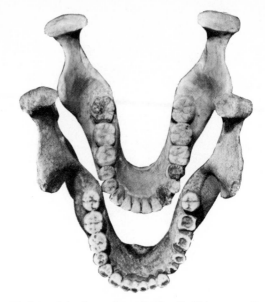

Models of the lower jaw of a South African gracile *(top)* and the jaw of Heidelberg Man, probably early *H. erectus*. Note the reduction in molar size and the change to a thinner, more parabolic jaw. (Courtesy of the American Museum of Natural History)

the braincase, and a series of buttresses developed on the surface of the skull. In the front, thick browridges stuck out over the eyes. They may have helped to distribute chewing stresses more evenly over the front of the cranium. At the back of the head, a bony swelling, or *torus,* developed, to which powerful neck muscles were attached. Both the torus and the neck muscles may have been necessary to counterbalance the massive faces of the early erectines (Bilsborough, 1976). (See Figure 3.)

Late Homo Erectus

The Fossils

The fossil record during the Günz glacial period, beginning about 700,000 B.P., is very fragmentary, but many hominid fossils are

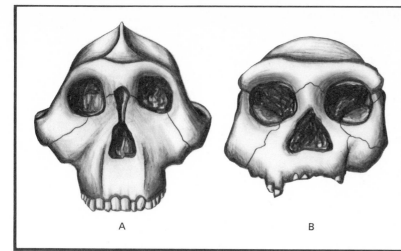

Figure 2 Faces of an East African robust (A) and an early H. erectus (B).
Enlargement of the braincase has led to an upper face much broader than even that of the East African robust, the broadest-faced of the earlier hominids.

found in strata dating to the Mindel glaciation, about 450,000 to 400,000 years B.P. The most spectacular discoveries from this period are skulls, jaws, teeth, and postcranial fragments from Chou-kou-tien, China.

For many centuries, enterprising traders had led annual expeditions to remote Asian caves and mountain gorges. They brought back tons of fossils of all sorts to supply the demand for "dragons' teeth" in Far Eastern cities. The fossils were sold to druggists, who ground them into powders thought to have great medicinal value. When paleontologists arrived on the scene in the nineteenth and twentieth centuries, they often did their "fieldwork" in drugstores. Among the fos-

silized bones waiting to be ground up was a humanlike tooth. Inquiries as to where it had been found led paleontologists to the site at Chou-kou-tien, near Peking. Workers dug through the debris there for 13 years during the 1920s and 1930s, unearthing 14 skulls, assorted other remains from at least 40 individuals, tools, and hearths where fires had been built. This priceless collection was somehow lost during World War II. Fortunately, however, detailed descriptions and good casts of the originals had been sent out of the country before the war. Recently, excavation of the cave has been renewed, turning up more hominid fragments.

The hominid represented by the Chou-

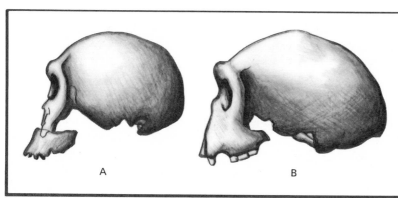

Figure 3 An East African gracile (A) and an early H. erectus (B).
Brow ridges have expanded in the latter to distribute chewing stresses over the front of the cranium. Note the torus at the back of skull B. It anchored the large neck muscles needed to balance the massive face.

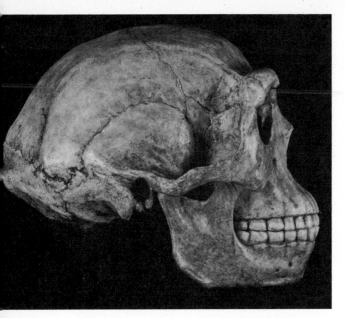

A side view of late *H. erectus,* from Chou-kou-tien. As in early *H. erectus,* the brow ridges are prominent, but cranial capacity is greatly expanded. (Courtesy of the American Museum of Natural History)

kou-tien fossils was once called "Peking Man." But it is now grouped by most anthropologists with similar African and European hominid fossils of about the same age. These include skull parts from Swartkrans Cave in South Africa that did not match those of the many earlier hominids found in the same cave. There are also many sites in the North African countries of Algeria and Morocco. And in Vertesszöllös, Hungary, in a valley cut by a former tributary of the Danube River, researchers have found ancient hearths, charred bones, a number of tools, and part of a skull and some teeth. They also seem to have belonged to a late *H. erectus* population (Kretzoi & Vértes, 1965).

Far more numerous than actual hominid fossils of this period are sites where late *H. erectus* populations left recognizable traces of their cultural activities. For instance, distinctive tools from the middle of the Mid-Pleistocene have been found in at least 31 locations, stretching from Spain and Morocco in the west to Java in the east (Collins, 1969). By the middle of the Holstein interglacial period (a time of fairly warm temperatures between glacial episodes) cultural sites were established all over Europe. Some have been found as far north as southern England.

The Environment

During the Middle Pleistocene, hominids continued to inhabit warm, open grasslands. But some began a definite tendency to live in more extreme environments. Both in Eastern Europe and at Chou-kou-tien in China hominids seem to have lived in the kinds of forests and steppes now found in cold areas farther north. When they were inhabited, the Chou-kou-tien and Vertesszöllös sites were about 1,000 miles from the ocean, thus subjecting them to the seasonal extremes of heat and cold typical of inland regions (Collins, 1969).

During the Holstein interglacial period, northern areas became warmer and more humid as the glaciers retreated. Silver firs replaced pines. These firs are now found mostly in the foothills of mountains in southern Europe. Their living requirements give us a good indication of what the Holstein climate must have been like. In what is now northern Europe, it was probably considerably warmer and wetter than that area is today. But the soils probably were not very rich, and the forests not very dense (Collins, 1969). In eastern Europe, forests expanded around the edges of the Eurasian steppe.

Physical Characteristics

Judging from the facial structure of late erectines, the stress of food-chewing continued to decrease. The front teeth of the late erectine fossils were smaller than those of the early erectines, and the trend toward smaller molars continued. The jaws became thinner and smaller, and the mouth area was reduced, giving the face a somewhat flatter appearance.

The chewing muscles also became smaller as did the skull areas to which they were attached. The neck muscles and the area at the back of the skull to which they were attached became smaller, possibly because they no longer had to counterbalance such a massive jaw.

At this time, the final adjustments to a fully magnum, at the base of the skull, ended its magnum at the base of the skull, ended its long-term movement in primate evolution. Rather than being located toward the rear of the skull base, as in quadrupedal animals, it is located toward the middle of the skull base, the most efficient position for balancing the head on the top of the spine. And muscle attachment points at the base of the skull became somewhat smaller, since the decreased mass of the jaws and face no longer required strong neck muscles for support, as in the early erectines.

Cranial capacity continued to increase. Only part of this growth can be accounted for by the increase in body size from early to late erectines. There were also structural changes that have nothing to do with body size. The most significant of these were in the frontal and parietal regions, which became higher in the skull as well as larger.

The marked changes in brain size and structure, as well as the smaller size of the teeth and jaws, suggest rapid evolution between the Lower and Middle Pleistocene as hominid populations radiated to new niches. Increasing cultural sophistication was probably the major factor making this possible.

Early Archaic Homo Sapiens

By the end of the Holstein warming trend, about 225,000 years B.P., the fire-using hunt-ers of the Middle Pleistocene had given way to a more highly evolved hominid, *H. sapiens.* The division between *H. erectus* and *H. sapiens* is arbitrary, for the latter group evolved slowly from the former. Nevertheless, there are sufficient evolutionary differences in the form of the jaws, face, cranium, and brain to warrant using a new species name. By giving it the same genus name, we recognize its descent from the *H. erectus* forms. *H. sapiens* is further divided into four rather arbitrary groups: early archaic, late archaic, early modern, and modern. The early forms differ only slightly from their erectine forbears. And the range of variation in the early forms is significantly different from the range found in modern human populations (Wolpoff, 1975).

The Fossils

Early archaic *H. sapiens* fossils are those that date from the latter part of the Holstein interglacial period (late Middle Pleistocene) to the end of the Riss/Würm, or Eemian, interglacial period (early Upper Pleistocene). The time span represented is roughly 275,000 to 75,000 years B.P. The oldest fossils from this period are probably those from Steinheim (a warped skull found in a German gravel pit) and Swanscombe (a skull cap uncovered in an English gravel pit). Both may have been females (Brace, Nelson, & Korn, 1971). They are about 250,000 years old.

Other European hominid fossils from this period were found at Montmarin, Fontechevade, Abri Suard, and Arago Cave in France; Ehringsdorf and Steinheim in Germany, Petralona in Greece, and Krapina in Yugoslavia. This last find is made up of assorted bone and skull fragments of 14 or 15 individuals, five of whom were probably infants or children (Brace, Nelson, & Korn, 1971). Early Archaic *H. sapiens* is also represented by 11 faceless skulls and two tibia from the Solo River in Java. These fossils cannot be dated definitely because of poor excavation techniques. But their structural traits seem to place them at about this point in human evolution. African hominids during this period are represented by fossils found in Rabat, Temara, and Casablanca in North Africa and at Broken Hill in Rhodesia (Wolpoff, 1975). (See Figure 4.)

The Environment

The geographic distribution of early archaic *H. sapiens* seems to be about the same as that of the late *H. erectus* populations. In Europe, however, glaciation did not force the hominid populations to move south. Instead, they remained on the tundra, exposing themselves to greater cold than their ancestors had ever endured. Some sites in England and Germany may have been lived in when the edge of the Riss glacier was only a few miles away (Collins, 1969).

As the ice sheets moved south, game animals migrated to warmer areas. Instead of following them, some of our Pleistocene ancestors apparently learned to hunt mammoths, for these woolly creatures thrived in the tundra or cold steppe environments at the glacier's edge (Collins, 1969).

The cold of the Riss glaciation was followed by a warmer period—the Riss/Würm interglacial period. Just as their predecessors had done during the Holstein interglacial several hundred thousand years before, the early humans moved north as the glaciers receded.

Physical Characteristics

Many of the trends already established in the evolution of the human skull continued during this period. For instance, the lower jaws, molars, and chewing muscles were still smaller among these fossils than in late erectine populations. Internal buttressing of the lower jaw was further reduced, and some fossils began to exhibit external buttressing in the form of a weak chin (Wolpoff, 1975). But a reversal of some other trends shows up in the fossil record. The front teeth, upper jaws, and

neck muscles of early archaic *H. sapiens* are noticeably *larger* than those of late erectines. This gives the newer forms a forward-projecting mouth area somewhat like that of more primitive hominids.

Wolpoff (1975) has an intriguing explanation for this enlargement of the front teeth. He speculates that these teeth were used as tools. In modern human groups, people have been seen using their front teeth to work animal hides, pull things, break thread, grip and twist objects, and even to pry the lids off gasoline drums. An uneven pattern of wear in some of these fossils suggests that the front teeth also were used to hold and manipulate objects. In doing so, new stresses were placed on their jaws. The crowns, roots of the teeth, and bones behind were pulled outward. The resulting projection of the upper jaw gave early *H. sapiens* a primitive look that their predecessors had almost lost. The need to counteract the pulling and gripping of the incisors and canines also apparently caused enlargement of the neck muscles. Larger teeth apparently were a selective advantage and became an increasingly frequent trait. Larger neck muscles, in part, probably developed during the life of the individual in response to stresses created by using the teeth as tools.

Despite the possible use of teeth as tools, cultural rather than biological adaptations seem to have been more important to the survival of the earliest *H. sapiens*. Evidence of complex hunting strategies, sophisticated tools, and semipermanent habitations suggests that human intellectual horizons were expanding. What anatomical evidence do we have that hominids were getting smarter? For one thing, the brain was clearly larger than in earlier hominids. Cranial capacity increased by about 21 percent over what it was in the later erectines (Wolpoff, 1975). Most of the difference seems to be associated with expansion of the frontal lobe. It began to expand above the browridges rather than behind them. And the whole skull became even higher and rounder to accommodate swelling in the occipital and

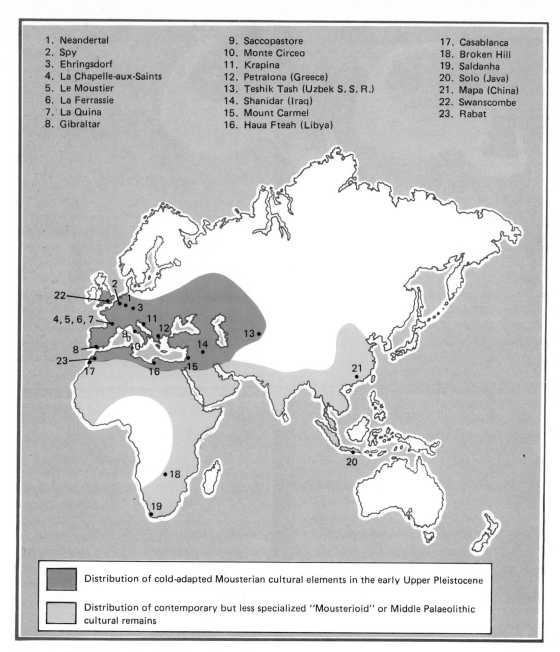

1. Neandertal
2. Spy
3. Ehringsdorf
4. La Chapelle-aux-Saints
5. Le Moustier
6. La Ferrassie
7. La Quina
8. Gibraltar
9. Saccopastore
10. Monte Circeo
11. Krapina
12. Petralona (Greece)
13. Teshik Tash (Uzbek S. S. R.)
14. Shanidar (Iraq)
15. Mount Carmel
16. Haua Fteah (Libya)
17. Casablanca
18. Broken Hill
19. Saldanha
20. Solo (Java)
21. Mapa (China)
22. Swanscombe
23. Rabat

Distribution of cold-adapted Mousterian cultural elements in the early Upper Pleistocene

Distribution of contemporary but less specialized "Mousterioid" or Middle Palaeolithic cultural remains

Figure 4 Distribution of archaic *H. sapiens* sites.
The colored area indicates the sites of Mousterian culture remains.

parietal lobes (Bilsborough, 1976). (See Figure 5.) The areas of the brain that were expanding most noticeably seem to be those that integrate sensory inputs and make speech possible. The frontal lobe coordinates muscle responses and conscious thought, and the occipital and parietal lobes integrate memory, perception, and vision.

EVOLUTION OF THE GENUS *HOMO*

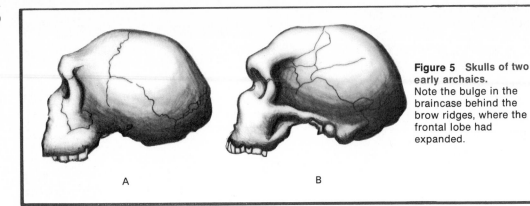

Figure 5 Skulls of two early archaics.
Note the bulge in the braincase behind the brow ridges, where the frontal lobe had expanded.

A   B

Late Archaic Homo Sapiens

The next hominid grouping covers only the first part of one glacial period—the Würm glaciation, which lasted from 75,000 to 10,000 B.P. Fossils of this age found in Europe have traditionally been referred to as "Neandertal." The label comes from skeletal fragments discovered in 1856 in a grotto in the Neander Valley, Germany.

The Environment

The geographic distribution of the late archaic fossils is close to that of the early archaics, although far more sites have been found from this period than from any earlier ones. Nearly 100 locations in Europe, Africa, the Middle East, and Asia have yielded specimens. And even more sites have contained tools, but no trace of the hominids that made them.

Within this broad area hominids were expanding into new environments. In Africa it seems that they were exploiting tropical rainforests for the first time. In Europe only a few early archaic sites have been found near areas that were never free from ice and snow. However, the tundra just south of the glaciers—from Spain and France in the west to the Ukraine in the east—seems to have been densely inhabited by the late archaics. Perhaps because of this advance into more marginal habitats, hominids were also more often making their homes in caves and rock shelters rather than out in the open.

Despite the cold weather late archaics must have faced in Europe during the Würm glaciation, the number of plant and animal remains found there suggests that the area was capable of supporting abundant life. In midsummer there were probably 16 hours of sunlight a day, and at least half that much in winter. In the south, great forests of pine and shrubs stretched from Southern Germany to Russia. In north central Europe the tundra was covered with a variety of plants that could exist in the cold, except in areas of perpetual snow. The tundra, like the savanna, supports few different kinds of plants. But because these few species were abundant during the Würm glaciation they supported large herds of mammoth, wooly rhinoceros, reindeer, elk, and bison. In the more forested regions south of the tundra, cave bears, hyenas, lions, and deer thrived. Although the hominids of this time fished and hunted game ranging from cave bears to small mammals and birds they must have been especially fond of reindeer. At one open-air site, almost three-fourths of the animal remains found are those of reindeer (Kennedy, 1975).

The Makeup of Archaic Populations

Since there are so many Würm fossils, we have enough data to apply population analysis techniques to extinct humans. Although we are not dealing with a biological population, enough individuals are represented to apply these techniques. Hominids from this period probably lived in bands of about 10 to 30 people. Some lived as nomads, following herds of game animals north into the tundra during the summer and south to the forests in winter. But in areas that had stable animal populations, hominids led a more settled existence.

Studies of age at death suggest high annual mortality rates and short lives. Very few lived to be older than 40; half of them died in infancy and childhood. Most women apparently died before they were 30, many in childbirth. Males probably outlived females, a trend that has been reversed probably only in industrial-age *H. sapiens* populations. It is possible that this sex ratio is inaccurate, however, because fragmentary skeletal remains make recognition of secondary sexual characteristics impossible. When analyzing such remains, researchers tend to assume that specimens with a heavy build are males rather than sturdy females (Kennedy, 1975).

Physical Characteristics

Although we shall refer to the late archaics as a single group with a single label, the fossils from this period show a broad range of anatomical variation. These are interpreted by some anthropologists as subspecific variations. Despite their broad geographical range and differences in environment, late archaic groups apparently had enough contact with one another and enough genetic similarity that they could still interbreed successfully. They did not become so genetically isolated that they evolved into separate species.

Some of the differences between late archaic fossils from Europe and those from other parts of the world may be related to time differences. For instance, while the early European fossils are over 50,000 years old, those from the Near East date mostly from 50,000 to 35,000 years B.P.

Some of the differences may also reflect anatomical adaptation to local environments. The late archaics from Europe—especially those from early in the Würm glaciation—may have developed specialized adaptations to the continual cold. The European fossils have extremely projecting faces, large nasal cavities, and somewhat short and stocky bodies. These characteristics were foreshadowed in earlier hominids and continued in other late archaic groups. But nowhere are they so noticeable as in the European fossils. All these characteristics can be seen as adaptations for retaining body heat. The projecting face, for instance, may have kept inhaled air as far as possible from arteries that supply blood to the brain, limiting the chance of chilling it. The large nose may have served to warm and moisten air as it is inhaled, and the large sinuses behind it may have acted as additional warming chambers. A short, stocky body would have reduced the amount of surface area over which heat could be lost (Wolpoff, 1975; Mann & Trinkaus, 1973).

Late archaics have, on the average, the largest front teeth of any fossil hominids. (See Figure 6.) This trend reached a peak during the first part of the Würm glaciation (about 65,000 to 50,000 years B.P.). During the middle part of the glaciation (about 48,000 to 40,000 years B.P.) the front teeth then began to get smaller. Neck muscles and their attachment points began to decrease in size even sooner.

According to Wolpoff's teeth-as-tools theory mentioned earlier, the development of specialized hand tools must have reduced the need to use the incisors to help grip and work

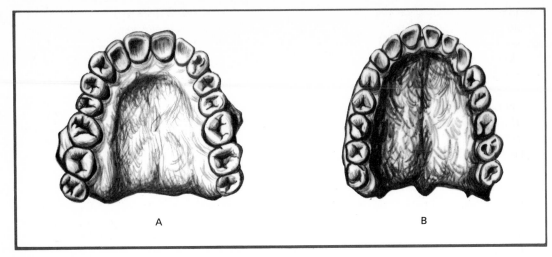

Figure 6 Dentition of a late archaic *(A)* and of a modern *H. sapiens (B).*
Incisors are larger than those of any other hominid. Molars of modern
humans are smaller. (*A* is from Brace, Nelson, & Korn, 1971)

objects. The shift away from the use of teeth as tools is reflected first in smaller neck muscles. These are more affected than teeth by what goes on during a person's lifetime. Tooth size, a trait controlled largely by genetics, changes more slowly, in response to evolutionary pressures. It may be that the problems caused by the crowding of large teeth in a shrinking jaw were beginning to outweigh the selective advantages of having big front teeth (Wolpoff, 1975).

Elsewhere, the back teeth and jaws continued their long-term trend to smaller size. A slight chin was beginning to appear on many of the specimens from both Europe and other areas. Browridges were reduced. And the brain became so large that the average cranial capacity found in late archaic fossils—1470 cc.—is even greater than the average cranial capacity of modern humans—1330 cc. Whether these numbers say anything about how the intelligence of these hominids compares to our own is an open question. Brain size cannot be strictly correlated with intelligence, so the late archaics may not have had our mental abilities. However, evidence of

burials and the appearance of ritual activity has prompted some anthropologists to argue that they were just as intelligent as we are.

Late archaics seem to have been able to use their hands independently—an indication of mental refinement of another kind. Tiny parallel scratches on their incisors suggest that they used stone knives to cut their meat before swallowing it. The direction of these cuts indicates that they habitually held onto the meat with their right hand, while cutting it with their left. Specialization in use of hands is a uniquely human trait. Some scientists associate it with the evolution of higher brain centers (Kennedy, 1975).

Another function of the higher brain centers is speech. Scientists are intrigued by the question of when language evolved. But as yet we have no way of knowing whether the late archaics could talk to one another. We know little of how their brain was structured, for only a few of their gross external features have been preserved as fossilized molds. Whether or not they had a localized "speech center" in their brains we cannot tell. However, some researchers have noted that these hominids had plenty of room to move their tongues around if they did try to speak, since the bony shelves had disappeared from the inside of their lower jaws. Philip Lieberman, a linguist, and Edmund Crelin, an anatomist, have determined that the larynx and brains of these early people were better equipped for speech than those of other primates. Their speech potential, Lieberman and Crelin suggest, was similar to that of modern human infants. And judging from their cultural advances, they probably used some primitive form of spoken communication. Lieberman and Crelin think that they could produce only a few vowel sounds, and their consonants were limited to *b*s, *d*s, and a few others. Fascinating as this theory is, however, it is based on very thin evidence—a single, possibly deformed, fossil. Alexander Marshack (1976) feels that Neandertal geometric designs indicate a symbolic ability that must have included a fairly sophisticated form of language.

Phylogenetic Interpretations

Although we have thus far treated late archaics as a single widespread group, anthropologists disagree as to how to interpret the variety within this group. Controversy centers on the late archaics. These fossils have been referred to traditionally as *Neandertals*. The use of this term has been particularly confusing. At different times, it has been used as a label for (1) the western European fossils contemporary with the Neander Valley skull, (2) an evolutionary grade (the "Neandertal" stage of biological and cultural evolution), and (3) the fossils from all over Europe, Asia, and Africa that date from the Würm glaciation. As a result, there is confusion as to which set of fossils the Neandertal label is being applied.

Why is "Neandertal" used for so many very different finds? Up to the mid-1950s, fossil collection and analysis was heavily influenced by a European bias on the part of western paleontologists. It seemed to them that the European fossils were the most important, since they were the most numerous. This is not surprising, because most of the fossil hunting went on in Europe. At any rate, the idea developed that Europe was central in hominid evolution. However, fossil finds accumulating from other parts of the world gradually made it evident that Europe was only a part of the evolutionary theater—and a rather isolated part, at that. Nonetheless, scientists continued to interpret these non-European fossils in terms of the European classification scheme. As anthropologist David Pilbeam has pointed out, calling fossils from Java "tropical Neandertals" makes no more sense than referring to modern populations living in Java as "tropical Europeans" (Pilbeam, 1970).

The lack of early data and often confused interpretations have combined to produce a number of theories for this period. The three major phylogenic theories are often referred to as the presapiens theory, the pre-Neandertal theory, and the single-lineage theory. In the past, the popularity of each has depended to a great extent on the popularity of its leading proponents.

The Presapiens Theory. This theory holds that the European Neandertals branched off from the hominid line at least as long ago as 250,000 years and finally became extinct, leaving no descendants. As the Neandertals evolved, another group of hominids was developing modern human anatomical traits. These hominids were the presapiens, for whom the theory is named. (See Figure 7.)

The presapiens theory has its origins in the end of the nineteenth century. Then, as now, interpretation of fossil discoveries was strongly influenced by the current climate of opinion. People were very unsympathetic to the idea that all life—including civilized Europeans—had evolved from more primitive forms. The newly found Neandertal remains, therefore, seemed to belong to a creature far more "brutish" than modern humans.

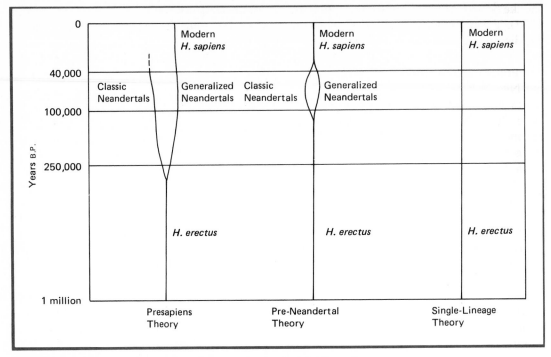

Figure 7 Theories of the evolution of early and late archaic *H. sapiens.*
The presapiens theory suggests that the European Neandertal lineage
diverged at least 250,000 years ago. According to the pre-Neandertal theory,
two groups of late archaics evolved from the early archaic form more
recently. The single-lineage theory proposes a single evolution line.

Since there was no known way to determine the age of the find, many scientists assumed that it was just an abnormal human.

As more European fossils resembling the Neandertal specimen were found, the notion that it was an isolated freak had to be discarded. But popular feeling still colored scientific interpretation. In 1908, the most complete set of bones of this type—the skeleton of an aging man found in La Chapelle-aux-Saints, France—was sent to Professor Marcellin Boule of the Museum of Natural History in Paris. The massive volumes this scholar turned out pictured the Neandertals as the kind of "cave men" we still see in cartoons. Very few people—including Boule—were willing to consider primitive creatures like the La Chapelle-aux-Saints fossil their ancestors. So Boule concluded that they were representatives of a line that had eventually died out, leaving no descendants. Their place was supposedly taken by more modern humans with "superior" traits, who invaded Europe from a hypothetical homeland somewhere else.

To support his theory, Boule presented evidence that the Neandertals and the modern forms that seemed to replace them in the geological record were far too different to be seen as evolutionary stages along a single line. Boule's theory influenced the classification of fossils for years. But in 1957 reexamination of the La Chapelle-aux-Saints remains showed that they had probably been distorted by a severe case of arthritis, making them seem more apelike than they were (Strause & Cave, 1957). Today the presapiens theory is generally discounted.

The Pre-Neandertal Theory. According to the pre-Neandertal theory, two groups of late archaics evolved from the preWürm early archaic form that had existed throughout Europe, the Middle East, and North Africa: the *generalized,* or *early, Neandertals* and the *classic Neandertals.* The traits of the generalized Neandertals were unspecialized enough that many experts think they evolved into modern humans. Holders of this theory believe that the modern form emerged everywhere except in Western Europe, where those who would become the classic Neandertals were isolated by glacial advances. Under the extreme natural selection caused by the cold weather, a specialized form that could survive in the harsh climate quickly evolved.

Supporters of the pre-Neandertal theory do not think that the classic and generalized Neandertals were different enough to warrant classification as separate species. They do, however, argue that with the retreat of the second Würm glaciation, modern-looking humans with new cultural techniques entered previously isolated Western Europe. There, they probably mixed with the classic Neandertals, and both groups contributed to the gene pool of modern humans.

The Single-Lineage Theory. The third theory—the *single-lineage theory,* proposes that in spite of some local variations, all hominids living around the world in the Würm glacial age are part of a single evolving line. The European Neandertals also contributed to the gene pool of modern humans, according to this theory.

What conclusion can we draw about these conflicting theories? There is a growing body of evidence that the presapiens theory is the product of a rather narrow focus on events in Europe, to the exclusion of the rest of the world. Reinterpretation of the fossil and archaeological data from the period suggests that European Neandertals were simply a localized population of a worldwide species, *H. sapiens.* The new evidence indicates that the Neandertals, along with other groups, evolved into early modern forms.

The presapiens theory was based on proving that rather modern humans appeared before Neandertals in the European fossil record. The traditional candidates for old but modern-looking humans have included the Piltdown skull and skullcaps found in Swanscombe, England, and Fontéchevade, France. Piltdown, of course, has been exposed as a hoax. Reexamination of the Swanscombe fossil shows that it is indeed older than the Neandertal finds. But its features do not fall within the range of variations seen in contemporary human populations as presapiens theorists had claimed.

As for the two Fontéchevade skullcaps, their apparent lack of browridges had been used as proof that they were closer to modern skull shapes than the Neandertals. But at least one of them belonged to a child and the other could have. Children at this time developed browridges as they aged. Therefore, the absence of browridges in these childlike skullcaps does not support the presapiens theory.

A fourth set of fossils—two individuals found in the Vertesszöllös cave—has recently been offered as evidence of a modern human line that predated the Neandertals. Again, these fossils are unquestionably older than the Neandertals. But their cranial characteristics are most similar to those of *H. erectus.* They cannot be interpreted as early *H. sapiens* (Wolpoff, 1971).

Finally, there is good biological and cultural evidence that the western European Neandertals gradually evolved in place into modern *H. sapiens* (Brose & Wolpoff, 1971). As Brose and Wolpoff point out, neither relative strata studies nor comparison of absolute dates reveal any signs that these people were suddenly replaced by more advanced forms. Instead, tools show a gradual improvement in technology at all sites. In anatomy, too, there appears to be a gradual transition from the Neandertal form to a more modern one. At both levels, however, there is a great deal of individual variation.

Early Modern Humans

During the latter part of the Würm glaciation, hominids having a nearly modern anatomy first began living in the Western Hemisphere and Australia. By 30,000 to 25,000 B.P., they had extended their range to all the areas now inhabited by humans. Though these people continued to live in rather small groups as hunters and gatherers, they rapidly advanced in both cultural and technological sophistication.

The Fossils

Far more fossils have been found from this period than from any that came before it. Because these hominids were often carefully buried, whole skeletons have been preserved. In Europe, for instance, twice as many fossils of early moderns have been found as fossils of late archaics. The density of archaeological sites from this period seems to indicate that population size had grown, too.

From modern-day France to the Soviet Union, early moderns hunted a wide assortment of game animals with a sophisticated variety of weapons—spears, harpoons, clubs, bows and arrows, and boomerangs. Their technology allowed them to survive in all but the most forbidding environments. Shelters ranged from caves and tents to skin-covered huts sunk into the ground.

Outside of Europe, there are not as many early modern fossils. A few have been found in Java, Japan, and China. Eastern Africa may have been heavily inhabited because it was a crossroads between the Nile Valley to the north, the rain forest to the west, and the grasslands to the south.

In Australia and the New World, hominid fossils appear for the first time during this period. How and when they got there we are not sure. Hominids may have island-hopped with small rafts or boats to reach Australia from the long-inhabited Java area. A fairly lengthy fossil record exists in Australia extending back to 25,000 years ago. Unfortunately, many fossils are hard to interpret. One find at Green Gully, near Melbourne, for instance, consisted of 3,900 scrambled bone fragments from a male and a female. As is still the practice among some Australian aborigines, their bodies had probably been left to rot for about a year before they were buried. Before being scooped into a single grave, their bones were probably mixed up and spread around by animal scavengers. Despite such paleontological nightmares, we are *certain* that there were fossil hominids in Australia before 24,000 B.P., and perhaps even as early as 32,000 B.P.

As in Australia, we have no direct evidence of how and when fossil hominids first reached the New World. Now, most scientists believe that they crossed a wide land bridge between Siberia and Alaska and then moved southward. When the Wisconsin glacier, the North American equivalent of the Würm glaciation in Europe, reached its peak about 40,000 years ago, it would have gathered so much sea water into its mass that the sea level might have been lowered by as much as 460 feet. This would have exposed a corridor of land across what is now the Bering Strait. This landbridge may have closed and reopened at times as the glacier periodically retreated and then advanced again, allowing migrants to cross in waves.

Physical Characteristics

These most recent of our ancestors looked very much like us. Their tooth structure and jaws are almost within the range of sizes seen in today's populations. Their faces became much flatter than those of earlier hominids. A chin was clearly in evidence on early modern fossils from all over the world. The cranial vault was higher but narrower than in earlier fossils, perhaps because reduced demands on the teeth allowed the skull to be shaped more by the expansion of the upper brain than by the need to provide robust anchor points for the jaw and neck muscles. (See Figure 8.) Finally, increasing use of specialized tools rather than muscle power in survival tasks decreased the need for heavy bone structure. All over their bodies, early moderns were generally less robust than their late archaic ancestors.

Although early moderns looked more like contemporary humans than any preceding group had, they were not fully modern. Compared to earlier groups, they had a higher incidence of "modern" characteristics (such as chins) and a lower incidence of "archaic" characteristics (such as strongly prognathous faces). In some traits, some of the fossils fall within the range of variations found in con-temporary human populations. But taken as a whole, they are as different from living humans as they are from the late archaics (Wolpoff, 1975).

As one generation followed another under conditions of increasing cultural control over the environmental pressures of survival, the frequency of these primitive traits gradually declined, and more fully modern-looking humans emerged.

Summary

1. The major anatomical changes in hominids during the Pleistocene Epoch were reduction of the chewing apparatus and expansion of the brain. Both changes are the product of interacting biological and cultural forces.

2. We have divided the Pleistocene hominids into five groups: early *Homo erectus,* late *Homo erectus,* early archaic *Homo sapiens,* late archaic *Homo sapiens,* and early modern humans. With the possible exception of the Upper Pleistocene forms, these hominids probably represent a single lineage.

3. During the lower Pleistocene (2 million to 700,000 years B.P.) early *H. erectus* forms

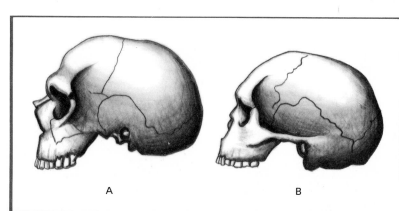

Figure 8 Skulls of a late archaic *H. sapiens* (A) and an early modern *H. sapiens* (B). Cranial capacity is similar, although the skull of *B* is shorter (from front to back), narrower, and higher (from top to bottom) than that of *A*.

A   B

174

spread from Africa to warm parts of Java, China, and Europe, perhaps in pursuit of migrating animal herds. Compared to the early African hominids, these hominids had a more erect posture, lighter jaws, smaller molars, and bigger brains. But their broad faces and heavy neck muscles gave them a somewhat primitive appearance.

4. Fossil hominids are scarce from the period following 700,000 B.P., but reappear as late *H. erectus* from 450,000 to about 250,000 years B.P. These hominids inhabited harsher environments, aided by improved technology and expansion of brain centers responsible for conscious thought and sensory-motor integration. Chewing apparatus was further reduced.

5. In early archaic *H. sapiens* (ranging from about 225,000 to 75,000 years B.P.), the trend toward smaller jaws, molars, and chewing muscles continued. But their front teeth, upper jaws, and neck muscles were larger again, an evolutionary reversal that may have been a response to the use of the front teeth as tools.

6. Hominids from the Würm glaciation period traditionally have been referred to as Neandertals, but we call them late archaic *H. sapiens*. Classic Neandertals from western Europe were shorter and had a more projecting face and a relatively large nasal cavity compared to the generalized forms found elsewhere. Perhaps this is partly because their features were adaptations to the cold climate.

7. Explanations of the presence of late archaic variation fall into three main theories. The *presapiens theory* (today generally discounted) holds that the European Neandertals branched off from *H. erectus* stock as long ago as 250,000 years and became extinct, while another group of hominids developed modern human anatomical traits. According to the *pre-Neandertal theory*, the earlier *generalized Neandertals* and the later *classic Neandertals* evolved from earlier preglacial archaics. The generalized form later evolved into modern humans. The *single-lineage theory* proposes that all hominids of the Würm glaciation contributed to the gene pool of modern humans.

8. Early modern human fossils have been found in the New World and Australia, as well as in the long-inhabited areas—for example, Africa and the Far East. These fossils show the loss of the primitive characteristics of their predecessors. But their range of anatomical variations does not quite match that of modern humans.

Genetics and the Study of Human Variation

9

THE fossil record can tell us part of the story of how we evolved. Looking at fossils, we can see some of the ways in which the hominid body has changed in the course of time. Natural selection is the primary force that caused these changes. But we can only theorize about how natural selection has been at work and why various traits have evolved, because the fossil record consists of a small group of individuals from different times and different places. To study the process by which traits are inherited and show the action of natural selection and other evolutionary forces, we must look at evolution among living organisms. In this chapter we shall discuss the nature of heredity and how it applies to humans and how the forces of evolution have been studied and illustrated in living human groups.

Mendel's Laws of Inheritance

In his theory of natural selection, Darwin explained the natural force that changes the physical makeup of populations from one generation to the next. Although Darwin understood that some traits increase the chances of survival in a given environment, he never discovered exactly how these traits are passed on to offspring. The real operation of inheritance was being worked out by Gregor Mendel, an Austrian monk, at the time Darwin was writing *On the Origin of Species*.

Mendel experimented with garden peas during the late 1850s and 1860s. Since seven characteristics of these plants—seed color, seed shape, leaf color, stem length, pod color, flower color, and pea color—exist in two alternative forms, Mendel was able to isolate inherited characteristics. Stem length, for example, is either long or short. Mendel cross-pollinated equal numbers of long-stemmed and short-stemmed plants. The first generation offspring were all long-stemmed plants. When he crossed these plants with each other, the second generation of plants was about 75 percent long-stemmed plants and 25 percent short-stemmed plants. (See Figure 1.) Mendel thought that these results suggested that separate particles exist in the plant cells and that each particle controls a specific trait. These particles, whose presence was still only guessed at, were later named *genes.*

Because stems of the first generation of cross-pollinated pea plants were not medium-sized—a blend of long and short—but were all long, Mendel concluded that each particle, or gene, controls one form of a given trait. The reason that all the first generation plants were long-stemmed was, Mendel explained, because one gene was dominant over the other and could therefore prevent the expression of the other, or recessive, gene trait. The

Figure 1   Results of Mendel's cross of long-stemmed and short-stemmed pea plants

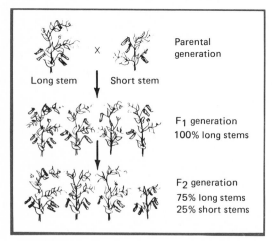

different forms of the same gene are now called *alleles.*

The alleles of an organism together make up its *genotype.* The interaction of the alleles (be they dominant or recessive) determines the physical characteristics of an organism, or its *phenotype.* A genotype that contains two alleles of the same type, whether they are dominant or recessive, is *homozygous.* A genotype that contains two different types of alleles is *heterozygous.*

To explain how genotypes are created, Mendel looked at the formation of *gametes,* the cells that join in fertilization to become the first cell of a new organism. He reasoned that when male and female gametes are formed, the paired alleles of the parent cell must divide so that each gamete will contain only one allele. Thus, the alleles *segregate* to form gametes that contain only one of the two alleles controlling a particular trait. The gamete from one sex then joins in fertilization with a gamete from the other to form the genotype of the new organism.

Mendel also explained that genes controlling different characteristics could be inherited independently of one another. He said that they were *independently assorted.* We have learned since that this is not always true and that some genes may be linked, rather than independent. But the genes for the traits Mendel studied were inherited independently of one another.

Inside the Cell Nucleus

In the nineteenth century it became possible to look at the internal workings of cells, the basic units of life. Using improved microscopes, scientists were able to study the *nucleus,* then known to be a structure encased in a membrane at the center of the cell. Staining revealed long, thin threads, which were named *chromosomes,* within the nucleus. Every body cell contains the same number of chromosomes. Since the sperm and the egg alone join to form a new organism and since the sperm is mostly nucleus, it was deduced that the genetic information was contained in the nucleus of the cells. In 1900, when they rediscovered Mendel's earlier work, scientists realized that the chromosomes carry the genes whose existence Mendel had proposed.

Mitosis and Meiosis

In the process of cell division, daughter cells receive a complete copy of the organism's genetic information. Scientists distinguish two types of cell division. The division of body cells to form other body cells is called *mitosis.* The division of sex cells to form sperm or ova is called *meiosis.* In mitosis, the exact duplication of the chromosomes passes on the same genetic information to every new cell. This genetic information controls the structure of the body's cells and allows the body to function correctly.

In meiosis, sex cells divide to form gametes that have only one-half the normal number of chromosomes. When male and female gametes unite, they form a new cell called a *zygote,* which contains a normal number of chromosomes. If this halving did not occur, two gametes, each having the normal number of chromosomes would combine to form a zygote with twice the normal number.

177

Figure 2 **Meiosis in an animal cell.**
Meiosis involves two sequences of cell division, creating four gametes. We shall explain meiosis in terms of six stages. Stage 1: Chromosomes have contracted, and homologous pairs have moved together. Stage 2: Each member of every homologous pair, having copied itself before Stage 1, becomes clearly double-stranded. The homologous pairs and their replicants line up at the center of the cell, and members of each pair and its replicant move to opposite poles. Stage 3: Two new cells form, each with one member of every homologous pair and its replicant. Stage 4: (Stages 4, 5, and 6 are a division exactly like that of mitosis.) The previously-formed duplicate pairs line up at the center of the cell. Stage 5: The pairs become unjoined, and the two copies move toward opposite poles of the cells. Stage 6: Each cell forms two identical daughter cells, which are gametes.

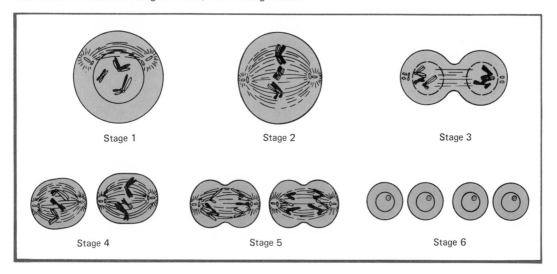

Stage 1   Stage 2   Stage 3

Stage 4   Stage 5   Stage 6

GENETICS AND THE STUDY OF HUMAN VARIATION

The zygote's chromosomes are matched, or *homologous*, pairs of chromosomes from the parental gametes. Today we know that humans have a total of 46 chromosomes, which function as 23 pairs in the body cells. Thus, meiosis not only reduces the number of chromosomes by one-half, but it also distributes one member of each of the 23 paired chromosomes to each resulting gamete. See Figure 2 for the details of meiosis.

An understanding of meiosis clarifies some of Mendel's observations of pea traits. When Mendel crossed long-stemmed plants with short-stemmed plants, all of the first generation (F_1) plants had long stems. But when he crossed these F_1 generation plants with each other, the short-stemmed variety reappeared. From these results, Mendel concluded that the factors controlling stem length acted as separate particles. Both contrasting traits could reappear independently in the F_2 generation: They did not blend together. Now we can see that the genes behave this way because the two alleles that controlled each trait existed on different members of the same homologous pair. Furthermore, Mendel's seven pea characteristics are located on seven different homologous chromosome pairs. This was the basis of his idea that traits are assorted independently of one another. Actually, traits located on the same chromosome are inherited together, so that independent assortment does not apply to them.

The Chemistry of Genes and Their Activity

Biologists first gathered the information about genes that we presented in the last section almost entirely by inference. Later, however, much direct evidence was found to support the early theories. This evidence included detailed knowledge of the chemical makeup of the genetic material, how the chromosomes copy themselves, how they direct the activities of the organism, and how they affect its characteristics.

Once scientists realized that the chromosomes must carry the genes, researchers began to find out the chemical composition of the genes by analyzing the chromosomes, which they could identify in their microscopes. As early as 1869, chemists studying the cell nucleus knew that it contains protein and an acid named *deoxyribonucleic acid,* or *DNA.* In the 1920s, researchers using a stain to color the DNA bright red found that a major portion of the chromosomes is DNA. But most researchers believed that the other main element of the chromosomes—protein—was probably the genetic material. Only it seemed to have the necessary complexity. By the early 1950s, however, experiments with bacteria had strongly suggested that DNA indeed is

Figure 3 The sugar of one nucleotide bonds to the phosphate of the next to form a long chain. (Moody, 1975)

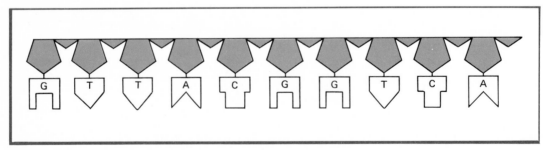

the source of genetic instructions. Finally, in 1953 James D. Watson and Francis H. Crick proposed the model for DNA that is commonly accepted today. Watson and Crick received the Nobel Prize for this model, which is considered one of the most important landmarks in the history of biology.

Proteins and DNA

Watson and Crick conceived of DNA as a large compound made up of a series of smaller molecules bonded together. The basic unit of DNA is a group of three molecules, called a *nucleotide.* The three molecules are a sugar, a phosphate, and an organic base. The organic base can be one of two different types, either a purine or a pyrimidine. There are two purines: adenine (A) and guanine (G) and two pyrimidines: cytosine (C) and thymine (T).

The sugar of one nucleotide is bonded to the phosphate of the next, forming a long chain, as shown in Figure 3. The DNA molecule is made up of two such chains, linked together like the two sides of a ladder, but twisted into a form more like a spiral staircase. (See Figure 4.)

Probably the only function of DNA is to direct the very complex task of making proteins in the cells. Proteins are more intricate than any known compound and are vital to the body's functioning and to its structure. Cell membranes are made up of proteins, as are many of the internal parts of the cell. Some proteins serve as *enzymes,* chemicals that are necessary to start or speed up vital chemical processes in the body. For example, enzymes control the breakdown of nutrients into energy compounds and the synthesis of nutrients into large molecules of body tissue. Enzymes also direct the development of the embryo.

The basic structural units of proteins are *amino acids.* A single protein can contain from 50 to 50,000 amino acids. The 20 known amino acids can form practically an infinite number of proteins, each with a different

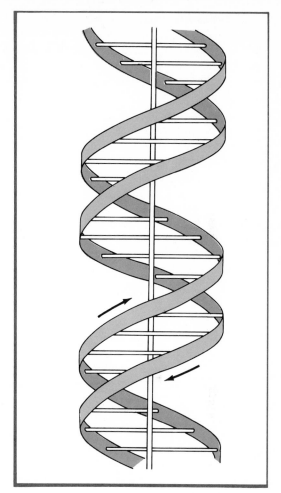

Figure 4 DNA molecule.
Measurements with x-rays led Watson and Crick to conclude that the DNA molecule is in the shape of a helix.

shape and different physical properties. There is strong evidence that DNA molecules control the sequence of amino acids in proteins.

Human Genetics

It is harder to apply the principles of heredity to humans than to pea plants. We cannot do experiments like Mendel's to determine the genetic control of human phenotypes. Most human genotypes are complex, and we have not yet studied changes in human genetics over several generations. Our knowledge of human genetics, therefore, has been built up very slowly.

We know most about *simple genetic traits* —those phenotypes controlled by only a few alleles at a single *locus* (or gene position) on one pair of homologous chromosomes. Blood characteristics, such as ABO blood groups, are simple genetic traits. We know much less about *complex genetic traits* —those phenotypes controlled by a large number of alleles at many loci. Most of the visible features of the body, such as height, weight, and skin color are complex traits. Our understanding of genetic control of these characteristics is incomplete for two reasons: (1) the number of genes involved cannot be known precisely, and (2) these phenotypes are strongly influenced by the environment. We shall examine how the genetic basis of simple and complex traits is studied.

Simple Genetic Traits

To study the genetic basis of simple traits, we begin by analyzing the phenotype of the trait. Phenotypes can be seen and measured, but we cannot directly observe the controlling genes. Once the various phenotypes are known, it is possible to figure out the number of different alleles that are involved in their inheritance by making up a *pedigree*. A pedigree is an analysis of the phenotypes of related persons. Often done in the form of a diagram, a pedigree shows the phenotypes and biological relationships of family members for at least two generations. Scientists can figure out the genotype of each individual by taking into account the number of alleles needed to explain the phenotypes and the possible presence of dominant and recessive alleles.

ABO Blood Groups. The ABO blood groups were among the earliest traits to be analyzed by pedigrees. In 1900, Karl Landsteiner isolated four distinct blood groups: A, B, AB, and O. He was able to identify these phenotypes by observing the pattern of clumping when one person's blood cells were mixed with the serum of another.

Once the phenotypes were known, scientists worked to determine the genes that governed inheritance of the different types. Mating between type O, type A, and type B individuals yielded more children of types A and B than of O. This indicated that the alleles controlling A and B phenotypes are dominant over the type O allele. Since children of a parent of type A and a parent of type B showed AB phenotypes, it was assumed that both A and B alleles are dominant. Ultimately, the existence of three alleles—A, B, and O—was proposed to account for the known phenotypes. There were thus six possible genotypes: AA, AO, BB, BO, AB, and OO. But there are only four phenotypes, because O is recessive to both A and B alleles, so that genotypes AO and BO are expressed as A and B phenotypes. (See Table 1.)

Human geneticists have used the same principles to identify the genetic basis of many other simple traits. Our knowledge is especially complete for blood characteristics. The genetic basis of the structure of hemoglobin in the red blood cells, and the structure of the white blood cells and of certain proteins in the blood serum are now fairly well known, for example.

Abnormal Traits. Research on the genetic basis of blood traits has greatly expanded our knowledge of the abnormal or pathological traits that threaten health and may even cause early death. Some pathological traits are caused by a dominant allele. In Huntington's chorea, mental deterioration goes along with uncontrollable movements. Because the trait is controlled by a dominant allele, persons who are homozygous for the allele, as well as

Table 1 Blood Group Phenotypes and Genotypes

Genotype	Phenotype
AA	A
AO	A
BB	B
BO	B
AB	AB
OO	O

those who are heterozygous, have the trait.

More often, abnormal traits are controlled by recessive alleles. This means that the disease will only appear if the person has two recessive alleles. Cystic fibrosis and a large number of metabolic disorders are caused in this way. In the case of metabolic disorders, an enzyme normally controlled by the dominant allele cannot be produced, and some bodily process is suppressed.

Mutation—The Source of New Traits. Genotypes are usually inherited. In rare instances, however, the genetic material is changed spontaneously during meiosis. The individual may then possess a feature controlled by an allele that is not part of either parental genotype. Such a change is called a *mutation.*

Changes in the nucleotide sequence of a DNA molecule are called *point mutations.* There are three kinds of point mutations, each of which effects a different kind of change in the sequence of nucleotides in the DNA sequence. One or more nucleotides replace others in *substitutions;* one or more nucleotides are added in *additions;* and one or more are lost in *deletions.* For example, a single amino acid substitution has been found to cause an alteration in the ability of human hemoglobin to bind oxygen. This abnormal hemoglobin causes sickle-cell anemia, a disease that shortens the life expectancy of its victims.

More common than point mutations, *chro-mosomal rearrangements* are changes in the structure or number of chromosomes. They can be seen with a microscope. One type of chromosomal rearrangement is *nondisjunction,* the failure of paired chromosomes to separate completely during meiosis. In Down's Syndrome (sometimes called mongolism), people inherit 47 chromosomes instead of the usual 46. *Translocation* is a rearrangement in which one chromosome is broken and then joined with a piece from another chromosome. In *inversion,* part of a chromosome is broken off, turned around, and reinserted backwards.

Radiation from medical and dental x-rays and from nuclear power plants and atomic bombs has caused concern because it is known to increase the mutation rate. And the effects of radiation are cumulative. Low dosages over a long period of time can have the same effects as large dosages occurring rapidly. Even so, they occur about once in every 1 million to 10 million gametes. Mutations are rather rare events.

Ultimately, mutations are the only source of new genes and, as a result, of the genetic variability underlying differences of phenotype in the members of a population. As we have mentioned earlier, natural selection reduces the variation within a population by eliminating the least adaptive traits. In times of environmental change genetic variety is essential. If no variants exist that allow survival in the new conditions, the population may become extinct.

Complex Traits

For complex traits there is no direct correspondence between phenotype and genotype. Since height and head shape, unlike blood type, are controlled by a number of interacting genes, researchers may never be able to define the genetic basis of these complex traits. Complex traits are shaped to a large extent by the environment. Height, for example, is partly a product of the quality of one's diet.

There are two kinds of complex traits. *Morphological traits* are part of the physical structure of the body and are measurable in terms of size, weight, and shape. *Physiological traits* are traits of body function, such as breathing or digestion. If we look at the lungs, for example, we can measure the dimensions of their tissues (morphological traits) and measure the amount of oxygen or carbon dioxide that passes through their membranes (physiological traits). Because function is so closely linked with structure, however, the distinction between the two is more an analytical convenience than a reality.

The Study of Human Populations

In the preceding pages we presented the genetic processes responsible for individual differences. In this section we shall turn our attention to patterns of these differences as they are seen in the members of whole populations. These patterns are the product of various evolutionary forces. Thus, to understand how evolution is occurring at the present time, physical anthropologists must identify the forces at work by studying the pattern of individual differences in a population.

Defining a Human Population

Among humans, a population can be defined as a group of individuals who are more likely to mate among themselves than among others of the same species. In human populations, mating with persons outside the group may be restricted for two reasons: geographic factors, and social factors. Geographic obstacles can limit mobility, thereby limiting the pool of potential mates to members of the

local group. The populations of many islands in the South Pacific are good examples of geographic isolation. Social factors such as marriage rules can prevent intermarriage with members of neighboring groups. Among humans, the breeding unit, or population, is always defined socially by a set of values, attitudes, and ideas of correct behavior. In India, for example, the caste system prohibits marriage between socially defined groups. Therefore, within even a very small geographic area, several populations may be identifiable by caste. It is no wonder that the ethnographic concept of culture as a group of individuals with shared ways of life is often the same as the biological concept of population.

Evolutionary Forces Acting on the Population

Because the human lifespan is long and relevant data for previous generations often do not exist, studies of human populations concentrate on short-term biological change, or *microevolution*. We can gain a fairly clear understanding of how genetic changes in populations can occur by studying *microevolution.* Studies of *macroevolution,* physical change over millions of years, tend, however, to be descriptive. We can describe what has happened over a long period of time, but not why it has happened.

Studies of microevolution have shown that biological differences among groups and among generations of the same group are the result of four different forces: (1) mutation, (2) gene flow, (3) genetic drift, and (4) natural selection. Of these processes, only the pattern of change produced by natural selection is influenced by the environment. Genes that control nonadaptive traits become less and less frequent in the population as individuals who possess these genes either die or fail to reproduce. Genes controlling adaptive traits become more and more frequent in the population because of the survival advantage of the trait. Changes in gene frequency caused by gene flow, drift, and mutation occur randomly with respect to the environment. Only by chance could these forces produce a group of genes of great survival value to a population in a given environment. Instead, these forces are modified by natural selection. Selection opposes a random increase in the frequency of maladaptive traits or strengthens the effect of a random increase in the frequency of adaptive traits.

Simple Genetic Traits

To assess the action of evolutionary forces, we must be able to measure change in a population. We know that simple traits are controlled by only a few alleles and that complex traits are controlled by large numbers of genes. When studying a simple genetic trait, we can determine the genotype responsible for the trait. Once we know the genotype of each person in the population, we can count the number of times a given allele appears. Changes in the frequency with which a particular allele appears from one generation to the next would be clear evidence of evolution.

Gene *frequency* is the proportion represented by a given allele of all the alleles that occur in a population at the same point on homologous chromosomes. To map frequency, all the genotypes possibly responsible for the observed phenotype are determined. Genotypes with two dominant alleles or two recessive alleles are easily determined. When the phenotype shows a single dominant gene, however, it is difficult to determine the genotype because a recessive allele may be masked. Genotypes must be established by figuring out a pedigree. It is not always easy to construct a pedigree, though, because many non-Western societies reckon kinship in cultural rather than biological terms. In some societies, all the kinspeople of one's mother's generation are called by the same term. If

degrees of biological relationship can be determined, pedigrees can be used to find genotypes.

Once all the possible genotypes have been determined and the genotype of each member of the population identified, the total number of each allele in the population is figured. Dividing the number of each specific allele by the total number of alleles gives us the frequency of each allele.

Changes in the frequency of alleles controlling for simple traits as a result of gene flow and genetic drift are the easiest to study. Mutation is harder to study, and showing the action of natural selection is the hardest. We shall discuss each of these processes subsequently.

Gene Flow. We define *gene flow* as the movement of genes across population boundaries. Members of one population who leave and mate with members of another population are likely to contribute alleles to the new gene pool in frequencies different from those already existing in the receiving gene pool.

The degree to which gene flow affects the receiving population depends on two factors: (1) the number of people who immigrate and (2) the degree of difference in gene frequencies between the two populations. In many societies, cultural rules promote marriage with members outside the group and ensure a steady flow of genes between populations. Male members of Bushman bands, for example, must seek mates in other bands. If mates are exchanged over a long time, then the two groups become genetically more similar.

Gene flow links all human populations together. Genes that are introduced into a population by migrants can be transported to still other populations by their descendants. Gene flow is only interrupted when natural or social barriers restrict migration. Because no group has been isolated totally, gene flow has been important in maintaining the unity of our species for the last million years.

Genetic Drift. *Genetic drift* is a random change in gene frequencies associated with small population size. Looking at a single trait controlled by two alleles, we can see that the greater the number of children a person has, the greater the chance that one of the alleles will be passed on. In small populations in which the number of children is relatively small, the chance that some alleles will *not* be passed on is greater (see Table 2). Random changes in the frequency of alleles may therefore occur from one generation to the next.

The simplest method for detecting genetic drift is to look at gene frequencies in small, isolated, but genetically related groups living in similar environments. If the frequency of a given allele changes from population to population, it is possible that drift is responsible. Neighboring populations in the New Guinea highlands often have dramatically different gene frequencies. Because the highland environment is uniform, the same selective forces would act on all. Therefore, natural selection is probably not the cause of the differences. Also, gene flow would increase similarity between groups, and mutation would not act quickly enough to produce such differences. By process of elimination, the genetic differences on New Guinea have been attributed to drift (Gajdusek, 1964).

It is much more difficult to show the process of genetic drift in operation, because data spanning many generations is lacking for conclusive evidence. Still, information on random changes within one generation do give evidence of special cases of drift.

The *founder effect* is one special case. It occurs when a natural disaster or migration decreases an original population sharply. The remaining population is called the founder group. If it is small, it may not accurately reflect the genetic makeup of the original group. Some alleles may be present in higher frequency than they were originally and others in lower frequency. Thus, the founder

Table 2 Number of Children versus the Chance of Inheriting a Given Allele

Type B Blood: Genotype BO		
Number of Children	Chances that B Allele Will Not Be Inherited	
1	$\frac{1}{2}$	$= \frac{1}{2}$
2	$\frac{1}{2} \times \frac{1}{2}$	$= \frac{1}{4}$
3	$\frac{1}{2} \times \frac{1}{2} \times \frac{1}{2}$	$= \frac{1}{8}$
4	$\frac{1}{2} \times \frac{1}{2} \times \frac{1}{2} \times \frac{1}{2}$	$= \frac{1}{16}$

group will probably differ biologically from the original population.

The Yąnomamö Indians of the Brazil-Venezuela border are an excellent example of the founder effect. Yąnomamö lineages are linked by exchange of mates because men can only marry certain relatives. As a result, different interbreeding pairs of lineages have unique gene frequencies. The Yąnomamö social system can only organize a certain number of people in a village structure. When the population grows beyond a certain point, rivalries split the village. After the split, pairs of linked lineages tend to remain together. When a village containing several of these pair lineages splits, new villages founded by each of the pairs will have markedly different frequencies from the original village.

Inbreeding, or the mating of biological relatives, has a genetic effect like that of drift. Inbreeding increases the frequency of homozygous genotypes. *Random inbreeding* occurs when a population is so isolated geographically that the pool of potential nonrelated mates is more and more limited with each generation. Even though there is no cultural preference for relatives, the degree of relatedness between individuals who may marry continually increases. When the offspring of related parents marry, they are very likely to pass on shared genes to their children. As a result, children of biologically related parents are more likely to be homozygous for any given allele. Several recessive genetic disorders, including dwarfism and rare types of anemia, have been documented among the Amish, a Mennonite sect living primarily in Pennsylvania. The Amish do not prefer to marry relatives; their potential mates, however, are often second, third, or even first cousins because they have been mating only within the small population for generations.

Nonrandom inbreeding happens when mating customs prescribe a close relative as the most desirable mate. In some societies, marriage between first cousins is preferred as a means of keeping valuable assets in the family.

Mutation. Mutation rates are hard to know with certainty. Changes in the DNA sequence do not always produce noticeable phenotypic expressions of mutation. Dominant mutation rates are easily determined by counting the number of persons whose phenotype reveals the presence of the mutation. Individuals with a phenotype variant known to be controlled by a dominant allele are counted if neither parent is known to possess the trait. A recessive mutation, when paired with a dominant allele, is much harder to detect because the dominant allele controls the phenotype.

The kind of change mutations produce is completely random. Mutations therefore have very little effect on gene frequencies. Once a mutation occurs, it is just as likely to change back into the normal form as it is to change in some new way. Although mutations do provide a continuing source of new variation, most mutations that affect the phenotype are not advantageous. More often than not, they disrupt normal body function and place the carrier at a definite disadvantage.

Selection. One of the main problems we face in the study of selection in human populations is that direct study over several generations is impossible. Some long-term studies of gene frequencies in single human populations have been begun, but the results are not yet clear.

We can, however, look for evidence of how the process of selection has worked in the past. There are two ways of doing this. *Trait distribution studies* use data from many populations to chart the frequency of a single gene. Researchers then look for correlations between the gene's frequency and different environmental factors. *Single population studies* attempt to establish the environmental advantages offered by particular genes to one population.

A Trait Distribution Study. This method has been used to study sickle-cell anemia, which is controlled by one of a number of alleles that regulate the making of hemoglobin. Hemoglobin molecules in the red blood cells help distribute oxygen to the cells of the body. We will be concerned with only two alleles: the allele for normal adult hemoglobin (Hb^A) and the allele for sickle-cell hemoglobin (Hb^S). The structure of the two hemoglobins differs in only one amino acid.

Three phenotypic and genotypic combinations of these two alleles exist. The homozygous normal genotype ($Hb^A Hb^A$) produces hemoglobin that can transport oxygen from the lungs to the tissues under all normal conditions. The heterozygous normal sickle-cell genotype ($Hb^A Hb^S$) produces a mixture of cells with normal hemoglobin and cells with sickle-cell hemoglobin. The homozygous normal and heterozygous normal-sickle-cell phenotypes are difficult to tell apart. Severe exercise or a low level of oxygen, such as occurs at high altitudes, may cause some of the cells with sickle-cell hemoglobin to collapse and form a sickle shape. The sickle-shaped cells may block small capillaries, cutting off the oxygen supply to the tissues. Though severe pain results, the attack subsides with rest and removal of the stress.

The final genotype is the homozygous sickle-cell ($Hb^S Hb^S$), which produces red blood cells with almost 100 percent sickle-cell hemoglobin. Homozygous persons suffer from sickle-cell anemia. They can undergo a crisis after any sort of physical or emotional stress. Massive blockage of the capillaries results in serious damage to the spleen, lungs, and brain, and most of these persons die very young.

Since the 1920s, it has been known that many American black people possessed the sickle-cell allele. In the late 1940s and early 1950s, when its worldwide distribution was mapped, it was noted that the distribution of the Hb^S allele in equatorial Africa seemed to coincide with the distribution of malaria in the same area. (See Figure 5.) Malaria is caused by a parasite that spends part of its lifecycle in the blood of human hosts. The parasite breaks down the amino acids of hemoglobin molecules and incorporates them into its own structure, destroying large numbers of red blood cells in the process.

Among people with normal hemoglobin who live in this area, malaria parasites multiply rapidly in the blood and often cause early death. Among heterozygotes, however, the level of parasites is greatly reduced. This is an advantage to young children and to pregnant women, whose placenta can be damaged by the infection. Homozygote sicklers experience the same grave disadvantage in malarial

environments as they do in nonmalarial environments. The reason for the heterozygote advantage is not entirely clear, but it seems to retard the spread of the parasite in the blood. Because more heterozygotes survive, there is a high frequency of the Hb^S allele.

There is an upper limit on the frequency of the sickle-cell allele, however, because heterozygotes who marry other heterozygotes will produce some homozygote sicklers (who die of anemia) and some homozygote normals (who die of malaria) in each generation. The stability of gene frequencies that occurs because the heterozygote is selectively advantageous (rather than either of the homozygotes) is called *a balanced polymorphism.*

There are three conditions that must be satisfied if the action of natural selection with respect to a given trait is to be shown: (1) the characteristic must have a simple genetic base so that we can measure and detect changes in gene frequencies; (2) the trait must give such an advantage or disadvantage that it directly affects the chances of survival of the person who has it; and (3) the trait must be studied easily, which in most cases means that it must be blood related.

Sickle-cell hemoglobin offers one of the few opportunities to study selection as out-

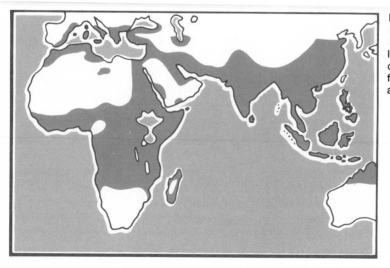

Figure 5 **Distribution of malaria in Africa and Southern Asia.** Its presence corresponds to high frequences of the Hb^s allele.

lined above, because: (1) the blood phenotype (hemoglobin) is controlled by a simple genetic system; (2) the presence of the sickle-cell trait among heterozygotes increases their chances of survival, while its absence often means death from malaria; and (3) the selective agent (the malarial parasite) lives in the bloodstream, where it is easily studied.

Single Population Studies. This method allows scientists to study natural selection by demonstrating the selective advantage or disadvantage of a particular trait in a single population. Studies of the relationship between smallpox and ABO blood groups in rural India, for instance, have shown a much higher incidence of the disease among people who have type A or AB blood (Vogel & Chakravartti, 1971). People who have type B or O blood show a lower incidence of the disease.

The Interaction of Evolutionary Forces. Although we have dealt separately with evolutionary forces, they normally act together. For instance, a mutant recessive allele for the Ellis-Van Creveld syndrome, a kind of dwarfism, was contributed to the Lancaster county Amish population by a person who immigrated to Pennsylvania in 1744 (McKusick et al., 1971). Thus, a mutation that occurred outside the population was added to it by gene flow. Once in the gene pool, this mutation increased in frequency because of the small size of the population—an expression of genetic drift. Inbreeding caused many people to be born homozygous for the syndrome. But because homozygous persons mated infrequently, selection placed a ceiling on the total number of alleles for dwarfism in the population.

Complex Genetic Traits

Complex traits are controlled by the interaction of a large number of alleles at different loci on different chromosomes. Complex traits are continuously distributed in the population. That is, they exist in as many forms as there are people. No two people have exactly the same skin color, for instance. There are two reasons for this: (1) the large number of alleles that contributes to complex traits produces a much greater range of possible genotypic combinations than existed with, say, two alleles; (2) most complex traits can be influenced by environmental factors during growth and development. The combination of these two phenomena makes it impossible to treat complex traits as if they fall into neat, easily definable phenotypes. In order to analyze complex traits, then, we cannot use any of the techniques used to study simple traits. Instead, we employ a number of different statistical models.

In the American population, for instance, the weight of males ranges from about 42.5 kg to about 105 kg. Most men weigh about 62.5 kg. A graph of all the weights in the population forms a bell shape, a pattern called a *normal distribution.* (See Figure 6.) We can compare two populations in terms of a complex trait by graphing the distribution of the trait in both populations.

Distinguishing Environmental from Genetic Influences. Because we cannot determine the genetic basis of complex traits, we can only assess indirectly the role of genes in forming them. We separate the environmental effects from the genetic effects by measuring the extent to which individuals' phenotypes are changeable. Studying the phenotypic ranges of individuals in the population begins to tell us the degree to which population differences may be due to environmental influence.

Acclimatization. The ability of a phenotype to change in response to environmental forces is called *acclimatization.* All humans can make quick adjustments to changes of temperature or diet, or to the presence of disease microorganisms. In general, physiological traits adjust rapidly to new environmental conditions. In hot weather, the circulation of the blood through the skin quickens,

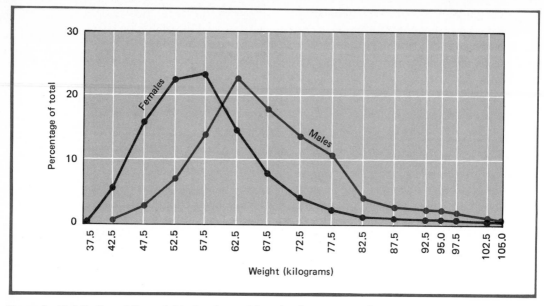

Figure 6 Distribution of the weight of males and females (average age is 17.5 years) in the United States.
Because weight is a complex trait, its distribution is in approximately a bell-shaped curve.

and the perspiration rate increases almost immediately to keep the internal temperature of the body constant. Morphological traits respond somewhat more slowly. After several weeks of hot temperatures, for example, weight loss will occur. Such short-term responses are most highly developed among mammals, probably because they live in varied environments that require many adjustments.

Other responses may develop over years of exposure to a particular stress. These *long-term acclimatizations* cause gradual changes that produce a phenotype more compatible with the environment. Among people who exercise heavily, changes in the tissues of the heart increase pumping efficiency and allow the low resting heart rates found among athletes.

Factors Affecting Acclimatization. Ability to adjust to stress varies with sex and age. Humans, unlike many other animals, are not marked by a high degree of sexual dimorphism. Before puberty there are few morpho-

logical or physiological differences between the sexes. Known physiological differences between adult males and females seem to be related to morphological differences that appear after puberty. Differences between the sexes in the capacity to do physical work and to adjust to cold temperatures and related to different patterns of daily activity and differing proportions of muscle and fat.

We know a good deal about how acclimatization varies with age. The growth period is the time during which humans are most shaped by the environment. This shaping is especially apparent when exposure to extreme conditions—such as high or low temperatures, poor nutrition, or disease—is prolonged. For example, one study showed that American children who grew up in the hot, tropical climate of Brazil were shorter and weighed less than those who grew up in the United States, even though nutrition and medical attention in Brazil were good (Eveleth, 1966). This developmental acclimatization occurred gradually, as the children grew up in the heat stress of the tropics.

As people age, their ability to acclimatize lessens. The elderly, for example, have rather poor metabolic responses to the cold. Since their bodies concentrate heat in the core, many older people suffer from cold hands and feet during the winter.

Control-Comparison Models. To tell to what degree a complex trait is genetically controlled and to what extent it is shaped by the environment, the most useful device is a control-comparison model. (See Figure 7.) One study, partly based on such a model, focused on the height of Japanese-Americans living in California and Japanese living in Japan (Greulich, 1957). The study showed that American born children of Japanese immigrants grew as tall as people of European descent living in the same area. This similarity suggests that differences in height are the result of developmental acclimatization, probably related to nutrition. Body proportions, such as limb length in proportion to height, remained the same after puberty in both Japanese and Japanese-American children. Thus, the control of limb growth must be associated more directly with genetic factors than is height. This study, however, represents only half of the control-comparison model. The other half would involve measuring children of Europeans growing up in Japan.

Evolutionary Processes. Only when we sort out the genetic and the environmental influences on a trait is it possible to see how evolutionary forces change the complex traits of a population. In the next section we shall discuss how each of the evolutionary forces is studied using complex traits.

Gene Flow. The flow of genes controlling some simple genetic traits can be measured precisely by counting the number of new alleles in a population that can be traced to migrants. No such precision is possible in the study of complex traits.

Physical anthropologist Ivan G. Pawson measures Tibetan refugee children in Nepal as part of a high-altitude study. (Courtesy of I. G. Pawson)

Nevertheless, the effects of migration on some complex traits such as head shape and height have been studied. A study of the people of the Swiss canton of Ticino, for example, showed that gene flow had resulted in an increase in height. During the twentieth century, the traditional custom of marrying within the village has fallen by the wayside. Those who have taken a spouse from outside the village have brought about gene flow, for the new spouse has introduced his or her genes into Ticino's gene pool. Sons of fathers who married outside the village are an average of 5 cm taller than are men whose fathers had married within the village (Hulse, 1968). Differences in height occurred independently of improved nutrition.

Genetic Drift. Random change in the frequency of a single trait is very hard to detect, especially when the trait is controlled by many genes at more than one location on the chromosome. It is best studied only when one gene can be shown to have a general effect on a complex trait. For instance, the lack of a single enzyme controlled at one point by one

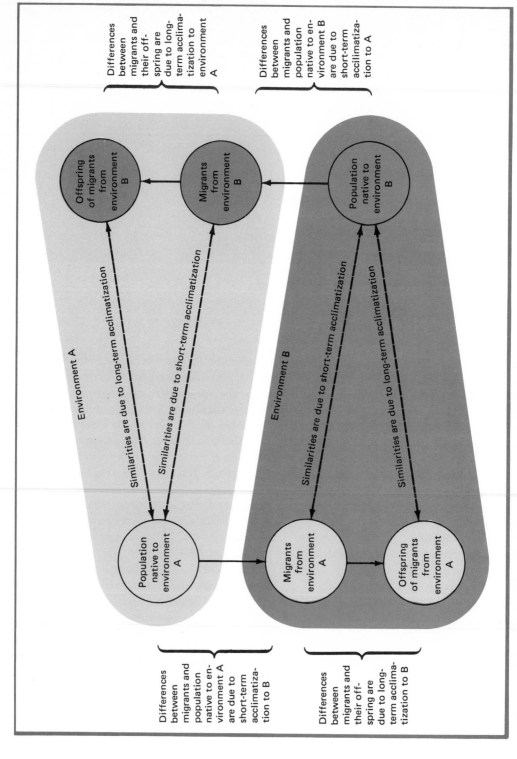

Figure 7 A control-comparison model. By comparing the traits of people native to an environment, migrants, and their offspring, physical anthropologists can distinguish genetic from environmental influences on complex traits.

allele can affect the production of the skin pigment melanin. This condition, known as albinism, is controlled by two recessive alleles. Small population size and inbreeding have combined to cause a high incidence of albinism among the Hopi Indians of New Mexico (Woolf & Dukepoo, 1959).

Mutation. Again, because we cannot count the alleles that affect complex traits, it is very difficult to figure out the rate of mutations that bear on their expression. A point mutation may have a strong effect if it prevents other genes that control the trait from functioning normally. In phenylketonuria, or PKU, for example, the presence of a single mutant allele prevents the formation of an enzyme that, in turn, prevents the normal functioning of a certain metabolic process. Information about the frequency of mutations among genes whose effect is not so obvious is scanty.

Natural Selection. The effect of natural selection on complex traits is the easiest evolutionary force to study. Researchers measure the variation in a population with respect to skin color, height, limb proportions, and other traits. They summarize their data in a graph like those in Figure 8. Most of the population will fall within certain limits for the trait in question. Researchers assume that those forms of a trait that are most common in a population have the greatest selective advantage in the given environment. The most common form has somehow allowed its possessors to pass on the genes for that trait more effectively than those who have a less common variant of the trait.

Because one form of a trait is more common in a population than another does not mean that this distribution will remain unchanged. To account for the possibility that environmental conditions could be changing a population while it is being studied, scientists define three types of selection. If natural selection is favoring the form of a trait presently found with greatest frequency in the population, it is said to be *stabilizing* (see Fig-

The bodies of marathon runners have adapted to the stress of their sport in many ways. Muscles have become stronger and more efficient, and the functioning of nearly every organ in the body is improved. The heart, for example, is stronger and more coordinated. But because genes and long-term acclimatization vary, some runners finish before others. (Gerhard E. Gscheidle)

ure 8). If some outside force upsets the equilibrium between the most common and the rarest forms of a trait, one of two patterns may emerge. *Directional selection* favors individuals at one end of the curve. A less common form of the trait becomes more adaptive, causing a gradual increase in the number of individuals having the advantageous form of the trait. Selection that favors forms of the trait at both ends of the range is called *disruptive selection.* Individuals in the center of the distribution are at a disadvantage in this case. Disruptive selection is thought to occur in varied environments, where one extreme is favored in one area and the other extreme is favored in another (Hartl, 1977).

As we saw in our discussion of natural selection with respect to simple traits, researchers can study the *results* of natural selection better than the actual process. Investigators have two choices in their studies of complex traits: They can study single populations or they can use a trait distribution approach.

Studies of Single Populations. Humans,

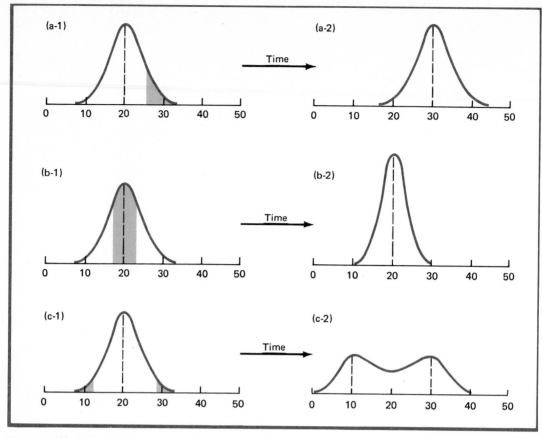

Figure 8 Natural selection can act on complex traits in three principal ways.
In *directional selection (a-1)*, persons in the right-hand tail of the distribution are favored by selection. Ultimately, selection shifts the average of the population to the right *(a-2)*. In *stabilizing selection (b-1)*, individuals near the center of the distribution are favored and become more common *(b-2)*. *Disruptive selection* favors extreme phenotypes *(c-1)* and increases their frequency *(c-2)*. (Hartl, 1977)

more than many other animals, can adjust their biological functioning according to the demands of the environment. Therefore, a great deal of stress can be placed on a population with absolutely no evolutionary effect.

When environmental stress is continuous and severe, however, there is a good chance that the distribution of complex traits will be influenced by selection. Therefore, many of the single-population studies of complex traits have focused on human populations living in harsh environments. These studies have cen-

tered on physiological as well as morphological characteristics. Testing the ability to adjust to cold temperatures by prolonged immersion of the hand in ice water has shown that groups that live in cold areas have physiological responses that keep the internal organs warm. Eskimos, for example, have high metabolic rates, which allow them to convert food into bodily warmth more quickly than many other groups.

Part of the difficulty of testing physiological traits is in separating genetic responses from those that are acquired during growth to adulthood. Many of the differences shown by the Eskimo, for example, can be explained environmentally. A diet that is high in fat and protein may be responsible for their higher rate of metabolism. And the responses of Eskimo children to cold are not the same as those of adults. This suggests that Eskimo adults' excellent responses to the cold are acquired during growth.

Another body of research has centered on the apparent adjustment of high-altitude dwellers in the Andes of South America and the Himalayas of Nepal to low levels of oxygen. When people used to low altitudes go rapidly to heights of 3,000 m or more, they suffer from altitude sickness for several days or longer. Symptoms include headache, shortness of breath, dizziness, and nausea. Pulmonary edema, which causes the air sacs of the lungs to fill with fluid, can be fatal. Even in the absence of such symptoms, lowlanders are unable to perform normal activities as well as highlanders. Peruvian and Nepalese natives are active and energetic. Peruvian children play running games, and adults walk as much as 30 km to market.

Close examination of the phenotype of these people reveals several interesting differences from that of lowland dwellers. Physical growth of the Peruvian Indians is slow, lasting into the early twenties. Sexual maturation is late as well. The mountain dwellers have larger chest and lung capacity, greater marrow capacity in the long bones, and the ability to deliver a larger amount of oxygen to the muscles than do sea-level populations (Little & Baker, 1976).

Some of these differences can be explained by poor nutrition and by the colder temperatures of high altitudes. But the primary influence was found to be the low oxygen content of the air. Research in Peru shows that increased chest and lung size and the ability to do work at high altitudes are not genetically controlled traits but develop during growth to maturity. Children who migrate from sea-level homes to the mountains, for example, developed larger chests than sea-level dwellers who remained behind (Little & Baker, 1976). There may, however, be a genetic factor in the growth and maturation pattern of Nepalese highlanders. Children of mountain-dwelling parents retain the phenotype of their parents even after growing up in a lowland environment with higher oxygen content.

The Trait Distribution Approach. Another way to study natural selection is to chart variation in the expression of a trait from one environment to another. Scientists using this approach have studied how the form of the body varies with the average temperatures of areas around the world.

In mammals, body tissue produces heat as a byproduct of metabolism. Animals with a large amount of tissue, or body mass, can generate more warmth. At the same time, the larger the surface area of the skin, the more quickly body heat escapes into the air. Because large animals have a smaller surface area in proportion to their body mass than do small animals, larger animals are probably better ad-

Natives of the Altiplano region of Bolivia. Because their bodies are adjusted to the low oxygen content of the air, they can be as active at 3,500 m as lowlanders are in their own environment. (Gerhard E. Gscheidle)

justed to cold environments than to warm climates. The principle that small animals will be found in warmer environments and large animals in colder environments is called *Bergmann's rule.*

Likewise, because disproportionately large amounts of body heat escape through the limbs, it was proposed that animals with shorter limbs would be more likely to be found in cold regions and that animals with long limbs would appear in warmer regions. This generalization is called *Allen's rule,* after J. A. Allen, who suggested it in 1877.

A number of studies have been successful in applying these rules to human populations. Eskimos, for example, have short, stocky bodies and short limbs that would seem to be adapted for mininum heat loss through the skin. Certain peoples of East Africa are exceptionally tall and thin and therefore have an ideal surface-area-to-body-mass ratio for their hot, tropical climate. In tropical areas the advantage of sweating is small since moisture will not evaporate in the humid air. Hence, even slightly lighter individuals may have a selective advantage because their bodies produce less heat compared to the potential for radiating it through the skin.

Despite the general conformity of human populations to these rules, we know that morphological traits that vary with temperature—weight, the proportion of fat, limb length, and surface-area-to-body-weight ratio—are also often influenced by local variations in nutrition and disease.

In recent years, the study of human diversity has become much more concerned with understanding the forces behind change than with cataloging human variation. For simple traits, studies of population genetics have demonstrated that genetic drift and gene flow have a very significant effect on the evolution of human populations. Researchers have not demonstrated the process of selection as successfully, although we can see its consequences in macroevolutionary terms. For complex traits, the most useful models involve natural selection. Many studies have also emphasized the importance of local acclimatization. But it is very difficult to demonstrate gene flow and genetic drift for complex traits.

We have talked about how the distribution of traits and sometimes the genes that control them can be measured in populations. Now that we have some idea how these measurements give clues to the evolutionary forces that are molding human populations today, we shall discuss ways in which the resulting human diversity has been conceived of in the past.

Race and the Attempt to Classify Human Groups

Human groups have long been aware of their biological and cultural differences. In their explorations and conquests, the ancient Greeks saw that all people in the world do not have the same physical characteristics. This awareness is reflected in Greek art, as well as in historical references to Pygmies, to black Africans, and to blonde Europeans. The Roman, Chinese, Egyptian, and other early civilizations also were aware of these differences. After the fall of Rome, however, European contacts with different cultures were sharply reduced, and Western ideas of human diversity became more limited.

Early Attempts to Define Race

At the beginning of the Age of Discovery in the sixteenth century, European explorers, merchants, and travelers once again made contact with different populations. At the same time, scientists grew restless with reliance on the word of classical writers and became interested in firsthand observation and classification of nature. Even so, most of the Europeans who first tried to classify humans did not venture abroad to study different populations. They relied instead on description and stories, aided by the study of skulls and by casual observation of the few foreigners who had found their way to Europe. Early taxonomies, like that of Linnaeus, were therefore based on limited data. Linnaeus' classification of *Homo sapiens,* published in 1735, divided the species into four groups according to skin color and place of origin: black Africans, red-skinned Americans, darkish Asians, and white Europeans. Linnaeus' categories still form the basis of popular ideas equating race and skin color.

In 1775, J. F. Blumenbach produced a racial taxonomy that influenced the scientific classification of race for over 100 years. His taxonomy paid particular attention to the measurement of human skulls, because he believed that skull features were the most important criteria for race. Blumenbach identified five races: Caucasian, Asiatic, American, Ethiopian, and Malay. Although he knew that some humans would not fit any of these types perfectly, his classification had the effect of dividing humanity into units with sharp boundaries. The idea of five distinct groups seemed reasonable to eighteenth- and nineteenth-century Europeans because they knew nothing of the subtle variations that occur between neighboring groups. As awareness of human variation grew, however, the arbitrary nature of racial classification became more apparent.

Blumenbach's precise measurement of skull features was the springboard for the systematic scientific description of human variation. In the late nineteenth century and through the first half of the twentieth century, the study of race had two basic goals: (1) to develop a systematic racial classification for *H. sapiens,* and (2) to trace human races back in time.

Skull shape and skin color were often used as the basis of racial classifications. But other features were also used. In 1889, for example, J. Deniker proposed that humans could be divided into 29 races by the texture and color of the hair. But the groups he identified on the basis of hair types did not seem to fall into the geographical patterns expected of racial groups. People with straight black hair exist, for example, in Asia, America, and Europe; and people living in one locality often have a variety of hair traits.

Recent Attempts to Define Race

To attempt to solve this confusion, scientists developed racial groupings based on more than one trait. In 1930, A. C. Haddon (1855–1940), a founder of modern British anthropology, published a multiple-trait analysis primarily based on hair texture, but also on skin color, height, and skull shape. Nordics were defined by their wavy hair, light skin and hair, blue or gray eyes, tall stature, and rounded heads. Negroes had curly hair, short or tall stature, dark skin, and relatively long, thin heads. It was only important that most— not all—of an individual's traits match the definition. A person with brown eyes could still be classified as Nordic if he or she fit the definition in all other ways.

Today there is great debate among those who still use the concept of race. The multiple-trait approach has led many scientists to propose a large number of small races, rather than a small number of large races. The larger the number of criteria, the fewer the people that satisfy them. One scientist who favors many small races restricts the definition of race to "a breeding population characterized by frequencies of inherited traits that differ from those of other populations of the same species" (Goldsby, 1977). This definition is practically useless as a means of classification, since it would result in as many races as populations—thousands.

Others see races as geographically definable

groups of people who share few physical characteristics. Stanley Garn for example, divides the world into nine races: American, Polynesian, Micronesian, Melanesian, Australian, Asiatic, Indian, European, and African (Garn, 1971).

Difficulties with the Concept of Race

There is never likely to be agreement on the number of races. The reasons for this strike at the heart of the concept of race. First, in light of our increasing awareness of the genetic differences among people, it has become apparent that the isolation necessary to produce identifiable races has not been part of human evolution. Migration and continual exchange of mates between groups have created subtle gradations that defy definition by means of racial boundaries. Second, it has become clear that variation in some features is caused by environmental influences that affect the growth process rather than genetic influences.

To explain why some people do not fit neatly into any of the existing racial categories, it has been suggested that migration may only recently have created mixed populations. In the past, human populations may have been more distinct, and isolation may have allowed basic differences among primary races to evolve. These groups supposedly remained distinct until humans developed the means to travel long distances, and composite races were created by mating between the primary races. Some racial classifications of the 1930s and 1940s expressly divided the world into primary races and composite races. We know, however, that migration and exchange of mates was probably always important in human evolution. The early hominids migrated out of Africa beginning about 2 million years ago, and there was a flow of people into the Americas during the end of the Pleistocene period.

Franz Boas, in a classic study in 1910, dramatized the point that most so-called racial features are shaped to a significant degree by the environment. He found that American-born children of East European immigrants had significantly different head shapes than did their parents. If skull features include such a large environmental factor, he reasoned, then they are not the genetically stable features on which racial classifications should be based.

Since Boas, scientists have attempted to find workable racial criteria among traits that do not reflect environmental influences. Blood groups were used as a means of racial classification in the late 1940s and early 1950s. Since blood type is directly controlled by a small number of alleles, there are no gradations caused by environmental influence. So it was thought that races could be distinguished on the basis of gene frequencies for the blood groups. But even with blood types it is impossible to draw racial boundaries. Maps of the frequency of alleles controlling blood type show only gradual shifts in frequency from one population to the next in some areas. (See Figure 9.) This gradual shift in gene frequency over a stretch of territory is called a *cline*.

In the last few years researchers have attempted to define how various groups differ in terms of a cluster of simple genetic traits. They have done multiple-trait analyses of national, ethnic, and religious groups. But because the groups are often large and are defined in cultural terms before the research begins, units of people who should be classed together on the basis of shared biological traits cannot be identified. Furthermore, this approach masks the variation within the groups it analyzes, reducing its usefulness as a scientific method.

During the first half of the twentieth century, many researchers turned to the fossil record for evidence of origins of apparent racial differences. If it could be proved that racial groups (however defined) had been isolated in

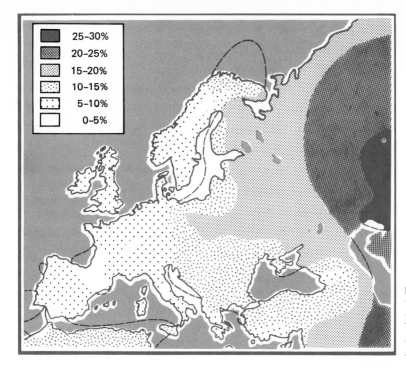

Figure 9 A cline of frequencies for the gene responsible for Type B blood. (Based on studies by A. E. Mourant)

the course of evolution, the idea of race would have a sound biological basis. Many notable physical anthropologists have been convinced of this idea. The most recent attempt to look for the ancestor of modern races in the fossil record is that of Carleton Coon, presented in his book *The Origin of Races* (1962).

We find, however, the same problems in identifying ancient races as we find in defining modern races. Even if these problems could be overcome, the fossil record is too incomplete to supply evidence of the quality needed to establish the presence of clusters of traits that might define a race. In addition, it would seem inappropriate to apply "racial" criteria derived from living humans to fossils from 1, 2, or 3 million years ago.

Race as a Cultural Concept

Why has it been impossible to agree upon a definition of race? The answer to this question lies in the fact that the racial categories people

use are often very revealing indicators of their social values. The way in which we see other people is culturally conditioned. Recognizing the race of another is something we learn in the process of growing up in a particular culture. Some cultures recognize many more shades of skin color than do Americans, who tend to lump people into the categories white and black. Brazilians have about 500 different racial labels (Kottak, 1974), each label corresponding to some phenotypical trait. Because the gradations are so subtle, one individual may have several different racial labels during the course of his or her lifetime.

Concepts of race are so ambiguous and so much a product of cultural bias that *race,* as the term is traditionally used, has no clear biological meaning. Thus, by using the term, one runs the risk of having it interpreted in ways that were not intended. No anthropologist would deny that race is an important way of organizing human variation in cultural terms. But culturally defined categories cannot be translated into objective, clear, biological categories. For this reason, physical anthropologists are gradually abandoning the use of racial categories in studying human variation.

Summary

1. Gregor Mendel's experiments with the cross-pollination of garden peas enabled him to explain the mechanism by which physical traits are passed on from one generation to the next. Thus, he extended the understanding of the forces of evolution outlined by Charles Darwin.

2. Mendel suggested that separate particles in the plant cells controlled specific traits, or *phenotypes.* Later, these particles were named *genes.* He explained that each phenotype is controlled by two forms of the same gene and that one form may be dominant over the other and prevent expression of the recessive form. The two forms of the same gene are called *alleles.* The traits that Mendel studied were determined by genes that were independent of one another. Now we know, however, that some phenotypes are controlled by linked genes.

3. In the nineteenth century, improved microscopes and tissue-staining techniques allowed researchers to see long, thin threads, called *chromosomes,* in the cell nucleus. The chromosomes, which divided before cell division, were found to carry the genes.

4. There are two types of cell division. *Mitosis* is the division of body cells to create new cells for growth and repair. Daughter cells produced by mitosis each receive an exact duplicate of the organism's genetic information. *Meiosis* is the division of parent cells to form sex cells, or *gametes.* Gametes receive one-half of the chromosomes in the parent cell. The union of two gametes, one from each parent, creates the first cell, or *zygote,* of a new organism, which has a full set of chromosomes.

5. Chemically, genetic material is identified with *deoxyribonucleic acid,* or *DNA,* which is found in the nuclei of cells. Watson and Crick won the Nobel Prize for their discovery of the double-helix structure of the DNA molecule in 1953. DNA is the source of hereditary information for all cell growth and coordination of body functions through the creation of proteins. DNA is copied by *ribonucleic acid* (RNA) molecules that are capable of causing amino acids to link together to form proteins.

6. Phenotypes controlled by only a few alleles at one gene position are called *simple genetic traits.* Simple genetic traits can be studied by using *pedigrees,* records of the biological relationship of family members. Pedigree studies of blood types have revealed that three alleles, A, B, and O, determine blood type and that the A and B alleles are dominant over type O.

7. Phenotypes controlled by a number of genes are called *complex genetic traits. Morphological* traits include size, weight, and shape. *Physiological* traits are related to body functions, such as breathing and digestion. Complex traits are more difficult to study than simple traits, partly because they may be affected by the environment.

8. Two types of mutations provide a source of new traits: point mutations and chromosomal rearrangements. *Point mutations* are changes in the nucleotide sequence of the DNA, such as substitution, addition, or deletion of part of the normal nucleotide triplet. *Chromosomal rearrangements* include nondisjunction, translocation, and inversion. Mutations have been linked to radiation and chemicals in the environment. The expression of a mutation is rare, because for a mutation to

appear, the mutant allele must be dominant or two recessive mutant alleles must appear on a gene together.

9. Applying the principles of genetic inheritance to populations can help to explain human evolution. A population is a group of interbreeding individuals bound together by social codes. Both geographical isolation and social factors such as class systems or marriage laws may define a population by limiting the choice of marriage partners.

10. Studying the changes in the frequency with which an allele for a simple genetic trait appears in a population gives evidence for evolution.

11. *Gene flow* is the movement of genes from one population to another through migration of individuals. Gene flow has maintained the unity of the human species over centuries.

12. *Genetic drift* causes random changes in gene frequencies because of small population size. The *founder effect* is a special case of drift in which a new population created by a split from a larger group is, by accident, very different genetically from the original group.

13. Inbreeding also limits the amount of genetic variation in a population. Because persons who are closely related mate with one another, inbreeding often causes an increase in the number of harmful homozygotes.

14. The process of natural selection is studied by two methods. Trait distribution studies determine the distribution of a single trait in many populations. Single population studies focus on the frequency of a trait in one population. A trait distribution study of sickle-cell anemia showed that this hemoglobin disorder occurs most frequently in areas of equatorial Africa where malaria is common. It was discovered that the sickle-cell trait increases the chances of a carrier's survival by protecting the individual from the malaria parasite. Similarly, single population studies on blood types have revealed that in some populations individuals with types A or AB

blood are more susceptible to smallpox. Thus, smallpox may be acting as a selective agent.

15. It is more difficult to study the effect of natural selection on complex genetic traits because it is hard to separate genetic from environmental effects. One way of distinguishing the two effects is to measure the ability of a phenotype to adjust to the environment. Human physiological traits generally adapt rapidly to new conditions, such as changes in temperature. Single population studies, however, show that Eskimos have the ability to adjust to cold temperatures through increased metabolic rates and that mountain dwellers have an expanded lung capacity. These morphological traits are evidence of a slowly developed adjustment to the environment called *long-term acclimatization.*

16. The study of human variation has led to attempts to classify human species into races based on certain physical characteristics. Early classifications, such as that of Linnaeus published in 1735, divided the species according to skin color. Other criteria used for racial classification have been skull features, color and texture of hair, and height. As scientists realized that variation within human groups could be great, they tried to construct multiple-trait classifications.

17. Some scientists have used geographical separation to define races into Americans, Polynesians, Melanesians, Australians, Indians, Europeans, and Africans.

18. Genetic traits, such as blood type, have also been made the basis of some racial classifications. But we do know that changes in blood types do not show sharp boundaries between populations.

19. Racial categories show two flaws. First, migration and the exchange of mates between groups has occurred throughout human evolution. Second, many complex genetic traits are affected by the environment. Racial categories are, in the end, not based on actual physical and genetic differences but on cultural definitions.

PART TWO

Archaeology

10
Early Hominid Cultures

IN past chapters we presented humanity's biological development up to the present. In the next few chapters, however, we will start over again with the early hominids, tracing the beginnings of their cultural traditions. Distinguishing culture from biology in this manner is somewhat artificial, but it is a useful way of organizing the material remains of past societies. Although artifacts are often not found with biological remains, they provide clues to such traditions as toolmaking, hunting, pair bonding, food sharing, labor dividing, social grouping, home building, clothes making, art, speech, and religion. Some of these—such as the making of crude tools and the presence of sex- and age-related activities—are found among certain other animals as well. But only humans, with their self-awareness, prolonged childhood, and their large and complex brains, have ever come to depend so much on learned behaviors to meet the problems of survival. And as knowledge and customs grew over the millenia, humans became so good at manipulating their environment that culture began to shape biological evolution in important ways.

The Stages of Prehistory

In the past, prehistoric cultures have been divided into four stages: the Paleolithic, Mesolithic, Neolithic, and Metal Ages. These terms for chunks of prehistory are often thought inadequate today, because they are based on the toolmaking sequence found in western Europe. They have little to do with what was going on elsewhere in the world or in other aspects of cultural evolution. But since they are so familiar, we will use them as a rough guide to major cultural stages.

The *Paleolithic,* a term still commonly used by archaeologists (literally, the "Old Stone Age"), initially referred to the stage in which humans made chipped stone tools. Now, however, it stands for the period of cultural development that began during the late Pliocene Epoch and lasted through the glacial advances and retreats of the Pleistocene Epoch. Since this covers such a long time span, it is often divided into thirds: the Lower, Middle, and Upper Paleolithic. These have no connection with the geological subdivisions Lower, Middle, and Upper Pleistocene. Instead, the long Lower Paleolithic is defined as simply everything in cultural evolution that preceded the Middle Paleolithic. The Middle Paleolithic, in turn, refers to the state of human culture in western Europe during Neandertal times. And the Upper Paleolithic has traditionally been defined as the time during which blades, long, thin stone tools with parallel sides, and burins, tools used to cut and shape wood and bone, were used. It is difficult to date this sequence because cultural evolution proceeded at different rates in different areas. Consequently, the dates presented in this chapter will be area specific.

In this framework, the *Mesolithic* (the "Middle Stone Age") refers to the gap between the Paleolithic and the Neolithic in Europe. It is less often used today. The period is transitional between the last Upper Paleolithic cultures and the first cultures having agriculture. In Europe and the Near East it is a very short period just before the emergence of agriculture. With the exception of the Archaic period in North America, it is doubtful that a similar sequence appears elsewhere. Once again, the dates for this period vary. In Europe and the New World, it began about 8,000 to 10,000 years ago. In the Near East, it began somewhat earlier.

During the *Neolithic* (New Stone Age), humans began making tools by grinding and polishing rather than by chipping. A more re-cent definition of this cultural stage is the period from the invention of agriculture to the invention of metalworking. This stage, or ones like it, have been identified in Europe, Asia, Africa, and the Americas.

The Neolithic was followed, at least in Western Europe, by the *Bronze Age* and the *Iron Age.* Bronze and iron were the chief metals used in the art of metallurgy, which developed at this time. Toward the end of the Iron Age, people began to keep written records, ending millions of years of prehistory.

Various other frameworks have been suggested. One is based on the means of food procuring. This framework divides prehistory into two chunks: the food-gathering stage and the food-producing stage. During the first, hominid societies were organized to efficiently gather plants and to hunt animals. In the second major phase, humans began to assert more control over resources by domesticating plants and animals. The larger populations that could be supported by this process eventually led to the development of complex political structures.

The question of which system is best to analyze cultural stages is subject to considerable debate. Many archaeologists switch back and forth, depending on the time and the archeological culture they are discussing. Both systems break up a continuous line of cultural evolution. Thus, as long as the types of cultures to which we refer are clear, it does not matter which system we use.

In this book we have chosen the traditional terms. The term *Paleolithic* will be used to mean that period during which humans hunted and gathered. It was during this long period that humans spread from their tropical origins to all parts of the world. The term *Neolithic* will be used to mean that period during which agriculture emerged. And *Mesolithic* will stand for the transitional episode between the Paleolithic and the Neolithic.

Table 1 Cultural Stages of Human Prehistory

Years (B.P.)	Geological Scale	Cultural Stage	Stone Industry	Cultural Achievements
3,000	Holocene	Iron Age Bronze Age		Writing in the Near East
10,000		Neolithic Mesolithic	Upper Paleolithic	First agriculture
	Upper Pleistocene	Upper Paleolithic	Mousterian	Blade technology begins Oldest burials
100,000		Middle Paleolithic		
200,000				Hand axes widely used
	Middle Pleistocene		Acheulean	Oldest dwellings made by humans
500,000		Lower Paleolithic		Oldest evidence of fire
				Oldest biface tools
1 million	Lower Pleistocene		Pebble culture	
2 million				
2.6 million				Oldest stone tools

Although we have given some rough dates for these segments of human prehistory in Table 1, cultural development did not proceed at the same speed everywhere. Agriculture, for instance, apparently appeared independently at various places at different times and then spread slowly. Some societies still have not adopted this means of feeding themselves. For Eskimos and people of the Australian bush, for instance, hunting and gathering is still the only means of survival in regions where crops will not grow.

In this chapter, we shall explore cultural evolution during the Paleolithic period. It is by far the longest of the major toolworking stages, for it lasted from about 2.6 million to 10,000 years B.P. in the Near East. It persisted even later in Europe and the New World. Its history can be seen as a tale of cultural diversification. At the earliest and simplest level, stone tool assemblages were remarkably similar at sites throughout Africa, Europe, and the Near East. In the next stage, there were two major toolmaking traditions. By the late Middle Paleolithic, traditions were still more diversified. And by the Upper Paleolithic, there were a large number of specialized local cultural traditions.

The Oldowan Culture

The first signs that primitive hominids had begun to shape their environment by learned patterns of behavior, rather than just adapting to it biologically, are the crude stone tools found at very ancient sites. We can barely tell some of them apart from ordinary rocks. Perhaps the deliberate making of stone tools was preceded by finding and using stones whose edges were sharp enough to be better than human hands for certain chores (Bordes, 1968). Just what these chores were is hard to say for sure, but it is widely assumed that they mostly involved food getting. Perhaps sharp stones were used in cutting up carcasses or splitting bones to get at the marrow. Perhaps they were used for making points on sticks so they could be used in digging. Whatever their use, the discovery that sharp stones made certain tasks easier was important for the survival of early hominids.

Stones were not the only material aspects of early cultures. Sticks and bones must have been available, too. But wood is rarely preserved, and crude bone tools are often hard to recognize as tools. The wood and bone tools that have lasted show that until rather recent times they were cruder than stone tools (Clark, 1977).

The earliest stone tools have been grouped together in the *Oldowan tradition,* so named because tools of this type were first uncovered in the lower beds at Olduvai Gorge. These tools were made by striking one pebble against another rock to knock off enough flakes to form a single crude edge.

The Range of the Oldowan Culture

The earliest Oldowan tools known do not come from Olduvai. They were found in another part of the great Rift Valley System of East Africa. Here 10 to 12 million years of prehistory have been preserved in natural basins by sedimentary deposits. Shifts in the tectonic plates below have since exposed them. Anthropologist Glynn Isaac recently discovered stone tools that may be 2.6 million years old at the Koobi Fora formation, a peninsula that cuts into Lake Turkana in the northeast corner of Kenya.

Tools found at Koobi Fora are similar to those found in sediments at Olduvai Gorge that date from 1.89 million to about 400,000 years B.P. (M. Leakey, 1975). Early stone tool traditions probably spread from East Africa to southern and northern Africa, and then were carried to the tropical and subtropical zones of Asia as hominids moved out of Africa. Later these tools were used by early inhabitants of temperate zones in Europe. By about 700,000 years B.P., the same kind of crude tools appeared in Vallonet Cave on the shore of the Mediterranean in southern France (Bordes, 1968).

Just who made these tools is not yet clear. There may have been several species of bipedal hominids on the African scene at the time the earliest tools appeared. At least one species began to carry stones about and to sharpen their edges when the need arose. Most anthropologists think the stone carriers and sharpeners were probably the East African gracile hominids, who may have been meat eaters. The unspecialized tooth pattern of the graciles is often cited in support of the notion that tools took over some dental functions, such as the preparation of food before eating it. Tools may also have expanded the number of different types of foods that could have been eaten. Their less-advanced neighbors, the robusts, were probably highly spe-

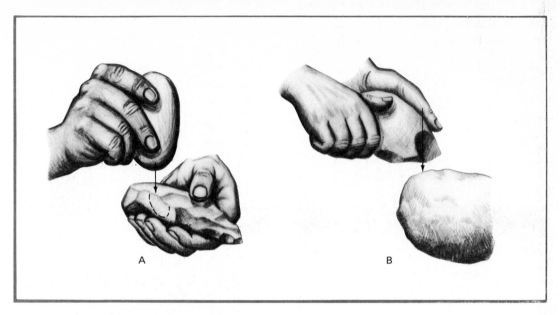

Figure 1 Two kinds of percussion flaking.
In *A*, a hammerstone is being used to strike flakes from another rock to form an edge. The finished tool will be a chopper. In *B*, flakes are chipped from a rock by striking it against an "anvil." (Adapted from Fagan, 1977.)

cialized vegetarians and therefore less likely to have made tools. As we mentioned in Chapter 7, their specializations suggest that the robusts were part of a separate evolutionary lineage that did not contribute to later hominid evolution. The presence of dental specialization suggests that cultural adaptations to the environment either were not made or were used in only a limited way. Although graciles seem to have been the stone toolmakers, the controversy over the number of gracile species and their names continues. It is therefore not possible to say for certain whether the toolmakers were gracile australopithecines or early members of the genus *Homo* (Isaac, 1978).

Technology of the Oldowan Culture

We know that early hominids carried stones suitable for making tools rather than gathering them on the spot. Many have been found in places where the naturally occurring stones are no larger than peas (Isaac, 1978). The favorite stones of these early hominids seem to have been water-worn pebbles about the size of a tennis ball (R. Leakey, 1977). These were given a sharp cutting edge by knocking a few flakes off one part of the rock with another rock, called a *hammerstone*. (See Figure 1.) Sometimes the stone being flaked was struck against another rock, called an *anvil*. Both methods of using one stone to strike off flakes from one or both sides of another are called *percussion flaking*.

The small flakes themselves make effective cutting or scraping tools if held between the thumb and fingers and were probably used this way. What is left of the pebble after the flakes have been removed is called a *chopper*. (See Figure 2.) We are not sure what they were used for, but modern researchers who have experimented with choppers find them very effective in cutting up game animals (Fa-

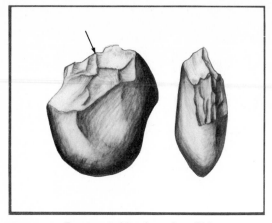

Figure 2 **Front and side view of an Oldowan chopper from Olduvai Gorge.**
The arrow shows the worked edge. The drawing is about ³/₅ actual size. (Adapted from Fagan, 1977.)

gan, 1977). As the period progressed, tools of quartzite, such as hide-scrapers and burins, increasingly appeared in the Oldowan assemblages as well (M. Leakey, 1975).

The Econiche of the Early Hominids

The hominids of the Oldowan culture seem to have been part of a savanna ecosystem. Although they did hunt animals that lived in the savanna-forest fringes and along watercourses, their diet included a large number of grassland plants and animals. These hominids usually camped near bodies of water—lakes, rivers, or streams. They may have preferred these sites for a number of reasons. For one thing, they offered a ready supply of water before anybody invented things to carry it in (R. Leakey, 1977). Water would have drawn many animals that could be preyed upon when they came looking for water (Butzer, 1971). And the trees around these areas would have provided shade, fruits, and a means of escape from predators. Isaac suggests that in using tree-lined streams for campsites, early hominids kept their ancestors' means of security in an arboreal envi-

ronment even as they began exploiting the more varied resources of the open grasslands (Isaac, 1975).

Food Resources. Our earliest ancestors were mainly vegetarians. They lacked the large flesh-ripping canines of other carnivorous animals. It was a cultural solution—toolmaking—rather than a biological change that allowed them to tear through the fur and skin of animals to get at the meat inside. The gradual switch from a diet of vegetation to one that included a variety of animals probably added to their success in making use of the food resources of tropical areas. It may also have made possible their later move to colder climates, where plant foods were only available in certain seasons (R. Leakey, 1977).

Meat probably became part of the early hominid diet in a gradual way. When hominids first began to eat meat, they ate mostly small, easy-to-catch animals. The bones of creatures such as rodents, birds, bats, lizards, turtles, and fish are most common at their living sites. Judging from the diets of modern hunting and gathering tribes, vegetation probably continued to provide about two-thirds of what they ate. But occasionally they seemed to have fed on big game, such as hippopotamuses. Some of the remains suggest that they chased large animals into swamps and then clubbed or stoned them to death. They may also have taken meat from carcasses killed by other animals, a practice still present in some primitive tribes (Butzer, 1971).

Social Patterns

Artifacts from the beginnings of hominid culture reveal very little about social behaviors. To help reconstruct such behaviors, archaeologists also draw on an awareness of the behaviors of modern primates and hunting-and-gathering groups. The evidence has convinced archaeologists that late Pliocene and early Pleistocene hominids must

East African savanna. The early African hominids exploited a similar environment, camping near tree-lined lakes and streams. (Cannon, Anthro-Photo)

already have been diverging from nonhuman primates in social *and* biological ways.

Like some modern primates, early hominids probably lived in small bands. The members of the bands were probably fairly young, for the probability of surviving until adulthood was low (Mann, 1968). Food sharing and the cooperative behavior in food getting may have been the forces most responsible for group cohesion. There are growing signs in the fossil record that systematic hunting was an important part of this behavior. Thus, the hunting hypothesis put forth over 10 years ago by S. Washburn and C. S. Lancaster seems more relevant than ever (Washburn & Lancaster, 1968).

According to this hypothesis, hunting may have given rise to division of labor, a behavioral trait that is unique in the animal world: males probably left a base camp to hunt in bands, while females gathered plants, shellfish, eggs, and the like. Care of the young, while probably still mainly a female activity, may also have been performed part-time by males. This is the case among many nonhuman primates and human societies. It is true that open-country primates such as baboons do have a highly evolved division of labor for defense and social control. But the cooperation involved in splitting up to gather different kinds of food and then bring them back to th base camp to share would be something new. Food sharing is almost unknown among the other primates, for they forage as individuals and eat as they go. Only chimpanzees share food, and they do so rarely. When they have meat, they allow some scrounging by other members of the troop. The hypothesis that hominid hunters and gatherers brought food back to camp to share with one another is supported by sites that have piles of the remains of many different animals. According to Isaac, it is unlikely that they were all killed and eaten at the same spot. Instead, they were probably killed here and there and then carried to a butchering or camping site for the group to eat (Isaac, 1978).

Some camps may have been built near lakes and rivers during the dry season when water elsewhere was scarce. While there, the hunters killed large numbers of turtles and grazing animals, the same kinds of animals hunted by modern bushmen during the dry season. During the rainy season, Oldowan hominids moved on to other areas, about which we know little.

Hominids may have evolved permanent pair bonds between males and females to reduce aggression between males and to allow their integration into a cooperating band. Pair

A female chimpanzee, whose arm is visible at top right, begs for a piece of bushbuck being eaten by two brothers. Chimpanzees tolerate scrounging for food and sometimes hunt and use tools. These behaviors, however, are not integrated into a coherent behavioral pattern, such as food sharing at a base camp. This pattern, together with a division of labor by sex, is thought by Glynn Isaac to be the most basic innovation of human society. (Nancy Nicolson, Anthro-Photo)

bonding presumably would have lessened sexual jealousies by limiting promiscuity. Males would also help to protect and get food for mothers and their offspring.

Finally, to make all this cooperative behavior possible, hominids may have developed a communication system that was more advanced than those of the other primates. Although we have no way of knowing when language appeared, it seems logical that group planning called for some way of talking about objects, times, and places. By contrast, primate communication is largely limited to responses to objects in the immediate environment. Nonhuman primates cannot express abstractions well enough to communicate about the future or make plans.

Forces for Change

Although the cultural achievements of these early hominids were limited, they repre-

sent a landmark in our evolutionary history. At this time, hominids began to assert conscious control over their environment. They could begin to change the environment with their behavior or, if this were impossible, change their behavior to suit the conditions. Culture, in effect, created a new niche for the hominids, in which natural selection began to favor the best culture users. Smart hunters and tool users were the most fit because of their better survival strategies.

These strategies in turn probably began to select for a more complex brain. Hunting depends for its success on the ability to remember the nature and location of environmental features, as well as the habits of animals. Refinements in the coordination of hand and eye facilitated the making and use of tools. And perhaps simple language was necessary for teaching the young the basics of culture, or to plan the hunt. All these activities required the culture bearer to process sensory data, to remember it, and to integrate new perceptions with those stored in the memory. Hominids with the best brains were probably also the most adept at using culture and therefore more likely to pass on their genes. Eventually these selective pressures produced the extremely complex brain of the members of the genus *Homo*.

Early Migrations from Africa

As we noted earlier, Oldowan tools have been found not only in Africa but in other tropical and subtropical areas of the Old World as well. It is possible that they were invented separately at each location. But since the tools found at Koobi Fora and Olduvai Gorge are older than any found elsewhere, most archaeologists believe that the earliest hominid toolmakers originated in East Africa.

The earliest hominids to exploit the plants and animals of grasslands outside Africa were probably *Homo erectus*. It is not yet clear what kind of pressure led to this expansion. One theory is that early hunters followed herds of savanna herbivores in their migrations to these new territories. Both in Africa and elsewhere, this movement was accompanied by increases in technological sophistication. These, in turn, allowed hominids to move into colder and colder regions. Probably during the Günz and during the Mindel glaciations of the Middle Pleistocene (from about 600,000 to about 400,000 years B.P.) some lived in temperate environments in Europe. And during the Riss glaciation (roughly 220,000–150,000 years B.P.) some populations seemed to have lived in perpetually cold areas of Europe.

During this time, the carriers of the Oldowan culture split into two different cultural and geographical groups. The two traditions were more or less separated by a mountain barrier made up of the Himalayas in the east, the Caucasus and Zagros Mountains in southwest Asia, and the Carpathians in southeast Europe. To the east and north of this mountain barrier was an elaboration of the Oldowan tradition called the *chopper-tool culture.* People to the west and south of this string of mountain ranges evolved the life-style and way of making tools, specifically hand axes, known as *Acheulean culture.* (See Figure 3.)

The Acheulean Tradition

The Acheulean toolmaking tradition first appeared about 1.2 million years B.P. at Olduvai Gorge, long before Oldowan technologies died out. It is also found throughout much of Africa, persisting until about 60,000 years B.P. at one Rhodesian site, Kalambo Falls. Acheulean tools have also been found in the Middle East, India, and Java. They are common in southern Europe as well, but were replaced there about 100,000 to 70,000 years B.P. by the beginnings of the next cultural tradition, the Mousterian.

Acheulean Technology

The tool most characteristic of Acheulean assemblages is the *hand ax.* It is considered a logical improvement over the Oldowan chopping tool, for instead of one sharpened edge it has two. These edges meet to form a point that added to the usefulness of the tool (see Figure 4). The base, or butt, is broad for easy gripping. We are not sure how *H. erectus* used the hand ax. Recent experiments show that these tools may have had a number of functions, such as skinning, butchering, and digging.

A variation on the hand ax, the *cleaver,* is also bifacially worked, but instead of a point there is a third cutting edge (see Figure 4). The cleaver could have been helpful in chopping, hacking, and prying apart carcasses. Retouched flake tools, made from stone flakes chipped from a core, commonly appear in Acheulean assemblages.

The transition from Oldowan to Acheulean stone-working technology seems to have happened in several stages. Some of the early Oldowan choppers had been worked on both sides. Gradually, however, early hominids flaked more and more of the surface of the stone, making the tool more slender and symmetrical. By the end of the Acheulean tradition, the whole tool, including the butt, was shaped, often to the point that the original shape of the stone is unrecognizable.

At first this flaking was done with a hammerstone, as in the Oldowan industries. But eventually Acheulean toolmakers discovered that they could control the size and shape of the flake better by using a bone or a stick as a hammer. This method is called the *soft-hammer* technique. In this technique, a bone, antler, or piece of wood was used to strike off shallow flakes from the sides of core tools. The use of this technique is marked by thinner axes, from which many more flakes have been removed to create a sharper edge (Bordes, 1968; Butzer, 1971).

A further development was an increasing

sophistication in the production of flakes. In Oldowan industries, flakes were merely useful by-products of making choppers. Probably recognizing that a well-designed flake could be more functional than one randomly struck, later Acheulean toolmakers prepared some stones with an eye toward the shape of the flake, rather than the shape of the parent stone, or core. The chief intent in this aspect of toolmaking was to prepare the core in such a way that flakes of predictable size and shape could be struck from it.

Stone was not the only material Acheuleans used for their tools. Bone and wood artifacts occasionally appear in their assemblages as well, but they are much rarer than stone tools. Bones were shaped and trimmed for specific purposes. They may have been used as picks, axes, and cleavers, or perhaps for activities that humans no longer carry on. Wood is oc-

Figure 3 **Distribution of cultures with and without hand axes.**
The two cultures are separated by a chain of mountain ranges extending from the Himalayas in the east to the Pyrenees in the west. Note the overlap in central Europe. (Adapted from Bordes, 1968.)

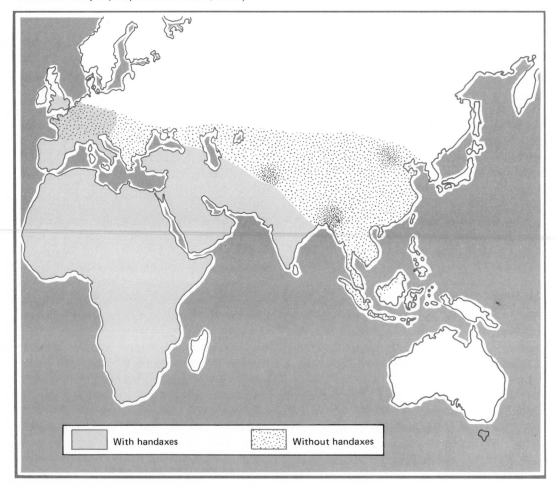

With handaxes   Without handaxes

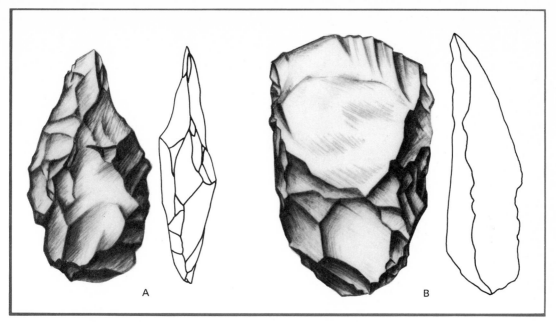

Figure 4 An Acheulean hand ax *(A)* from Olduvai Gorge and an Acheulean cleaver *(B)* from Baia Farta, Angola.
The hand ax is ³/₄ the actual size; the cleaver is ¹/₂ the actual size.
Acheulean toolmakers worked a much greater portion of the stone than Oldowan people had. (Adapted from Fagan, 1977.)

casionally preserved in the shape of what appears to be a spear. The Acheuleans may also have used wood as clubs, throwing sticks, and tools to dig for roots and bulbs, as primitive peoples do today (Butzer, 1971).

Econiche

In the main, Acheulean sites seem to have been located within grassland environments. These grasslands probably provided an optimal environment for the large and medium-sized animals that they regarded as food. Until the end of the middle Paleolithic, Acheulean groups avoided both the dense tropical rainforests of west-central Africa and the barren deserts elsewhere on that continent. For most of this time, they lived in tropical or subtropical latitudes, rarely venturing farther north than southern Europe, which had a warm-temperate environment. But toward the end

of the Acheulean period, particularly during the Riss glaciation (220,000–150,000 years B.P.), they moved into progressively colder regions. In some cases, the cold came to them, in the form of advancing glaciers. For instance, instead of retreating southward ahead of the European ice sheets, as did the elephants they had been hunting, the Acheuleans in southern Europe stayed in place, culturally adapted to the cold, and started hunting the mammoths that thrived on the tundra (Collins, 1969).

One cultural innovation that would play an increasingly important part in humans' ability to survive in cold climates was the controlled use of fire for warmth and cooking. Fire clearly was used at a chopper-tool site, Vertésszöllös, about 450,000 years B.P. It can also be seen in the bits of charcoal and charred bone at Torralba, in Spain. The use of fire spread slowly to warmer climates, not reaching Africa until the end of the Pleistocene.

Shelter, too, was becoming more important as another cultural adaptation to the cold weather. In Europe, signs of crude windbreaks and huts with stake walls reinforced by stone piles have been found. There is also evidence that caves were being occupied. But some sites seem to have no shelters at all, suggesting that people did not build them unless the weather was bad or a long stay was expected. Judging from the lack of debris at their campsites, the Acheuleans seem to have moved about a great deal, possibly because they followed the seasonal movements of animal herds. But a few of the sites seem to have been occupied for weeks or months by bands of about 20 to 30 adults plus children.

The dismembered carcasses and smashed animal bones that litter Acheulean sites leave little doubt that these bands were also becoming increasingly systematic hunters. Animal protein was probably very important in cold climates where vegetation was seasonally scarce. Although Acheulean hunters may have eaten scavenged meat, as the Oldowans did, they had more refined methods of downing large animals. For instance, stone bolas on hide thongs were probably hurled at the legs of running prey. Prey varied from elephants and rhinos to baboons and reptiles, but some local populations seem to have concentrated on a single species (Butzer, 1971).

The Chopper-Tool Culture

Another distinct cultural tradition seems to have existed during roughly the same period as the Acheulean. Dates for this chopper-tool culture are not as well determined, however. Chopper-tool assemblages lacked hand axes, and are found over a different geographical and environmental range than the Acheulean. Except for northern Europe, where they were intermixed somewhat with the Acheulean, chopper-tool culture sites are all located north and east of the Acheuleans—in east Asia, southeast Asia, and in India east of the Indus River.

Technology. Non-Acheulean tool kits are

Figure 5 A chopping tool *(A)* and a cleaverlike tool *(B),* both of the chopping-tool culture.
These implements were found in the same bed as *H. erectus,* at Chou-kou-tien. (Adapted from Bordes, 1968.)

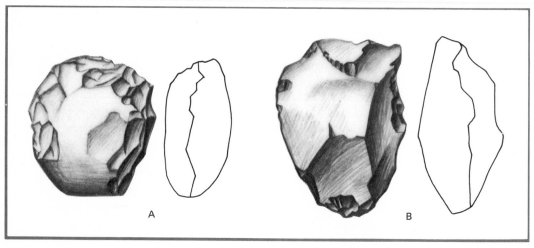

A   B

easier to define by what they lack—the hand axes that are so typical of Acheulean assemblages—than by what traits they have. Some assemblages seem to consist mostly of flakes removed by striking a stone held against an anvil. This was *bipolar* working, for it produced percussion effects at both ends of the flake. The edges of some of the flakes were then chipped to form a variety of rather refined tools, some with teeth and notches. Choppers and chopping tools (with cutting edges worked on both sides) were also present. (See Figure 5.)

The origins and spread of this toolmaking tradition are obscure. But French archaeologist François Bordes suggests that it may have appeared first in southeast Asia 475,000 to 425,000 years B.P. as an elaboration on the Oldowan tradition and then spread to the west as far as England. Chopper-tool sites there have been dated to the Holstein Interglacial, which began about 425,000 years B.P. (Bordes, 1971).

Food Resources. Despite the relative crudeness of their tools, Eurasians of this period managed to kill and butcher a great variety of animals. The bones of deer are most common in their food debris, but elephants, rhinos, bison, water buffalos, and many other animals were eaten as well. They may even have enjoyed an occasional meal of their own species. At Chou-kou-tien, near Peking, cannibalism may have occurred. Some of the long bones of hominids found there were split, possibly so that the marrow could be reached. Some skulls seem to have been cracked open so that the brains could be removed (Clark, 1977).

Econiche

The chopper-tool complex is found at sites that are on the northern edge of the Eurasiatic mountain chain. Compared to Acheulean sites, they were located in more wooded and colder areas, farther from the ocean.

Acheulean and chopper-tool sites were, for the most part, clearly separated. In northern Europe, however, they do overlap in time and, in some cases, space. One explanation is that the sites attributed to the two different cultures simply represented different activities—and therefore different types of tools—of the same population. But a closer look at the environmental range and toolmaking technology of these two cultures shows that they were really quite different. Desmond Collins (1969) has suggested that the chopper-tool complex was organized to exploit wooded terrain and a greater variety of food resources than the Acheulean. The latter specialized in the sorts of game herds that lived in more open, grassland environments. Because of this difference, the chopper-tool culture was the first to colonize northwestern Europe sometime during the Holstein Interglacial (420,000–220,000 years B.P.). Until the Riss, the glacial period following the Holstein Interglacial, Acheulean populations may only have existed in open areas or during warmer periods in larger river valleys in the north. During the Riss, however, Acheulean populations seem to have adjusted to the tundra parkland near the glaciers—particularly exploiting the large mammoth herds. But even at this time the types of environments exploited by the two cultures would have remained distinct. Because of this aparently distinct adaptive difference, it is likely that two separate culture types existed at this time.

Cultures of the Late Middle Paleolithic

By the beginning of the Würm glaciation, at about 80,000 years B.P., and perhaps even a little before then, populations in many parts of the world began to make a greater variety of more specialized, more sophisticated tools. Hominids intensified their efforts to exploit the environment, managed to survive in extremely cold conditions, and showed many social features of modern human cultures.

This late middle Paleolithic cultural period is roughly contemporary with the archaic *H. sapiens* (or Neandertal) period of human biological evolution. In Europe, where the time sequence is best known, it lasted from 80,000 or 100,000 years B.P. to about 40,000 years B.P. The major tool tradition associated with this time period is the Mousterian. Its characteristic assemblages are found throughout Europe and in the Near East, western Russia, south Asia, and northern Africa.

Technology

Mousterian assemblages are not identified by a single tool—as Acheulean sites are characterized by the presence of hand axes—or even by a single toolmaking tradition. Different sites may have very different tool kits. Perhaps these differences represent increasingly sophisticated adaptations to differing environments. Or they may indicate different sets of cultural notions about how tools should be made, and what kind. In general, though, they are more complex than anything that existed before.

Mousterian artifacts are often *composite tools,* having several parts. Earlier tools were made in one part from a single piece of raw material. A Mousterian spear might have a wooden shaft, a stone point, and a bone handle. Another indication that the toolmaker's art was becoming more advanced was careful preparation of a core so that flakes could be struck in precise, preshaped forms. This method, called the *Levallois technique,* produced longer, sharper cutting edges than previous methods. (See Figure 6.)

There was considerable local variety in Mousterian assemblages. Bordes (1968) sees five distinct general toolmaking traditions in Mousterian France. They correspond to some extent to assemblages found in similar environments elsewhere in the world.

Figure 6 The Levallois technique.
During the Middle Paleolithic, stoneworkers refined the technique of preparing a stone core from which many flakes of a given shape could be struck. One such form was a Levallois core. The worker first trimmed the sides of a piece of flint *(1),* then the top *(2).* Next, an edge was chipped at one end *(3)* so that a flake could be struck from the top *(4).* The process was repeated to produce additional flake tools. (Adapted from Fagan, 1977.)

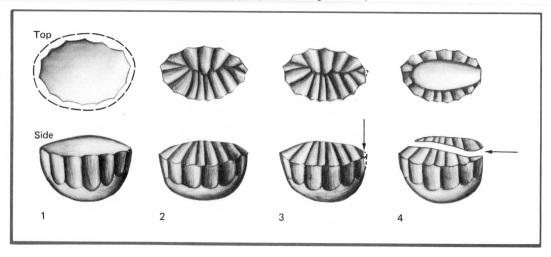

Top

Side

1   2   3   4

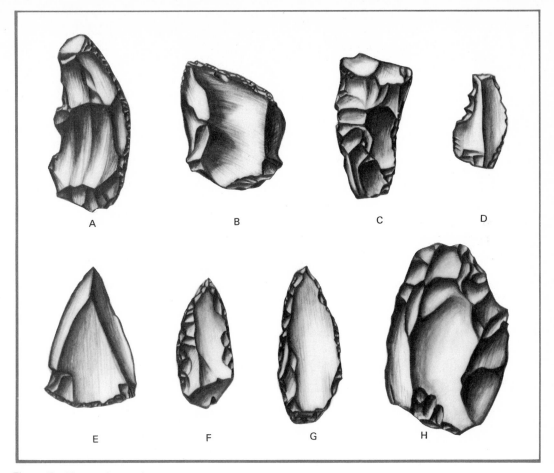

Figure 7 Mousterian tool types.
A–C are scrapers, *D* is a notched tool (notches are along the upper left edge), *E–G* are points, and *H* is a Levallois flake. (Adapted from Bordes, 1968.)

1. *Typical Mousterian* assemblages rarely contain hand axes. Tools probably used as scrapers are plentiful, and points on other tools are made with care.
2. *Quina-Ferrassie* (or Charentian) assemblages are dominated by scrapers. Some are apparently designed for extremely specialized functions.
3. *Denticulate Mousterian* assemblages are rich in fine-toothed (or "denticulate") tools. But hand axes, points, and scrapers are either altogether lacking or of poor quality.
4. The fourth tradition, *Mousterian of the Acheulean tradition,* evolves from an earlier to a later form. Type A has numerous hand axes and varied flake tools, including a number of scrapers. Type B, on the other hand, has few hand axes or scrapers, but many denticulates and knives.
5. The last tradition, *Micoquian,* is characterized by lance-shaped hand axes, often with concave edges and thick bases.

Although Bordes interprets the differences among these assemblages as distinct cultural traditions, some archaeologists see them as the products of a single culture, occupying varying environments and carrying on different activities.

Econiche

The econiche occupied by the late archaics is best understood in Europe, which was densely settled during Mousterian times. Sites dating from the Würm have been excavated intensively in modern times. Despite the cold weather that hominids must have faced in Europe during the peak of glacial activity, the number of plant and animal remains found there suggest that the area could support abundant life. Ample amounts of sunlight helped. In midsummer, there were probably 16 hours of light a day, and at least half that much in winter. Except in areas of perpetual snow, northern Europe was covered with a variety of plants that were adapted to the cold. Wooly mammoth, wooly rhinoceros, elk, bison, and many other animals were numerous. The environment must have been like the tundra meadow and forest areas of northern Canada and Alaska—a region that today supports large herds of elk and moose.

The European hominids of this time apparently took full advantage of the high biomass of the tundra. Although they seemed to be capable of bagging everything from cave bears to fish, they must have been very fond of—or good at following and killing—reindeer. At one open-air habitation site in northern Germany, for instance, almost three-fourths of the animal remains found are those of reindeer (Kennedy, 1975).

To make use of this rich ecosystem, humans continued to rely on traditional hunting tools such as spears and bolas. Bows and arrows, fishhooks, and harpoons were still unknown. It is possible, though, that since Mousterians made graves with digging sticks, they also probably used pits to trap game. And the increasing inventory of tools may have been used to fashion a variety of weapons made of wood, bone, and plant fibers.

Adaptations to the cold may have included anatomical changes, as we saw in Chapter 8. (The larger noses of the Neandertals may have helped them to bear better the bitterly cold air of the glacial period.) Cultural solutions included continued use of fire. Rock shelters and caves were now systematically used for dwellings for the first time, sometimes on a semipermanent basis. Branches or skins may have been draped across the openings to keep out the cold, and fires were burned for warmth. And even in open-air sites some groups seemed to have built weather-tight shelters covered with skins. The many scrapers found in Mousterian assemblages suggest that these people were also scraping animal hides, possibly for use as blankets or clothing, though we cannot be sure of this (Clark, 1977).

Another way in which some of these archaic humans adapted to the Würm cold was to migrate with the seasons, as did the animals they hunted. In the summer they traveled north into the open tundras; in the winter they came south to take refuge in the forests. This kind of life continued to favor small group size. Campsites are not large enough to suggest any social organization more complex than a band.

Outside of Europe archaic *H. sapiens* populations were expanding into new ecosystems, from tropical rainforests to subarctic regions. They were also developing technologies more specifically aimed at making use of local food sources and building materials. In the African rainforest, for instance, there was a seeming emphasis on tools for working wood, for this material was abundantly available (Butzer, 1971).

Glimmers of Modern Culture

At the same time that they were refining their toolmaking arts and living in new ecosystems, some groups seemed to be developing a more modern capacity for self-awareness and symbolic thought. We know that their brains were large, at least as large as ours, though this trait cannot be directly linked with intelligence. By this time, their cultural traditions were so rich that they must have been using some form of speech. Our only evidence of their ability to speak, however, is indirect. We know little of how their brain was structured, for only a few of their external features have been preserved in endocranial casts. Whether or not they had a localized "speech center" in their brains we cannot tell. Some researchers have noted that these hominids had plenty of room in which to move their tongues if they did try to speak, since the bony shelves had disappeared from the insides of their lower jaws. Philip Lieberman, a linguist, and Edmund Crelin, an anatomist, determined that the larynx and brain of these early people were better equipped for speech than those of other primates. The two scientists built a model of the vocal tract of a European fossil dated to the early part of the Würm. They then designed a computer program to analyze what kinds of sounds it could have made. The result: although the late archaics could make more differentiated sounds than other primates could, they could produce only a few vowel sounds, and their consonants were limited to *b*s, *d*s, and a few others. Fascinating as this theory is, however, it is based on very thin evidence—a single fossil of a very old male.

In some areas, the late archaics had begun to practice such uniquely human social customs as ritual burial. Sixty thousand years ago, in a cave located in modern-day Iraq, a child was buried on a bed of flowers. A youth found buried at Le Moustier, France, was buried with animal bones and stone tools. And at La Chapelle-aux-Saints, another individual was laid to rest in a small grave carved out of the rocky floor of the cave. The body was surrounded by bits of quartz, jasper, and red ochre. Perhaps these were personal possessions; perhaps they were symbolically linked with a belief in an afterlife. We have no way of knowing. We do know, however, that ochre was increasingly used in burials and other rituals, suggesting that it carried some kind of symbolic meaning. One anthropologist thinks that the red of the ochre was linked to the life-giving connotations of blood (Wreschner, 1976).

Some of the earliest ornamental objects yet found may have been made by Mousterian groups. Most were things worn on the body—necklaces and beads made of animal teeth, bones, and even 50-million-year-old fossilized shells. Whether these were used as ornaments, symbols, or perhaps even as magical tokens is not clear (Marshack, 1978; Clark, 1977). But strange groupings of cave bear skulls and bones have been interpreted as strong evidence for some kind of magical or religious beliefs (Kennedy, 1975). For some reason, the Mousterians also made symbolic marks—such as zigzags—on bone plaques and then covered them with red ochre (Marshack, 1976).

Such rare discoveries are extremely exciting to contemporary archaeologists, for they push back by tens of thousands of years the possible beginnings of symbolic, rather than strictly functional, behavior. And for all we know, Mousterians may have had elaborate myths, songs, and dances that will remain forever lost to us because they have left no material traces (Marshack, 1976).

The Upper Paleolithic

Up to about 40,000 years ago, culture had evolved rather slowly. The Oldowan tradition lasted 1.5 million years, overlapped to some extent by the Acheulean, which persisted for

220

over a million years. The pace of change increased somewhat during the Mousterian, which in Europe lasted only 40,000 to 60,000 years (Butzer, 1971). By the Upper Paleolithic, people apparently had the technology and the background of accumulated knowledge to rapidly improve and specialize their toolmaking techniques. They organized themselves into larger groups and translated their perceptions of one another and the animals they hunted into surprisingly good works of art. And, exploiting many different environments, they crossed geographical barriers to enter the last frontiers of the habitable world: the Americas and Australia.

Technology

Upper Paleolithic toolmaking traditions are complex and confusing. The best-known sequences exist in Europe. But even there, they are poorly worked out except in France. Some archaeologists speculate that southeastern Europe and southwestern Asia may have been areas in which for some reason there were many cultural innovations. These traditions then spread to other regions (Klein, 1974). Others, like Bordes (1968), suspect that technological changes were taking place independently at many different locations, rapidly increasing cultural diversity throughout the world. Rather than try to follow the changes in each region, we will focus on only two: France and the Paleo-Indian cultures of the New World.

In France, deposits show a gradual transition from Mousterian to *Perigordian* industries. This culture existed from about 35,000 to about 18,000 years B.P. It probably evolved from the Mousterian of Acheulean tradition. At about the same time, however, another culture appeared in France that did not seem to have originated there. This was the *Aurignacian,* which lasted from about 33,000 to 25,000 years B.P. Its origins and spread are still a mystery, though some archaeologists

suspect that it may have been introduced from the Middle East. During the third Würm glaciation (Würm III), these two cultures seem to have coexisted without affecting each other much more than the various Mousterian traditions of the earlier Würm did.

Whatever the relationship between the Perigordian and Aurignacian, only the former existed between about 25,000 and 18,000 years B.P. After 18,000 years B.P. the late Perigordian was replaced in France by the short-lived *Solutrean.* The Solutrean lasted only 2,000 years, but during that time flintworking techniques advanced to a new peak. The origin of the Solutrean is not at all clear. It may have been a holdover from some Mousterian tradition that had continued to evolve in an isolated region before it spread across a rather limited area of Europe.

Roughly 16,000 years ago, the Solutrean vanished as mysteriously as it had appeared. It was quickly replaced by the very different tools of the *Magdalenian* tradition. The Magdalenian lasted until about 10,000 years ago, when it was replaced by the so-called Mesolithic Period (or Middle Stone Age). As we shall see in the next chapter, the Mesolithic lasted until the onset of agriculture in Europe (Bordes, 1968).

Despite their differences through time, Upper Paleolithic assemblages have one unique technological feature: They are rich in *blades.* These are long, thin flakes with parallel sides. Blades may have been produced in at least three different ways: (1) hammering a chisel-like instrument against a stone that was steadied on top of a large rock (see Figure 8), (2) punching vertical slices out of a prepared rock with a long pointed tool steadied against the toolmaker's chest, or (3) traditional stone-against-stone percussion flaking. The blades that resulted were of predictable, standardized shapes. With a little retouching, they could readily be made into specialized tools. The keen edge of these tools probably made it

A blade, characteristic tool of Upper Paleolithic assemblages. (Courtesy of the American Museum of Natural History)

possible to work material other than stone, such as hides, wood, and bone.

Among the specialized Upper Paleolithic blade tools are what archaeologists call *borers.* Their sharp points were probably used to drill holes into wood, shell, bone, or skins. The flattened ends of burins may have been used to chisel grooves in wood, bone, and antlers. *End scrapers* were sharpened on both ends, rather than one side (as in the Mousterian side-scrapers). They were probably used in hollowing out bone and wood or removing bark, as well as in scraping skins. *Notched blades* may have been used to shave wood in fashioning the shafts of arrows or spears.

Upper Paleolithic assemblages also contain *backed blades,* with one purposely dulled edge and one sharpened one, useful in general cutting and scraping. Bows and arrows appear for the first time during this period. *Shouldered points* were probably affixed to spears or arrows for fighting or hunting. Laurel-leaf blades were so delicately chipped and thin that they may have been used as ceremonial items, rather than as weapons.

Figure 8 (From Fagan, 1977.)

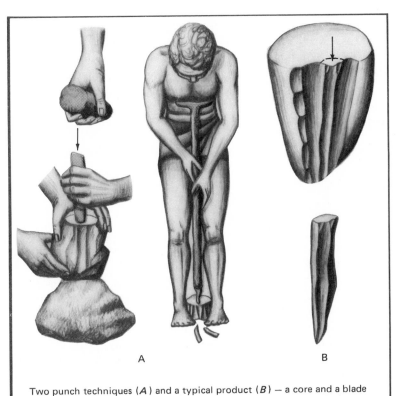

A

B

Two punch techniques (*A*) and a typical product (*B*) — a core and a blade struck from it. The dotted line and arrow show the point at which the next blade will be struck off from the core

A Solutrean laurel leaf blade.
(Courtesy of the American Museum of Natural History)

In addition to blade tools, Upper Paleolithic assemblages—especially the Magdalenian—contain elaborate tools made of bones and antlers. Magdelenian bone and antler spear-throwers, barbed fish-hooks, harpoon heads, thong or shaft straighteners, and needles testify to the specialized uses to which materials other than stone were put. These objects were not only efficient tools but also showed the artistic talent of their makers. Many are even handsomely decorated with engraved pictures (Fagan, 1977; Butzer, 1971).

Econiche of European Upper Paleolithic Populations

Upper Paleolithic tools made possible a more efficient use of food resources. In Europe, Upper Paleolithic populations occupied roughly the same tundra and forest ecosystem in which Mousterian populations had lived. But there are far more Upper Paleolithic sites, some apparently the ruins of permanent or semipermanent camps of over a hundred people. This suggests that more successful adaptations to extreme cold allowed population density to increase greatly. Their more settled existence and larger group size probably called for some form of political authority, a theory that is borne out by evidence

that some people were buried with greater ceremony than others. The informal political structure of small bands becomes a less effective way of organizing large groups of people. In larger groups leadership roles were probably performed by persons who could influence others through the force of their personalities.

Like their predecessors, the Upper Paleolithic peoples of Europe continued to rely on tundra and forest game. There is no sound evidence that they were beginning to domesticate the herds that they followed, though herd management may have appeared at about this time in the Middle East with selective killing of the young (Patterson, 1973). But their ways of capturing game were becoming far more effective than ever before. Spear-throwers and bows and arrows increased the accuracy and speed with which projectile points could be directed at prey. Judging from large piles of bones at the base of some cliffs, herds apparently were driven over precipices to their death. Cave drawings show the use of various traps, pitfalls, and enclosures. And fishing was greatly improved by the invention of harpoons and primitive fishhooks. All these advances led to what was probably the highest standard of living ever known anywhere before the onset of agriculture (Butzer, 1971).

For the first time, humans were having a significant effect on the environment. The increasing use of large game animals like the mammoth may have contributed to their extinction, though climate changes undoubtedly played a part in this, too. Upper Paleolithic groups may have changed the vegetation as well. Frequent evidence of forest fires in layers of this age has been interpreted by some archaeologists as an indication of intentional burning by humans. Fires may have made it easier to sight and trap game. Fires also caused plants eaten by game species to grow, and helped the growth of berries and other vegetation probably eaten by humans (Butzer, 1971).

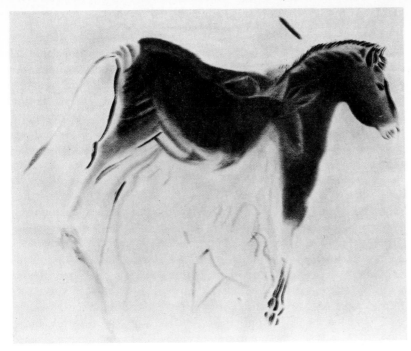

An Upper Paleolithic cave painting from Altamira, Spain, showing a horse with a deer superimposed on it. (Courtesy of the American Museum of Natural History)

Art

Improved hunting-and-gathering techniques may have provided Upper Paleolithic peoples with enough free time to develop artworks of extraordinary quality. Especially in France and Spain, engraved bone and antler implements, low-relief clay sculptures, carved statuettes, cave drawings, and multicolored paintings reached a peak of sophistication during the Magdalenian.

Observers once tended to dismiss these pieces as bored cave dwellers' way of distracting themselves. But the current trend is to see the paintings as meaningful products of a patterned intelligence. Some of the realistic representations of game animals might have been used repeatedly in rituals designed to encourage the success of the hunt, cure sickness, mark births or deaths, or celebrate the onset of spring. Exquisite "Venus" statues of women—many of them apparently pregnant—might have been fertility symbols. Various abstract signs—such as rectangles, rows of dots, barbed lines, and ovals—might have symbolized males, females, and their re-

lationships. Some marks might be attempts to keep track of time, distance, or quantity. If so, they predated by thousands of years the first recognizable calendars, rulers, and systems of writing and arithmetic. Consistencies in the location of various animals in the cave paintings suggest that whatever the explanation, it was intentional and orderly rather than random. Many archaeologists are now excitedly studying them as symbolic traditions that, if deciphered, could provide a wealth of clues to how these early people lived, thought, and perhaps spoke (Leoroi-Gourhan, 1968).

Migration to the New World

Except for its bitterly cold climate, eastern Siberia was probably fairly attractive to Stone Age hunters. With open park vegetation feeding an abundance of animals, it probably supported more people than it does today. By late Paleolithic times, humans apparently had adjusted to cold by wearing warm, fitted clothing and shoes (Bricker, 1976) and by living in rather large heated dwellings.

Perhaps because of the increasingly successful adaptation to this environment, Upper Paleolithic groups may have increased in number beyond the ability of the area to support them. At any rate, about 30,000 years ago various groups began to migrate into the previously untapped ecosystems of *Beringia,* the land mass that connected eastern Siberia and western Alaska.

This continental land mass was temporarily exposed as expanding glaciers trapped normally circulating water as ice and caused sea levels to drop. The first human immigrants probably followed grazing herds onto Beringia and eastern Alaska not long after their ancestors reached Siberia, perhaps between 32,000 and 28,000 years ago. These migrations were cut off about 10,000 years B.P., as the last glacial maximum ended and sea levels rose, covering the landbridge.

Alaska and the Yukon were probably even richer in plant and animal life than Siberia. This new area had never been covered by glaciers. Instead, it was dotted with streams, lakes, and a variety of forest, grassland, and tundra ecosystems. A similarly rich and varied environment lay to the south, and when gaps appeared between the major eastern and western Canadian ice sheets, some humans followed animal herds down through these unglaciated corridors. They probably reached what is now the continental United States by at least 18,000 years B.P. and South America by at least 16,000 years B.P.

The Paleo-Indian Hunters of North America

The earliest known humans in the New World—the so-called *Paleo-Indians*—brought with them technologies and living patterns taken from Old World cultural traditions, especially those of eastern Siberia. After they made their way south of the ice sheets, they spread rapidly and diversified as they adapted to new ecosystems.

The unusually rapid movement into these new ecosystems may have been caused partly by sheer human curiosity to see what lay over the horizon. But perhaps it can also be explained by the dynamics of population growth in a new environment. According to one model (Patterson, 1973), populations probably increased as they moved into areas of previously untapped resources. As their numbers grew, the Paleo-Indians began to exhaust some of these resources—food, water, fuel, shelter, toolmaking materials—making it necessary for some of the population to migrate. The rest probably stayed behind to live at a density that could be supported by the resources of the area. Those who moved out probably settled in virgin territory nearby, increased in number, and then split again. At each stop, the features of the environment changed to some degree. Therefore these migrants would have had to abandon the use of traditional resources and invent ways to make use of the new ones.

As a result of this continuing process, the material cultures of the New World became very diverse. The *Llano* culture, for instance, first appeared among mammoth hunters in what is now the western United States. Llano people soon spread across the northern United States to the northeast coast, hunting mammoths. But as mammoth populations declined, those back in the temperate grasslands of the Great Plains and Rocky Mountain valleys began hunting bison instead, using smaller points called *Folsom points.* In the East, on the other hand, Paleo-Indian groups turned to more intensive fishing and plant gathering and to hunting smaller mammals such as deer, which were plentiful in their temperate forest ecosystem (Butzer, 1971).

Paleo-Indian tool assemblages of North America are classified by age and projectile-point style into three traditions—the Llano, Folsom, and Plano. The Llano tradition, for instance, is identified by what seems to be an American innovation in stone tool technology: a small blade at either side of the base of a lance-shaped projectile point, perhaps designed to improve the way it fit into a wooden shaft (Bordes, 1968). Characteristic of this tradition are the so-called Clovis and Sandia points. Clovis points in particular are widespread in the American West and Northeast. The Llano tradition lasted from about 11,600 years B.P. to about 10,900 years B.P. in the West and until 10,500 B.P. in the East.

The Llano tradition was replaced in the area just east of the Rocky Mountains by the Folsom culture. It lasted from 10,800 to 10,000 B.P. and seems to have marked a shift from dependence on mammoth to bison.

About 10,200 years B.P., the Folsom gave way to the Plano tradition, which existed between Mexico and Canada and from the Rockies to the Midatlantic Coast. It reflected a growing diversity of local traditions, suggesting great cultural complexity (Butzer, 1971).

A major area of controversy in the study of Paleo-Indian cultures is whether or not they were responsible for the widespread mammal extinctions that occurred not long after their arrival. Almost a third of the genera of mammals in North America became extinct at the end of the Pleistocene, from about 13,000 to 7,500 years B.P. They covered a wide range of econiches, from open-country grazers (mammoths, wild horses, camels, llamas, bison, antelopes, yaks) to forest browsers (such as mastodons and ground sloths).

It is hard to blame their extinction on climatic or environmental changes, partly because they had such differing habitat requirements and partly because in many cases their favorite habitats never disappeared and are still widespread in North America today. But as Butzer (1971) points out, it is hard to see how Paleo-Indian groups could have caused this much damage, either. They moved in relatively small bands spread over an enormous area, never staying in any one place for long and never hunting any animals intensively except mammoths and bison. And even the far more numerous and efficient Indian hunters of later times killed many fewer buffalos each year than the herds' annual increase in population. Instead of accusing the Paleo-Indians of single-handedly causing "Pleistocene overkill" in America, some archaeologists now think that human hunters simply pushed already precarious animal populations over the brink of extinction. There is evidence that even before human predators appeared, these animals' numbers were already marginal. Better-adapted competitors, and animals newly arrived from Beringia and Alaska by way of the Canadian corridor, may have reduced the native fauna. Severe reduction of grazing lands caused by glacial advances or arid periods and the loss of young when bitter cold occurred in the springtime may also have contributed to the mass extinctions.

Human hunters in the Americas adjusted to the loss of these animals by making use of a large number of different food resources, including many plants. Except for a limited number of agriculturalists, most North Americans were still following this diversified food strategy when European settlers arrived.

Summary

1. Prehistory can be divided into four cultural stages. The *Paleolithic* lasted from the late Pliocene, when the first tools were made, almost to the end of the Pleistocene, about 10,000 years B.P. It is often divided into three parts: the *Lower Paleolithic,* which preceded the *Middle Paleolithic*—the state of culture in Neandertal times—and the *Upper Paleolithic,* during which *blades* appeared in large numbers. The *Mesolithic* Age is transitional between the Paleolithic and the first appearance of farming. During the *Neolithic,* humans made tools by grinding and polishing stone rather than solely by flaking and began to pro-

duce food as well. Finally, the *Bronze* and *Iron Ages* of the *Metal Age* were marked by the smelting of the metals for which they are named.

2. Experts think that the earliest stone tools that form the *Oldowan tradition* were made by one of the early gracile hominids, although they do not know by which one. Percussion flaking—the process of using one stone, a *hammerstone,* to strike flakes from another—was employed to make the *chopper,* the characteristic tool of the tradition. A chopper is a pebble of which one edge has been sharpened.

3. The early hominids were probably part of a savanna ecosystem, ate more vegetable matter than meat, and lived in small bands that shared food that was probably gathered by the women and hunted by the men.

4. As the carriers of the Oldowan tradition migrated into Europe and through southern Asia to the Far East, two new tool traditions evolved: the *Acheulean tradition* and the *chopper-tool culture.* The Acheulean lasted from about 1.2 million years B.P. in Africa to about 100,000 years B.P. in Europe and is marked by the common use of the *hand ax* and the *soft hammer technique.* The chopper-tool culture, generally found to the north and east of the Acheulean, may have arisen 475,000–425,000 years B.P. and lacks a hand ax. The two cultures are probably the separate adaptations of different populations to different environments.

5. The major tool tradition of the late middle Paleolithic is the *Mousterian,* which in Europe lasted from about 100,000 to about 40,000 years B.P. Mousterian tools vary greatly but are more complex than earlier tools. The *Levallois technique* was used to prepare stone cores so that preformed flakes could be struck.

6. The European Mousterians adapted to the tundra by hunting big game and probably by building open-air shelters and sewing clothes from animal hides. Aspects of modern culture began to appear at this time. Limited speech may have been possible, and Neandertals buried their dead, made ornaments, and may have engaged in rituals.

7. During the *Upper Paleolithic,* (40,000–10,000 years B.P. in Europe) population densities increased, making necessary more efficient use of food resources. As a result, tool types and styles became more complex in response to the demands of local environments. *Borers, end scrapers, notched blades, backed blades, bows and arrows, spear throwers,* and *fishhooks* are among the new tools. Like the Mousterians, Upper Paleolithic peoples exploited a forest and tundra ecosystem, but they lived in larger groups, possibly of greater political complexity than those of earlier people.

8. Sculpture, drawings, and painting became advanced during the Upper Paleolithic. Art may have played a role in ritual, though consistencies in the location of cave art can only tell us for sure that its placement was often not random.

9. Some time between 32,000 and 28,000 years B.P., Siberian hunters, whose numbers may have increased beyond the ability of eastern Siberia to support them, probably followed herds of big game into the New World. These people migrated across *Beringia,* a land bridge now covered by the Bering Strait. By at least 18,000 years B.P. they had reached the continental United States.

10. The three major early archaeological cultures of North America are the *Llano,* the *Folsom,* and the *Plano* traditions. The Llano precedes the other two and was adapted to hunting mammoths. The Folsom was designed for smaller game and was succeeded by the diverse and widespread Plano tradition.

11
The Origins of Agriculture

BETWEEN the end of the Paleolithic Age, with its Pleistocene big-game hunting and stone-tool traditions, and the beginning of the Neolithic Age, with its sedentary farming villages and pottery traditions, there was a transitional period. Archaeologists have named this period the Mesolithic Age.

The Mesolithic Age

While not clearly defined in all areas of the world, there is evidence of the Mesolithic in Europe, the Near East, and North America. In general, the Mesolithic Age coincided with the warming trend that followed the retreat of the last glaciation some 10,000 years ago.

Along with the post-Pleistocene warming trend came the extinction of the animals that had lived together in large herds on the *tundras* that had covered most of Europe. These game-rich tundras were gradually replaced with modern temperate forests. The new forest ecosystems supported a larger number of different species, but the density of each species was less than in the Pleistocene period.

Smaller, and in some cases less abundant, game animals caused people to live and hunt in smaller social groups, or bands, and to use new weapons and tools. A greater variety of food was consumed, and each source of food was exploited more fully. In the Near East, Mexico, and probably China, as we shall see later in this chapter, these Mesolithic adaptations ultimately led to the domestication of plants and animals. Traditionally, the beginning of food production marks the end of the Mesolithic Age, so its length varies in different parts of the world. Perhaps the best-studied Mesolithic period is that from Europe.

In fact, the term *Mesolithic* was originally used to describe the European remains from the end of the Magdalenian, or "reindeer" period, about 10,000 years ago, until the adoption of agriculture about 6,000 years ago.

The game available to European Mesolithic peoples included elk, wild pig, bear, small mammals such as wild cat, fox, and marten, and wild fowl. These people also leaned heavily on fresh- and saltwater fish and shellfish (Clark, 1977). One unusually well-preserved site at Starr Carr in England includes a birch platform at the very edge of a lake. There, the inhabitants may have fished through holes cut in the ice while preying on the red deer that wintered not far from the site (Clark, 1972).

The tools of the European Mesolithic dif-fered greatly from the long, fluted, leaf-shaped stone points of the Paleolithic. Small blades usually less than an inch long, called *micro-liths,* were used especially as tips and barbs for arrows. These weapons were well suited to hunting the small game of this time. Other tools included flint and polished stone adzes for breaking earth and chopping trees, antler and bone-headed spears and harpoons, bone fishhooks and needles, and nets, dugout canoes, and paddles (see Figure 1). The artifacts left by different peoples in different environments show great variety and suggest to some archaeologists that Mesolithic peoples lived in very specific econiches (Binford, 1968).

Some experts see the Mesolithic as a "cul-

Figure 1 **Some Mesolithic tools.** Mesolithic people developed implements designed for hunting small game. One such tool was the bow *(A)* and arrow tipped with a microlith *(B)*. In Northern Europe heavy stone tools designed for felling timber were produced. Some, such as this adze *(C)*, were chipped, and others were ground *(D)*. Bone tools, such as the Natufian needles *(E)*, fishhooks *(F)*, and harpoon point *(G)* shown here, were fashioned. And people wore bone ornaments such as this Natufian necklace *(H)*. *(A–D* from Braidwood, 1975; *E–H* from Clark, 1977)

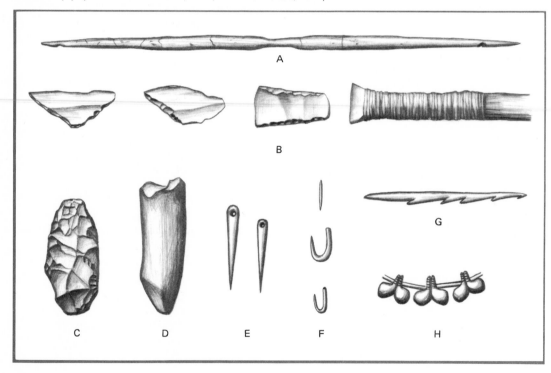

tural degeneration when compared with the Upper Paleolithic" (Binford, 1968). They cite the fact that there was no representational art as evidence. Others, however, remind us that the highly stylized drawings of humans and animals common in the art of this time are not inferior to representational art. Clark (1977), for example, suggests that the abstract drawings may have been the forerunners of Neolithic pottery designs.

North America

In North America the Mesolithic Age has been divided into two parts, according to time and place: (1) the *desert tradition,* which began about 9,000 years ago in the arid western regions of North America and lasted until European contact; and (2) the *archaic tradition* of the Eastern woodlands, which began about the same time and lasted until about 4,000 to 3,000 years ago.

The Desert Tradition. The desert tradition evolved in the extremely arid Great Basin, an area that includes Nevada and parts of Utah, California, Oregon, Idaho, and Wyoming. There, American aborigines, especially the Paiute, roamed while making use of seasonal resources such as piñon and other nuts, seeds, and berries, as well as bison, deer, antelope, and other smaller animals (Willey, 1966).

The people of the desert tradition are considered Mesolithic because they depended on modern plants and animals, used microliths, and lived in bands. Small, seminomadic bands were most effective in making use of scarce resources. At most, any one location could support only 25 to 30 people at a time. The wide variety of resources called for a variety of portable, easily made tools. These included microlith projectile points for hunting, and baskets and milling stones for collecting and grinding up plants (Willey, 1966).

The Archaic Tradition. The archaic tradition

of the Eastern woodlands and river valleys arose in an environment more like that of Europe. Like the European people, the Indians of the archaic tradition also relied on fish, shellfish, small game, and wild plants. This tradition extended as far west as the Great Plains, where its remains are somewhat like the tool assemblages of the desert tradition. However, ground- and polished-stone tools, especially adzes, axes, and gouges for working wood, were specifically an archaic adaptation. Like members of the desert culture, archaic tradition peoples were seminomadic. But later, perhaps due to a greater wealth of resources, they gave up their seasonal wandering for a more settled existence (Willey, 1966).

In Europe, and in North America north of Mexico, the Mesolithic did not lead to the independent development of agriculture. It is likely that plants and animals that could be domesticated were absent in these areas. In addition, population densities may never have been so high as to make food production necessary (Clark, 1967).

The Neolithic Age

The story of plant and animal domestication is the subject of the so-called *Neolithic Revolution.* This term is used to describe the change from a hunting-and-gathering economy and a flaked-stone-tool technology to an economy based on farming and a technology that included polished stone tools, pottery, and weaving (Clark, 1977; Perkins & Daly, 1974).

The Neolithic Revolution has been considered as important as the Industrial Revolution. Indeed it is probably more so, since without agriculture there never would have been an Industrial Revolution. But the use of the word "Revolution," while helping to show the importance of the change, is misleading. The Industrial Revolution spanned about 100 years, but the Neolithic Revolution took at least 3,000-4,000 years. And although we associate the Industrial Revolution with specific inventions, such as the steam engine, the domestication of plants and animals was not an invention, but a very gradual process in which humans began to manipulate the traits of plants and animals for their own advantage. Unlike a political revolution, with its abrupt, often violent change, the development of agriculture production was a slow, continuous change.

In what ways, then, was the development of food production revolutionary? The answer lies in its profound impact on all other aspects of life. The domestication of plants and animals allowed people to produce more food on a given area of land and thus to support larger populations (Clark, 1977). Permanent settlements were formed near the fields, and people began to hold title to pieces of land and call them their own. Conflicts arose over property, territory, and resources. And some groups within a farming society came to have higher prestige and more property and benefits than other groups. Food production may have begun over 10,000 years ago, but we are still dealing with its effects today.

Not only did agriculture begin fairly recently, but it also spread very rapidly, compared to the rate of change in the Paleolithic and Mesolithic. Between about 10,000 and 2,000 years ago, agriculture had almost everywhere replaced hunting and gathering as the main way of life. Modern studies of living hunters and gatherers suggest that this change did not occur because agriculture provided a better standard of living than hunting and gathering. Despite old myths of half-starved hunters scrounging from day to day, anthropologists now know that contemporary hunting-and-gathering peoples frequently eat better, work less, and live more securely than farming people, to whom a blight or a drought spells disaster and the waste of countless hours of labor. Why, then, did most human beings change from hunting and gathering to agriculture? Before answering this question we shall first study the nature of domestication and its effects on wild plants and animals. Then we shall look at some of the cultures in which agriculture first arose.

The Domestication of Plants and Animals

When humans first began to cultivate wild plants and raise wild animals, they caused a kind of evolution, a change in gene frequencies over time, to occur. Perhaps the most potent force causing changes in genetic makeup is selection. In the case of domestication, humans were the selective agent.

Plants or animals with small chance of success in the wild but with features desirable to humans were often chosen for sowing or breeding by early domesticators, thus increasing their presence in the population. As a result, the frequency of genes responsible for these traits increased. Plants and animals whose traits were an advantage in the wild, but a liability under domestication, however, may have been less well protected by humans or purposely prevented from reproducing.

Human beings may have produced some of these changes without knowing it at first. Merely changing the environments of plants and animals by moving them to different areas or by protecting them from weeds, drought, or predators permits more mutants and variants to survive and reproduce. Deliberate saving of seed for future crops may have been a major step in domestication, since it probably led to planting in new environments and to further changes in the selective pressures acting on the crops' genetic composition (Patterson, 1973). The soil of a new environment could differ in terms of moisture and nutrients. Such changed conditions might favor traits not previously selected for.

Obstacles to Domestication. Wild plants and animals are adapted to surviving and reproducing in their natural environment. Often they have traits that make it difficult for human beings to use them effectively.

Plants. According to archaeologist Kent Flannery (1965), wild grains posed three major problems:

1. The brittle *rachis* of wild wheat and barley breaks easily and helps scatter seeds. The rachis is the fiber by which the seed is attached to the stem of the plant. This adaptation helps the wild plant survive and multiply, but makes harvesting very difficult.
2. Wild grains have tough, inedible *glumes,* or husks, which hold the kernels tightly, despite vigorous threshing.
3. Wild grain grows in scattered patches on hillsides, not in concentrated stands suitable for easy reaping.

According to one expert (Helbaek, 1959), the earliest farmers overcame the problem of a fragile rachis by selectively reaping grains with a tough rachis. But the argument can be made that selective reaping of grain with a tough rachis would favor an increase in the number of the brittle-stemmed plants. Grain with a tough rachis would be eaten, while the grain from the brittle-stemmed plants would remain in the field to sprout. Only deliberate sowing of the tough-rachis plants could lead to their domestication.

The problem of the tough glumes was solved in two ways. First, roasting the grains made the husks brittle enough to be ground off on stone slabs. Also, early farmers could have sorted out and planted certain mutant forms. For example, polyploidy, a genetic trait of many plants that permits the number of chromosomes to increase from one generation to the next, may have created new strains of easily harvested wheat. Hybrid forms, created by crossing two different kinds of plants, may have produced grain having "naked kernels," which are easily threshed free of their husks (Flannery, 1965).

The problem of grain being difficult to harvest was overcome through a mutant form of barley better adapted to the drier spring weather of the level Mesopotamian plain. This mutation resulted in a barley with six fertile kernel rows instead of only two. The harvesting of barley therefore became both easier and more productive when it was planted in dense stands in lowland fields. (See Figure 2.)

Mutations and human-directed changes in the frequency of genes controlling valued traits resulted in domesticated species that were physically different from wild species. As they became adapted to new, human-dominated environments, they became dependent upon human intervention for survival. In the case of wheat and barley, the tough stems that made harvesting easier also made natural seed dispersal impossible. Modern corn is also totally dependent on human beings for its reproduction. Unlike the extinct tiny wild maize from which it evolved, modern corn has seeds entirely enclosed by husks. Thus, it cannot reproduce itself without human help. Both consciously and unconsciously, human beings became an important selective agent in the evolution of domesticated plants.

Animals. Early domesticators had to overcome several problems in keeping wild animals. First, animals must be either aggressive or good at escaping to survive in the wild. Wild cattle, for example, were large and powerful, and had long horns for protection (Isaac, 1971). Nor were adult boars and sows particularly docile. Other animals, such as fowl, could easily escape their human captors. The earliest would-be herders, then, had to handle animals that could be quite dangerous or difficult to keep.

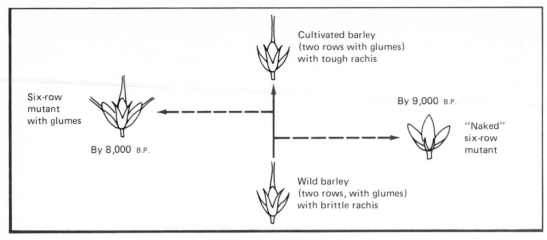

Figure 2 Diagram showing some of the changes in barley after it was first domesticated. Each of the three domestic forms shown represents the elimination by early farmers in the Near East of an obstacle to the domestication of the original wild barley. (Flannery, 1965)

Furthermore, some animals that were kept probably competed with humans for food. It is likely, for example, that pigs were never economically important in the Near East because, unlike cattle, goats, and sheep, they competed with humans for grain. The other animals ate fodder (Perkins & Daly, 1974).

By studying the archaeological record and comparing wild strains with domestic strains scientists have found that domestication has changed certain plant species in a number of ways.

Captive animal herds in the Neolithic Near East had sex and age compositions different from those of wild herds. Early farmers slaughtered young animals for food, while keeping the adults for breeding. More young males were butchered, since females would be valuable for breeding. An excess of female goats and sheep may have proved a further boon in later winter and early spring when the lambing season brought forth a flow of milk (Flannery, 1965).

Other differences between wild and domestic strains are known primarily by comparison of living varieties. Sheep and goats have two kinds of hair follicles: *primaries,*

which produce the straight hairs of the visible coat, and *secondaries,* which make up the wooly undercoat. Wild animals have mostly straight hair. Mutation and selective breeding resulted in animals having many more secondaries, thus producing the familiar wooly coat of domestic sheep and goats. (See Figure 3.) Wooly hair probably first appeared as a random mutation some 2,000 years after sheep had been domesticated. We know that wool may have been spun as early as 8,000 years ago in Turkey.

Some genetic changes in domesticated animals seem to have no adaptive advantage. For example, the twisted horns of domesticated goats are unknown in the wild variety (Flannery, 1965). In addition, just as domesticated plants become more and more dependent on humans for their survival, so, too, do domesticated animals. Animals lacking powerful defensive traits could also only survive in domestication (Isaac, 1971). Thus, although domesticated animals (unlike grains) have retained the ability to reproduce without help from humans, they cannot protect themselves from predators as well as wild animals can.

Theories of the Origins of Agriculture

Why did people start sowing wild plants and go to the trouble of subduing unruly animals in the first place? This is a hard question to answer, because to do so we must imagine the thoughts and motives of Neolithic humans.

Archaeologists have nevertheless developed a number of hypotheses explaining the kinds of pressures that may have motivated the earliest farmers. In this chapter, we shall discuss a few of the most prominent of these theories and then briefly review the evidence of agricultural development in the Near East, China, and Mesoamerica.

Childe's Oasis Model

V. Gordon Childe (1892–1957), one of the most distinguished British anthropologists of the early twentieth century, spent much of his life studying the Neolithic people of the Near East. In his *New Light on the Most Ancient East* (1952), he published a theory linking the drying trend that presumably affected much of the world as the glaciers withdrew at the close of the Pleistocene period to the domestication of plants and animals. His theory, unlike previous ideas, presented a series of hypotheses specific enough to be tested by archaeological data. According to Childe, as the Mesopotamian climate grew drier, already dry grasslands turned into deserts, dotted here and there with oases. People, animals, and plants were concentrated in these areas. This climatic crisis forced humans to domesticate plants and animals, since killing them would have left the oasis-dwellers with no sources of food. These inhabitants of the oases domesticated animals by (1) letting

them eat the fodder remaining in their fields after harvest, (2) protecting them from predators, and (3) selecting for docility by killing aggressive animals for food.

In the long run, archaeological data has not supported this theory. Rainfall and vegetation in such key early agricultural sites as Jarmo and Karim Shaher were at least as heavy at that time as they are now. Moreover, these and many other early villages clustered not in Childe's alluvial oases, but in upland areas, where there was enough rainfall for cultivation.

Finally, Childe's theory has been attacked as being logically unsound. As Braidwood (1967) has remarked, "There had also been three earlier periods of great alpine glaciers, and long periods of warm weather in between. Thus, the forced neighborliness of men, plants, and animals in river valleys and oases must also have happened earlier. Why didn't domestication happen earlier, then?"

Braidwood's Nuclear Zone Theory

Braidwood believes that when people had acquired an in-depth knowledge of the environment they lived in, they were ready to begin food production. They were culturally receptive to domestication. The other prerequisite for food production was an area rich in animals and plants that could be domesticated. In such an area, called a *nuclear zone*, people worked out the techniques of domestication. Braidwood identified several possible nuclear zones in the hills of the Near East. Knowledge of agriculture later spread from these zones to surrounding areas.

Unlike Childe, Braidwood does not explain agriculture as a new adaptation in the face of environmental pressures. Instead, Braidwood believes that the ability to experiment with and manipulate the environment has long been part of human nature. These abilities were gradually being improved in the course of human evolution, and only the right envi-

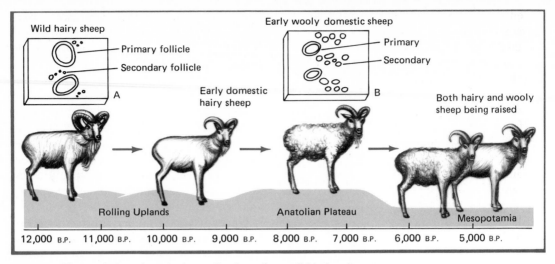

Figure 3 **The evolution of wooly domestic sheep from wild hairy sheep.**
(A) is a section of the skin of a wild sheep, as seen through a microscope,
showing the pattern of primary (hair) and secondary (wool) follicles. *(B)*
shows a magnified section of the skin of a wool-bearing domestic sheep.
Note that there are many more secondaries and that they form clusters
away from the primaries. (Adapted from Flannery, 1965)

ronment, that of a nuclear zone, was needed to stimulate agriculture. As Braidwood admits, however, it is very difficult to see the archaeological traces of an "atmosphere of experimentation" (Braidwood, 1967).

Braidwood's hypothesis has been attacked because it does not explain enough. He implies that the various events of cultural evolution were the natural expression of emerging human traits. The evolution of human qualities controlled the sequence of culture history. To explain why agriculture had not occurred in between periods of glaciation in the Pleistocene, he said that "culture was not ready to achieve it" (Braidwood & Willey, 1962). Thus the reason that agriculture developed is that culture was ready for it to develop. But, as archaeologist Lewis Binford has pointed out, "Trends which are observed in cultural evolution require explanation; they are certainly not explained by postulating emergent human traits which are said to account for the trends" (Binford, 1968).

Population Models

Over the past 20 years, several theorists have suggested that population growth beyond the land's ability to support the human biomass is responsible for the development and spread of agriculture. In other words, when there were not enough preferred foods, people were forced to experiment with and eat secondary (and probably less desirable) foods.

Archaeologists disagree as to the most likely source of disruption of preagricultural human ecosystems. Some think that environmental changes reduced food supplies, while others believe that an increase in human populations came first.

Lewis Binford has suggested that the balance between the food resources of the land and the needs of a given population can only be disturbed by a change in the environment. He argues that long before people in a group whose numbers were expanding would have allowed themselves to starve for lack of food, certain cultural restraints would have been placed on fertility. The killing of infants, abortion, and taboos on intercourse during lactation have all been used by twentieth-century hunter-gatherers as a brake on population growth.

If preagricultural groups did limit population growth to numbers below the carrying capacity of the environment, then outside conditions that could have led to food production are of two kinds: (1) a change in the physical environment that reduced the available food; and (2) an increase in population density beyond the environment's carrying capacity, as a result of immigration. The first condition is essentially Childe's oasis theory, with which Binford disagrees (Binford, 1968). In favoring the second option, Binford suggests that people from relatively sedentary, heavily populated areas in which fish and shellfish were very plentiful migrated to less favored inland areas already populated by more mobile groups. In this "tension zone," the balance would have been upset, and people would have had to use new methods of getting food, such as agriculture (Binford, 1968).

There are two main problems with Binford's theory: First, it is too specific in requiring sedentary forager-fishing villages as the "donor groups." Secondly, by specifying that the source of imbalance must be population pressure caused only by immigration, it seems too restrictive.

Another group of theorists believes that human populations naturally increase to the limit of the ability of the environment to support them. William Sanders and Barbara Price (1968), for example, suggest that in the Tehuacán Valley of Mexico, *geographical circumscription*—the condition occurring when a population is surrounded by physical features of the land that make emigration difficult—may have led to food production. High mountain walls and tropical jungles block the exit of the valley into the coastal plain. The growing population in the valley turned to farming to increase the food supply because the excess population could not leave (Sanders & Price, 1968).

Esther Boserup (1965) has suggested that on a worldwide basis, human populations have grown steadily, and that growth has forced changes in technology and subsistence—in particular, the development of agriculture. Anthropologist Mark Cohen (1972) offers detailed archaeological evidence from the Old World and North and South America to show that by the end of the Paleolithic, hunters and gatherers had spread to all parts of the world that could support them. In doing so they had expanded the number and variety of wild resources used for food in order to feed growing populations. As migration became more difficult, Paleolithic peoples had to gather a wider variety of less preferred foods.

In the period between 9,000 and 2,000 years ago, populations around the world were using nearly all the available edible foods. But their numbers continued to increase relentlessly. As a result, people were forced to increase the supply of those foods that could be domesticated. These were not necessarily the most tasty foods to be had. In fact, Cohen thinks that the earliest plants to be sown and harvested were generally undesirable foods. Hungry populations used them because other food sources were not enough (Cohen, 1977).

The Development of Agriculture

Argument continues on the question of why agriculture began. Most archaeologists would agree, however, that some combination of population pressure, ecological change, and population movement is responsible for its origin. In the next section we shall look at

Table 1 Selected Sequences at the Beginnings of Food Production

Years Ago	Near East	China	Tehuacán	Central Peru
3,000				Pottery enters region
			Purron Phase: Pottery	
4,000				Permanent agricultural villages
			Abejas Phase: Larger, more permanent settlements; agriculture firmly established	
5,000				Domestication of alpaca, llama, and many plants
			Coxcatlán Phase: Early cultivation of maize, beans, aramus, squash, and chili	
6,000		Cultivation of millet; domestication of pigs and dogs; small settlements		Early cultivation of quinoa and squash
7,000				
			El Riego Phase: Intensive plant gathering	
8,000	Ceramic Jarmo pottery	Intensive plant gathering		Seasonal pattern of intensive plant gathering
	Prepottery Neolithic B: domestication of plants and animals			
9,000				
10,000	Prepottery Neolithic A: early cultivation of barley and wheat; permanent settlements			
11,000	Natufian: intensive plant gathering; possible early herding			
12,000				

three areas in which the archaeological sequences are well worked out: the Near East, China, and Mesoamerica. To a significant degree, archaeologists working on the origins of food production in these areas have oriented their research to test different aspects of the preceding hypotheses. When it is appropriate, therefore, we shall point out data that support or refute the different theoretical models.

The Near East

We shall begin with the Near East, where agriculture first developed.

Environment. For the purposes of this discussion, we can limit the geographical extent of the Near East to modern-day Iran, Iraq, Turkey, Syria, Lebanon, Israel, and Jordan. Within this area, it is possible to distinguish several ecological zones, as shown in Figure 4:

1. The *Levant,* the narrow eastern and southern coasts of the Mediterranean, containing evergreens and plants adapted to this warm, temperate environment.
2. *Mesopotamian alluvium,* the swamps, desert, and desert-steppe surrounding the Tigris-Euphrates river systems, much of which is unsuitable for agriculture.
3. *High mountains and the Iranian plateau,* the high Zagros mountains, too rugged for normal farming; and, to the north and east, the central plateau of Iran, a desert basin.
4. Foothills and valleys in between mountains, *the oak and pistachio woodland belt* of foothills and valleys that flank the Zagros mountains to the southwest. In this zone, with its ample streams, rivers, and rainfall, were present all plants and animals that could be domesticated, such as wild emmer wheat, barley, oats, and wild sheep, goats, pigs, cattle, and horses.
5. *Steppe-piedmont,* rolling hills and natural winter grasslands that lie between the Zagros foothills and the Mesopotamian alluvium. This zone includes wide, farmable floodplains and pastures that could have supported wild or domesticated herds (Flannery, 1965; Braidwood et al., 1960).

The Developmental Sequence. In the Near East, there were both wild plants (emmer wheat and barley) and herd animals (sheep and goats) that could be domesticated. Near Eastern Mesolithic populations migrated from area to area as resources became available seasonally. As a result, they could make use of food resources of different habitats. Compared to the Paleolithic big-game hunters,

Figure 4 **Map of the Near East, showing the environmental zones mentioned in the text.** (Flannery, 1965)

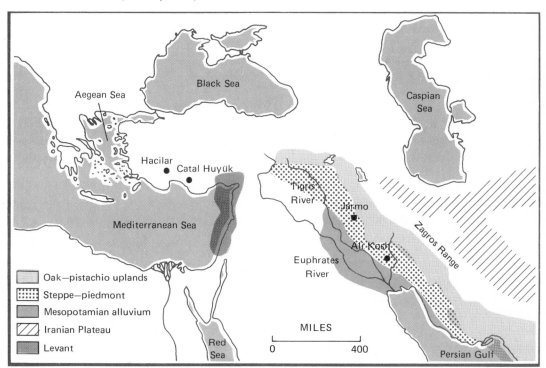

Near Eastern Mesolithic populations depended on smaller animals and more plants. These adaptations occurred at the same time as increasing population densities, a tendency to settle in one place, and, finally, about 9,000 years ago, the development of agriculture (Cohen, 1977).

Domesticated plants and animals did not develop at the same time in each of the Near East's major geographic zones. The earliest evidence of changing patterns comes from the Levant and from the Zagros highlands. As early as 13,000 years ago, populations seem to have been concentrating on a few animal resources. Wild goats and gazelles seem particularly favored at sites associated with the *Kebaran* culture in the Levant; wild cattle, goats, and sheep are associated with the *Zarzian* culture in the Zagros highlands. It is possible that this reflects a subtle shift toward herding—perhaps to ensure a constant source of food for a growing population. People still lived in caves or in open-air camps, with no sign of permanence (Mellaart, 1975).

The Natufian Culture (12,000–10,000 Years B.P.). About 12,000 years ago in the Levant, the Kebaran culture gradually gave rise to the *Natufian* culture. The Natufians seem to have preferred to live in the belt of oak and pistachio forests that was bordered by the Mediterranean coast to the west and the desert to the east. This area of coastal foothills had more water than it does today and supported stands of wild emmer wheat and barley. As during the Kebaran culture, there is some evidence that herds were being kept (Mellaart, 1975). Natufian sites show a high proportion of bones from immature gazelle and goats. This is a sign that Natufians slaughtered young animals for food, while keeping the adults for breeding (Clark, 1977).

The Natufians seem to have lived in large settlements on cave terraces, near springs, or alongside lakes and rivers. Although there is evidence of growing *sedentism,* or settling in villages, archaeologists disagree about the extent to which this was happening. Clark (1977) regards their sites as base camps from which the Natufians migrated to follow seasonally available animal and plant resources. Perkins and Daly (1974), however, argue that the Natufians lived in permanent villages, with large populations supported by much wild grain and other crops.

Whoever is correct, the archaeological evidence makes it clear that the Natufians did harvest and grind grains, possibly wild barley and wheat. The many reaping-knife handles made of bone and antler, and flint sickle-blades showing the sheen that comes from cutting stalks, indicate that cereal grasses were harvested. Stone mortars and pestles were used to grind these and possibly other plant foods. Other stone tools included many microliths, burins, borers, and scrapers. Antler and bone fishhooks suggest that the Natufians also fished (Clark, 1977).

Pre-pottery Neolithic A and B (10,000–8,000 Years B.P.*).* Between about 10,300 and 10,000 years ago in the Levant, experiments with plant domestication led to the first farming communities (Mellaart, 1975). Excavation of a number of Near Eastern sites shows that during the next 2,000 years humans came to depend almost entirely on domesticated plants as well as animals. By about 8,000 years ago, for example, the farming village of Jarmo depended on domestic sheep and goats for 95 percent of its meat.

Because it is used to prepare and store food, pottery generally appears in the same strata as the first signs of agriculture. In the Near East, however, early domestication of wild plants and animals occurred for at least 2,000 years before the appearance of pottery. Archaeologists break up this span into the pre-pottery Neolithic A and B.

Pre-pottery Neolithic peoples manufactured a large number of stone tools, especially of flint and obsidian. These included microliths and flaked and side-notched points. Barbed spearheads and projectiles tipped and

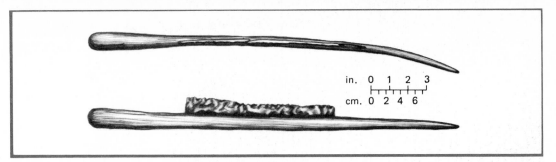

Figure 5 Mesolithic sickle made by fitting flint blades into a wooden haft. Sickles such as this were used by Natufian people to harvest stands of wild grain. (Cole, 1965; reprinted by permission of the trustees of the British Museum of Natural History)

barbed with microliths were used for hunting.

Domesticated emmer wheat and barley appeared in the pre-pottery Neolithic A level of Jericho, and during the B period domesticated einkorn wheat and legumes such as lentils, peas, and horse beans were added. In Syria and Turkey the earliest evidence for farming villages occurs at dates contemporary with pre-pottery Neolithic B in the Levant (Mellaart, 1975). Here and in the Zagros mountains, people began to grow many of the same crops at about the same time.

Fully Developed Village Farming. Beginning at about 8,000 years B.P., there were fully developed farming villages and small towns in the Near East. Most of these permanent communities held several hundred peasants, a considerable increase over the approximately two dozen households that normally made up pre-pottery Neolithic settlements. The relative uniformity of house size, construction, and layout show an absence of social hierarchies, although there may have been some specialized crafts. In general, houses had a main living space with sitting and sleeping benches, a fireplace, a corner or wall oven, a nearby mortar, and several small storage areas. Buildings were usually one story, although two-story kilns were used to fire the high-quality pottery that came out of this region. Passages, yards, and courtyards separated houses, but with the later building and

rebuilding that occurred in these villages, such spaces tended to fill up.

The outstanding addition of this period to the Neolithic tool kit was pottery. The people of the pre-pottery Neolithic period had used clay in ritual cults to make figurines, and to coat skulls that were buried separately from bodies. But they did not use clay to take the place of their stone, wooden, and woven vessels. The appearance of pottery probably is linked to a fully sedentary lifestyle. Pottery is well suited to the storage and preparation of grains and vegetable foods. However, pottery is fragile, and thus is liable to break if moved from place to place. It is not surprising, then, that it first developed in various areas of the Near East, usually by 8,000 years B.P., when fully developed village farming arose.

Pottery is an especially useful clue for archaeologists, since they can trace the spread and sometimes origins of various cultures by the styles of pottery manufacture and especially decoration. The earliest Near Eastern pottery was both plain and decorated, and found at such sites as Jericho in the Levant, Çatal Hüyük and Mersin in southwest Turkey, Jarmo in the foothill zone, and Hassuna in the steppe-piedmont zone. The earliest pottery included dishes, bowls, flasks, and some vessels with bucketlike handles (Clark, 1977).

In this period there was less and less hunting as domesticated animals made more populations self-sufficient (Perkins & Daly, 1974). Some sites, such as Erbaba in Turkey, show a complete absence of hunted animals such as pig or red deer. But at other sites, such as Djeitun in the U.S.S.R., north of Iran, antelope and goat were still an important part of the diet (Clark, 1977). In areas with enough rainfall, such as northern Mesopotamia, grains were cultivated without irrigation. Primitive irrigation was used near the Zagros foothills, and, in the Sumerian south, elaborate irrigation projects were undertaken.

China

Archaeologists know much less about how agriculture began in China. Although it evolved about 2,000 years later in China (around 7,000 years B.P.) than in the Near East, archaeologists believe that it was an independent development. The idea of domestication probably was not imported from elsewhere.

Paleolithic people to the north in Siberia had hunted the mammoth, bison, rhinoceros, and other big-game animals common in the Pleistocene. By about 12,500 years B.P., however, much of the big game had become extinct, and human populations had begun to move south from the *steppes* (vast, level, treeless plains) into the *taiga* (a forest region dominated by spruce and fir). Here they made use of a wide variety of food resources. Mesolithic people of China relied on fishing and the hunting of single forest animals. Vegetable foods also became important, and after about 7,000 years B.P. permanent settlements appeared, often near streams and bays. Tools from this preagricultural period include grindstones for vegetable foods, fishing equipment, and stone spades (Cohen, 1977; Clark, 1977).

The Yang-Shao Culture. The earliest Chinese farming took place on the fertile loess soil

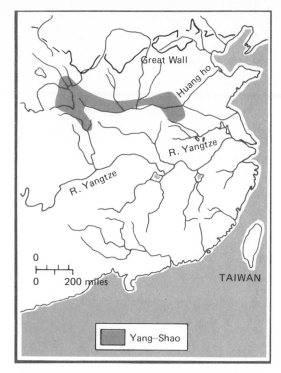

Figure 6   The distribution of the Yang-shao, the first food-producing culture of China. It arose in the valley of the Wei and Huang-ho Rivers. (Clark, 1977)

along the Yellow (or Huang Ho) River in the Chung-yuan region of north-central China. (See Figure 6.) By about 6,000 years B.P., peasants of the Yang-shao culture were raising millet (a hardy, drought-resistant cereal grain) and brown corn. Rice was first domesticated in Thailand, and was not grown in China until several hundred years later—about 5,000 years ago. Archaeologists believe that the Yang-shao farmers engaged in slash-and-burn agriculture—a type of shifting agriculture involving the periodic clearing and burning of forest land to create new fields. Thus the terrain, the crops grown, and the agricultural techniques that arose in China were quite different from those in the Near East. However, like the Near Eastern agriculturalists, the Yang-shao peasants also kept dogs, hunted wild cattle, horse, deer, and other animals, fished, and collected wild seeds and plants. Later Farmers also raised cattle, sheep, horses, and water buffalo (Clark, 1977).

Yang-shao villages consisted of some 50 round or rectangular dwellings. Often built partly underground, these shelters had wattle-and-daub (woven twigs and plaster) walls, thatched, slanted roofs, stamped-earth or plastered floors, and hearths. As in the early Near Eastern Neolithic settlements, no sign of social hierarchy is evident from these structures. Yang-shao villages also lacked elaborate defensive works, suggesting that important village differences in wealth did not exist (Clark, 1977).

There is evidence from at least one site that pottery may have occurred before agriculture among settled hunting-and-fishing populations. By Neolithic times Chinese pottery was already impressive. The Yang-shao peasants made ceramic bowls, dishes, jars, and other vessels, and probably used them for cooking, serving, and storage. Yang-shao peasants also engaged in weaving, basketry, leather-work, and carpentry. Stone was worked into axes and adzes for cutting and shaping wood, and projectile heads and knives, especially reaping blades, were made of polished stone. Fish-hooks, arrowheads, and a variety of craft tools were fashioned out of bone (Clark, 1977).

Mesoamerica

Domestication of plants and animals also arose independently in Mesoamerica—central and southern Mexico and the northern part of Central America. As in China, it occurred at least 2,000 years later than in the Near East. Domestication did not begin with one population in one area. Instead, it first appeared separately at various times and places in Mesoamerica.

As in the Old World, New World peoples domesticated local wild plants and animals. These were different from Old World types

and included corn, squash, peanuts, potatoes, chili peppers, and kidney beans. In all, as many as 150 different kinds of plants may have been cultivated. Also unlike the Old World, the New World had far fewer animals that could be domesticated. Consequently, animals were much less important to farming in the New World. Only the Andean populations, which raised llamas and alpacas, made heavy use of animals. Four other species of animals were domesticated in the New World—dogs, turkeys, guinea pigs, and ducks.

The Tehuacán Valley. Among the most important regions for early agriculture were the central highlands of Mexico. The Tehuacán Valley, located about 150 miles southeast of Mexico City, has provided vital data about the beginnings of agriculture in the highlands. Here archaeologists have painstakingly reconstructed the sequence of events leading to the development of agriculture and have provided detailed information about its origins.

The valley itself, at an elevation of about 6,000 feet above sea level, is surrounded by mountains rising about 5,000 feet above the valley floor. These peaks block precipitation and restrict annual rainfall to about 20 inches. The valley is not only dry but also quite warm, with temperatures ranging from 55° to 92°F. The floor of the valley is semiarid and spotted with scrub and cactus (Willey, 1966). Once it contained a mesquite grassland inhabited by deer, jackrabbits, gophers, and quail. Along the edge of the valley, small side canyons extend in among the mountains. Here deer lived and wild avocados and maguey (a fleshy, spiny-leafed plant) flourished.

Archaeologists have been able to trace a sequence of continuous habitation in the Tehuacán Valley, from a Paleo-Indian hunting-and-gathering culture to full-fledged settled villages and ceremonial centers supported by irrigation agriculture. As in the Near East, agriculture developed very gradually in Mesoamerica. Archaeologist Richard MacNeish (1964) has described nine phases in the Tehuacán Valley sequence.

Ajuereado Phase (12,700–9,200 Years B.P.*).* During this time, wandering bands of no more than four to eight persons lived a hunting-and-gathering life. Hunters, trappers, and food gatherers moved from place to place, as resources in different parts of the valley became available. They hunted big game such as antelopes and horses, as well as rodents, turtles, and birds. Wild plants were a smaller part of their diet. Tools included leaf-shaped flint knives and projectile points, choppers, and scrapers. Life must have been difficult, for these valley dwellers had fairly few resources on which to draw in the hot, dry environment.

El Reigo Phase (9,200–7,200 Years B.P.*).* The population of the valley grew slightly larger, and there was a greater emphasis on collecting wild seed plants than there had been in the earlier phase. The culture at this time has been likened to the desert culture tradition of the American Southwest. Various wild plants were available only in certain seasons, which determined the activities of the *tehuacanos,* the inhabitants of the valley. During the dry winter months (from October to March) small bands hunted game animals, which gathered around the springs and streams that did not dry up. These bands also trapped smaller animals and collected maguey leaves and roots from certain other plants. Plants were scarce during this time of the year. As a result, deer and peccary, a nocturnal animal related to and resembling the pig, made up about 75 percent of the total food eaten at this season.

During the rainy season, from mid-March through mid-September, the *tehuacanos* gathered in larger groups and harvested various plants as they ripened. Prickly pears were gathered first, then wild grasses and mesquite, and toward the end of the rainy season wild fruits could be picked. Wild varieties of squash, chili, and avocados were collected as well. Plant foods probably made up about 65 percent of the diet during this season.

The *tehuacanos* of this period used pestles and mortars to grind seeds. They also fashioned wood and wove baskets and blankets. Scrapers and choppers were used to work skins and to process vegetable foods.

Coxcatlán Phase (7,200–5,400 Years B.P.*).* It is from this phase that we have the earliest clear evidence of agriculture. In the past only 10 to 20 people had lived in the valley; during this time the population increased tenfold. Domesticated plants took on a minor but important role in meeting the added need for food.

In an excavation of a cave located in the valley wall, Richard MacNeish uncovered the oldest maize cobs, the forerunner to modern strains of corn, known anywhere in the world. The ears are tiny and podlike, looking vastly different from the foot-long cobs of today's hybrid corn. The cobs have been dated to about 7,000 years B.P., a date that strongly suggests that the maize plant was first domesticated in Southern Mexico (Willey, 1966). The Coxcatlán cobs are thought to represent the very earliest stages of domestication of this species.

There is also evidence that chili peppers, squash, beans, and gourds were being planted at this time. The canyons opening on the valley were favored planting grounds. Later wild fruit trees, such as avocados, were planted around springs and along the banks of streams and rivers. The first trees and maize planted in the valley were probably native to the area. Later arrivals such as gourds and squash, however, were imported from neighboring areas (Patterson, 1973).

The shift from hunting and gathering to agriculture involved a fundamental change in the way the *tehuacanos* saw their environment. Before, they had thought about the land in terms of the kinds of plants they could find there. Now, however, they evaluated the land in terms of its ability to support the various

Corn as we know it today evolved from the tiny maize cob at the left. This cob, the earliest known domesticated maize, was uncovered in Coxcatlan Cave of the Tehuacán Valley in a layer dating from 7,000 years ago. Selective breeding over the course of about 4,000 years increased the number and size of cobs on a plant and resulted in more fragile husks. (Courtesy of Paul Mandgelsdorf & R. S. MacNeish)

with larger cobs. Pumpkins, beans, cotton, and dogs were domesticated for the first time, as well.

Purron (4,300–3,500 Years B.P.*) and Ajalpan (3,500–1,100 Years* B.P.*) phases.* Agriculture increasingly became a fulltime job carried out by the people living in settled villages during this time. The appearance of the earliest-known pottery in Mesoamerica dates from the Purron; it made possible long-term storage of vegetable foods. During the Ajalpan, settled villages of 100 to 300 grew hybrid corn, various squashes, gourds, amaranths, beans, chili peppers, avocados, and cotton.

These crops were planted during the spring and the early summer, and harvested in the fall. In autumn, however, the *tehuacanos* ate the newly ripened fruit, thus saving their crop plants for the dry season in the late fall and winter. Eventually, they became good enough farmers to supply themselves with adequate food to last year round (Patterson, 1973). More productive strains allowed more people to settle permanently in small villages.

During the next three phases, the population of the valley increased dramatically. Irrigation enlarged the land area on which crops could be farmed, and, by the later phases, commerce with other areas supplemented the domestically produced food supply. Villages with temples expanded into citylike ceremonial centers, dominated by monumental architecture. At this time sedentism and almost total dependence on agriculture had long been established.

plants they could transport and farm there (Patterson, 1973).

Agriculture also brought with it a tendency for people to remain in one camp for a longer period of time. Although the valley dwellers still followed their ancient pattern of wandering with the seasons in search of food, their groups were becoming larger and their base camps more permanent.

Abejas Phase (5,400–4,300 Years B.P.*).* The trend toward sedentism continued during this phase. Less dependence on hunting and gathering was made possible by genetic changes in maize and other crops that resulted in a higher yield. Maize was crossed with a variety of wild grass to produce a hybrid corn

The Spread of Agriculture

Some ecosystems cannot easily maintain the sort of changes required by agriculture or herding. As mentioned earlier, it is a myth

that simple farming is necessarily more productive than hunting and gathering for any
given population. Had certain Indian groups
in central California adopted agriculture, they
would have had less—not more—food to eat.
Small wonder, then, that they resisted its introduction (Patterson, 1973).

Today, of course, sophisticated irrigation
networks and refined fossil fuels used for
tractors have made the central valley of California one of the most productive agricultural
areas in the world. Without this technology,
the soil would be easily depleted, and crops
would soon die in the semiarid environment.

In some areas, so much food grows wild
that food production is simply unnecessary.
People tend to choose the economic strategy
that is most effective in their area.

There is good reason to believe that population pressure led to the widespread diffusion
and acceptance of agriculture practically
throughout the world, and in a relatively short
period of time. According to Mark Cohen
(1977), populations at the end of the last
glaciation throughout the world had become
as large as the resources of their ecosystems
would allow. In his view, population growth,
which first resulted in territorial expansion
and the entering of untapped areas, gradually
made farming necessary when there were no
more virgin areas to which to migrate (Cohen,
1977). In this section we shall look at how
agricultural know-how was spread throughout
Europe, Africa, and coastal Peru.

Europe

Agriculture probably was brought to
Europe from the Near East. Many of the
plants and animals that were eventually
domesticated were introduced from Asia. And
not only did the earliest farmers use reaping
and milling tools similar to those that were
used in the Near East, but they also raised

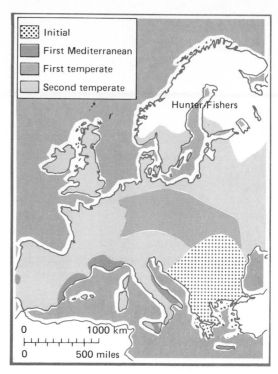

Figure 7 **The four stages of the spread of
agriculture in Europe.** (Clark, 1977)

livestock that had no wild ancestor in the
region (Clark, 1977).

The most important route for the spread of
agricultural ideas was by way of Greece into
central, south, southeastern, and northern
Europe. No doubt sailors and traders who
came to Europe by way of the Mediterranean
also helped spread seeds and the techniques of
agriculture. Greece and the south Balkans
were farmed first, about 8,000 to 7,000 years
ago. They are the closest to the Near East, and
because climate and soil there were most similar to those of the Near East, it was easier for
the imported plants and animals to survive
(Clark, 1977).

During this first phase in the spread of
farming across the continent, peasants lived
year-round in settlements consisting of a small
cluster of shelters made with sun-dried mud.

They grew barley, lentils, beans, and several kinds of wheat. They also raised sheep, goats, and pigs. These early peasants made pots, baskets, polished stone axes, and adze blades for felling timber and woodworking. They reaped crops using knives of chert, a flintlike mineral, and obsidian blades set in antler or wood handles. This way of life continued for 2,000 to 3,000 years without any major changes. The population and settlement density grew steadily, and farming gradually spread into nearby areas (Clark, 1977).

Between 7,000 and 6,000 years ago, European agriculture expanded beyond its early zone into several areas along the Mediterranean coast and into Central Europe as far west as France and as far east as southwest Russia (see Figure 7). In this temperate area, the peasants practiced slash-and-burn agriculture. After harvesting crops for a few years, the clearings lost their fertility and the small villages were temporarily abandoned, to be reoccupied some years later. Centuries of this activity were probably the major force responsible for the reduction of the forests that once covered most of Europe.

Between about 6,000 to 5,000 years ago, a second phase of expansion spread agriculture throughout the rest of Europe's temperate zone. However, the inhabitants in the North, beyond the deciduous forest, kept a hunting, fishing, and foraging economy. In Western Europe, the earlier Mediterranean settlement seems to have expanded into Spain, France, part of Switzerland, and the British Isles. In these areas, peasants grew wheat and barley and raised cattle and pigs. In south Britain, a crude plough was used to till the soil. Hunting became fairly unimportant except in rugged Alpine areas (Clark, 1977).

Farther east, in the south Balkans and central Europe, the peasants developed a copper industry. In south Russia, the use of wheels on ox-drawn carts and wagons eased the burden of peasant transportation, and between 5,000

to 4,000 years B.P. such vehicles spread to northern and western Europe. Later, the domestication of the horse in south Russia made it an important military tool (Clark, 1977).

In northern Europe hunting, fishing, and gathering remained the basic economy. Because the climate north of the deciduous forest did not favor agriculture, hunting, fishing, and gathering remained the basic source of food (Clark, 1977).

Africa

Knowledge of agriculture in Africa is limited by a lack of research and, because of climatic conditions, poor preservation of archaeological clues. Consequently, firm evidence is lacking as to whether agriculture arose there independently or spread southward along the Nile from the Near East. The earliest reliable evidence of domestication in Africa is in the Fayum Oasis in Egypt, where grains of emmer wheat, barley, and flax were preserved from about 6,500 years B.P.

The earliest certain evidence of African agriculture outside Egypt is from Dhartichitt in Mauritania. There, due to a drying trend, hunting and fishing became impossible. As a result a farming economy grew up within a few hundred years around 3,000 years B.P. The lateness and speed with which the grains raised there took hold point to the introduction of a grain that had been previously domesticated elsewhere (Cohen, 1977).

A number of African food crops may have been domesticated independently at several places in the zone south of the Sahara and north of the Equator. These crops include African rice, millet, yams, and watermelon. This domestication might have resulted from high population densities and the southward expansion of the Sahara Desert. Displaced peoples may have placed pressure on the carrying capacity of the savanna south of the desert. Domestication may have been the solution to this problem (Cohen, 1977).

Other archaeological evidence of domestication in Africa south of the Sahara, especially in West Africa and eastern and southeastern Africa, is relatively late—sometime around 1,500 years B.P. Crops included several types of wheat, melons, legumes, and cowpeas. It is thought that the spread of agriculture south of the Equator occurred with the movement of iron-using, Bantu-speaking peoples (Cohen, 1977). Possible reasons for the late occurrence of Neolithic technology in West Africa include: (1) lack of incentive due to an environment rich in meat and plant food; and (2) ecological obstacles, such as a heavy tropical summer rainfall unsuited to the crops grown in Egypt and North Africa. A long period of experimentation was needed to transform local wild varieities into crop plants (Clark, 1970).

Coastal Peru

In South America, food production arose independently in Peru and diffused gradually into neighboring areas. The first clear evidence of the domestication of plants dates from between 7,500 and 6,200 years ago in the Ayachucho region of Central Peru. Here, the seeds of domesticated quinoa (an Andean grain) and squash have been uncovered. By 4,500 years ago, the list of domesticates had expanded to include potatoes, corn, gourds, common beans, and perhaps cocoa. All except corn appear to have been domesticated indigenously (MacNeish, Patterson & Browman, 1975). About the same time crop plants appeared, tamed llamas and probably alpacas seem to have existed in the Huancayo region of Central Peru, which, like Ayachucho, is an area of mid-altitude. One region to which the idea of food production diffused was the Ancón-Chillón area of the desert coast of Peru.

The Consequences of Agriculture

Within a few thousand years after people first began to raise animals and crops, agriculture had set in motion a series of events that completely changed human culture and altered the natural environment. Much of this transformation can be traced to one fact: Agriculture supplied enough food to make it possible for larger groups of people to live in smaller areas. A hunting-and-gathering way of life had usually meant moving in small groups with the seasons in search of food. But when people evolved to a more settled existence in villages, more complex governments were required for social control. Trade and conflict grew, health worsened, and new technologies were invented.

Demographic Effects

During the Mesolithic Age, most environments could support only small groups of people. It is true that some environments rich in resources have fed hunting-and-gathering settlements with large populations. The best-known examples are the large communities of the American Northwest coast, which thrived on fish and shellfish. But the carrying capacity of most environments kept human groups small. The population of the entire Tehuacán Valley before about 9,000 years ago, for instance, is thought to have been no more than 12 to 24 people (MacNeish, 1964). Twelve thousand years ago, the world population was perhaps 5 to 10 million. When seen against the background of the gradual increase throughout the 2 million years of the Pleistocene, the last 12,000 years represent a population explosion.

Agriculture led not only to population

growth but also, far more importantly, to increased population density. Hunter-gatherers generally needed a large range in which to draw on a variety of foods. Agriculture concentrated the food in nearby fields in the form of crop plants that were much more productive than wild varieties. This allowed settlements to become larger and closer together.

The adoption of agriculture not only raised the ceiling on population size, but also may have reduced the death rate among infants and the elderly. Soft foods such as animal milk and cereal mush added to the possible diet of the toothless. There is not, however, any firm evidence that life expectancies improved during the Neolithic. Men lived an average of 31 to 34 years, and women lived an average of 28 to 31 years (Smith, 1972).

Changes in Social Organization

The advantage of being able to store surplus food tended to lead, according to some theorists, to increasing inequality in agricultural societies. In early agricultural groups there was a change in the way food was gotten and surplus food redistributed among the members of the group. Hunter-gatherers tend to have less complex political systems—members of the group have more equal access to available material and social rewards (Harner, 1970). Among hunter-gatherers food sharing is based on kinship. But in agricultural groups some people, perhaps on the basis of their age or position within the kin group, began to take charge of food distribution. The more productive the society, the more complex the redistribution system, and the more control the leader(s) attained. As populations grew, the leadership, because of prestige and power associated with the role, became more powerful. The position also became institutionalized—that is, the leader became dependent for power not on personal traits, but on custom and the office itself.

With agriculture came not only more complex governments and economies, and greater differences in power within a society, but also a change in the division of labor. In hunting-and-gathering societies sex, age, and natural ability were probably the only factors affecting how work was divided. In larger groups, however, other factors, such as inherited status, began to play a role. Some people in farming groups spent part of their time at crafts such as pottery making or woodworking. In more complex societies the most skilled workers became full-time specialists.

Agriculture ultimately influenced the role of the sexes in society, as well. At first the division of labor by sex was probably not much affected. Men continued to perform the most strenuous tasks such as hunting and adopted forest clearing, herding, and plowing. The women probably added weeding, harvesting, and food preparation to the task of plant collecting (Smith, 1972). But as population pressures increased the need for more intensive cultivation, the role of women in agriculture decreased. With it, status may have fallen as well. The status of women tends to be high when they do most of the agricultural work, as among the Iroquois Indians of the American Northeast before the European invasion. Where women are less active, they are valued as mothers only (Smith, 1972). One study (Sanday, 1974) suggests that when women's contribution to subsistence is about equal to that of men, their status is highest.

Conflict and Trade

As population densities increased, and people began to produce more food and goods, war and trade among different groups became more common. Although there was almost certainly conflict in prefarming days, groups were too spread out for the violence to become systematized warfare. But the massive walls of Jericho, probably built soon after it became a farming settlement, and the cliff dwellings in the American Southwest show how much early farmers felt they needed to be defended. For warriors, the incentives to launch raids were greater than ever before. The spoils of war took the form of food, slaves, animals, and resources such as mines and irrigated land (Smith, 1972).

As the demand for the products of farming communities increased, so did peaceful means of obtaining them. Trade became more elaborate and, for the first time, institutionalized. Markets were set up, and middlemen, who sold the goods carried by others, appeared on the scene. It was not long before flint, amber, obsidian, food, and manufactured goods such as pottery were traded between regions and communities (Smith, 1972).

War and trade both helped bring about radical changes in the distribution of the physical traits of the world's populations. More contact between people increased gene flow and began to break down group differences. The trend heightened as food producers grew in number and expanded their territory, displacing or intermingling with other cultures.

Inventions and New Technologies

Continual population pressure resulting from the production of more and more food provided an incentive to find still more efficient ways of using the land and other resources. News of discoveries and breakthroughs spread relatively quickly because of the increased travel of this time due to trade and war. As a result, the rate of innovation rose dramatically (Smith, 1972).

Inventions of the age include the wheel and sails, both of which were present by at least 5,300 years B.P. in Mesopotamia. Animals were harnessed for transportation and for plowing the fields. And pottery allowed long-term storage of some foods. It also expanded the variety of foods that could be eaten, since they could now be prepared and cooked in a number of new ways.

Numerous new technologies were developed at this time, as well. Irrigation greatly improved crop yields. In canal irrigation, channels several feet deep brought water from rivers to the field. In pot irrigation, pots were used to draw water from shallow wells for use in watering the crops.

In some regions, new, heavy cutting and chopping tools such as axes, adzes, hoes, and other tools used in felling trees and tilling the soil were developed. And just about everywhere, new ways of changing the properties of natural substances were found. Kilns transformed clay into wear-resistant pottery. Metals were produced after the basics of smelting were learned. And people discovered how to change fruit and grain into delightful drinks by allowing the raw materials to ferment.

All of these inventions and technologies, except possibly the last, contributed to an enormous increase in the efficiency with which humans could change their environment to support themselves. As this ability increased, so did population, thus redoubling the pressure to invent and to discover.

Summary

1. The *Mesolithic Age* coincided with the warming trend and the extinction of herds of large game animals following the retreat of the last glaciation of the Pleistocene Epoch. The period is distinguishable in Europe, the Near East, and North America. Smaller game animals were hunted with small blades called *microliths*. The relative scarcity of food caused Mesolithic people to exploit a greater variety of food resources.

2. The *Neolithic Age* is marked by a change

from a hunting-and-gathering economy and a technology dominated by flaked-stone tools to an economy based on farming and new technologies, such as polished stone tools, pottery, and weaving.

3. In *domestication,* humans, acting as a selective force, brought about evolutionary change in the frequency of traits of plant and animal populations. Domestication not only made plants and animals more productive sources of food, but also made them dependent on humans for their existence.

4. Kent Flannery has proposed three obstacles to the domestication of grain: (1) the brittle *rachis* of some grains broke easily under the impact of the sickle, scattering the grain and making it hard to harvest; (2) wild grains had tough husks, or *glumes,* which encased the edible kernels; (3) wild grain grew in difficult-to-harvest patches scattered on hillsides. These obstacles were overcome in the Near East when early farmers deliberately began to sow plants with a tough rachis, developed "naked kernel" hybrids, and planted mutant six-row barley in lowland fields.

5. The primary obstacle to the domestication of animals was the aggressiveness of the wild forms and the ease with which they could escape. By breeding less aggressive animals, herders reduced the number of unmanageable animals in their flocks and herds. Other changes resulting from domestication were the rise in frequency of wooly-haired sheep and goats and of goats with twisted horns.

6. The major theories explaining the origins of farming covered in the text are *Childe's oasis model, Braidwood's nuclear zone model,* and various *population models.*

7. V. Gordon Childe proposed in his oasis model that a drying trend in Mesopotamia during the Mesolithic turned grasslands into deserts dotted with oases. Humans were forced to domesticate the animals and plants concentrated in the oasis, since killing them would have eliminated all sources of food.

Archaeological data have discredited this theory.

8. According to Braidwood's nuclear zone theory, the human ability to experiment with and manipulate the environment had by the Neolithic advanced to the point that, given a zone rich in domesticable species, humans would naturally begin to produce food. This theory has been attacked for its lack of explanatory power.

9. Various population models propose that an imbalance between population size and food resources provided the stimulus to produce food. Some experts feel that populations tend culturally to limit their numbers to a level beneath the carrying capacity of the environment. Lewis Binford, for example, argues that external factors such as a change in the physical environment or immigration create pressure for food production. Others, however, like Esther Boserup and Mark Cohen, argue the populations have tended to grow large enough to exceed the food supply, making farming necessary.

10. Archaeological sequences pertaining to the origins of food production are well worked out in the Near East, China, and Mesoamerica.

11. Food production first appeared in the *Near East* in the Levant between 10,300 and 10,000 years ago, although signs of herding predate this by at least 2,000 years.

12. In *China,* farming settlements began to appear by about 6,000 B.P., when people of the *Yang-shao* culture were planting millet and keeping pigs and dogs.

13. In *Mesoamerica,* native plants and a few animals were domesticated separately at different times and places. Natives of the Tehuacán Valley of central Mexico hunted and gathered in seasonal patterns until around 7,000 years B.P. Then, steady population growth may have forced the planting of *maize,* the ancestor of modern corn.

14. Persistent worldwide population growth among hunter-gatherers is the most

likely reason for the spread of agricultural techniques. Agriculture spread from the Near East throughout Europe in several stages. Farming did not reach parts of northern Europe until some 3,000 to 4,000 years B.P. By 6,500 years B.P., wheat, barley, and flax were being planted in North Africa, but southward diffusion was slow due to already plentiful food supplies and ecological obstacles. And in the Ancón-Chillón coastal area of Peru a rising population forced domestication of some plants by about 4,000 years B.P.

15. Agriculture transformed human life by allowing people to live permanently in much larger and more densely settled communities than ever before. Higher densities made necessary more complex forms of social control, and some groups gained greater access to wealth and prestige than others. Demand for the goods and food of settlements was satisfied peacefully by means of trade and violently in wars. Growing populations provided an incentive to use resources more efficiently. Inventions such as sails and the wheel, and technologies, including irrigation, pottery-making, metalworking, and brewing helped bring about more effective exploitation of resources.

12

The Emergence of Cities, States, and Civilizations

OR more than 99 percent of our history, humans have lived in simple egalitarian societies (societies whose members were nearly equal in prestige and access to resources). As the population of agricultural societies grew, increasingly complex political structures evolved to coordinate the activities of a larger number of people. The first societies in which some groups had more power than others appeared in the Near East about 5,500 years ago. In some parts of the world the change from a egalitarian social structure to more complex forms is still occurring, spurred by pressures from more advanced states.

Before we begin to explore where, how, and why complex societies emerged, we must define three basic terms: *city, state,* and *civilization.*

Some Definitions

The City

A *city* can be defined as a central place that performs economic and political functions for the surrounding area. The first cities probably developed around political bureaucracies that became the seat of political power in a region. When the bureaucracies began to attract people who performed special services for rulers and people who wanted to become part of the ruling structure, the first true cities probably were formed. The process by which cities are formed is called *urbanism*. As urbanism progresses, cities become composed of new people with more diverse talents and cultural backgrounds.

Not everyone, however, agrees to this reconstruction of how cities arose. Jane Jacobs (1970) holds that cities emerged before rural settlements, and that they in fact stimulated the development of agriculture. The first cities, she believes, were trading centers. The basic techniques of agriculture arose as city dwellers experimented with wild plants and animals brought in by traders in return for obsidian or other valuable items. The techniques that came out of such experimenting later diffused to nearby farming villages, which exchanged food for the goods of the city. Jacobs' theory is considerably weakened, however, by traces of agricultural activity that have been dated back to between 10,000 and 9,000 years B.P., well before the earliest cities.

The State

A *state* can be defined as an independent political unit that includes many communities in its territory, with a centralized government that has the power to collect taxes, draft citizens for work and for war, and enact and enforce laws (Carneiro, 1970). States are socially *stratified*—some groups of citizens have greater access either to wealth, status, or both than do other groups. States are also economically diversified, which means that only a part of the population produces food—other members may be artisans, traders, priests, rulers, or other specialists (Flannery, 1972). In early states, organized religion merged with the state and its leadership, making both objects of worship.

Civilizations

Civilization is the most difficult of the three concepts to define, partly because it is used in so many different ways. A precise definition has been offered by E. R. Service (1975): Civilization "can be accurately used to mean that the society was characterized by the presence of cities or large towns and that the inhabitants were citizens of some kind of legal commonwealth." But civilization carries with it many connotations other than that of cities of people bound together in a government based on laws. Some think of civilization as a flourishing of the arts. Others associate it with the development of philosophical concepts to a very high level. Others have identified writing as the distinguishing feature of civilization.

Perhaps the best-known list of criteria for civilization is that of V. Gordon Childe. It is presented here in Service's summary (1975):

1. Urban centers (of between 7,000 to 20,000 people)
2. A class of full-time specialists working in the cities
3. A ruling class of religious, civil, and military leaders
4. A surplus of food produced by the peasants for use by the government
5. Monumental public buildings, symbolizing the concentration of the surplus
6. Use of numbers and writing
7. Arithmetic, geometry, and astronomy
8. Sophisticated art
9. Long-distance trade
10. An institutionalized form of political organization based on force, called the *state*

Excavation has turned up evidence against Childe's list. Seldom have all of these traits appeared together in the earliest cultures that we think of as civilizations. It is often argued, for instance, that cities do not have to exist for there to be civilization. Most people would agree that the Maya were a civilization, in spite of the fact that cities did not exist. And while the Inca culture did display most of Childe's characteristics, there was no system of writing.

The term *civilization* has become more and more vague as it has been applied to societies that have different characteristics. Because *state* can be more clearly defined, we shall treat this concept as the center of our discussion. Nevertheless, *civilization* is often useful as a word meaning a society with sophisticated artistic, architectural, philosophical, economic, and political features.

The development of states and the emergence of cities are the main consideration of this chapter. We shall explore different types of political organization and then consider a number of theories of state formation. Finally, we shall present some of the archaeological data that are the basis of the definitions and theories we have presented.

From Bands to States

States did not spring fully formed from anarchy. Archaeologists have identified several stages through which human societies passed before states appeared. Our knowledge of these stages comes from the archaeological record and from observations of present-day societies. Unfortunately, in trying to distinguish the earliest states from less complex societies such as chiefdoms, we must arbitrarily break up what was a continuous process of evolution. But with this in mind, the contrasts between three different levels of pre-state social organization can be seen.

The Bands

Before about 12,000 years B.P., the basic unit of human social organization was a small, egalitarian society called a *band.* The only subunit of the band was the family, or a group of related families held together by kinship and marriage bonds. Leadership was informal, probably not resting for very long with any one person. The leader's power came from force of personality rather than from laws or traditions defining the role and naming the

person to assume it. Bands were and are the usual form of society among hunting-and-gathering people, who do not have a strong sense of territoriality (that is, the need to define and defend one's own land). Owning and defending land would not make sense for people who were often moving from one area to another.

The Tribes

About 9,000 years B.P., a slightly larger, more complicated form of social organization called the *tribe* can be inferred from the archaeological record in the Near East. It appeared in Peru about 5,000 years B.P., and in Mesoamerica by 3,300 years B.P., The *tribe* was larger than a band; it was made up of groups of families related by common descent or by membership in a variety of kinship-based groups such as clans or lineages (Flannery, 1972). The power of leaders was weak, with individual family heads being more important than any one leader. Kinship groups seem to have been bound together for different reasons in different cultures. Among primitive farmers, the kin group probably held land in common. Farming brought with it territoriality, since land was now an important resource. Lines of ancestral descent were becoming an important part of tribal life—evidence includes the skulls of many generations found buried under the floors of their descendant's houses in Near Eastern villages (Flannery, 1972). There was little or no stratification, and division of labor was still largely by age and sex.

The Chiefdom

A third stage of pre-state social organization, the *chiefdom,* first appeared in the Near East around 7,500 years B.P. Chiefdoms were probably theocracies, with the ruler or a member of his family serving as a high religious official (Service, 1975). For the first time, the position of leader existed apart from

Table 1 The Cultural Evolution of Societies

Type of society	Some institutions, in order of appearance	Ethnographic examples	Archaeological examples
State	(Local group autonomy, Egalitarian status, Ephemeral leadership, Ad hoc ritual, Reciprocal economy, Unranked descent groups, Ranked descent groups, Redistributive economy, Hereditary leadership, Elite endogamy, Full-time craft specialization, Stratification, Kingship, Codified law, Bureaucracy, Military draft, Taxation)	France; England; India; United States	Classic Mesoamerica; Sumer; Shang China; Imperial Rome
Chiefdom	(Local group autonomy, Egalitarian status, Ephemeral leadership, Ad hoc ritual, Reciprocal economy, Unranked descent groups, Ranked descent groups, Redistributive economy, Hereditary leadership, Elite endogamy, Full-time craft specialization)	Tonga; Hawaii; Kwakiutl; Nootka; Natchez	Gulf Coast Olmec of Mexico (3,000 B.P.); Samarran of Near East (7,300 B.P.); Mississippian of North America (3,750 B.P.)
Tribe	(Local group autonomy, Egalitarian status, Ephemeral leadership, Ad hoc ritual, Reciprocal economy, Unranked descent groups)	New Guinea highlanders; Southwest pueblos; Sioux	Early formative of inland Mexico (3,400–3,000 B.P.); Pre-pottery Neolithic of Near East (10,000–8,000 B.P.)
Band	(Local group autonomy, Egalitarian status, Ephemeral leadership, Ad hoc ritual, Reciprocal economy)	Kalahari bushmen; Australian aborigines; Eskimo; Shoshone	Early Archaic of United States and Mexico (12,000–8,000 B.P.); Late Paleolithic of Near East (12,000 B.P.)

Flannery, 1972. Reproduced with permission from the *Annual Review of Ecology and Systematics*, Vol. 3. © 1972 by Annual Reviews, Inc.

the person who occupied it. That is, his power came not from his personality, but from his position or role as leader. When a chief died, the role was filled by someone from a particular line of descent.

No longer were all family groups or lineages of equal rank. There is further evidence that some kin groups may have owned the best farm land or enjoyed other marks of status. Perhaps the best evidence that certain groups enjoyed higher status from birth is the discovery of the remains of children who had been buried much more elaborately than most other people at the time. At Tell es Sawwan, Iraq, from about 7,500 to 7,000 years B.P., children were buried with alabaster statues and turquoise and copper ornaments. At La Venta, Mexico, from about 800 B.C., children were buried with jade articles in basalt-columned tombs. These children, having died so young, could not have achieved a status worthy of such attention. Their status had to be inherited (Flannery, 1972).

Chiefdoms were characterized by large villages, among which some craft specialization existed. Some villages in the Near East, for example, worked only on pottery; others produced large amounts of copper goods. In Mesoamerica, some villages made magnetite mirrors, while others made shell ornaments. But within each village, there were no groups of people who worked only on these goods. All villagers seem to have worked part-time at crafts as well as at farming: Signs of both activities can be found in the remains of houses whose members were part of a chiefdom.

Chiefdoms exist today in many parts of Africa, as well as in South Pacific Islands such as Fiji and Tahiti. Until they were disturbed by Europeans, the Hawaiians and the Kwakiutl and Nootka of the Pacific Northwest were also chiefdoms (Flannery, 1972).

The Emergence of States

Why some bands developed into tribes and others did not, or why some tribes became chiefdoms and others did not are questions that concern many anthropologists. In this chapter we shall limit our discussion to the transition from chiefdoms to states. Along the way, we shall examine the role the formation of cities has played in this transition.

The first question we must ask is what features allow us to distinguish a chiefdom from a state. The answer lies partly in the types of changes that occur as states emerge. Most anthropologists would agree that the following events mark the transition from chiefdom to state.

1. Complex chiefdoms break up and collapse.
2. Regulatory organizations change, and a formal, centralized, legal apparatus for governing emerges.
3. Specialized economic activities become the function of particular groups.

4. Territorial expansion follows the emergence of the state.

This list may tell us what happens in the state formation and provide clues that archaeologists can look for. But it cannot tell us why the process occurs in the first place. Since we were not present to observe these causes, their nature can only be approached by hypothesis. Two basic types of hypotheses exist. Some experts have proposed universal causes of state formation. These so-called *prime mover* theories tend to focus on single causes. Others have decided that such a complex evolution cannot be explained in terms of a single cause. They look to a combination of factors. We shall examine some of the most important theories of state formation in this section.

Irrigation

In his *hydraulic theory,* Karl Wittfogel (1957) has suggested that states first arose in dry areas when large-scale irrigation became a necessity. The body of officials needed to manage the building of canals and to operate them evolved into the strong government of the state. Wittfogel assumes that village farmers saw the advantages of large-scale irrigation and chose to join in a larger political unit to get them. The state grew larger as it took over the functions of smaller administrative units.

The hydraulic theory has been weakened by evidence uncovered since it was put forth. Excavations in China, Mesopotamia, and Mexico—three areas originally cited in support of the theory—have shown that these states arose long before there was large-scale irrigation. Furthermore, some states, such as the ancient Mayan, grew in areas where irrigation was always of minor importance.

Trade

In some areas of the world, the lack of certain vital raw materials required that communities trade with one another. For example, southern Mesopotamia needed building stone, wood, and metal. The Petén region of Guatemala lacked salt, obsidian, and stone for maize-grinding tools. To get such goods, these communities had to trade with people outside their immediate areas (Flannery, 1972). This trade called for a way to organize the production of the resources traded, as well as communication and recordkeeping. All of these activities are thought to be important in the formation of states.

Unfortunately, not all emerging states depended on trade. Raw materials were abundant in the Valley of Mexico, for example. There trade began after the state had already developed.

Population Growth

As we mentioned in the last chapter, many experts feel that population growth was the prime mover that gave rise to farming and to complex societies. Excavation has clearly shown that population increases are linked with (1) the beginnings of food production and (2) the appearance of complex societies. There is a great deal of disagreement, however, as to whether population growth preceded or followed the other two trends.

Some authorities hold that the development of agricultural techniques caused population growth. Knowledge of how to produce food led to food surpluses, which made possible concentrations of people and gave some the time to specialize in nonfarming pursuits. One such pursuit was government. Full-time administrators dependent on the food produced by others supervised the activities of an increasingly powerful central government in the emerging state.

In the 1960s another group of experts, foremost among whom was Esther Boserup, proposed (1965) that population growth itself forced humans to look for more and more efficient means of supplying food. Population growth preceded farming, in their view. The class of officials who oversaw food production and other activities formed the basis of the state's bureaucracy.

It remains to be shown, however, why population increased in the first place. Studies have revealed that many human groups behave in such a way as to keep their numbers below the resource limits of their environment. This is especially true of hunter-gatherers. Sexual abstinence and socially prescribed killing of the young and old may have occurred during periods of environmental stress. But these may only have proved effective within limited periods. Over the longer periods archaeologists deal with, some gradual population increase may have occurred.

Circumscription and Warfare

Robert Carneiro's *circumscription theory* (1970) can be seen as a modification of the idea that population pressure acted as a prime mover in the rise of the state. According to him, there is evidence of war during the early stages of the formation of all the major states. Growing populations fought one another for land, and in some cases states were formed. But, because war does not necessarily lead to the birth of a state, it must do so only under certain conditions. To define these conditions, Carneiro sought factors common to the times and places in which states have formed.

The one common condition he found is *circumscription*. In *geographical circumscription* an area is set off by mountains, seas, or deserts, which severely limit the land that people can occupy and farm. In Egypt, for instance, the state arose in the narrow strips of fertile land that flank the Nile River. The river valley was virtually isolated by deserts and other geographical features.

Similarly, in *social circumscription* people may be prevented from moving by the surrounding populations. Napoleon Chagnon found social circumscription in a study (1965)

This relief, from Persepolis, the capital of ancient Persia, shows a procession of officials from Media, a territory that was conquered and incorporated into the empire. The officials are paying tribute to Darius, the founder of the empire. Here, as elsewhere, government grew and became more complex as the state expanded. (Georg Gerster, Photo Researchers)

of the Yąnomamö of the Amazon River Basin. He observed that at the center of Yąnomamö territory, villages are much closer together than elsewhere in the territory. Migration from these central villages is difficult, because to do so would mean encroaching on another village's territory.

According to Carneiro, war produces greater centralization and, eventually, states. As populations in the circumscribed Nile River Valley increased, crop-producing land became more scarce and valuable. Consequently, villages began to war with one another for land. Because defeated villages could not move, they had to choose between death or political subordination. As chiefdoms collected taxes, drafted armies, and administered more and more villages, they grew stronger. Warfare among the two great chiefdoms of the upper and lower Nile ultimately led to state formation.

At the same time warfare need not inevitably lead to state formation. Although the Yąnomamö are socially circumscribed and have probably engaged in warfare for many generations, they are clearly not a state—or even a chiefdom.

It should be clear that each of these prime-mover theories explains more in some areas than in others. This fact is not lost on many archaeologists, who feel that different combinations of factors caused state formation in different areas.

Flannery's Process Model

Kent Flannery (1972), for instance, feels that different combinations of the prime movers we have just discussed act in different areas to set in motion the processes of state formation. When a society is subjected to stress—as it is, for example, during war or as a result of population pressure, the demands of large-scale trade, or any combination of prime movers—it either collapses or changes. Flannery believes that the mechanisms of change leading to state formation are universal, although the events and conditions that set them in motion are not. For this reason, none of the prime movers alone is enough to explain the rise of states.

An understanding of Flannery's view of society is helpful in comprehending his model of the processes that make societies more complex. He sees human society as a series of subsystems arranged hierarchically, from lowest and most specific to highest and most general (Flannery, 1972). Each level controls the one below it by comparing the performance of the latter to goals defined by the needs of subsistence and to ideological and religious values. A low level of government, for instance, might direct the planting and harvesting of crops in the field with specific commands. A middle level might control the distribution of harvests and surpluses by means of rituals or general policies that set goals and guidelines.

Flannery's explanation of the rise of the state centers on the processes by which such a system becomes more complex. He defines complexity in terms of the degree to which two processes have occurred. The first, *segregation,* is the extent to which various administrative tasks are split up among separate units of the bureaucracy. The second, *centralization,* is the "degree of linkage between the various subsystems and the highest-order controls in society." He then proposes two mechanisms that affect the level of segregation and centralization in a society. *Promotion* is the elevation of a preexisting institution to a higher level or the elevation of one role of an existing institution to the status of a new institution. *Linearization* is the bypassing of lower-order controls by higher-order controls.

Promotion may embody one aspect of the function of an earlier institution in a new institution specializing in that one task. Thus, aspects of the office of the director of public works might be split into several offices. The director of irrigation and the director of public monuments, for example, might be promoted to become heads of their own departments. As more administrative units are created, each function becomes regulated more closely. Promotion, therefore, adds to increasing segregation, because it creates new institutions.

Linearization typically occurs when higher-order systems have to take on the regulatory activities of a lower level because the latter fails to perform its function. For instance, states may initially tax only local chiefs, who then assess their followers. If this arrangement is later replaced by direct payment of taxes by each citizen, linearization has occurred. As you can see, linearization increases centralization.

Modern archaeologists recognize that the main value of each of these hypotheses is that they can be tested in the field. That is, the data that archaeologists find can be used to support, reject, or modify hypotheses so that a clearer understanding of what underlies the formation of states can be developed. With this in mind, in the rest of this chapter we shall review the archaeological evidence from four ancient states—Mesopotamia, Egypt, China, and Mesoamerica. As we describe the evidence, we shall take note of which, if any, of the theories we have just presented is the most applicable.

State Formation in the New and Old Worlds

Mesopotamia

The first state emerged in the area between the Tigris and Euphrates Rivers in what is now Iraq, Syria, and Iran. In our account of its rise we shall draw primarily on the work of Robert Service (1975).

Bands of hunters and gatherers had roamed

Table 2 The Chronology of State Formation

Years Ago	Mesopotamia	Egypt	China	Mesoamerica
1,000	Militaristic period	Militaristic period	Militaristic period	Militaristic period
2,000				Initial empire
				Regional centers
3,000			Initial empire	Formative
4,000			Regional centers	Early agriculture
5,000	Initial empire	Initial empire	Formative	
	Regional centers		Early agriculture	
6,000	Formative	Early agriculture		
7,000	Early agriculture			
8,000				
12,000				

the highlands of the Zagros mountains since Neolithic times but had rarely wandered into the arid lowlands to the southeast. Around 10,000 years B.P., however, some of these people began settling as herding and farming tribes on the Assyrian steppe between the mountains and the lowlands. There, as we mentioned in the last chapter, during the late Neolithic they developed a basic knowledge of irrigation, which in time allowed them to move into and farm the arid lowlands.

Formative Era (7,000–5,000 years B.P.). Before irrigation, lowland inhabitants had depended to some degree on hunting and gathering. This, of course, made some seasonal migration necessary. After upland peoples introduced irrigation, the dry lowlands of the

Tigris-Euphrates lowland system could for the first time support settled villages.

Several geographical factors also influenced the social evolution of lowland culture. Many villages lacked certain basic resources, forcing them to acquire these materials through trade. They traded food for wood to build boats and stone for tools and construction with people living in the highlands. The easily navigable rivers aided the movement of goods and people, and, equally important, the movement of ideas, inventions, and discoveries.

Another important trend of this period is the gradual evolution of a separate herding culture in the highlands. Highlanders became more specialized as herders, trading with lowland people for what they could not grow. At times the herders raided lowland communities, and their mobile way of life led to a military superiority that later became an important factor in the social evolution of the area.

The most advanced culture of the late formative era appeared in the far south, on the alluvial plain of Sumer. Here, farmers lived in self-sufficient, politically independent villages. Excavation of a site named Al Ubaid shows the presence of an advanced chiefdom. As in other chiefdoms, religion and government fused in the chief. At Al Ubaid, imposing temples built during the late formative period served as a place of worship, a palace, a storage place, and a center for the gathering and redistribution of goods. The Sumerians were clearly placing the temple and its priests at the core of their social and political organization.

There is also evidence of full-time specialization in the crafts. The building of temples alone probably required the full-time labor of a large number of people. As the class of specialists grew, so did the power of the temple administrators who saw that they were fed and controlled the trade of the goods produced.

Formation of Regional Centers (5,500–5,000 years B.P.).

During this time large towns, each controlled by a chiefdom, became the religious and economic focus for whole regions. Warka, on the Sumerian plain, is typical of these regional centers.

The Warka site is dominated by a temple that was probably the religious and economic life of the settlement. The temple was a 40-foot-high ziggurat—a stepped pyramid with outside staircases and a shrine at the top. Adams (1966) estimates that if all the hours spent by those building the temple were added together, the total would come to 7,500 years worth of work. Evidently, the priestly administrators could command enormous amounts of labor. There is evidence that the temple redistributed both manufactured goods and raw materials over wide distances. Wood and metals brought from distant areas

are among the evidence found at the site. The ability of the chiefdom to control the distribution of goods may suggest that, at this time, economic influence was more important than political controls.

Still, loyalties seem to have been to local political and social institutions. A centralized bureaucracy, which is typical of states—specialized to administer a number of governmental functions at several levels—had not yet emerged.

Era of Multiregional States (5,000–3,500 years B.P.).

The development of multiregional states out of regional centers was gradual. The first step is a fairly brief but important dynastic era (4,900–4,500 years B.P.). It was characterized by a lessening of the influence of religion in the government, the build-up of cities, and an increase in the social differences among various classes of people. Warfare was almost constant. Highland dwellers and herders living on the fringe of settled lowland areas stepped up their raids on the cities. And the expanding cities fought one another over land needed for farming, water, and trade routes. Military leaders replaced priests as the most vital decision makers. In time, these military leaders were able to keep power within their families, resulting in the first dynastic kingdoms. Because of the constant threat of warfare, many villagers moved into the larger towns, which were more easily defended. As a result, major cities grew up. Warka, for instance, may have had 20,000 to 30,000 inhabitants at this time.

The growth of social stratification is evident from burial sites. Before 5,500 years B.P., such sites show almost no distinction in the wealth or prestige of the deceased. As Warka became a regional center, differences become more apparent; during the dynastic era, they are marked. At the bottom level were slaves, who as captives of war were assigned work such as weaving cloth. Most of the population were farmers, some of whom owned their own land. There was also a class of craft work-

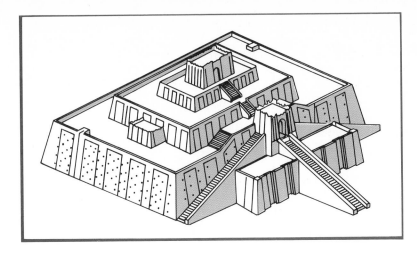

Figure 1 The Ziggurat of Ur. Temple-towers such as this required the organization of large labor forces over a long period of time—a feat most easily accomplished by a state. (Adapted from Mallowan, 1965)

ers, who are difficult to describe in terms of status because it varied from one craft to another. The ruler and his family were the leaders of the society, although we cannot tell for sure to what degree wealth was concentrated among them.

The first empire uniting all the separate regional centers of Mesopotamia was founded around 4,500 years B.P. by Sargon, who, it was said, began his political career as a cupbearer to the king of Kish, in northern Sumer. After becoming a successful military leader, he founded and set himself up as ruler of the city of Akkad, which was in a strategic location between the steppes and the lowlands. Further conquests brought the sophisticated, theocratic regional centers of Sumer to the south under his control.

Akkad attracted a diverse population—older, more refined, religious Sumerians and rougher, secular Semites from the hill country. Akkad of course was a secular city, having been founded by a military leader instead of evolving from a long period of priestly rule. Under Sargon, farming techniques such as irrigation were applied by managers who had been tribal chieftains. These men had once been in charge of flocks but now directed the activities of workers in the irrigation system. Thus, the combination of government by chieftains and the technologies of Sumer led to a bureaucratic government unlike any other previous system. As the empire changed during the four generations that it existed, local rulers and priests were replaced by members of the royal family and trusted friends, thus making the bureaucracy more and more loyal to the ruler.

The local loyalties upon which the earlier city-states were based were replaced by loyalties to the larger, more impersonal, multiregional state. At the top of the bureaucracy was the hereditary ruler (the king, or emperor) who performed judicial, administrative, and legislative functions. Sargon himself took important steps toward a rule by law, one of the characteristics of the state, as we have defined it. He gained the right to enforce agreements and oaths among people in the empire.

Examining the Theories. It is hard to pinpoint the precise period at which a Mesopotamian state emerged. By the time regional centers were being formed (5,500 years B.P.), however, all 10 of Childe's characteristics of civilization were, in varying degrees, present in Mesopotamia. Least evident were full-time specialists, except the priest-rulers and other temple officials. Political organization based on force was not very evident until the dynastic era. True states probably did not emerge until the beginning of the dynastic era.

No one factor can explain the emergence of the state in Mesopotamia, which makes it necessary to think in terms of a multiple-factor theory. Without irrigation, significant settlement—let alone the formation of a state—could not have occurred in the arid lowlands. But irrigation began in the steppe region long before the formation of states. Thus, irrigation was a necessary precursor to state formation but did not directly cause it. Gradually, irrigation became an important source of the state's control of the population, until control of irrigation was taken over completely by the state. Flannery's idea of centralization by linearization is helpful in describing this process.

Circumscription and warfare did not bring about state formation, but they played crucial roles in building nonreligious rule and in the later emergence of multiregional states. Nor can agricultural surplus explain the creation of the state. The soil of Mesopotamia was fertile because annual floods deposited silt in the floodplain. The resulting abundant harvests produced a food surplus that enriched the state but was not a primary factor in creating it.

Trade was vital because of the lack of raw materials, and its control undoubtedly also added to the development of central authorities. The larger empires, like that of Sargon, included varied geographic areas, and the planned exchange of certain goods was clearly important to the integration of these areas.

Population growth during the formative period probably caused some important changes in the structure of the society. Growth may have led to increasing competition for resources, which finally resulted in the increasing militarism and secularization of the dynastic period (Adams, 1972).

Thus, it is obvious that a number of factors contributed to state formation in Mesopotamia. Population growth, leading to circum-

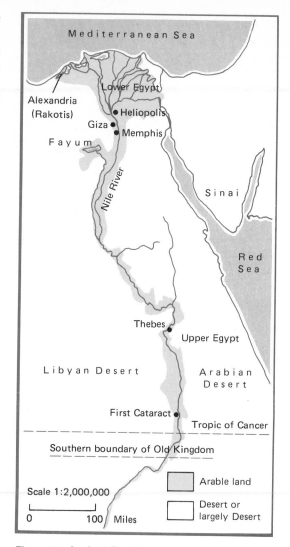

Figure 2 Ancient Egypt

scription and warfare, may have started the process. But along the way trade, agricultural surpluses, and management of irrigation enlarged the scope and power of the state.

Egypt

Egypt is rightly called the Land of the Nile, for that great river dominates the area through which it flows. For most of its length the Nile is bounded by deserts to the east and west. Waterfalls limit travel south into the interior of Africa, while to the north the broad delta of the Nile fans out into the Mediterranean. Every year the Nile floods its narrow valley. The rise and fall of the river takes place over a period of months, renewing the soil without eroding it. The Nile also provides easy transport for raw materials, goods, and information. All these factors eventually helped shape the state that arose there.

Formative Era (6,000–5,350 years B.P.). People first began to farm in Egypt by at least 6,000 years B.P., when scattered villages supporting themselves by floodwater farming appeared throughout the Nile's floodplain. These villages were organized into local districts called *nomes*. Although these local governments were independent, like those of the cities of Sumer, they were much weaker. Small temples seem to have been a major feature of these nomes, but religious leaders did not command much political power, because the local chieftain, priest, or priest-king was not looked on as the earthly representative of the local gods, as was the case in the cities of Sumer. Later, after the state arose, the pharaoh could be seen as the unrivalled god of the whole valley, Unification of the valley was made easier than if localities had been strong. Finally, complex urban bureaucracies did not develop, partly because there was not yet any long-distance trade that needed regulation by bureaucrats (Service, 1975).

Formation of Regional Centers (5,350–5,050 years B.P.). At this time the difference between Lower Egypt (the delta region of the north) and Upper Egypt (the southern Nile valley) became important. The two regions shared a common language, a similar culture, and a political structure based on the nome. Lower Egypt, however, was more culturally advanced, while Upper Egypt was more disciplined politically. The ambition of the rulers of the southern region led them to extend their power over more and more of the Nile area, until they had joined the rival nomes under a unified government.

Era of Multiregional States (5,050–3,970 years B.P.). Tradition holds that Menes, a chief of Upper Egypt, conquered the lower Nile around 5,200 years B.P. and established the First Dynasty of the Egyptian empire. Most likely the unification actually occurred over several generations. Even so, it appears to have been accomplished with relative ease, probably because of the weakness of the nomes.

In many respects Egypt during the first few dynasties was more like an elaborate chiefdom than a state. The pharaoh held sway over all the nomes of the valley, with little if any bureaucracy in between. Unlike the earlier chiefs, he was both emperor and god. It was not until the Fourth Dynasty that a separation of powers in the theocracy appeared. Then a top official took over secular matters such as trade, the treasury, and food production.

Apparently the organization of communal projects such as land reclamation, flood control, and irrigation did not come about on a really large scale in Egypt until a political system of centralized rule under the pharaoh had been established. The attitude of awe felt toward the pharaoh by his subjects continued during much of the Old Kingdom (established with the Third Dynasty and lasting from 4,636 to 4,110 years B.P.) and helped to make possible the enormous projects (such as pyramid-building) the state undertook for its rulers. It was believed that the pharaoh could make those officials who pleased him immortal. Their devotion created peace and made possible a powerful state (Service, 1975; Aldred, 1965).

The Old Kingdom started out with a fairly simple governmental structure. But by the Fourth Dynasty, which began about 4,563 B.P., the pharaoh governed by means of a vast

Seated figures of Aemonophis III, the only remains of his funerary temple. The awe pharoah's subjects felt toward him helped make possible the enormous undertakings of the Egyptian state. (George Holton, Photo Researchers)

bureaucracy. The structure of Old Kingdom society resembled a pyramid, with the pharaoh at the top. Members of the royal family held the top positions in the bureaucracy. This structure controlled all important trade of the country, collecting and redistributing goods in accordance with the wishes of the royal court. The pharaoh held a virtual monopoly on the trade of the empire. Some pharaohs expanded trade routes to reach along the Mediterranean coast to the Levant.

Below the bureaucrats were the artists and craft workers, who were organized into guilds on a hereditary basis. The vast majority of citizens, however, were simple farmers. They worked in the fields during part of the year and supported the bureaucracy with the surplus they produced. At other times, they were drafted to help in the huge building projects of the state.

Examining the Theories. The history of the rise of the Egyptian civilization seems to contradict Childe's idea that cities are essential to civilization. Although most of Childe's 10 characteristics of a civilization were present, even in the times when regional centers were being formed, the most notable exception is the presence of cities. In Egypt, urbanism neither preceded nor accompanied the formation of the state: It came long after. The first true cities did not appear until after the Old Kingdom.

The theory of geographical circumscription seems to provide the best explanation for Egyptian development. The Nile River Valley can be seen as an area circumscribed by deserts and the sea. As a result, the unification of the South and the North by Menes was easier than it would have been otherwise. The nomes never produced strong leaders because the need for strong bureaucratic control of irrigation and defense never arose. Annual floods made extensive irrigation projects unnecessary. And enemies could not easily reach Egypt early in its history. Thus, there was little need for local military organization. As a result, the weak nome leaders could offer little resistance to the northern conquerors. Because the area was circumscribed, the people had little choice but to accept the rule of Menes. Gradually, the dynastic rulers provided the centralization from which the state emerged.

China

Complex political organizations first grew up in northern China around the lower and middle Huang Ho River. The area is a basin bounded on the north and west by plateaus, and on the south by plateaus and mountains. To the east it opens on a large plain. As in Egypt, the state that arose here seems to have been formed without the influence of outside forces.

Formative Era (5,000–4,600 years B.P.). Farming villages were first established during this time. Each village apparently was a moderate-sized, self-contained tribal community. Social stratification was not pronounced, nor was warfare frequent (Chang, 1976).

Formation of Regional Centers (4,600–3,850 years B.P.). During this stage, the people of the Lung-shan culture were able to increase rapidly their agricultural production. This seems to be associated with increased population density, and larger, more permanent settlements.

Because basic agricultural methods do not seem to have undergone any great improvement during the time of the Lung-shan culture, the growing productivity must be explained in terms of a social change. The archaeological evidence points to increasing specialization and to the beginnings of differences in status among the population. The presence of potter's wheels and excellent craftsmanship suggests that there were full-time potters. And jade objects concentrated at one site indicate the presence of specialists in jade-working. Activities, when performed by specialists whose work is directed by officials, are carried out much more efficiently than when done on a part-time basis. Thus the rate at which goods and food were produced rose.

Population pressure probably caused farmers from the original settlements to spread out into new territories. Then, for several reasons, the Lung-shan culture split into a number or regional stylistic traditions. One of the traditions, probably the Honan, was the base of the earliest Chinese state (Chang, 1976).

Period of Multiregional States (3,850–3,050 years B.P.). At the beginning of this period the communities of the lower and middle Huang Ho River were joined under the control of the Shang dynasty.

The change from Lung-shan culture was gradual and was marked by an intensification of long-term trends. Population density increased, and status and role differentiation became greater. Increasingly, central settlements governed political and economic affairs of the surrounding area. Communication was no longer a haphazard process carried out by individuals. Institutions put their messages into writing, and trade was carried on by organizations, which made communication between groups more regular and dependable.

Perhaps the most evident trait of the Shang dynasty is the presence of networks of build-

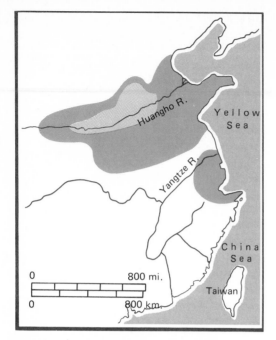

Figure 3 The distribution of the Lung-shan (darker-shaded areas) and Shang cultures (lighter-shaded area)

ing clusters. The networks were most concentrated at the center, and spread out to fill an area of between 30 and 40 square kilometers. The Lung-shan communities had been self-contained, with little contact with other villages. During the Shang dynasty, however, these villages became part of the administrative web that surrounded central clusters. From these centers officials and priests directed and organized political and economic activities. They in turn obeyed the ruler-god, whose position was inherited. Local villages were administered by relatives of the ruler, other high officials, or local leaders under the control of the ruler (Chang, 1976).

Examining the Theories. Early in the development of regional centers, China showed evidence of all 10 of Childe's characteristics of a civilization, except possibly monumental

buildings. Many of the early Chinese structures were made out of wood, apparently a preferred material. Because they did not survive, we have little information about the kinds of structures that were built.

In the development of the state, circumscription and warfare were significant factors. It appears that state formation and development could not have occurred without the use of force. The people of the Huang Ho River Basin were not geographically circumscribed, but they may have been socially circumscribed. Land was either controlled by urban centers or left undefended to nomadic invaders. As populations increased, warfare among neighboring populations in competition for resources increased. In order to migrate, a defeated village would have to enter the territory of hostile neighbors. Instead, they were absorbed into expanding states.

Neither irrigation nor other technologies were crucial to the development of the state in China, although flood control and irregular rainfall could have brought about some river control. Trade, although widespread, was not well developed, probably because there were no great regional differences in goods that were produced.

Mesoamerica

Archaeologists use the term *Mesoamerica* when referring to the area in Central America in which several native Indian civilizations arose. The region consists of the highlands and lowlands of central and southern Mexico and Guatemala, and the lowlands of San Salvador, Belize, and part of Western Honduras. (See Figure 4.) The highlands, centering around the Valley of Mexico (where Mexico City now stands), are dry, with irregular rainfall. The lowlands, particularly the Yucatán Peninsula of Mexico and the Petén region of northern Guatemala, are covered by dense tropical rainforests. Mountain ranges, large lakes, and the Gulf of Mexico produce great

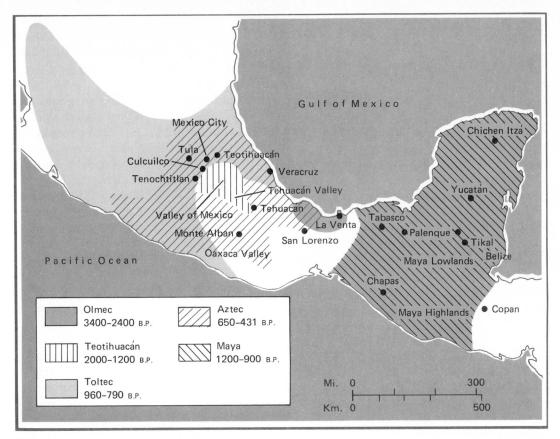

Figure 4 The major civilizations of Mesoamerica

geographic and climatic variation within both of these regions.

The best way to understand the complex societies that emerged in Mesoamerica is to consider the area as a unit. In this way we can gain a perspective and ability to generalize that is not possible in a discussion limited to one regional center. We shall use the same framework we used to describe the development of the state in the Near East, in Egypt, and in China.

The Formative Era (3,450–2,750 years B.P.). Complex societies first emerged in the Mesoamerican lowlands and spread from there to the highlands. The earliest complex society of the lowlands was that of the Olmecs, who lived on Mexico's southeastern Gulf coast, north of the Yucatán Peninsula. The Olmecs, with their distinctive art forms, imposing architecture, complex calendar, and writing, foreshadowed the more sophisticated states of the highlands.

The Olmecs are best known for their *ceremonial centers,* clusters of earthworks that seem to have been designed for religious purposes rather than as dwelling places. The largest of these centers, at a site named La Venta, took an estimated 800,000 days of human labor to build (Coe, 1962).

The ceremonial center appears to have been separated from the villages in which the population lived. There is no evidence that people lived in the centers, except perhaps a small number of priests. People probably grew their crops elsewhere and supported the priests with the surplus.

The extent of the power the priests had can be seen in the labor force they could get for the construction of sites like La Venta, which was redone, expanded, and repaired over a period of 400 years. The stone carvings of the Olmecs are striking as well. Characteristic of the art style are "baby-faced" sculptures and jaguar motifs. These motifs are seen at many Mesoamerican sites and are testimony to the influence that the Olmecs must have had on other Mesoamerican cultures. Moving huge stones upon which human faces were carved offers further testimony to the priests' power to mobilize people for work. But, in both cases, there must have been a strong element of religious activity in this work. Time and effort were probably gladly given to fulfill religious obligations.

Formation of Regional Centers (2,750–1,850 years B.P.). Three main regional centers began to emerge at this time: one in the Valley of Mexico, another in Oaxaca (a valley to the south of Mexico City), and a third in the Mayan lowlands of Yucatán.

The Valley of Mexico. The earliest farmers of the Valley of Mexico (probably migrating from the South) seem to have been organized into large tribal villages. In time, however, population size grew, and chiefdoms seem to have arisen. The largest of the chiefdoms were at Teotihuacán, a village in the northeastern part of the Valley, and Cuicuilco, a village at the southwestern part of the Valley. Around 2,150 years B.P., both Teotihuacán and Cuicuilco had at least 4,000 inhabitants, and both used irrigation to aid farming (Sanders, Parsons, & Logan, 1976).

Oaxaca. Oaxaca is a flat-bottomed, semiarid valley with three wings (see Figure 4). In each of these three parts of the valley independent, theocratic chiefdoms were developing during this time. The leaders of these growing societies were powerful enough to draft workers to build large monuments. They also controlled populations that lived in the mountains surrounding the valley, regulating the trade that had grown between the mountain and valley people. Like the centers of the Near East, the ceremonial center probably functioned as a regulator of trade, a religious center, an administrative center, and a center that redistributed the surplus produced by the area's farmers. Also like other chiefdoms, those in Oaxaca supported a growing number of craft specialists (Service, 1975; Wright, 1977).

Mayan Lowlands. Before this period began, Mexico's Yucatán Peninsula and northern Guatemala and Belize were settled by people who were related to the Olmecs. The first people in this area to live by farming, they practiced a slash-and-burn system, as did the Olmecs. At the beginning of this period the Maya were beginning to form themselves into political groups and to build the type of ceremonial centers that were to characterize their later development.

The Mayan ceremonial centers were arranged in a hierarchy. Each hamlet had a small ceremonial center or platform at which the important local rituals were performed. These small centers also acted as the administrative centers for the hamlets. Ten to 15 hamlets together would support a minor ceremonial center, which probably coordinated the activities of the local inhabitants. Major centers were supported by the inhabitants of 10 to 15 minor centers. The major chiefs probably lived in or near these larger centers. But at this time, large ceremonial centers were inhabited by only a few people. The bulk of the population lived in scattered settlements (Bullard, 1960).

Formation of Multiregional States (1,850–1,300 years B.P.). This is really the story of

Teotihuacán—of its growth and ultimately its influence or direct rule (we do not know which) over the rest of Mesoamerica.

About 1,900 years ago, Teotihuacán's rival for dominance in the Valley of Mexico, Cuicuilco, was destroyed by a volcano. Teotihuacán may have absorbed some of the displaced population. In any case, its population increased rapidly. By 1,850 years ago, the city contained at least 10,000 people, about half the population of the Valley (Parsons, 1976). By about 1,800 years ago, the city's broad north-south and east-west avenues had been laid out, and the Pyramid of the Sun—the largest construction in Pre-Columbian America—was built. Traders from as far away as Tajin, a center in the northern Veracruz lowlands, came seeking obsidian (which was mined nearby) and other products of Teotihuacán.

Whether or not Teotihuacán was actually an empire is open to question. It did not conquer other communities in the Valley of Mexico: It swallowed up their populations like the center of a vast whirlpool. There is also little evidence of militarism at Teotihuacán, so that military conquests probably did not occur. More likely, cities far beyond the Valley of Mexico were attracted to Teotihuacán as a religious and economic center. The influence on them was probably like the effect that powerful modern economies, such as that of the United States, have on other nations.

By 1,350 years B.P., perhaps as many as 200,000 people lived within the 8 square miles of Teotihuacán (Millon, 1976), making it one of the largest and most populous preindustrial cities of the world. Aside from the city itself, the Valley contained only a few small villages that served special functions. Some were salt- or lime-mining towns, and there were three ceremonial centers of no more than 3,000 inhabitants each. Possibly these were used only in certain seasons (Sanders, Parsons, & Logan, 1976).

The central role of religion in the Teoti-huacán state never faltered. The priesthood was as powerful, if not more powerful, than the aristocracy. Militarism and the secularization that often were associated with power in other states did not develop until perhaps the very last stage of Teotihuacán's influence. Military figures do not appear in art until about 1,300 years ago (Millon, 1976).

Militaristic Period (1,300–430 years B.P.). The urbanism that was part of Teotihuacán's greatness also added to its decline. The city had become too large to be supported by local or even valley-wide farming. Drought years must have had terrible effects. Cutting down the forests for firewood, boats, and building materials may have caused soil erosion (Patterson, 1973). Competition in trade may also have eroded the city's economic base. Finally, nomadic raiders from the north may have sacked the city around 1,150 years B.P. (Service, 1975). The city was not abandoned, but the population gradually moved away into smaller communities. None of these towns developed into a major city.

The collapse of Teotihuacán also had an effect on its tributaries. Work on the structures in some Mayan sites seems to have been stopped between 1,416 and 1,352 years B.P., perhaps signaling the end of Teotihuacán's influence in the lowlands (Willey, 1977). The Oaxacan state collapsed around 1,050 years B.P.

The Maya. For a time, the power vacuum left by the decline of Teotihuacán was filled by Tajin. However, the major state in Mesoamerica after Teotihuacán's collapse appeared in the Mayan lowlands. For about 300 years, until about 1,050 years B.P., the Mayan civilization was able to support a number of extremely elaborate ceremonial centers. Some of these centers, like Tikal, were apparently "supercenters" that were supported by a large number of other major centers (Sanders & Price, 1968).

The centers themselves and the Mayan re-

The temple of the Giant Jaguar at Tikal, one of the large ceremonial centers of the Maya. It was built about 1,300 years B. P. by piling up rubble and encasing it with limestone blocks. (George Holton, Photo Researchers)

ligion were directed by a highly organized priesthood. Priests played a major role in government and were custodians of astronomy and astrology. Relationships between centers were also controlled by the priests. The members of the ruling class at this time differed from those of earlier periods in that they were probably hereditary secular leaders. These leaders were probably involved in the growing militarism that is apparent after 1,300 years B.P. Wall murals and stone carvings show that conflicts between the supporters of different ceremonial centers had become a fact of life at this time.

In the eleventh century B.P., the lowland Mayan sites were abandoned one by one. The most satisfactory model of the "collapse" of Mayan civilization emphasizes the fact that the Mayan social-political system was too rigid to deal with the onset of a number of problems, including disease, drought and soil depletion, trade disruptions, and war. By 1,041 years B.P., the last of the great Mayan centers had been abandoned to the jungles (Willey, 1966; Willey & Shimkin, 1973).

The Toltecs. Toward the end of the twelfth century B.P., the Toltecs emerged as the dominant power in Central Mexico. Their capital, Tula, about 60 kilometers north of the Valley of Mexico, became the center of an empire that covered a large part of the same region that was earlier controlled by Teotihuacán. Unlike Teotihuacán, whose influence was primarily economic, there is no doubt that the Toltecs captured and kept their empire by force. At Chichén Itzá in the northern part of the Yucatán Peninsula, murals and carvings show Toltec warriors defeating, capturing, and being honored by Mayan warriors (Willey, 1966).

The Toltecs were probably brought down by a combination of internal rebellion and a series of disastrous droughts (Coe, 1962). After Tula was abandoned, the Valley of Mexico once again returned to a collection of city-states.

The Aztecs. The last of the great militaristic empire-builders, the Aztecs, migrated into the Valley of Mexico beginning about 750 years ago, and for at least 100 years were vassals of the existing city-states. They settled on a series of islands in the middle of Lake Texcoco.

About 550 years ago they began to sys-

Part of a mural at Bonampak. Two Mayan chiefs dressed in jaguar tunics pass judgment on captives. These murals supplied the first evidence that warfare played a role in the formation of the Mayan state. (Avis Tulloch, in Thompson, 1954)

tematically conquer and control their neighbors. Within a century they controlled most of Mesoamerica, except for the Yucatán Peninsula. Among the Aztecs, as among the Toltecs, warfare was of great importance. One of the most important of the Aztec gods was the fierce Huitzilpochtli, the god to whom perhaps 25,000 people a year were sacrificed (Harner, 1977).

When the Spanish arrived (431 years B.P.), the great Tenochtitlan, with perhaps 300,000 inhabitants, was a thriving city. It was dotted with pyramids and plazas interspersed between masonry apartments and even parks.

The social order of the Aztecs was rigid. At the top were the nobility, chief priests, and war officers. Together these groups ruled society. This class elected the emperor, who reigned for life. In the eyes of the Aztecs, the emperor was linked to the gods. And in a more secular sense he was also the richest of the Aztecs. Below the nobility were the commoners. This, by far the largest group, was organized into 20 clans that lived in separate parts of the city. Each clan erected a small temple and built and maintained markets in their section of the city. Below the commoners were serfs and bondsmen who worked on the lands of the nobility. At the bottom of Aztec society were slaves and war captives, many of whom were ritually sacrificed and often eaten (Harner, 1977).

When the Spanish finally conquered Tenochtitlan in 431 B.P. they brought an end to the indigenous development of the state in Mesoamerica.

Examining the Theories. Trade probably contributed to the multiregional aspect of Teotihuacán culture. Its importance as a trading center probably grew as a side effect of its importance as a religious center. Why and how Teotihuacán grew as a religious center is still being investigated by archaeologists.

Because the city was located in a small side arm of the Valley of Mexico, it may have been geographically circumscribed. The organization of local resources could have created the bureaucracy that coordinated the state. As elsewhere, the process of urbanization was linked with population increases and increasing cultural diversity. The society may have failed ultimately because agricultural production failed to keep pace with population growth. It has been learned that irrigation systems had been developed while Teotihuacán was competing with Cuicuilo—probably to cope with a growing population in a geographically limited area. The state did not survive partly because it could not develop a truly complex irrigation system, as the Aztecs would do in the same area many centuries later.

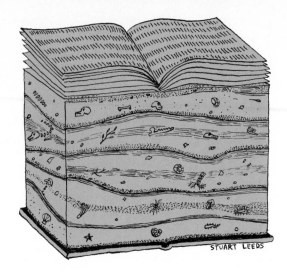

STUART LEEDS

We have already observed that warfare did not play a major role in the formation of the Teotihuacán state. But some sort of conflict may have been significant in the evolution of the early state in Oaxaca. Wright (1977) notes that the collapse of chiefdoms in the three arms of the Oaxacan valley occurred before the first Oaxacan state emerged—the same thing that happened in Mesopotamia.

We know that Teotihuacán was a highly segregated city and that centralization would have had to increase as the city grew. But it is not clear how much promotion and linearization occurred over time. Perhaps the city's internal structure was too rigid to be able to react positively to the problems of expansion. In spite of its enormous size, in the end it was unable to overcome internal shortages, competition, and hostile forces.

Of the other civilizations that emerged in Mesoamerica, the Mayan has most intrigued archaeologists. The lowlands were neither geographically circumscribed nor dependent on irrigation. Warfare, while common during the height of the civilization, was little in evidence as the basic features of Mayan life were being formed. Population growth did not lead to urbanism—indeed, there may have been no true urbanism. But trade was important,

perhaps crucial, to state formation. The organization of long-distance trade may have required the sort of bureaucratic structure from which more complex political organizations could have emerged (Rathje, 1970). In addition, contact at the formative stage with the Olmecs and at later stages with the Valley of Mexico was vital in introducing and encouraging the centralization that would have affected state formation.

In using a process model for studying the Mayan state, it would be especially interesting to analyze what went wrong in the period of their collapse. Besides two constructive mechanisms, Flannery's model proposes two destructive mechanisms. These include *usurpation,* in which a subsystem is elevated to a higher status for self-serving purposes, and *meddling,* the unnecessary, unproductive bypassing of lower-order controls (Flannery, 1972). An increasingly ingrown, withdrawn, insular elite, perhaps more concerned with achieving greater power and prestige, could have caused great damage to the traditional Mayan political system, and thus made it unresponsive to changing social and economic conditions.

Summary

1. A *city* is a central place that performs economic and political functions for the surrounding area. The process by which cities are formed is called *urbanism*.

2. A *state* is an independent political unit that includes many communities in its territory, with a centralized government that has the power to collect taxes, draft citizens for work and for war, and enact and enforce laws. States are *stratified* (some groups of citizens have greater access to wealth and status, or both) and *economically diversified*.

3. *Civilization* refers to a society having large cities or towns whose residents are bound together in a legal commonwealth. Some authors, such as Childe, have defined the term more broadly, and it remains an ambiguous concept.

4. Archaeologists have arbitrarily defined the stages of human social evolution from simple to complex as follows: band, tribe, chiefdom, state.

5. Before about 12,000 years ago, humans lived in small egalitarin groups called *bands*. Force of personality is the basis of the leader's power, and there is probably little if any sense of property.

6. *Tribes* appeared in the Near East about 9,000 years B.P. A tribe is made up of groups of families related by common descent. The leader is weak. In tribes that farm, land is considered property, though stratification is minimal.

7. *Chiefdoms* were present by 7,500 years B.P. in the Near East. Chiefdoms are often theocracies, and the position of chief is institutionalized. Stratification is present in some degree, as are large villages and part-time craft specialization.

8. As states are formed (1) chiefdoms collapse, (2) centralized legal apparatus for governance emerges, (3) certain activities become the full-time function of particular groups, and (4) the emerging state expands its territory.

9. Holders of *prime-mover* theories think state formation stems from a single cause.

10. Karl Wittfogel, in his *hydraulic theory*, proposes that the state arose from the body of officials needed to manage irrigation works in dry areas. The state grew as surrounding areas opted for extension of irrigation into their land.

11. Other theorists think the state grew out of the need to organize and regulate *trade* and production of goods in areas that lacked vital raw materials.

12. Still others think *population growth* has been a prime-mover. Expanding populations led to food production and eventually to a food surplus, upon which a group of officials could draw, while administering more and more political and economic activities.

13. According to Robert Carneiro's *circumscription theory*, growing populations in areas that are geographically or socially circumscribed, making migration difficult, collide and war over resources. Because defeated people cannot migrate, they are absorbed into an expanding state.

14. Kent Flannery's *process model* is one theory that allows for a number of interacting factors in state formation. Flannery believes that the mechanisms of change that produce a state are universal, but the events and conditions activating the mechanisms are not. Flannery names two mechanisms of state formation: *promotion* and *linearization*. The first produces greater *segregation*, and the second increases *centralization*, both of which are present to a high degree in states.

15. The first multi-state empire emerged in *Mesopotamia* about 4,500 years B.P., when Sargon united Sumer and northern Mesopotamia. Before this time, villages in the Tigris-Euphrates river valley expanded as trading centers and were governed by chiefdoms. By

5,000 years B.P. multi-regional centers such as Warka redistributed goods and administered other activities over a wide area. In the next 500 years some of these centers developed a strong enough political organization to be called states.

16. Unlike in Sumer, large independent cities were not present before the formation of the *Egyptian state.* Tradition holds that Menes united upper and lower Egypt to form the first empire there about 5,200 years B.P. Scattered villages had appeared by 6,000 years B.P. and were organized into weak political units called *nomes.* These units were easily united, first in regional governments and then in the empire. Irrigation, circumscription, and warfare seem to have contributed to state-building in Egypt.

17. About 3,850 years B.P., villages along the lower and middle Huang Ho River were united under the Shang dynasty, *China's* earliest known state. Tribal farming villages, which had first appeared about 5,000 years B.P., gave way to larger, partly stratified and economically diversified settlements during the Lung-shan culture (4,600–3,850 years B.P.). By the time of the Shang, settlements had become urban clusters controlling large surrounding regions. Circumscription and warfare were certainly factors in the rise of the Shang.

18. In Mesoamerica, the *Olmecs,* with their ceremonial centers, their ability to draft large labor forces, and their arts, foreshadowed later Mesoamerican societies. Several regional centers emerged in the period 3,750–1,850 years B.P. after the Olmec decline: Teotihuacán and Cuicuilco in the *Valley of Mexico, Oaxaca,* and the *Mayan lowlands.* Populations grew, and chiefdoms were able to organize the building of elaborate ceremonial centers. Between 1,850 and 1,300 years B.P., *Teotihuacán* emerged as the dominant religious and economic force in central and southern Mexico. After the city's collapse, which occurred around 1,150 years B.P., the *Mayan state* became strong, supporting a number of large ceremonial centers directed by priests. First the *Toltecs* and then the *Aztecs* succeeded the Maya as empire builders after the decline of the Maya, beginning about 1,100 years B.P.

PART THREE

Perspectives on Anthropology

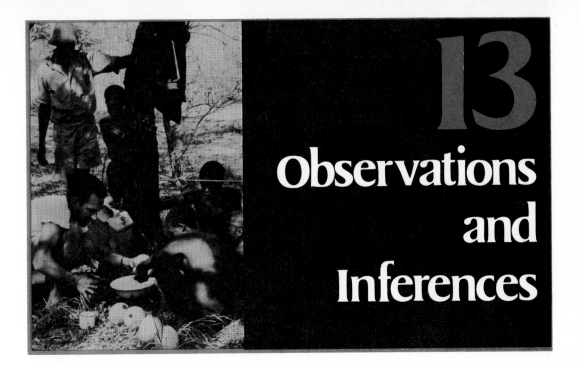

Observations and Inferences

ANTHROPOLOGISTS study both the characteristics that all humans share and those that are unique to a specific social group. Shared characteristics include such phenomena as kinship and language use. Unique aspects of these phenomena are, for example, the clan organization of the Bororo Indians of Brazil and the jargon of Americans talking over citizens band (CB) radio. Anthropology considers people from all times and places, from the earliest apelike human ancestor to the baby born this morning, from isolated hunters and food-gatherers of the Amazon to professionals in large urban centers.

Cultural, or social, anthropology concerns itself with living populations. It examines the beliefs and practices that make social life possible. These features—religious beliefs, political, economic, and legal institutions, arts and crafts, to name a few—comprise the *culture* of a particular society or population. The

next chapter will discuss this key concept in detail.

Another key concept utilized by anthropologists is that of *society*. This term refers to a group of human beings that is organized in various ways in order to accomplish common purposes. The notion of society calls attention to the interaction of humans in various social settings, whereas culture refers to the common bond of understanding that makes such interaction possible. In this chapter we look at the methods and techniques used by cultural anthropologists in their work. To discover the patterns of organization within a society, its development and change, and its relations with other societies, cultural anthropologists have adopted various techniques of observation, description, comparison, and analysis. These techniques enable researchers to record in detail the various practices they observe. Anthropologists use their recorded data to compare what they have learned with the

279

findings of other observers of the same culture. They also compare the features of one culture with those of other cultures.

Ethnography and Ethnology

The collection of information on societies and cultures by anthropologists is called *ethnography*. Anthropologists must often spend months in the field observing and interacting with their subjects of study. They provide detailed descriptions—*ethnographies*—of the activities, values, and thought of a given social group. *Ethnography* literally means the "description of a people." It records in careful and minute detail the social and cultural phenomena observed by the anthropologist in the field. Although such phenomena may be of interest in themselves, anthropologists are primarily interested in the relationships and patterns that exist among them. It is these patterns that are disclosed through the analysis and interpretation of ethnographic accounts. Anthropologists analyze these accounts by seeking out the patterns in the activities they describe, and they then compare these patterns with those of different cultures. *Ethnology* is the study of culture on a comparative basis. Ethnology traditionally has been considered more theoretical in nature than ethnography. Because ethnography is usually a slow process and less theoretical in orienta-

Different observers attach different interpretations to the same set of phenomena. (Twohy)

tion than ethnology, it has in the past been held in lower esteem by many cultural anthropologists who preferred the theoretical side of the discipline. Recently, anthropologists have come to understand that ethnography and ethnology are not completely separate activities, but, rather, interrelated and even interdependent stages in a single process of investigation.

Differences in Observation

Anthropologists cannot begin their fieldwork without some background in theory, since theory enables them to classify and interpret what they see. It is important, though, that anthropologists be as aware as possible of their theoretical preconceptions. Above all else, they must be prepared to abandon any theoretical framework that does not fit the facts discovered in fieldwork. They must also be aware that other observers, with different theoretical views, may disagree completely about the meaning of the same set of phenomena. An example will serve to illustrate this point.

A classic instance of differing interpretations is found in the studies of the Mexican village Tepoztlan published by Robert Redfield (1930) and Oscar Lewis (1951). Redfield, who visited Tepoztlan in 1926, believed that the character of tribal and peasant societies is completely different from that of modern urban communities. According to Redfield's theory, tribe members and peasants—the inhabitants of folk communities—have direct contact with one another, feel strong group solidarity, and behave in predictable and "traditional" ways. Modern city dwellers, on the other hand, he believed to be less friendly, more isolated from their fellows, and less likely to act in predictable ways. Because of his preconceptions, Redfield's study, *Tepoztlan— A Mexican Village,* offers a harmonious picture of rural existence in which social life is seen as peaceful and well integrated.

Oscar Lewis visited Tepoztlan in 1943 to see firsthand the workings of the folk community that Redfield had described. He published his observations in *Life in a Mexican Village: Tepoztlan Restudied* (1951). What Lewis found, however, was a village seething with personal tension and discord. Lewis's conclusions were so different from Redfield's that other scholars wondered at first how the Tepoztlans could have changed so radically in only 17 years. The change, anthropologists soon realized, was not so much in the people as in the opposing perspectives of Redfield and Lewis. One looked in Tepoztlan for a peaceful folk community, the other for the problems of daily life. Tepoztecan society, like all societies, was sufficiently complex to contain both harmony and stife, integration and conflict.

To imagine any observer as a mere recording eye and ear, then, is misleading. Every observer inevitably colors what he or she sees according to personal background, education, interests, beliefs, and values. In fact, it has been pointed out that the topics treated in ethnographic accounts, as well as the manner in which they are analyzed, frequently reflect the prevailing intellectual climate of a given period. British anthropologists, for example, emphasized integration and conflict resolution during a colonial period when these topics were on the minds of people in administrating nations. Thus, an ethnographic record cannot be separated from the ideas and theories that influence a particular fieldworker. The more clearly fieldworkers identify their own premises and beliefs—for themselves as well as for their readers—the more clearly their observations will be understood for what they are—observations from a particular perspective.

Alien Observers

When cultural anthropologists engage in fieldwork, they are generally aliens or outsiders in a society that may not share their inquisitiveness about local beliefs and practices. Anthropologists' special interests, after all, are shaped by the values of their own cultures. These values and understandings in turn influence the manner in which social and cultural phenomena are perceived.

For example, when living among the Toba Indians of northern Argentina in the late 1950s, the author noticed that the villagers reacted with great excitement to an early manufactured satellite that passed overhead. The villagers were divided as to its significance, but all agreed that it was a powerful sky spirit carrying a message or omen that could be interpreted only by a shaman (a religious and medical specialist). After a long discussion of the object, several Toba asked the author what he thought the "sky being" was. He confidently explained that the object had been placed in orbit from the earth by a powerful machine and carried the message of extraordinary technological achievement. His companions, however, were unconvinced by this explanation and stuck to their original story. Furthermore, they pressed their visitor until he acknowledged that the "sky being" did appear to be a moving star and that he could not prove that it had not been set in motion by a powerful shaman who could also interpret the meaning of its heavenly trajectory.

Both the author and his Toba companions had seen the same phenomenon, but each had interpreted it differently. The anthropologist, familiar with aerospace technology, recognized an orbiting satellite. The Toba, accustomed to magical signs and omens, detected the presence of a sky spirit. Conditioned by different traditions and bodies of knowledge, each saw, in effect, a different object. This disagreement between the anthropologist and the Toba Indian villagers was due, at least in part, to the vast differences between them in culture and education. But anthropologists themselves, although they may share similar backgrounds, cultural systems, and educa-

tions, sometimes draw opposing conclusions from virtually identical phenomena, as did Redfield and Lewis.

In the course of doing fieldwork, anthropologists frequently revise and reformulate their field of inquiry. Unexpected developments or discoveries make such modifications virtually unavoidable. But the changes themselves are always limited to a degree by what the ethnographer already understands—that is, by his or her own culture and education. This is the dilemma: anthropologists attempt to record living societies in all their diversity, but the record is ultimately made in terms and categories that have meaning primarily for members of their own culture, and especially for those who have studied anthropology. In an attempt to make sense out of what he or she observes, the anthropologist discovers that one's own ready-made categories often do not fit the field data. For some anthropologists, therefore, the most enduring and central aspect of fieldwork is not the encounter with another culture nor the data collected but deeper insights into one's own culture that often follow. Having acknowledged this problem and its challenge, we should stress that ethnography nonetheless forms the foundation for all work in cultural anthropology.

Ethnographic Fieldwork

Early Fieldwork

When anthropology emerged as a discipline in the late nineteenth century, the influence of evolutionary theory was encouraging the belief that human existence had followed a pattern of "progress" from lower to higher forms of life. Social scientists believed that there existed orderly "stages" of cultural evolution, from more simple to more complex forms. The main goal of anthropology, they thought, was to reconstruct the patterns of development in technology, kinship, and religion. They assumed, too, that so-called "primitive" societies found today represent remnants of an earlier stage of human social development. So, early anthropologists were interested in the collection of data on so-called "primitive" cultures which would exemplify early stages in this pattern of progress. One of the best known early anthropologists was Sir James Frazer. The research that Frazer undertook in 1887 consisted of sending a questionnaire to missionaries and colonial administrators around the world. It was entitled *Questions on the Manners, Customs, Religions, Superstitions etc. of Uncivilized or Semi-Civilized Peoples.* Frazer apparently did not use much (if any) of the material that was sent to him (Leach, 1961). Instead, as he wrote some years later,

I made a practice of noting in a book the passages of authors who seemed to me of particular significance in their descriptions of the manners and customs, the beliefs and practices, of the various races of men, especially of those races of backward culture, an understanding of whom is of special importance for a knowledge of our race. (Frazer, 1938, p. vii)

Although early anthropologists such as Frazer catalogued and recorded the customs of exotic peoples, they made no attempt to see these customs as part of a consistent whole in which single activities could be understood in relation to others within a system. The materials collected were analyzed from an armchair position rather than from firsthand observation in the field. Perhaps for this reason, the interconnections of cultural phenomena were more readily ignored.

In contrast to early evolutionists, prominent anthropologists in America such as Franz Boas (1858–1942) and Alfred Kroeber (1876–1960) stressed the study of particular societies over specified periods in order to construct their cultural histories. Boas and Kroeber studied chiefly North American Indian groups whose cultures had been drastically altered and sometimes threatened with extinction by the European settlers of the New World. They attempted to record in detail the features of these cultures. Their desire, of course, was to record for posterity those cultures before they lost all resemblance to their original forms or disappeared altogether. But by the time early culture-historians such as Boas and Kroeber began their work, the changes were in some instances already so great that it was possible to find only a handful of individuals who could recall the traditional practices and beliefs. These informants were chosen because their ages or social positions suggested that they could describe fully and accurately the earlier social and cultural life of their people. But they were sometimes unreliable or misleading. Led more by the inclinations of the informants than by the shape of the culture they thought they were preserving, anthropologists often accumulated fragmented accounts of language, folklore and mythology, ritual, technology, and political systems; but these accounts also rarely if ever reflected the full range of a people's thought and activity.

Modern Fieldwork: Participant Observation

Bronislaw Malinowski's research in the Western Pacific during World War I marked a radical development in the nature of ethnographic research and laid the foundation for modern anthropological fieldwork. Malinowski firmly believed, as did Boas, that ethnographers must take up residence among the subjects of their study and learn the native language. They must not only participate in daily activities but also learn to act as members of the community insofar as possible. This method, which came to be known as *par-*

ticipant observation, is now accepted as a prerequisite to responsible fieldwork. Only by moving into a local community, involving oneself in the daily life of the people, learning the language, and settling down for a period of months can the ethnographer begin to recognize the ordinary but vital texture of village life. Living with the people themselves helps the fieldworker to overcome the suspicions of his or her hosts and to be tolerated (if not accepted fully). As Malinowski remarked about the attitude of the Trobianders to him: "as they knew that I would thrust my nose into everything, even where a well-mannered native would not dream of intruding, they finished by regarding me as part and parcel of their life, a necessary evil or nuisance" (1922, p. 8).

An anthropologist "going native"—in tennis shoes. (Napoleon Chagnon, Anthro-Photo)

Malinowski gave attention to every detail of social life, stressing the patterns in the behavior observed. In place of the loose, fragmentary data that had been a feature of earlier work, modern fieldworkers consider the structure and function of social and cultural phenomena. They conceive of cultures and societies as complex wholes in which the patterns of relationships, and not merely isolated phenomena, must be studied. Despite the fact that recent fieldwork has gone beyond Malinowski in precision and completeness, he is recognized as having pointed the way to modern fieldwork methodology.

Thus, modern fieldworkers recognize that the object of study is not the *place* itself (the village, settlement, or city neighborhood) but *what happens within it*—the events of daily life, the development and expression of values and attitudes. Anthropologists choose one place rather than another because they believe it to be a promising source of information about the processes in which they are interested. Obviously, not every village or every society offers the same sort of data in equal abundance and richness. For this reason, choosing a place of study is important. If one wished to investigate the relation between national political parties in the United States and local factionalism, one presumably would not go to a Mennonite community, whose members neither vote nor participate in national politics.

It is important to note, too, that the gender of the fieldworker can be a factor in terms of establishing rapport and collecting information. It is difficult to believe that any male could have collected the data that Margaret Mead did on child rearing in the Pacific or have been privy to the kinds of activities that Elizabeth Fernea (1975) reported in her study of women in Morocco. On the other hand, female anthropologists sometimes find it difficult to acquire information from males who are not accustomed to communicating with women on given topics.

Measures of Fieldwork

The task of ethnographers continues to be to observe everything that occurs in the social life of a people, their public transactions, and their personal dealings, together with their comments on them. Ethnographers must record their observations systematically and clearly. To ensure credibility of their observations, anthropologists have been concerned with problems of reliability and validity. *Validity* is the degree to which observations actually record what they are intended to record. To illustrate, Pelto (1970) offers the example of a door-to-door interviewer soliciting intimate details about respondents' sex lives. The information gathered in this way is not likely to represent accurately real behavior and would therefore lack validity if presented as data about sexual practices. If the responses were said to reveal the ways in which people answered questions on a sensitive subject, however, their degree of validity might be quite high.

Reliability, on the other hand, is the degree to which the result of an experiment or a set of observations can be obtained on another trial by a second experimenter or observer. If repeated door-to-door interviews produced similar sets of responses to questions about respondents' sex lives, the observations would have high reliability (Pelto, 1970). The responses may be reliable without being valid, if, for example, the respondents lied consistently to all interviewers.

Use of Informants

In many instances, the most dependable ethnographic descriptions are characterized by high degrees of both validity and reliability. This correlation is easier to obtain when informants describe ideal behavior—how things ought to be. High degrees of validity and reliability are more difficult to achieve when in-

Individual informants are the primary source of field data. Here, a village chief in Kenya is interviewed by a fieldworker. (Georg Gerster, Rapho/Photo Researchers)

formants describe real behavior—the ways things actually happen. In such cases, there is a strong likelihood that the researcher's data will be less reliable, since an informant may not trust the fieldworker completely and may consciously mislead him or her. Many times, this misdirection is not deliberate, since native descriptions often are rationalizations of a given activity. Other times, in order to satisfy the anthropologist's desire to learn about some unobserved custom, informants may pretend to remember more than they actually do. Informants continue to be the primary sources of data in fieldwork, but it is crucial to avoid depending too heavily upon too few, unconfirmed sources. Pelto and Pelto (1973) mention one ethnographer who interviewed a single Ingalik Indian for 500 hours. This informant may have been a remarkably knowledgeable person—or simply a great storyteller. For this reason, one must question the reliability of information until it is confirmed by more than one member of a society. Experienced ethnographers learn to confirm whatever information they record by checking it with other informants who, by virtue of the positions they hold or have held, can comment on the activities in question.

Whatever the limitations of informants in specific instances, their necessity to fieldworkers is beyond question. They help teach fieldworkers to speak the local language; to master native skills; and to behave in appropriate ways. Without such instruction, a stranger might linger indefinitely on the fringes of society, unable to gain acceptance. One's first informants are often marginal members of the society themselves and therefore more easily approached and more eager to give information. They may be, for this reason, less initiated into the inner workings of the group than others closer to the center. But with the introduction provided by initial informants, anthropologists usually soon establish rapport with others in the group. They may sometimes even achieve this access unaided, if they are already adept at some important local skill. Freilich (1970), for example, reports his quick acceptance by his Creole subjects in Trinidad because he was adept at cricket: "The British had introduced cricket to Trinidad, and the sport was popular with young and old. My knowledge of the game soon brought me into contact with Mr. Ed . . . [whose] house was a hang-out for many of the Creole peasants. . . . After cricket practice we would all stop at Ed's house." Anthropologists frequently find that they can collect valuable information at such informal gatherings. One's simple observations of who is present and who is absent in themselves provide insights into local relations and groupings or, more important, into changes in them.

Field Data

Maps, Inventories, and Census

One of the major problems encountered in the early stages of fieldwork is simply one of settling into the society—setting up housekeeping and some sort of work schedule, finding one's way around the community, learning the language and the daily routine of the people—not to mention the physical adjustments to changes in temperature, food, and water. From the beginning, most anthropologists keep diaries in which they note as many details of each day's events as possible. They try to record only what they have observed and not to generalize about their experiences. Eventually, of course, many small items from these diaries work their way into broader understandings. Therefore, the writer tries to omit nothing, no matter how poorly or incompletely he or she may understand an observation. For example, when the author had returned home from Argentina and was in the process of analyzing his field data on Toba religious leaders, he found references in his diary to places and dates that proved helpful in separating out distinctive attitudes of various Toba communities toward their leaders. In fact, a chance comment about the action of one chief led to a major reconsideration of the widely held distinction between religious and political leaders.

While ethnographers are still relatively unfamiliar with their subjects and as yet unable to speak the native language, they usually take the opportunity to collect certain information about the local community. They gather data that are easy to compile without much fluency in the language or help from native* infor-

*To anthropologists, the term *native* refers simply to indigenous people, those belonging to the region. Thus, natives may be primitive people living in the wild, or the most sophisticated urban dwellers, depending on what region is the subject of fieldwork.

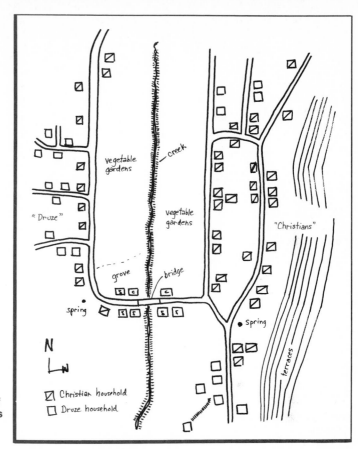

A map drawn in the course of fieldwork in a Lebanese village shows physical features of the area, as well as the religious affiliation of households. A census of who lived in the "Druze" (a Moslem sect) and in the "Christian" parts of the village showed the inaccuracy of the native model of the village as rigidly divided on the basis of religion. (Robert W. Fredericks)

mants but which will be useful later in interpreting other materials. This early period is very often spent in mapping the physical features of landscape and habitat and making inventories of material goods. Among the physical features the ethnographer would note are the locations and types of fields and forests and sources of water—streams, springs, or wells. In the local community itself, the anthropologist would record the presence of paths and streets, the arrangement, density, and construction of buildings, and the like.

Inventories of material goods also can be extremely informative. They can reveal differences—by local standards—between the more and the less materially successful members of the community. Some of the items that an anthropologist might consider in an inventory of material goods are house style; materials used in house construction; source of water and lighting (if any); amount and kinds of furniture; numbers of animals owned; landholdings; means of transportation; tools; food; clothing (Pelto, 1970). By plotting this data, the fieldworker discovers not merely who is rich and who is poor, but also how different individuals and groups live and are employed. An inventory also can highlight what equipment is technically useful and what items are connected to status and prestige in that society. Since people sometimes enjoy showing off their possessions, taking inventory can often serve as a pleasant introduction of the ethnographer to the community.

In addition to maps and inventories, anthropologists use photography as a means of collecting field data. Photographs and films themselves often serve as documents of anthropological fieldwork. In recent years, anthropologists have sought professional assistance in filming ceremonies and other types of social interaction. These films have proved to be useful not only for descriptive purposes but also when analyzing aspects of social interaction. Some people, in fact, consider use of photography in fieldwork a specialized subfield of the discipline, which they call *visual anthropology.*

Once the ethnographer can speak easily to the people under study, he or she customarily attempts to take a census of each household. The purpose of the census is to map, among other things, the residence patterns of individuals, recording changes of residence throughout their lives. The age, marital status, and education of each member and his ownership of land or other property or forms of wealth also are recorded.

At this point the fieldworker usually proceeds to collect data on kinship and marriage. Such work frequently begins with the collection of genealogies (descent charts). In some societies, genealogies provide insights into the entire social system. Anthropologist Napoleon Chagnon discovered in studying the Yąnomamö Indians of Venezuela and Brazil that "accurate genealogies are fundamental to an understanding of Yąnomamö social organization, intervillage political relationships and past history. . . . [Genealogical]

In an area where the supply of water is a problem, Irven DeVore and a Bantu interpreter measure the amount of water used in a day by a group of !Kung bushmen hunters. (Stan Washburn, Anthro-Photo)

data have constituted the most important single source of information on many different aspects of the culture" (1974, p. 89).

In recent years, anthropologists have begun to include a number of other items in their census. To shed light on the problems of food production and distribution, for example, some fieldworkers have recorded the number of individuals who participate in the production of food, the length of the working day, seasonal variations in the routine of food production, the number of years men and women are thought capable of contributing to food production, and other related factors. Consumption goods are weighed and measured in each household in order to determine how much value a given household places upon accumulation rather than consumption.

When the community under study is too large to be canvassed completely by direct interviews and surveys, different methods are required. In this case, the ethnographer must master the techniques of sampling. They will ensure, as far as possible, that the data collected and conclusions reached are representative of the community as a whole and the groups within it. To generalize from data carelessly compiled can lead to serious distortion—and sometimes has done so. Despite the fact that anthropologists have moved increasingly to the study of urban communities, it does not mean necessarily that they are always working with large populations. In fact, many of their studies continue to be with small groups, such as skid-row drunks or minorities of one sort or another.

Whether the community is large or small, however, there are many reasons to collect reliable quantitative information. Mitchell (1967) provides an example of marriage between clans. If two clans have no preference for intermarriage, the incidence of marriage between members of the clans would be determined by the number of eligible marriage partners. If the anthropologist finds there are more intermarriages than chance would dic-

tate, he or she has discovered a preference for interclan marriage. If there is less intermarriage than chance would dictate, one may have discovered an aversion to interclan marriage. Thus, quantitative data may reveal the patterning of certain phenomena. Demographic features—birth and death rates, frequency of marriage and divorce, age distribution, and kinship categories—may reveal the basic organization of a community. When a report of the fieldwork is written up, demographic features are often used to support the fieldworker's analysis of the social structure.

Organizing and Using Field Data

From this discussion, we have seen what kinds of material anthropologists gather in the field and the sequence in which they are collected. We have yet to learn how they go about organizing their data into categories or framing questions about these materials. In compiling a genealogy, for example, how do anthropologists identify particular members of a kinship group? Should they use the native categories and terms or kinship categories from their own culture? Should they attempt to formulate a uniform, comprehensive system that permits them to describe and analyze not only the kinship system under study but other kinship systems as well and to compare one system with another? From whose point of view should anthropologists attempt to view a kinship system—or any other social phenomenon—the natives' or their own? Will one's own categories hold any meaning for the natives? Anthropologists who enter the field with their survey questions already rigidly drawn up sometimes find that the natives cannot make sense of the questions and are unable to answer them since the questions seem irrelevant.

Even when anthropologists agree about terminology, disagreement may arise over its application. For example, two surveys of residence patterns on Truk, an island in the North

290 Pacific, done only 3 years apart by John Fischer (in 1944) and Ward Goodenough (in 1947), differed considerably. Goodenough's results indicated that Truk residence was overwhelmingly *matrilocal,* meaning that when a couple married, the groom moved to or near the home of his bride's parents. Fischer, however, found the residence pattern to be *bilocal,* meaning that the couple lived with or near either the husband's or the wife's parents. Fischer found that although in more than half the cases residence patterns were matrilocal, another third of the newlywed couples lived at or near the home of the groom's parents (a residence pattern termed *patrilocal*). After comparing their divergent findings, Goodenough concluded that the differences arose "from an honest difference in how to interpret the data" (1956, p. 24). That is, Goodenough and Fischer did not agree on what was a case of patrilocal residence. Goodenough himself stated that they had probably "been working in practice with somewhat different concepts of residence" (p. 24). He further concluded that all too often anthropologists do not routinely gather enough census data to permit them to identify residence patterns with any degree of certainty.

In the 1950s, *ethnoscience,* or cognitive anthropology, emerged as an approach to studying other cultures. It claimed that by employing the language categories of native speakers, one could identify the native—or insiders'—points of view. Ethnoscientists argued that a valid description of a society could be made best by a fieldworker who learned to speak the native language fluently and to understand its terms (such as those of kinship or residence) well enough to behave in a local setting as if he or she were native to it. Social behavior, according to the ethnoscientist, should always be studied from the point of view of the native, and the categories applied to the social activities should always be native categories. Ideas should never be imposed by

anthropologists upon their material; ideas should be allowed to surface from within by means of procedures attuned to native thinking and terminology. Although this approach is relatively recent, its origins can be traced back half a century to the writings of Edward Sapir, a culture-historian. Sapir warned of the pitfalls of externally describing cultural behavior:

It is impossible to say what an individual is doing unless we have tacitly accepted the essentially arbitrary modes of interpretation that social tradition is constantly suggesting to us from the very moment of our birth. Let anyone who doubts this try the experiment of making a painstaking report of the actions of a group of natives engaged in some form of activity, say religious, to which he has not the cultural key. If he is a skillful writer, he may succeed in giving a picturesque account of what he sees and hears, or thinks he sees and hears, but the chances of his being able to give a relation of what happens in terms that would be intelligible and acceptable to the natives themselves are practically nil. He will be guilty of all manner of distortion. His emphasis will be constantly askew. He will find interesting what the natives take for granted as a casual kind of behavior worthy of no particular comment, and he will utterly fail to observe the crucial turning points in the course of action that give formal significance to the whole in the minds of those who do possess the key to its understanding. . . . Forms and significances which seem obvious to an outsider will be denied outright by those who carry out the patterns; outlines and implications that are perfectly clear to these may be absent to the eye of the onlooker. It is the failure to understand the necessity of grasping the native patterning which is responsible for so much unimaginative and misconceiving description of procedures that we have not been brought up with. It becomes actually possible to interpret as base what is inspired by the noblest and even holiest of motives, and to see altruism or beauty where nothing of the kind is either felt or intended. (Sapir, in Mandlebaum, 1949, pp. 546–547)

The declared aim of ethnoscience has been to discover and employ the cognitive processes by which members of a society organize and understand their own knowledge of the world.

Critics of this approach make the point, as we have, that the anthropologist's overall theoretical framework controls much of his or her mode of observation. They also point out that although the native models of reality may often offer insight into their social life, this view cannot be relied upon to explain all its aspects. The native view often fails to illuminate important relationships and processes; at times native explanations even obscure or distort aspects of social *processes*.* Anthropologists frequently find, for example, that such explanations may serve to mask tension or conflict between individuals or groups. More frequently the anthropologist finds that the natives' purpose is *opposed* to that of the anthropologist, which is to make clear the patterning of relationships and the cultural processes involved. Nevertheless, because native explanations often point to the most significant aspects of a phenomenon, they do frequently offer valuable clues to the anthropologist. Among the Toba, for instance, it is widely believed that a man will lose his ability to hunt if a menstruating woman touches his bow or arrows. One adult male, in particular, insisted that he had lost his luck as a hunter because his wife had handled his weapons during her menstrual period. Further analysis of the culture demonstrated that hunting was one of several activities where male and female roles were clearly differentiated. Hunting was the domain of males, and women were expected to have no association with it. The Toba explanation served to perpetuate this separation of roles. Furthermore, it turned out that the male in question had never been a good hunter; his complaint was an excuse to cover his own ineptitude.

*Anthropologists use the term *process* to refer both to the internal mechanisms within a society that provide the impetus for its peculiar character (one society might stress competition while another might value cooperation), and to the conditions of culture contact that produce change.

Inference

Generalizing from Observations

In any ethnographic study, generalizations are based on hundreds or, more often, thousands of observations of the practices of a single social group. As the anthropologist begins to identify behaviors and attitudes that seem to form a pattern, he or she begins to make tentative inferences about possible relationships. The anthropologist quickly tests these hunches against further observations in order to confirm the tentative conclusions. In this manner he or she begins to make generalizations and to discover patterns.

We should note, however, that the anthropologist usually arrives in the field with a specific problem in mind and maybe even a proposed solution as well. In order to meet the requirements of a degree and to acquire funds to do fieldwork, the anthropologist has already defined a problem and considered its theoretical and methodological implications. It would be misleading, therefore, to imply that the problem under study is derived strictly from observations in the field.

Finding Patterns. The simplest level of generalization involves the description of a single pattern or regularity found to exist in the social life of people under study. Sometimes ethnographers document these patterns with supporting field data. More commonly, they simply state the patterns as fact, with little or no documentation. The next task is to link a pattern with others in order to show how they are interrelated.

Thus, when anthropologists are able to make firm generalizations about one or more aspects of the social life of a group, they are tempted to create a pattern of generalizations based on those key points, and then to make other related generalizations from them. This method is logical, but it can lead to problems. For example, the anthropologist may have dependable data from a single culture about the patterning of relations among kinspeople but less information about the patterning of relations within voluntary associations (groups of people not related by kinship but united by common interest). The anthropologist may wish to offer a generalization that will link the patterning of relations in these two groups. But he or she may not be able to decide whether to regard voluntary associations as a pattern similar to, and perhaps derived from, the kin groups in the society, or as a reaction against such groups. If the anthropologist stresses similarities, he or she might suggest that voluntary associations derive from or attempt to simulate kin groups. If he or she stresses differences, the logical inference might be that voluntary associations arose in reaction to the demands of kinship (Cohen, 1970).

The manner in which anthropologists go about generalizing from field data continues to be an important matter for debate in the discipline. The problem can best be illustrated by a specific example.

Marriage in the Middle East. The example concerns marriage relations in Middle Eastern societies. In many of these societies, marriages between the children of brothers (or those classified by the society as the children of brothers) is widespread. Anthropologists call these unions *patrilateral parallel-cousin marriages,* and considerable attention has been paid to them in the literature. Many anthropologists conducting research in these societies act as if there were no other forms of marriage practiced. By ignoring all other forms of marriage, they imply that everything one needs to know about marriage is exemplified by patrilateral parallel-cousin marriages.

Hilma Granqvist (1931), a Danish anthropologist, was one of the first to study marriage relations in the Middle East. In her analysis of the social life of a Palestinian village, she does mention that several forms of marriage are practiced, but she considers in her study only those marriages between persons classified as patrilateral parallel-cousins. Accounting for 47 percent of the marriages in the village, this is the most prevalent form, although of course more than half the marriages are not between such cousins. According to Granqvist, the popularity of patrilateral parallel-cousin marriages is rooted in the desire to keep the ownership of land and other property within the family. Since, in these societies, property is inherited through one's father, if a man's daughters marry his brothers' sons, then their inherited property remains within the kin group. This one factor—the desire to keep property, particularly land, within the family—is, to Granqvist, solely responsible for determining the preference for marriage forms in the village.

This is a questionable explanation at best. Critics point out that the loss of property through women who have married outside the kin group would, in many cases, be balanced in the long run by property gained through women from other groups who married into it. Regardless of such criticisms, what is important for our purposes is the methodology used by Granqvist to construct her patterns of generalization. First she listed all forms of marriage practiced in the village. She then isolated the one form—patrilateral parallel-cousin marriage—that was statistically most common. Finally she identified the single feature—namely, the retention of property by the kin group—shared by all cases of such marriages. In other words, Granqvist looked only for similarities among the group of marriages, not for point of contrast or differences.

A study of marriage relations among the Bedouin of Cyrenaica (Libya) by Emrys Peters (1963) reveals a different approach. The Bedouin economy has been primarily pastoral.

Thus, the rights to pasture lands and sources of water have been of great value to the Bedouin. Peters points out that one of the major social distinctions the Bedouin make is between *patrons* and *clients*. Patrons may claim the use of pasture and water as rights, whereas clients may not. Although both patrons and clients practice the same forms of marriage, the social implications of marriage between patrilateral parallel cousins are quite different for patrons than they are for clients. When a patron marries within his kin group, he increases his access to pasture and water by virtue of his wife's rights in the kin group. He therefore is able to increase the size of his animal holdings. Clients have no rights of access to pasture and water, and therefore they cannot increase the size of their herds and flocks by marrying within their kin group. On the basis of this one difference, Peters proceeds to construct a pattern of generalizations that has implications in many fields of activity, showing the differences in potential of kin-group marriages for patrons and for clients. In particular, Peters shows that patrons are able to exchange access to pasture and water for political loyalty. Clients cannot make transactions of this kind since they have no rights in the resources they use.

By examining differences as well as similarities, Peters has revealed a pattern through which he can make sense of patrilateral parallel-cousin marriage among both patrons and clients. He is able also to use the pattern to illuminate a number of other fields of activity and, in the process, show some of the implications of this marriage form throughout Bedouin social life. In contrast to Granqvist and most other anthropologists who have written on marriage in the Middle East, Peters does not dwell upon a single marriage form exclusively. Through his analysis, he sheds light on the total pattern of marriage among the Bedouin. Again, had Peters looked only at similarities, he would have ignored many important features of Bedouin social life.

In looking at patterns of social behavior, anthropologists consider the ways in which various activities interrelate. A yearly festival is the only occasion these Moroccan nomads have for a marriage ceremony. Their entire tribe meets once a year, at which time young people are married off, camels are traded, and divorces are available. (Stephanie Dinkins, Photo Researchers)

The Comparative Method

A major approach in anthropology has been *cross-cultural comparison,* or what has come to be termed the comparative method. There is, in fact, no single comparative method but a series of them. In the nineteenth century, anthropologists demonstrated the development of societies by comparing selected aspects of culture according to their relative degrees of sophistication. Thus, among means of transportation, for example, the horsecart might be judged more advanced than the sedan chair but less advanced than the stagecoach. The belief in ancestor spirits was considered more advanced than the belief that all natural phenomena are inhabited by spirits (animism) but less advanced than the belief in one supreme being (monotheism). Such comparisons of separate elements were measured along a scale from more simple to more advanced.

In the twentieth century, the comparative method came to mean comparing instances of culture change within a specified geographical area. In American anthropology, this involved studies of North American Indian communities; in British anthropology, the focus was mainly on African societies. In 1954, in an address to the Association of American Anthropologists, Fred Eggan proposed a method he called *controlled comparison*. To Eggan, this meant making comparisons between similar social groups or similar cultural types. He suggested, for example, first comparing the lineage structures of Australian aboriginal tribes and then comparing these findings with the results of a similar study of the Indians of Southern California, whose social structure resembles that of the Australian aborigines. Still further comparative studies could be made with other similarly organized groups. This method has not been widely used, but it demonstrates the range and variety of the comparative method.

A more ambitious version of the comparative method was introduced by George Peter Murdock, who in 1937 initiated the Cross-Cultural Survey, later converted into the Human Relations Area Files (HRAF). The purpose of HRAF is systematically to gather information on every known human society and to arrange the data in categories that permit anthropologists to take a single element of one culture and compare it with its counterparts throughout the world. For example, habits of dress, marriage customs, or table manners could be examined and compared for every society for which there is information. Already a *World Ethnographic Sample* has been compiled, based upon a representative sample of cultures and using the available data. This sample can provide information for cross-cultural study of any anthropological topic. It is to date the most ambitious attempt to organize ethnographic data on a global scale.

One achievement of the quantitative studies that have come out of uses of the *World Ethnographic Sample* has been to identify a group of elements that occur together in a number of cultures and to ascertain what principles link them. For example, Guy Swanson (1960) found that monotheistic beliefs tend to originate in societies with a hierarchy of three or more independent social groups. Witchcraft was found to be prevalent in societies in which sovereign social groups interact without legitimate mechanisms for social control. Such comparative studies have been criticized for trying to compare incompatible data, but their findings often are provocative.

Structural Models

In their continuing attempts to compare social phenomena, anthropologists have shifted their attention increasingly from the level of observable social behaviors to the level of models. A *model* is a system of relations that is thought to be parallel to, or a simulation of, a set of relations under study. It can be thought of as a kind of analogy. There are many types and varieties of models used in anthropology. The most characteristic feature of a model is its reduction of a state of affairs to the most simple and logically determined level. This simple and logical state can then be reapplied to more complex and elusive aspects of social life in order to generalize on their nature. A model must satisfy certain requirements. First, it must be a system composed of interdependent parts, so that a change in one element will cause changes in the other elements. Second, it should enable one to predict what will happen if one or more elements of the model are modified. Third, the model as constructed should explain all the observed social phenomena (Lévi-Strauss, 1953). Once an anthropologist has constructed a model, he or she will usually compare it to other similar models, letting the relationships of one social structure shed light upon another. It is the structural similarity that is sought, rather than a similarity of content in terms of data. Those who construct structural models for the comparative analysis of social phenomena are called *structuralists*.

Two major types of structuralists are found in anthropology. The first type, represented by the works of Radcliffe-Brown and his students, finds structure at the same level as observable social interaction. These structuralists look at social interaction and infer from it a model that may account for the activities concerned. A different type of structuralist approach is found in the writings of Claude Lévi-Strauss, who derives his models not from conscious social activities but from logical properties associated with the human mind. The kind of structure sought by Lévi-Strauss is found in unconscious reality, which cannot be discovered by observation but can be demonstrated by models that are used to uncover structure. The underlying structure can be called upon to interpret social relations as they appear at the level of observation. Thus, Lévi-Strauss took attention away from the *content* of social relations to focus on their underlying structure.

Microcosmic Models and the Bigger Picture

Anthropologists have been largely content in the past to confine their observations and inferences to the local community. In other words, they have taken a microcosmic approach to their fieldwork. In the microcosmic approach, the local community, be it a camp or village, is considered to be the entire society in miniature or, conversely, the society is thought to be no more than the local community much expanded. Not only is the local community treated as "typical" of other communities in the society, but it is also believed somehow to "typify" the society itself. The problem with this approach is that it is extremely unlikely that the local community is representative of anything except itself.

Thus, generalizations about the larger unit tend to be meaningless. It is therefore extremely difficult to imagine a case in which the microcosmic approach would be sufficient to explain the variation within a single society.

The chief shortcoming of the microcosmic approach is that it has led some anthropologists to believe that the focus of their study is more or less isolated, capable of being studied in and of itself as a complete system. They assume that every important influence on the beliefs and practices of the community under study is to be found within the physical limits of the community. Any outside influences that clamor for description are given "secondary" status or, in some cases, no status at all. But no social unit, no matter how small, simple, or seemingly isolated, is bounded in such a clear and absolute fashion. The boundaries of any community are ill defined and constitute merely thresholds of intensity in kinds of interaction. For example, when the Argentine government required military training of all aboriginal populations, it opened up contact

Few cultures today remain untouched by either urban society or tourists. Here, Western tourists watch a New Guinea ceremonial dance. (Philip Jones Griffiths, Magnum Photos)

with the broader society that had far-reaching implications. Young men who had stayed close to their native communities now had the opportunity to go to new places and have new experiences. Were one to study the Toba without taking into consideration government policies toward Indians, the resulting enthnography would be limited in scope and devoid of valuable information necessary to understand life among the Toba.

Cultural anthropologists now recognize that events and activities outside the boundaries of the local community influence what happens, or what people think and do within it. What at first glance appear purely local activities and ideas cannot be fully interpreted without reference to regional, national, and even global frameworks. When anthropologists insist upon too narrow a focus, they necessarily limit the validity of their findings. Growing acceptance of this viewpoint makes current anthropology more realistic and illuminating and facilitates its relevance to pressing problems and issues of the day.

"Truth" in Anthropology

We have discussed the methods of cultural anthropology—fieldwork involving participant observation, the use of informants, compilation of field data and their comparative analysis—and have noted the problems of some aspects of anthropological method. But we have still not answered the question of what constitutes "truth" in anthropology. Lévi-Strauss (1968) has suggested that anthropological truth may not be "factual evidence" of the sort to be found in the natural sciences but may "consist in a special kind of relationship between the observer and the observed" (p. 351). One resemblance between modern anthropology and the natural sciences, however, may explain why data collected as recently as the early twentieth century often no longer seems adequate or valid. Just as advances in the natural sciences have rendered invalid a great quantity of early theory and experimental data, so have advances in anthropology robbed many earlier observations of their "truth." In some cases, the questions themselves are no longer relevant. Nevertheless, much of what early anthropologists accomplished continues to serve as the basis for new developments in the field. As Lévi-Strauss has written, "in anthropology, as elsewhere, progress will never result from destroying what has been previously achieved but rather from incorporating the past of our science into its present and future, enriching the one with the other and turning the whole process into a lasting reality" (p. 352). Every piece of work in anthropology is limited—by the constraints of the situation, the shortsightedness of the observer, lapses in the field, and the limits of the age. Multiple observers, working together or at different times, can improve the quality of our knowledge and understanding, but they can never tell us all there is to know. In other words, because issues and interests change from period to period, we may approach but never arrive at the "truth." Every student of anthropology realizes that his or her work offers only partial and fleeting insights into the nature of cultural phenomena. There will always be new ideas to consider, as well as new ways of looking at what we think we already know.

Summary

1. *Ethnographers* observe in detail the social and cultural life of a people. To accumu-

late material for their ethnographies, they usually live with their subjects of study for a time. During this period they observe, question, and even adopt the customs of the people. *Ethnologists* analyze the information gathered, looking for patterns, processes, and signs of change. These findings are subsequently compared with other ethnographies in an attempt to contribute to a larger understanding of humankind. The dilemma faced by anthropologists is that they seek to comprehend an alien social and cultural system, but their own categories of understanding influence the degree of comprehension possible. No matter how effective their adaptation, they always remain "marginal natives."

2. Modern ethnography begins with the work of Malinowski. Earlier fieldwork was often fragmentary, misleading, and based upon unreliable reports. Malinowski insisted that fieldworkers make long, patient, and thorough studies, taking notice of the smallest aspects of social life. Modern ethnographers are *participant observers,* living among their subjects, speaking their language, and gathering facts in order to discover the underlying patterns of their society and culture.

3. The ethnographer aspires to make descriptions that are not only detailed but *valid* and *reliable* as well. A valid scientific observation is one that records the facts it claims to record. A reliable observation is one that can be repeated by other experimenters or observers. The most useful observations possess high degrees of both validity and reliability. While informants are a major source of data for the anthropologist, they sometimes can be unreliable.

4. Mapping is useful for recording the physical landscape and residence patterns. Genealogical data and a census of individual households help the anthropologist learn about social status, size of population, occupations, and ownership of land and other property, among other things. Some anthropolo-

gists fail to collect quantitative data, but such data have proven valuable to most researchers.

5. *Ethnoscience,* or cognitive anthropology, claims that observers should adopt the natives'—or insiders'—perspective. Categories, ideas, and judgments should emerge from the phenomena observed and not be imposed on them. Critics of ethnoscience argue that this is an impossible aim.

6. Every ethnography makes many generalizations based on thousands of observed acts. A single generalization signifies very little, so anthropologists often relate one generalization to another. A *pattern method* of generalization permits the anthropologist to show the relationship of a number of social and/or cultural phenomena. Any pattern should consider differences as well as similarities between the elements of comparison. To ignore differences may lead to distorted or misleading conclusions.

7. There are many applications of the comparative method. One early use involved studying cultural change in a single geographic area. Through *controlled comparison,* anthropologists study only groups or elements that show strong social or cultural similarities. The Human Relations Area Files (HRAF) were developed so that anthropologists could compare cultural phenomena around the world. Structuralist anthropologists make their comparisons based on models of social structures derived from what they have observed in the field. Some models are at the level of observable social phenomena; others at the level of the unconscious workings of the human mind.

8. A regional perspective is gradually replacing the microcosmic approach to field work. According to the microcosmic approach, a single community can be considered a miniature version of an entire society. The observer may thus confuse the focus of study, the local community, with the true point of study—the patterns of interaction in the community. Anthropologists are coming to agree

that no single place should be studied in isolation.

9. Anthropological truth is hard to define, because the "truth" of anthropology may "consist in a special relation between the observer and the observed." That is, it may be more experiential than factual in nature. The truth itself is so complex that there can be no final, definitive statement about cultural phenomena.

14
The Culture Concept

WHAT does the word *culture* suggest to you? Is it a special quality you can somehow develop by visiting book-lined studies, opera halls, and museums? Can you "catch" culture by listening to Mozart, studying poems, or appreciating paintings? According to anthropological definitions of culture, none of these activities is necessary—we all have culture already by virtue of having been raised in a society. We express culture in such everyday activities as eating, shopping, and going to school. For *culture,* to an anthropologist, is something shared to a large extent by everyone in a particular society, something we learn from each other and from past generations, something that influences how we think and act. It refers to that which is learned and shared, in contrast to what is genetically transmitted among humans. When it comes to applying the concept of culture to actual situations, however, anthropologists find themselves in fundamental disagreements.

The history of cultural anthropology can be seen as a series of attempts to define and use the concept of culture. On each definition, different anthropologists have built very different ways of examining the human condition. In this chapter, we describe eight major theoretical approaches in anthropology by looking at how the concept of culture is defined in each of them.

From Speculation to Science

Attempts to understand and explain the nature of human existence and behavior are probably as old as humankind itself. For as long as written records have been kept, people have speculated about the origins of their institutions and their relationship with the outside world, each other, and supernatural beings. In the classical civilizations, they often credited supernatural beings with creating social institutions and beliefs. The ancient Egyptians, for instance, created elaborate myths to explain the facts of the human condition in terms of intervention by the gods. It was Osiris, for example, who taught people how to grow crops and trees and who gave them the gifts of wisdom and appreciation for the arts. He made laws that enabled humans to live together harmoniously, explained the origin of the earth and humanity, and taught people about the gods and how they were to be honored (Colum, 1930). The Mesopotamians, on the other hand, thought the gods had created humans to do their earthly chores. A cosmic council was said to have chosen a human king and charged him with establishing social order on earth. Social phenomena—such as laws, kinship patterns, or food getting—were thus considered human-made features of life and not the work of gods (Wright, 1960).

Such explanations increased over the years. It was not until the late nineteenth century that the study of humanity was clearly defined as a science, a methodical attempt to explain the human condition through the use of theories (White, 1949). A theory, according to Freeman (1968), is simply "the expression of a series of hunches about which things go together in the world of our experience" (p. 193). An anthropologist might, for instance, suspect and demonstrate a relationship between a group's treatment of certain animals and the group's religious beliefs. The treatment of cattle in India and the position of cattle in Hinduism is a case in point.

A basic problem in formulating theories is knowing where to look to find the things that fit together. There are so many things we might observe about people—a person's hairdo, one's depression over turning 40, the choice of clothing, the arrangement and presentation of food, a country's treaty-making practices—that to generate theories we have to focus on only those phenomena that will tell us most about human behavior in society. This was difficult until someone suggested how to limit the field of inquiry.

Edward B. Tylor first did so in 1871, by defining the subject matter for a new science of humankind. He called it "culture." The science he fathered became known as anthropology. Ever since then, anyone who has proposed a different way of looking at human behavior has begun by redefining this subject matter. This is why we have so many definitions of culture today: different theorists have chosen to focus on different aspects of the human condition. Although the variety of approaches is confusing, each has contributed to our total understanding of humanity.

Culture as Evolutionary Progress

Tylor set forth his classic definition of culture in the first sentence of his 1871 book, *Primitive Culture:*

Culture, or civilization . . . is that complex whole which includes knowledge, belief, art, morals, law, custom, and any other capabilities and habits acquired by man as a member of society. (1958, p. 1)

Learned Behaviors

One of the key words in Tylor's definition is "acquired." It focused attention on the aspects of human behavior which can be traced to social learning rather than to biological heredity or individual experience. According

Culture consists of socially learned understandings. Elements of culture include the stories and myths people learn and how they learn them; the clothes they wear; the kinds of art with which they are familiar; the social groups in which people participate; the buildings in which they live and work, and their furnishings. (Marc and Evelyne Bernheim, Woodfin Camp; Alan Harbutt, Magnum)

to Tylor, the biological facts of the human condition—such as cutting teeth and having the urge to eat—are not the sorts of things anthropologists should study. But *learned* ways of expressing these biological features—customs and beliefs surrounding the eruption of the first tooth, for instance, or the use of chopsticks or silverware or other eating utensils—are. Likewise, the characteristics that individuals develop from their own unique experiences—the fear of worms, for instance, or the ability to play the piano—are not cultural phenomena unless they can be shown to be socially transmitted to a large segment of the population.

Culture, then, for Tylor, consisted of such things as knowing how to make a dug-out canoe (knowledge); feeling that supernatural beings are aware of your every move (belief); painting designs on clay pots (art); thinking it acceptable to cheat in order to gain personal advantage (morals); forbidding a community to enter into economic transactions on Sunday (law); and sharing the first piece of wedding cake with your spouse when you marry (custom).

The Complex Whole

Another important part of Tylor's definition is the phrase "complex whole." It suggests that culture traits are not isolated, random characteristics, but instead that they bear some kind of relationship to each other. A group's size, for instance, might bear a complicated relationship to its ways of obtaining food, its kinship practices, and a number of other social arrangements as well. The idea that culture traits form a "complex whole" foreshadowed the later notion of culture as an integrated system of related elements.

The Notion of Progress

Tylor's emphasis on socially learned characteristics and his notion of culture as a complex

whole still provide the general framework for the science of anthropology today. But his tendency to equate the term *culture* with *civilization* and to view human history as progress is no longer accepted.

In Victorian England, Tylor was immersed in a society that saw progress everywhere—in advancing industrial technology, increasingly enlightened politics, an ever-expanding economy. Swept up by the general feeling that life was getting better and better, Tylor looked at what was known of the history of humankind and saw in it an evolutionary progression from primitive existence to the peak of civilization—his contemporary England. As he saw it, all human groups were moving in the direction of increasingly rational thought and practical behavior, though some had progressed farther than others.

This notion of evolutionary progress gave Tylor a way to organize his thoughts about culture. Another evolutionist writer, L. H. Morgan, had proposed that humankind was moving upward through three stages: savagery, barbarism, and civilization (1877). The traits in a "savage" society included small groups, simple tools made of wood, stones, or bones, and a hunting and gathering mode of subsistence. Progress into the "barbaric" stage was to have been heralded by the development of either agriculture or animal raising. People in this stage were thought to live in settled villages, to establish political institutions, and to begin to build things from metal. The onset of the "civilized" stage, Morgan proposed, was signaled by the use of writing. Along with the advent of writing, there developed trade with other societies, formal government and courts of law, specialization in occupations, and the growth of social classes (Freeman, 1968).

Leslie White: A Return to Evolutionism

Since Tylor, in particular, saw humankind as progressing toward a state of civilization, he thought of culture in the singular. To him, culture was something all humans shared, though some had more of it than others and were therefore more "cultured." Anthropologists gradually dropped this notion, preferring to study the differences among groups as just that: differences, not lags in development. But the notion of culture as evolutionary progress in humanity as a whole reappeared in the middle of the twentieth century, in the writings of Leslie White.

Symboling. To White, author of the influential book *The Science of Culture* (1949), culture is:

a distinct . . . class of phenomena, namely those things and events that are dependent upon the exercise of a mental ability, peculiar to the human species, that we have termed "symbolling." . . . Culture consists of material objects, . . . acts, beliefs, and attitudes. . . . It is an elaborate . . . organization of . . . ways and means employed by . . . man in the struggle for existence and survival. (1949, p. 363)

By "symbolling," White meant people's use of symbols, such as words, to represent the things in their experience. With symbols, people can pass on knowledge and beliefs without having to use the actual things they are talking about as demonstrations. A mother can, for instance, tell her daughter the "proper" way to act toward her husband-to-be without producing the fiancé and acting out mock domestic scenes.

Through the use of symbols, people also give meaning to their experiences. In some societies, for instance, a woman may see her fiancé as a symbol of love and companionship; in others, he may symbolize authority, protection, and material security. This possibility of differing interpretations of the facts of social existence allows considerable variations in world views.

Progress as Energy Harnessing. To explain the development of variations in the ways

people in different societies live and think, White returned to Tylor's view of history as evolutionary progress. All people, he thought, are moving toward the same goal through adaptation; some have simply gone farther than others. Like Tylor, White therefore asserted that we can think of all cultures as composing a single unit—the culture of humankind—and trace its development from the past to the present.

When White did so, he found evidence that human progress depended not on such things as writing or legal codes but primarily on a technoeconomic factor—the harnessing of energy. Culture, to White, was a system for capturing energy to aid people in the "struggle for existence and survival." He stated that the increased harnessing of energy represents progress because it produces changes that enable people to adapt themselves more efficiently to their environment.

The earliest human groups, according to White's theory of the history of culture, depended on human energy alone. Averaging the contributions of children, men, and women, including the aged, this would probably amount to only about 1/20th of one horsepower per person. Fire might have been used for warming the body, cooking, and scaring away wild beasts, but it was rarely used as a substitute for muscle power.

Whereas the most primitive groups subsisted solely on wild plants and animals, the domestication of crops and herds gave people greater control over nature and released a considerable amount of human energy for what White called "culture building" (1949, p. 371). Within a few thousand years (a relatively short period compared to the hundreds of thousands of years of slow and limited development during the Stone Ages), cultures mushroomed into great civilizations. From China to Egypt to Mexico, cities and empires replaced small-scale, isolated social groupings. Progress in industry, art, and knowledge was rapid. There were huge engineering projects,

PYRAMIDES ÆGYPTIACÆ.

A. Die größte Pyramide, woran 360000 Menschen 20 Jahr gearbeitet, B. Die andere, welche etwas weniger an Umfange hat C. Die kleineste, in welche, wie in die andere gar kein Eingang ist D. Das überbliebene von dem Colossalischen Sphynx E. Dessen sonst vollkomne Gestalt. Anson.

A. La plus grande des Pyramides, qui a été l'ouvrage de 360000 hommes pendant 20 Ans. Pion B. La seconde, qui a un peu moins de circonference C. La plus petite, qui a nulle ouverture, comme la Seconde. D. Le reste du Sphynx Colossal. E. Le Sphynx dans sa forme entiere. Anson.

Culture historians believe that domestication of plants and animals released human energy that led to the development of the great ancient civilizations of China, Mexico, and Egypt. (From the collection of Dr. N. T. Gidal, Monkmeyer)

great architectural efforts, and impressive accomplishments in the arts. Writing, mathematics, astronomy, and medical science appeared and developed.

But after this mushrooming of the great ancient civilizations on the basis of agriculture and animal husbandry, progress reached a peak and then leveled off or, in some areas, even declined until about 1800 A.D., when a new way to harness energy was found—the engine. With this advance, others quickly followed. Population increased; cities and political units expanded in size and scope; wealth accumulated; and the arts and sciences developed more rapidly than ever before.

Writing in 1949, White speculated that the new harnessing of atomic energy might start humanity on a fourth great spurt of culture building.

Today when it is apparent that the high control and utilization of energy can be counterproductive, in that it can destroy the very environment that provides humankind with its basic means of subsistence and survival, the notion of progress is considered much more problematic. The idea of culture as a single thread of development could not withstand intensive scrutiny, and it had to be replaced with a more flexible and relativistic approach.

Culture as Historical Processes

An argument against looking at culture in terms of progress appeared around the turn of the century in the works of Franz Boas; he has sometimes been labeled the father of American anthropology. He replaced the evolutionists' sweeping generalizations about the history of culture as a whole with ways of examining specific cultures which are still apparent in American anthropology (Stocking, 1974).

Boas felt that anthropologists did not yet have enough information to develop general theories about culture. He argued that the "laws" that govern cultural change can only be discovered by intensive investigations of the histories of specific cultures. In his words,

before we can build up the theory of the growth of all human culture, we must know the growth of cultures that we find here and there. . . . We must, so far as we can, reconstruct the actual history of mankind, before we can hope to discover the laws underlying that history. (1898, p. 4)

To put this plan into practice, Boas chose to search out detailed histories of human groups in a limited geographical region. He first studied the northern regions of Asia and North America which bordered the Pacific Ocean. His goal was to figure out whether people on either side of the Bering Strait had contacted and influenced each other and, if so, what kind of historical processes had been at work in shaping these cultures.

Diffusion and Integration of Traits

Boas's North Pacific expedition came up with these results: at some time in the past, there was probably considerable contact be-

tween the East Siberians and the Indians of British Columbia, because a number of the same complex myths were found on both sides of the ocean. These myths were *not* found in the Eskimo tribes which had later migrated into the area, forming a wedge between the other two groups (Lowie, 1937).

In painstaking plotting of the distribution and elaboration of the myths, Boas found evidence of two important historical processes: diffusion and integration. *Diffusion* is the spread of culture traits—such as the use of shredded bark in religious ceremonies or the presence of nature-spirits in myths—from one group to another by historical contacts. *Integration* is the modification of these borrowed elements to fit the local cultural, social, and environmental contexts.

Indians of the Great Lakes area, for instance, tell of a terrible flood that occurred long ago. According to one version of the myth, several animals escaped in a canoe and tried repeatedly to dive under the floodwaters to bring up some mud. One of the animals, a muskrat, was at last successful in dredging up a bit of mud, and it expanded magically to form the earth. This tale has been found throughout a large area, including the Mackenzie River Basin in Canada, the Great Lakes watershed, the mid-Atlantic and southern parts of the United States, and several places on the Pacific Coast. But in each area, it is told somewhat differently. The Cherokee, for instance, say that in the beginning all the animals were in the air. Nothing existed below them but a great spread of water until a little water beetle and a water spider began to dive under the water to bring up some mud, thereby forming the earth. While the earth still was soft, a buzzard flapped its wings about the new land and created mountains.

According to Boas's analysis, this account of the creation of the earth was carried from one tribe to another by the process of diffusion. He argued that the spread of the myth by diffusion is more likely than its having developed independently in all these different societies. As it diffused throughout the various areas it was altered to fit each group's unique characteristics through the process of integration (Boas, 1940). We could probably account for the spread of the St. Nicholas legend from Russia (where he is a patron saint) to the United States (where he is a kindly symbol for merchants) by the same two processes in much the same way.

The Uniqueness of Culture

The process of integration, Boas felt, ties cultural traits into a coherent, though changing whole. This whole and the circumstances that have formed it may differ considerably from one group to the next. Each must therefore be studied in its own terms, rather than be compared with a single standard of comparison. For instance, Tylor looked at various societies to see how they measured against Victorian English standards. But his approach did not provide a way to understand a society that emphasized other standards. If a society considers capacities such as the power to heal the sick or to obtain the blessings of divine beings more important than the ability to grow more food than the people need, then traits in that society should be considered as choices based on spiritual beliefs rather than as failures to make technological progress.

Boas and his students thus came to view a given culture as the result of specific, often complex, historical processes. Instead of considering human culture as a whole, they focused on specific cultures in order to better understand how they had developed. Evolutionists had thought of culture as a series of stages (such as savagery-barbarism-civilization or humanpower-domesticated plant and animal power-fuel power-atomic power). Anthropologists who followed Boas saw culture as a number of historically molded units. They approached these cultural units as integrated wholes that could be evaluated and understood in terms of their own internal principles.

Cultural Relativism

It was in this context that the twentieth-century American view of *cultural relativism* emerged and took shape. Cultural relativism is the principle that all cultural patterns are equally valid. It takes form in the attempt to understand other cultural systems in their own terms, not in terms of one's own cultural beliefs. Sometimes this is not easy because the practices one encounters (such as human sacrifice or infanticide) may seem so different from the fundamental ideas or practices of one's own culture. For example, when the author first traveled among the Toba of Argentina, he was shocked to discover that the food items that he had taken with him in the jeep were not considered his personal property. Upon arriving at a settlement, he was informed by the Toba host that times were hard and that there was no food on the premises. "That's no problem," announced a Toba companion who had requested a ride to the community, "we have bread and oranges in the jeep. Brother Elmer, how about getting them some." Not only had the author lost control over his emergency food supply, but he was being ordered about by someone who had begged a ride from him in the first place! Further experience in the community made it clear when it was acceptable to horde food and when one was obligated to share, as well as when it was advisable to follow or to contradict the advice of a colleague. By withholding judgment, the author was able to learn about an elaborate system of food sharing and about the expression of opinion, which provided an important background for interpreting Toba behavior.

Although the historical view of culture contributed some important insights into the nature of the human condition, it failed to provide a clear-cut rationale or a coherent theoretical approach that could guide the discipline through the twentieth century. Failing to find generalizing principles at the level of unique cultures, it turned increasingly to the individual and to psychological processes to account for cultural phenomena. This led to the development of the culture and personality approach that will be discussed subsequently. The concept of society was underdeveloped and largely ignored by the historical approach.

Culture as Functionally Related System

While reaction in America to a nineteenth-century evolutionary view of culture was changing into concern with the details of individual cultures, opposition to Tylor's approach was taking a different course in England. There, anthropologists stopped trying to re-create the history of humankind, either as a whole or in pieces. Instead, they thought they would learn more by looking at living societies and cultures, analyzing them as systems in which every relationship or institution has a function and is understood as a part of the larger whole that is society. Two principal proponents of this *functional* or *structural-functional* approach were Bronislaw Malinowski and A. R. Radcliffe-Brown.

Malinowski viewed culture as an instrument for fulfilling human psychological and biological needs, such as reproduction, nutrition, comfort, and safety. For him, certain cultural institutions—such as those involved in obtaining food—exist to satisfy these basic needs. Others, he argued, satisfy the secondary needs that arise from them. The primary need for bodily comfort, for instance, may be transformed by one culture into a need for the manufacturing of inner-spring mattresses and upholstered furniture.

While Malinowski looked at cultural phenomena as mechanisms that meet individual needs, Radcliffe-Brown focused on the needs of society. To him, the purpose of any social relationship was to ensure the integration and stability of the social structure that formed the basis of society. He equated a society or social system with the total ensemble of social relations, the social structure that he saw as observable in the everyday life of a people.

Structural Principles

Radcliffe-Brown's chief interest was in discovering certain fundamental principles that contribute to the coherence of society, such as the divisions of people on the basis of generation and sex, or the closeness of sibling groups. This kind of analysis has become quite sophisticated, with studies that try to uncover the mechanisms that allow societies to maintain their structure, even though maladaptive. Of the two, Radcliffe-Brown's influence has been more persistent and extensive.

S. F. Nadel (1960), for instance, has demonstrated that witchcraft in four African societies is a mechanism that allows tensions between people occupying certain social roles to continue, without disrupting the social structure. Among the Nupe people, for instance, witches are always women; their victims are invariably men. The sex antagonism this reveals—with evil intentions ascribed to females and kindly ones to males—can be explained as a result of tensions built into the relationship between Nupe husbands and wives. The women are usually better off financially than their husbands, which the men consider to be contrary to the traditional way of things. Among the Nupe, it is often the mother, rather than the father, who puts up the bride price that their son needs in order to marry. She also finances big feasts and pays for

307

THE CULTURE CONCEPT

the children's education. Women often earn their income as itinerant traders. To do so, they may leave their children when they are 4 or 5 years old, refuse to have any more children, and accept the image of having loose morals which is associated with the trading profession in Nupe society. Men deeply resent these reversals of what they feel are the proper sex roles, but they are helpless to change them. Their hostility toward domineering and independent women, resentment of their own powerlessness, and wishes of having the upper hand, Nadel argues, are transformed into witchcraft beliefs in which men are both the victims of women's immorality but also the only ones who can develop the magical power to block their witchcraft.

In another group, the Mesakin, the tensions that cause witchcraft beliefs seem to revolve around older men's envy of younger men's virility and youth. The Mesakin divide male adolescence and adulthood into three highly formalized age classes. The first class includes all prepuberty boys. The second class consists of boys who have reached puberty and is characterized by the right to engage in certain sporting contests. The third class occurs around age 24; at that point a man is considered to be already old and is grouped with physically old men.

The first sporting contest, which is allowed when a boy reaches puberty, is an occasion of much celebration among the Mesakin. It is expected that the boy's uncle will honor the occasion with an important gift—an animal from his herd. According to the descent rules of the Mesakin, the boy will some day inherit this herd; thus, the animal given at puberty is a sort of anticipated inheritance. The demand of the inheritance while the older man is still very much alive aggravates the existing tension between the young boy and the uncle. Having a relative old enough to claim the inheritance is a pointed reminder of growing

old. The older man, therefore, refuses to give the inheritance, and the young man is expected to take it by force. Quarrels over the inheritance are common, and if any misfortune befalls the youth, the older man is suspected of having used witchcraft against him. Accusations of witchcraft are frequent, and it is always the older man who is accused. According to Nadel (1952), the witchcraft beliefs of the Mesakin are obviously related to the stress that Mesakin society puts upon men as they age and to the hostility of the older men toward the younger.

What purpose, then, do witchcraft beliefs serve in these situations? Some theorists might say that they channel social hostilities into outlets that are relatively harmless, thus enabling society to continue functioning in as much harmony as possible. But Nadel points out that witchcraft beliefs, instead, fan these hostilities, adding to the stresses in society by causing bloody acts of revenge. They deflect tension from the real cause of the problems—in Nupe, for instance, the marital and economic situation; in Mesakin, the failure to distinguish between social old age and physical old age. The function of witchcraft beliefs in these societies, then, is to control social conflict but not to resolve it, since the conflict is rooted in the very structure of society. According to Nadel, witchcraft beliefs

enable a society to go on functioning in a given manner, fraught with conflicts and contradictions which the society is helpless to resolve; the witchcraft beliefs thus absolve the society from a task apparently too difficult for it, namely some radical readjustment. (Nadel, 1960, pp. 418–419)

In functionalism, the focus of research shifted from the concept of culture to that of society. It also shifted from that of history and change to that of static equilibrium. Not only did functionalism fail to account for change, it also failed to explain how any supposed system came to be what it was claimed to be. Since any social phenomenon was explained in terms of its relationship to another one, there was no logical place to begin and end the systemic analysis. Its reasoning appeared to be circular. Society and culture were treated as mirror images of each other, and no dynamic interaction between the two concepts was proposed.

Culture as Personality Configuration

At the same time that the structural-functional approach was taking form in England, the students of Boas in the United States were coming around to a similar view of culture as an integrated system. Compared to the British, though, they gave more attention to the limitless possibilities for cultural variations and put more stress on the psychological reasons for differences between cultures.

Cultural Diversity

The classic example of this approach is to be found in *Patterns of Culture* (1934) by Ruth Benedict, a student of Boas. She pointed out that the various aspects of social life—concepts of ownership, relations of production, trade, sexual activities, religious beliefs and rituals—may be endlessly varied and combined into different patterns. Each culture selects only certain elements for its pattern and emphasizes some more than others. As Benedict wrote, "one culture hardly recognizes monetary values; another has made them fundamental in every field of behavior. . . . One builds an enormous culture superstructure upon adolescence, one upon death, one upon after-life" (Benedict, 1934, p. 22).

The basis for variations in cultural patterns, Benedict decided, lies not only in history or the functioning of social institutions but also in the temperament of a people. A whole society, she wrote, may develop a typical pattern of emotions and attitudes, or what she called a personality configuration. For instance, people in one culture might tend to be aggressive, passionate, and proud, whereas those in another might typically be easy-going, loving, and modest. Benedict held that such personality configurations determine which cultural elements will be selected, rejected, or modified to be integrated into the cultural pattern of a society. According to Benedict, you cannot really understand a culture unless you are aware of the underlying pattern that holds everything together. To illustrate this point, she explained the contrasts between two American Indian groups on the basis of their personality differences.

The Pueblo and Plains Patterns. Benedict used two personality configurations borrowed from the Greek tragedies to describe the two groups of Indians. She characterized one group, the Pueblo Indians, as "Apollonian," and the other group, the Plains Indians, as "Dionysian." The "Dionysian" character of the Plains Indians was expressed in excess, frenzy, and heightened individual experience. To achieve supernatural power, for instance, men of the Plains tribes subjected themselves to terrible tortures—slicing skin off their arms, cutting off fingers, swinging from poles by straps run under their shoulder muscles, denying themselves food and water, among others. They sought religious ecstasy in trances induced by fasting, cactus beer, peyote, or marathon dancing, sometimes with snakes. This tendency to value excesses was expressed in other customs as well, from abandoned mourning behaviors to violent reactions to adultery.

The "Apollonian" character of the Pueblos stressed moderation and cooperation in all things, according to Benedict (who has been accused of ignoring evidence to the contrary to make her point). For instance, their funeral rites were simple and undramatic; disagreements were handled without violence; and initiation of boys into manhood was supportive rather than humiliating. Whereas a Plains Indian husband would react violently to his wife's adultery and cut off part of her nose, a Pueblo husband would respond mildly to such a discovery. Pueblo institutions allowed easy divorce, and adultery might simply be seen as the first step in this direction.

Although some of the same cultural elements can be found in both Pueblo and Plains tribes, Benedict argued that these elements were used differently according to the temperamental type around which each culture was integrated. Fasting, for instance, supposedly was used by the Plains Indians to produce visions. The Pueblo peoples fasted, too, but primarily to purify themselves for religious ceremonies (Benedict, 1934). However, subsequent investigation has shown this observation to be oversimplified and superficial.

The French "National Spirit." This search for an integrating principle or personality type below the level of cultural expression has been used to understand technologically developed, diversified cultures as well as simpler ones. Edward Sapir, for instance, analyzed French cultural institutions as embodiments of what he called the French "national genius": "clarity, lucid systematization, balance, care in choice of means, and good taste. . . [but also] overmechanization, . . . emotional timidity or shallowness, . . . exaggeration of manner at the expense of content" (Sapir, 1949, p. 312). Among the cultural traits Sapir

traced to this French national spirit are the formal nature of classical French drama and the tendency to intellectualism in French art, philosophy, and literature. Other attempts to capture national character have been equally vague and impressionistic. For this reason, national character studies have come to be abandoned completely.

Psychoanalysis of Cultures

Scholars associated with this approach to culture, known in anthropology as the "culture and personality school," turned increasingly to psychology and psychiatry for descriptions and explanations of how various configurations developed. Often, explanations were sought in early childhood experiences that were thought to be typical. Tight swaddling of Russian infants, for instance, was said to produce manic-depression in Russian adults (Gorer & Rickman, 1950). Strict toilet-training of Japanese babies was pinpointed as the cause of compulsiveness in the Japanese national character (LaBarre, 1945). Anthropologists who took this approach began to see whole cultures as sick personalities. The Kwakiutl of British Columbia, for instance, with their obsessive potlatches (ceremonies in which large quantities of various possessions are given away or destroyed to enhance status) were considered to be "megalomaniac"; the magic-stressing Dobus of New Guinea were thought to be "paranoid" (Benedict, 1934). Such characterizations have not proved to be particularly useful; consequently, they have been largely abandoned in the discipline.

Much as the functionalist approach to society made culture a mere reflection, so the configurationist approach to culture viewed society as generated by culture patterns. Instead of deriving culture from social interaction, the nature of society was derived from cultural configuration. In either case, no means was provided for considering the manner in which the variables in society and culture might operate independently of each other.

The personality configuration approach to an understanding of culture focused on the *emotions* that were thought to be characteristic of a people. We will now turn to three twentieth-century approaches that are based, instead, on the *ideas* that characterize a culture. The first of these views culture as a cognitive system.

Culture as Cognitive Systems

In the "cognitive" approach, cultures are defined as systems of knowledge—the things that people have to know or believe in order to behave in ways that are acceptable to their group. Nowhere, except perhaps in asylums, do people perceive their world as completely disorderly and meaningless. The reason is that in all societies, children are taught how to view their experiences and how, on the basis of these views, to interact with one another. In our society, for instance, a child learns that certain pieces of green paper are valuable and can be used in exchange for material goods and that a funeral is an occasion calling for dark clothes, sober looks, and soft speech. Although people within our culture may not agree precisely on these matters, they agree with each other more than they agree with people from another culture who may, for instance, find in death an occasion for shouting and dancing.

For cognitive anthropologists, these ready-made models of reality are what constitute the local culture. They feel that if one can discover the models that a people use to interpret their experiences, one can begin to explain their various patterns of behavior (Scheffler, 1970). In this view, culture does not consist of customs, habits, or any other forms of concrete behavior, but of the concepts that lie behind them. It is the cognitive models people use for "perceiving, believing, evaluating, communicating, and acting" that constitute culture (Goodenough, 1970, p. 99).

Native Categories

Anthropologists using the cognitive approach try to discover native ways of thinking as a means of understanding the various activities of a society. Rather than approach an alien culture with predetermined categories—such as upper, middle, and lower socioeconomic classes, a classification system based on our own money-oriented way of thinking—they try to discover the classification systems that natives themselves use to order their experience of the world. On the Pacific island of Tikopia, for instance, all spatial relationships are perceived in terms of the classification system "inland" and "seaward," since the island is so small that people can hear and often see the sea from any point on it (Firth, 1963). A Tikopian might say, "It's on the seaward table," rather than, as we might, "It's on the table to your right," or "It's on the table against the east wall." Notions of left and right, north, east, south, and west are part of our geography system, but not of theirs.

To discover the classification scheme of a culture, cognitive anthropologists often focus on its language. While they admit that analysis of language does not yield everything to be learned about native ways of thinking, they feel that as its main communication device, language, should reveal a culture's most important cognitive features (Frake, 1974). An important part of their fieldwork therefore consists of formal interviews that are designed to reveal the language categories and subcategories that people carry in their heads.

For instance, those of us who get our food from grocery stores and supermarkets might

312

walk through the woods seeing only "trees" and "plants." But an ethnographer's observation and questioning of a tribe that subsists by hunting and gathering wild foods will reveal that these people perceive their natural environment in quite different terms. The Wanindiljangwa, who live on an island near Australia, can name and identify over 120 kinds of trees and plants that are either edible or otherwise useful. This is what they "see" when they walk through the woods. In addition to perceiving vegetation as useful or nonuseful, they also classify the useful things differently than our botanists do. To the Wanindiljangwa, living things are divided into four categories: things in the air (a group which includes not only birds but also insects, bats, and flying foxes), things in the sea, land animals, and trees and plants (Brain, 1976).

From Categories to Behaviors

Once anthropologists have painstakingly elicited the details of a native classification system, they still cannot predict what behaviors natives would think appropriate unless they know how these categories are combined and applied in different situations (Basso, 1973). For example, hunters and gatherers do not grab every useful plant they see. Whether they pick something probably depends not only on whether it is considered edible but also on other factors, such as whether it is considered ripe for harvesting, how much food they already have, whether the food is a choice item not often found, and whether it is for an ordinary meal or a ceremonial one.

The jump from drawing out native linguistic categories to understanding what ideas govern which behaviors is a big one (Keesing, 1974). So far, cognitive analysts have only been able to map the classification systems necessary to operate successfully in a few rather limited situations. Frake (1961), for instance, has carefully analyzed how the

Subanun (of the Philippines) categorize and diagnose human illnesses. Of the 186 named disease categories of the Subanun, Frake concentrated primarily on skin diseases. He argued that the disease categories were mutually exclusive, and despite occasional confusion in diagnosis, the Subanun considered the categories discrete. He subsequently extended his study to include ecology and settlement patterns (1962), social interaction (1964a), and religious behavior (1964b).

In another case, Basso (1973) has carefully analyzed the 13 labels the Slave Indians of northern Canada give to different kinds of ice. He has also identified the situational variables that determine whether the Indians would consider trying to travel across the ice. These variables include the mode of travel—walking in canvas shoes or snowshoes, traveling by dog sled—and the speed at which they need to travel.

After much questioning and the playing of a game by which the Slave fathers teach their sons what different kinds of ice "mean," Basso learned how to define types of ice as the natives do. "Tevu," or "hollow ice," for example, is ice that is more than 4 inches thick, is neither melting nor cracking, but has large air pockets under the surface. Considered strong enough to support a man on foot or snowshoes, it might not be safe for a dog sled and would be carefully checked if this were to be the mode of travel.

The cognitive models that have been constructed thus far are still too limited to provide any general understanding of why people in a specific culture behave as they do in even the most basic, everyday situations. Rather than pursue broader research, cognitivists are trying to determine how people in a particular culture separate what is relevant in their experiences from what is irrelevant; how they code information; how they anticipate events; and how they evaluate and choose among possible courses of action. In doing so, cognitive anthropologists are gathering data toward some long-range goals. They hope to contribute to anthropology an understanding of the relationships among language, cognition, and behavior; a way to make useful cross-cultural comparisons by discovering universal principles that classify the outside world; and descriptions of what a person must know in order to behave appropriately in any given culture (Frake, 1961).

Some anthropologists have pointed out that it is a big step to assume that the formal properties of a cultural code reveal the workings of the human mind. Burling (1964) has also argued that the total number of alternative analyses of any given cultural domain is so great that no single analysis can be considered definitive. In the cognitive approach, culture is again the dominant analytic concept, and it is assumed that social relations are generated by the cognitive system.

Culture as Structural System

While cognitivists analyze native cognitive processes to discover universal similarities in the ways people of various cultures construct categories of understanding, "structuralists" also look for universal principles of thought. Despite obvious differences in ways of life from one culture to the next, structuralists believe that the minds of people in widely different circumstances function according to the same basic structural principles. According to French anthropologist Claude Lévi-Strauss, the most prominent of the contemporary structuralists, the thought processes of people in simple societies are as complex as those of people in more "advanced" societies. For Lévi-Strauss and most structuralists, in addi-

tion to being constrained by the mind, social relations are also confined by the ecology in which a society is found. As such, they cannot be said to be either purely mental or purely material phenomena.

Lévi-Strauss's writing and his theories are not always easy to communicate to introductory students. But in general, he feels that cultural elaborations—kinship systems, myth, music, art, and so forth—are merely superficial elements that can be analyzed to find the underlying structural properties of the human minds that produce them.

Oppositions

One of the basic structural principles Lévi-Strauss identified is that of contrasts in a natural world that is often changing and random (Keesing, 1974). The difference between nature (which is random, changing, meaningless) and culture (which imposes order and meaning on experience) is itself one of the contrasts people in all societies have noticed and worked into their mythologies and ways of behaving. Other such universal contrasts, or oppositions, include life/death, male/female, animal/plant, individual/group, and friend/enemy.

These contrasts may not be perceived as clear black-and-white oppositions. For instance, we do not divide the people we know into only two groups—great friends and great enemies. But oppositions give us a scheme for sorting out and classifying our experiences (Lévi-Strauss, 1963). You may think of your acquaintances as falling along a continuum that runs from best friend to worst enemy. Most of them probably fall somewhere in between, but it is the friend/enemy contrast that gives you a way to organize your perceptions of them.

Edmund Leach (1970) used traffic signals to illustrate the structuralist notion that relations which exist in nature are repeated in the formation of cultural phenomena. He points out that the colors red and green are universally seen as opposites of a sort (except by those who are colorblind), because of the differences in their wavelengths and intensity. The human brain interprets these colors as oppositions, even though the color spectrum is a continuum rather than a series of distinctly different colors. Red and green are then transformed to another set of opposites: danger/safety. In our own culture, for instance, red is given the value of a danger sign: traffic lights, hot water taps, live electric wires, and debit entries in account books. A similar pattern appears in other cultures as well. Leach suggests that seeing the color red as a danger signal may have something to do with the association of red with blood. In any case, the use of green to mean "go" and red to mean "stop" in our traffic lights shows how relations which exist in nature are transformed into cultural phenomena patterned on those same relations.

Unconscious Logic

To a structuralist, then, the task of cultural analysis is to identify the structural principles that underlie the cultural elaborations of a people. Since people are largely unaware of these principles, which operate mostly on an unconscious level, asking them to describe their ways of perceiving and classifying things does not do much good. Lévi-Strauss recommends, instead, techniques such as analysis of myths or language to discover the hidden logic behind them. The object is to break down the particular social phenomena in order to reconstitute them in a way that shows the rules by which meaning is produced from raw perceptions of the natural world. Here linguistic models serve as a guide for analyzing the messages of myths.

The logic by which Lévi-Strauss moves from basic structural principles to various expressions of cultural behavior and vice

versa has not been easy for anthropologists to duplicate. Perhaps his greatest contribution has been to open anthropology to a range of considerations that it might otherwise have ignored. Here, again, the distinction between society and culture is insignificant in terms of analysis.

Culture as Symbolic Systems

A third approach to culture as ideas has been proposed by a group of scholars who treat cultures as fundamental systems of shared symbols and meanings. This point of view is most clearly expressed in the works of American anthropologist Clifford Geertz.

According to Geertz, anthropologists can use observable public events as their subject matter. Whereas Lévi-Strauss looks at cultural phenomena as isolated puzzles to be deciphered by finding their underlying structure, Geertz holds that more meaning can be extracted from these phenomena if they are examined in the broader context of social life. He finds culture not in people's heads but in public scenes of social interaction. Geertz tries to figure out what is going on in such events as sheep raids, cockfights, mass festivals, and priest-consecrating ceremonies.

In such situations, Geertz holds, people both tell and learn something about themselves. They are expressing, through symbolic acts, various themes in their social life. At a Balinese religious festival, for instance, Geertz thinks the people are acting out a friendly feeling of spiritual unity despite their differences in earthly status and interests. This symbolic meaning is shared by the actors but may not be readily apparent to an outside observer. What a native observer might see as a mere contraction of the eyelid, for instance, might be a wink full of meaning for two mischievous conspirators (Geertz, 1973).

Interpretation and Explanation of Social "Texts"

How, then, can an anthropologist make any sense of the puzzling behaviors of people of another culture? According to Geertz, to get at the meaning behind socially established patterns, an anthropologist can interpret them as "texts" of a sort, models of and for reality and social interaction. Using social action rather than printed words, anthropologists try to read a "text" over the actors' shoulders to see how they interpret it. This involves *thick description*—understanding the meaning of social patterns to those who take part in them. The term *thick description* refers to the fact that a single activity may consist of various layers of meaning. Different messages may be conveyed at different layers. Thick description means calling things "conspiratorial winks," if that's what they mean to the actors, rather than "contractions of the eyelid." The second step is explanation—trying to see overall themes in thickly described events, what it is that they demonstrate about the culture and perhaps about social life in general.

The Balinese Cockfight. To illustrate how this works, Geertz (1973) presents a lengthy analysis of Balinese cockfights, important social events which the ruling Javanese have tried unsuccessfully to outlaw. Geertz sees the fights as complex embodiments of many themes in the Balinese view of life. For one thing, the roosters are obvious masculinity symbols; their male owners passionately identify with them. But in their mindless rage when fighting, the birds are also symbols of animality, the dark natural powers that so many Balinese customs are designed to thwart. Infants, for instance, are not allowed to crawl since this behavior is too animal-like; the chief puberty rite consists in filing the

child's teeth to keep them from looking like animal fangs; and emotions are kept under careful control. Identification with one's rooster thus has something of the fascination with the forbidden about it. After winning one of these bloody struggles, a victorious bird owner goes home not only with the loser's carcass but also with what Geertz calls "a mixture of social embarrassment, moral satisfaction, aesthetic disgust, and cannibal joy" (1973, p. 421).

Because of these ambivalent feelings, those watching a cockfight do so in utter silence, constrained by an elaborate system of rules handed down through the generations. There are no disputes. An extremely well-trusted, solid citizen acts as umpire. Under his direction, the violence of what the roosters are doing to each other takes place in a carefully ordered human setting.

There is a great deal of intricate betting. Large sums of money are wagered by the birds' owners and their supporters in even-money "center bets"; lesser sums are exchanged in unbalanced side bets. The fact that the center bets may involve up to about 200 times as much money as an average worker earns in a day makes the game highly risky but also deeply fascinating for the participants. Since they have bet well over their heads, the Balinese feel that more than money is symbolically at stake. What they really stand to gain or lose, temporarily, is their social status. Bets thus oppose people who are opposed in social life, either those of different descent groups within a village or even a whole village against another.

Despite the dramatic clashes taking place on all these levels at a cockfight, nothing really happens to anyone except the birds. People humiliate each other, but only symbolically. No person gets killed, or castrated, or turned into a beast, or raised or lowered in social status. No one even becomes dramatically richer or poorer, because cockfights take place every few days and the roosters are matched

Geertz saw cockfights as multilayered "texts" that revealed important patterns in Balinese social life. (Elizabeth Reeve, Magnum)

so evenly by convention that exchanges of money tend to even out over a period of time.

According to Geertz, the cockfight takes a number of themes in human life—masculinity, status, rivalry, pride, loss, chance—and focuses them in an ordered social structure. This structure neither heightens nor relieves the passions evoked by these themes. But it gives the participants a chance to see them for what they really are. Emphasis on prestige, for instance, is everywhere apparent in Balinese customs. But only in events like the cockfight, Geertz writes, are the emotions upon which the social hierarchy rests revealed in their true colors.

Enveloped elsewhere in a haze of etiquette, a thick cloud of euphemism and ceremony, . . . they are here expressed in only the thinnest disguise of an animal mask. . . .
Jealousy is as much a part of Bali as poise, envy as grace, brutality as charm; but without the cockfight the Balinese would have a much less certain understanding of them. (Geertz, 1973, p. 447)

Discontinuity

All cultures, Geertz feels, can thus be approached as collections of "texts" (like the cockfight) that demonstrate to people what their emotions look like when expressed collectively, though symbolically. Geertz holds that these texts do not always fit together neatly to form a coherent whole. Contrary to those who try to explain cultures as higly integrated sets of elements, Geertz sees cultures and cultural symbols as disconnected, and often contradictory (Keesing, 1974).

It was Geertz who called attention to the useful distinction between the social and cultural aspects of life, suggesting that they may be treated as "independently variable yet mutually interdependent factors" (1957, p. 33). In making this conceptual distinction, Geertz proposes that culture be viewed as "an ordered system of meaning and symbols, in terms of which social action takes place," and that society refer to "the pattern of social interaction itself" (1957, p. 33). It is this distinction between symbolic meanings (which allow humans to interpret their experience and guide their actions) and social structure (which analyzes the form social interaction takes) that makes symbolic anthropology an engaging enterprise.

Culture as Adaptive Systems

The last definition of culture circles back past all the other definitions based on ideas or emotions, all the way to Tylor and the biological notion of evolution. Anthropologists taking this approach look at cultures as expressions of people's adaptation to their environmental setting. Julian Steward, who is usually credited with developing this contemporary approach to cultural analysis, calls it *cultural ecology*. Since we will later devote a whole chapter to cultural ecology, we will merely outline its main ideas here.

When he studied the aboriginal cultures of the North American Great Basin Area (which

includes present-day Nevada and parts of the surrounding states), Steward began to focus on what he called the *culture core*. This consisted primarily, in each society, of the economic and subsistence activities that seemed most directly involved with making it possible for the people to survive in their particular environment. The culture core in one group, for instance, might be its use of hunting and gathering to extract food from the environment, plus a number of other cultural elements—such as group size and political organization, or lack of it—that can be seen as functionally related to this adaptation. To understand the reasons for these core activities as well as the secondary elements that are related to them, Steward held that one has to understand in detail features of the environmental setting.

As Keesing (1974) has pointed out, there is a great range of opinion today among those who view cultures as adaptive systems. But they do hold in common at least four ideas about how cultures develop and why they change:

1. Cultures are systems for relating human groups to their environmental settings.
2. Culture change is largely a means of adaptation, a process by which individuals respond to changing conditions in order to function in a given environment.
3. Most central to cultural adaptation are technology, subsistence activities, and means of organizing the society for production.
4. The ideas that dictate cultural behavior —such as religious beliefs—may have adaptive purposes, too, such as controlling population growth or keeping people from overexploiting and thus destroying their environment.

The Cattle Complex

As an example of the kind of interpretation the cultural ecology approach can yield, con-

317

THE CULTURE CONCEPT

Cultural ecologists have explained the cattle complex of East Africa as an adaptation to the harsh environment of the area. (Yoram Lehmann, Peter Arnold Photo Archives)

sider the so-called "cattle complex" in East Africa. There, it appears that a number of tribes lovingly raise cattle for seemingly nonutilitarian purposes. Cattle are normally neither eaten nor used to pull things. Though they supply milk and are occasionally killed for ceremonial feasts, they are more often considered a means of displaying status, validating weddings, making friendship contracts, and providing a legacy for one's sons.

In the past, these uses have been explained simply as an expression of a reverence for cattle. But a number of recent researchers have found that the value placed on cattle keeping can be explained as an adaptation to the East African environment.

For one thing, agriculture is impractical in the mountainous areas of irregular rainfall where people keep cattle instead of growing crops. Keeping animals that can be moved from one sparse grazing area to another gives people a way to utilize the available plant energy without being hampered by the possibility of localized water shortages and danger-ous insect infestations. The animals are thus able to follow the rainfall and may graze over an area as large as 500 square miles in the course of a couple of years (R. Dyson-Hudson & N. Dyson-Hudson, 1969).

Energy stored in the cattle is then used selectively for adaptive purposes, with each cattle owner offering his neighbors at least one meat feast a year. The immediate consumption of a whole steer prevents spoilage of fresh meat in the absence of refrigeration, sets up reciprocal obligations which will later help feed one's own family, and enhances community cooperation. One support of this explanation is found in the fact that meat feasts are likely to take place when other foods are in short supply. These adaptive functions may be hidden beneath a maze of cultural elaborations and may not even be suspected by the cattle keepers themselves. A Karimojong boy, for instance, "is given a specially named male calf to identify himself with, to care for and to decorate, to commemorate in song at dances and beer parties, and to incorporate into the style of his most formal name as an adult" (R. Dyson-Hudson & N. Dyson-Hudson, 1969). Cultural ecologists can demonstrate that such cultural elaborations have developed and persisted because of the value of cattle for the survival of the people (Netting, 1971).

The concerns of anthropologists who take an adaptational approach focus primarily upon the material nature of human existence. Thus, the approach provides an important balance to those that concentrate on ideas and mental activities. It also ties in with investigations of hominid evolution and ethological research which relates culture to biological processes. It integrates the subdisciplines of physical anthropology and archaeology with cultural anthropology better than do the idealist views of culture.

Designs for Living and Designs for Research

These eight approaches to the concept of culture by no means exhaust all the possibilities. In their book *Culture, a Critical Review of Concepts and Definitions* (1952), for instance, A. L. Kroeber and Clyde Kluckhohn discuss more than a *hundred* views of culture that have been advanced. Each one is significant because it has shaped (1) the questions posed in research, (2) the inferences the researcher makes about data collected, and (3) the results obtained. Many of the old definitions—such as those based on a view of culture traits as genetic variations—are no longer in use today. But those at which we have looked represent an overview of most of the ways of looking at culture that are found in contemporary anthropological studies.

It would be nice, for the sake of organizing the large body of cultural information, if we could somehow combine all the definitions of culture and say that all anthropologists are dealing with essentially the same subject matter. But it is not possible to follow this strategy very far, since some definitions vary greatly in what aspects of human social activity they emphasize.

Some approaches are obviously more compatible than others. The adaptive and evolutionary views, for instance, fit together fairly well since both emphasize the material conditions of human existence. These two approaches are characteristic of the materialistic view of culture that we discussed earlier. The structural-functional and evolutionary approaches are also compatible, since both are concerned with systems of cultural characteristics—cultural elements that influence one another—and they both search for cause-and-effect relationships. Although structuralists stress stable patterns while evolutionists stress change, there is little basic conflict between the two approaches (Freeman, 1968). The cognitive, structural, and symbolic approaches are consistent with the idealist view of culture. They all stress the mental processes behind cultural forms.

Although some approaches are compatible, great differences remain. In writing textbooks, as in designing research, anthropologists must therefore choose from the available definitions instead of trying to synthesize them. In this book we treat culture as "designs for living,"* the conscious and unconscious understandings that natives use to interpret their experiences and to guide their actions.

Using the Native Model: Designs for Living

Of what value to us is the native's understanding of his or her experiences? As we pointed out earlier, the native's conscious models of reality tend to be poor ones for an anthropologist to rely on in *analyzing* society

*The expresssion "designs for living" was coined by Clyde Kluckhohn. See Kluckhohn & Kelly (1945).

and culture. They are intended, as Lévi-Strauss points out, neither to explain nor comprehend social phenomena but rather to "perpetuate" them. However, Lévi-Strauss also notes that native models may provide substantial "insights into the structure of the phenomena" (1963, p. 282). The idea that the anthropologist must begin with native concepts of things in order to arrive at an anthropological understanding of them is very old and well established in the discipline. Thus, native models provide some of the basic materials for any anthropological analysis; without them, no reconstruction of a cultural system would be possible.

Every functioning member of a society carries in his or her head a design for living which is similar to that of others in the society. These behavioral expectations do not need to be shared fully in order for a human society to operate efficiently. They must be shared sufficiently, however, so that people can understand and communicate with one another (Wallace, 1961). People in our society, for instance, share the assumption that property disagreements that cannot be resolved by discussion must be settled in courts of law. The opponents may differ in their interpretation of the law. But they can communicate with each other better than if one believed in settling property disputes by gunfight, or if one did not believe in property ownership at all. It is these areas of mutual understanding—such as belief in a judicial system and in private ownership of property—that the anthropologist seeks to discover in his or her fieldwork.

Choosing an Anthropological Model: Designs for Research

Every textbook has a bias that is reflected in the materials chosen for presentation and the manner in which they are discussed. Since the purpose of an introductory text is to offer an overview of the discipline, however, it is important that the student be introduced to a variety of conceptual approaches. The important thing is to make sure that the bias of the approach in question is clearly stated. Unfortunately, not all case studies in anthropology do this. While some anthropologists rely on native models for basic raw material, some fail to get beyond this raw material in their analysis. The preference in this text is to select studies in which anthropologists have removed certain elements from the native model and clearly regrouped them according to one or more of the analytic models described before, that is, models constructed by the anthropologists themselves. Among these, those works written from an idealist view of culture will be relied upon most heavily.

Separating cultural phenomena from the observable flow of social life frees us to see relationships between different kinds of activities (between food getting and religion, for instance) that are not apparent in the everyday life of a people. It allows us to move beyond the interpretations and justifications for their actions put forward by the natives themselves to find explanations that are not apparent to them. It is this reorganization and reinterpretation of raw data that we refer to here as "designs for research."

In some cases, one will find that the same social phenomena have been studied through more than one analytic model. The potlatch ceremony of the Kwakiutl Indians of the Pacific Northwest, for example, is on first sight a ceremony in which the chief wantonly destroys or gives away many of his possessions to an assortment of invited guests. This puzzling practice has been explained by Ruth Benedict according to her personality configuration approach as an expression of megalomania, a mental disorder characterized by delusions of grandeur, wealth, and power. She interpreted the destruction and giveaways as ostentatious attempts on the part of a chief to prove that he is wealthier and superior to his guests (Benedict, 1934).

Other anthropologists have come up with different explanations of the potlatch as they fit it into different analytical models. Some, for instance, have analyzed it in terms of environmental adaptation. They have suggested that the practice could be seen as an adaptation to changes in the food supply. Food shortages existed periodically in all parts of the region, but not necessarily at the same time. The real function of the potlatch, according to this model, was to redistribute food, to spread it out more equally within the tribe. Anthropologists who came up with this interpretation acknowledged that the Kwakiutl drive for prestige certainly had something to do with it. But for them, prestige was a secondary basis for the potlatch—one which had developed and lasted because it motivated people to keep having potlatches—rather than as the primary one (Suttles, 1960).

The choice among analytic models and the explanations they suggest is sometimes difficult. But anthropologists usually try to choose research designs that allow them to understand the most social phenomena. Can the adaptational approach to the cattle complex, for instance, account for the fact that herds are often so large that they overgraze their range, for the timing of meat feasts, for the characteristics of the pastoralist personality? Often a combination of perspectives provides the most insights and the most interesting studies. In Gregory Bateson's classic study *Naven* (1936), for example, we find the analysis of a New Guinea tribe from three points of view. Bateson analyzed the Iatmul ceremony in terms of (1) its social structure, as understood by structural-functionalists; (2) its cultural structure, much as cognitivists would see it today; and (3) its personality structure, as elaborated by Benedict and Mead.

Whichever approach anthropologists choose, the concept of culture is the key analytic tool that allows them to interpret and compare their data with that from other so-cieties. The very ambiguity of the term, which sometimes frustrates beginning students of anthropology, turns out to be a major strength for those who pursue the discipline. It permits them to systematize their understanding of the social patterns they are studying from several perspectives. And in seeking to understand others, they place themselves in a better position to understand themselves, to pose relevant questions about their own social life and their own view of the world.

Summary

1. The age-old attempt to explain the human condition became a science in 1871, when Tylor set forth a definition of culture as a complex whole that is learned and passed on to succeeding generations. Tylor tended to view culture as a universal effort toward a "civilized" condition. In the end, he identified culture with civilization.

2. The Victorian view of culture as evolutionary progress was echoed in the twentieth century by White. He saw in human history a pattern in which the increased harnessing of energy leads to advances in all other spheres of social life.

3. Boas rejected these sweeping generalizations about human history, preferring to concentrate instead on what could be learned about the histories of specific cultures. Each culture is uniquely shaped, Boas thought, by historical processes such as the *diffusion* and *integration* of traits and should not be judged by standards developed in another culture.

4. Malinowski and Radcliffe-Brown defined culture as *functionally integrated systems.* In such systems, each institution has a purpose and is related to other institutions. Malinow-

ski tended to see institutions as satisfying individual needs, whereas Radcliffe-Brown thought their function was to keep the social structure intact.

5. Benedict emphasized the seemingly unlimited diversity of cultural phenomena. She felt that each society had developed a typical *personality configuration* which could be seen as the integrating principle behind its elements.

6. The *cognitivists* define culture as a system of categories. They try to uncover native models for classifying the things they experience. They do so in order to see how people of the culture perceive life and how they make decisions about how they should act.

7. Lévi-Strauss seeks to reduce the apparent discontinuities of society and culture to underlying *structural* invariants. He looks for universal features in the way the human mind works. Among the unconscious mental structures he has found in all cultural systems is the fact that people think in terms of oppositions and contrasts.

8. Geertz and others have defined culture as *symbolic systems.* They feel that people in a society share an understanding of what their actions mean. These meaningful behaviors are most clearly expressed in public performances, where people are acting out social dramas that express the basic themes in their social lives.

9. An eighth definition of culture comes from *cultural ecologists,* like Steward, who see it as an *adaptive system.* They focus on a core of activities that are most closely linked to survival and on the cultural features that support the basic adaptation of people to their environment.

10. In this book, the term *culture* will be used in two ways. On the one hand it will refer to the models of and for experience shared by a particular social group. These can be thought of as *designs for living.* On the other hand, the term *culture* must also be recognized as an analytic tool used by anthropologists to understand social life on a comparative basis—their *designs for research.* The two ideas are intricately intertwined, of course, since native designs for living can only be grasped by non-natives through the designs for research constructed by social analysts.

PART FOUR
Cultural Variation

15
Culture and Language

LANGUAGE, more than any other attribute, distinguishes human beings from other animals. In many cultures, a child is considered fully human only when he or she has begun to speak. Then the child is given a name and initiated into truly social existence. All physically normal humans possess the innate capacities to learn to speak and to communicate through language. The structure of the vocal tract and the physics of sound wave activity are the same among all peoples and in all places. Differences between the sound systems of one language and another are the result of factors other than the speakers' ability to produce sounds. A classic joke among linguists concerns a British couple who adopted a French baby and then proceeded to study the French language so they would understand the child when she began to talk. In fact, any human being can learn to utter the sounds of any human language.

Language is the most characteristic pattern of behavior that distinguishes one social group from another and is often considered the primary mark of its identity or its connection to other similar groups. For example, we consider as "Latin America" all those countries south of the United States in which Romance languages are spoken, despite the cultural differences among them. People who speak the same language are thought to be able to communicate with one another. Although this is not always true, certainly little communication of any consequence is possible between two people who cannot understand each other's languages. Several languages, however, can coexist within a single group, even if its members do not all speak every language.

The purpose of this chapter is to show how an investigation into the nature of language contributes to our understanding of the nature of culture. Since language is the primary means by which humans communicate with each other, it becomes the primary target for understanding how designs for living are understood and shared among humans. In order to show this, we will first consider how anthropologists have viewed the relationships of language and culture. Next we will look at the structure of language and its unique representational quality. Finally, by placing language in a broader area of communication, which demonstrates that not all language is coded in linguistic form, we will discover the extent to which models for analysis of language also contribute to the analysis of culture.

The Relationship of Language to Culture

Linguists and anthropologists agree that human language and culture are closely related, although they disagree as to the nature and extent of these relationships. Both culture and language, after all, are the results of human activity and are expressions of the human mind. If they were not related at all, we would have to conclude, with Lévi-Strauss (1963), that there is no connection between what goes on in the mind from one level to another. If this were true, the consequences would be disastrous not only with regard to the connection between language and culture but also for the entire fabric of beliefs and activities that we think of as culture.

People in some societies talk a great deal, even making a cult of conversation or communication and recording much of what is said or written. Our own society is one such group. In contrast, other social groups speak very little and then only in specific contexts that require it. Spoken language in those societies may be for the purpose of instruction, indoctrination, or the performance of rituals.

Nevertheless, every society requires language for its existence. Other animals possess social organization—families and larger groups such as herds or colonies—but only human beings are able to formulate, prescribe, and compel obedience to rules governing incest, marriage, divorce, inheritance, and many other areas of social life by means of speech. Without language, human beings could not have developed political, economic, or religious traditions. They would be unable to transmit their beliefs and values, bodies of law, knowledge and literature, ceremonies and social customs. These require the use of symbols, the ability to employ abstractions for absent or nonmaterial things. For example, it is not unknown for other animals to make

Writing is a more mysterious communication system in some cultures than it is in ours. Here, a Moroccan letter writer records a message. Although the woman may not be able to read what is being written for her, her posture and attention convey the importance the communication has for her.
(Joel Gordon)

what can be called spontaneous use of tools. Apes have been observed to grasp at a stick lying nearby in order to reach for a more distant object or to pick up a rock to break the hard shell of a piece of fruit. But only humans have shown the capacity for setting the stick aside in order to use it again in the future. To plan in this way requires the ability to abstract the general or symbolic utility of the stick from its immediate usefulness—in other words, to get the idea of the stick's potential value as a tool.

Language Independent of Culture

Language, then, makes the development of culture possible. But the question persists: Is language itself a part of culture or is it an external, independent phenomenon? Many linguists have preferred to analyze language with reference neither to its social nor to its cultural context. Leonard Bloomfield's example is sometimes quoted to illustrate how the linguist narrows the focus to exclude social context from what he or she studies: "If a beggar says 'I'm hungry' to obtain food and a child says 'I'm hungry' to avoid going to bed, then linguistics is concerned just with what is the same in the two acts" (in Hymes, 1974)—that is, with the statement "I'm hungry." According to this view, what is in the speaker's mind when speaking is largely irrelevant to the linguist.

When we reflect upon how we ourselves communicate—how a speaker gets meaning across to an audience, for instance—we realize that in order to express our private thoughts, feelings, and experiences we must often use terms that do not quite seem to fit. For example, when a speaker uses the word "house," he or she may be referring to a specific idea of house quite different from anything the listeners have ever thought of by the term. Nonetheless, in order to speak and be understood, the speaker will simplify his or her private sense of things, will

throw whole masses of experience together as similar enough to warrant their being looked upon—mistakenly, but conveniently—as identical. This house and that house and thousands of other phenomena of like character are thought of as having enough in common, in spite of great and obvious differences of detail, to be classed under the same heading. (Sapir, 1921)

Even the most personal utterance is conveyed through words that do not depend upon the speaker's thoughts for their meanings. Speakers express meaning in large measure only by making use of the concepts that are available in language.

Individual words or concepts alone, of course, do not constitute language. In order to make ourselves fully understood, we must string our words together in patterned units. Some linguists, notably Noam Chomsky, suggest that the pattern or structure of a given language results chiefly from "factors over which the individual has no conscious control and concerning which society may have little choice or freedom" (1965). Although individuals are free to say many things, they are not free to choose just any form in which to express a given utterance. For example, in English we can say, "John smoked a pipe," but not "A pipe smoked John." No individual speaker is free to choose his or her own patterns, except at the risk of being misunderstood or speaking nonsense.

Correspondence of Language and Culture

Most contemporary anthropologists no longer accept the view that culture and language are completely separate phenomena. They do not believe that either culture or language can be studied in isolation. Anthropological linguists have come to see that language tells us a great deal about culture itself. Malinowski (1935) asserted that the chief role of language was to take active part in human behavior and not to serve merely as a vehicle for the expression of thought. Most anthropologists have come to agree with this statement. They see that a speaker not only makes a statement about something, but performs an action—that is, does something—as well. To illustrate, we may return to Bloomfield's remark cited earlier. The little girl who says "I'm hungry" in order to put off going to bed may be appealing to her parents' good natures, challenging their authority, or struggling to cope with fear of the dark. The beggar's identical remark may be an attempt to protest his misery, or it may be a bid for a handout.

Language, then, is one of a number of codes that each culture uses in order to communicate. Its unique status as the means by which many—if not all—phenomena in a culture are expressed and understood does not place it outside the confines of the culture. Quite the contrary. The presence of language and its service in every area of culture from law making to love making point to the critical role of language in cultural life. The words we speak when we are introduced to someone for the first time express our culture as surely as do our customs of shaking hands upon meeting and parting, standing when we are introduced, and keeping a comfortable distance from people we are not intimate with.

Benjamin Lee Whorf, a student of Edward Sapir, made a number of bold, original speculations about the interrelations of culture and language. Whorf's work refined in many ways the work of Sapir and Boas. Boas, especially, asked how cultural behavior is a cognitive classification of experience. He left as an open question the extent to which these classifications are conscious or unconscious. Whorf proposed that in any language, speakers would be most aware of word categories and unaware of the way in which linguistic structure shaped their understanding of their experience. His theory, called the *Sapir-Whorf hypothesis,* was that the grammar of any language is not merely a way of speaking about the world but that it embodies a model of that world as well. Whorf believed that language reflects the way in which speakers of the language perceive and think about the world. Whorf compared a number of the features of Western languages (which he referred to as Standard Average European) with those of the Hopi language. He discovered, for example, that the great stress on nouns as things in Standard Average European (SAE) encouraged a quantitative view of time. An SAE speaker says, "ten days"; a Hopi says, "until (or after) the tenth day." The Hopi view of time is of "becoming later and later," whereas the SAE view is of a series of units. An illustration of the SAE view is the film portrayal of the passage of time as a series of leaves torn from a calendar (Whorf, 1956). Whorf concluded that cultural and environmental influences in Hopi society interacted with Hopi linguistic patterns "to mold them, to be molded again by them, and so little by little to shape the Hopi world-outlook" (1956, pp. 157–158). The relationship between language and culture, as Whorf saw it, was bidirectional.

Current inquiry by anthropological linguists often involves the attempt to place language in the cluster of various elements that figure in communication and to clarify the functions of language within the cluster. Dell Hymes (1974) has shown that a study of a community and all its means of communication reveals the frames of reference of its speakers. For example, the !Kung Bushmen of the Kalahari Desert customarily belittle the size and worth of the game they kill, despite their dependence upon the game for subsistence. They explain their behavior as intended to discourage arrogance among those who supply meat to the community. An uninitiated outsider, however, would think their behavior very odd, indeed. It seems calculated to deny !Kung hunters the recognition and gratitude due them for their service to their fellows (Lee, 1969). No account of !Kung language habits that ignored their economy and their belief that the hunter must be kept humble could hope to make sense of their speech.

Most contemporary anthropologists see the relationship between language and culture as one of correspondence. But they stop short of suggesting that either one influences the other. Instead, they see the two as moving along parallel tracks. There is correspondence, not because there is any certain connection between the two, but because both language and culture are creations, largely unconscious, of the human mind.

Language Is Culture

A third view about the relationship of language to culture suggests that the two do more than parallel each other—that, basically, language *is* culture. People who hold this view focus their study on the functions of language.

One function of language is the referential, the act of describing or telling about something. But few statements are merely referential. Michael Silverstein (1977) has recently called attention to a second (and to him, more important) kind of meaning in language, its indexical function. Indexing reveals through speech the culturally understood contexts of speaking and its purposes: the roles and social positions of speakers and hearers, the setting and the occasion of a communication, the purpose of a statement, and so forth. The fact that the referential function is essential to a communication explains why so much attention has been given it in linguistic analysis. But context-defining functions are important as well.

Influenced by the work of Roger Brown (1957; 1970), many scholars point out that in order to understand any statement containing a personal pronoun, we must know something about the speaker, the audience, and the social situation. Silverstein (1977) illustrates this with the English sentence *You went away happy,* which might be spoken to one or more persons, to its equivalent in French. If the French speaker is addressing more than one person, he or she uses the plural pronoun *vous.* In speaking to only one person, there is a choice between *tu* and *vous,* depending upon the age, social status, and degree of intimacy between speaker and listener. Furthermore, the full meaning of the sentence would not be clear to anyone who did not also know all these things. This distinction is a feature of many languages, including German, Russian, and Spanish. English usage is simpler because the singular *thou* has disappeared, and the plural *you* now is used in all cases. Nevertheless, English is capable of indicating this sort of distinction, though perhaps in a less formal way: an English speaker decides whether to address someone by first name or title (for example, Mr., Ms.) on much the same grounds as the French speaker chooses *tu* or *vous.* Other languages are a great deal more complicated. Geertz (1960) shows the elaborate indexical system of the Javanese speaker who must control many levels of style including words, phrases, and grammatical patterns, to show deference to the listener and to the topic of discourse. The delicacy with which a speaker does this, on the other hand, shows his or her own social status.

Other indexing devices include accent and vocabulary. Whether a person intensifies or minimizes an accent that relates to a particular region or social class, for instance, depends on the status of the audience relative to the speaker. Secretaries sometimes take on an "upper-class" accent when doing business on the telephone, but abandon it when doing something less publicly self-conscious, such as ordering lunch. Or a famous ballplayer may emphasize his street dialect when giving a clinic in his old neighborhood, to make himself seem more like a "regular guy." Individuals also are likely to choose different words in communications with different people—your peers versus your grandmother, for example —even when the message to be communicated is the same. Thus, linguistic behavior is seen as an inseparable part of cultural behavior.

The Structure of Language

Language is the medium through which human thought is expressed. The medium of language, in turn, is sound; sound constitutes the basic element of speech. *Phonology,* the study of human speech sounds, is generally subdivided into two parts: *phonetics,* the study of speech sounds from a physiological point of view, and *phonemics,* the manner in which sounds are used to communicate meaningfully in a given language.

The Sound System

Phonemics deals with the sets of sounds employed by speakers of specific languages. It does so by identifying *phonemes*—distinctive but meaningless sounds heard by native speakers of a language. Each language has a limited number of phonemes, usually 30 to 50, and each phoneme represents a single sound in that language. Infants younger than 12 months of age seem to produce in their babbling the sounds heard in various human languages, including pronunciations from languages that English speakers find difficult. As babbling continues, children begin to reproduce the sounds of the language they hear around them. They eventually limit themselves to the sounds of their own languages and cease to produce "foreign" sounds.

The phonemes of various languages are so different that adult speakers who pronounce effortlessly every phoneme of their own language may have trouble pronouncing or even distinguishing phonemes lacking in their native tongue. For example, [th], as in *thin,* and [th], as in *then,* are recognized and pro-

nounced without difficulty by most speakers of English. Both these sounds, however, are missing from the phonemics of French. A speaker of French attempting to speak English will likely pronounce them as [s] (thin/*sin*), [z] (then/*zen*), or [d] (then/*den*). This appears less astonishing, perhaps, when we realize that there are dialects of American English with the same kind of phonemic system. A visitor to a working-class bar in an American city might hear one of the regulars tell the bartender to "trow da bum out" when a patron grows unruly.

Various sounds are produced by the different positioning of the lips, teeth, and tongue. Different kinds of articulation identify the way in which a sound is produced. They include stops, fricatives, resonants, and vowels. *Stops* are produced by momentarily blocking the flow of air, as in the sounds *p* or *b*. *Fricatives* require impeding the flow of air, but not completely shutting off its passage; the sounds *v* and *th* are examples of fricatives. *Resonants* require a partial obstruction of the air flow (as in *m* and *w*). *Vowels* are produced without obstructing the passage of air at all.

To determine all members of the phonemic inventory for a given language, the phonologist looks for *distinctive features.* These are the differences in sound that speakers recognize unconsciously in minimally different words, called *minimal pairs.* English *pat* and *bat* constitute such a minimal pair. Both [p] and [b] are stops, produced when the flow of air through the vocal tract is momentarily impeded by compressing the lips, but [p] is voiceless, whereas [b] is voiced. To produce a voiced sound, the vocal chords must vibrate as air passes through the throat. When the sound is voiceless, the vocal chords do not vibrate. By such analysis we discover that voicing is a distinctive feature in English.

In order to identify the truly distinctive features in a language, we must pay attention to *complementary distribution* of sound. Several sounds in a language may differ from one another, but speakers of the language may treat them as a single phoneme because they never contrast in the same sequence of sounds. For example, [p] in *pine, spine,* and *sip* is a single phoneme, although it is pronounced differently in each case—aspirated, unaspirated, and unreleased, respectively. But because each [p] sound occurs in a unique environment (aspirated when it falls initially; unaspirated after an *s;* and unreleased as the final sound), these phonetic differences are ignored by the normal speaker of English. We therefore speak of only a single /p/ phoneme.

Discussing the phonemes of a language and their rules for sequencing, we find that the sound system of any language is systematic and regular, and that languages conform to similar principles. In addition, linguists formulate rules to account for the way language is structured into larger units of meaning. These rules are known as the *grammar* of a language.

The Grammatical System

The study of grammar has traditionally been divided into two parts: morphology and syntax. *Morphology* analyzes the combination of *morphs*—the smallest units of meaning in a given language—into words. *Syntax* is concerned with the rules for combining words into larger units of meaning, such as phrases or sentences.

The more we study grammatical systems, the more we realize that the structure of language does not consist of letters, words, and sentences, since parts of words, or morphemes, are frequently directly meaningful parts of whole sentences. For example, the sentence "The girl loves baseball" may be altered to "The girl love*d* baseball." There is but one simple difference in sound between these two sentences, yet this difference changes the meaning of the entire sentence.

Morphology and syntax share several important linguistic processes: selection, arrangement, and modification. We select the words we use in a sentence from the appropriate word groups; we arrange them in a meaningful order; and we modify the forms or pronunciation as necessary to their surroundings. In a language such as English, in which the normal word order of the sentence is subject-verb-object, speakers select nouns or nounlike words for subject and object and arrange them before and after the verb. Speakers modify the form of a word as well as the pronunciation when the grammatical surroundings require it. In the sentence "We like him," for example, *him* is a modification of *he* and in that position is pronounced [im] rather than [him]. Examples of morphological selection include the adding of affixes (prefixes or suffixes), as in *pre*pay or pay*check*. Morphological arrangement often also involves affixes. We say *mouth*piece and piece*meal,* for example, and not piece*mouth* or *meal*piece.

Instead of attempting merely to define morphemes, we can now give an inventory of the possible types of morphemes:

1. A single sound, like the plural morpheme *-s* in *cat-s*
2. A single syllable, like *child, girl,* and *-ish,* in *childish* and *girlish*
3. Two or more syllables, as in *aardvark, crocodile,* or *salamander*
4. No sound (zero-form), as in the plural of *sheep* and the past tense of *hit*

Different morphemes may be represented by the same sound, as in the plural *boys* and the possessive *boy's*. The sounds that constitute a morpheme in one place may not do so in another. The unit *-er,* designating a doer, is a morpheme in *singer* and *fisher,* but not in *butcher*. In the word *nicer, -er* is not a morpheme at all. In other cases, the same morpheme may be presented by different sounds. *Sign* and *signature* are examples of this class of morphemes.

Transformational Grammar. These observations about grammar tell us a good deal about how the words and sentences we speak may be classified. They do not tell us how every normal speaker develops the ability to "create" such a wide variety of sentences. The theory that we learn to speak by imitating what we hear others say, although undoubtedly partly true, fails to account for a speaker's ability to utter a vast number of sentences that do not resemble anything he or she has previously heard. *Transformational grammar* attempts to account for the phenomenon of creative language use.

Transformational grammar was introduced by Noam Chomsky, whose own research in descriptive linguistics was unable to offer any clue as to how speakers learn to use language in a creative way. Of course, no speaker is totally conscious of the system of grammar he or she has mastered, and every speaker, in practice, makes frequent errors. Those errors, though, are much less frequent than is usually supposed (Labov, 1972). Further, they often support the notion of linguistic competence, as when a child gives the past tense of *buy* as *buyed* instead of *bought*.

The key elements in Chomsky's theory of language are found in his idea that every sentence consists of both a surface structure and a deep structure. The *surface structure* of a sentence corresponds to the sounds we hear. An example of surface structure may be shown by the sentence "A wise man is honest." (See Figure 1.) The *deep structure* represents the underlying meaning of the sentence, which is more abstract than the surface structure. (See Figure 2.)

Every English sentence or surface structure is generated according to the rules of a deep structure found in English grammar. The relationships between deep and surface structure—the ways in which one can be "translated" into the other—are explained by rules called *grammatical transformations*. A set of "rewrite rules" breaks the units of the deep

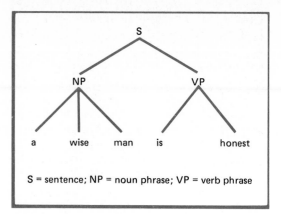

S = sentence; NP = noun phrase; VP = verb phrase

Figure 1 Surface structure

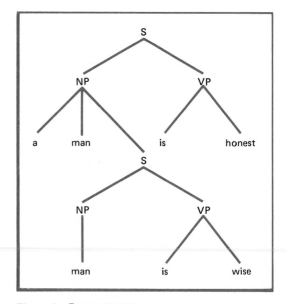

Figure 2 Deep structure

structure into noun phrases and verb phrases. Then appropriate operations, such as replacement, deletion, inversion, or negation, are performed to result in the surface structure. In Figure 2, for example, we saw the following noun and verb phrases:

a man	*[man is wise]*	*is honest*
NP_1	NP_2	VP_2	VP_1

The first operation that occurs is a replacement of NP$_2$ with *who*:

a man who is wise is honest

The next transformation is the deletion of *who is,* thus:

a man wise is honest

The final operation is an inversion, which completes the transformation from deep to surface structure:

a wise man is honest

Universal Grammar. Chomsky's theory of *universal grammar* or *linguistic universals* has been called his most daring speculation about the nature of language. This theory, which he concedes exists thus far only in the barest outlines, asserts that all known languages "rest on the same basic principles" and that children are born with knowledge of these principles (Chomsky, 1965, 1972). Universal grammar is thought to be a substructure of rules or properties common to all languages. Two such "universal" properties are the processes of negation *(I do not like beets)* and interrogation *(Do you like beets?),* which exist in all human languages (Elgin, 1973). The ability of children to learn any language to which they are exposed early in life and to emerge as creative users of the language despite a limited exposure to it, lends strong support, in many linguists' opinion, to the theory of universal grammar.

The Semantic System

Semantics, the study of meaning, is of greater interest to anthropologists who study human thought and communication than any other area of linguistics. One of the reasons that Chomsky's work was of such interest to anthropologists is that his first notion of underlying structure was close to semantics, or logical structure. Hence, it served as a window on human cognition, independent of culture or language use in communication. Semantics may also be the most elusive area of linguistics. Just as we often disagree about the "meaning" of a single statement, so there is considerable disagreement about what is meant by the term *meaning* itself. To anthropologists, meaning refers not merely to the lexical (or "dictionary") sense of words or morphemes. It also includes knowledge agreed upon by speakers of a language about the objects and events signaled by language. This knowledge may not be shared equally by all speakers of the language, but a sufficient amount of meaning is shared in order for members to communicate.

An analogy may help explain the anthropologist's view of semantics. Almost everyone has had the experience of going to a party with a friend and finding that most of the people present—except yourself—know each other very well. They may all have been in the same school or neighborhood or office, and they have a number of acquaintances and experiences in common. Eventually—despite efforts to include you—conversation will turn to people or events about which the members of the group share knowledge: "Sandy lost 50 pounds." "Can you believe that Sam is office manager?" You know the lexical meanings of the words you hear, but you do not have sufficient knowledge to understand their significance. Did Sandy weigh 120 or 230 before the weight loss? Did Sam start his career in the mail room, or is he the boss's son-in-law?

The anthropologist faces the same problem of interpretation when trying to make sense of meanings in alien cultures. Meaning includes the lexical meaning of vocabulary items, as well as situational and expressive components in native statements. For the anthropologist, the object of inquiry is more important than Sandy's weight or Sam's career path. Semantics concentrates on the aspects of language most closely associated with thought processes. The anthropologist seeks to discover the entire system of ideas that exists behind the statements he or she records. Thus, it is an area of primary concern to cognitive anthropologists, who attempt to identify underlying meaning systems of various cultures.

Sociolinguistics

From what we have discussed to this point in the chapter, it is clear that language is a social phenomenon. Language is learned only within social communities. Children raised in isolation, for example, do not learn to speak, although the *capacity* for learning language appears to be carried by the genes. The study of language use within a speech community is generally called *sociolinguistics*. Scholars have often suggested other terms to describe this research. A few of these terms—including "the ethnography of speaking" and "the sociology of language"—may express more clearly, perhaps, the particular focus of the field.

Sociolinguistics studies the variety of languages within speech communities, the elements of those languages, and the relationships and differences among them in usage and structure. The ways in which people actually speak is of great importance, although sociolinguists search for specific varieties of language rather than for particular speech patterns of individual speakers.

The diversity of language within a speech community is a mark of the social and cultural diversity of the community itself. The various languages therein may represent differences of national, geographic, or ethnic origin; economic or educational status; occupation; or personal interests. The range of possible languages within a single community, therefore, may often be considerable. But what emerges in speech is not at all a Babel of competing tongues. Each speaker selects from his or her own repertoire according to the hearer, the size and social makeup of the group, the setting, the topic of discussion, and many other factors (Fishman, 1970).

For instance, high-school friends or old army buddies who meet after many years of separation may automatically revert to the language of their old neighborhood or teenage or service slang. Yet when their spouses, who share none of these things from the past, approach to be introduced to these old friends, the group inevitably returns to a more standard, less specialized language.

Sociolinguistics seeks to discover the makeup of speech communities and to measure the interactions of subgroups with the larger community and with each other. Sociolinguistics also analyzes the speech event itself in the fullest possible context. It is here that the term "ethnography of speaking," introduced by Dell Hymes (1971b), has its greatest relevance. Just as the anthropologist describes and analyzes a number of social phenomena, so the sociolinguist must describe and analyze the use of language in its social context. Hymes points out that the sociolinguist must pay as much attention to the social behavior of speakers as to what they say. This social behavior includes the functions as well as the structure of language; the speech act as performance and as information; and the impact of speakers upon language and social life. The participants in speech events must be considered: senders and receivers, speakers and hearers, even messengers. Language itself can be seen in the kinds and forms of communications, verbal and nonverbal, and in the attitudes and meanings that may be conveyed. Above all, Hymes stresses the importance of "socially constituted linguistics"—identifying social functions, analyzing their influence upon the actual workings of language, and placing language in the larger context of social action (1971a, 1974).

Sociolinguists study how language is used in various social contexts. One area of study is the sacred quality of language used in communicating religious belief. Here, Indian boys are being taught from the Koran.
(George Rodger, Magnum)

The work of William Labov falls squarely in this area. His work depends upon actual speech over a period of time for its data. Labov focused on everyday speech in an effort to observe directly the shifting of styles by speakers responding to changes in social context and topic, and the degree of monitoring performed by speakers upon their own speech. He thus attempted to reveal the processes by which variation arises in a community's speech and how it is absorbed into the language.

In addition to these contributions, Labov improved the means by which linguistic data are gathered. In particular, he found solutions to what is called the Observer's Paradox. The paradox is that the very presence of the observer inhibits the speech of the subjects, although the observer's chief purpose is to find out how people normally talk. One solution is to arrange definite breaks from the interviewing, during which the subject relaxes and assumes that he or she is no longer being interviewed. Another solution is to introduce topics that involve the speaker in strong emotions or dramatic incidents. Labov cites as a successful example the question, "Have you ever been in a situation where you were in serious danger of being killed?" People answering this question almost always seem to shift style from the careful, conscious style they use when being interviewed to common, everyday language (Labov, 1972). It should be noted that Labov's linguistic methods have a sociological flavor, since he relies on the statistical manipulation of large bodies of linguistic data.

Sociolinguists use the superior data now available to identify subtle attitudes held by speakers toward their languages. For example, a given speaker may be ambivalent about the language of her ethnic ancestors. She may be proud to speak it among her family and close friends but embarrassed by using it among relative strangers. Values associated with various languages are themselves not fixed, but change in response to many personal, social, and demographic factors (Fishman, 1970).

As we have seen, the most useful way of viewing the relationship between culture and language is to view the two as intricately linked phenomena. Linguistic behavior of all sorts is part of cultural behavior more generally. We have looked at the properties of language that are shared with culture. But human beings are by no means the only animals capable of communicating with others of their own kind. We will now turn to animal communication studies to consider what relationships might exist between human language and that of other animals.

Language and Communication Studies

Human Speech and Animal Communication

Anthropologists study the languages of animals and the capacities of animals to learn human language in order to understand more fully the fundamental nature of language. Humans have long believed that only they possess language and that language is what distinguishes our species from the beasts. Yet we now know that other species are also highly intelligent, with sophisticated systems of communication. Ours is a single, extremely refined form of a general system of languages.

Much of the research in animal communication has focused on the capacity of animals to learn human language, and much of this work has been done with chimpanzees. In captivity, chimpanzees have learned to understand clas-

sifications and to sort pictures into classifications: fruit-vegetable, young-old, small-large. They also show the ability to classify the same object in more than one way. For example, they can recognize a watermelon as *fruit* in a fruit-vegetable grouping, and as *large* in a small-large grouping. Chimpanzees can learn not only the names of members of a class of objects but also the names for the classes of objects themselves (Premack & Premack, 1972).

The earliest attempts to teach chimpanzees human language were made in the 1930s and 1940s. The chimps were raised with human families and did learn to understand a large number of words. But, they did not learn to speak. A chimpanzee named Vicki did manage to combine several sounds and pronounce what seemed to be human phoneme combinations—such as the words "mama," "papa," and "cup"—with apparent human meaningfulness. But it has been demonstrated that apes lack the physical means of making human speech sounds. More recent experiments have therefore switched to sign languages. Washoe, a female chimpanzee, learned over 80 finger and hand signs by the time she was 4 years old. Her use of these signs, moreover, showed that she understood the concepts behind them. For example, after learning the sign for "open" with reference to a particular door, she then applied it to other doors. She finally applied it to other objects—drawers, jars, and the like.

Sarah, a chimpanzee in the laboratory of Ann and David Premack, has acquired a vocabulary of 130 terms using pieces of plastic of various shapes and colors. She can read and write in the language, selecting from pieces representing "apple," "banana," "red," "give," "color of," "pail," and many others. In addition to sentences like "Red color of apple" and "Mary give raisin Sarah," she was also able to read, write, and act upon utterances such as "Sarah insert apple pail banana dish" (Sarah inserts apple in pail and banana in dish). This was an important test, because it showed that Sarah understood the component structure of the sentence. She did not confuse either member of the pair "apple pail" with "banana" or "dish" of the other pair, although the terms were lumped together. And she realized that the verb ("insert,") and the subject ("Sarah") applied to both of the pairs in the sentence.

Sarah's achievement—the development of vocabulary and mastery of the elements of sentence organization—is impressive. She achieved a competence in language roughly equivalent to that of a 2-year-old child. Despite her obvious skills, it is not yet known whether she is able to use her plastic-word language to store information or to solve problems otherwise beyond her grasp. If Sarah were able to think "apple" without requiring that an apple be present, she would possess a crucial element of human language use: the ability to think and talk about things that are not actually there. Further studies may reveal whether chimpanzees can learn to do what human beings take for granted—to talk about absent friends, a trip one is looking forward to, or even things that are imaginary or fictional (Premack & Premack, 1972).

The language that Sarah learned was a very simple one, and it was necessary to teach her more directly and persistently than would have been necessary with a human infant. Each phase of instruction had to be broken down into simple steps. But, according to the Premacks, Sarah learned a simple form of human language. Moreover, the system that was used to teach Sarah has been employed in teaching brain-damaged people to speak, suggesting that Sarah's capacity to communicate may merely be weaker than—but not different from—that of humans. She would not have learned without being taught, but neither do human children who are completely isolated learn to speak. Future research will continue to explore the fascinating boundary between human language and the languages of animals.

In recent years, researchers have focused not only on language but on other signaling systems as well. They concluded that any one of these systems can be studied in the context of the others. As a result, nonlinguistic communication has become an area of growing interest. Two fields of study—proxemics and kinesics—focus on codes of nonlinguistic communication that exist in various human groups.

Edward Hall has studied the ways in which various societies use physical space. This field, called *proxemics,* borrows concepts from ethologists, who study territoriality among animals. The focus of proxemics is wide ranging; it considers how humans use space in such matters as architecture, furniture arrangement, interpersonal distance, listening behavior, and notions of privacy. Hall has found that space can be organized either to be conducive to communication or to produce "solitarity" (Hall's word for the state of being alone). A library in which people sit together at tables to study, for instance, tends to encourage more communication than does a library with individual carrels for reading and study. Hall found that notions of physical space differ by culture: "An Arab colleague has noted, for instance, that his small paneled recreation room was "cozy" to German friends but had just the opposite effect on Arabs, who found it oppressive" (Hall, 1968, p. 91).

Understanding proxemic distinctions is important in encounters with people of cultures different from one's own. Interpersonal distance, especially, tends to be dynamic and to vary widely from culture to culture. Latin Americans typically engage in more eye contact during conversation than do Americans; our tendency to let our eyes wander often seems to them like lack of attention (Hall, 1968). Also, two Latin American individuals engaged in serious conversation seem to talk

A subject for study in proxemics—spacing of telephones in our society and our attendant notions of privacy. (Kent Reno, Jeroboam)

chin to chin. The amount of space between them is significantly less than the space between two Americans would be. Proxemics reveals that items such as eye contact, posture, voice loudness, amount of physical contact, and personal space between speakers engaged in conversation are ingredients by which various groups measure interpersonal distance.

Other researchers, principally Ray Birdwhistell, have studied body movement and gesture as means of communication. This field, called *kinesics,* relies heavily on linguistic models. Just as linguists reduce speech sounds to morphs, so kinesicists seek to reduce body motion to least perceptible units, called *kines.* For example, Birdwhistell identifies brief raising and lowering of the eyebrows as a kine. He argues that differences in high or low eyebrow placement among various regional and economic groups can be identified. Many Englishmen, he asserts, position their eyebrows high; Americans tend to associate such

eyebrow position with a look of surprise. Kinesics has argued that brow and scalp behavior, facial expression, and posture—like spoken language—are learned behaviors that communicate messages, and thus form an important part of culture.

Metacommunication

In virtually all societies, spoken language is the official communication system, but features other than spoken language may determine the way we understand the social effectiveness of language. By placing language in a broader context of communication, anthropologists call attention to messages that are communicated beyond the confines of what is normally considered language. Messages may be communicated not only by language but by gesture, expression, tone of voice, and spatial movement. Such nonlinguistic messages put a "frame" around another

How we interpret extralinguistic messages depends on the system of nonverbal "language" by which we communicate. These, like spoken language, are learned behaviors that differ in various cultures. (Laima Druskis; Carl Frank, Photo Researchers)

message to tell the receiver how to interpret it. For instance, one's tone of voice and facial expression can tell a listener whether the statement "Thanks a lot" is an expression of gratitude or a sarcastic expression of displeasure. Gregory Bateson coined the term *metacommunication* to refer to a message that tells the receiver how another message is to be understood.

Metacommunications are different from nonlinguistic elements of communication studied in proxemics and kinesics in that metacommunications accompany spoken language. They are, therefore, so tied to the spoken message that they would have little or no

meaning without it. Unlike proxemics and kinesics, they cannot be studied as a *system* of communication, but only as an adjunct to it.

Uses of Language and Linguistics in Anthropology

The three views introduced earlier of the relationship of language to culture—language independent of culture, the correspondence of language and culture, and language as culture—can be seen in anthropological studies of language over the years.

The study of language has been an important feature of the practice and development of anthropology, especially of American anthropology. From its first use as a means of analyzing the history and nature of American Indian tribes, the linguistic method has served the broader aims of the study of culture. The work of early anthropologists was primarily to classify peoples according to their language, race, and/or culture. Since then the scope of anthropology has broadened considerably. As linguistics developed, the range and number of its contributions to cultural anthropology multiplied.

The contribution of language to the earliest anthropological work can hardly be said to have been linguistic in nature. As we have said, cultures were classified according to the languages their members spoke. But language was considered to be independent of culture. It was merely convenient to the researcher to have some knowledge of native languages. Such knowledge served to help the anthropologist gain admittance to and a degree of acceptance by the people being studied. Once anthropologists began to collect ethnographic data, however, the great advantage of competence in native languages became obvious. Fieldworkers who spoke directly to the people they studied had a great advantage over those who were forced to work through interpreters. They could gather data more easily, were likely to collect superior data, and were in a position to validate their findings.

Linguistic methods began to play an active part in anthropological research when interest turned to native languages as cultural entities and not as mere conduits of information. Anthropologists saw that the grammar of a language and its terminologies could reveal a great deal about the world view and patterns of thought of a culture. Earlier studies, ignoring the language itself, often had failed to penetrate these. More recent studies have focused specifically on all aspects of native grammars, both for linguistic purposes (to learn more about the nature and structure of languages) and anthropological ends (to see, for example, how the tense structure of a language affects the perceptions of speakers of that language) (Hymes, 1971).

Contemporary anthropologists are aware of the difficulty of discovering the underlying principles of organization of the cultures they study. Formerly, native informants were assumed to be qualified sources of reliable information about their social institutions. But it is now understood that though a member of a culture is an invaluable source of information, he or she cannot be depended upon to explain the culture as a system. Just as a competent speaker of a language may not know the grammatical rules governing use of that language —except implicitly—so a native may have little knowledge of the rules governing the social life of his or her people.

Other recent research has stressed the usefulness of language as a model for other cultural systems. The organization of various cultural phenomena may be seen as similar to a language, possessing a vocabulary and a grammar. In the study of kinship, for example, one begins with the terms of kinship and then passes on to its "grammar," the rules that regulate various areas of kin behavior, such as marriage, inheritance, roles within families, and so forth. The conduct of these processes and their interactions constitute the "syntax" of the system. As anthropology has matured from a discipline concerned chiefly with taxonomy (the classification of terms and features) to one that observes and analyzes the complex process of interaction among related elements, the models of language and grammar have been of great value.

Although linguistic models may be useful, not all cultural phenomena are organized in the way that language is. We have seen that language is closely bound up with many of the other cultural phenomena anthropologists study. It can be a valuable model for analysis of many of these phenomena. But not all data collected in fieldwork can be interpreted or analyzed by means of methods modeled on linguistics. Anthropologists therefore look for appropriate cultural entities, those that can be organized according to their distinctive features and analyzed according to rules. Although their value is great, linguistic models are only one of the tools essential to anthropological research.

Summary

1. Language is the distinguishing attribute of human beings and a precondition of human society. Since language is a primary means by which humans communicate, it is the prime target for understanding how cultural designs are understood and shared.

2. Linguists and anthropologists agree that human language and culture are closely related. They do not agree on the nature and extent of the relationship. Linguists tend to see language as an independent phenomenon, separate from social or cultural context. According to this view, the function of linguistics is to describe a statement, but not to explain its meaning. Most contemporary anthropologists, on the other hand, see the relationship between language and culture as one of correspondence. Because both are creations, largely unconscious, of the human mind, they parallel each other. The *Sapir-Whorf Hypothesis*—that language reflects the way in which its speakers perceive and think about the world—is an example of the correspondence view. A third view suggests that language *is* culture, that linguistic behavior is inseparable from social context and cultural behavior.

3. Sound is the medium through which language is expressed. *Phonology* (the study of sounds) consists of *phonetics* and *phonemics.* Each language possesses a limited number of *phonemes,* the distinctive but meaningless sounds heard as the same by native speakers of a language. Children learn to use only the distinct sounds of their language, although their babbling consists of many sounds that are foreign to an adult speaker's phonemic system.

4. From an analysis of speech sounds, phonologists formulate rules that govern the ordering of language into meaningful units. This set of rules for a particular language is its grammar. Grammar is divided into morphology and syntax. *Morphology* analyzes the combination of *morphs* into words. *Syntax* deals with the rules for combining words into phrases and sentences. Morphology and syntax share the processes of selection, arrangement, and modification. *Transformational grammar,* introduced by Chomsky, attempts to explain how speakers develop linguistic competence and become creative users of language. Sentences consist of *surface structure,* corresponding to the sounds we hear, and *deep structure,* representing the underlying structure by which meaning is generated. Grammatical transformations change deep into surface structure. *Universal grammar,* according to Chomsky, is the set of rules or principles governing all languages that explains basic resemblances between languages as well as the child's ability to master any language.

5. *Semantics* is the study of meaning; it involves attempts to define "meaning" and classifies kinds of meaning. Semantics is of special interest to cognitive anthropologists because it concentrates on aspects of language most closely associated with thought processes.

6. *Sociolinguists* study language use within a speech community. Topics on interest to sociolinguists are the varieties of languages within speech communities, the elements of

those languages, and the relationships among them to usage and structure. Speakers select language according to their audience, the setting, and the topic of discussion.

7. Anthropologists study animal communication in order to understand more fully the nature of human language. Chimpanzees have learned to communicate with humans using simple vocabulary and basic sentence structure.

8. Two fields of study—proxemics and kinesics—focus on codes of nonlinguistic communication in human groups. *Proxemics* studies the ways in which various groups use physical space. *Kinesics* studies body movement and gesture as means of communication.

It has found that such things as brow movement, facial expression, and posture—like spoken language—are learned behaviors.

9. Some messages are transmitted beyond the confines of what is normally considered language. A message that tells the receiver how another message or behavior is to be interpreted is termed a *metacommunication*.

10. Language has always been important to anthropology, but early research ignored the cultural elements of language. When language was seen to be related to culture, anthropological interest in it increased. Recent research has employed the categories and methods of linguistics as one of a number of tools by which to analyze cultural phenomena.

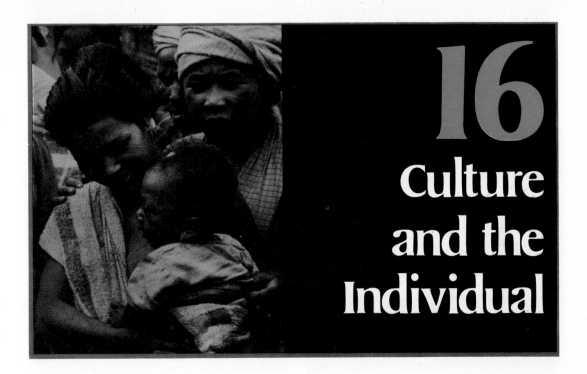

16
Culture and the Individual

I T has been said that every human being is in some ways like every other human being, in some ways like some other human beings, and in some ways like no other· human being (Kluckhohn & Murray, 1962). Although each of us is an individual with a distinct personality, it is clear that most of us agree on what are desirable personality characteristics, many of which we share. Our general sharing of such values as outspokenness and competitiveness makes us quite unlike inhabitants of Acoma Pueblo or Soviet Armenia. Indeed, our very insistence upon "rugged individualism" is a characteristic that would be quite alien, if not downright revolutionary, in a Pueblo Indian or an Armenian.

We saw earlier that culture involves understandings about life experiences shared by members of a human social group. In their inquiries into the designs for living of human groups, anthropologists deal directly with the individual participants in a given culture, whose activities are expressions of the cultural system. Of course, no one individual can express every aspect of a cultural system. Nor is any single member capable of knowing or communicating all the designs associated with that system. However, most people are able to understand their own society sufficiently well to function within it as "normal" members. A Navajo sheepherder, for example, does not have the knowledge that the singers in his culture who heal the sick through elaborate song cycles and traditional sand-painted designs possess, but he is able to explain many of their functions in his community as well as his understanding of interactions with them.

The relationship of the individual to society is the subject of this chapter. This field of investigation has traditionally been known in anthropology as "culture and personality." More recently, the term *psychological anthropology* has come into use. Psychological anthropology analyzes culture as expressed in the actions, thoughts, and feelings of its individual members.

The Concept of Personality

Personality may be thought of as the organized response patterns within every human being. These patterns shape the actions,

Personality is molded by an infant's earliest experiences as well as by the cultural designs of the group in which he or she lives. (Ken Heyman)

thoughts, and feelings of the individual in various situations. Within each individual, these patterns are more or less consistent with each other throughout life.

Personality directs us to act, think, and feel in certain ways. It is our particular style of facing and dealing with life events. Because one's personality is generally predictable, it allows us to say confidently, "If such-and-such were to happen, I would do thus-and-so." Each of us can be reasonably certain whether we would stand up and fight; cope with an emergency; evade an issue; prefer science fiction films or romantic novels; and so on. In these and countless other details we hourly acknowledge the consistency of personality. We do so also in our expectations of others' behavior, in such expressions as "She's the kind of person who . . . ," or "He's always doing things like that."

Personality may be thought of as the substantially consistent "blueprints" within each of us that allow us to respond to the world around us in predictable ways. This definition parallels our definition of culture as the designs that allow individual members of a group to interact with one another in expected ways. Cultural designs are, of course, intersubjective in nature and, in existence, well before the birth and development of any individual. They are themselves significant factors in the development of every human personality. Culture is, however, only one of the determining factors in the formation of personality.

We do not know at what age human personality is formed—6 months, 6 years, and every age before, between, and after have all been advanced by one authority or another. There is, however, general agreement that some aspects of personality are set very early in life, long before one is able consciously to do anything much about them. Although personality may be modified somewhat throughout life, our earliest experiences are influential in personality formation. "As the twig is bent, so is the tree inclined," goes an old saying—

and so the starting point for our discussion is those elements that go into bending the twig. In addition to culture, other significant factors in personality development include physical characteristics, environment, and the life experiences that are unique to every individual.

Physical Factors and Personality

Human physiology is surely one of the most obvious contributors to the formation of personality. It involves two aspects of biological characteristics: inherited physical and mental capacity on the one hand, and the health and functioning of the human organism on the other. Physical factors in personality thus include everything from the age, sex, and complexion of the individual to various endocrine disorders (such as diabetes) and other biochemical malfunctions. Mental attributes, too, are factors in personality. Personalities of the gifted, the talented, the average, and the retarded all reflect their inherent abilities. They reflect, as well, the extent to which peoples' capacities are utilized, recognized, frustrated, or looked down on in their cultural setting.

Clearly, the appearance of an individual's body has an influence on personality. However, body build is not evaluated equally in all cultural systems. In American culture today, obesity is considered unattractive (and unhealthy) in adults. Elsewhere in the world—and even at an earlier time in the United States—stoutness may be prized as a sign of prosperity and considered esthetically pleasing. So strong is the link between appearance and personality that some people reshape their physical characteristics to fit cultural norms and values. Certain traditional Polynesian cultures prized obesity, and the ruling class was force-fed to meet the standards for royal plumpness. Other physical characteristics that mold personality, and that may be subject to differential cultural appraisal, include health and strength. Consider, for ex-

Body build is evaluated differently in various cultures. Sumo wrestlers in Japan are honored for their size, as are some professional athletes in our own society. (Fred Mayer, Woodfin Camp)

ample, a girl with a healthy constitution and athletic bent in Victorian England, when daintiness and inactivity were the fashion for females.

An early study of the relationship between physiology and personality was done by W. H. Sheldon, who took detailed measurements and made tests on Harvard students and other American males. Sheldon assigned his test subjects to three categories on the basis of body build and claimed that there was a consistent personality within each category. Thin individuals (ectomorphs) were likely to be nervous, introverted, and have skin ailments and insomnia. Husky, muscular men (meso-morphs) were usually energetic, lively, and athletic. And heavyset individuals (en-domorphs) tended to be extroverted, lazy, and luxury-loving (Sheldon, 1940 and 1942). Similarly, E. A. Hooton correlated the body builds of convicts with the kind of criminal activity in which they had been involved. He found that, for example, short, heavy men were more likely than tall, thin ones to have engaged in crimes of violence such as assault and sex offenses (Hooton, 1939).

This type of evidence, however, has been fragmentary and inconclusive. Yet there is no doubt that some inherited traits do play a significant role in personality development and expression. As Kluckhohn and Murray express it, "biological inheritance provides the stuff from which personality is fashioned and . . . determines trends and sets limits within which variation is constrained" (1962, p. 57).

Environment and Personality

Folk wisdom or "common knowledge" has long believed that physical environment and climate shape personality. It has been suggested that people raised in the tropics are likely to be slow-moving, indolent, uninventive, and unambitious, whereas mountain dwellers are energetic, tough, and individualistic. No careful research has been carried out to support or disclaim such impressions, but individuals in every clime have been found with abilities and characters different from those proposed by such theories. Today it is generally accepted that such notions are without foundation.

Nevertheless, it *is* recognized that physical environment does influence human personality in specific ways. For example, the environment provides the materials for human handcraft or other production—from rocks, grasses, lumber, cave walls, and ocher for making paints to diamonds, petroleum, and

uranium. Technology allows for the use of these materials. Thus, human occupations, choices, and the utilization of human abilities (with all of their implications for personality) are clearly dependent upon the facilities provided by, or nonexistent in, a particular setting.

But the most important influence of the environment on human genetic potential is nutritional. The environment, of course, provides the materials for human diet. It has been shown that individuals whose diets lack key nutrients never achieve their maximum growth or optimal body functioning. In addition, they are likely to succumb to illness more frequently, to experience illness more severely, and to recover less completely than individuals with good nutrition—all factors which affect personality. Further, prolonged lack of various nutrients is itself a cause of disease. Dietary deficiency diseases are characterized by personality change as well as physical deformities.

Arctic Hysteria. Cross-cultural studies of nutrition are beginning to illuminate the role of minerals and other dietary factors in personality development. The outbursts of agitated behavior known as Arctic hysteria have recently, for example, been shown to be related in part to calcium deficiency. Arctic hysteria takes the form of wild running to and fro, screaming, and even convulsions. Such behavior occurs with significant frequency in Greenland, Lapland, Siberia, Alaska, and other polar areas. There, as Foulks (1972) has shown, the distinctive environment is responsible in several ways for limited calcium intake and use. For one thing, the irregular alternation of daylight and darkness directly interferes with the body's use of calcium, which is needed for the functioning of the central nervous system. In addition, the lengthy winter and the cold climate, requiring heavy and extensive body covering much of the year, allow only a minimal amount of solar ultraviolet radiation to reach the Eskimo's body. Ultraviolet light is required by the body for vitamin D production and utilization, which in turn affects the body's use of calcium (Foulks, 1972). And not least, the Arctic environment further limits the available natural food sources of calcium.

But environmentally produced calcium deficiency is not the sole cause of Arctic hysteria. Eskimos now live less in igloos and more in wooden shacks heated by coal stoves. In the wooden shacks, the heated air is not humidified, as it was by the melting and dripping of the frozen igloo walls. This change resulted in an increase in respiratory infections among the Eskimos. One consequence of such infections was that many individuals had chronic middle ear disease, symptoms of which include central nervous system disorders that may resemble Arctic hysteria. The introduction of a cash economy has led to the purchase of inexpensive starchy foods, bringing such dietary changes as an increase in carbohydrate intake and a corresponding decrease in the protein and mineral content of their food. And as part of the Eskimo cultural tradition, there was a social model for hysteria. In contests held during certain festivals and in the institution of shamanism, frenzied behavior similar to that of Arctic hysteria was considered appropriate (Foulks, 1972). Thus, Arctic hysteria as a personality trait has been shown to be the product of both environmental and cultural influences.

Personal Experiences and Personality

Without any doubt, personality owes much to factors and events particular to the individual. Every person has a unique history, composed of experiences that are never exactly like those of anyone else. This holds true even for identical twins brought up in the same household. One twin is older than the other, even if only by minutes; one may weigh less or be otherwise less sturdy or healthy than the other, and perhaps thus get more caretaking attention from parents; one may have a better appetite and consequently get more affection from the parent; and so on. Recent studies have shown that not only whether one is male or female but also aspects of the family into which one is born—such as age and the educational, occupational, and socioeconomic levels of one's parents—all contribute to the uniqueness of individual development. Then, too, there is the contribution to personality of the character and severity of illnesses and the age at which these occur. Similarly, we may have our share of those experiences labeled "traumatic"—a serious accident, hostility on the part of peers, the death or departure of a parent or other close family member.

Cultural norms and social conditioning may work to equalize certain types of experiences, but they cannot succeed in erasing or "normalizing" all of them. For example, Operation Head Start has attempted to provide enrichment for very young children from so-called "culturally deprived" backgrounds; months or years of psychotherapy may rid an individual of the aftereffects of a traumatic series of events. Yet the original experience can never be removed after the fact. The individual may learn in various ways to minimize or control its effects, but once experienced, an event or situation has been an influence.

Personality, as an organization of forces within the individual, is the cumulative result of all the factors just discussed. But of them all, culture is by far the major influence on the formation of any given personality. The rest of this chapter discusses in detail the cultural factors in personality development. First, we will survey contrasting views of personality to get some perspective on the studies that will follow.

Contrasting Views of Personality Formation

There are a number of different ways of looking at how personality is formed. Salvatore R. Maddi (1968) describes three major ones: conflict theory, fulfillment theory, and consistency theory.

Conflict Theory

The *conflict theory* of personality formation states that personality is formed as a result of constant conflict between the desires or instincts of the individual and the constraints imposed by society. Freud's articulation of the gratification/punishment principle is a statement of the conflict theory of personality formation. According to this view, the natural human instinct for gratification is inevitably curbed and frustrated when it comes up against the needs or demands of other persons in society; the individual must constantly compromise and adjust. All children learn sooner or later, for example, that food is not always promptly or adequately available on demand; that the rights and needs of others must be considered and respected; that bodily functions must be controlled. Freud believed that this process of adjustment is accompanied by varying degrees of frustration, repression, guilt, resentment, and anxiety, with consequent effects on personality. In response, all individuals develop self-protective personality mechanisms. These mechanisms may be healthy (such as the substitution of an acceptable activity for one that is taboo), or neurotic (such as ascribing to others unacceptable tendencies one cannot acknowledge in oneself).

Fulfillment Theory

Fulfillment theory, on the other hand, holds that conflict is not continuous but, rather, a periodic occurrence, and that the main stimulus to personality development lies within the individual. According to this point of view, all living things strive to realize the full measure of their genetic potential. For humans, self-actualization always requires the approval of others (one's family, for example, or community) and of the self as well. We develop a positive self-image in response to the image of ourselves reflected from others. The lack of a positive self-image is profoundly disturbing to the individual and severely interferes with his or her functioning within various reference groups (possibly resulting in a mental breakdown). The fulfillment model of personality formation is the theoretical foundation for the collection of current therapies and related activities known as the Human Potential Movement. In general, it emphasizes ways for the individual to become free from the influences of others in order to achieve optimal self-realization.

Consistency Theory

In contrast to both of these views of personality formation, *consistency theory* emphasizes the continuity of life experiences; each experience is filtered through the world view built up by the individual on the basis of prior experience. Personality within each individual, then, is largely consistent, since the individual processes new information and events in terms of the outlook that has resulted from the sum of past experience. The consistency model is based on the need of individuals for organization of various feelings and attitudes into one integrated and harmonious personality.

However, consistency theorists recognize that personality formation is a lifelong process and that an individual may well encounter situations and information that are inconsistent with his or her earlier personality construct. When this happens, the individual may experience anxiety to a greater or lesser ex-

Contact with other cultures introduces experiences and behaviors that may be totally different from one's own. Here, a Pygmy woman watches the application of lipstick with bemused fascination. (Monkmeyer)

tent. If the inconsistency is sufficiently significant, the individual may be driven to a reappraisal of his or her situation and world view, leading perhaps to changes in outlook and personality. We sometimes hear of a person whose life took a different course after a specific event or as a result of a new influence. Such dramatic reversals can be due to changes in the society as well as to events unique to the individual. The phrase *cognitive dissonance* has been applied to a situation in which an individual's outlook or self-image comes up against an opposite or inconsistent experience. In a sense, all of us experience cognitive dissonance as we go from one stage of life to the next. The role dependencies of childhood

must give way to the responsibilities of adulthood and the various roles associated with it. The individual's personality makes the adjustment during the transition period of adolescence (and, in more complex societies where assumption of the full adult role is delayed, in young adulthood).

Barnouw (1973) notes that each of these three theoretical views of personality formation takes a different attitude toward the relationship between personality and culture. For conflict theorists, culture is an inhibiting, controlling factor. Some of them hold that cultural complexity increases human frustration and that people in simpler cultures are less likely to develop neuroses. For fulfillment theorists, culture provides the means by which self-actualization can take place and human needs be fulfilled. The consistency model takes a more balanced view of the role of culture, making it neither an adversary (as in the conflict model) nor a primary determinant (as in the fulfillment model). Rather, culture is seen as an ever-present, but essentially neutral, factor. It is there to shape one's interactions with other individuals (Barnouw, 1973).

Of the three theories, the consistency view best fits the approach of this text. Just as the individual must integrate new developments into a preexisting personality structure, so too cultures attempt to incorporate new influences with minimal dislocations. The consistency of culture provides security within which the individual can develop. At times, inability to integrate new developments may result in what is called *culture shock*. This is a psychological response to an unfamiliar culture and is characterized by disorientation, anxiety, and sometimes mental breakdown, depression, or even suicide. But the formation of personality is a lifelong process, and most individuals in most cultures learn to integrate their accumulated experiences so that their self-image is not too incompatible with reality.

However, the other points of view about personality formation are also relevant to our purposes. The conflict model has been the starting point for the development of psychoanalytic theory. It underlies, as we shall see, studies that emphasize the role of childhood training in personality development and national character. Similarly, aspects of fulfillment theory underlie assumptions about the relationship of individuals to their society, as we shall see in our examination of role theory.

Socialization and Enculturation

The primary focus of psychological anthropology has been directed to the question

Socialization involves learning skills that enable one to function as a competent member of society. The Hoti Indians of Venezuela learn spear throwing at an early age by playing a game in which they throw spears through a hoop. (Jacques Jangoux, Peter Arnold Photo Archives)

of how a personality type characteristic of a given culture is continually recreated in each generation. The means by which the individual learns in the earliest years to become a functioning adult within a specific society and culture has been called both "socialization" and "enculturation." These terms involve essentially the same processes—absorption of a culture's values, world view, life styles, and skills. However, there is an implied shade of difference. *Enculturation* refers to the process whereby individual members of a society acquire the characteristics of a given culture, learning its language and generally acquiring competence in the culture. *Socialization* refers to the more general process whereby someone new to a society learns to function as a member of that society; it includes the learning of social roles such as that of wife or elder, and of occupational roles, whether through example or through more structured training, as in school.

In real life, of course, both processes happen together and are inseparable. "Socialization" is used most frequently by sociologists and psychologists and comprises all aspects of learning to grow up, including control of bodily functions, learning to relate to others, assuming adult responsibilities, and so on. Many anthropologists, on the other hand, tend to prefer "enculturation" because it comprises total learning of cultural expectations and does not imply undue emphasis on social roles. In this text both terms are used interchangeably.

Role Theory and Socialization

The nature of society's influence on individual identity is the subject of *role theory*. The pioneering work of social psychologist George Herbert Mead in the early part of this century laid the foundation for role theory. Mead's research and teaching established that identity is socially constructed and sustained. Children first learn the social roles of their group from those individuals with whom they deal most intensively—parents, siblings, other close relatives, teachers, and peers. Mead termed this important group of people *significant others.* After a while, the child discovers that the social roles learned from significant others are also those recognized by members of the society at large. This more distant and less intimate entity takes on a character of its own. It becomes a person's mental representation of the expectations of society; Mead termed it the *generalized other.* Referring to the generalized other enables a person to see things from the perspective of his or her entire group. Mead showed that a child takes on an image of self during the same time that he or she forms opinions about society. By combining the demands of significant others and of the generalized other, the child develops an image of self and comes also to understand the social roles that exist in his or her particular society.

Within every culture, identifiable social roles are assigned on the bases of age, sex, and occupation. Individuals learn what is expected of them by patterning their behavior on *role models.* These models are provided by members of the society who are already engaged in the role the individual can expect to assume. Regardless of what society one lives in, the criteria of age, sex, and occupation serve to create role models. In every society, those members of the next older age group provide models for behavior. Seven-year-old children get their notions of what it will be like to be 12 by observing the behavior and experiences of 12-year-olds, just as 12-year-olds watch teen-agers for an understanding of what is to come. As we shall see in a later chapter, some societies have clearly demarcated age categories in which certain defined roles and behavior

"**Son, someday all this will be yours.**" (Jack Kohl)

are prescribed. Individuals also pattern behavior on the basis of sex. In most societies, girls pattern after their mothers, boys after their fathers. Sometimes other adult men or women may also serve as models. Among the Haida of British Columbia, for example, a boy will live with, learn from, and model his behavior after that of his mother's brother (Murdock, 1934). Similarly, observed occupations may serve to shape behavior. Children may not know exactly what the work connected with a particular occupation is like on a day-to-day basis. But they do form general notions of the roles connected with such occupations as medical/religious practitioner (doctor and witch doctor, clergy and shaman), political leader, teacher, housewife, farmer or herder, artisan. Occupational role models define not only roles available in a particular society but also expected relationships among various people.

Childhood Determinism

Whereas G. H. Mead's work focused on the influence of social roles on identity, Freud's theories of personality formation emphasized the encounter between infant and early childhood instincts and the necessary restraints imposed by society through parents and other caregivers in the socialization process. Freud stressed in particular the influences of weaning, toilet-training, development of various sexual inhibitions and controls, and the resolution of oedipal feelings.*

*The oedipal conflict is the child's early attachment to the parent of the opposite sex, and concurrent resentment or hostility toward the parent of the same sex. These feelings must be resolved through identification with the same-sex parent in order for the child to progress to an adult relationship with a member of the opposite sex.

Our culture is so familiar with the notion that childhood training shapes adult personality that we easily accept the idea as a basis for our study of culture and personality. This general approach is known as *childhood determinism.* In emphasizing the early stages of life as crucial to personality formation, Freudian theory has been a stimulus to anthropological studies of child training in diverse cultural settings. Field studies and theoretical analyses have examined the role of early experiences in shaping adult personality. One type of inquiry looks at differences in enculturation processes in various societies. It attempts to answer the question, "How do children learn their culture?" A second kind of study is concerned with the influences of child-care practices on the sequence of human development. It addresses the question, "How do infants in different cultures develop in comparison to one another?" A third approach focuses on the correlations between childhood training practices and adult personality with the question, "What traits in adult personality can be attributed to experiences in one's childhood?" A fourth type of study relates child-rearing practices to other aspects of a specific culture. It considers the question, "What child-rearing practices reflect general patterns of a particular culture?" (Bourguignon, 1973). The key research projects that are described below are studies that examine these various aspects of the connections between culture and personality.

Margaret Mead: Enculturation and Child-Care Studies

Margaret Mead was among the first anthropologists to organize field research centering on a specific problem, in contrast to earlier studies which had attempted to be all-encompassing in scope.* Her first study dealt

*This discussion is based on Barnouw (1973), pp. 129–147.

with the constraints and limitations imposed by culture on adolescents. In this study, published as *Coming of Age in Samoa* (1928), Mead posed the question, "Are the disturbances which vex our adolescents due to the nature of adolescence itself or to civilization?" In Western cultures, adolescence is generally characterized by emotional tension, intergenerational conflict, and rebellion against authority. Mead intended, through comparison of different cultures, to discover whether these characteristics were due to physiological changes occurring at puberty. If so, Mead reasoned adolescence should present similar problems in all places and at all times, regardless of how different the cultures might be.

Mead found that on the South Pacific island of Samoa adolescence was very different from the tension-ridden experience she had known in the United States. Instead, for various social and cultural reasons, it was a period of relative calm, stability, and even intergenerational cooperation. Moreover, Mead felt that the social interactions of adolescent Samoans generally were characterized by a high degree of casualness and ease. She found that even premarital sexual relationships were accepted in Samoa as a natural part of adolescence, since the individuals involved did not invest a high degree of emotion in these relationships. In this study, as in the two that followed it, Mead showed that characteristics of personality are not a simple and inevitable consequence of biological processes common to human beings in all places and at all times. They are, instead, influenced by various social and cultural factors. Mead's work here illustrates the second inquiry of field research mentioned above, focusing on the ways that cultural differences influence personality development.

Mead's next effort was a pioneer work in the influence of childhood training on personality development. Here, she was concerned with the upbringing of children among the

Manus of the Admiralty Islands off the coast of New Guinea. In *Growing Up in New Guinea,* Mead (1930) observed that Manus children were not closely supervised by adults. Except for being instilled with a certain respect for property, they were left pretty much to their own devices. Among the Manus, children lived in a world populated by their peers. They spent most of their time in play and had few responsibilities and little contact with their elders. When they were young

the adults give the children no storytelling pattern, no guessing games, riddles, puzzles. The idea that children would like to hear legends seems quite fantastic to a Manus adult. . . . Where we fill our children's minds with a rich folklore, songs which personalize the sun, the moon, and the stars, riddles and fairy tales and myths, the Manus do nothing of the sort. (M. Mead, 1930, pp. 125, 130)

Mead concluded that the imagination and creativity we tend to associate with childhood must be cultivated through adult guidance and instruction. Without such a pattern for fantasy, this tendency will be kept from manifesting itself. Here Mead called attention to the beneficial side of our social tradition, which

can be seen not only as a constraint but as thought-provoking and creativity-inspiring as well.

Mead's third study compared three tribes in New Guinea—the Arapesh, the Mundugumor, and the Tchambuli—which, though living within the same general area, were significantly different in many aspects of their society and culture. In particular, Mead focused on the influence of culture on sexual roles and attitudes; she found that personality is not sex-linked, but culturally derived. In *Sex and Temperament in Three Primitive Societies* (1935), Mead discussed the evidence that led her to state that "many, if not all, of the personality traits which we have called masculine or feminine are as lightly linked to sex as are the clothing, the manners, and the form of head-dress that a society at a given period assigns to either sex" (p. 280). Sexual roles and attitudes, she concluded, are not biologically determined.

Although a number of questions have been raised about Mead's research, her studies remain landmarks in the field of culture and personality. They emphasize the importance of cultural influence on personality formation. As she concludes, "the differences between

Margaret Mead doing fieldwork in Bali in 1957. (Ken Heyman)

individuals who are members of different cultures, like the differences between individuals within a culture, are almost entirely to be laid to differences in conditioning, especially during early childhood, and the form of this conditioning is culturally determined" (1935, p. 280).

Basic Personality, Modal Personality, and Childhood Training

The concept of basic personality structure was articulated by Abram Kardiner as a means of relating childhood training to adult personality in a specific culture. *Basic personality structure* consists of the cluster of tendencies common to the personalities of all individuals who shared early childhood experiences as a result of being brought up in the same culture. Kardiner was a psychoanalyst who came into contact with Edward Sapir, Ruth Benedict, Ralph Linton, Cora Du Bois, and other anthropologists of the so-called "culture and personality school" in a seminar at Columbia University in the 1930s. He came to see traditional Freudian ideas of personality formation as strongly tied to Western society and theorized that other societies might have different ways of dealing with problems of personality.

Kardiner believed that some life experiences naturally have more impact than others. Those that are most responsible for disciplining, restricting (inhibiting), and gratifying the child he termed *primary institutions*. They consist of family and kinship arrangements; institutionalized activities associated with feeding, weaning, and sex training; and subsistence patterns. Primary institutions shape basic personality structure. *Secondary institutions* are those that serve the "needs and tensions" generated by the primary ones; that is, those through which basic personality structure is expressed. They include taboo systems, religion, the arts, mythology.

For anthropologists, Kardiner's approach

has proved both problematic and useful. A basic limitation is, as Singer (1961) points out, the lack of adequate proof of causal connections among child-rearing practices, personality traits, and forms of culture such as art, religion, and folklore. The approach has been useful to anthropologists because it looks at both cultural institutions and personality traits common to members of a society. It has prompted anthropologists to do studies using various psychoanalytic techniques and has led to other productive concepts.

Foremost among these was the notion of modal personality proposed by Kardiner's colleague, Cora Du Bois (1944).* *Modal personality* consists of the characteristics or tendencies shared by *most* members of a given culture. In a field study that was exceptionally thorough and, at that time, novel, Du Bois spent a year in general ethnographic inquiry on Alor, an Indonesian island. She followed this by psychologically oriented research. In this second phase, Du Bois obtained detailed life histories and materials such as the drawings of children, and she administered various projective tests to the people of Alor.†

When her field research was completed, Du Bois submitted the various psychological materials to a number of specialists, including Kardiner. They analyzed them independently of one another, and without knowledge of the cultural background of the people tested. So

---

*This discussion is based on Barnouw (1973), pp. 153–162.

†Projective tests present subjects with a visual stimulus—inkblots, for example, in the Rorschach tests. In response, without cues from the test administrator, subjects must express freely what they see or think is happening. Their responses are categorized by psychoanalysts according to the personality traits they indicate. Because the range of projective test responses has been standardized within contemporary American-European culture, a built-in culture bias can skew the interpretation of results from subjects with non-Western cultural backgrounds. One must understand the culture very well for a useful interpretation to be made. For this reason, projective tests are seldom used in anthropological research at the present time.

striking was the correspondence between the findings of the various specialists that Du Bois was convinced that each specialist, herself included, was correctly describing some general tendencies of Alorese personality.

Du Bois found that, among the Alorese, the sexual divison of labor was an important influence on personality development from infancy on. Men spent their time in such economic transactions as the exchange of pigs and ceremonial goods; women were the main producers of food and spent most of their time in its cultivation and collection. They spent so much time and energy in this activity that they had to leave their infants at home with a relative. Du Bois argued that for this reason, young children experienced various forms of stress, which multiplied as their lives proceeded. The initial stress took the form of oral frustration when the infant was left to be nursed by women other than the mother. Often a child simply was deprived of milk because no other lactating women were available; the child waited to nurse until the mother returned at day's end. Other frustrations followed when, after a year or so, the child began to walk and was no longer carried about, thus losing the security of physical contact with a caregiver. Feeding continued to be highly irregular as the child grew older. These frustrations were compounded by the custom of teasing, in which mothers showed preference for the children of other women or either parent pretended aggression toward the child. Du Bois felt that, as a result, the world appeared threatening to Alorese children. Consequently, she did not find it at all surprising that before the age of 5 or 6, children often throw rather intense and long temper tantrums.

During adolescence, Alorese boys and girls followed different sets of daily activities. Boys gathered together for idle play or, at times, intermittent periods of work in the fields; girls joined their mothers in most of their activities. Courting began toward the end of adolescence.

Marriage seemed to be a very tense relationship among the Alorese, who divorced an average of twice during a lifetime. As Du Bois saw it, this tension derived from the conflicting feelings of love and hate toward their mothers that Alorese males developed in early childhood. These attitudes were then transferred to their wives. A man, continuing to seek nurturance and other forms of attention, continued to be frustrated; the wife, like the mother, did not have time to satisfy his needs and desires. Men were consequently much given to jealousy and continued feelings of inadequacy. Du Bois was told, interestingly, that a man's wife should have the qualities of a mother, and she recorded instances when analogies between wives and mothers were drawn. The specialists analyzing her data noted suspicion, apathy, insecurity, and lack of emotional involvement among the personality traits of the Alorese (Malefijt, 1974). Through her wide-ranging research techniques, the evidence amassed by Du Bois seems to support the conclusions she and her consulting specialists reached, even though, as Du Bois is well aware, factors other than child training are also involved in shaping the modal personality of any culture. Furthermore, the agreement among the analysts of the Alorese data may have been as much a reflection of their common cultural understandings as it was of the situation on Alor.

National Character Studies

During World War II, the need arose to know more about the people of several nations, both enemies and allies. This need presented something of a problem because field study was not possible under wartime conditions. Nor were subject societies the "primitive" societies studied by ethnologists in the past but, for the most part, modern nations.

Under the guidance of Margaret Mead, Ruth Benedict, Geoffrey Gorer, and others, anthropological culture and personality study methods served as a starting point for the development of new techniques for analyzing "culture at a distance" (M. Mead & Metraux, 1953).

The techniques used for indirect culture study included interviewing former residents of or visitors to the nation under study; analysis of the history, economy, and geographical setting of the nation; and the careful inspection of such cultural materials as films, paintings, sculpture, architecture, literature, and speeches (Singer, 1961).

Of the national character analyses made during World War II, Ruth Benedict's classic study of Japan, *The Chrysanthemum and the Sword* (1946), is an outstanding example using the culture pattern (or configuration) approach. Earlier we looked at Benedict's notion that cultures are more or less consistent clusters of themes or patterns. This view was described as configurational theory. Child rearing is one of the patterns in the overall cultural configuration. It constitutes the means of communicating the configuration to the next generation. Benedict ascribed the themes running through Japanese culture and the personality traits of Japanese adults to early child-training practices, including teasing and strict toilet-training (Singer, 1961).

But in configuration theory, other cultural patterns combine with child rearing to influence personality. Attention has been called, for example, to the common characteristics or themes of interpersonal relationships in a culture. Relationships between interacting groups or individuals may be complementary, eliciting opposite behavior—dominant/submissive, for example—from both parties. Or they may be symmetrical, with both parties responding similarly to one another. Gregory Bateson (1942), for one, conceives of national character in terms of patterns in interpersonal relations; national characters differ according to combinations of specific themes in a given culture. For example, the Balinese seem to combine dependence, exhibitionism, and high status; Europeans seem to combine high status with social service (Singer, 1961).

National character can be seen as an element in a circular system of personality formation. Parents and child constitute a "mutually interactive system" (Singer, 1961, p. 48) with the parent responding to the child and in turn stimulating responses from the child. Other cultural patterns also have circular interactions with the individual. So, configuration theory moves beyond linear or direct causal relationships in its view of childhood training and adult personality. As Mead has written, in a circular system "the method of child rearing, the presence of a particular literary tradition, the nature of the domestic and public architecture, the religious beliefs, the political system, are all conditions within which a given kind of personality develops" (M. Mead, 1951).

Child Rearing and Culture Patterns: The Six Cultures Study

In the 1950s a vast quantity of ethnographic material was being assembled in the Human Relations Area Files at Yale University. Because the raw data had been accumulated over a long period of time by different researchers using different methodology, there were gaps in this cross-cultural record. Although it was the most comprehensive correlation of cultural material ever undertaken, the Human Relations Area Files contained only occasional material on child rearing and often sketchy descriptions of childhood experience. Because of such deficiencies, John W. M. Whiting devised an outline to guide field researchers, whose resulting studies would then be comparable. The result is known as the Six Cultures Study.

Each of six teams trained in the Whiting

approach studied a community of from 50 to 100 families, concentrating in each on a group of 24 mothers and their children between the ages of 3 and 10. The research reports were to follow a specific outline: the first part contained detailed descriptions of specific ethnographic material—ecology, kinship, architecture, and so on—and the second part focused on maternity and child-rearing practices. An aim of this coordinated cross-cultural survey was to identify any recurring correlations that might exist between specific child rearing practices, childhood experiences, and cultural institutions.

The materials from the six cultures were sorted according to comparable categories of data. Observations of children's behavior, for example, sorted out into two quite separate clusters. One cluster consisted of groups emphasizing cooperation; the second cluster was characterized by individualism. Children in the first, or Type A, group offered more support and help; children in the second, or Type B, cultures more often sought help and allowed themselves to be dominated. Other similarities in the Type A cultures included subsistence farming as the economic basis, along with lack of economic role specialization, egalitarian social organization, and lack of buildings for purposes other than dwelling. Type B cultures, on the other hand, were more complex and were characterized by a cash economy, division of labor, some class or caste hierarchy, specialized buildings, and a centralized political organization (Barnouw, 1973).

Because of the standardized and detailed methodology employed in the Six Cultures project, it has produced some of the most useful culture and personality studies. Research using Whiting's approach has continued in other cultures. Further, the material has proved fruitful for additional analysis and speculation about the applications of some of the findings to problems in American society. For example, the influences that produce the typical male aggressive-hostile personality

among the Gusii of East Africa have been compared to studies showing that the "macho" culture of lower-class American males was related to their growing up in predominantly female households, lacking effective male role models (Barnouw, 1973).

All of the approaches to personality formation discussed in the preceding pages have in common an emphasis on childhood experience as a determinant of adult personality. They also consider the accompanying role of culture in making certain possibilities available, restricting other opportunities, and generally providing the framework for the development of the individual. But childhood experiences, as some anthropologists have pointed out, can have a paradoxical relationship to adult personality. A society may raise its children in so permissive a manner as to "be ideal from a Freudian point of view" (Barnouw, 1973, p. 34) and yet wind up with neurotic, anxiety-ridden adults. Some would argue that we have seen this happening in postwar United States where permissive child-rearing practices apparently created an institutionalized counterculture that was, in its determination to undermine the establishment, exactly counter or against the previously prevailing cultural themes. Making a similar point, Wolfenstein (1955) has shown that the tension experienced by children in France under rigid behavioral restrictions and enforced hard work in school and other training for adulthood, nevertheless somehow produces adults with characteristic *joie de vivre*.

Altered States of Consciousness

Consider the following statements:

A Zuni woman remarks, "Sometimes when I have to paint a pot, I can't think what design to put on it. Then I go to bed thinking about it all the time. Then when I'd go to sleep, I dream about designs." (Bunzel, 1929/1953, p. 270)

The bandstand was only a foot high but when I went to step down it took me a year to find the floor, it seemed so far away. I was sailing through the clouds, flapping my free-wheeling wings, and leaving the stand was like stepping off into space. Twelve months later my foot struck solid ground with a jolt, but the other one stayed up there on those lovely clouds. . . .I was up in a plane, soaring around the sky, with a buzz-saw in my head. Up and around we went, saying nuts to Newton and all his fancy laws of gravitation (sic), but suddenly we went into a nosedive and I came down to earth, sock. . . .When I went back to the (band)stand I still heard all my music amplified, as though my ear was built right into the horn. (Mezzrow and Wolfe, 1946, pp. 71–77)

A Polar Eskimo can become a shaman only if he has received a call, which he recognizes when he sees or hears a spirit. He then undergoes certain supernatural experiences, receives his own familiar spirit and learns how to use it. His power as a shaman will come from this spirit or torn-guang, which may be an animal or nature spirit or a human ghost. When healing the sick, the shaman speaks to his familiar spirit in a dialect unintelligible to onlookers, sings a spirit song, and dances about wildly. The shaman trembles, groans, and works himself into an ecstatic state during which the tornguang is commanded to recover the lost soul of the patient so that he will become well. (Murdock, 1934, p. 217)

These passages describe three different altered states of consciousness—dream,

trance, and spirit possession, respectively. Different cultures deal with these experiences in different ways and attribute varying degrees of significance to them. The same behavior that in one cultural context is interpreted as conferring leadership ability may be seen elsewhere as abnormal. What is acceptable in an Eskimo shaman would indicate to people in our society a need for medical help. The drug-induced experience described in the second paragraph above was within the social norms of a cultural subgroup, American jazz musicians. Such hallucinations would be terrifying to the vast majority of other Americans.

Bourguignon (1972) has organized altered states of consciousness into a continuum with REM (Rapid Eye Movement) sleep during which dreams occur at one end and possession trance at the other end. Hallucination and vision trance fall at the midpoint. (See Figure 1.) Other altered states of consciousness occupy various positions on the same continuum. Daydreaming, for example, falls between sleep dreaming and trance. Glossolalia (or "speaking in tongues") approaches very near to possession. Altered states are frequently considered to be the work of forces or even beings outside one's self (Bourguignon, 1972). Culture provides the framework within which these states are experienced. For example, the Bagobo of Malaya believe they have two souls, a good or right-hand soul, and

Figure 1 Altered states of consciousness. (Adapted from Bourguignon, 1972, p. 424)

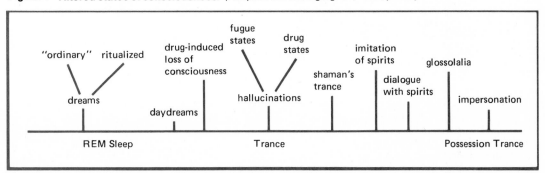

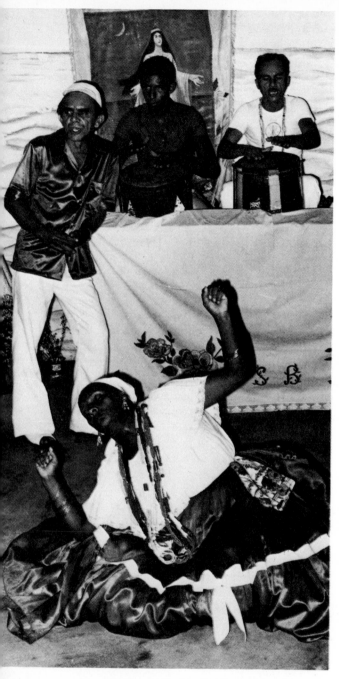

At a religious festival in Brazil, a woman is possessed by a spirit. Where possession is culturally sanctioned, it generally becomes a public performance. (Jacques Jangoux, Peter Arnold Photo Archives)

a bad or left-hand one. It is the left-hand soul that often leaves the human body and wanders about having adventures that are experienced as dreams or nightmares (L. W. Benedict, 1916/1953).

Possession, of course, is the ultimate altered state in which an individual is apparently taken over or inhabited by an external force. In traditional Jewish folklore, it is believed that a *dybbuk* (the soul of a dead person) can appropriate the body of a living person; in Christian belief, witches are said to be possessed by a devil. Ritual exorcism to get rid of the invading spirit is the prescribed solution to both of these cases of negative possession. Illness is often believed to be the result of possession by evil forces.

But ethnographically speaking, most examples of possession, as with the Eskimo shaman described above, are seen culturally as positive forces. They are believed to enable the one so possessed to deal with the supernatural forces that cause illness or some kind of social crisis. Modern Western societies view as psychopathological the behaviors associated with possession. It should be noted that where possession is culturally sanctioned, it becomes a public performance, as well as a ceremony. When it takes place, possession reinforces the cultural norms that prescribe it in the first place.

Trance, hallucination, or visionary states are a different kind of consciousness alteration, characterized by relatively inactive outward behavior and a great deal of internal activity. Such states are often experienced as the self looking on at the adventures of another self. Many peoples use a two-souls explanation for this, in which one soul is believed to part from the body temporarily; the remaining soul is an inactive observer. The person in trance may stare into space or go through normal activities in slow motion. The person in trance seems "spaced out," "not there," or to use the phrase spawned by the drug culture of the 1960s, "on a trip." Trances can be induced by suggestion, as is done in hypnotism; by a large variety of drugs; or by subjecting the body to severe stress.

Hallucinations can be auditory, visual, kinesthetic, or olfactory. The hallucinatory experience of "Mezz" Mezzrow described at the beginning of this section had several of these elements; it was induced by his first experience with marijuana. Use of natural plant substances to induce hallucinations is widespread; in the Americas, especially in Mexico, peyote and mescal have been widely used.

Among the Crow and other Plains Indians, visions are considered of prime importance. They are the source of songs and rituals; of designs to be painted on tepees or shields; of contents to put into a medicine bundle; of wealth, prestige, and success in warfare and hunting. Therefore visions are sought by all, but they do not come to everyone. Most try to bring them on by rites of self-torture intended to win the good will of the spirits (Murdock, 1934).

Even an ordinary dream can be induced, as the Zuni potter quoted at the beginning of this section would agree. So would the American woman who, about to begin psychotherapy, read an article about psychiatric uses of dream material. Concerned because she seldom dreamed, she fell asleep—and next morning was able to recall vividly a complex dream to present to her analyst.

Dreams occur to every human being (and to nonhuman animals as well). Research over the last two decades has established that sleep consists of repeated cycles composed of definite stages: light sleep, deep sleep, and REM (Rapid Eye Movement) sleep. It is during the REM stages of sleep that dreams occur; the eye movements observed in sleep laboratories signal that the sleeper is literally watching the events that constitute a dream. Dreams have always held great fascination and are often accorded significance. They are often considered to foretell the future or to reveal something hidden, such as the source of

illness or the identity of a witch. Dreams are also believed to confer special powers on the dreamer.

Although anthropologists have often recorded dreams—in particular those dealing with religion or other aspects of supernatural power—few studies have been specifically directed to this subject. Since Freud, the studies that have been done have focused on psychoanalytic aspects of dreaming. Freud saw dreams as wish fulfillment, providing release for the individual who has consciously to restrict behavior during waking hours. He believed that the latent content, or the symbolic meaning, of the images and events experienced in the dream represent the real longings and needs of the subconscious. The latent content, unique for every dreamer, has to be interpreted in the context of the individual's psychic history.

The Iroquois have a very similar concept. They believe that the symbolic content of dreams must be translated by specialists who can see into "the depths of the soul."

One of the techniques employed by these Iroquois seers to uncover the latent meanings behind a dream was free association, a technique employed by psychiatrists today. . . . The Iroquois still pay attention to hints given in dreams when they have to choose a curing ceremony, select a friend, or join a particular association; they still bring their more vivid dreams to a clairvoyant, usually a woman, for interpretation. (Farb, 1968, pp. 103–104)

The actual content of dreams appears to be culturally determined. In several hundred dreams collected among the Hopi, the water serpent was a frequent motif. This serpent is a fertility figure and, as such, has obvious sexual import; but it is also a deity controlling social antibehavior including gossip, quarreling, physical aggression, and sexual misconduct (Eggan, 1966, pp. 260–261).

The cultural content of 149 dreams collected by Sharp from 43 men and 8 women of the Yir Yoront of Australia was analyzed by

Schneider into four categories: sexual intercourse, aggression, death, and dreams of whites and white culture. In the dreams with sexual content, the sex partner of the male dreamer was usually from the group considered by the society as an appropriate source of mates. When this was not the case, the dreamed sexual activity was interrupted and "the magnitude of the interruption correlates with the strength of the prohibition of sexual relations" (Schneider & Sharp, 1969, p. 51). In the aggression dreams, the dreamer was the target of aggression in 56 percent of cases and the instigator in only 19 percent. The mother's brother and the dreamer's elder brother were usually the aggressors, in dreams as in real life. Death dreams and cultural contact dreams likewise reflected realistic situations. Bourguignon remarks that "the correspondence between cultural reality and the manifest content of these dreams, taken as a group, is striking" (Bourguignon, 1972, p. 407).

Cultural patterning of dreams is not alien to twentieth-century America. Many adults, for example, dream of being back in college and taking a test for which they did not prepare adequately; they vividly reexperience the anxiety of this stressful situation, which may reflect current feelings of anxiety or helplessness. The important point is that although dreams, trances, spirit possession, and other kinds of altered consciousness are highly individualistic experiences, they are shaped in a cultural context. They express certain social norms and are interpreted according to cultural values. In some cultures, as we shall see below, altered states have provided opportunities that may lead to social action and change.

Anthropologists are particularly interested in the relationships between culture and altered consciousness. What altered states of consciousness characterize a given society? Which individuals are likely to experience them? What use or interpretation are these experiences given? And what can cross-cultural comparisons of these phenomena add to our knowledge of human psychic and behavioral capacity? These are questions for further research and study.

The Individual and Culture Change

Every individual is born into a society with its characteristic designs for living, but everywhere these designs are subject to change. Among the agents of change are the actions of individuals. Every society contains people who deviate from the norm, but what is considered deviant behavior varies from one culture to another. Often it is the deviant who tries out new ideas, establishing a movement toward possible change in the designs of a particular culture.

Deviance frequently is rejected at first, but subsequent events may make the deviant acceptable. Noah, Moses, Jonah, Jesus, and Joan of Arc are all examples within the Judaeo-Christian tradition of visionaries (literally) whose experiences led them to undertake missions with both spiritual and pragmatic components. All of these prophets were at first seen as deviants, scorned and "without honor in their own land." Eventually they were accepted in a leadership capacity by significant numbers of their fellows (and/or posterity). However, some deviants are so charismatic, and make their appearance on the scene at a moment so crucial in the life of their society, that they capture the imagination of followers. These leaders serve as the focus of social movements aimed at promoting change in the social or cultural system. Jesus and Moses, for example, after initial setbacks, were able to influence people on a significant scale through their charismatic leadership. Mohammed is another example of how a prophetic leader changed the direction of social life to a significant extent.

A more recent example of the role of an individual who contributed to culture change is Wovoka, a Paiute from Nevada who became known as the Indian Messiah. In the 1880s, his message of peaceful response and even submission to white domination promised the eventual resurrection of all Indian people, who would then live on the earth in peace, following their old ways of life. Wovoka, while recovering from an illness, had had a revelation vision during an eclipse:

When the sun died, I went up to heaven and saw God and all the people who had died a long time ago. God told me to come back and tell my people they must be good and love one another, and not fight, or steal, or lie. He gave me this dance to give to my people. (Mooney, 1892/1953, p. 412)

The Ghost Dance, accompanied by specific songs, was to be performed 5 nights in a row every 6 weeks. Other tribes adapted Wovoka's teachings, and the movement spread across the Plains. The Indians came to believe that the white ghost shirts they wore during the dance would make them impervious to gunfire. Performed in a frenzied trance, the dance spread from reservation to reservation. White authorities became concerned. In December of 1890, Sioux adherents of the movement, with their leader Sitting Bull, were massacred at Wounded Knee, South Dakota. This massacre effectively halted Indian resistance for almost a century, but it has served as a rallying point for Indian activism in the 1970s.

Further discussion of the role of individual leadership in social movements will be discussed in the chapter on politics and leadership. The point we want to stress here is that individuals can change the direction of social life, and prophetic leaders often do so through use of dreams and other forms of altered states of consciousness.

As we stated at the beginning of the chapter, no individual can experience the total designs for living found in a culture. Furthermore, an individual can recognize expressions of these designs by observing the experiences of others, even though he or she may not experience them directly. (The designs themselves, however, are held largely at an unconscious level.) As we have seen, though, the individual can have an influence on the construction of new designs or the reformulation of old ones. It is the individual that anthropologists deal with most frequently in the field. And it is individual behaviors that provide the basic raw material for the initial inferences that lead to statements about a given cultural system.

Summary

1. Every individual is born into a culture whose preexisting designs for living are communicated from one generation to another. No individual operates with every one of a culture's designs, but most individuals understand their own cultural system sufficiently to function within it. The relationship between individuals and the larger social groups of which they form a part is the concern of psychological anthropology, known traditionally as the study of culture and personality.

2. *Personality* may be thought of as the organized response patterns within every human being. These patterns determine the behaviors of the individual in various life situations, and within each individual are more or less consistent with each other throughout life.

3. Culture is a major factor in the formation of personality, but it is not the only one. Among other influences are human physical factors; the environment; and personal experiences unique to each individual.

4. The *conflict theory* of personality for-

mation, formulated by Freud, states that personality is formed as a result of constant conflict between the desires of the individual and the constraints imposed by society. *Fulfillment theory* holds that all beings strive for optimal self-realization and that culture provides the framework within which potential can be attained. *Consistency theory* sees personality formation as a lifelong process in which new information must be integrated into the world view accumulated through prior experience. *Cognitive dissonance* refers to the situation in which an individual's outlook comes up against an inconsistent set of experiences. The inability to integrate such experiences into one's life may result in *culture shock.* The approach of consistency theory is most useful in anthropological contexts, although the other two have validity also.

5. *Socialization* and *enculturation* describe, slightly differently, the processes whereby an individual becomes a functioning member of a specific society.

6. *Role theory,* which came out of the work of George Herbert Mead, showed that children's concepts of self develop concurrently with their growing understanding of society. The child is first influenced by *significant others,* those people who interact most intimately with the child. The child soon learns that the larger society, which becomes a *generalized other,* expects much the same things as did the intimate agents. Children learn the social roles of their society by observing *role models* in areas of age, sex, and occupation.

7. The earliest years of life are generally considered to be crucial for personality formation; this belief is known as *childhood determinism.* Studies by Margaret Mead, Cora Du Bois, and others have contributed to our understanding of the interactions of culture and the growing child. Mead found that culture was more influential than biology in the development of sex role behavior.

8. *Basic personality structure* was postulated by Kardiner as the shared personality tendencies common to members of a given culture. Basic personality is shaped by *primary institutions* and is expressed in *secondary institutions.* Du Bois's concept of *modal personality* derived from the frequency with which specific traits appeared in individuals of a given culture, as determined by projective psychological tests and ethnographic research.

9. National character studies during World War II were primarily concerned with modern nations. They developed techniques using interviews and cultural materials such as history, art, films, and literature for analyzing "culture at a distance." Benedict's classic study of Japan, derived from this methodology, approaches national character as cultural character and notes the association of culture patterns or configurations with patterns of individual personality traits.

10. The Six Cultures Project was a culture and personality study using standardized and detailed methodology for observation of various cultures. Anthropologists engaged in the study looked for cross-cultural correlations among child-rearing practices, childhood experiences, and cultural institutions. They found, among other things, relationships between subsistence method and child behavior and between family type and child behavior.

11. Altered states of consciousness, such as dreams, trance, hallucination, and spirit possession are highly individual experiences regarded differently in different cultures, and may be accorded great significance. Analysis of dreams indicates that actual dream content appears to be culturally patterned.

12. The behavior that in one cultural context is interpreted as conferring leadership ability may be seen elsewhere as abnormal. One can become an agent of social change, sometimes as a result of an altered state of consciousness, often through some degree of deviance. Often looked at as "prophets without honor," deviants may still rise to positions of leadership through personal charisma, the force of events, or both.

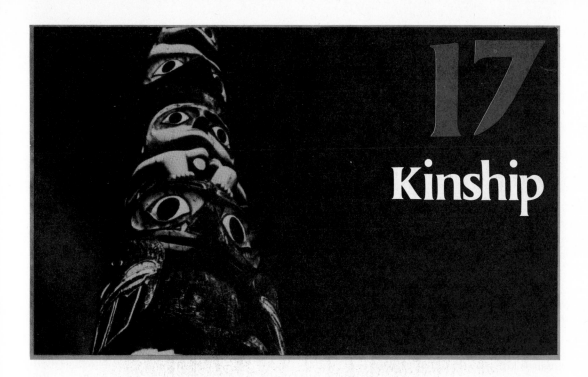

17
Kinship

THE preceding chapter was concerned with the relationships between the individual and culture. In this chapter our focus shifts to social activities and the formation of social groups. In societies usually studied by anthropologists, kinship is often the major organizing principle for social grouping. *Kinship* refers solely to the relationships based on descent and marriage. Kin, or relatives, are of two types: *consanguineous* kin, individuals who are thought to be biologically related by "blood," and *affinal* kin, individuals who are related legally through marriage. The study of kinship identifies and describes the relationships that individuals have with consanguineal and affinal kin and the social systems that are built around these relationships.

Kinship, marriage, and *family*—terms that we will be using in this chapter and the next—are part of everyone's daily experience.

Therefore, we might think that we know exactly what the terms mean and that the issues involved are quite simple. This is not the case, however. Some of the most complex and most debated issues in anthropology lie in the realm of kinship. Careful analysis of a variety of kinship systems, including our own, reveals that kinship is a remarkably intricate invention with widely different solutions to common biological givens.

Kinship has two essential implications for all individuals. First, it is one of several basic attachments that all people have, a fundamental tie. As Geertz (1963) puts it: "One is bound to one's kinsmen . . . as the result not merely of personal affection, practical necessity, common interest, or incurred obligation, but at least in great part by virtue of some unaccountable absolute import attributed to the very tie itself" (p. 109). Second, kinship permeates the social life of most peoples in a number of ways. In any society, individuals assume a variety of social roles. A man, for example, may be son, husband, father, landowner, provider, religious observer, and political supporter. Although he may not act in all these roles at any one moment, he may assume a number of them in the course of a single day. Kinship is the idiom by which many people, particularly in small-scale, traditional societies, comprehend these roles and activities. Gluckman (1962) refers to this overlapping of roles as "muliplex" relationships. He points out that when individuals interact intensively in a variety of roles, each of their actions takes on a larger moral significance. That is, the moral judgment that is applied to a man who is negligent in his work as cultivator may be applied not only to his roles as husband and father, sibling and son, but to his political role in the social group as well. On the other hand, if he quarrels with his immediate kin, they may fail to cooperate with him economically and politically. Thus,

every activity is charged with complex moral evaluations, and defaults strike not at isolated roles but at the integral relations which contain many roles. (Gluckman 1962, pp. 28–29)

Kinship is, of course, a construct, a cultural artifact created in every human society. But because kinship touches upon many areas of social life, it is an artifact that primarily shapes people, rather than one that is shaped *by* them. Although kinship relations and even the rules on which they are based may be consciously challenged by an individual or group, these relations generally involve understandings and ideals that act on the life of the individual rather than vice versa. Kinship relations are, as we have said, some of the most basic attachments an individual has in any society, traditional or otherwise. For this reason, kinship relations are generally unquestioned and unquestionable.

The Atom of Kinship

Any discussion of kinship naturally considers the family. Contrary to what we might think, the type of family with which we are most familiar—the *conjugal* (or *nuclear*) *family,* consisting of two mates of opposite sex and their offspring—is not a universal arrangement.

Until early in the twentieth century, it was widely held that the conjugal family structure was a "higher" form of family, since it was (and still is) characteristic of our civilization. It was believed that "simpler" peoples had family forms that were holdovers from an earlier stage in human evolution. Forms different from the conjugal family were pointed to as remnants of an earlier type of social organization. As anthropologists have accumulated more information on kinship, they have found that the conjugal family also exists among such technologically and economically simple groups as the Bushmen of South Africa and the peoples of the Andaman Islands (southwest of Burma), and of Tierra del Fuego (off the southern tip of South America). All of these groups are seminomadic bands, having minimal technology and little or no political organization. Thus, the conjugal family appears at various levels of civilization, in the most primitive hunting-and-gathering bands as well as in the most modern industrial states.

In most societies of intermediate complexity, family arrangements of other types are common. Among the Nayar of the Malabar Coast of India, for example, adult males at one time comprised a warrior caste living for the most part at a distance from their native community. Adult women, belonging to a different caste, were married in a symbolic ceremony to these men. Once married, a woman would leave the village of her husband and return to the home of her mother, where numerous lovers could freely visit her. Any resulting children belonged to the mother and her family line. This arrangement permitted adult males to perform their military functions without interruption. Authority over the family, including land tenure, was exercised by the woman's brothers.

This family arrangement of the Nayar was highly specialized and adapted to a peculiar situation, but it represents an extreme example of arrangements that are more common than might be expected. In the United States at present there are a number of situations in which nonconjugal family arrangements occur: single parenthood; divorced parents; parents separated for professional purposes. But in all of these cases there usually is at least an occasional affiliation of a "father" with the mother-child unit. The Nayar, in establishing a situation in which the father was consistently absent, represent a rare and extreme instance. Nevertheless, male authority figures were present in the form of the woman's brothers.

A very different nonconjugal family arrangement was found among the Toda of Tibet and Nepal. Among the Toda, polyandry (the marriage of a woman to more than one husband at one time) was a common practice. Several men, usually brothers, shared one wife. Within this system, the legal father of the children was considered to be the man who participated in a special ceremony with the woman upon her first pregnancy. Although he might not have been the biological father of any of her children, he continued as their legal father until one of her other husbands replaced him by participating in the same ceremony with her.

Toda polyandry required a greater number of males than females, a situation which was maintained by means of female infanticide. After the British colonial administration interfered with this practice by making it illegal, the Toda experienced a female population boom. To maintain their polyandrous family

organization, a group of brothers, instead of sharing one wife between them, married a group of sisters—an apparently genuine case of group marriage, but one that has followed rather than preceded other marriage forms.

One must also consider those family arrangements at the other extreme, in which men have a high degree of involvement by playing continuous and significant roles in the formation of family groups. Throughout most of Western Europe of a century or two ago, for instance, the major social unit was a family in which land ownership and all economic and parental authority was exercised by the oldest male or set of males. This grouping consisted of the oldest male (or set of brothers from the senior generation) and his wife (or their wives), the married sons with their wives, all the unmarried daughters, and the young

The minimum social unit is the mother-child relationship, to which various combinations of individuals may be added to form families. (Picatti, Jeroboam)

dependent children of all the married pairs. This form is often called the *extended* (or *joint*) *family*. It would be misleading to think of these larger groups merely as a series of conjugal families. To do so would ignore the very reasons for the formation of such an extended group.

Thus, it is increasingly clear that the irreducible minimum social unit, or atom of kinship as Lévi-Strauss (1963) calls it, is the mother-child relationship. Everywhere, this primary bond forms the basis of kinship. To the mother-child unit, as we have seen, a number of individuals may be added in a variety of combinations to make a family. Sometimes these additions are extended to include three or more generations within a single household. Such combinations have led anthropologists to conclude that, beyond the mother-child bond, kinship has little to do with the facts of biology and that it is, first and foremost, a cultural construct.

Thus the study of kinship is concerned with the familial *relations* that cultures add to the primary mother-child unit, and not with the *kinds* of families per se.

Forms of Kinship Extension

Although the mother-child relationship is the atom of kinship, nowhere and at no time has it stood alone. In every society other kin relationships are grafted onto it. Recruitment of additional kin is necessary in order for the basic unit to function effectively as a domestic unit. Ways must also be devised to transmit property and other functionally valuable rights (such as names and occupations) from one generation to the next. This is done by *descent* —the principle which links one generation to another in a systematized manner. In various descent systems, certain links are stressed whereas other links are ignored.

Kinship relationships are commonly illustrated by means of diagrams such as that shown in Figure 1. Ego is the person who serves as the point of reference for the diagram; the square representing Ego means that Ego's gender is unspecified. Where gender is specified, triangles designate males and circles represent females. A generally accepted notation of kinship terminology consists of the following abbreviations:

Ego: the person who is the point of reference for the diagram
 Fa: father
Mo: mother
 Br: brother
 Si: sister
Hu: husband
Wi: wife
So: son
Da: daughter

A group of kin related by common descent —by certain specified rights and obligations across generations—is called a *descent group*. A descent group may share a name, jointly own property, and participate together in economic and other social activities. In terms of defining who is and who is not a member of a descent group, one must consider the rules of membership as they are defined within the society. These rules include or exclude people on the basis of genealogical distance, gender, and whether the relationship occurs through marriage or through parentage.

Unilineal Descent

The most common rule of descent— *unilineal descent*—traces relations through one line of parentage, either the father's or the mother's line. Unilineal descent is termed *patrilineal* (or *agnatic*) when links through males are recognized; it is called *matrilineal* (or *uterine*) when links through females are counted. In theory, unilineal descent is a

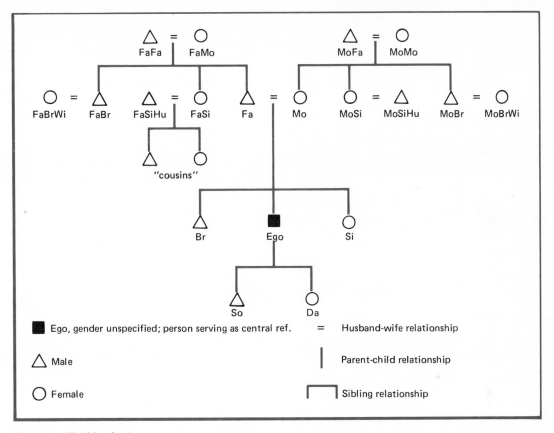

Figure 1 Kinship chart

"neat" concept. It is easy to determine who is and who is not a member of one's descent group, since the individuals concerned are clearly specified, generally by common names. Anthropologists recognize various sorts of unilineal descent groups.

Lineage and Clan. The criterion for membership in a descent group may be known and demonstrable relationships between individuals; such a group is called a *lineage*. When the relationships between the members of a descent group cannot be demonstrated and are simply assumed, the group is called a *clan*. The members of lineages generally trace their descent to a common ancestor who is known to have lived a number of generations back. The members of clans, on the other hand, frequently trace their descent to an ancestor who is thought to have lived at some time in the distant past and thus lies at a much greater genealogical distance. Clans sometimes claim a symbolic association with a plant or animal. This symbol or emblem—called a *totem*—is considered a sacred object to the group. It cannot be killed or eaten except under special circumstances. Further, the totem identifies who is and who is not a member of the clan. If the totem of your group were Fox, you would know right away that individuals whose totems were Eagle, Horse, and Snake were not members of your clan. The totem also identifies whom one may or may not marry, as well as serves as a symbol

A totem pole from Sitka, Alaska, showing various totemic figures. (Fred A. Anderson, Photo Researchers)

and focus for the group. Because both lineages and clans trace descent to a common ancestor, they are termed *ancestor-focused* groups. Anthropologists point out, in examining these groups, that they exist independently of their individual members and that they therefore continue in perpetuity, since they do not depend on the life spans of individuals.

Phratry. Sometimes a clan subdivides over a period of time, with each segment still claiming descent from the original common ancestor. The several clans that make the claim of common descent are together known as a *phratry.*

Moieties. Sometimes a society as a whole is subdivided into two groups for purposes of exchanging women through marriage. Each of these groups consists of a number of other large groups, either clans or phratries. These dual groups are called *moieties.* Among the Miwok Indians of Central California, for example, every lineage belongs to one of the two moieties, Land or Water (Gifford, 1926). See Figure 2 for an illustration of a society divided into lineages, clans, phratries, and moieties.

Patrilineal Descent. *Patrilineal descent* traces ancestry through the male line. A patrilineage, then, consists of a man (the founder); his sons and daughters; his sons' sons and daughters; his grandsons' sons and daughters; his great-grandsons' sons and daughters; and so on. Women such as the founder's daughters and the founder's sons' daughters, and so on are part of the patrilineage. But these women cannot pass on their rights and duties within their lineage to their offspring. These rights and duties can only be transmitted through males in the line. A simplified example of patrilineal descent is illustrated in Figure 3.

In patrilineal descent systems, relations of

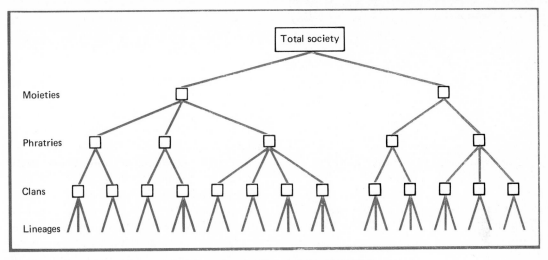

Figure 2 Subdivision of a society into various unilineal descent groups

Figure 3 **Patrilineal descent.** The solid color indicates those members of the patrilineage through whom descent passes. The stripe of color indicates individuals who are members of the patrilineage but who cannot pass on the descent affiliation.

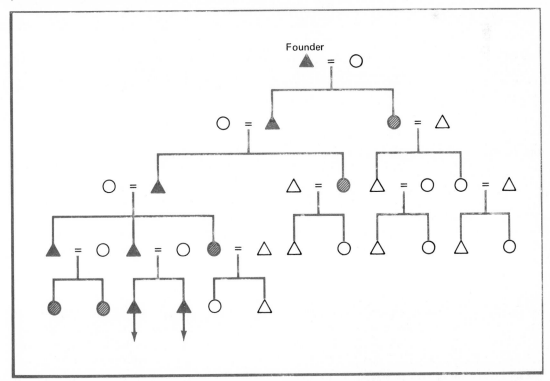

descent, authority, and residence reinforce one another. Among the Yoruba of Western Nigeria, for example, social order depends on the integration of political, economic, and religious activities through the system of patrilineages, known as *idiles*. The oldest male member of an *idile* is its acknowledged head. He exercises religious and political authority over his lineage mates. Female members of the lineage must marry men from *idiles* other than their own, and invariably they move to the communities of their husbands. Most of the male members of an *idile* reside in a single community with their wives. Members of other lineages may reside in that community as well, although in lesser numbers. But for all practical purposes—political, economic, and religious—a community is identified with its predominant *idile* (Schwab, 1955). The pattern of residence in which a married couple lives near or with the husband's family is called *partrilocal*. It usually goes hand in hand with patrilineal descent, ensuring that the men of the lineage will be a physically close-knit group so as to maintain their control over valuable resources.

In patrilineal systems, marriage is of considerable importance. In matrilineages, as we shall see, marriage is less significant, and a casual male attachment may accomplish the biological purpose. The women who marry into a patrilineage are important to the system, since they produce the heirs that allow the lineage to perpetuate itself. A patrilineage is exogamous, that is, the men choose as wives women born into other lineages. They may not impregnate the females in their own lineage to provide heirs. But the women from other lineages bring with them more than their capacity to bear children. They bring rights and privileges held in their own patrilineages; the claims they are able to make on the basis of these rights can be significant in a number of fields of activity. In many instances, the marriage of a woman into a man's lineage creates an alliance between her lineage and that of her husband. Often, too, the woman's children will, by virtue of the link with their mother's lineage, have access to its resources and other assets.

Segmentation of the Patrilineage. As generations pass, the patrilineage expands. It may acquire so many members that it outgrows the resources available to it. When this happens, some of the members must seek other resources and move to another location, sometimes traveling long distances. The patrilineage then subdivides. One group splits off from the original lineage and moves elsewhere. Or, after the death of the father, who served as a unifying factor, the sons sometimes separate from the group or from each other to head subgroups of their own. The subdivision of a clan or lineage into subgroups is known as *segmentation*. Large descent groups, whether lineages or clans, are candidates for segmentation.

Segmentation can be compared to the branching of a tree. The original lineage or clan is the main stem or trunk. Sublineages, created as segmentation is repeated over a period of time, form the branches, twigs, and even leaves (Fox, 1967, p. 12). In a later chapter we will review the political implications of segmentation; here we examine the various mechanisms by which it takes place.

To return to the Yoruba, a male may leave his *idile* to become the founder of a new segment. Likewise, any of his male descendants may create yet other groups once the demands and claims of its members cannot be met. But the members of all these segments continue to recognize their descent from a common male ancestor and can trace their genealogy back to the original lineage. Due to segmentation, an *idile* can consist of as few as 15 members or more than 500 (Schwab, 1955).

If segmentation results in a permanent break between two or more lineage segments, the process is known as *fission*. Fission would occur if each of the sons, with their wives and descendants, went off on their own to begin a

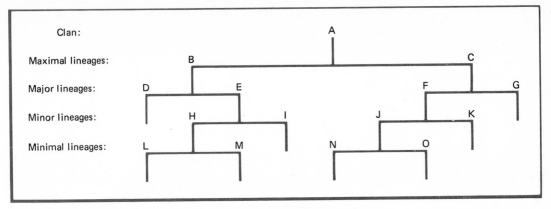

Figure 4 Clan segmentation. Adapted from E. E. Evans-Pritchard, The Nuer of the Southern Sudan, p. 285, in M. Fortes and E. E. Evans-Pritchard, *African Political Systems*. Oxford University Press, 1970.

new sublineage. Among the Nuer of the southern Sudan, for instance, the primary political structure centers on the clan. Each clan consists of an interrelated network of lineage segments and subsegments. Evans-Pritchard (1970) describes clans segmenting into maximal lineages which, in turn, segment into major lineages, each of which may subdivide further, forming minor lineages and each of these in turn into minimal lineages. Figure 4 illustrates such segmentation of a clan. Members of each group are loyal to their group against the members of other equivalent groups. Thus there may be competition among the maximal lineages of a single clan. Or hostility may erupt among members of the major lineages that segmented from a maximal line.

The process of recombination of segments also takes place at times. This recombination, called *fusion,* is usually temporary and occurs as a response to a specific need. For certain purposes, such as seeking vengeance for a homicide, several minimal lineages may find it necessary to consider themselves as one minor lineage. Or two minor lineages may combine and regard themselves as the major lineage from which they sprung. In certain circumstances, this process may repeat back up

again to the level of the clan (Evans-Pritchard, 1970).

Among the Nuer, the fission of larger kingroups into lesser segments occurs constantly. But, in practical terms, the fusion of all groups into larger groupings from which they sprung may also operate. Both fission and fusion operate most markedly in groupings where there is a high degree of correspondence between authority, residence, and descent relationships. As we shall now see, they therefore occur more often in patrilineal than in matrilineal systems.

Matrilineal Descent. *Matrilineal descent* traces ancestry through the female line. A matrilineage consists of a woman (the foundress); her sons and daughters; her daughters' sons and daughters; her granddaughters' sons and daughters; her great-granddaughters' sons and daughters; and so on. It is only through the foundress's female offspring that the rights and duties of the matrilineage can be passed on to the next generation. Figure 5 illustrates matrilineal descent.

In matrilineal systems, women must mate with men from other groups. Although inheritance rights are transferred through females, authority is vested in the males in many in-

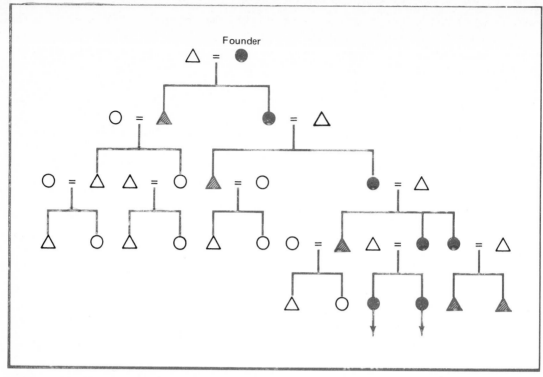

Figure 5 Matrilineal descent. The solid color indicates those members of the matrilineage through whom descent passes. The stripe of color indicates individuals who are members of the matrilineage but who cannot pass on the descent affiliation.

stances, giving brothers control over their sisters' children. They provide competition to any relationship she may have with a husband, who is an outsider in her family group (when he is in it at all). The crucial relationships in a matrilineal system are between mother and daughter, brother and sister, and mother's brother and sister's son. Consequently, the conjugal relationship is relatively unimportant, and the matrilineage has little need for the social roles of husband or father. Thus the biologically necessary male role may be fulfilled as casually as is socially possible.

Matrilineal and patrilineal descent are not simply opposites. Whereas patrilineal descent generally combines residence and authority with the descent group, this patterning of relations is seldom effected in a matrilineal

system. Authority relations usually pose a problem. Matrilineal organization does not necessarily mean high status for women within the matrilineage. Although primary rights and duties are transferred through the female line, authority is often vested in the males of the matrilineage. Problems arise as a result of the discrepancy between relations of residence and descent, on the one hand, and authority relations on the other.

Matrilineages, which are exogamous, must establish relationships with men from outside in order to reproduce. But the rule of descent keeps rights and duties out of the hands of the males marrying into the group. In matrilineal systems, then, men generally retain power and control within the lineage of their mothers and sisters, but inheritance passes to their sisters' sons. Consequently, it is the relationship between a man and his sisters' sons on which we must focus. There are three possible solutions to the problem of male control in a matrilineal system (Fox, 1967). The first and most complete solution is represented by the Nayar.

The Nayar Solution. Among the Nayar, as we have already seen, there were at one time no significant marital alliances, nor did significant father-child interaction take place. Hence, the men of the matrilineage had no divided loyalties. The family home (or *taravad*) was the center of the matrilineage. Nayar brothers returned to it after their military service. The women remained there, except for the brief duration of their symbolic marriages to men of another caste and village, and their children lived there with them. This residence pattern is called *natolocal;* that is, members reside in the houses in which they were born. Within the *taravad,* the eldest brother was the authority figure. He directed the other male members of the group in working the land and tending the livestock which were the lineage's property. On occasion, population pressure within the *taravad* led to segmentation. However, the sublineages maintained close relationships and shared in religious ceremonies.

The Navaho Solution. The second solution is represented by the Navaho. In Navaho society, a man went to live with his wife and her matrilineal relatives after marriage. This pattern of residence is called *matrilocal.* The man's own property and powers remained in the matrilineage of his mother and sisters and sisters' children. The senior brother was the male head of the matrilineage, and the children of his sisters were his heirs. In such an arrangement, marriage tends to be a weak institution, and a woman is easily able to divorce a husband who is no longer wanted. In the case of Navaho divorce, the man simply returned to his matrilineal home (the home of his mother or his sisters). Here the relationship between brothers and sisters was crucial,

and it was likely to come into conflict with the relationship between the sisters and their husbands.

The matrilocal solution of the Navaho maintains the unity of the females of the lineage. But it does not solve the problem of male control, because the men of the matrilineage are scattered. Most matrilineal descent groups are in fact matrilocal, and this arrangement can work fairly well, with two provisos. First, the matrilocal units should be close geographically so that the men can commute readily between their homes and wives and the homes of their sisters and maternal nephews. Second, the lineage should be relatively weak, with few specific functions to perform and with the ownership of property vested in its women, while men engage in hunting and warfare (Fox, 1967, pp. 103–104). If the property and political rights of the matrilineage become significant, the men of the matrilineage need a more structured connection to the source of the family's power. This leads to the third solution, as exemplified by the Trobriand Islanders.

The Trobriand Solution. In the Trobriand Islands in the Pacific, upon marriage a woman goes to live with her husband, whose home is in the village of his own matrilineage. A village centers around the men of the matrilineage—the mother's brothers and sisters' sons—since the mothers, sisters, and daughters of the matrilineage live in the villages of their husbands' families. When a son reaches puberty, he goes back to the village of his mother's brother. This combination of residence with the husband's family (*virilocal residence*) and residence with the uncle (*avunculocal residence*) results in a community that consists of all males who are matrilineally related along with their wives and dependent children.

The Trobrianders believe that a woman's husband is not an equal procreative partner but is simply the "opener of the way" for the child, whom the woman conceives in

377

KINSHIP

378 a "spiritual" manner (Malinowski, 1929). Whereas the Nayar eliminate the father altogether, the Trobrianders retain him but minimize his biological role. Both explanations, however, serve to reinforce the matrilineal descent ideology in the respective societies.

An avunculocal solution, or the viriavunculocal combination of the Trobrianders, keeps the men of the matrilineage together in order to exercise authority and to control property. But at the same time the solution creates a situation in which a man loses his sisters and his own children as well. Malinowski (1929) reported that as a result there was frequent hostility between a man and his wife's brother. The matrilineal problem is not completely solved by the avunculocal solution. There is inevitable conflict between the role of a man in the matrilineage and the role of a man with his wife and children. As Fox puts it,

On the one hand [the man] is a husband and father and wants to have his wife around, while on the other hand he is a maternal uncle with lineage responsibilities to his maternal nephews and hence needs to keep some control over them and their mother, his sister. (1967, p. 108)

To summarize, matrilineal systems can take one of several possible forms. In one form, emphasis is placed on the relationships between blood-related kin in the lineage —mother-daughter, brother-sister, mother's brother-sister's son. The men (sons and brothers) maintain their control over the group's affairs and retain authority. In another form the mother-daughter-sister relationships are emphasized by means of matrilocal residence. The women of the lineage are the property holders, and they provide lineage continuity, as their brothers commute between the home of their lineage and that of their wives. In still another form, the brother-sister-sister's son relationships are central. Avunculocal residence or some other mechanism provides the sister's brother with

control over his nephews. Male authority is a very real factor in all three of the solutions, although it is minimized in the second (the Navaho) form. In an avunculocal society, such as that of the Trobriand Islanders, female status is lowest.

Advantages of Unilineal Descent. In most societies, political and economic control is vested primarily, if not totally, in males. We have examined the problem that this creates in matrilineal systems, in which various arrangements are worked out to deal with the conflict between male authority and female line-of-inheritance. This problem does not exist in patrilineal systems in which relations of authority, residence, and descent are conveniently combined.

The members of a patrilineage have a different problem: they must secure females from outside the group in order to produce heirs. Consequently, the patrilineage must lose its own women—sisters and daughters—to other groups. It appears that as a compensation for the loss of their female kin, the men of the patrilineage have more complete rights over their children. In a patrilineal system, the father-son and brother-brother relationships are of prime importance, but a man's relationship to his wife cannot be ignored. In patrilineal systems, marriage is highly significant since only the acquisition of a wife or wives from outside the group makes possible the male heirs on which the system depends. As already indicated, marriage also serves to establish alliances between groups that exchange women. These alliances can prove useful during warfare or other times of difficulty.

The various complications of patrilineal and matrilineal systems are relatively minor in view of the overall efficiency of the unilineal descent principle. Where group membership is assigned to individuals through a single line, it is clear who is and who is not a member of the group. Where individuals belong to more than one group, problems such as divided

"I told you you'd regret getting all involved with this 'roots' business." (Bill Maul)

loyalties and conflicts of interest, or competitive claims on property or nonmaterial rights, are likely to crop up. As a way of transmitting rights from one generation to the next, both matrilineal and patrilineal systems provide for inheritance in as clear a manner as possible. Inheritance is restricted to specific categories of kin. Rights transmitted through kinship are attached not only to land and other forms of property, but also to other things such as game and fish, political and ritual offices, craft or other occupations, and cult membership.

Unilineal systems specify which rights are to be acquired through males and which through females. Although a system may be defined as either matrilineal or patrilineal, it does not mean that relationships through the other kinship line are ignored or unimportant. On the contrary, people seldom, if ever, follow one pattern exclusively in all aspects of their social life. They may follow varying modes of inheritance for such different aspects as group name, property, ritual rights, residence, and so on. One can tell whether a descent system is matrilineal or patrilineal by determining in which line the most important rights and duties are transmitted.

In virtually every unilineal descent system, however, certain secondary rights and duties, complementing the primary ones, pertain to kin in the other line of filiation. In a patrilineal system, then, one might be able to obtain access to a variety of resources and/or services from the relatives on one's mother's side (one's *matrilateral* relatives). Such access might determine survival during a period of drought, for instance. Then, one's matrilateral relatives, whose area of residence has not been affected to the same degree, could be a dependable source of sustenance. Or, in a matrilineal system, one's *patrilateral* kin (the relatives on one's father side) might provide assistance in time of emotional or political conflict.

In unilineal systems, then, one has affiliations to one's father's group *and* to one's mother's group.* Relationships through the parent who does not determine descent is called *complementary filiation.* In a patrilineal system, for example, one's complementary affiliation is to the mother's group. In unilineal systems, there are variations in what particular rights and duties are defined as being of primary importance for each group. The fact that one has affiliations with both father's and mother's kin introduces flexibility into any social system based on unilineal descent.

There is another way in which an individual might obtain access to resources and services not his or hers by right of descent, and that is through the claims of marriage, or *affinity.* Affinal relations usually set up exchanges of resources and services between the groups involved. These exchanges occur usually at the time the marriage is proposed, when it takes place, or when a child or children are born. Frequently, one can, through one's spouse, make additional claims in various areas of activity. It is generally assumed that what one may receive during one season will be returned in another if and when one's affinal kin are in need.

Double Descent. There is still another type of descent, called *double descent,* that uses a variation on the unilineal principle. Double descent differs from matrilineal and patrilineal descent by recognizing lines of descent

*Possible exceptions are the Nayar and any similar groups where there is, to all intents and purposes, no father.

through *both* males and females. The operation of double descent can best be understood in terms of the affiliation of an individual with his or her grandparents. In a unilineal system, an individual traces descent through only one of the four grandparents. In a matrilineal system, descent is traced through the mother's mother. In a patrilineal system, descent is traced through the father's father. In a system of double descent, the individual traces descent through both the mother's mother and the father's father (Murdock, 1940).

In a double descent system, each line of kin usually serves specifically different functions. Among the Ashanti of West Africa, for example, property and authority are inherited in the female line. The relationship between the mother's brother and her son is crucial, because it is the line of inheritance of crucial resources. The matrilineal group, generally the more important one in Ashanti life, also participates in an ancestor cult and performs various funerary and other rituals. At the same time, "spirit" is the primary inheritance through the male line. Residence among the Ashanti is patrilocal. Upon being married, a woman goes to live in the household of her husband's patrilineal extended family (Rattray, 1923). Thus both lines of descent are recognized culturally and are used for distinct purposes.

Elsewhere in Africa, the Herero, a southern Bantu people, have matrilineal kin groups that have primarily economic functions, alongside patrilineal groups that have primarily religious functions. Real property is inherited matrilineally, but access to sacred knowledge and resources is transmitted in the male line. Still another African example is provided by the Venda, who define descent, succession, and property inheritance patrilineally. The matrilineage is important in social and religious aspects of life, involving participation in an ancestor cult (Murdock, 1940).

Double descent has been described in other parts of the world as well. The Toda of southern India, the Aranda and other Central Australian tribes, and the Manus of Oceania all have both matrilineal and patrilineal descent groupings. With few exceptions, wherever double descent has been described, both patrilineal and matrilineal kin groups are exogamous. Property inheritance and succession are usually patrilineal, and residence is usually patrilocal (Murdock, 1940).

Parallel Descent. There is yet another possible form of unilineal descent—*parallel descent,* which is extremely rare. In parallel descent systems, males trace ancestry through males and females through females. Many anthropologists have considered this variation to be possible but, not having found a verified instance of it, they usually conclude that it does not exist. However, Jane Safer (1975) has recently described a parallel descent system as she observed it among the Saha, who live in the Santa Marta mountains near the Caribbean coast of Colombia, close to the Venezuelan border. Here, boys belong to the descent groups of their fathers, and girls to those of their mothers. These descent groups, called *sana* and named for certain animals, have both male and female members. The *sana* itself owns certain ritual property, such as songs and dances, and has an alleged place of origin to which members go to give offerings. Among the Saha both women and men may own property, which includes livestock, houses, and land. But the property of a wife is not merged with that of her husband. Males inherit from males, and females from females. All property is inherited within the *sana* except that, before death, a man with no sons or a woman with no daughters may elect to leave his or her property to a child of the opposite sex—and therefore of a different *sana*—rather than to his or her own same-sex sibling.

Cognatic Descent

Not to be confused with double descent is *cognatic descent,* a system in which the individual reckons his or her ancestry through lineal relatives of both sexes with little or no formal distinctions among them. This is the descent system used in our society. In this system, all four of Ego's grandparents count, as well as all eight great-grandparents, and so on as far back as one can go. In a cognatic system, all the descendants of the same ancestors are considered relatives as well, regardless of their sex. That is, the individual acknowledges a relationship to all of the descendants of his or her grandparents, great-grandparents, and so on—the uncles and aunts, great-uncles and great-aunts.

This nonexclusive mode of tracing descent seldom provides the clearcut access to rights, duties, and resources that a unilineal system can, due to the fact that any given individual belongs at the same time to a number of descent categories. The problem in cognatic descent is to find a means to include some individuals for purposes of mutual cooperation and benefit, while at the same time excluding others who are eligible. Rights to inheritable positions and property can be maintained and responsibilities can be assigned according to the cognatic principle of descent without the necessary formation of formal corporate groupings. Circumstances of life history (such as living closer to some kin than to others), as well as economic considerations or simple affection and attraction, may operate to include some eligible members in such transactions and to exclude others. At the same time, though, if the local situation demands it, formal groups as tightly organized and as efficient as any found in a unilineal system, can also be formed according to the cognatic principle.

The Kindred. The most commonly recognized form of kin grouping found in cognatic descent systems is that of the *kindred.* A kindred is composed of any group of consanguineal relatives without reference to either maternal or paternal line of descent. In our society, a kindred tends to be the group of relatives we might see with some frequency at family re-unions, weddings, funerals, holiday celebrations, and so forth. The kindred consists of people closely related to oneself, rather than to an ancestor. Thus, a kindred is considered an *ego-focused group,* in that it begins with oneself and works outward. Membership in a kindred group is based on one's degree of relationship to a given individual. Some people, for example, belong to "cousins' clubs." These clubs may consist of first and second cousins of the founding individual, along with their spouses and children. The members of ego-focused kindred are linked to each other by relationship to the central member, but (except for full siblings) they are not necessarily related to each other.

There is a potential kindred centering on every person in a society, and every individual is also a possible member of a number of kindred centered around other relatives. One may receive birthday and holiday cards or gifts from members of one's kindred and will owe cards or gifts in the other kindreds of which he or she is a member. Since the kindred is an ego-focused group, it exists only for the life span of the individual at its center. It is not generally a corporate group in that it does not hold property or exclusive rights to be passed on from one generation to the next. Groups mobilized according to kindreds tend to be temporary and come together for specific ritual or ceremonial occasions such as weddings, funerals, christenings, and the like.

Much of the literature on cognatic descent groups has been generated from materials collected in the Pacific where examples of corporate cognatic groups seem to be clearly found. Fox (1967, p. 156) defines three kinds of cognatic descent groups: unrestricted, restricted, and pragmatically restricted. A group is *unrestricted* when all descendants, both male and female, of an acknowledged ancestor are included. Every individual will be a member of as many unrestricted groups as he or she has ancestors (Goodenough, 1957, p. 197). In a *restricted* descent group, all of the founder's descendants have a *right* to membership, but some limitation is placed on the ways in which they may claim this right. For example, they may be obliged to reside in the founder's territory or on his property in order to exercise their rights to membership in his descent group. Individuals thus are obligated to choose with which of several possible groups to reside. Once the individual has made a choice, his or her rights to other lands are surrendered. In a *pragmatically restricted* cognatic system, individuals retain rights of membership in all groups to which they are entitled to belong, even though they are affiliated for practical reasons with only one such group.

Kindreds are loosely organized groups of persons related to a central individual. They come together for ritual or ceremonial functions such as weddings, as has this group of Spanish gypsies. (Josef Koudelka, Magnum)

We must not lose sight of the fact that although cultural features are studied by anthropologists independently of one another, they *are* highly interrelated. Thus, the distinctions between different kinship patterns are not abstract or arbitrary. Rather, they have to do with property ownership and the economic-productive organization of the community, along with other factors. A lineage or other group will live on land it owns or is economically bound to in some way. Kinship and residence determine not only which individuals see each other daily but also who works alongside of whom and to what purpose.

One of the most complex kinship systems is found on Gilbert Island in the Pacific. There, five different types of kinship groupings, including three separate cognatic groups, may be found. All three of these groups are connected in some way to land. The multiple cognatic system of the Gilbert Islanders illustrates an adaptational advantage of such groups: flexibility in coping with inevitable demographic fluctuations. Where a unilineal descent group must inhabit a prescribed and limited territory, the population of the lineage may become too great to be supported by its land, or a lineage's membership may decrease. A run of female children would result in substantial loss of membership to a patrilineal group, for example. Or through good management or good fortune a lineage may acquire more land than its members can work efficiently. In a cognatic system, on the other hand, an individual will be a member of several groups and can claim rights elsewhere in response to land or population pressures. Under demographic pressures, a unilineal descent group that is also property-owning may be helpless because of its rigidly prescribed membership qualifications. A cognatic group can redistribute both land and population in a relatively rapid response to demographic pressure (Goodenough, 1957).

Many anthropologists believe that the need for a redistribution of property can lead to a restructuring of descent groups. In particular, patrilineal systems tend to become cognatic. Cognatic groupings frequently have, in fact, some patrilineal elements. There is a fairly universal tendency toward keeping the males of a family—the fathers, sons, and brothers—together for work, property ownership, defense, or other purposes. Thus, residence is frequently patrilocal even in a cognatic system.

Kinship Terminology

Thus far our discussion of kinship systems has focused on the ways in which people organize their relationships with kin and some of the social uses that kin groups can serve. We now turn our attention to kinship terminology, the terms that people use to classify or categorize their relatives.

At the outset, it must be understood that the set of kin terms provided by our culture is neither exhaustive nor universal. As we shall see, many other categories of relatives—and ways of establishing such categories—exist. The system of kin groupings with which we are familiar is in a minority position in the ethnographic world.

Kin everywhere are given names designating certain categories of relationship. A people specify the kinds of relatives it is possible to have in their society by classifying them into categories. By designating the categories of kin in a given society, the kinship terminology system maps the social universe of a people.

Kin terminologies seem to constitute a precise and self-contained set of data with which to work. As such, kinship terminology has for over a century provided anthropologists with a domain in which to apply their various theoretical points of view. Over the years,

384 perhaps more controversies have raged over the analysis of kin terms than over any other aspect of the study of kinship.

As a topic for anthropological analysis, the significance of kinship terminology was recognized more than a century ago by the American ethnologist Lewis Henry Morgan. In the course of his pioneering fieldwork among the Iroquois of New York State, Morgan noticed the same word, *hanih,* was used for father and father's brother but not for mother's brother. He also noted that the word for mother and mother's sister was the same, but different from that for father's sister. This terminology was strikingly different from his own father-uncle, mother-aunt terminology, which does not distinguish between the brothers of father or mother, or between the sisters of father or mother. Morgan became more intrigued when he found a similar usage among the Ojibwa Indians. To learn about the kin terms used elsewhere, he devised a questionnaire which he sent out to hundreds of travelers, missionaries, and colonial administrators in all parts of the world. His analysis of the terminologies that were collected in this way was published in 1871 as *Systems of Consanguinity and Affinity in the Human Family.*

Approaches to Kinship Terminology

Over the years, different approaches have been taken in the analysis of kinship terminology. One approach is historical. It sees kin terms as a set of clues to relationships that have existed in the past, and then compares cultures in a given region in terms of the linguistic similarities in their terms. This historical approach is based on the premise that language is more resistant to change than are social institutions. Therefore, the words used to define kinship would be older than the customs of the period in which the terms are collected, and can thus tell something of past cultures.

The second approach is that of the functionalists. It is concerned with the ways in which kin terms relate to actual behaviors of individuals, and with the correlation of terminology with such social institutions as marriage, descent groups, and residence patterns.

A third approach is that of the cognitivists. This approach investigates kin terms as a set of classificatory categories organized on the basis of a limited number of distinctive features or components, such as age, gender, and generation. The cognitive anthropologist analyzes these components in an attempt to discover the underlying set of principles that a society uses to place individuals into particular categories. Analysis of distinctive features thus becomes a means of investigating cognitive processes by seeking to explain cultural categories.

Some anthropologists have questioned whether one should view kin terms as referring primarily to biological relationships or to social roles. For example, the Trobriand term *tama* refers to the father, father's brother, father's sister's son, and all male members of the father's matrilineage in the same generation as the father and in succeeding generations (Keesing, 1976). Does this mean that the individual cannot distinguish between his or her mother's husband and other male kin? Some early investigators believed so and built whole theories around the fact that some peoples seemed unable to distinguish among their fathers, uncles, and cousins. When we examine the *social* role of the individuals designated by the single word *tama,* though, it becomes clear that this word is used to distinguish a specific category of individual. Keesing (1967) suggests that it should really be translated as "domiciled man of my father's subclan hamlet" (p. 268). Similarly, the term *tabu* refers to all males and females of the grandparent or preceding generations; it also refers to all females of the father's, the father's father's, or the mother's father's clans. *Tabu* is a reciprocal term like our word "cousin"; someone whom I describe with this term also uses it to describe me. Keesing suggests that, in the context of Trobriand life, those classified by the term *"tabu* are in fact classed together not because of some positive feature they share in common, but because . . . they are distant and marginal to [the individual]" (pp. 268–269). The term has a functional purpose as well: it indicates the category of persons from which a man may find a wife. In the matrilineal system of the Trobrianders, the term *tabu* identifies women who are outside the matrilineage and who, by the rules of exogamy, are therefore possible marriage partners.

The meaning of a society's kin terms must be understood in conjunction with an analysis of the society's social structure and institutional frameworks. It is one thing to call your mother, your mother's sisters, and your mother's brothers' daughters by the same term (which is done in the Omaha system, as we shall see below), but it is quite another thing to treat them similarly. The view of culture that we have been expressing in this book fits better with this emphasis upon group interactions and alliances than with a biological-genealogical orientation toward kinship terms. Emphasis on the social significance of kinship terminology is a relatively new development in anthropological studies. From the beginning, Morgan's breakdown of the data he had gathered focused on terminology as it described biological relationships.

Kinship Terminology Systems

Morgan divided the terminologies he collected into two categories, descriptive and classificatory. In a *descriptive* terminology system, only primary terms referring to what Morgan took to be direct biological relationships are used: terms such as father, mother, son, daughter, grandmother, grandfather, brother, and sister. Those people related in other ways are called by combinations of the primary terms: mother's brother, sister's son, and so on. A *classificatory* system uses one term to refer to a class of relatives in both ascending and descending generations. Thus, *lineal relatives* (those in a direct biological line, such as father or mother) may be included in the same term as *collateral relatives* (relatives such as father's brother or mother's sister who are not related in a direct biological line). The Iroquois use of one name for both father and father's brother is an example of a classificatory system.

The distinction between descriptive and classificatory is now seen as only one of a variety of kinship factors. Other factors that are considered in classifying kin terminology were identified by Kroeber in 1909. These include:
- *generation*—the difference between Ego's generation and that of the relative in question;
- *gender*—whether the person is male or female;
- *affinity*—whether the relationship is affinal (through marriage) or consanguineal (through direct biological lines);
- *bifurcation*—the incorporation of lineal and collateral relatives in one line but not the other (for instance, FaBr and Fa comprise one term that is distinct from MoBr);
- *polarity*—reciprocity, or whether the same terms are applied by the relative or group of relatives to the speaker, and vice versa.

Three subsidiary factors noted by Kroeber include relative age, speaker's gender, and decedence (whether the person through whom the relationship occurs is living or dead (Kroeber, 1909).

Working from the Human Relations Area Files at Yale University, Murdock classified the relationship terms used by 250 societies. He identified six distinct types of kinship terminology systems. They focus particularly on the ways in which cousins are distinguished. There are four possible kinds of cousins: the father's brother's child; the father's sister's child; the mother's brother's child; and the mother's sister's child. *Parallel cousins* are children of the same-sex siblings of one's parents. Thus the children of one's father's brother and one's mother's sister are parallel cousins. *Cross cousins* are children of the opposite-sex siblings of one's parents. Thus one's cross cousins are the children of one's father's sister and one's mother's brother.

The six kinship terminology systems identified are Eskimo, Hawaiian, Crow, Omaha, Iroquois, and Sudanese. They are named after societies that exhibit the systems most clearly.

Eskimo System. The Eskimo system of terminology is the one used in our own culture. (See Figure 6.) It centers on the nuclear family—father, mother, brothers, sisters. Unlike the other systems we will look at, no other relatives are referred to by the terms used for these family members. Descent in cultures that use Eskimo terminology is based on the cognatic principle. Since both sides of Ego's family are of equal importance, the terms used for sisters and brothers of mother and father are the same (aunt, uncle). Similarly, no distinction is made between cross cousins and parallel cousins; a single term is used to identify all cousins.

Hawaiian System. Of the six systems we will look at, the Hawaiian system of kinship terminology uses the fewest number of terms. (See Figure 7.) Relatives of the same sex in the same generation are referred to by the same term. Thus, father, father's brothers, and mother's brothers are grouped together, as are mother, mother's sisters, and father's sisters. Brothers and male cousins are denoted by a single term. Likewise, sisters and female cousins are called by one term.

Crow System. Crow kinship terminology is usually associated with matrilineal descent systems. Because the line of matrilineal descent is emphasized, matrilineal relatives are differentiated across generations. (See Figure 8.) In a matrilineal system, mother's brothers are likely to be Ego's most important relatives (other than mother and father) because they control the rights and privileges associated

Figure 6 **Eskimo kinship terminology**

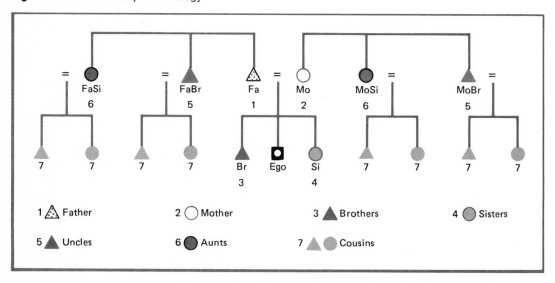

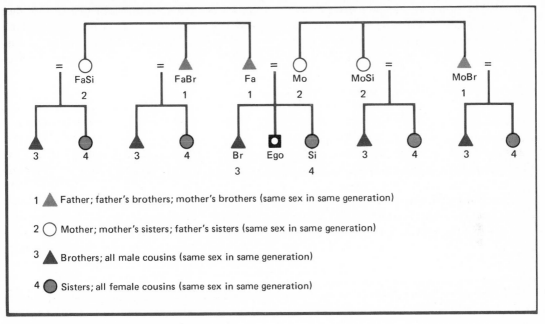

Figure 7   Hawaiian kinship terminology

Figure 8   Crow kinship terminology

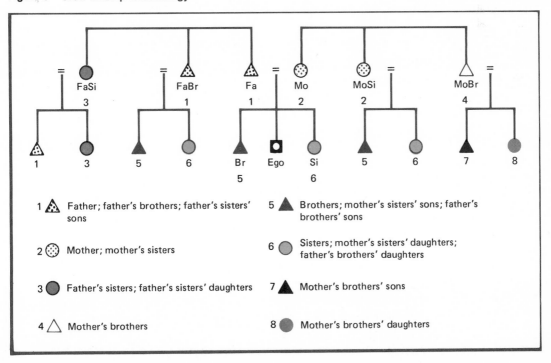

with the matrilineage. And because of the close connection with mother's brother, there is also likely to be a close connection between Ego and mother's brothers' children. Thus, there are unique terms for mother's brothers and for matrilineal cross cousins (mother's brothers' sons and daughters). Because they are of less importance, patrilineal relatives in the Crow system are grouped together across generations. That is, father, father's brothers, and father's sisters' sons are denoted by the same term. A single term also identifies father's sisters and father's sisters' daughters. Finally, notice that in the Crow system, mother's sisters are called by the same term as mother, and father's brothers are called by the same term as father. Consequently, the children of mother's sisters and of father's brothers (Ego's parallel cousins) are called by the same terms—"brother" and "sister"—as are used for the children of Ego's mother and father. In other words, parallel cousins are re-

ferred to in the same way as Ego's brothers and sisters.

Omaha System. The Omaha system of terminology is usually found in patrilineal descent systems. It is, therefore, the mirror image of the Crow system. (See Figure 9.) Patrilineal relatives are distinguished across generations. Separate terms identify father's sisters and father's sisters' sons and daughters. In the less important matrilineal group, mother, mother's sisters, and mother's brothers' daughters are grouped together under the same term. Likewise, mother's brothers and mother's brothers' sons are referred to by a single term. Again, parallel cousins are called by the same terms as those for Ego's brothers and sisters.

Iroquois System. The Iroquois system of kinship terminology is similar to the Crow and Omaha systems at the level of Ego's own generation. (See Figure 10.) As in the Crow and

Figure 9 Omaha kinship terminology

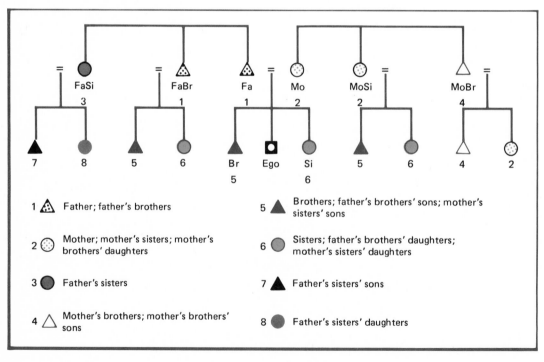

1 ⬖ Father; father's brothers

2 ⊙ Mother; mother's sisters; mother's brothers' daughters

3 ● Father's sisters

4 △ Mother's brothers; mother's brothers' sons

5 ▲ Brothers; father's brothers' sons; mother's sisters' sons

6 ● Sisters; father's brothers' daughters; mother's sisters' daughters

7 ▲ Father's sisters' sons

8 ● Father's sisters' daughters

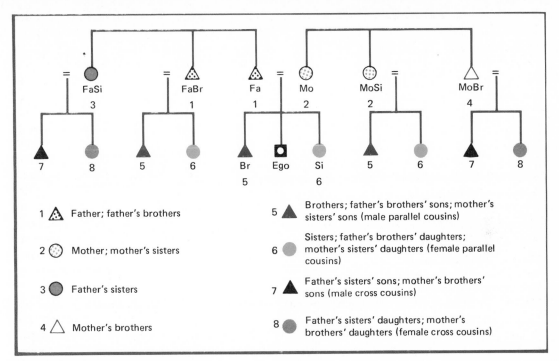

Figure 10 Iroquois kinship terminology

Omaha systems, mother and mother's sisters are denoted by the same term. Similarly, one term is used to identify father and father's brothers. The opposite-sex siblings of Ego's parents—that is, mother's brothers and father's sisters—are called by separate terms.

In both the Crow and Omaha systems, though, one set of cross cousins was grouped with the generation above. The difference in the Iroquois kinship terminology is that there are separate terms for female and for male parallel cousins. Usually the term for brother is applied to male parallel cousins. The term for sister usually is used to refer to female parallel cousins. Sometimes, though, separate terms exist for brothers, male parallel cousins, sisters, and female parallel cousins, as well as for male cross cousins and for female cross cousins.

Sudanese System. The Sudanese is the ultimate descriptive terminology. It differs from the other five systems we have looked at in that it has a different term for each of the 16 relatives on the chart. (See Figure 11.) No relatives are grouped with any others in their own or in a different generation. Societies with Sudanese terminology tend to have patrilineal descent systems, with a great deal of class stratification or political complexity, which the kinship terminology reflects.

These categories are useful pigeonholes in which to tuck away certain types of data. But they represent merely one attempt to organize the available information on kinship terminological systems, which is admittedly unwieldy. The categories should not be seen as a rigid typology into which all kinship systems can be placed. Indeed, the data do not always fit the categories neatly. Nevertheless, much of the literature on kinship refers to these systems, and for this reason they are presented here.

Murdock's typology represents a genealog-

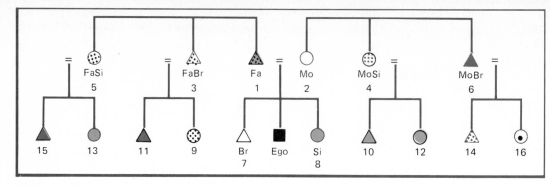

Figure 11 **Sudanese kinship terminology.** (1-16: separate terms for each of the 16 relatives)

ical approach to kin terms. That is, the relationships and terminologies as he views them refer to kinds of genealogical connections rather than kinds of people. But what kinship is all about is the interactions among people. Kinship terminologies are of significance in cultural studies because they ultimately concern the relationships between individuals. As Bohannan reminds us, "kinship terms refer not merely (and often not even primarily) to the facts of biological relationship but also to the cultural image of them—that is, to the social facts of role expectations" (Bohannan, 1963, p. 67). All societies place kin into categories that are recognized and given names. Behind the categories and the terms for them, there is always a set of relationships which must be investigated.

The Significance of Kinship

It is not always easy to determine which type of descent category—matrilineal, patrilineal, or cognatic—describes the actual situation in a given culture. Under some circumstances, a patrilineal system can seem more similar to some cognatic systems than to other patrilineal systems. The way in which one classifies a kinship system depends not

only on an analysis of the rights and obligations people have toward one another, but also on how the people understand the workings of their own system (Bender, 1970). We have spoken in previous chapters of the importance of considering the native's understanding of his or her society. With this in mind, we must not overlook the natives' consciousness of kinship and how it operates for them.

"Matrilineal" and "patrilineal" are categories devised by anthropologists to describe certain observed similarities in the patterning of kinship in various societies. Such categories exist for *our* convenience; we should not make the mistake of assuming that these categories necessarily have reality for the people whose groupings we so describe. A Navaho man, for instance, does not go around saying "I belong to a matrilineal, matrilocal society which creates certain problems for men." The typologies we have been discussing allow *us* to describe and compare kinship patterns. But peoples everywhere—with the exception of anthropologists and their students—simply *live* their kinship arrangements and do not try to categorize them for comparison with other kinship systems.

When it comes to kinship, people can be surprisingly pragmatic. For example, it is not unusual for people to misstate or try to alter their biological connections in order to take better advantage of a given situation. In our own society, numerous people have made claims about biological relationships in order to profit from someone's will. The economic and political demands of a particular time and place frequently lie behind such manipulations. Also important is the significance that people give to descent and kinship in their conversation and daily activities. Bender (1970), for instance, points out that the Ondo are not usually very conscious of their relationships with kin. The subject of kinship only comes up for them on occasions when people may derive some practical benefit from it. When this is the case, the reckoning of relationships is geared to the specific situation and may be ambiguous to some extent. A wider range of claims can be made on kin when the rights and duties defining their relationships are not well-defined. This lack of definition of kinship roles or of one's rights and duties can be beneficial in allowing for flexibility, both in making claims and in responding to them once they are made.

When it comes to determining how kinship fits into a people's scheme of things, anthropologists look, first, to what extent descent groups dominate their social structure. Second, they observe whether there is a correspondence between relations of descent and the patterning of residence and to what extent the membership of a descent group lives in a particular area. It usually takes quite a bit of probing to determine the functions of any particular kinship arrangement in the social organization of a people.

Summary

1. In the societies traditionally studied by anthropologists, kinship is often the major organizing principle for social grouping. *Kinship* refers to relationships based on marriage and descent. Kin acquired through marriage are *affinal* kin; biological or "blood" relatives are *consanguineal* kin.

2. The irreducible "atom of kinship" is the mother-child unit. To this unit, a number of individuals may be added in a variety of combinations. Our society typically adds a father, to form the *conjugal* (or *nuclear*) *family*. Some societies minimize the role of the father, even to the point of eliminating him altogether, as do the Nayar. Elsewhere, as with the Toda, sociological fatherhood may have absolutely no relationship to biological fatherhood. At the other extreme from the mother-child minimal family unit is the *extended* (or *joint*) *family*. The variety of observed family forms leads to the conclusion that beyond the mother-child bond, kinship is a cultural construct.

3. Recruitment to the basic mother-child unit is necessary in order for the kin group to perpetuate itself and to pass on rights and property. *Descent* rules recognize links between generations. In various descent systems, certain links are stressed whereas other links are ignored. A group of kin related by common descent is called a *descent group*.

4. *Unilineal descent* traces ancestry through either the male or the female line. Descent is *patrilineal* when men are the linked relatives and *matrilineal* when women are. Unilineal descent groups are exogamous —that is, their members must marry members of another group. There are several types of unilineal descent groups. *Lineages* are groups in which descent may be traced to known and demonstrable relationships between individuals. *Clans* are descent groups in which descent cannot be demonstrated and is simply assumed. Clans frequently trace descent to a mythological figure and often claim symbolic association with a *totem*. A *phratry* consists of the several descent groups that claim common descent from a particular clan or lineage. *Moieties* are the two groups into

which a society may divide, each consisting of a number of kin groupings.

5. Patrilineal descent is relatively uncomplicated; it provides a tidy package of descent, authority, and residence for male members of the patrilineage. As a patrilineage expands, it may outgrow its resources and thus have to segment into smaller groups. *Fission* refers to a permanent break between lineage segments. *Fusion* describes the temporary recombination of segments in reaction to a specific need.

6. Matrilineal descent creates a problem regarding the relationship of men to the lineage. Although inheritance takes place through the female line, authority in a matrilineage tends to rest with a woman's brothers. The Nayar, the Navaho, and the Trobriand Islanders each have separate solutions to the problems of male control in a matrilineal system.

7. All unilineal systems specify which rights are to be acquired through the father and which through the mother. The basis for defining a system as matrilineal or patrilineal is the line through which primary rights and duties are transmitted. Everywhere, though, certain secondary rights and duties are received through one's *complementary affiliation,* the parent who does not determine descent.

8. *Double descent* is a type of unilineal descent that recognizes lines of descent through *both* the mother and the father. In double descent systems, specific properties or rights are transmitted by each lineage to which an individual belongs.

9. Another possible form of unilineal descent is *parallel descent,* in which males trace ancestry and inheritance through male lines and females through female lines. Recorded cases of parallel descent are extremely rare.

10. *Cognatic descent* is the system used in our own society. It traces ancestry through lineal relatives of both sexes. Any group of close blood relatives, without reference to either the paternal or maternal line of descent, constitutes a *kindred,* an *ego-focused group* that is unique to a given individual.

11. Kinship terminology refers to the names that people use to identify their relatives. There are many ways of grouping kin. Kin terms specify the kinds of relatives recognized in a given society. There are a number of ways of looking at kinship terms, and many typologies have been worked out. More than a century ago, Morgan divided terminology systems into *descriptive,* in which only primary terms referring to direct biological relationships are used, and *classificatory,* which combine *lineal* and *collateral* kin under one term. Murdock's six-part typology—Eskimo, Hawaiian, Crow, Omaha, Iroquois, and Sudanese—focuses on terms for parents' siblings and on different categories for cousins.

12. The true importance of kinship terminology is as a guide to cultural behavior. All human beings are born into a kinship structure of one kind or another, and the social ways in which a given society utilizes kinship have consequences for the ways in which individuals live.

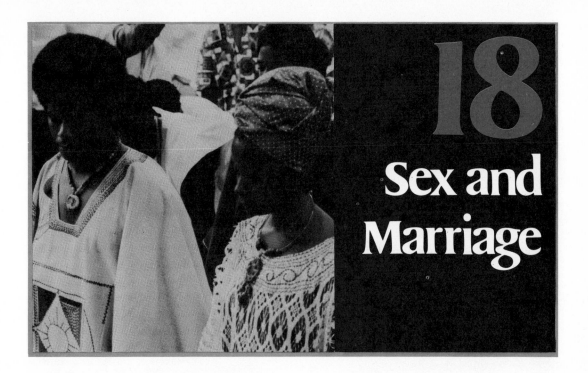

18
Sex and Marriage

As we pointed out in the preceding chapter, in all human societies kinship bonds and networks are based on two types of relationship: consanguineal and affinal. Different societies use these relationships in a wide vareity of ways. In the previous chapter, we examined the bonds and groupings, including those of descent, that develop through consanguineal ties. Here we will complete the study of kinship by examining relationships based on affinity.

The central concern in any study of affinal relationships is, of course, marriage. In the course of our discussion, it will become apparent that the understanding of marriage by most Europeans and Americans is not universal. Many characteristics of our marital arrangements are, in fact, rare among the cultures of the world.

Males and females are the single universal components of the relationship we call mar-

riage. Every society makes some provision for this relationship between the sexes. But, as we shall see, monogamous marriage in the form we know it is neither universal nor predominant in human societies. What is necessary is some sort of socially approved relationship between adult males and females. Such a relationship serves a number of functions. It provides for the fulfillment of human sexual needs; furnishes domestic and economic services; gives children a legitimate standing in society; specifies property rights and lines of inheritance; and may establish group interdependencies and rights. However, the particular functions served by marriage vary from one society to another, although sexual union and legitimate parenthood seem to be nearly universal characteristics. Marriage is, though, only one form of relationship between men and women. The universal fact of human sexuality provides the starting point for an examination of the relationships between males and females that are found in any given society.

Human Sexuality

Human sexuality and marriage are closely related in virtually all human societies on which we have information. Nevertheless, the cultural norms governing sexual relationships are different from those governing marriage. This was as true for the Victorian English as it is for the Nayar of India, as valid for the ancient Greeks as for the modern Japanese. Everywhere, a description of marriage involves inquiry about sexual relations, and everywhere, sexual arrangements exist that do not involve marriage. Before we discuss marriage itself, then, it will be useful to consider human sexuality in order to comprehend how it is channeled by means of culture.

In any discussion of human sexuality, there are at least two categories of comparisons to

Differences in ideas of beauty and attractiveness vary from culture to culture, as can be seen from the body painting of an Asurini girl of Brazil (note her rubber thongs) and scarification of the face of a Makonde woman from Tanzania. (Jacques Jangoux, Peter Arnold Photo Archives; Lynn McLaren, Rapho/Photo Researchers)

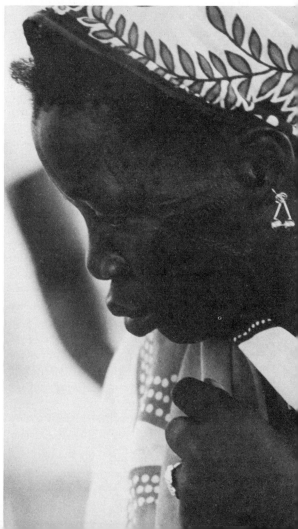

be made. The comparative perspective is one from which we may judge the forms and uses of human sexuality. But we also compare human sexuality with that of other animals, so that we can appreciate the extent to which we participate in the basic mammalian sexual heritage and can note ways in which we differ.

For most mammals, sexual activity is restricted to the periods during which fertilization is possible. Sex is thus linked directly to species reproduction. Generally, lower mammalian females offer themselves to males only when they are "in heat"—that is, during the limited periods, perhaps only at one time during the course of a year, when increased production of hormones stimulates the female. Among all but the simpler primates, however, female sexuality is less specifically tied to hormonal activity. Female chimpanzees, for example, have been observed during infertile periods making advances to, and receiving the attentions of, males.

Obviously, human sexuality is not controlled solely by hormones. This is not to say that humans are not influenced sexually by biological factors, including hormones, although the extent to which this is true is not clear. There is assuredly a high level both of individual variation among humans as a species and of variation for a given individual over time. However, most postadolescent individuals have direct experience of the fact that being aroused is usually a case of mind over matter. Human sexuality may have more to do with mental set and social environment than with any biologically measurable factors.

There are a number of other aspects of sexuality shared by humans and other mammals. Self-stimulation or masturbation is general in mammalian species. Juvenile sex play is found in many species; its frequency and variety tend to increase from the lower mammals to the higher. The specifics of the sex act—male erection and ejaculation, genital stimulation by means of rhythmic pelvic thrusting—are reflexes found in all mammals. Mutual grooming, a characteristic of precoital behavior in a number of human societies, is common to all subhuman primates that have been studied (Ford & Beach, 1951).

Thus, human beings bring to sexual behavior a heritage shared with other mammals, and especially with the higher primates. Certain basic sexual behaviors appear to be universal to human beings as a consequence of biological evolution. But, for *Homo sapiens,* the forms with which these behaviors are expressed are shaped largely by learning and through the cultural experience.

Sexuality and Culture

Not even the necessity for sexual learning, however, is unique to humans. Behavioral studies have shown that "at least some, and perhaps all, male chimpanzees have to learn how to copulate" (Ford & Beach, 1951). There are indications that sexual learning is required by other primates as well.

There is a surprisingly large range in which sexual behavior can be learned. At an early age, Marquesan males (of Polynesia) learn to maintain erections and delay ejaculation for prolonged periods. It is not clear to what extent males are capable of achieving this in our society, but there is much evidence to show that such practices are not universal. The influence of culture on sexual behavior is particularly evident in the topics of childhood sexuality, precoital stimulation, extramarital sexual activity, and homosexuality.

Childhood Sexuality. The degree of freedom that children and young people have to explore their bodies and experiment with their developing sexual capabilities varies enormously. Among the Toba Indians of northern Argentina, for instance, children touch their genitals and play love-making games with dolls and other play objects, showing intercourse between the objects of play with no objection from adults. The play is ignored rather than reprimanded or laughed at. Similar adult indifference is found among the Trobriand Islanders, where children listen to ribald conversations and observe adults engaged in intercourse. Early childhood sex play, including mutual stimulation of genital organs, is casual and frequent. Older Trobriand youths and girls are encouraged to form sexual attachments. By midadolescence they have graduated from a series of frequent but casual liaisons to a more permanent relationship that may culminate in marriage.

Precoital Stimulation. In virtually all societies, some form of precoital stimulation is practiced. However, its extent and nature may be quite different from one society to the next. The kind of mutual grooming practiced by most primates and some human societies may be stimulating in some groups, but in our own society it would most likely be counterproductive. Among the Sirionó, the Truk, and Trobriand Islanders, both men and women learn early to interpret certain hair pulling, or being scratched or bitten, as a signal of sexual arousal. These sensations, elsewhere considered painful and unpleasant, here become erotic stimuli, a form of grooming (Ford & Beach, 1951). A minority of Americans and Europeans, however, have learned to associate the infliction and/or reception of pain with sexual pleasure. Sadomasochistic practices are more generally considered "sick" or "kinky" and have been the subject of numerous psychiatric studies.

The human ability to respond to symbolic stimulation may reduce the amount of direct physical stimulation preliminary to intercourse. But the nature of the symbols that may have the desired effect is highly variable, perhaps even within a given culture. This is certainly true within our own culture, where the sight of the naked body of the sex partner may be sexually stimulating, or where the sight of the clothed or partially clothed body may be equally so. What causes physical arousal in some individuals may be offensive or distracting to others. The degree to which symbolic stimulation substitutes for actual physical stimulation may be uniquely human.

Extramarital Sexual Activity. Similarly, wide variation is found in the extent to which extramarital sexual activity is permitted, condoned, or prohibited. In one study of 139 cultures, 39 percent approved of some form of sexual liaison outside of marriage (Ford & Beach, 1951, p. 113). The Toda allow a woman to have not only more than one husband but a number of lovers as well. This pattern should be seen as a convenience for males rather than as a license for females since the Toda have a disproportionately low number of adult females, due to female infanticide. At the other extreme was the culture of early New England, where adulterers were physically punished or exiled. Hester Prynne, with her scarlet letter "A" in Hawthorne's novel, constitutes a mild example. In other societies certain liaisons are approved. The Sirionó permit a man to have a sexual relationship with his wife's sisters and his brothers' wives and their sisters. Sirionó women are not discriminated against in this regard and are permitted sexual activity with their husbands' brothers and their sisters' husbands. The Marquesans similarly permit men and women to have extramarital intercourse with siblings-in-law.

A particular form of extramarital relationship is wife-exchange or wife-lending, practiced by the Eskimo and related cultures. Since the Siberian Chuckchee reindeer herders must travel widely, a man will arrange for the services of his host's spouse in each village on his route and will permit the same exchange when these men visit his community (Ford & Beach, 1951). A total range of wifely services, including but not primarily sexual ones, is provided in this way. A wife is valued as an economic asset and literal helpmate. No northern man can deal with the environment without such absolutely essential wifely services as boot-chewing and clothing repair (LaBarre, 1954).

Homosexuality. There is no society in which homosexuality is the sexual preference of the majority of adults, but the extent to which it may be encouraged, tolerated, or tabooed varies widely. Homosexuality does occur among a minority of people in every society, and wherever it is found, it is more prevalent among males than it is among females. Homosexual relationships were accepted among all males in ancient Greece and Rome. Among the Keraki of New Guinea all men are expected to have homosexual experience before marriage and are considered abnormal if they do not (Ford & Beach, 1951).

In some societies, specific provision is made for individuals who have a homosexual preference. For example, among the Chuckchee of Siberia, certain shamans "marry" a spouse of the same sex. These shamans are called upon in their early youth by various tribal spirits to undergo a change of sex, a call that is "much dreaded" but heeded nonetheless (Bogoras, 1953). The transformation takes place in stages, beginning simply with the adoption of a female hair style. But in the third and final stage, the young man

leaves off all pursuits and manners of his sex, and takes up those of a woman, [which he learns to use] quickly because the "spirits" are helping him all the time . . . . Generally speaking, he becomes a woman with the appearance of a man. . . . The "soft man" begins to feel like a woman. He seeks to win the good graces of men, and succeeds easily with the aid of "spirits." Thus he has all the young men he could wish for striving to obtain his favor. From these he chooses his lover, and after a time takes a husband. The marriage is performed with the usual rites, and it forms a quite solid union, which often lasts until death. . . of one of the parties. The couple live much in the same way as do other people. . . . (Bogoras, 1953, p. 108)

This custom of homosexual marriage, called *berdache,* is found also in some American Indian groups. The Nuer have a similar but reverse practice, in which women become the "wife-husbands" of other women (Evans-Pritchard, 1940). Our own culture seems to be in a state of transition from total aversion to moderate tolerance of homosexuality.

In our own culture in general, the range of socially acceptable sexual behavior has changed vastly in the twentieth century alone. Between the "spooning" of the turn of the century and the "living together" arrangements of the 1970s lies a multigenerational chasm.

Incest

No matter how permissive a society may be in sexual matters, there is always some rule limiting the category of appropriate sexual partners. Prohibitions usually apply to varying categories of relatives, and almost universally to all members of the conjugal family (except, of course, the husband and wife). The term *incest taboo* is applied to the prohibition of sexual access to certain categories of kin.

The relationships that are tabooed vary widely. In our own culture, incest taboos extend from members of the nuclear family to include aunts, uncles, and usually first cousins (the laws on this vary from state to state). In previous chapters, we mentioned a number of societies in which marriages between those relatives we call first cousins are in some cases preferred and in some abhorred. In many cases it is considered desirable for cross cousins (the children of one's mother's brothers and father's sisters) to marry; in such cases parallel cousins (children of one's mother's sister and father's brother) come under the same incest prohibition as siblings. However, we also have mentioned the Bedouin Arab preference for marriage between patrilateral parallel cousins. The ancient Egyptian practice of mating between brothers and sisters in royal families, found also among the Inca of Peru, is a classic example of the extent of incest variation.

An example of a preferred marriage between relatives who in most cultures would be forbidden access to each other occurs among the Saha of Colombia, South America. Here, every person is expected to have at least two marriages in a lifetime. The preferred second wife for a man is the daughter, by an earlier husband, of his first wife. Such a marriage is termed a mother-daughter marriage. In general, the Saha prefer marriages between close kin, who must be members of different but linked clans. Therefore, marriages occur between individuals already having a number of relationships to each other.

The topic of incest has attracted considerable interest in anthropology, and numerous theories have been proposed to account for the presumed universality of incest prohibitions. One theory assumes strong sexual attraction among family members and postulates, therefore, that equally strong societal controls are necessary. Thus, it has been suggested that the control of sexual impulses at an early age is essential for the socialization of the child. Other anthropologists, taking a complementary view, have argued that mating outside of the family is required for broad-based cooperation and group survival. According to still another theory, sexual access would be appropriate within the family except for the fact that when one family member reaches sexual maturity there would not likely be available an individual of the opposite sex and appropriate age.

Psychoanalytic Theory. A different explanation of the incest taboo was offered by Freud. According to his theory, a strong sexual attraction exists between mother and son and between father and daughter. In the course of socialization, the child learns to repress his or her feelings out of fear of punishment or injury from the parent of the same sex. Although repressed, the sexual attraction continues to exist in the unconscious mind of the child. The incest taboo is, therefore, another line of defense against the forbidden impulse.

Childhood Familiarity Theory. Even though Freud's theory can account for some observable situations, many anthropologists find it an inadequate explanation for both the origin of the taboo and its many cultural expressions. In the 1920s, Edward Westermarck proposed an alternative explanation that has come to be known as the childhood familiarity theory. Westermarck held that the intimacy existing among family members resulted in sexual aversion among them. This theory was vulnerable on two points. First, cases could be found in which family members *were* sexually attracted to each other. Second, if familiarity caused lack of interest, why was an incest taboo needed in the first place?

Recently, Arthur Wolf set out to test Westermarck's hypotheses. He considered various data, including verifiable gossip, for several hundred marriages in two Chinese villages in Taiwan. Two types of marriage—major and minor—occur there. "Major" marriages are contracted between partners whose relationship was initiated in adulthood. "Minor" marriages take place between a man and a woman who was adopted into his family at an early age to be raised as his potential marriage partner. The partners of a minor marriage are, therefore, "a couple whose experience of one another is as intimate as brother and sister" (Wolf, 1970, p. 504). Wolf hypothesized that if sexual aversion results from childhood association, that aversion should show up in a minor marriage and mar the relationship between husband and wife. In fact, the minor marriages did consistently result in fewer children than did major marriages. The lower fertility rate also correlated with higher rates of infidelity, separation, and divorce. Wolf believes that "there is some aspect of childhood association sufficient to preclude or inhibit sexual desire" (p. 515). The incest taboo, he concludes, is a formal statement on the general sexual aversion among close kin.

Inbreeding Theory. David Aberle and colleagues (1963) examined inbreeding in animals in an effort to determine the sociobiological roots of the human incest taboo. They found behavior ranging from no matings among family members (except the parents) to intensive family matings. In the Canadian goose and a few other species of birds, individuals raised in the same brood appear to instinctively avoid mating with each other. Among mammals that avoid inbreeding, the reason may be connected with competition between a parent and a child of the same sex. The parent usually is sufficiently strong to force the child to leave the family—and find another pool of mates—as it nears sexual maturity.

Aberle and his colleagues theorize that the incest taboo originated in the time lag between sexual maturity and self-sufficiency of offspring. Human parents do not generally force children to leave home upon reaching sexual maturity. They therefore need to solve the problem of sexual competition among family members and still maintain an organized family life. The incest taboo serves this purpose. However, in the long run, the taboo proves to be a selective advantage to the species in avoiding the genetic ill-effects of repeated inbreeding (Aberle et al., 1963).

A variety of studies have been undertaken to explore the alleged ill-effects of inbreeding. Reid, for example, interviewed several hundred married couples in Sri Lanka, Ceylon, where there is a high percentage of marriages between first cousins and other close relatives. He found that the closer the consanguineal relationship of the conjugal pair, the fewer the pregnancies, live births, and living offspring. However, the consanguinity of married couples does not seem to affect the rates of spontaneous abortion, stillbirth, or later death of offspring. Reid concluded that consan-guineous couples had significantly lower fertility levels and that "this result remains consistent with the belief that inbreeding reduces Darwinian fitness" (Reid, 1976, p. 144).

The foregoing theories are only a few of the approaches taken by anthropologists in the study of incest. As in the story of the blind men and the elephant, no one has grasped this subject in its totality, but each has contributed something toward an understanding of the sizable whole. Taken together, all the points of view represent useful keys to improve our knowledge of this phenomenon—or these phenomena, as Needham (1971) would perhaps urge. He holds that because incest prohibitions differ from one society to another, no general theory can apply to them all. The cultural meanings of incest taboos differ for every society although incest regulations have in common the prohibition of sexual access. However, with the exception of the mother-son relationship, there is no truly universal proscription. From the perspective of a study of marriage, the significance of incest taboos lies in their opposites. Since they list categories of persons not available as sexual partners, they make implicit statements about acceptable sexual and marital unions.

Defining Marriage

But what is marriage? In the previous chapter, we examined a variety of marriage arrangements:

- A situation in which several men obtain both sexual and domestic services from one woman, but only one man legitimizes her offspring (the Toda)
- Situations in which one man may have all of these rights and obligations toward several women (the Yoruba and others)

An African wedding rite, performed by a couple in New York City. (Katrina Thomas, Photo Researchers)

- Situations in which a man may have all these rights and obligations to one woman but virtually none of her children even though they be recognized as his (the Navajo)

Since there is a wide variety of marriage arrangements, a definition of marriage has to be broad enough to accommodate them all. One key point is recognition of sexual relations between the sexes. Since we have come across cases in which a man takes the role of a wife and a woman the role of a husband, we shall use male and female to refer to sex *roles* rather than to biological differences. Marriage gives primary sexual rights to the partners in the marriage, in that it is accepted that a sexual relationship of some sort will exist between them. As we have seen, the sexual rights that accompany marriage are not everywhere necessarily considered exclusive, as they are for the most part in our own society. A second important consideration is that, although formalized by different means in various societies, marriage is publicly recognized and socially sanctioned. It is entered into with some expectation on the partners' parts that it will endure for some period of time, if not forever. Third, marriage brings with it certain other rights and obligations between the husband and wife. These may be domestic cooperation or exchange between groups, practices and understandings of the society in question.

To sum up these factors, we will use the following definition: *marriage* is a socially recognized and relatively stable union providing sexual access, legitimating offspring, and establishing other rights and obligations between the marriage partners and other units of society.

The Nayar Case

Although the above definition of marriage has almost universal application, there is one major exception—the Nayar from the Central Kerala of India. The marriage customs of this group differ markedly from those of any other group known and studied to date.

The only marriage ceremonies among the Nayar are group affairs held every few years for all the girls who have not yet attained puberty. These prepuberty marriage rites for girls, aged 7 to 12, are essential for establishing the girl's place in the community.

Preceding the marriage ceremony, the neighborhood assembly meets and, on the advice of the village astrologer, selects the ritual bridegrooms for all the girls. For 3 days prior to the ceremony itself, the girls are secluded in an inner room of a nearby house. On the appointed day, the ritual bridegrooms arrive in a procession at the house where, after various ceremonies, each ties a gold ornament (*tāli*) around the neck of his ritual bride.

Then, each couple is secluded in private for 3 days, during which time sexual relations may take place but often do not. At the end of the 3 days of seclusion, each couple is purified from the pollution of cohabitation by a ritual bath. Following this, the ritual husbands depart.

After the 4 days of ceremonies, the ritual husbands have no further obligations to their brides. The brides have only one further obligation to their ritual husbands: they and all their children by whatever father have to observe rites upon the death of their ritual husbands.

Although the *tāli* rite does not establish husband and wife as an institutionalized, legal, residential, or economic unit, it is absolutely essential for establishing the woman's place in the community. The ritual bride's life actually depends on the ceremonial marriage because, if she is not ritually married before puberty, she faces excommunication and even death. The *tāli* rite endows a girl ceremonially with sexual and procreative functions and confers upon her the status of a woman. After the rite, when she reaches puberty, a girl can receive visiting husbands. A woman usually has a small number of visiting husbands at one time. Among them could be her ritual husband, if both are willing, but he has no special priority over other men.

A husband visits his wife after supper at night and leaves before breakfast in the morning. He places his weapons at the door of his wife's room, and if others arrive while he is there, they are welcome to sleep on the veranda of the woman's house. At the beginning of the relationship, the visiting husband usually gives the woman a cloth of the type worn as a skirt, although it is not essential. Later he is expected to make small personal gifts to her at the three main festivals of the year. Failure to do so is a sign that he has ended the relationship. A passing visiting husband, a man who does not live in the same or nearby community, gives the woman a small gift at each visit. Both husband and wife are free to terminate the relationship at any time with no formalities.

When a woman becomes pregnant, it is necessary for one or more men to acknowledge fatherhood. This is done at the time of the birth of the child. At that time, the "father" pays the midwife, which is considered an open acknowledgment that the child has a father who is a man of the required rank. If no man comes forth to pay the midwife, it is assumed that the woman has had relations with a man from the wrong caste, and she can be banished or killed. Once the birth fees are paid, the father has no economic, legal, or ritual rights or obligations to his children. Women and their children are maintained by the matrilineal group.

All of a woman's children call all her current husbands by the same word, a term meaning "lord," and no particular ties distinguish a direct father-child relationship. A woman's ritual husband is the only one who has any rights in her children: they are expected to mourn his death even if he has not fathered any of them. Although the Nayar marriage ceremony does not create an institutionalized family unit, it does provide ritual and legal recognition of both the woman's and her children's status in the society (Gough, 1959; Leach, 1955).

Marriage Rules

All societies have restrictions on whom one may or may not marry. Through incest taboos, as we have seen, societies prohibit sexual access between certain categories of kin. While incest taboos provide negative regulations regarding choice of marriage partners, certain other positive regulations specify which categories of females are to be considered marital preferences (or even prescriptions) by the males in a society, and vice versa. These regulations constitute the other half of the marriage coin.

Whom May One Choose as a Mate?

As we have said, in every society the choice of potential marriage partners is in some way restricted. Some societies go further and specify which persons one *will* have as a mate. Two forms of restriction are endogamy and exogamy.

Endogamy and Exogamy. *Endogamy* refers to the expectation that a marriage partner will be chosen from within the social group of which one is a member. *Exogamy* refers to the expectation that the choice of a marriage partner will be from a social group of which one is not a member. In every society there are both endogamous and exogamous groupings. The Toda of India, for instance, are divided into two endogamous groups (or moieties), each of which has separate economic and ritual functions. Each moiety is subdivided into a number of exogamous clans. Marriage is exogamous—that is, a woman must marry a man from another clan of her own moiety (Murdock, 1934). In our own culture, although the nuclear family and close kin are exogamous, ethnic, racial, religious, and/or economic class considerations may be (explicitly or implicitly) endogamous. In every society, individuals come of age knowing pretty well what is expected of them in the choice of a spouse.

It has often been theorized that exogamy developed as an extension of the incest taboo covering various categories of relatives. But exogamy is more than merely the extension of incest prohibitions. Marrying outside one's group has the functional advantage of bringing to one's group certain benefits. Exogamous groups are often well aware of this advantage.

In European royal marriages over the centuries, the importance of contracting political alliances appeared to take precedence over personal considerations. Americans are also aware of marriages that unite families that are socially prominent. The possible benefits to all concerned are matters of public speculation. Apparently anthropologists are not the only persons who are aware of the benefits of exogamy.

Another reason for the practice of exogamy may be group survival. The notion of marrying outside of one's group or dying out has been pervasive ever since the earliest anthropological writings on marriage. Exchange of marriage partners between groups establishes alliances between them. This is not to say that marital exchange necessarily brings peace. But the rule of exogamy forces two groups to depend on each other for continued reproduction, and the knowledge of this fact helps to regulate relations between the groups.

We should keep in mind when discussing exogamy that there may be differences between the requirements of incest taboos and of exogamy. That is, incest taboos restrict sexual relations—whether outside of or within marriage. Exogamy regulates only the choice of potential marital partners. In terms of this distinction, two individuals might be prevented by rules of exogamy from marrying each other. Yet they might be allowed a sexual relationship if there were no incest prohibition operative between them. The Toda demonstrate this difference: marriage between individuals of different moieties or within the same clan is not permitted. However, sexual relations between members of the two moieties, and also between members of the same clan, are tolerated (Murdock, 1934, p. 122).

Cousin Marriages. In some societies, restrictions on marital partners are also accompanied

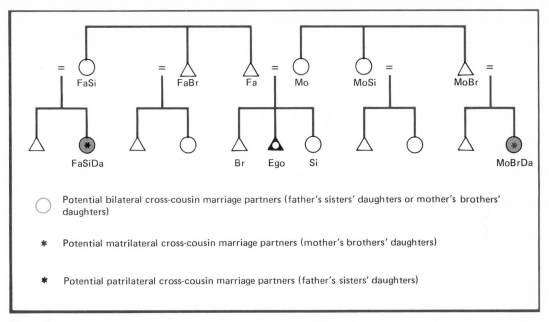

Figure 1 Possible cross-cousin marriages for Ego who is male

by a preference for marriage with certain other relatives. The most usual preference is for marriage between cross-cousins. *Cross cousins* are children of the opposite-sex siblings of one's mother or father. Specifically, one's cross cousins are the children of one's mother's brothers and one's father's sisters. In some cases, the obligation involves more than a preference—it is required. Societies in which such obligations apply are said to have *prescriptive marriage rules.*

Theoretically, there are three possible kinds of cross-cousin marriages: bilateral, matrilateral, and patrilateral. Figure 1 shows the possible cross-cousin marriage for Ego who is male. In bilateral cross-cousin marriage, a man marries from among either his mother's brothers' daughters or his father's sisters' daughters. In matrilateral cross-cousin marriage, he marries one of his mother's brothers' daughters only; and in the patrilateral cross-cousin marriage he finds his wife from among the daughters of his father's sisters.

Figure 2 shows the cross-cousin marriages allowed Ego who is female. Bilateral cross-cousin marriage is an exchange arrangement that requires only two reciprocating kin groups, although more may be involved. Matrilateral and patrilateral cross-cousin marriage (both of which are relatively rare) require at least three intermarrying groups, and may involve many more.

Rare also is a preference for parallel-cousin marriage. *Parallel cousins* are children of the same-sex siblings of one's mother or father. That is, one's parallel cousins are the children of one's mother's sisters and those of one's father's brothers. As we have mentioned in previous chapters, this is considered one of the ideal arrangements among the Middle Eastern Bedouin. In their case, parallel-cousin marriage serves the practical, and stated, purpose of keeping property within the landholding group.

Clearly, if prescriptive marriage rules are followed generation after generation, rela-

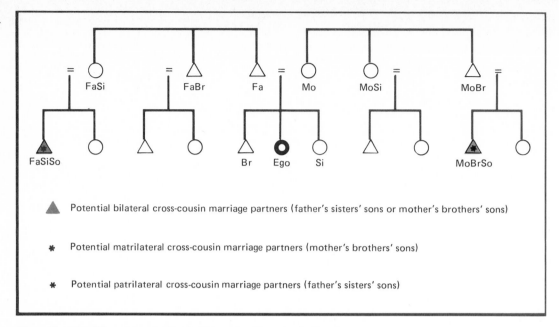

Figure 2   Possible cross-cousin marriages for Ego who is female

tionships among family members will operate on several levels at the same time. For a male Bedouin (Ego) about to marry his patrilateral parallel cousin, his father's brother (already his "uncle") will become his "father-in-law." Such relationships become more complicated over several generations.

The Kareira are among the several indigenous Australian groups practicing bilateral cross-cousin marriage. Here, Ego's father's sister, who is one of his potential mothers-in-law, is probably married to his mother's brother. And so while it might seem that Ego could at least choose between his father's sister's daughter and his mother's brother's daughter, these females might be one and the same person, as well as the sister of his own sister's husband.

Kin groups that regularly exchange spouses are likely to interact in a number of other areas as well, each of which reinforces the others. Marital reciprocity is only one of a number of relationships—in the economic, ritual, and political spheres—that exist between descent groups in a society with prescriptive marriage rules.

Levirate and Sororate. The levirate and sororate involve special cases of marriage regulation. They go into effect following the death of one member of a married couple. *Levirate* is the practice of requiring or permitting a man to marry the wife of his deceased brother. A good example is found in the Old Testament:

> If brethren dwell together, and one of them die and have no son, the wife of the dead shall not be married to a stranger; her husband's brother shall go in unto her, and take her to him to wife and perform the duty of a husband's brother unto her. And it shall be that the first-born that she beareth shall succeed in the name of his dead brother that his name be not blotted out of Israel (Deuteronomy 25:5–6).

The wording of this command indicates that the need for a legal heir for the deceased is a prime concern. Elsewhere, the Old Testament indicates the property and other rights that might be involved. In early Biblical times, women had little say in the matter; all members of a household were subject to the authority of its oldest male head. But later, when the Israelites were a settled agricultural people with some degree of political organization, women had the right both to complain about and publicly humiliate a brother-in-law who refused to comply with the levirate (Patai, 1959, pp. 92–96).

The levirate often coincides with polygyny (the marriage of one man to two or more women), patrilineal descent, and patrilocal residence. These conditions result in an extended patriarchal family, as they did in the early Old Testament days. The levirate is still permitted throughout the Middle East to this day, though it is now found only rarely. Patai (1959) has shown that a man's exercise of his levirate duties establishes his claim as his brother's heir in property and other rights. In the past, such claims also applied to a father's property. In this case, the heir of a deceased man might inherit his father's wife or wives (exclusive, of course, of his own mother) together with the father's other property.

In the Old Testament version of the levirate, any children born are considered to be the heirs of the deceased husband. A variation is found in the so-called "ghost marriages" of the Nuer. The brother of a man who had died without children could marry a woman "to the name of" the deceased. The offspring of this union would be regarded as children of the dead man and, thus, as his heirs (Evans-Pritchard, 1940).

Another variation on the levirate is found among the Kadara of northern Nigeria. There, a man may be required to marry the widow of his elder brother or the widow of his father's father (Smith, 1968). Marriage to one's elder brother's widow is the most frequent type. In reality, the second situation would occur only when the father's father left no surviving junior siblings and, therefore, no one else to provide for his widow. Again, the importance of the levirate for the raising of heirs is em-

phasized. A man's lineage mates would usually object to a marriage with his *maternal* grandfather's widow, since the offspring of such a union could be claimed by the lineage of the maternal grandfather. But if a man married either his brother's or his *paternal* grandfather's widow, children would belong to his patrilineage, and the patrilineage would lose neither members nor property as a result of the marriage (Smith, 1968).

The *sororate* is a complementary practice to the levirate, in which a man marries the sister of his deceased wife. The term also sometimes applies to the situation in which the husband of a childless woman is given her sister also in marriage, in which case some of the children born to the sister are counted as those of the childless wife. The same principle applies to each: the services agreed upon at marriage remain an obligation between the groups. As with the levirate, the sororate occurs with patrilineal descent, patrilocal residence, and polygyny, since an important alliance has been established between the wife-giving and the wife-receiving groups. Sometimes, it is the natural extension of *sororal polygyny,* the marriage of a man to two or more sisters at the same time. Marriage to one woman may give a man the right to marry her unwed sisters as well. If a woman dies, her family may be expected to provide a replacement, especially if the man and his kin provided a sizable bridewealth at the time of the original marriage.

Among the Arapaho and other Plains Indian groups, levirate and sororate both provide a widower and widow with a new spouse. These practices maintain the alliances set up by the original marriage between two exogamous kin groups. This differs somewhat from the emphasis in the Middle Eastern version of levirate, where the original marriage may well have been endogamous. Endogamy introduces differentiation within the lineage and serves to segment groups within it. In this case, provision for a second marriage is clearly tied to providing an heir for the dead as well as

406

to ensuring the continuity of the descent group for the purpose of property inheritance.

Both levirate and sororate are widespread in one form or another. Well over half of the societies in Murdock's (1949) study practiced levirate marriage to a significant extent (127 out of 185 groups for which there was data on this point). Nearly as many practiced the sororate.

How Many Mates Does One Choose?

One of the areas that consistently interests anthropologists is the question of how many persons one may marry at a time in various societies. Our society is so decidedly monogamous—pairing one man and one woman at a time—that different patterns are a matter of some curiosity. Once again, the possible patterns are these:

1. *Monogamy:* the marriage of one man to one woman at a time
2. *Polygyny:* the marriage of one man to two or more women at a time
3. *Polyandry:* the marriage of one woman to two or more men at a time
4. *Group marriage:* the marriage of two or more women to two or more men at the same time.

Polygyny, polyandry, and group marriage are all forms of *polygamy,* or plural marriage. We will look at each of these marriage patterns in turn.

Monogamy. Anthropologists who took an evolutionary approach to the study of culture once believed monogamy, like monotheism and industrialism, to be a sign of progress and civilization. Most anthropologists now view social and cultural differences simply as differences and not as lags, evolutionary or otherwise. Whether a society permits one marriage partner or a number of partners at a time is no way related to that society's level of civilization.

Monogamy occurs worldwide with less frequency than many Westerners expect. In their sample of 185 societies, Ford and Beach (1951) found that 29 of them (or less than 16 percent) were monogamous. Of those, fewer than a third approved of extra- and premarital sexual liaisons. Recent analysis of a much larger cross-cultural sample had much the same result: of 854 societies, 16 percent were exclusively monogamous (Bourguignon & Greenbaum, HRAF, 1973). However, an additional 39 percent of the societies sampled practiced monogamy with occasional polygyny. Polygyny is permitted (or even preferred) in these societies, but in practice monogamy is more frequent there. Economic and population factors tend to limit the number of polygynous marriages. In some cases, only the most powerful or wealthy men can afford to have more than one wife. In other cases, there simply are not enough women to allow for two or more wives to every man.

The form of monogamy that characterizes Western society has been referred to as *serial monogamy.* This consists of a pattern of marriage, divorce, and remarriage. Thus, although the individual is married to only one person at a time, over a number of years he or she may have had a number of spouses.

Polygyny. Worldwide, polygyny is certainly the most popular form of marriage. Of the societies analyzed by Bourguignon and Greenbaum, 44 percent (or 379) were predominantly polygynous. As we have noted, nearly as many—39 percent (or 335)—were monogamous with occasional polygyny (1973, Table 27, p. 51). The incidence of occasional polygyny was broadly scattered, but occurred in half or more of the societies of east Eurasia, the Insular Pacific, North America, and South America. By comparison, polygyny is the predominant form of marriage among 85 percent of the groups studied in sub-Saharan Africa; in over a third of the groups in the

The number one wife of the deji (king) of the Yoruba of West Nigeria is being greeted by other wives of the king. (Marc and Evelyne Bernheim, Woodfin Camp)

circum-Mediterranean region; about a quarter of the societies of the Insular Pacific and South America; and in only 13 percent of the groups of east Eurasia. Almost everywhere, however, monogamous unions are more numerous than polygynous ones, even where polygyny is preferred.

Typically, a husband in a polygynous marriage has the same rights and obligations to each of his wives, and will be the legitimate father of all children born to them (even though the wives may sometimes be permitted to have sexual relations with other men). In some instances, a first or a last or a favorite wife may have rights in addition to those of the other wives. She may serve as an economic or labor supervisor over the secondary wives, or have social and/or ritual obligations and recognition that subsequent wives lack. In such cases, this may form the basis for segmentation in the lineage at a later time. Usually, "each wife considers herself the guardian of her children's rights within the family created by the polygynous marriage" (Marshall, 1977). This can also create conflict and cleavages within the lineage.

A common form of polygyny is *sororal polygyny*. In marrying one woman, a man may acquire the right to claim her sisters in marriage as well, with or without additional payments or ceremonies. People in polygynous societies frequently verbalize approval of sororal polygyny. They believe that sisters get along well together as wives of the same man, since they are used to cooperating and being together in the same household. A well-known Biblical instance of this practice was the marriage of Jacob to Leah, the older sister, and then to her younger sister Rachel, the woman he had chosen originally (Genesis 29). (Both women were, incidentally, his mother's brother's daughters—his matrilateral cross cousins.) In this case, however, there was a good deal of envy between the sisters: Leah envying Rachel, who was preferred by Jacob, and Rachel envying Leah, who was able to bear children (Genesis 30). Despite expectations to the contrary, sisters in sororal polygynous marriage do not necessarily cooperate as co-wives. Marriage creates new interpersonal relations that may interfere with cooperation, as it did for Leah and Rachel.

The Baganda of Uganda represent a good case of the preference for polygyny so widespread in sub-Saharan Africa. Sororal polygyny is preferred, but unrelated women may be married to the same man as well. A man must accumulate a substantial amount of property—several goats or a cow and thousands of cowrie shells—to give to the family of his prospective bride. A Baganda king can afford to have hundreds of wives; chiefs may have dozens; even a commoner may have two or three. A wife is an economic asset, since the fruits of her labors go to her husband. Because a wife has a very heavy work load, she may gladly welcome additional spouses for her husband, especially if she is the first or second wife, since the first two wives have higher status than succeeding ones. Women not married to the head of the household, such as unmarried female relatives and slaves, may also be attached to it. After a man dies, the first wife must tend his grave. Other wives may be claimed by relatives, and those remaining go, along with the rest of his property, to an heir designated by the clan of the deceased. (Sons do not inherit directly from their fathers.) The first wife may remarry also, but her brother will have to refund to her deceased husband's relatives the payment made by the groom when the couple were married. A widower may take a new wife from the clan of his former wife, but must, again, reciprocate the appropriate goods (Queen & Habenstein, 1974, pp. 72 ff).

Polyandry. Polyandry is a rare form of marriage. Only four instances were found in the Bourguignon and Greenbaum (1973) sample of 854 societies. Murdock (1949), citing two cases in his sample of 238 societies, regarded polyandry as "an ethnological curiosity." The Toda of India, who practice *fraternal polyandry*—marriage of a woman to two or more brothers—are considered the classic example. Fraternal polyandry is the counterpart of sororal polygyny in that an arrangement is made for a category of males rather than females. A similar instance is the Sinhalese of Sri Lanka (Ceylon), where two brothers may live in a household with one wife, although there are also households where two or more brothers each live with a separate wife. Polygyny is also permitted among the Sinhalese (D'Oyly, 1929, p. 129). In Sinhalese polyandry, unlike the Toda version, the first husband must consent to his wife's successive husbands and to her sexual activities with them. And unlike the Toda case, each Sinhalese husband legitimizes the children he has fathered. Inheritance is bilateral, in that all of a woman's children have an equal claim on her property in addition to the right to inherit from their respective fathers.

Among the Toda on the other hand, inheritance is patrilineal, and there is a preference for cross-cousin marriage. So no matter which husband legitimizes the children, the property stays in the family; the several husbands of a Toda woman are likely to be brothers, and therefore her child would belong to the same patrilineage as all of them (Murdock, 1934, pp. 114–122). One would therefore expect less conflict over rights and less fissioning among the Toda.

Nonfraternal polyandry is found among the Marquesans of Polynesia, who are the only people outside of the Indian subcontinent known to practice this form of marriage. There, a number of unrelated men join the household of a woman of high status and participate jointly in economic responsibilities and sexual privileges (Murdock, 1949, p. 26).

The "visiting husband" of the Nayar women may be seen as a variant of nonfraternal polyandry. It should be emphasized that these relationships are not casual liaisons. Rather, they are mateships, since they are on-going and of some durability. The woman is free to receive casual visitors, as long as they belong to the appropriate subcaste. Furthermore, when she becomes pregnant, one of a woman's visiting husbands must acknowledge paternity by providing a fee of cloth and vegetables for the midwife who delivers the baby (Gough, 1959).

Group Marriage. Group marriage appears very seldom, even as a minority practice, although early ethnologists believed that it was characteristic of an early stage in social evolution. Murdock (1949) found group marriage occuring more frequently among the Kaingang of Brazil than in any other culture. Yet, in a statistical analysis of that group's genealogies for over 100 years, he found that only 8 percent of all Kaingang marriages were group marriages. Of the remaining marriages, 14 percent were polyandrous, 18 percent polygynous, and 60 percent monogamous. Murdock concluded that group marriage does not exist anywhere as the prevalent marriage form. However, as we noted in the preceding chapter, fraternal-sororal group marriage was succeeding or supplementing polyandry among the Toda of southern India, as the prohibition of female infanticide altered the demographic imbalance of the sexes.

Where Does One Live after Marriage?

When a marriage occurs, either or both parties must change residence. As Murdock puts it, "the possible alternatives are few in number, and all societies have come to adopt one or another of them, or some combination thereof, as the culturally preferred rule of residence" (Murdock, 1960, p. 16). The possibilities are

1. *Neolocal residence:* the newly married couple establishes its residence without regard to the residence of either partner's family of origin.
2. *Patrilocal residence:* the bride goes to live with the groom in the household headed by his father. (This pattern is sometimes called *virilocal residence,* to indicate that the bride goes to live with the groom in the vicinity of his kin group or family of origin, rather than in the father's household per se.)
3. *Matrilocal residence:* the groom goes to live with the bride in the household headed by her mother. (This pattern is called *uxorilocal residence,* to indicate that the groom goes to live with the bride in the vicinity of her kin group or family of origin, rather than in the mother's household per se.

4. *Bilocal residence:* the couple has a choice of living with or near the parents or kin group of either bride or groom.

5. *Ambilocal residence:* the couple is expected to live for a period of time with or near the bride's parents and for another period of time with or near the groom's parents.

6. *Avunculocal residence:* the couple lives with or near the groom's mother's brother.

In some cultures, the pattern includes change from one type of residence to another after a specified period of time. Thus, there may be an initial period of matrilocal residence, followed by patrilocality, or there may be a shift from patri- to avunculocality (Bourguignon & Greenbaum, 1973, p. 53; Goodenough, 1956, p. 25). Among the Toba, for example, the couple traditionally lived with the wife's family until the first child was born, after which they were free to join the husband's group, a form of ambilocal residence.

Worldwide, an overwhelming majority of societies favor patrilocal or virilocal residence. In the Bourguignon and Greenbaum study (1973), these patterns together characterized nearly 70 percent of all societies. Matrilocal or uxorilocal and avunculocal societies combined accounted for only 17 percent of the 854 societies in the sample.

The location of postmarital residence is neither an isolated nor an idle choice. It is deeply bound to other facets of the social and economic system with far-reaching political and psychological consequences for the individuals and families involved. Leach argues

A Bedouin bride in Libya rides hidden from sight on the way to her husband's village, where the couple will live. (Dr. Georg Gerster, Rapho/Photo Researchers)

that one can draw correspondences between the nature of the marriage institution and the principles of descent and rules of residence in a given society. For instance, patrilocality correlates with patrilineal descent. Among patrilocal societies with patrilineal descent, Leach finds that concern with legal fatherhood "is far and away the most important element." Among the Trobriand Islanders, on the other hand, where virilocality is associated with matrilineal descent, giving a husband the property rights of his wife is more important than legal paternity (Leach, 1955).

One might expect that residence choices would be a simple and clear-cut issue, but this is not the case. The interpretation of residence rules, as you may recall from an earlier chapter, was the subject of some disagreement between Goodenough and Fischer. In 1947, Goodenough found a predominantly matrilocal pattern in his study of residence patterns on the northern Pacific island of Truk. Three years earlier, Fischer had concluded that residence on Truk was bilocal.

Comparing their findings, Goodenough determined that the difference between their interpretations was the result of each ethnographer having utilized somewhat different concepts of residence. As an example of the ways in which data can be misinterpreted, Goodenough cites a family unit consisting of an elderly man with his second wife, his three sons by his first marriage, and the wife of his eldest son. On the surface, this appears to be a typical patrilocal extended family. However, on closer examination, it turned out that the family was residing in a house and on land belonging to the matrilineage of the older man's first wife, to which his sons also belonged. Thus the real situation was that of an initial uxorilocal residence by the father and avunculocal residence by the son (Goodenough, 1956).

Goodenough proposes that anthropologists investigate the conditions and considerations that influence the decisions concerning resi-

dence after marriage. He states that it is necessary to examine a sufficiently large number of cases before a statement can be made about the residence rules of society. Census data alone are insufficient to discover the rules, and what may be relevant information for one society may be irrelevant for another.

Some studies have attempted to correlate residence patterns with other cultural patterns. Perhaps because data in various studies are not always comparable, the correlations are not clear-cut. Ember and Ember (1971) found, for example, that female dominance in subsistence activities was associated with matrilocal residence in North America but not anywhere else. They have also attempted to correlate viri- or patrilocal residence (male localization) with a number of factors that Murdock believed to be associated with high status for males, but their findings are inconclusive. Only herding and intercommunity political organization "turned out to predict more than half of the cases in which males are localized after marriage. . . .Two other conditions— polygyny and slavery—predict male localization weakly. And the last two conditions— warfare and division of labor—do not predict male localization at all" (1971, p. 593). However, the Embers did find some evidence that warfare is distinctive when one contrasts matrilocal with patrilocal residence. The presence of warfare *within* a society tends to be accompanied by patrilocal residence. Matrilocal residence tends to characterize societies that are engaged in warfare only with *other* societies. In this case, while the men are engaged in warfare, the labor needed to maintain subsistence is performed by women. Thus, residence tends to center around women where cooperation and family arrangements make for the smooth operation of the domestic unit. (1971, p. 593). The nature of various other social conditions that might affect residence patterns is an open question and one that calls for further research and discussion.

Marriage Transactions

In nearly all societies, as we have seen, anthropologists find certain correspondences between the character of marriage institutions and such other features as rules of descent and residence. These features focus on the intergroup relationships that marriage brings with it. In most places, the importance of marriage is tied to its implications for the social group as a whole, and marriage can be viewed as a contract between two groups rather than simply between two individuals. Here, we will look at the variety of transactions and exchanges that accompany marriage, especially with regard to property distribution and group alliances.

Marriage as Exchange

Marriage arrangements can best be interpreted in terms of the theories of alliance and exchange proposed by Lévi-Strauss. Rules of exogamy and endogamy set up social boundaries, thus clearly defining and limiting the types and intensity of exchange between social groups. Within the appropriate boundaries, exogamy sets up the exchanges that tie social groups together. Marriage exchanges focus on women and the ways in which a given society circulates women in marriage. This exchange corresponds to other types of exchange among the groups concerned.

Elementary systems of marriage specify the categories or groups from which spouses must be chosen; complex systems (such as our own) only specify those ineligible to be spouses. Elementary systems circulate women in two

A groom in Israel signs the marriage contract just before the wedding ceremony, while his future father-in-law, *right,* looks on. (Dan Porges, Peter Arnold Photo Archives)

ways: by direct (or symmetric) exchange, in which two groups simply take wives from one another. Thus, men of group A take wives from group B, and men of group B take wives from group A. In indirect (or asymmetric) exchange, women circulate in one direction only. Women from group A marry men of group B; women of group B marry men of group C; and women of group C marry men of group A. As Figure 3 illustrates, direct exchange requires only two exogamous intermarrying groups, whereas indirect exchange requires at least three (and theoretically could involve an infinite number of) exogamous groups.

In elementary systems, marriage links kin groups together. The groups involved in an elementary system may be as minimal as small family bands. Usually the groups are on the order of lineages, clans, or moieties. Repeated marriages between two groups over several generations perpetuate alliances. Thus, the groups with which one's own group has such long-term marital exchanges becomes recog-nized and identified. This relationship may be acknowledged verbally or ceremonially, or may have more far-reaching implications for political alliance and economic cooperation.

Even where the forms of marriage are somewhat atypical, these intergroup relationships are recognized. The Saha of Colombia have descent groups, *sana,* that customarily follow certain intermarriage patterns. Each *sana* is associated with an animal, believed to be ancestral to its members. Thus, the Saha say that "jaguars must marry armadillos" (Safer, 1974). Among the Nayar, there are linked lineages with specified ceremonial responsibilities to each other. A woman's ritual husband must come from an appropriately linked lineage. Even though, in this instance, the husband's role is minimal, the linkage between lineages is highly significant (Gough, 1959, p. 173).

Property and Service Transactions

Gifts and exchanges of property and other related transactions serve as public recognition of the transfer of rights that takes place at marriage. In elementary systems of marriage, alliances between linked exogamous groups are solidified by such formal transactions. In complex systems, which do not set up such alliances, marriage exchanges symbolize the temporary associations between two groups.

The most frequently found property and service transactions are

1. *Bridewealth:* goods given to the bride's kin group by the groom or his kin group.*
2. *Dowry:* goods given to the bride or the newly married couple by the bride's kin group.

*The terms *bride-price* and *bride-service* used to be used to refer to *bridewealth.* They are no longer preferred because they carry the implication of payment made for the acquisition of a woman at marriage.

Figure 3 Circulation of women in elementary systems of marriage

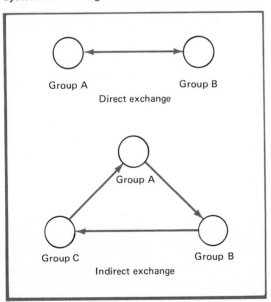

Group A ⟷ Group B
Direct exchange

Group A
Group C
Group B
Indirect exchange

414

3. *Gift exchange:* exchange of gifts or goods by each of the two kin groups being linked to each other by a marriage.
4. *Suitor service:* a period during which a groom lives with and works for the kin group of the bride.

In only a few societies is there an absence of any property or service transaction at or around the time of marriage.

To view these transactions as payments by a male or his kin group for the person or services of the female is not merely an oversimplification but also a distortion of the facts. Fortes (1962) points out that the exchanges of goods and services made during the course of marriage arrangements are a "means of winning and preserving the goodwill of those with the power to transfer marital rights" (p. 10). These are not one-sided transactions but, rather, exchanges in which valuable goods are passed both ways. Marital rights may simply be given in exchange for cattle, cowrie shells, coins, or whatever. But there may also be an exchange of material goods in *both* directions. In this case, the goods given by the kin group of the woman usually are of no more than

token value; in surrendering the woman herself, this group is parting with its most valuable commodity. Figure 4 illustrates the usual movement of goods and services in various marriage transactions.

Bridewealth and Dowry. Bridewealth and dowry, although given by the kin groups of groom and bride respectively, are not opposites. Bridewealth is given by the bridegroom and his kin group to the kin group of the bride in return for certain rights to the bride. The bridewealth is not given to the newly married couple but is kept by the bride's kin group. It is sometimes seen as compensation for the loss of her productive services or of a potential heir, since in patrilineal systems where bridewealth is most often given, a woman's child will become a member of her husband's kin group. In most cases, the bridewealth becomes a sort of circulating capital investment. It is used, in turn, to make the bridewealth payment when a brother of today's bride takes his own wife tomorrow (Tambiah, 1973, p. 61).

Dowry, on the other hand, is not a payment to a man or to his kin group. Nor is it to be understood as an exchange for his services in marriage. Rather, a dowry is the woman's share of her inheritance, which she takes with her at the time of marriage. As a sort of early inheritance, the dowry is available to the newly married couple for their own use (Tambiah, 1973, p. 64).

Bridewealth is a custom particularly widespread throughout Africa, where the amount of goods exchanged can be quite elaborate. Generally, the higher the amount, the higher the social status of the bride, and the higher the economic worth of the groom. Among the Baganda, the bridewealth may consist of several goats or a cow, and thousands of cowrie shells. If a man can accumulate enough property, he will invest it in bridewealth payments in order to secure additional wives and, thereby, raise his status even higher.

Figure 4   Marriage transactions. (Goody, 1973)

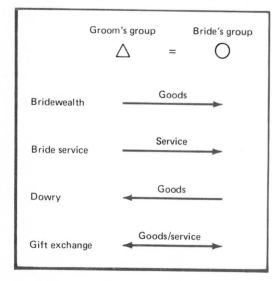

An Arab woman, wearing part of her dowry.
(Thomas Hopker, Woodfin Camp)

will reimburse him for these gifts and services, and the arrangement is terminated. If the marriage is to take place, however, the suitor gives the bride's father a further gift. This gift "includes as its essential element the precise sum in cowries that was paid to the midwife who brought her into the world, [signifying] that the bride has belonged to the groom's family, as it were, from birth" (Murdock, 1934, p. 580). The gift reinforces the alliance between the groups. After a third gift of livestock, palm oil, vegetables, and liquor, which is sacrificed to the bride's ancestors, the marriage is finalized. In poorer families, sister exchange replaces the midwife fee and fulfills the requirements of intergroup alliance.

In a second type of Dahomey marriage, which takes place when the "girl's clan is depleted in numbers," the payment of the midwife's fee is omitted. The bride then remains at her ancestral home, and her children are considered to belong to her clan (Murdock, 1934, p. 581).

When bridewealth is given, women and property move in opposite directions; when dowry is paid, both women and property move together in the same direction (Tambiah, 1973). Although bridewealth and dowry are different, they need not be mutually exclusive. In India and Ceylon, for example, both are given. In these societies, where property is transmitted through both males and females, these two different kinds of transactions coexist within a complex network of marriage transactions (Tambiah, 1973).

Bridewealth may also be considered a guarantee on the part of the groom and his kin group that the wife will be well treated in her new home. If she is not well treated, she may return to the home of her parents, and the husband will lose his investment in her (Murdock, 1960, p. 21). An important difference between bridewealth and dowry shows up in the case of divorce. In theory, when a divorce occurs, either all or part of the bridewealth that has been transacted must be returned by

Among the Dahomey of West Africa, there are various bridewealth exchanges, each indicating a different form of marriage. Usually the prospective suitor gives a betrothal present of cowrie shells, cloth, and grain to the father of the bride-to-be. This gift, which may be arranged while the two are still infants, commits the male to participation in funeral rites and performance of certain services for the female's kin group. If, when the female is older, she refuses to marry him, her family the wife's kin group to the kin group of her husband. But if the wife has received a dowry, she will be able to take the remaining portion of it away with her when the marriage ends, since it has always been legally her property (Tambiah, 1973).

Gift Exchange. Gift exchanges may range from a competitive attempt to outgive the new kin group to a token exchange of customary

"Pin money"—actually pinned to the bride and groom—is given by friends as gifts at this wedding on Cyprus. (Paul Conklin, Monkmeyer)

presents. Gift exchange accompanies marriage in our own society. Usually both kin groups and friends of the bride and groom give gifts to the bridal couple. In some instances, there may also be gift exchanges between the two nuclear families. Frequently, there is an attempt on the part of relatives to outdo the other group. The emphasis is on helping the newlyweds off to a comfortable start, but often there is also concern about giving gifts commensurate with those received on previous occasions. And, like many other peoples, we also offer gifts that are primarily symbolic in nature. The double ring ceremony popular in the United States symbolizes the vows taken by each new spouse; it also serves to symbolize the equality with which, at least theoretically, a man and woman enter into marriage in our society.

Suitor Service. In a number of societies, the groom must live with the bride's kin group for a particular period of time, which may range from a token few days to several years. During this time, he works with or for the bride's kin group. Sometimes he must produce a definite quantity of food supplies or give specified gifts. In some cases, his kin group must also supply gifts during this period. After the required period of service has been completed, the couple either returns to the husband's kin group or sets up housekeeping on their own.

A combination of suitor service and bridewealth was found among the Hupa and Yurok Indians of California. Postmarital residence was usually patrilocal, but a man who could afford only half the customary bridewealth would reside with and work for his father-in-law for a special period of time in lieu of the remaining bridewealth (Murdock, 1960, p. 21).

Among the matrilineal Hopi, there was a token form of marriage service, but in this case the bride lived with her husband's family for 3 days immediately preceding the wedding. She carried to her prospective mother-in-law a gift of cornmeal that she had ground. In the course of her 3 days' stay, she had to work industriously to grind additional cornmeal as well. During this time, her future mother-in-law had to defend her from mock attack for "laziness" by the paternal aunts of the groom. After the wedding, the couple continued to live with the husband's kin group for a few weeks, until he had finished weaving the special wedding clothes for his bride; she could not return to her home without them. When she did return home, both kin groups exchanged gifts and the marriage was consumated. Thereafter, the couple lived with the bride's kin group, and the husband worked for them (Queen & Habenstein, 1974, pp. 57–58).

All of these marital transactions may be spread out over a substantial period of time. Certain gifts or payments may be offered at the time the marriage is first considered. Sometimes additional payments must be made when a child of the couple is born or, later, when a child reaches puberty. The different payments or stages in property transactions usually represent stages in the process of allocating different rights. Among the Zulu, a particular payment (the *mfuko*) gave a husband exclusive sexual rights to his wife. If the *mfuko* had been paid, a wronged husband could claim compensation for adultery. Claims against an adulterer were not valid, though, if the payment had not been made. Other payments (in the form of cattle) transferred the rights to the couple's children to the father's kin group. Until this payment was made, rights to the children still belonged to the mother's kin group (Mitchell, 1962).

The types of property transaction accompanying marriage in any given society depend on several factors, among which are the nature of the prevailing economic system and the way in which descent and inheritance are determined. Leach contrasts situations in which property rights are vested solely in men, and situations in which property rights are vested

in women as well. In the latter case, marriage establishes a unique bundle of property rights; the children of any one marriage have a different total inheritance potential from the children of any other marriage.

In many societies, even where women may hold property, there exists the ideal that landed property should remain intact in the hands of male heirs. This creates a dilemma: on the one hand there is the notion that full brothers and full sons of full brothers *ought* to remain together in their ancestral home and work the ancestral land. On the other hand, when the wives of these men join the household, they bring with them property that will be inherited by their own children but not by their husband's nephews and nieces. Thus, each new marriage creates a new block of property interests, vested in its offspring, which is in conflict with the ideal of maintaining the social solidarity of male siblings.

There are several ways of resolving the dilemma. Leach mentions endogamy and fraternal polyandry as two different ways to keep property in the man's kin group. Fraternal polyandry seems to be particularly effective, for as Leach states:

If two brothers share one wife so that the only heirs of the brothers are the children born of that wife, then, from an economic point of view, the marriage will tend to cement the solidarity of the sibling pair rather than tear it apart, whereas, if the two brothers have separate wives, their children will have separate economic interests, and maintenance of the patrimonial inheritance in one piece is likely to prove impossible. If the ethnographical evidence is to be believed, polyandrous institutions, where they occur, are deemed highly virtuous and tend to eliminate rather than heighten sexual jealousies. (Leach, 1968, p. 79)

In the case of nonfraternal polyandry, as sometimes occurs among the Sinhalese, children inherit from their mothers and from the appropriate genitor/husband. The matrilineal Nayar avoid the predicament altogether by

417

SEX AND MARRIAGE

keeping children and property in the woman's kin group, where her brothers are in control.

Divorce

Now that we have considered marriage in some detail, we will look briefly at attitudes and practices that surround the dissolution of marriage—divorce. Discussions of divorce in other social sciences tend to regard its occurrence as a kind of breakdown of or deviance from socially acceptable norms. The comparative perspective of anthropology provides a useful corrective to such culture-bound views. In most of the world's societies, marriage is not considered to be the sacred once-and-for-always bond that our Judeo-Christian culture makes it out to be. Rather, marriage is usually recognized as being a fragile relationship that individuals may attempt a number of times before settling into a permanent arrangement. Riviere comments, "permanency in marriage. . . is certainly not a necessary characteristic of the union," and cites the *expectation* among the Irigwe of Nigeria "that a woman will move from husband to husband" (Riviere, 1971, p. 70), perhaps never achieving a permanent relationship, or perhaps achieving it only late in life.

Similarly, among the Toba of Argentina, it is expected that several trials will be necessary before the right combination is found to work. The right combination involves not only compatibility between husband and wife but also agreement of the wife's kin in particular. According to traditional sources (and confirmed by contemporary accounts), the customary rule of residence among the Toba has been matrilocal, particularly until the birth of the first child. After that, the couple might reside with the husband's kin. There is still a marked tendency to reside with or near the wife's family. This kin group often will bring pressure to bear on a relationship, ultimately deciding whether a man should stay or leave. A Toba woman with one or more children is a highly desirable commodity, and she can readily remarry if her husband should leave. No formal arrangement is necessary to dissolve a marriage union; the man simply leaves the residence and indicates that he has no intention of returning. He might return to his own kin group or take up residence with a new woman. This latter form of "trial" marriage has occurred frequently, but it is not necessarily considered desirable or preferable. Although those cases in which a couple's first marriage has lasted a long time have been relatively few, the husbands report proudly to a researcher that they are living with their first and only wife. Today Toba marriages appear to be in the process of becoming both less readily formed and less easily dissolved. Legal marriage documents are now required by Argentine law. These documents have an influence on marriage stability, but more importantly, residence changes due to land tenure problems and job opportunities seem to be playing an important role in the change.

But what exactly is marital stability? Many of us know of couples in our own society who stay together "for the sake of the children" or who, for some other reason, are never counted in the divorce statistics, even though their lack of compatibility or extramarital activities are common knowledge. We will consider *divorce* as the lawful dissolution of the legal ties established at marriage. Thus, separation and other breaks in marital relations, although they may occur with fair frequency, will not here be considered as divorce. Our society, which traditionally provided relatively greater accessibility of extramarital sexual relationships than of divorce, is not alone. Among the Nuer, for example, divorce, which is signified by the return of bridewealth, is rare, but conjugal separation is relatively frequent (Evans-Pritchard, 1940).

It is not unusual for the initiation of divorce proceedings to be a male prerogative. Among the Aranda of Australia, "a man may easily dispose of his wife. A woman, however, cannot secure a divorce; she can only run away" (Murdock, 1934, p. 39). Among the Baganda of Uganda, "a man can divorce his wife whenever he wishes." The primary reason for divorce here, as in many places, is a wife's barrenness. However, instead of divorcing an unwanted wife, a man will usually simply neglect her. Women are not without resources in this situation; a neglected or otherwise ill-treated wife will run away to her relatives. Her husband must then

explain his conduct to the men of her clan, give them a goat and a pot of beans, and, if proved in the wrong, make his wife a present and promise to reform. If she runs away repeatedly, he usually lets her stay and demands the return of the bride-price from her clansmen, thereby leaving her free to marry again. (Murdock, 1934, p. 541)

Among the Toda of India, "a man may divorce his wife on the grounds that she is lazy or a fool, not, however, for barrenness or adultery. He pays her family a fine of one water buffalo and receives in return any buffaloes he has given as funeral contributions" (Murdock, 1934, p. 121).

In Samoa, on the other hand, divorce is easy for both parties. Either of them may decide at any time to end their marriage, and do so by dividing up their property, including their children. Younger children go with the woman; older children go with the man (Murdock, 1934, p. 75). And among the Semang of the Malay Peninsula, partners can be changed with great frequency, especially when a couple has no children:

The husband simply leaves or is told to leave the shelter, which is the woman's property. If the wife terminates the union, her father must restore the bridal gifts or their equivalent to the husband, but if a man leaves his wife he forfeits the bride-price. The children normally remain with their mother. Either party may remarry, except that marriage between a man and the divorced wife of his younger brother is forbidden. (Murdock, 1934, pp. 99–100)

Divorce among the Hopi is similarly simple. A man may simply leave and return to his mother's house. A wife who wants to end her marriage announces this by placing her husband's belongings outside the door of their home (Queen & Habenstein, 1974, p. 68). Because of the strengths of the extended matrilineal household, the conjugal family can break up without disrupting the household very much. Nearly one out of three Hopi marriages ends in divorce, a rate that is, as Queen and Habenstein point out, roughly the rate in American society today.

In some societies, the position of women is far from being weak or vulnerable. For example, in a Dahomey marriage in which the full bridewealth has been paid,

the wife can obtain a divorce if the husband fails to perform his ceremonial duties toward her ancestors, or neglects his annual services to her father, or commits adultery with the wife of one of her near relatives. The husband, however, has no right to initiate a divorce. If he wishes to terminate the union, he can only neglect his spouse, insult her relatives, and resort to petty annoyances in order to force her to take action. A council of her kinsmen then assembles, reviews the evidence, and announces the divorce, which usually involves the return of the bride-price and other presents. (Murdock, 1934, pp. 582–583)

Full-bridewealth marriages among the Dahomey are less likely to be terminated than those in which the midwifery payment has not been paid and the wife continues to live with her kin group. Either party to the marriage can end this type of union, probably in recognition of the additional pressures that living with the woman's clan and kin in a predominantly patrilocal society can create (Murdock, 1934, pp. 582–583).

The role of extramarital sexual relationships in contributing to divorce is variable. It depends, naturally, on whether marriage in a particular society also confers exclusive sexual rights. It may depend somewhat on the kinship system of the society as well. Among the Haida of British Columbia, for instance,

> either party may have relations with a clansman of the other, and the injured spouse, though he may object, can take no action. But adultery—a liaison with anyone else—gives adequate grounds for divorce. A husband can take personal vengeance against neither his adulterous wife nor her lover. The latter, nevertheless, must pay damages—not, however, to the husband, but to the wife's mother. (Murdock, 1934, p. 252)

Among the Yao of Nyasaland, women can sue for divorce only on the grounds that their husbands are impotent; most divorces are granted at the suit of men who take action following a wife's adultery. The adulterer is considered to be a thief who has stolen the husband's rights, and compensation is paid to the husband for loss of these rights (Lloyd, 1968).

Within a given society, the degree of marital stability is influenced by a variety of factors. Gibbs (1963) identifies characteristics of the social system that tend to contribute to marital stability:

1. Clear marital norms. The social system spells out clearly just what is expected of a husband and wife, assigning specific rights to each and formalizing the marriage in some more or less official manner.
2. Rewarding of conformity to marriage norms. The personal rights accorded to married individuals are considered highly desirable and are not available outside of marriage. Sexual or reproductive rights, for instance, may be limited only to married people. Or, in some societies, where women are an important source of labor, a wife may significantly add to her husband's economic and social status.
3. Punishment of deviance from marriage norms. Through various sanctions, especially the removal of personal rights or by subjecting the spouses to group controls, or both, individuals are strongly discouraged from nonconforming behavior.

Gibbs predicts that relative marital stability is also connected to kinship organization and descent. The relationships between marital stability and type of descent system and kinship organization are, however, far from clear. Matrilineal systems usually give women ready access to means of dissolving undesirable marriages, and matrilocality certainly makes the procedure easier. But, at the same time, these conditions place exceptional pressures on the marriage by surrounding the husband with his wife's kin at every step. And Gluckman (1950) has hypothesized that marital stability would be extremely high in strongly patrilineal societies where women were completely transferred into their husbands' lineages. These and other possibly relevant factors still remain as questions for further study and research.

Summary

1. Marriage as we know it is neither universal nor predominant in human societies. But some sort of socially approved relationship between adult males and females, providing for the fulfillment of sexual needs and the legitimacy of children, *is* necessary and universal.

2. Human sexuality and marriage are related in virtually all known human societies. Sexuality provides the biological basis of

human reproduction and the preservation of the species. Many characteristics of sexuality are shared by *Homo sapiens* and other mammals, but for humans the forms in which these behaviors are expressed are shaped largely by learning and cultural experience. The influence of culture on sexual behavior is particularly evident in the areas of childhood sexuality, precoital stimulation, extramarital sexual activity, and homosexuality, all of which are expressed in a wide range of forms in different societies.

3. No matter how permissive a society may be in sexual matters, there is always some rule limiting the category of appropriate sexual partners. The term *incest taboo* is applied to the prohibition of sexual access to certain categories of kin. The existence of incest prohibitions in some form is almost universal for all members of the nuclear family (except the husband and wife). But the tabooed relationships vary widely. Many theories have been proposed to account for the universality of the incest taboo—among them Freud's psychoanalytic theory, Westermarck's childhood familiarity theory, and the inbreeding theory.

4. *Marriage* is a socially recognized and relatively stable union providing sexual access, legitimating offspring, and establishing other rights and obligations between the marriage partners and other units of society. This definition has almost universal application—except for the case of the Nayar of India.

5. All societies have restrictions on whom one may or may not marry. *Endogamy* is the expectation that a marriage partner will be chosen from within one's own social group. *Exogamy* is the expectation that the choice of a marriage partner will be from a social group of which one is not a member. In every society both endogamous and exogamous groups exist. Anthropologists recognize that marrying outside one's group brings certain benefits to one's group. It also may be related to the necessity for group survival.

6. In some societies, restrictions on marital partners are also accompanied by a preference for marriage with certain other relatives. The most usual preference is for marriage between *cross cousins*. Societies in which such preferences are considered to be obligations are said to have *prescriptive marriage rules*. If such rules are followed generation after generation, close ties between the intermarrying groups will develop. The levirate and the sororate are special cases of prescriptive marriage rules. The *levirate* prescribes that a man marry his brother's widow. The *sororate* prescribes that a man marry the sister of his dead wife.

7. The possible patterns regarding how many persons one may marry at a time are *monogamy,* the marriage of one man to one woman; *polygyny,* the marriage of one man to two or more women; *polyandry,* the marriage of one woman to two or more men; and *group marriage.* Polygyny, polyandy, and group marriage are all forms of *polygamy,* plural marriage.

8. When a marriage occurs, either or both parties must change residence. Possible residence patterns are *neolocal,* in which the couple establishes residence without regard to the residence of the kin group of either partner; *virilocal,* in which the couple lives with or near the groom's family; *uxorilocal,* in which the couple lives with or near the bride's family; *bilocal,* in which the couple may live with or near the parents of either the bride or the groom; *ambilocal,* in which the couple is expected to spend time with the relatives of both the bride and the groom; and *avunculocal,* in which the couple lives with or near the groom's mother's brother. The location of postmarital residence is deeply bound to facets of a society's social and economic system, and it has far-reaching political and psychological consequences.

9. Various exchanges and transactions accompany marriage. Exchanges of women among social groups serve to tie the groups together in economic and political matters.

422 The property and service transactions that may accompany marriage are *bridewealth,* goods given to the bride's kin group by the groom or his kin group; *dowry,* goods given to the bride by her own kin group; *gift exchange* between the two kin groups; *suitor service,* in which the groom lives with and works for the family of the bride for a period of time. All of these marital transactions may be spread out over a period of time.

10. From the comparative perspective of anthropology, *divorce* is the lawful dissolution of the legal ties established at marriage. In many societies, marriage is recognized as a trial-and-error period, and series of marriages are not unusual. Grounds for divorce, economic transactions that accompany divorce, disposition of children, and rules regarding remarriage vary significantly from group to group.

19

Non-kin Groups and Associations

I N the preceding chapters, we discussed some of the social implications of kinship and marriage in small-scale, traditional societies. Although the organization of these societies is dependent more upon the structuring of kinship and marriage, perhaps, than upon any other pattern of social relations, the principles governing kinship, residence, and marriage constitute fundamental building blocks for the formation and maintenance of social institutions in virtually every human society.

We now will turn our attention to other patterns that also contribute to ordered social life. These patterns include ritual kinship ties, the criteria of age and sex in forming groups, secret societies, voluntary associations, and ethnicity. In this chapter, we shall investigate the ways in which all of these are organized, the place each of these plays in ordering social life, and their contributions to social integration and/or conflict. In a later chapter, we will consider caste and social class as other patterns of social organization.

The Nature of Social Groups

First, we must understand the nature of social groups generally before we look at specific instances. *Social groups* are composed of individuals who interact over a period of time in relatively consistent and predictable ways. A group comes into existence for the purpose of achieving certain common aims or goals, and individual members are expected to act in ways that best serve the interests of the group. Even though many social groups form purely for some temporary purpose—such as providing relief for a group of disaster victims—they are distinguishable from crowds, gatherings, and other collectivities that arise spontaneously and dissolve just as quickly after brief, unpredictable interaction. Thus, the members of a religious congregation who gather to worship together every week may be considered a social group, but those individuals who fill a football stadium to urge the home team to a play-off berth are merely members of a crowd.

A social group whose membership is based on face-to-face interactions is called a primary group. Naturally, primary groups are usually relatively small—for example, the members of a conjugal family or the religious congregation mentioned above. *Secondary groups,* on the other hand, are generally large—for example, a clan or all the members of a college's alumni association—although size alone is not a reliable indicator of the nature of a given group. The employees of a small factory, some working days and others nights, would be a secondary group because not all of its members interact on a firsthand basis.

Some of the descent groups discussed in the chapter on kinship are primary groups. Others have become secondary groups, because they are geographically scattered and have been segmented for so long that their members do not always know one another and often will never meet. A social group, then, is defined by its internal organization, that is, according to the ways in which its members are related to one another.

Recruitment to Social Groups

The key to the formation and persistence of any social group is recruitment. If membership in the group is voluntary, there must be ways to encourage prospective members to join. Even if membership is involuntary, there must be some means to compel members to act in the group's best interests. Culture plays a crucial role in encouraging recruitment to social groups.

The rules and procedures of recruitment rarely are so clearly defined or so potent that the individuals involved have no choice over whether they will participate or, conversely, that those nominally excluded may never arrange to become members. Instead, recruitment designates who is *eligible* to join a specific social group. It is often left up to the individual to decide whether to participate in the affairs of the group and, if so, to what degree. There are cases, of course, of groups whose membership is predefined and automatic, such as societies which organize their members into age sets or age grades where no choice is possible to the individual. In a society organized into special age categories, an individual enters the youngest age grade upon reaching a certain age and passes successively to more senior grades as he or she grows older.

Anthropologists who take a structural-functional approach believe that every social group serves an adaptive function in that it enhances the chances of survival for the larger community. For example, among the Masai of East Africa, the age-grade system provides for community defense and protection of herds, communication with neighbors, and maintenance of public order. But the functions of societal institutions and arrangements may change as social needs change. If the Masai were to cease to be herdsmen and turn to agriculture, the economic function of their age grades would either shift to the agricultural sphere or, if this proved impossible, would significantly decline. Similarly, in nineteenth-century America, when horses supplied the chief means of transportation and agricultural power, blacksmithing was a thriving trade, and blacksmiths' associations were numerous and economically powerful. When automobiles and tractors replaced horses and mules, the blacksmith became economically marginal, and his associations vanished because they no longer served a significant function. Thus, technological change as well as function influences the formation and persistence of social groups.

Ritual Kinship

Ritual (or fictive) kinship serves as a bridge between the kin group and the larger society. *Ritual kinship* describes the formalized relationship modeled on kin relations that one may have with a nonkin individual. A common form of ritual kinship is *compadrazgo,* or godparenthood, which itself shares many features both with kinship and with other kinds of social relations. By examining several of the forms ritual kinship may take, we shall be able to see how and why this kind of relationship has come to play an important role in some societies.

Godparenthood is the example of ritual kinship par excellence. Individuals become godparents by agreeing to "sponsor" a child, usually when he or she is baptized. Although the apparent focus of this relationship is on the godparents and the child, the primary focus is on the relationship between the parents and the godparents. The godparents agree to become coparents with the child's actual parents. In other cases of fictive kinship, "brotherhood" is entered into by means of a ritual performed by the individuals themselves. This ritual may involve the mixing, exchange, or ingestion of some ritual substance—blood, saliva, semen, food, alcohol. A weakened form of such ritual may be detected in the sealing of a bargain between two parties with a drink, the drinking of toasts, and the division

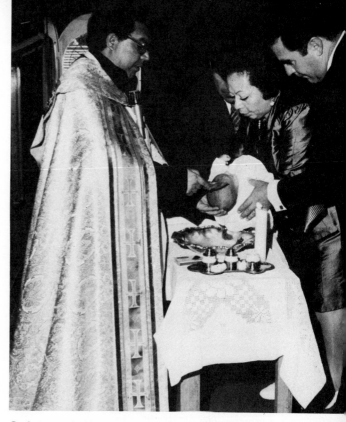

Godparents in Mexico participate in the baptism of their godchild. (Herb Taylor, Editorial Photocolor Archives)

of a large cake for the celebrants at a birthday, wedding, or holiday feast. In some cultures, no direct or formal exchange is necessary. Among the Eskimo, delivery by the same midwife establishes a bond of brotherhood. In fact, children delivered by the same midwife are subject to an incest taboo, perhaps because the Eskimo stress roles (as brother and sister) rather than position in such matters.

From the point of view of the community, there are advantages of *compadrazgo* and other forms of ritual kinship. The system of obligations and prestige placed upon the parties to such a relationship makes "the immediate social environment more stable, the participants more interdependent and more secure" (Mintz & Wolf, 1950, p. 344). It does this by linking in a relationship of mutual obligation and trust members of society who would not otherwise be related. In some cases, it serves as a social leveling device by which the poor have access to more wealthy members of the community. In other cases, ritual kinship may serve to unite individuals for other purposes. For instance, two men may establish a *fictive kin* relationship in order to avert a possible adultery (and the jealousy and hostility that might ensue) between the wife of one and a close male friend of the family. In small societies, such jealousy is not only disruptive but can lead to fission of groups into population levels that may make subsistence difficult. By establishing a ritual kinship that entails sacred privileges and obligations, possible trouble is nipped in the bud (Pitt-Rivers, 1973). Ritual kinship serves as an addition to actual kinship in most cases. An adopted kinsman does not give up the association with his or her real kin. Because ritual kinship may serve functions and needs that actual kinship does not, the two relationships may coexist.

The most striking contrast between ritual and actual kinship involves the matter of choice, already noted. Parents are free, at least in theory, to ask any other members of the community to serve as godparents to their children. Sometimes godparents are chosen from a social group that has higher prestige and/or wealth than the social group of the infants' parents. This ensures access to—and the possibility of help from—the social group represented by the godparents. Mintz and Wolf (1950) point out that parents choose godparents from outside their own social group only when there is cultural or economic reason to do so. For example, a local peasant who has no hope of achieving upward mobility either for himself or his children is unlikely to seek godparents outside the peasantry. Instead he would seek, by his choice of *compadres,* to solidify his position within his own group or community. Mintz and Wolf (1950) provide several other examples that serve to illustrate this point.

The Maya Indians of Tusik, in the Yucatan Peninsula, comprise an agricultural society, raising maize, which they consume, and chicle, the only cash crop. No member of the society enjoys inherently higher economic status than the others, although some may accumulate more wealth by extracting more chicle than their neighbors. They carry on their trade with traveling merchants, with whom they enjoy good relations. But they make no effort to bind the merchants to the community by choosing them as *compadres,* preferring instead to employ the child's grandparents or tribal chiefs for this purpose. The reasons for this seem to lie in the fact that there are no social means of mobility between the Tusik Maya community and the broader society. Since the Tusik Maya apparently lack any effective mechanism for improving economic relations with the merchants or an acceptable means for attaining prestige with members of an outside group, they are content to confer *compadrazgo* upon their own folk.

The sugar cane fields around Barrio Poyal, a rural community on Puerto Rico's southern coast, were formerly owned by local plantation owners. Residents of the barrio who make up the labor force once chose compadres for their children from among these wealthy landholders, but now that the land is owned by large corporations, the workers pick as *compadres* their neighbors and fellow workers. Members of the managerial and entrepreneurial class—foremen, administrators, public officials, shopkeepers—are shunned because they no longer interact with the workers. Furthermore, many workers migrate to the United States and no longer provide a stable working-class community. Today, if a worker seeks a wealthy *compadre,* he is criticized by his compatriots. In this case, the lesson seems clear: unless there are social and economic advantages to *compadre* relationships, these will disintegrate and disappear.

A contrasting example is provided by the practice of *compadrazgo* in Moche, a community on the coast of Peru. The Mocheros, who are native to Peru, are rapidly assimilating a Spanish way of life, owning land individually, taking jobs outside the community, and entering the professions. But although many native customs have died out, *compadrazgo* has grown stronger than ever before. Godparents are sought not only among the Mocheros but from outside the community as well. According to Gillin (1945), parents aspire to secure godparents who are well-off, influential, and socially well-connected and who will help both child and parents to achieve social and economic advancement. Thus, ritual kinship serves to support social mobility when it is already present, but it cannot establish social mobility in and of itself.

The case of Moche reveals the attempts of a community to reduce as much as possible the friction between itself and the larger society with which it seeks to merge. By this means, the process of assimilation is facilitated. Other examples provided by Mintz and Wolf, such as San José, a coffee and farming community in Puerto Rico, reveal how *compadrazgo* may stabilize relations between landholders and agricultural workers or between large and small landholders in an area where little or no social mobility is possible. Large landholders serve as *compadres* for small landlords, and small landholders for landless workers. In this manner, important social links are provided in a society where inequality of wealth could produce friction and potential conflict.

Social Categories Recruited by Age

Age Grades

All known societies differentiate members according to age. Our English terms infant, child, youth, teen-ager, adult, and elder, among others, all indicate age categories, however imprecisely defined. They differ from the age terms found in other societies by lacking clearly defined boundaries. Except for teen-ager, we would be unable to set with certainty the chronological limits of any of these terms. If we were to try, we would discover a good deal of overlapping adjacent terms. For example, youth and teen-ager appear to refer to similar age periods, but for many they are probably not identical. We might think of some preteens as youths and some teen-agers as adults. In fact, we would be unable to agree on the age at which a member of our society becomes an adult, although a number of possibilities suggest themselves, such as the minimum age for voting or entering military service, marrying without parents' permission, or even viewing an X-rated film.

So much imprecision and variance in our classification of age categories may lead us to suspect that our society lacks *age grades*—categories of persons arranged according to age only. This suspicion is correct, for, in fact, our society does lack a specific, uniform set of terms designating age grades, and we do not designate age grades at all. Of the terms we examined earlier, some have fairly precise definition, but others do not. For example, how should we refer to the newborn: infant, baby, or child? The law, whose terms best approach the technical precision of age grades in our language, uses only the term infant for anyone who is not an adult. This state of affairs may be contrasted with the Masai, for example, who divide their males into uninitiated youths, young men or warriors, elders, and ancient elders (Gulliver, 1965). Every male in the community belongs to one of these grades—and over the course of his life, he may belong to all of them. The roles and behaviors of each grade are so specific that every male knows what is expected of him both in public and private life as a member of the age grade.

These boys of the Namba tribe have been initiated into puberty by a rite of passage, which consists of circumcision, a period of segregation, a washing ceremony, and a feast, after which they return to the community. (Kal Muller, Woodfin Camp)

A system of age grades is characterized by orderly sequence of membership from one grade to another and specific behavior required of members of a given age grade toward members of one's own and of other grades. Entry into the lowest grade occurs at a specified age. Members of younger grades pass into progressively older ones at certain times, usually either when they, as individuals, reach a particular age or when an entire age grade is initiated into the next grade in the sequence. Whether shifts of grade are done on an individual or on a group basis, they are usually accompanied by some rite of passage or some other ceremony such as a feast.

The Jie of Uganda appear to have a rather straightforward age-grade system. Generations are established at approximately 25-year intervals, when members of the junior generation begin to be initiated. There are, in theory, only two generations, senior and junior, though in fact there are generally a number of young men and boys too young to go through the initiation ceremony with the current junior generation. They will be held over to form part of the next junior generation. Each generation adopts a name, usually of some animal—buffalo, jackal, snake, leopard—and small groups form within generations, also according to age. The age-grade system of the Jie serves to perpetuate traditional ritual activity and to establish ranking and leadership according to seniority. Seniority is precisely established and carefully maintained. Within a group, any member of a senior group is senior to all members of junior groups.

However, the actual operation of the Jie age-grade system is not as straightforward as it sounds. Seniority may not be determined simply by chronological age. For example, A may be senior to B because his father was senior to B's father, though A himself may be younger than B. This determination of seniority is a common feature of age-grade systems. It is also common for entry into one's age grade to be postponed for a number of reasons. If the initiation period is long, a prospective initiate may be held back by his family if his labor is needed at home. If initiation is expensive, it may be postponed because a family cannot afford the fees. In other cases, initiation into age grades may be accelerated. A man may marry young, thus graduating from the bachelor grade to the grade of married men. Or a young man may be suddenly promoted to the status of head of family because his father has died, although his coequals continue to be members of the "boys" grade. There are thus many cases where the age grade of an individual may be at odds with the chronological age (Gulliver, 1965).

Many age-grade systems are organized around specific biological or developmental events rather than other features of age. The age-grade systems of the Kayapó of Brazil are an example of this sort of developmental classification. Unlike the Jie, the Kayapó rank both males and females according to age in a number of grades ranging from infancy to old age. The stage representing infancy lasts up to approximately the age of 4. A single term is used to refer to both boys and girls in this grade. From about 4 to 8 years old, children are referred to as "little boys" and "little girls"; and from then until they are approximately 12 years of age as "boys" and "girls."

The next stage, the initiation into manhood or womanhood, shows clearly the developmental properties of Kayapó age grades. Initiation into adulthood takes place when the youth becomes capable of producing children, sometime between his or her twelfth and sixteenth years, and is a true puberty rite. The initiation period of young women is quite brief, but that of young men consists of a 4-month isolation in the forest. This difference between the sexes is typical of age grades in many societies. Initiation into manhood involves a number of other individuals of the same age, whereas initiation into womanhood tends to occur without so much public recognition. Thus, initiation into adulthood tends to

430 be a more public and social occasion for young men than for young women.

By the time they are 18, most Kayapó young men and women have already married, thereby passing into the adult age grade. At this point, terminological distinctions between male and female vanish (as they were absent in infancy). The Kayapó use different terms for childless adults, adults with one child, and those with two or more children. Another term designates grandparents or people old enough to be grandparents.

At his initiation to manhood, a young man joins the men's society to which his nonkin guardian, or "substitute father," belongs. However, he does not become an active member of the men's house until he marries and his wife has borne a child. He is therefore excluded from participating in the important political activity of the society and village. But he may engage in sporting events such as wrestling and field hockey with senior members and participate in village rituals, singing, and dancing. Thus, the men's houses allow for

the expression and resolution of hostility among members, especially between younger and older members, by creating certain traditional modes of rivalry (Bamberger, 1976). By the time the young man joins the adult age grade in his society and begins to participate in village affairs, he will have successfully integrated his own interests with those of the community.

Age Sets

As we have seen, the term *age grade* refers to a category of people ordered according to age. An *age set,* on the other hand, identifies the group of members of a given age grade who pass together through various life stages. Age sets are usually given names and take on a group identity. The name may be a traditional one, used on a rotating basis with a number of others. Or it may be used once, then retired and never repeated. To illustrate, although we do not specify age grades and age sets in our society, we might roughly consider the cate-

Masai warriors of Kenya, with heads freshly shaved, assemble inside the circle of huts built especially for the ceremony in which they move into the junior elder age set. (Jen and Des Bartlett, Photo Researchers)

Figure 1 Nandi age-set system. (Adapted from Huntingford, 1953)

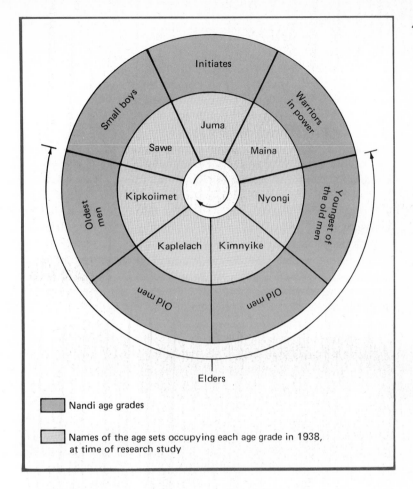

☐ Nandi age grades

☐ Names of the age sets occupying each age grade in 1938, at time of research study

gory "college freshman" as an age grade, while a particular freshman class—(say, class of 1984)—would be somewhat equivalent to an age set.

Members of a single age set enjoy certain privileges and have certain duties in relation to other members. They may be expected to offer one another support in arguments or fights, to lend money or offer other economic help as necessary, and in general to be generous and helpful to one another. Toward members of older age sets they must usually be respectful and obedient, but at the same time they often have the right to expect indulgence and favors from their seniors. One age set may exert some control over younger

age sets, but its members must usually present an example of proper behavior.

An example of an age-set system of some complexity is provided by the Nandi of Kenya. The influence of the age-set system upon military and political life is profound, and it plays an important role in regulating social and kinship behavior as well. Every Nandi male is a member of one of seven age sets; each set consists of the males born during a period of approximately 15 years. Each set, identified by a name that is kept throughout the lifetime of its members, passes through the following age grades: small boys (uncircumcised), young men (circumcised), warriors in power, and four sets of elders. (See Figure

1.) The changeover of each set from one grade to the next is marked by ceremonies, the most important of which is the circumcision ceremony. Each set moves through the various age grades; finally, the name of the age set of the oldest men passes around to the bottom of the cycle to the next set of small boys. In addition, each age set is subdivided into four *mats,* or associating groups, which remain constant as the members pass through the various grades. Huntingford explains these groups as follows: "The word *mat* . . . means 'fire,' and the term is derived from 'the fire that roars in the seclusion huts . . . of those who are being circumcised, and those who share such a hut are of the same mat.'" Members of the set of young men (initiates) gradually assume the duties of the warriors in power, thus allowing for gradual retirement of older members and continuity of power (Huntingford, 1953). Thus, age may serve as an important criterion for incorporating members of society into significant groups that share common identity and purpose.

Social Categories Recruited by Gender

Just as all societies establish social categories according to age, so gender is universally employed as a means of sorting people in one form or another. Mothers are distinguished from fathers in all societies purely on the basis of the biological differences between them, although the role of a mother in relation to her child and husband is not identical in every case. Here we will focus on the ways in which gender serves to recruit individuals into groups and categories of various sorts all over the world.

Groups consisting solely of men are more common the world over than those with entirely female membership. The men's houses of tropical South America, various parts of Africa, and Oceania are common examples of groups recruited according to gender. In many cases, the men's houses or societies have important ritual functions. But these practices often seem to do little more than mask the groups' role as the principal economic, political, and social force in the community.

In most societies in which it appears, the men's house serves as a meeting place and the area for preparation and storage of ritual paraphernalia. It may also serve as a dormitory for village men who must avoid becoming impure or polluted by living with women during their menstrual periods, for visitors, or for young bachelors. The chief purpose of the men's house, however, is to provide a place where men may discuss trade and hunting expeditions, warfare and politics, and everyday affairs. Affiliation with a men's house confers considerable prestige upon a male.

In a typical village containing them, the men's houses stand in the center of the community, surrounded at the periphery by the family dwellings and any other village buildings, such as the chapel or school. Distinguished by its position and size—the men's house is invariably the largest building in the village—it is a physical reminder of the significance of the social, economic, and political activities conducted there. Women are generally forbidden to enter the men's house and are confined to the domestic dwellings on the periphery of the village.

It might be expected that the men's houses and the societies that conduct their business within them would reduce the factionalism in the social group at large that often results from kinship loyalties and interests and thus produce social harmony. However, this is not necessarily the case. The Ge of Brazil, for example, promote aggressiveness, rather than harmony, as a virtue (Maybury-Lewis, 1974). Women in particular seem to be the targets of

Men's houses are familiar features of communities in South America, Africa, and Oceania. Here, Kamayara men of Brazil sit in front of their men's house. (Loren McIntyre, Woodfin Camp)

aggression in many men's societies among the Ge, but the aggression is not by any means confined to them. Aggressive relations are the rule between men of different factions within the same group, as well as in relations with outsiders. Maybury-Lewis attributes this antagonism to the strong sense of difference between a member's feelings about his own group and all other groups. Even in societies like that of the Sherente of Brazil, which are not organized around men's houses and associations, each village reveals a two-faction system and a strong sense of opposition

between factions. Those societies that stress aggression between age sets or genders express this aggression in open hostility.

Although men's groups are more common than are groups composed solely of women, some societies—the Plains Indians, for example—organize both men's and women's social groups. The Cheyenne had men's societies devoted to the making of shields and women's groups specializing in weaving. Membership in each was similarly restricted, and each group's work was equally guarded by secrecy and ceremony (Grinnell, 1962).

Virtually every society recruits members to social groups according to gender, and this preference is variously explained by each society. The important point to note here, however, is that gender constitutes a means whereby some members are included and others are excluded from a given social group.

Secret Societies

Another type of nonkin social grouping—secret societies—exists in one form or other all over the world. Much of what we know about their organization and function derives from studies of the secret societies of West and Central Africa. In these areas, secret societies have flourished, serving ends accomplished elsewhere by age grades and other nonkin groups. In West Africa, for example, secret societies superintend training in social conduct, teach local crafts and traditional lore, determine and enforce sexual and marriage codes, play key roles in tribal trade and politics, perform medical services, serve as local judiciary, conduct religious affairs, and provide entertainment and recreation. They also establish a social bond among members who may otherwise be loyal to different tribes, families, or territories and thus integrate a much larger population.

One of the key activities of any secret society involves the initiation and indoctrination of new members. The activities of the initiated group may vary slightly from those of other social groups in societies without secret organizations. But the fact that here it is accompanied by secrecy serves to strengthen new members' obedience to the authority of the group.

The initiation rites of the Poro society of the West African Mende show the breadth of the education received by initiates as well as the emphasis that is placed upon the group's social and spiritual nature.

The Poro

The initiation period of the Poro commences with a ceremony of feasting and ritual during which the young boys are marked or scarred on their backs in a manner symbolizing that they have been "swallowed" by the snake spirit, the marks having been made by the spirit's teeth. After a period of training in the bush, the boys emerge as if reborn and are granted full adult status in the community.

The training period consists of lessons in lore, crafts, politics, and law. The boys are expected to endure hardship in the bush, to cooperate with their companions in providing for the group, to participate in tribal ritual on cue, and to learn various points of lore and crafts from local specialists who instruct them. In Mende society these specialties include native law and practices, agriculture, building, weaving, fishing and trapping, drumming, singing, and acrobatics.

One important effect of the initiation practice and a source of its value to the community—as well as a key to the survival of the secret societies themselves—is the attachment that it engenders among members of the initiation group. Torn from their families at a rather early age and subjected to an experience that is exciting, strange, and somewhat terrifying, the initiates rapidly develop a sense of loyalty to their cohorts—a "corporate sense," as Little (1949) expresses it—that transcends local feelings arising from family, village, tribe, and even religion. A different secret society among the Mende regulates marriage and mating in the community. This society, called the Humoi, is headed by a woman. It determines to whom marriage is permissible, what constitutes forbidden and incestuous intercourse, rules of sexual hygiene, and punishment and compensation for infraction of its rules. If a trial or hearing were necessary in the event of a sexual transgression, however, it would be conducted by the Poro, which is the judicial body of the Mende. The courts of the Poro are composed of senior members of the society, who are usually also political leaders and whose authority and influence, especially when they sit in judgment masked as *jamu* (Great Masked Figure), is considerable.

Although the importance of secret societies such as the Poro has waned because of persecution from colonial governments, their influence continues to be strong. Initiation continues to be practiced, although it is briefer than it once was. Political leaders among the Mende invariably belong to one of the secret societies. The Poro determines the seasons for fishing, planting, and harvesting; sets rates for labor; regulates trade in certain areas; and even issues its own currency. It is no wonder that there is some tension and conflict between formal colonial governments and the powerful secret societies that serve many of the functions that governments seek to control.

Secret societies serve ritual and entertainment functions as well. Important events in the community are often marked by celebrations featuring the spirits of the secret societies, one of whose purposes is to amuse and entertain. Each spirit is impersonated in these celebrations by a member of the group who is hidden entirely behind a wooden mask. The "spirit" dances through the town accompanied by attendants, pausing to perform in front of the houses of prominent villagers. On occasion it dances to the beating of a drummer or, if the event is unusually important, to the singing of a group of women and the percussion of rattles and drums. Members of the community eager to achieve or maintain prominence throw money at the dancers (Little, 1949).

Secret societies are not confined to tribal cultures but may be found in every type of social organization. In our own society, secret societies may develop when other legal and educational institutions fail to accomplish what a number of individuals desire. They operate in secret, sometimes because their activities are outside the law, at other times because secrecy permits the members to carry out their objectives more easily, especially if those objectives could not gain approval from the larger society. In every society, whether or not formal secret societies exist, some forms of knowledge or skill are kept secret and remain the special province of a single group. Although secrecy is universally held to be advantageous, some societies do not form secret organizations to achieve their goals. Rather, they form age grades, associations of other sorts, or even informal groupings.

Voluntary Associations

In the United States in 1968 there were close to 11,000 national associations devoted to everything from sports, religion, and education to science and business. The diversity of these groups reflects the range of interests in our society. From the American Society of Golf Course Architects to the American Vegetarian Union and the Society of Descendants of Colonial Clergy, people join social groups whose interests and needs in some way match their own. Such groups are called voluntary associations.

A *voluntary associaton* is any group that one joins by choice in order to accomplish a common purpose. It contrasts with kinship and age groups to which one belongs by virtue of birth and maturation and with other groups in which membership is compulsory. In general, the more developed and urbanized the society, the greater the number and importance of voluntary associations. For example, in small, technologically simple societies, voluntary as-

Voluntary associations to help and protect migrant farm workers have grown in power as they have changed into modern trade unions. (Mimi Forsyth, Monkmeyer)

sociations often provide only recreation and may indicate distinctions in social rank. In larger, more complex societies such as our own, they also tend to serve political, economic, and even military functions.

One example that provides an excellent contrast between the organization of a small group on the basis of kinship and the more complex organization made possible through the formation of voluntary associations is offered by the Blackfoot Indians, who roamed the Great Plains in the nineteenth century and subsisted mainly by hunting buffalo. From autumn through early spring, grazing was poor and the buffalo divided into small herds. The Blackfoot correspondingly banded in small kin groups to hunt. In late spring and summer, however, the buffalo formed huge herds because grazing was abundant. The Blackfoot then organized on a larger basis by forming associations that migrated, hunted, and cele-

brated together. The choice of association was, within limits, up to the individual, so these large communities were voluntary in nature, even though every Blackfoot joined one or another of them (Banton, 1968).

Such voluntary associations were more closely connected to matters of survival than are voluntary organizations in technological societies. Yet, voluntary associations may fulfill similar functions today. The Blackfoot availed themselves of voluntary groups in order to solve problems that arose cyclically or periodically. Nowadays, an association may be formed to deal with a problem that arises rather suddenly as the result of rapid technological change or the migration of people from villages and towns to large cities. Industrialization in many societies has presented workers with unprecedented problems with which they deal by forming workers' associations that, in many cases, evolve into modern trade unions. But the problems of the worker who comes to the city from the countryside may not be confined to the work place. In some instances, workers' associations have become involved in matters of health, death, legal aid, unemployment, and savings. We recognize in these the health plans, burial insurance, legal aid groups, funds for workers who have been laid off, and credit unions that are frequent adjuncts of trade union organization. In small-scale societies, functions similar to these are served by kinship.

Similar organizations, in this country and elsewhere, are based upon the geographic or ethnic identity of their members rather than upon common occupation. In Sierra Leone, these groups are known as dancing *compins* (Creole for companies) and serve as mutual aid and protection societies as well as means to bridge the gap between small-town and urban life. Membership is sometimes open, but most members of a single association come from the same region or social group. Equivalent groups also exist in Ghana and Nigeria (Little, 1967).

Among the functions served by such voluntary associations are the following: financial assistance to members, especially those who must make the transition to an economy based chiefly on money; orientation to an environment consisting of diverse cultural and racial groups; teaching members how to dress and act in their unfamiliar surroundings; and protection of members, especially women, while they adjust to new social and sexual customs. These associations often have rules protecting the female members against seduction; they may fine members who are found guilty of adultery or other behavior detrimental to the good reputation of the society. On the other hand, members who run afoul of the law are assisted by the association, and members are encouraged to settle their differences through the association.

In general, voluntary associations such as these in Africa try to foster the feeling of an extended family among their members; to encourage the intimacy and generosity that is more characteristic of families than the formal, legal relations of the city; and to offer comfort and sociability. These practices foster feelings of solidarity among members and provide protection from other groups who are not sympathetic to them. They also help to form a base of self-interest from which political power may often be pursued by members of the association.

The common thread that runs through organizations of migrants to West African towns and cities extends also to associations of migrant laborers and squatters in the United States and elsewhere. In several parts of Latin America, and in North Africa, Turkey, and Iraq, residents of migrant settlements have organized committees aimed at providing electricity, running water, and other amenities of urban life. Many of the features of traditional "neighborhoods"—visiting, mutual aid, and benevolent relations—are in evidence despite the relative deprivation of individual residents and the absence of similar relations with people outside the immediate vicinity. Studies have suggested that life in the migrant settlements is usually less desperate and predatory than slum life in the same city or town.

As we have just seen, voluntary associations are often organized for the purpose of achieving specific, often temporary, goals. They thus reveal a flexibility that other social groups may lack and may be formed and disbanded when it is convenient to do so. Task forces formed to attack a single social or political problem, tenants' groups organized to force a landlord to make needed repairs, volunteers who collect food and clothing for people left homeless after a flood, or concerned citizens who respond to the mayor's call for volunteers to clean up a local park—all are examples of the kinds of voluntary associations that form briefly in our own society, accomplish their goals, and then pass just as quickly into oblivion.

"Ethnicity" and Ethnic Groups

Ethnicity is one of those terms that has come to mean all things to all people and is consequently impossible to define with any precision. Nevertheless, it is used here because it does call attention to group identity that cannot be distinguished on any other clear basis. Although it includes kinship, ethnicity is wider and larger in its reach than any arrangement of kinship. It is generally agreed among anthropologists that an *ethnic group* is a population with the following traits: it is biologically self-perpetuating; shares fundamental cultural values which are expressed in unified cultural forms; is charac-

terized by internal communication and interaction; and is considered by itself and others to have particular identity (Barth, 1969). The features of this particular identity are cultural similarities and differences that the members of the ethnic group itself consider significant. These are not necessarily features that individuals outside the group would regard as identifying characteristics. Barth finds such identifiers to be of two types: (1) overt or obvious signs that people everywhere use to show identity, such as language, dress, or housing; and (2) basic values, the standards by which performance and activity are judged. Again, it is the individual members of the group—and not people outside the group—to whom these features are meaningful. Membership in an ethnic group, then, results from the individual's self-identification as part of the group. By emphasizing their similarities to

The Amish are a still-recognizable ethnic group within American society. (David Strickler, Monkmeyer)

the overt features and basic values shared by others in the group, individuals declare "allegiance" to the ethnic group (Barth, 1969, pp. 14–15).

The Amish are an example of a recognizable ethnic group within the larger American society. They retain a distinctive appearance, pursue a life style that is at odds with increasingly technological habits, and insist upon their own educational system in order to teach their young people Amish values rather than those of the society at large. Thus, the Amish have managed "to maintain cultural continuity and cultural integrity, to remain a discrete minority, steadfast to their own vision of the good life" (Hostetler & Huntington, 1971, p. 116).

In addition to those communitarian societies like the Amish which maintain their identity by living in relative isolation from the larger community, there are ethnic groups which are not geographically isolated. Some degree of concentration and communication must be maintained, however, in order for ethnicity to persist. Identifying another person as a member of one's own ethnic group allows for further expansion of the social relationship between the two, especially in communities (such as large cities) where ethnic groups are not geographically isolated. Two such people recognize that they are, as Barth puts it, "playing the same game" (1969, p. 15). Thus, they are more likely to share understandings, judgments, and interests than they would be if they were not of the same group.

Likewise, one of the functions of ethnicity is that it structures interactions between groups. Specifically, ethnicity may facilitate successful commerce, especially for a group that is itself reluctant to engage in trade. In Thailand, for example, where the belief that commerce is "crooked" persists, the native population is ill-disposed to involvement in trade. "Crookedness" has been exemplified by villagers as "selling for more than the purchase price" (that is, making a profit) as well as giv-ing short weight and offering goods of poor quality. Much of the commerce in Thai society is, therefore, conducted by foreigners and particularly by the Mon, a prominent minority group that began to emigrate from Burma in the sixteenth century.

In many respects, the Thai and Mon are culturally and racially similar, but the Mon practice elements of Buddhism borrowed from India and retain their own language as well. They engage extensively in Thai trade, especially in the manufacture and sale of bricks and pottery, the selling of thatch and firewood, and the hauling of these and other goods on boats and barges. They are able to engage in commerce because their ethnic differences permit them to minimize the friction inherent in trade, by ignoring the cultural discouragements from trading found among the Thai (Foster, 1974).

Ethnic groups often do not share the goals and objectives either of the larger community or the other ethnic groups who are their neighbors. As a result, multiethnic communities often experience conflicts and tensions among groups. The nature of these conflicts and the importance of resolving or controlling them will be discussed in the next chapter. Non-kin groups and associations, then, serve common purposes within the broader social system of which they form a part. They provide group identity and give a means for expression of common values.

Summary

1. A *social group* is distinguished from a casual gathering by its organization, duration, and predictability. Although kinship is the basis for organizing social relations in small-scale traditional societies, other groups are re-

cruited on the basis of age and gender. Still others are formed on the basis of voluntary association. Every social group, if it is to persist, must serve a useful function in society, and thus may change or disappear as social needs change. In industrialized, large-scale societies, an increasing number of social functions are served by voluntary associations.

2. *Ritual kinship,* of which *compadrazgo* is a classic example, serves to unite unequal elements of a larger social unit when other mechanisms in the society do not do so. It may function among members of the same group, as well as different groups, to increase interdependence and mutual security. Social or economic gain may be intended as well. Ritual kinship provides person-to-person relationships in an increasingly impersonal social structure and is a transition from kin-based to urban, industrial-based societies.

3. All societies categorize their members by means of age, but some more than others. An *age grade* refers to a category of people grouped according to age, through which members of a society pass at some stage of life. An *age set* is the specific group of people occupying a given age grade at a single time. A strict age-grade system entails orderly sequence and a code of rules governing relations between grades. Age grades participate in the conduct of important affairs including economic, political, military, and ritual activities.

4. Categorization according to gender is also common to all societies. Gender often serves to promote male control of the community. Men's societies are often identified with a men's house placed at the center of the village, from which women are excluded and where political, economic, and military discussions are held. Men's societies frequently serve ritual functions as well; their rituals commonly express hostility toward women and outsiders. Although men's groups are more commonly found than women's groups, many societies contain both.

5. Secret societies often develop to accomplish some objective not served by the broader society. These objectives may include education, the settling of disputes and legal questions, determination of political and economic policy, ritual expression, and entertainment. Secret societies almost always require lengthy, arduous initiation of new members, which serves to instill respect for authority and ensure their continuance in power. Initiation also binds those initiated together. Even cultures lacking secret societies usually reserve some knowledge or skill for a select few.

6. *Voluntary associations,* including many nonkin groups, are those which members join freely. In general, voluntary associations are more numerous in more complex societies, as they are better suited to promoting the political and economic goals of those societies. They often provide assistance to immigrants who are unfamiliar with the new environment and who join associations, often consisting of members from their native region, which assist their adjustment to their new experiences. In many instances, trade unions were originally workers' associations that served health, financial, legal, social, and educational needs of members. Migrants and squatters often form similar organizations.

7. *Ethnic groups* are biologically self-perpetuating, share and express common cultural values, demonstrate internal interaction, and are considered by themselves and others to be a distinct group.

20
Social Control

IN the preceding chapter, we focused on the various rules that govern the formation of social groups in small-scale, traditional societies, as well as on some of the functions that these groups perform. In this chapter, our emphasis shifts to the topic of how social order is maintained. That is, we will look at the question of what makes people in a society act in the ways they are expected to act. How does any given society get its members to conform to its expectations and requirements? These questions were touched on in an earlier chapter where we discussed the relationship between the individual and culture. It will become apparent, also, that many of the non-kin groups that we discussed in the preceding chapter play a significant role in maintaining social order, and that many of their functions will also be pertinent here. Politics touches on the topic of social control as well. We will look at politics in a separate chapter later in the book; here we will focus on the kinds of control mechanisms that operate independent of political processes per se.

Conformity, Deviance, and Social Order

The problem of social order is basic in all of the social sciences. All consider principles of integration—that is, explanations of why and how humans interact with one another in meaningful and practical ways. The most basic integrating principles in a society are its rules, which govern such minor matters as table manners, and important ones such as trade and litigation. Many of these rules operate at an unconscious level. Individual members of a group are often unable to express in specific

Imprisonment is a formal means of social control that occurs most frequently in large nation states; small-scale societies tend to use other kinds of sanctions. (Paul Conklin, Monkmeyer)

customary, or they may be formally expressed as law.

Every society not only defines what it considers to be deviant or unacceptable behavior but also provides means for dealing with individuals who behave in deviant or unacceptable ways. The means of dealing with such behavior are known as *sanctions.* If, for instance, you take off all your clothes on a public beach and go swimming in the nude, you may be arrested, or at least get strange looks from the other bathers, depending on the beach. But sanctions take many forms besides strange looks or a night in jail. They are, in fact, some of the most diverse institutions studied in anthropology, as we shall see in this chapter.

Why Do People Conform?

Freud argued that social standards or rules are often at odds with individual drives and desires. The result is that people must block and sometimes suppress some of their basic drives. In recent years, this point of view has been modified somewhat. Society is increasingly regarded as channeling rather than blocking individual urges. But whether basic drives are blocked or channeled, the question that remains is, why do individuals conform to the rules of a society? Why don't they simply ignore what is expected of them and act totally in accord with their own desires and interests? What makes a person wear a bathing suit on a deserted beach when he or she could probably get away with swimming in the nude? Why does the driver of an automobile stop and wait through a red light at 3 A.M., when there are no other cars in sight? These are the kinds of questions that interest anthropologists and others involved in the control of human behavior.

terms the nature of the rules they are following. When rules *are* known and individuals are able to comment on them, anthropologists have frequently found that the rules are not always clear or unambiguous. Whether they operate at conscious or unconscious levels or both, rules embody a society's norms, its notions of acceptable and unacceptable behavior. As we shall see, rules may be unwritten and

Consensus Versus Coercion

In a discussion on social conflict, Ralf Dahrendorf (1959) presents two models that social scientists have used to account for the order and coherence of society: consensus and coercion. The *consensus model* is based on the idea that social order results from the general agreement of the members of a society on a set of values that are more important to them than any differences of opinion they may have. In short, it focuses on social commonalities. This model assumes that

1. every society is relatively stable;
2. every society is a system of interrelated or integrated position and roles;
3. each element in the system has a function (that is, it contributes something to the continuation of the system); and
4. the system is based on agreement among its members as to fundamental values and goals.

This model, as exemplified by the theories of Talcott Parsons and Radcliffe-Brown, dominated sociological and anthropological thought in the mid-twentieth century. As we discussed in an earlier chapter, one way by which individuals reach general agreement as to values and goals is through socialization. This is the process by which an individual internalizes the rules of his or her society. It provides the person with a recognizable identity as a group member. Internalization leads individuals to act the way they are expected to act without being fully aware that they are doing so. If, for example, you are convinced that it is wrong to steal, you will not steal even when it is clear to you that you would not get caught. Socialization is an important element in social order.

The *coercion model* presents a sharp contrast to the consensus model. It focuses on differences among members of society. The model is based on the belief that social order is a product of force and constraint. Its central idea is that there must always be some people who dominate and some others who are dominated. The assumptions of this model are that

1. every society is continually undergoing change;
2. every society displays disagreement and conflict;
3. each element in the structure of a society contributes to its disintegration; and
4. every society is based on coercion of some members by others.

Karl Marx, among others, held a conflict model of history.

These two models of social order are basic to all social thought, and both are widely used. They have generally been considered to be mutually exclusive. That is, if a society is stable, it cannot be continually changing; if every element in the society is contributing to the continuity of the whole, it cannot at the same time be contributing to its disintegration; and so on. Dahrendorf suggests, however, that it is not necessary to adhere to one model and reject the other entirely. There are some questions that fit the framework of the consensus model while others can be explained only in terms of the coercion model. Still others can be analyzed using either model. In short, the two models may be seen as complementary rather than alternative. As we have seen, some models may apply more to particular problems than do others.

How can these apparently contradictory models be viewed as complementary? According to Dahrendorf, every society is characterized by all the factors we have mentioned: stability coexists with change, integration with conflict, consensus with coercion. In fact, none of these factors can exist in the absence of its opposite. There can be no conflict if there is no integrated system within which conflict may occur. For example, conflict is unlikely between American hockey players and Tibetan monks because they do not share a common frame of reference. When conflicts do occur, as they often do in hockey matches, the source of the conflict is the differing interests of those involved.

Formal Versus Informal Control

Yehudi A. Cohen (1971) uses both the consensus model and the coercion model in accounting for the maintenance of social order. In his view, consensus is more prevalent in societies operating under informal control mechanisms such as customs. Coercion is found more frequently in societies that have specialized legal institutions and roles. Since this distinction between formal and informal mechanisms will serve as the framework for the rest of this chapter, it is worth discussing it in some detail here. Before we continue, however, we should mention the problem of relativity encountered in any comparison of social control mechanisms in different societies. As we have seen, not all societies hold people liable for the same acts. Even when they are held liable for the same acts, they may not be punished in the same way or to the same degree. Killing, for instance, is not always considered criminal in all societies. When killing *is* considered a criminal act, in some societies the guilt must be shared by the kinsmen of the murderer, whereas in other societies only the murderer is subject to punishment.

With this warning about relativity in mind, we will turn to the definitions of informal (or customary) control and formal control. *Informal control* consists of traditional or customary rules, beliefs, and procedures that are not arranged systematically. In some cases, as we mentioned earlier, some of these customary rules operate at an unconscious level. Cohen points out that resolution of disputes by informal control occurs in face-to-face, interpersonal contacts. *Formal control,* on the other hand, is characterized by a systematized set of rules and procedures—laws—for managing disputes. In systems of formal control, institutions and individuals emerge to interpret and enforce the law. This distinction between formal and informal systems of control is largely artificial. It does not mean that informal techniques are no longer in use in complex societies, nor does it mean that fairly formal control cannot be achieved without formal institutions. The distinction is useful, however, in that it helps us to identify the legal forms used in any given society. The distinction is purely analytic made for the purpose of understanding the differences and similarities among the ways in which social order is maintained in various societies.

Types of Informal Control Mechanisms

There are many informal means by which a society can get its members to act in expected ways so that the social system will function smoothly. Informal mechanisms are many and varied, as the following examples show.

The Reference Group. The concept of *reference group* has been developed most fully in social psychology and sociology. It refers to groups with which individuals either identify themselves as members or aspire to be identified. By adopting the values and interests of the group, individuals not only increase their chances of becoming a member of that group but also make it easier for themselves to adjust to the group once membership has been achieved. The reward for conformity—group membership—is so desirable to the individuals that it controls their behavior.

The role of the reference group can be seen clearly in many societies. The age grades and age sets studied in the previous chapter all act as reference groups. In such groups, the individual's sense of relatedness to the group is stronger than any sense of loyalty to abstract laws. If a person commits a serious crime—particularly theft or adultery—the group takes punitive action. The guilty person may be fined, ostracized, or perhaps banished from the group. The group's moral code may be reinforced by religious beliefs. It may be held that a person who commits a crime, and possibly other members of the group as well, may suffer bad luck, sickness, or some other misfortune.

When a member of a reference group commits a crime outside the group, the group remains important, though it usually acts differently than it would if the crime were committed within the group. This is because to outsiders, the criminal represents not himself or herself but the group as a whole. The group will usually try to defend and aid the offender. If a crime is committed by an outsider against a member of the group, the group often makes sure that proper compensation is made to the wronged member.

The Ndembu of Zambia, in particular, illustrate the role of the reference group as a form of social control. Victor Turner (1957) has shown that the ties that bind the Ndembu together as a group are not based solely on kinship or on politics but also on ritual system. Two kinds of rituals take place in Ndembu society: life-crisis rituals and cults of affliction.

Life-crisis rituals recognize significant points of biological and social development in Ndembu culture. The most important of these rituals signal puberty in girls, circumcision of boys, and death. Performance of rituals upon these occasions serves to reaffirm ties among various groups within the society. The rituals also recognize and deal with the changes in the social structure that will occur as a result of the life crises—the death of the head of a family, for instance.

Cults of affliction are performed to rid individuals of sufferings supposedly caused by various infractions of socially acceptable behavior. These afflicted persons are said to have been "caught" by spirits that have been made angry. An individual may be "caught" for forgetting to honor ancestors with small gifts or prayers at village shrines or for quarreling with his or her kinspeople. A man who is "caught" may be afflicted by bad luck in hunting (the Ndembu's primary mode of food getting). A woman who is "caught" may suffer from reproductive disorders, or, she may simply become ill.

The spirit that does the afflicting is a deceased relative, known and named, of the afflicted person. The treatment is carried out by a number of people—called "doctors"—who have been involved in performance of this ritual in the past. The status of the participant within the cult becomes higher the more he or she participates in the rituals.

An important function of the rituals connected with the cults of affliction is to revive the memory of dead relatives and thus remind the living of their kinship connections. During the ritual, the "doctor" with the highest status of those present frequently speaks to the afflicting spirit, mentioning its kinship connections with the participants. The "doctor" also discusses the unacceptable behavior that is believed to have caused the spirit's anger. In this way, the society as a whole (represented by the participants, of whom there may be a great many from various villages in the community) is involved in the resolution of the conflict. Thus, the group simultaneously reinforces its feelings of kinship and social unity and deals with behavior that violates the group's norms.

Social Pressure and Gossip. Another informal mechanism of control is social pressure. An example is found among American teenagers, who often experience heavy pressure to conform to group norms. Those who do not or cannot conform often are ridiculed and made to feel like outcasts. Social pressure can be a major tool of control everywhere; it is especially so in Far Eastern societies such as Japan. The Japanese make extensive use of shame as a way of punishing individuals who do not live up to expectations. Attempts to shame are so effective that they sometimes drive people to suicide.

Gossip is a common form of social pressure. Particularly in small-scale, face-to-face social groups, it can effectively shape social behavior. Gilmore (1978) found that in a rural Spanish community, for example, no woman could resist joining the group of gossipers in her street, for fear that she herself would become the subject of the gossip. Nor did any woman spend less than an hour making a purchase in the local shops "because of the polite necessity to chat with the salesgirls" (p. 91). The same fear of being gossiped about also applies to the men, who hang out in the bars and barbershops. The fear of gossip has a tremendous impact on the everyday lives of the members of this community. Most women in the community do not allow neighbors into their houses for fear of the gossip that might follow the visit. Even the most private decisions are based on "what people will say." Thus, most newly married couples have their first child right away so that the husband's virility will not be open to question. Gossip can clearly be a powerful technique for controlling social activity.

Gossip can be an effective form of social control in small-scale communities, as in this small village in Spain. (Mathias T. Oppersdorff, Photo Researchers)

Ostracism. Another informal control mechanism is *ostracism*—the rejection or exclusion of an individual by the general consent of the group of which he or she is a member. Many groups use ostracism to some extent. In a recent case, an Old Order Mennonite was involved in a dispute with his wife's brother, who was also the minister of the church, the center of the social life of the community. As a consequence of the dispute, the man's wife and family, as well as the other members of the community, ostracised him. Their refusal to communicate with him in any way ranged from not eating with him to not engaging in everyday economic transactions involving him ("Mennonite Dissident Shunned by Church and Wife," 1973). In this case, the informal mechanism of ostracism was joined by the formal mechanism of the church supporting the ostracism. The threat of ostracism and its uncomfortable effects on the individual may in some societies serve to control behavior along socially acceptable lines. Ostracism is more likely to be an effective control mechanism in a small community than in a large one. A large community offers alternatives to the ostracized individual that do not exist in smaller communities. Such alternatives make ostracism seem less powerful a force.

Song Duels. The song duel is a rare form of social control found both among the Eskimos and in central Nigeria. Among the Tiv of Nigeria, it takes the following form: a person who feels that he has been wronged hires a song maker and brews a large quantity of beer. When both the beer and the songs are ready, he has a party at which the song maker teaches the songs to all the guests. The songs, which attack the character of the supposed wrongdoer, are then sung loudly and with gusto. Because the community is so small, the wrongdoer cannot avoid hearing them. The only honorable thing for the subject of the songs to do is to hire his own song maker, brew some beer, and have a competing party. This situation continues until the elders of the community invite the competing groups to submit both the songs and the original dispute to them for a decision on the merits of both. The person who wins the case may not necessarily be the person who wins the song duel.

Economic Adaptation and Social Control

Why do some societies tend to use customary control while others tend toward formal control? Cohen believes that the answer to this question depends on the way a given society has adapted to its environment. As we shall see, the control systems of hunting-and-gathering societies, horticultural societies, and modern nation-states differ according to the way each society distributes its resources and goods and the hierarchical organization that forms on the basis of this distribution. In other words, every society has rules governing the relationships between people and things. Anthropologists have observed that when these relationships change, legal institutions and codes also change.

Hunting-and-Gathering Societies. Hunting-and-gathering societies hunt game, fish, and gather wild plant foods as their primary means of subsistence. In hunting-and-gathering societies, no single member has exclusive control over the group's resources. Every member of the group has an equal right to hunt and gather within a given territory. As a result, there are no individuals with the power to enforce decisions by denying others access to resources. Therefore, coercion is less apparent, and formal law does not develop in these societies.

A hunting-and-gathering group generally is small. Relationships within the group are close and personal; in fact, the members of the group are highly interdependent. Almost all of their activities take place in the open. Such conditions are conducive to customary rather than formal techniques for settling disputes since customary techniques are based on face-to-face interactions. Examples of such informal techniques are the mechanisms of witchcraft accusations, sorcery, joking, and teasing.

If these methods fail, there is another possible solution: one or both of the disputants may leave and join another camp. Since the members of a hunting-and-gathering society have few possessions and do not own any particular territory, this is relatively easy to do.

Besides, intermarriage with other groups is so widespread that any individual can usually find kin in another camp and use affinity as a basis for joining these camps. This technique for settling disputes shows adaptive behavior in that it is necessary for hunting-and-gathering groups to divide periodically in any case in order not to put excessive pressure on available resources.

In hunting-and-gathering societies, every person frequently is expected to settle his or her own disputes. A person must serve as his or her own lawyer and judge, using the customary standards of the group as the basis for the ultimate decision. Thus, in these societies there is no particular specialization of roles—legal or otherwise—nor is there any differentiation of institutions—such as courts—for settling disputes.

Horticultural Societies. Horticultural societies are those that use plant cultivation, usually with rather simple tools, as their primary means of subsistence. In a horticultural society, individuals are tied to the land and depend on it for their sustenance. As a result, particular groups acquire exclusive rights to particular territories, and individuals within the groups are given the right to use portions of that territory. Membership in the group and the right to use its land are both inherited.

It follows that a horticultural society will develop rules of property—techniques to protect the cultivator's right to continuous use of the land. In addition, the fact that land suitable for cultivation is usually in limited supply means that the group—not the individual—must control the distribution of land. Since the group is usually a kin group (such as a lineage or clan), it is likely that the head of the group will become a headman or chieftain who may resolve disputes among the members.

The system of social control in horticultural societies is more impersonal than that in hunting-and-gathering societies. Although individuals no longer solve all of their disputes on their own and some submit to the chief for arbitration, informal techniques continue to be used in most cases.

The Nation-State. According to Cohen, the replacement of customary control with formal control is an outcome of the establishment of a nation-state. State formation occurs as the result of a mixture of political, economic, and historical circumstances. Simply put, a state is formed when one group gains centralized political control over all the other groups within the society, usually by means of coercion. The ruling group is then faced with the problem of maintaining that control, and for this a formal legal system is essential.

The shift to formal law does not occur all at once, however. In newly formed state societies, informal techniques continue to be used in personal and village relationships, between neighbors and among kinspeople. Formal law is used in matters relating to the central government, in taxation, military service, and the like. The two types of control can exist side by side because informal control involves continuous face-to-face interaction while formal control does not.

Centralized authority is almost always achieved at the expense of local autonomy. The rulers are continually attempting to gain more power while local authorities try to retain as much autonomy as they can. A successful state is one that has managed to persuade or coerce local leaders to transfer their loyalties from the local community to the ruling group. The state continues to be divided into local areas, but this is primarily for administrative purposes. The benefits of such a system are efficiency and equality of treatment. But it results in a highly impersonal and often complex relationship between the individual and the state.

Law and Legal Processes

Whatever the specific definition of law, it is generally agreed that it involves some form of social control—some way of responding to deviations from the society's norms. In our society, social control through law takes the form of a complex system of police, lawyers, judges, and juries. In other societies, there may be no courts or policing, but there is law, nonetheless. Consider the following example:

A Florida Seminole kills one of his fellows and, according to Seminole law, the oldest member of the victim's family is supposed to take revenge by killing the murderer. In one case, an old Seminole of more than ninety years had to be propped up with a gun and told to pull the trigger. The state of Florida, of course, has its own law and in accordance with this law the old man was arrested and brought to trial. The point is that by acting in accordance with his own law, the Seminole violated the law of the white man. (Dundes, 1968, p. 253)

When does customary law, such as that of the Seminole, become formal law? When there are courts and judges? When the laws are written down? What happens when dif-

Legal proceedings may be more or less formal depending on the size and character of the society in question. Here, a woman of the Kpelle tribe in Liberia is being tried in a village court; the "town chief," at right, presides.
(Jacques Jangoux, Peter Arnold Photo Archives)

ferent legal systems come into contact with one another, as they do increasingly in the modern world? There are almost as many ways of looking at law as there are students of law. In this section, we will discuss some of the approaches to law and present an illustration of a society that is in the process of substituting formal law for customary law.

Approaches to the Definition of Law

The "Reasonable Man." Max Gluckman (1963) sees legal systems as being based on what the "reasonable man" would consider fair. He illustrates this principle with a discussion of a case involving a marital dispute that was decided by a Barotse court (the Barotse are a Bantu people who live in Rhodesia).

In Barotseland, men can divorce their wives simply by sending them home. But in order for a woman to divorce her husband, she has to prove in court that he has not behaved as a reasonable husband. Thus, Barotse judges have to decide what is involved in being a "reasonable" husband. This is not easy under any circumstances, but in Barotseland it is complicated by the fact that in order to provide material goods for his wife, the man must go away to European settlements to earn wages. However, if he does so, he is unable to sleep with his wife or be a companion to her. The Barotse have therefore passed a law stating that a husband cannot be away for longer than a fixed period. If he is absent for a longer time, his wife is entitled to a divorce.

In the case in question, a woman brought suit for divorce, stating that her husband had been away longer than the period fixed by law; the court granted the divorce. It turned out that her husband had been on his way home when the divorce was granted. The woman wanted to go back to her husband, but her father claimed that this would be a new marriage and that he should therefore receive a new marriage payment. The court ruled that it

would not have granted the divorce if it had known that the husband was on his way home. It interpreted the law's phrase "return home" to mean "leave place of employment," because the purpose of the law is to maintain marriages, not to encourage divorce.

The point here is that the Barotse judge has to interpret what is reasonable in each case that arises. Basically, the definition of reasonableness is derived from the standards of the community as a whole, from its opinions and customs. When these standards change (as they have been in Barotseland since the advent of European influence), the judge's interpretations change. Thus, a reasonable Barotse husband has always been expected to provide both material goods and companionship. When it became necessary for the husband to be absent for long periods in order to continue providing material goods, a law was passed to put reasonable limits on such absences. When the letter of the law was violated, the court made a decision on the basis of what was now reasonable under the new circumstances. Most members of Barotse society would agree with the court's interpretation.

Submission to Authority. In the preceding chapter, we discussed the Poro of the West African Mende as an example of a secret society. Such secret societies are instruments of social control in that they function to maintain the status quo and to enforce adherence to traditional norms. James Gibbs (1962) points out that the Poro of the Kpelle also requires unquestioning acceptance of authority. This respect for authority carries over into Kpelle political life, in which authority is exercised by elders and chiefs.

In Kpelle society, disputes are settled in a court presided over by the chief. The settlements reached are usually satisfactory, particularly in cases dealing with assault, theft, or possession of illegal charms. When it comes to marital disputes, however, the decisions of the court are less effective and often seem arbitrary. The coercive nature of the court's rulings often add to the tension among the parties rather than restore harmony. Thus, according to Gibbs, the respect for authority learned in the Poro leads the Kpelle to accept arbitrary decision making in the courts. This makes it possible for the courts to serve as a powerful force in sanctioning deviant actions, but it also limits the courts' effectiveness in certain matters.

From the Personal to the Impersonal. We have just described a legal system that appears to be based on consensus (the Barotse) and

Formal law tends to be impersonal and to involve specialists—judges and lawyers such as these in an Algerian courtroom—whose relationship with the disputants of a case extends only to interpreting the legal code of the society. (Coster, Monkmeyer)

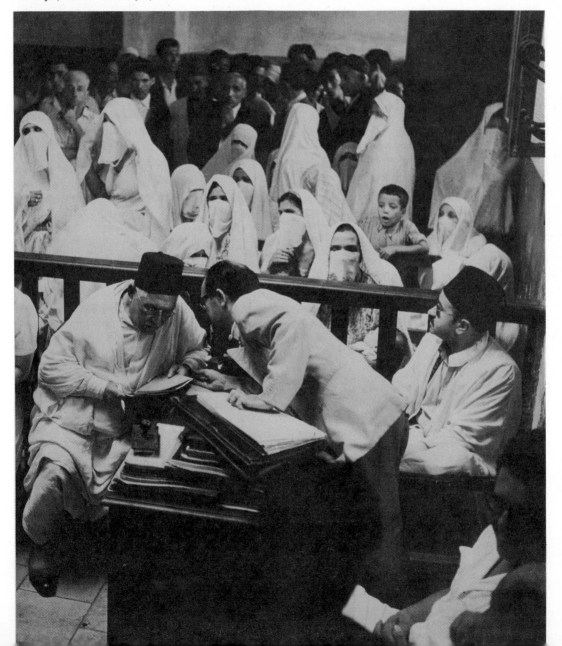

one in which coercion seems to dominate (the Kpelle). In both systems, we find courts and judges, but neither is entirely "formal." Customary law continues to play an important role in both Barotse and Kpelle life. Clearly we need a different standard than the presence or absence of law courts for determining whether a legal system is formal or informal.

In their discussion of social control and law in African societies, the Ottenbergs (1960) point out that the legal system in many African societies is concerned at least as much with reconciling the disputants as with arriving at a settlement. Since the members of these small-scale societies tend to be in frequent contact with each other, it is as important to restore social harmony as to exercise social control. Reconciliation between the parties can be even more important than determining blame or guilt. The speed with which a matter is settled is not as important, though, as thorough presentation and discussion of the information. Verbal recall of similar cases by the elders is highly valued: "In many parts of Africa there is great admiration for the well-tried case, for the speaker who summarizes a dispute or gives the judgment with clarity, for the elder who is able to cite past cases of significance or quote proverbs to make a legal point" (Ottenberg & Ottenberg, 1960, pp. 59–60).

The Ottenbergs' discussion illustrates an important point: informal law is personal, whereas formal law is impersonal. The legal process itself is specialized and specific. The disputant's relationship with a lawyer or a judge is to the case at hand and carries with it no other commitments or obligations. The relationships involved are simple in nature; the individuals' various roles do not overlap and are not juxtaposed. Where control mechanisms are more informal, as in the societies described by the Ottenbergs, this is not the case. The disputants and the elders have dealings with each other every day on a wide variety of matters. Their relationship is not limited to the settlement of a particular case in a specified field of activity. In other words, the relationship is multiplex.

The Sebei in Transition

When economic shifts occur in societies, laws and legal systems must change as well if they are to be useful in dealing with the new circumstances. Goldschmidt (1967) describes such an adaptation in the legal system of the Sebei of western Kenya. The Sebei were originally a pastoral, herding people. Their legal system was based on the fact that in pastoral societies land and water must be freely available to all the members of the group. Over time, though they did not give up pastoralism entirely, they became a horticultural people. In a horticultural society, as we have seen, the legal system is based on the relationship of people to the land—land ownership—since people depend on having the right to use the land continuously and to exclude others from its use.

But legal systems do not change all at once. The history and attitudes of the members of a group have a significant effect on the new situation. They place limits on the changes that may be made and the speed at which those changes may take place. Thus, the legal system of the Sebei shows a mixture of the more customary law of pastoralism with the more formal law of horticulture.

The Sebei approach to land ownership is adapted from their notions of livestock ownership. The men own the land, even though it is cultivated by the women. The men are obligated to supply their wives and their sons with land; they allocate land to their wives, just as they used to allocate cattle. However, the meaning that cattle had for the Sebei has not been transferred to land. Land is not used in paying a bride-price, for example. Yet the

Sebei value land: they have boundary markers, they argue over land rights, sometimes they build up large personal landholdings.

Along with the formalization of land ownership have come more or less formal ways of dealing with disputes over boundaries and the sale and purchase of land, as well as various contractual arrangements for its utilization. At the same time, however, the Sebei have developed an unusual technique of controlling individual behavior, a ritual called *ntarastit*. It consists of an oath that tribesmen take, indicating one's intention to behave lawfully and one's acceptance of punishment for unlawful behavior. Walter Goldschmidt (1967) describes this ritual as follows:

All circumcized men gather naked at the specified location, and before an altar of implanted branches of certain specified plants of ceremonial significance, swear as follows: "Anybody who kills anybody passing by (or who takes things belonging to others, etc.), may the earth eat him." They thrust their spears at the altar in unison each time they recite this formula, naming a different kind of offense. (p. 125)

Ntarastit thus consists of calling upon supernatural authority to punish individual offenses and thereby maintain peace in the community. It has several interesting features. *Ntarastit precedes* the deviant act and is thus the group's statement of the law. Furthermore, it is backed up by the group's readiness to act. If a member of the group commits one of the offenses named in the oath, he will be punished by the group after an informal hearing. (The punishment, incidentally, takes the form of destruction of the offender's property.)

Ntarastit is clearly a customary or informal method of social control. But it coexists with a more formal legal system having to do with land. In a nation-state, both the offenses covered by *ntarastit* (murder and theft) and matters of property would be settled in the courts—that is, by formal methods of control.

The Impact of the Nation-State on Traditional Means of Control

The development of a nation-state entails, in part, the coming together of a number of different groups under a single political umbrella. This can be a long and complicated process, since the various groups do not always share the same values and interests. The problem of forming a nation is not a simple one, since it involves political, economic, and legal changes in the organization of a society.

The Problem of Identity

One of the most difficult problems facing the leaders of a nation is how to persuade its citizens to identify with the nation as a whole rather than with their particular linguistic, religious, or tribal subgroups. Pandit Nehru, who guided India from 1947 to 1964 while it was becoming a nation after winning independence from Great Britain, was forced to recognize the linguistic variety of his people and to organize the nation along linguistic lines, despite his personal dislike of such an organization. He feared that the "narrow loyalties, petty jealousies, and ignorant prejudices" of the subgroups based on language would threaten the potential for the country's political unity (quoted in Harrison, 1956). Divisive contrasts in various countries throughout the world are based on racial or tribal groupings, language, religion, social customs, and region.

Clifford Geertz (1963) explains the problems of the coming together of old societies and new states as arising from two distinct and often opposed motives: (1) the desire to retain one's identity, which is often defined in terms of race, language, or tradition; and (2) the desire to be part of an efficient, modern state, which implies a rising standard of living, political order, and greater social justice. How can such opposing impulses be reconciled? Sometimes a new regime simply will ride roughshod over the attachments of individuals to their groups. This course of action may have the opposite effect from the one intended: feelings of identity with one's way of life may actually be stimulated or sharpened by the formation of a nation-state. At the same time, people and groups feel vulnerable and unsure of what will result when their old attachments are threatened by new influences in the nation-state.

Legal Pluralism

Apparently, then, the ties of individuals to their own language, religion, and so forth need to be recognized in some way by the leaders of a new state. Such recognition is often expressed in the newly formed legal system. The existence within a society of more than one legal system at the same time, some of which may actually be in conflict with one another, is referred to as *legal pluralism*. In many African nations, for example, there are European groups, Africans who have adopted "modern" European life styles, and many Africans who have begun to abandon their ancient traditions and accept European values but who have not done so entirely. The law for Europeans often is different from the law for Africans, and among Africans the law varies from one tribe to another.

As new states have been formed out of a number of tribal communities, a uniform set of "territorial" laws has been superimposed on the "personal" laws of the various tribes. But in many cases the tribal law is still in use. According to Max Rheinstein (1963), if this legal pluralism is used cautiously and wisely, it can be a valuable tool for integrating different groups into a new nation. However, it should not be expected to work by itself, for pluralism has educational, economic, and cultural aspects as well. Native courts can handle cases involving matters such as the sale of cattle or payment of bride wealth, or even bodily injury resulting from a fist fight or damage done by stray cattle. Murder and transactions involving large amounts of money or property are increasingly handled by some sort of higher court.

But what happens in cases of intertribal conflicts? Rheinstein lists three possible ways of handling them:

1. simply applying the law of the court in which the case happens to come up;
2. developing a special set of laws for intergroup conflicts;
3. developing a set of rules for deciding which of the several sets of laws already in existence should apply to specific types of intergroup conflicts.

The first approach is unsatisfactory because it is unsystematic and may result in widely different decisions. An example of the second approach was found in the legal system of the Roman Empire. Originally, Roman law was the law of the city of Rome. When the Romans conquered Italy, Greece, and surrounding regions, they did not impose Roman law on their new subjects. Rather, they allowed each city or region to retain its own law. But as commerce and other contacts developed among different parts of the empire, disputes arose that had to be settled by the Roman authorities. The technique used by the Romans was to apply to such cases neither the law of any subject region nor the law of Rome itself but a new law of their own creation, the *ius gentium* "law of nations," as opposed to *ius civile,* or "civil law," of the city of Rome). Over time, the *ius gentium* swallowed up the *ius civile* as well as the laws of the various subject regions and became the universal law of the Roman Empire.

As Rheinstein points out, it would be difficult to develop such a universal legal system in many African nations. This would require law schools, libraries, knowledge of legal language, and long years of study. Even if such a legal system were developed, it would not apply to all kinds of intergroup conflicts. Some would still require the third approach—the development of rules governing which set of tribal laws should apply in any given case. This is also a very difficult task. Thus, there is a strong tendency for national leaders to favor uniformity over pluralism in the legal system of the new state.

Summary

1. Every society has rules governing the interactions of its members. These rules are often unconscious and may be ambiguous, but they are nonetheless effective in maintaining social control. Every society has means of dealing with individuals who deviate from its rules. These means are known as *sanctions,* and they take many forms.

2. Anthropologists are interested in what makes individuals conform to the rules of their society. The *consensus model* assumes that all the members of a society agree on that society's values. The *coercion model* assumes that social order is a result of force and constraint. These models can be seen as complementary rather than contradictory if it is assumed that the members of a society agree on its basic values but often have interests that are in conflict.

3. Techniques of social control may be seen as *informal,* or customary, and as *formal,* categories that are roughly equivalent to the consensus and coercion models. This is an artificial distinction, however; informal techniques can sometimes be highly coercive, and both formal and informal techniques may be used within the same society.

4. The *reference group* is the most important informal technique of social control. Because an individual's ties to the group are stronger than his or her loyalty to abstract laws, this serves to control the individual's behavior. Other informal control techniques include social pressure and gossip, *ostracism,* witchcraft and sorcery, and the song duel.

5. Anthropologists have found relationships between economic adaptation and social control. Hunting-and-gathering societies tend to use customary law because they have no central authority and can split up easily if a conflict cannot be resolved by other means. In horticultural societies, individuals are tied to the land they cultivate, and rules of property become important. In such societies, formal and informal techniques of social control may coexist. A nation-state is formed when one group gains control over all the other groups in the society and develops formal, impersonal means of maintaining that control.

6. It is difficult to draw a line between customary law and formal law. Societies that have courts and judges may have a legal system based on either consensus or coercion and still use relatively informal techniques of control. More formal legal systems are less interested in restoring harmony among the disputants; moreover, they entail impersonal relationships between the disputants and the legal authorities.

7. The leaders of a new state face a major problem in trying to persuade its members to transfer their loyalty from their local groups to the state itself. The desire of the individual to retain an identity that may be defined in terms of race or religion often conflicts with the desire to be a member of a modern state.

8. *Legal pluralism,* a system in which tribal law continues to be used in some cases and territorial law in others, could be a valuable tool for integrating the people of a new nation. However, the resolution of intergroup conflicts presents a problem. Should such cases be settled by the court in which they happen to come up? Should a new set of laws be developed for settling them? Or should a set of rules be developed to determine which of the sets of laws already in existence applies to a given type of case? The first approach is unsatisfactory, but either of the other two is very difficult.

21

Culture and Ecology

WE are all by now as familiar with the word ecology as we are with the problems that first brought it to our attention: lakes and rivers polluted by industrial wastes, cities blanketed by smog from automobile exhausts. By dumping pollutants into the waters or discharging them into the air, people put the ecology of their cities and their regions out of balance. Environmentalists have been trying to correct the damage done by this exploitation or destruction of natural resources. When we look at ecology in this way, humans often appear as selfish, sometimes unconscious, meddlers with environments that would do quite well without them. For example, human communities require energy for heat, light, and other basic needs. A nuclear power station might be built for the purpose of supplying the energy required by a large population. Such a power station requires large quantities of water for its cooling opera-

tion. When the water is returned to its source, it will be considerably hotter than when it was withdrawn. The resulting thermal pollution may seriously affect the capacity of this body of water to support plant and animal life. Thus, in order to provide for human comfort, the ecology of a region may suffer.

Ecologists, however, do not view the human role in the natural scheme as so limited. Humans are part of a larger community that includes plants and animals as well as the physical features of the environment. This community is called an *ecosystem*. A single ecosystem may be quite small—a drop of pond water and the micro-organisms that live in it—or it may be considerably large—the earth and its plant and animal life. Whenever humans are part of a given ecosystem, they are its most dynamic members.

Ecology studies the ways in which all living organisms interact within the environment. The concept of ecology and its relation to cul-

457

458 ture will be the focus of this chapter. The interaction between culture and environment (or, more precisely, between specific cultural phenomena and environment) has always been a primary concern of anthropologists. The nature of the relationship between human populations and given ecological niches (that is, the totality of the natural habitat within which a population is located) continues to merit discussion and debate. We shall examine some early theories regarding these interactions, and then go on to survey more recent investigations of ecosystems and human populations.

Culture and Environment

Implicit in all ecological studies in anthropology is the notion of adaptation. That is, a human population adapts to its habitat when it is able to survive and perpetuate itself. Culture is the means by which humans make this adaptation. Some populations are better adapted than others; they are, in Darwinian terms, "winners" in the struggle for existence.

Culture and environment studies have generally attempted to deal with two different kinds of problems. First, they seek to explain why particular elements or sets of elements exist at particular times and in particular places. Second, they attempt to interpret how these particular elements function within a given cultural and natural habitat.

Environmental Determinism

The early generations of anthropologists, around the turn of this century, believed that the cultural features of a group were caused by the environmental setting in which the group was located. *Environmental determinism* (or *environmentalism*) held that the reason for the

presence of a specific culture feature could be traced to the habitat in which it occurred.

Environmental determinism has a long tradition in Western thought. Some of the earliest histories of ancient Greece, particularly those of Aristotle and of Pliny the Elder, were based on similar notions. In the early eighteenth century, Montesquieu wrote of ancient Greece in a like manner. He believed that "the sterility of the soil of [Athens]" was responsible for the development there of popular government, while "the fertility of [Sparta]" fostered "an aristocratic ruling class" (quoted in Sahlins, 1964, p. 132). Even less convincing today is Montesquieu's notion that weakness and timidity, as well as indulgence in extraordinary sexual practices, were sure to be found among those who inhabit a warm climate (Netting, 1971, p. 2).

Environmental Possibilism

As comparative cultural data accumulated early in this century, the theory called *environmental possibilism* began to displace environmentalism. Possibilism claimed that environmental factors limit the adaptive possibilities for a given culture but do not determine which adaptations or choices a society makes. For example, arable land makes it possible for a society to practice agriculture but does not guarantee that it will. Aided by the growing number of studies of various cultures, anthropologists noted that quite different cultural phenomena frequently arose under identical environmental conditions. In a famous instance, Kroeber (1923) observed that in the same region of the American Southwest lived Pueblo Indians, who farmed and lived in highly concentrated settlements with sizable populations, and the Navaho, who followed a nomadic way of life, dependent largely upon hunting.

Kroeber argued that cultural phenomena are caused only by other cultural phenomena (1939, p. 1). He cited as an example the spread of agriculture through the Americas, carried by cultural contact from its origins in southern Mexico or Guatemala, first to the American southwestern tribes and eventually across the entire continent to Indians of the East Coast:

> . . . the Southwestern Indians did not farm because nature induced them to make the invention. They did not make the invention at all. A faraway people made it, and from them it was transmitted to the Southwest through a series of successive tribal contacts. These contacts, which then are the specific cause of Southwestern culture, constitute a human social factor; a cultural or civilizational factor. Climatic or physical environment did not enter into the matter at all, except to render agriculture somewhat difficult in the arid Southwest, though not difficult enough to prevent it. (Kroeber, 1923, pp. 185–186)

Kroeber acknowledged, of course, that the environment did play a limiting role: "Had the Southwest been thoroughly desert, agriculture could not have gotten a foothold there." But within these limits, societies chose freely from a number of possibilities. The Pueblos, as mentioned, farmed while the Navaho hunted. Thus, although the natural environment made agriculture possible, it was the human environment—contact with people from agricultural communities—that made farming a way of life for many tribes of the Southwest and, over the years, for other native populations on the continent.

The possibilists recognized the importance of such environmental features as climate, topography, and available natural resources, but they gave greater stress to historical and cultural factors. Drucker (1963), for example, observed of the Northwest Coast Indians: "In a sense, the natural environment favored the development of the woodworking craft, for the towering trees of the Northwest contained a number of useful and readily workable woods" (p. 61). The most useful of these woods were the red and yellow cedar. Even

the northerly Tlingit, though they lived beyond the cedar forests, insisted on importing cedar bark for clothing, containers, and other items of everyday life. This is clearly an example of a cultural choice that goes beyond what the immediate physical environment has to offer. The environmentalist, who expected a society passively to accept the limited available resources, would perhaps be surprised by this early instance of significant trade. The possibilist, who assumed that humans actively select, develop, adapt, and retain elements from the environment, would not.

Possibilism advanced but did not resolve the environment-culture question. By the middle of the twentieth century, anthropological thought was moving toward a more balanced concept of the interplay between the physical environment and cultural systems. This latter approach, which has become known as cultural ecology, concerns itself with the ways in which particular environmental features are interwoven with specific aspects of culture, selecting only those environmental characteristics and those particular cultural arrangements which can be functionally related.

Cultural Ecology

Cultural ecology focuses on the relationship of specific cultural features to a group's adaptation to its total habitat. Julian Steward, the primary advocate of cultural ecology, was interested in the patterns of activity adopted by social groups in order to exploit a particular ecological niche. He was especially concerned with ascertaining whether specific adaptations were associated with particular environments, or whether a society could in effect select from a range of possibilities in its adjustments to and utilization of a given environment.

To illustrate the concept of adjustment, Steward cited the differences between two groups of hunting tribes, each sharing a common technology but living in different environments. One group hunts large herds of migratory animals—bison or caribou—that can be followed efficiently by a large group of people over a great distance. The other hunts smaller game which neither migrates nor gathers in large herds. The roving group of hunters will form a mobile social group that is potentially large, given the nature of the food supply and the technology needed to exploit it. The second will remain rather small in size and range over a limited territory. The type of leadership and the units of production will vary significantly in the two groups.

Kroeber had emphasized that various cultural adaptations were possible within a given environment. Steward argued instead that the role of environment goes beyond merely permitting certain cultural adaptations and that there is a degree of inevitability in such adjustments. Steward believed, for instance, that the Arctic winter virtually required the more or less isolated conjugal family to be the effective social group. This is because herding requires a degree of nomadism and a small-scale social organization, and because wild vegetation necessitates food gathering on an individual or family basis. Cultural diffusion may be of enormous value in enhancing the ability of a people to exploit their environment—as the use of the horse aided the Plains Indians or the nomads of Central Asia. But it can also be of no value at all—a horse would be of little use to an Eskimo. Only specific cultural traits that serve the adaptive strategy of a given population are assimilated.

As set forth by Steward (1955), the study of cultural ecology involves three basic procedures:

1. Analysis of the interaction between the environment and the technology that uses it. Some environmental features may be

Cultural ecologists point out that features of the environment, including available natural resources, affect the tools and techniques used in various societies. Canoe-making in two different cultures illustrates this point. At left, young men of the Abruré tribe of the Ivory Coast carve a dugout canoe out of a large forest tree. At right, two Njemps men of Kenya shred saasevlera into rope-like strips to be used in canoe construction. (*Left:* Marc and Evelyne Bernheim, Woodfin Camp; *right:* Jen and Des Bartlett, Photo Researchers)

more crucial than others in influencing culture and technology. No society (including our own highly technological one) can make use of every aspect of its ecological niche. The features of the environment that are utilized depend upon the culture. Steward held that simpler cultures are more directly affected by the environment than complex ones. Thus, our culture has softened the effects of climate with heating and air-conditioning devices and has overcome the limitations of geography by constructing railroad tunnels, superhighways, aircraft, and space satellites.

2. Analysis of the patterns of activity required by the exploitative technology used in a given area. Does the technology require cooperation? Does cooperation result in more efficient utilization of resources? Through invention and diffusion, new tools and techniques become available, but the social activities these bring about depend upon the adaptive strategy of the group found in a given environment. Cultural ecology must study not only "the habits concerned in the direct production of food and of goods but [also the] facilities for transporting the people to the source or supply of the goods to the people" (Steward, 1955, p. 41).

3. Description of how the behaviors involved in exploiting the environment affect and are affected by other aspects of the culture. The organization of kin groups, sociopolitical organization, population density, architecture, and lore are only a few of the areas of social life that may be involved. These questions have proved to be as valid for modern industrial states as for traditional hunting-and-gathering bands.

Stewards's formulations helped move anthropology away from the preoccupation with issues of origins that was characteristic of the earlier evolutionary outlook. Instead cultural ecology came to focus on how a wide variety of factors work in their specific cultural contexts, without regard to their origins. On the basis of cross-cultural comparisons, Steward observed that certain interrelationships between cultural and environmental variables recurred in cultures that were not in contact with each other. These recurring patterns led him to the tentative conclusion that there are certain "essential features" of particular groups (such as patrilineal bands) that are found universally. Consequently, certain ecological factors may be considered causative. Peoples as diverse as the Bushmen, Congo Negritoes, Australians, Tasmanians, and Fuegians, all of whom inhabit very different environments, have similar cultural inventories and patrilineal band organization. Steward argued that these similarities exist "because the nature of the game and therefore of their subsistence problem is the same in each case" (Steward, 1955, p. 38).

For example, among hunters and gatherers such as the Shoshone Indians, the unpredictable supply of food, the lack of means for harvesting and storing it in quantity, and the fact that cooperative action on the part of large groups could not improve efficiency in collecting wild seeds and roots, all combined to make scattered nuclear families the effective food-producing units (Steward, 1955, pp. 105–107; Vayda & Rappaport, 1968, p. 484). Or again, sparse distribution of game, inefficient transportation, and low population density produce patrilineal, patrilocal bands:

Were individual families to wander at will, hunting the game in neighboring areas, competition would lead to conflict. . . . (But) as the men tend to remain more or less in the territory in which they have been reared and with which they are familiar, patrilineally related families would tend to band together to protect their game resources. The territory would therefore become divided among these patrilineal bands. (Steward, 1955, p. 135)

Since Steward pioneered the concept of cultural ecology, others have used it in their

Irrigation canals and terraces in Bali. (Klaus D. Francke, Peter Arnold Photo Archives)

research, but they have developed it somewhat differently. In Geertz's comparison of irrigation in Bali and Morocco, for example, he shows that each culture is so much part of its ecological niche that it is difficult, if not impossible, to think of the cultures independently of their ecological settings. Although these two societies have many things in common—among them "Islam, poverty, nationalism, authoritarian rule, overpopulation, clean air, spectacular scenery, and a colonial past" (Geertz, 1972, p. 24)—they are very different. The differences are exemplified by the patterns of irrigation in each society. In southeast Bali, irrigation canals, divided and subdivided in measured fashion, form a neat and complex network down every mountainside. These canals are maintained and controlled by a corporate organization known as a *subak*, which allots water equally to all holdings in its territory. So well organized is the system that the times set for each of nine specified stages of rice cultivation are staggered in every area in such a way that the *subak* highest on the mountainside opens its water gates earlier than the one directly below it. "The result is that, at any one point in time, the drainage area as a whole shows a step-by-step progression in the cultivation sequence as one moves downslope" (Geertz, 1972, pp. 30–31).

In contrast, the workings of the east-central Moroccan irrigation system, rather than being strictly ordered and supervised, are the subject of constant squabbling among individuals over the allocation of so many hours of water rights in each of several canal systems. In Morocco, the canals are diverted frequently —perhaps every 3 hours, or as often as every hour—to water the several fields of different owners. Water in Morocco is only one of several kinds of property held in private ownership, and one's water rights may be loaned or rented out to others.

Geertz shows that the patterns tied in with irrigation and cultivation are repeated in the respective climates of Bali and Morocco. Not only are the climates totally opposite in terms of water availability—Bali receives heavy rainfall and Morocco is semiarid—but the predictability of the Balinese climate and the extreme variability of Morocco's weather seem to be paralleled by the behavioral patterns associated with cultivation. Irrigation in Bali is predictable and regular; in Morocco, it is variable and dependent on individual efforts. For Geertz, then, ecology plays such a central role in the joining of all the elements that constitute a culture, that the separate analysis of ecology and culture as set forth by Steward would be meaningless. As he puts it, nature is not just a stage upon which culture performs:

a society tunes itself to its landscape, mountainside, river fan, or foothill oasis, until it seems to an outside observer that it could not possibly be anywhere else than it is, it could not be otherwise than what it is. (Geertz, 1972, p. 38)

Steward's formulations are fundamental to the ecological approach in anthropology, which strives for descriptions of the functional relations or interplay between specific environmental features and cultural traits. Vayda and Rappaport (1968) rightly criticize Steward, however, for failing to test his model with adequate cross-cultural samples. They point out that Steward was content to select those examples that fit his thesis. Further, they believe he failed to show to what extent similar adaptations may occur without the cultural traits in question, or to note instances where the same traits may be present but not accompanied by the same adaptations. They also point out that even where certain correlations between cultural traits and given adaptations can be shown, the task remains of showing which is cause and which is effect. They suspect that such correlations are more intertwined than directly causal. However, it must be noted that Steward realized that the interactions between culture and ecology are complex; he only suggested that cause-and-effect relationships might have prevailed in those situations where parallel developments were unusually striking in geographically separated cultures with no contact. His classic example was the effects of the adaptation of the horse among the Plains Indians and among Indians of the pampas in Argentina, where parallel developments in tribal organization could be recognized.

The notion of "inevitability" of cultural characteristics is also challenged by Vayda and

Rappaport, who point out that functional relationship is not identical with inevitability. They suggest broadening the bases of environmental features to be studied by considering nonhuman interactions as well as human ones. This approach led Rappaport to consider a systems approach to human populations and ecology, which will be considered in more detail below. Nevertheless, Steward's principal contribution has endured. Social activities are now studied not in isolation or in relation to arbitrarily selected environmental factors but as part of an ecosystem, where the internal dynamics of these activities, biological transactions, and physical processes may be recognized most clearly.

Tools, Technology, and the Harnessing of Energy

Technology—the production and use of tools—is the means by which human populations at all times and in all places exploit the environment in order to satisfy their basic needs for food and shelter. In fact, some anthropologists have insisted that the primary defining feature of humanity is the creation and use of tools. Kenneth Oakley (1959) proposed such an argument when he defined culture as "the ability to make tools and communicate ideas" (p. 1). All other physiological distinctions of *Homo sapiens*—upright posture, bipedalism, opposable thumb, conceptualizing brain—are significant, Oakley believed, because of their contribution to the human ability to construct and use tools.

Two anthropologists who have placed great stress on tools and technology in the growth and development of culture are V. Gordon Childe and Leslie White. Childe (1951) argued that tools are the principle means

463

Through the use of tools—even very simple ones such as that being used here by a cultivator in Spain—humans are able to increase their control over nature. (Rick Windsor, Woodfin Camp)

whereby any society adapts to its natural and social setting. As such, tools are the critical factors in human history. Through the invention and spread of increasingly efficient tools, humans were able to increase their control over nature and to bring about technological achievement. A recent example comes from a developing region on the edge of the Indian desert. One Indian camel can carry a 600-pound load; if it is harnessed to a two-wheel bullock cart, the carrying capacity of one beast increases to more than a ton. But the bullock cart, familiar elsewhere in India, cannot be used on the sandy ground in this area because of its narrow wheels. When discarded heavy aircraft tires are used, however, the two-wheel

cart with camel dramatically increases the transporting facilities of the region (Borders, 1978). However, societies have not always perceived such progress as advantageous. In many instances, opposition and conservatism has had to be overcome before new tool inventions were accepted.

White (1949; 1959), on the other hand, saw technology in even more deterministic terms. He divided culture into three subsystems: a technological system, a sociological one, and an ideological one. He saw the three systems hierarchically layered, so that the technological layer determined the nature of the other two systems, while the reverse was not true.

For White, the technological system includes tools of production, subsistence technology, materials from which shelter is constructed, and the instruments by which people protect themselves and wage war. The sociological system consists of the networks of interpersonal relationships and activities for all facets of social life—kinship, political, religious, occupational, recreational, and so on. The ideological system is the collection of ideas and beliefs expressed through mythology and theology as well as "legend, literature, philosophy, science, folk wisdom, and common sense knowledge" (White, 1949, pp. 364–365).

As White saw it, these three subsystems do not make equal contributions to culture. The technological system—through which humans adjust to the natural environment in terms of food, shelter, and defense—is the primary influence. If technology is the pri-

mary determinant of the course of culture, White reasoned, energy is the primary influence on technology. Through technology, energy could be harnessed and used to satisfy human needs. White saw all life as a struggle for effective control of free energy. Some technologies are, naturally, more efficient at harnessing and using energy than are others (White, 1949).

White developed a formula to show the relationship between tool efficiency, energy, and cultural growth and progress: $E \times T \rightarrow C$. The three variables in this formula can be found in every cultural system. E represents the amount of energy harnessed per capita per year. T represents the efficiency of tools used to control and direct energy. C stands for the degree of cultural development, as determined by the production of "human need-serving goods and services" (White, 1949, pp.

The harnessing of animal energy is thought by White and other cultural ecologists to contribute to the development of culture. (Marc and Evelyne Bernheim, Woodfin Camp)

368–369). Thus, White held that the development of culture—cultural evolution—takes place in proportion as energy utilization and tool efficiency are both increased and act upon each other.

White's stress upon the capture of energy is useful and applicable to human culture everywhere. However, his confidence in the positive aspects of technology and his evolutionary premises came to be questioned in the 1960s and 1970s, when it became apparent that instead of being life-enhancing, new forms of energy developed by Western technology could destroy human—and other forms—of life.

White's belief in the primacy of technology and energy, the material aspect of cultural systems, was taken up by Marvin Harris. His analysis (1974) of the multiple role of the cow in India uncovers and makes sense of the cultural importance of cattle to the energy and technological needs of that country. Although sacred cows symbolize life to the Hindus, some observers have alleged that cow worship is at the root of India's extreme poverty and hunger. They point to as many as 100 million "useless" beasts competing with humans for available food while contributing little to the economy. Indeed, the sight of cows wandering about and stalling traffic in city and countryside and helping themselves from gardens, marketplaces, and garbage bins is a familiar one throughout the country.

The cows do provide milk, although only a small amount by Western standards. The average Indian cow gives under 500 pounds of whole milk a year, compared to more than 5,000 pounds for an average American dairy cow. Moreover, in any year about half of the Indian cows are dry and give not a drop of milk. Any available beef is eaten only by some members of the untouchable caste, as well as by non-Hindu Indians. However, a beef-raising industry in India is unthinkable, but not alone because of the widespread taboo on the eating of beef. Rather, a shift to beef consumption would be nutritionally counter-productive because it would, as Harris explains, "strain the entire ecosystem." When vegetable products are directly consumed by humans, more calories are available per capita than when vegetation is fed to domesticated animals which are then eaten by humans. In India, the per capita calorie intake is already substandard. Thus, using crop lands to feed animals, in order to feed humans, would result in higher food prices and poorer diets for most families (Harris, 1974).

What critics also fail to realize, Harris points out, is that India's special relationship to the cow is at the core of a complex economy that ultimately makes possible human survival in this low-energy, animal-based, labor-intensive ecosystem. For example, the cattle of India are put to a number of uses—plowing, carting, and supplying milk, meat, leather, fuel, and fertilizer. Some of these uses are apparent, but others require explanation. Milk, meat, and leather are not the only things produced by cattle. The most plentiful product of all is dung—some 700 million tons per year—and little of it is wasted. In Harris's words, "cows and oxen provide low-energy substitutes for tractors and tractor factories . . . [while] carrying out the functions of a petrochemical industry" (Harris, 1974, p. 18). The collection of manure gives employment to many who would otherwise lack cash-earning jobs in the present economy. About half the total dung output is left in place or scattered in the fields, for use as fertilizer. Combined with water, dung forms a paste that converts a dirt floor to a hard, durable surface. Dried in cakes, it is the ideal cooking fuel for Indian cuisine, which requires the clean, slow, long-burning flame dung provides. Annually, dung provides "the thermal equivalent of 27 million tons of kerosene, 35 million tons of coal, or 68 million tons of wood," none of which is avail-

In India, cow dung is collected and dried in cakes, like those on the roof of this dwelling; it is then utilized as a long-burning cooking fuel. (Norman Weiser)

able in India in significant quantity (Harris, 1974, p. 19).

In addition to having all these uses, Harris points out that the Indian cow is a hardy, energy-storing, disease-resistant animal, able to survive with scant water and food over long periods of time. Far from competing with humans for a meager supply of food, the cow is a scavenger, consuming primarily inedible portions of food grains such as rice husks and wheat bran. From a cultural ecology viewpoint, then, a belief in the sacredness of the cow is technologically functional in India. By this example, Harris was able to demonstrate

the extent to which culture and technology become intertwined.

(heat energy) when an animal eats vegetation, and an even greater loss when one animal eats another.

Human Populations and Ecosystems

Ecosystems contain a number of interconnected food chains. But feeding is only one of the processes of an ecosystem. Many ecosystems are relatively simple, consisting of a limited number of interacting populations and a limited range of inorganic features. Such a simple ecosystem is quite fragile, being vulnerable to the slightest alteration in any one of its few components. But most ecosystems are quite complex. Our own—that of the western world—is almost infinitely so. The more complex and diversified an ecosystem, the more stable it is and less likely to change. Its very diversity provides a cushion against disruption (Little & Morren, 1976). In New York City a few years ago, for example, it was found that trees located under certain newly installed street lights were not developing to their full leafy potential, nor did birds come to rest on the leafless branches. After only one or two growing seasons, many of the trees died. But—except for the aesthetic sensibilities of apartment dwellers who appreciated even the minimal plant life and bird song under their windows—no other parts of the ecosystem were significantly affected. In contrast, any interference in leaf development in an area inhabited by hunter-gatherers would be disastrous, since the foliage provides a cover for hunting activities, nourishment for some game animals, materials for the construction of homes, and many useful artifacts, including cord for trapping, plaited sleeping mats, and other necessities.

The complexity of an ecosystem is determined not by the inclusion within it of a human population but by the number and types of interacting populations. Even within a simple ecosystem, human beings interact with other populations with other ecological features, as the analysis of the Arctic Eskimo shows (Little & Morren, 1976).

The Arctic Eskimo. The Eskimos, a hunting society, inhabit the Arctic tundra along the coasts of Alaska, Canada, and Greenland. This habitat consists of a shallow soil level covering permafrost; relatively few species of plant or animal life; a short, cool, summer growing season lasting only 2 or 3 months; low temperatures year round; little annual precipitation (rain or snow); and low levels of solar radiation. Even in summer the soil is usable only to a depth of less than 1 meter. This not only limits root and plant growth but, because of poor water drainage, also creates a marshy landscape over which travel is difficult. The Arctic winter is long and intensely cold, with nearly complete daytime darkness for months at a time. The surface water, thawed in summer, freezes again beginning in early fall when slush starts to form along the coastline. Then the spread of ice into the sea begins; it continues until late March. At this time traditional Eskimo technology—dog sleds and kayaks—provides the most effective means of transportation (Little & Morren, 1976).

Description of the living components and energy exchanges of the tundra ecosystem might well begin with the spring thaw, which makes available water and soil to nourish the sparse growth of lichens, flowering herbs, shrubs, and grasses. This vegetation is eaten by such herbivores as the brown lemming and the caribou. Lemmings are, in turn, eaten by carnivores such as the fox and snowy owl. The Eskimo population functions as a higher-level carnivore, utilizing foods from the vegetation and herbivore, as well as the carnivore, levels. In addition, Eskimos consume marine resources—fish, seals, beluga whales, and walruses—which also provide fuels.

To exploit this environment, human populations follow available food resources by

An Eskimo woman hangs strips of whale meat on a log to be dried for later consumption. (Paolo Koch, Photo Researchers)

moving to the shore regions in fall and winter, gradually working their way inland during the thaws. In the short summer season, some vegetable products and small terrestrial game such as birds and rabbits are available. Then population reaches its greatest concentration in inland settlements. Population scatters with the onset of fall, when small groups follow the sea ice to hunt marine foods most effectively. The available food resources in the tundra ecosystem result in a high-protein, low-carbohydrate diet that is among the most specialized of any in the world.

Inevitably, contact with other cultures has brought changes to the balanced tundra ecosystem. The rifle, motor-powered boat, and snowmobile are replacing the harpoon, kayak, and dog sled. Store-bought ammunition and petroleum fuels are necessary for this new equipment, and continuous participation in a money economy is essential. Even those Eskimos who remain in their traditional communities participate in craft production, receive money-transfer payments from the United States or Canadian governments, and may also for part of the year be employed in low-level service positions in urban communities. These changes, in turn, have created other alterations in life style. Disruption of closeknit family life has occurred, as some members of the family leave to attend government schools or move to seek work in a nearby town or city. The customary high-protein diet has been replaced by one consisting of purchased high-carbohydrate foods.

The long-range effects of acculturation on the tundra ecosystem may well tip the ecological balance. Expanded snowmobile use is likely to degrade the landscape. Moreover, this greater mobility combined with the use of firearms may result in the killing of a greater quantity of game, perhaps beyond the point at which natural increase will compensate. At the same time, the introduction of improved health care has reduced infant mortality and is

already creating population pressure as the birthrate remains high.

In this case study, we see overexploitation of the ecosystem becoming apparent. Everywhere, human intervention produces changes in the environment. Sometimes a new balance is created, but sometimes the environment becomes damaged beyond short-range redemption.

The Eskimo case study demonstrates the varieties of interaction that take place in an ecosystem and is a good illustration of the comprehensive ecological approach as it is practiced today. Such studies—well-rounded considerations of human and cultural interactions with nonhuman and inorganic features of the ecosystem—take Steward's notions of cultural ecology and broaden them in accord with the suggestions of his critics. In the section that follows, we shall examine the twin problems of adaptation and change in an ecological context.

Ecology, Adaptation, and Evolutionary Theory

Adaptation refers to the ability of a living system—organisms, populations, and/or communities, in an ecological context—to maintain or regain stability under conditions of environmental change. Physiological adaptation by genetic means has been the mechanism for biological evolution of all living species. Darwin's "natural selection" and "survival of the fittest" are principles which scholars have used to explain why successful adaptations have survived and nonuseful or inadaptable forms perish. But, from the point of view of anthropological studies, adaptations can be social and cultural as well as physiological and genetic.

The concept of cultural adaptation within an ecosystem provides a framework within which social relations can be viewed. Cohen (1971), for example, has applied the idea of adaptation to marriage and the family. He constructs an evolutionary framework for viewing family arrangements, from those typical of hunting-and-gathering bands to those of modern industrial societies.

Marriage and family arrangements everywhere change in response to changing needs for acquiring a livelihood. We see this in our own society as two-job families adapt their child-care, food preparation, and house-keeping responsibilities to fit the changing demands made on them. Cohen points out that relationships within families have effects on relationships between families; these, in turn, are connected with the adaptive strategy of a society.

In the simplest hunting-gathering societies, marriage alliance for purposes of exchanging women is a particularly characteristic adaptation according to Cohen. These arrangements, including especially the Australian aborigines' elaborate exchanges, have long-term adaptive utility in an ecological niche in which

local groups do not have exclusive rights to particular territories or resources. . . .The abundance of food in their habitats varies from year to year, and flexible organization enables people to move from area to area and to join with other groups in coping with this variability. . . . As a result, there develops a system of mutual and reciprocal access to resources incorporating many groups.
. . . Systems of marital exchange that have developed among hunter-gatherers are a result of their unique territorial relationships. . . . Each hunting-gathering camp becomes dependent on others for a supply of wives and is allied with others through. . . (marriage. [This] contributes to the maintenance of peaceful relations among the groups that move around, camp with each other, and exploit overlapping territories. (Cohen, 1971, p. 25)

Cohen's argument here is that hunting-and-gathering families tend to follow similar patterns everywhere. Food tends to be distributed along kinship lines, and the relationship between family type and economic adaptation can be fairly easily established.

In horticultural economies (those in which simple plant cultivation provides most of the food), however, the relationship of the human population to its habitat changes. There, Cohen argues, "the notion of exclusive rights to territory claimed by a group [is] probably designed. . .to protect investments of time and effort in particular plots" (p. 26). But the transformation to sedentary horticulture does not take place overnight. Archeology and history demonstrate that this evolution proceeded slowly: "At each step along the way, cultivated foods make up a larger proportion of the diet [and] kin group organization becomes progressively stronger" (Cohen, 1971, p. 26). That is, instead of loose family ties, clans and lineages are formed. According to Cohen, horticulturists are more likely to exchange material payments such as bridewealth than to exchange women directly. Territorial alliances become less important, but economic cooperation among households expands. Cooperative landowning and work-organizing groups, such as clans and lineages, are better adapted to exploitation of the environment in a horticultural economy than are the band and named territorial groups. Postmarital residence patterns as well as marital arrangements themselves take on new and more rigid form. The lineage, a corporate land-allocating group usually also involved in social control is, according to Cohen, never found among hunter-gatherers, whereas it is widespread among horticulturists.

For pastoralists, among whom the welfare of flocks and herds is the basic technological requirement, there are seasonal changes in kinship organization. During rainy seasons, there is more likely to be water and vegetation close to home. Kinfolk are then able to live together in large numbers and still provide for the animals in their herds. But during dry seasons, animals must graze over a wider area, and kin members must disperse in order to care for the herd. These seasonal patterns of kinship organization have important implications for the sorts of social institutions that are formed.

Greater variation occurs in the family organization of industrial societies:

In industrial society, where every person barters or sells his labor individually. . . .the household ceases to be a productive unit [and] the cooperative labor of kinsmen is no longer required. . . . Traditional kin groups and ceremonial kinship systems tend to dissolve. . . . (Cohen, 1971, p. 281)

We might take Cohen's sequence one step further, into postindustrial or technological society. Here we see that "strategies of adaptation"—such as long-continued education, mobility for educational or occupational reasons, "retooling" for new occupations as traditional fields become outmoded—tend to isolate the individual from family and other kin groups and to create fragmented work and social units that lack continuity over time. Further, such adaptations tend to remove much of the process of enculturating children from the family. They transfer social controls to a shifting peer group and postpone or lead to the dissolution of marriage. Such changes put increasing strains on family and kin organization.

Too often, the view of culture as consisting primarily of adaptive processes had led to an evolutionary perspective that places social and cultural systems in a hierarchy, with Western civilization generally located at the top. While discussion of adaptation cannot be separated

from the idea of evolution, it must not be confused with progress. An evolutionary perspective is one of several useful ways to organize data about human life. But the linkage of evolution with the notion of progress presents a serious problem, and the concept is used with increasing caution in contemporary studies. Where Steward had seen adaptations as being caused by ecological similarities, Cohen views them as being successful in a kind of Darwinian "cultural selection" process. When presented in terms of survival mechanisms found in human populations, the concept of adaptation is useful. But when too closely tied to evolutionary theory, it becomes an ideological statement about one way of life being superior to another, a notion that is contrary to an anthropological perspective.

For this reason, Rappaport's argument—that modern "civilization" may represent an aberrant form of adaptation, one that might destroy the ecosystem of which it is a part—becomes important. Whereas White (1949) had considered improved energy-harnessing ability an indication of progress, Rappaport suggests that today's high-energy technology has "accelerated" maladaptations. Consider, for example, the different but equally harmful effects of two recent technological innovations: napalm, which devastates a landscape, preventing growth of vegetation for substantial periods of time, but injures relatively few humans; and the "clean" neutron bomb, which destroys organic life over a wide area but leaves structures and habitat otherwise intact.

It is, of course, impossible to describe a culture and its subsystems without discussing the ecological niche inhabited by the population, or the technology and associated activities involved in its exploitation. Whatever the primary interest of the anthropologist—family and kinship organization, religion or whatever—the study of subsistence activities and their related social organization is relevant. The climate can no less be ignored than the house types, the available flora and fauna no less than the systems of material exchange.

Thus, no serious ethnography can today ignore the ecological setting of the culture under study. Those anthropologists who feel that ecology is a primary focus allow it to inform their research at all levels. Even those who find it limiting, so that it is not central in their analyses, must also refer to the ecological concept at some point in study.

Summary

1. The term *ecology* refers to the interrelationships of all living organisms within a total environment. The concept of interaction between culture and environment has always been a primary concern of anthropologists.

2. Implicit in all ecological studies is the notion of adaptation; human populations adapt to habitats by means of culture. Some studies seek to explain why particular cultural traits or sets of traits have originated and existed in particular times and places. Others focus on how these traits function in a given cultural and natural habitat. Early analysts were *environmental determinists,* holding that cultural characteristics were caused by the environmental setting in which a given society was located. *Possibilism,* as expounded by Kroeber, held that the environment made possible a range of cultural responses, but that cultural traits and development were due to culture contact and transmission.

3. The concept of *cultural ecology* appeared around the middle of the twentieth century, with Julian Steward as its primary advocate.

Steward was concerned with the ways in which particular environmental features interact with specific features of culture, and in the patterns of activity adopted by social groups to exploit a particular ecological niche. All organisms interact with their environment but, in the case of humans, the factor of culture is added to the ecological mix.

Steward has been criticized for not giving adequate consideration to the nonhuman aspects of the ecosystem, for concentrating on a limited number of factors, and for failing to provide sufficient empirical data to support his conclusions. However, his emphasis on the crucial relationship between certain ecological conditions and the form that social relations and culture may take has been a major influence in anthropology.

4. *Technology*—the production and use of tools—is the means by which human populations exploit environments for food and shelter. Leslie White emphasized the importance of energy for technology, since the harnessing of energy makes possible all ecological exploitation and adaptation. He developed the formula $E \times T \rightarrow C$ to communicate that culture *(C)* develops as both energy *(E)* and total efficiency *(T)* are increased. Following White, a number of studies, such as those of Harris, have concentrated on the material aspects of culture-technology-ecology interactions.

5. The primary energy exchange in an ecosystem is through the food chain, which represents a series of individual feeding relationships. Human populations, because they are superbly equipped through culture and technology to exploit the resources of an ecosystem, usually dominate the ecosystems of which they are part. The interaction of a human population with its ecosystem is intricate. Any change in human behavior may trigger a chain reaction of consequences spreading throughout the system.

6. Adaptation is the ability of living sys-

474 tems to maintain or regain stability under conditions of change. Adaptation is a process of evolution. But evolution is not necessarily progress. Recent studies, such as those by Cohen, have argued that different stages of technological adaptations affect social systems. Adaptation implies the possibility of maladaptation, and there is a real question whether "advanced civilization," with its high-energy technology and enormous destructive power, may prove to be maladaptive in the long run.

22
Systems of Production

THE study of ecology and the study of economics are closely related. They even have the same Greek root—*oikos,* meaning "house"—which implies that they both have something to do with household management. And indeed both ecology and economics are concerned with the material aspects of survival. One important factor for survival is the availability of material goods necessary to sustain life. Economics is the field of study dealing with human activity in which persons interact with their physical and social environment in order to produce and distribute those necessary materials. Thus, the systems of production and distribution adopted by a society to provide life-supporting materials form an integral part of that society's economy. Economics, therefore, encompasses every aspect of activity that is directed toward provisioning society, including the integration of society with its natural environment. Yet cultural ecologists and economic anthropologists sometimes organize their research and develop their terminologies as if the two fields of study were completely separate. Cultural ecologists, relying heavily on biological ecology, treat humankind as a species and view culture as that species' principal mode of adaptation. Economic anthropologists, recognizing that *Homo sapiens* is the only species that transforms natural materials into life-sustaining products, tend to emphasize social relations at the expense of ecological factors.

Although the sciences of ecology and economics have different goals, they are similar in many ways: they emphasize cyclical processes—or *flows*—of materials, energy, and information. They portray their respective systems as tending toward an optimal state of equilibrium but never actually reaching that state. In short, both ecology and

476 economics are dynamic rather than static in nature.

Economic Anthropology

In this chapter and the following one, we will be concerned with *economic anthropology.* What is the relationship between economics and anthropology? At first it would seem that they have very little in common. Economics is a well-established social science with well-developed conceptual formulations. Cultural anthropology, by contrast, is a younger discipline and less theoretically unified. The data used by economists are largely statistical and usually come from official records and large-scale surveys rather than from individual research. Economists use equations and models to show relationships among the data they collect. Anthropologists use concepts from economics in their attempts to explain aspects of the material conditions of human existence, but their more diversified interests do not always match up well with traditional explanations offered by economics.

Yet each field of study can contribute to the other. Where the economist uses the term *ceteris paribus* ("other things being equal") to cover noneconomic phenomena, anthropologists can fill in the blanks with information not usually considered by economists. And where anthropologists have concentrated on the social framework of economic activity without fully considering the economic process itself, economists can contribute supply-and-demand analyses, techniques for measuring transactions, and general ideas about allocation of resources.

What, then, is the task of economic anthropology? It is, first of all, to describe the variety of economic arrangements developed by humankind in different times and places. Economic anthropologists then sort these diverse arrangements into classes, and attempt to fit them with different types of societies and cultures. As Manning Nash (1966) puts it, economic anthropology must

develop a body of theory which will explain the gift giving of the Plains Indians, the pig exchanges of the New Hebrides, the circulation of valuables in the Solomon archipelago, the persistence of hundreds of separate pottery producers in a single Mayan Indian community, the effects of wage labor and cash cropping in New Guinea, . . . and a host of other real, significant, and puzzling economic and cultural facts. (p. 16)

Anthropologists provide different perspectives on these economic activities than are provided by economists. To the anthropologist, it is the *total* cultural system, the *total* society, that provides the context for investigating and interpreting systems of production and exchange. Take, for example, a simple monetary transaction such as, "I will give you $1.00 for a dozen eggs," or a nonmonetary transaction such as, "I will give you a kilo of rice for a dozen eggs." There is more going on in such transactions than simply an exchange of commodities. Anthropologists are interested in finding out such information as where the commodities come from, who produces them, how they are produced, what is the relationship between the parties involved in their production, who can participate in their exchange, and so on. In comparison to the economist, the economic anthropologist takes a more *holistic* approach.

Formalist Versus Substantivist Approaches

Economic anthropology has been characterized by two fundamental approaches. The *formalist approach* takes traditional economic theory as its point of departure, and stresses the scarcity of resources and the importance of rational decision-making (for example, economizing). The *substantivist approach,* on the other hand, denies that there is any such thing as an "economic sphere" and insists that economic relations can be identified only in the context of each society studied. Substantivists emphasize the ways in which economic activities are intertwined with other social activities in any given society. Their emphasis is on the various ways in which economic relations are embedded in other, broader social relations.

These two approaches present us with a dilemma. According to the substantivist approach, preindustrial social systems have no economic institutions as such, but the social institutions of such societies (such as marriage) have various economic aspects (such as bridewealth). According to the formalist approach, the economy consists of all decisions that have to do with economizing, which means a large portion of all the decisions that are made in any society.

It can be argued that *both* the formalist and the substantivist approaches must be taken into consideration in any empirical study, and that, indeed, what is required is a synthesis of these two approaches. For example, if we wanted to understand how corn is produced and distributed in a society where corn is the staple of the diet, we would want to look at the law of supply and demand (formalist approach) as well as how politics, religion, kinship, and other social patterns and processes (substantive approach) affect the production and distribution of corn. Neither approach on its own would provide all the information we would need, since traditional economic theory alone would not shed any light on the other social factors that influence production and distribution in most societies, and social theory alone would not take into account the formal economic imperatives that exist. We will pursue such a synthesis in this and the following chapters.

The Nature of Economic Relations

In this section, we will examine economic relations in general before turning to a discussion of several specific types of economic systems. Economic activity can be viewed as "activity in which (people) interact with their physical and social environment in the calculated attempt to acquire . . . a living" (Cook, 1973, p. 810). It can be viewed as "a sort of strategy of matching limited means with alternate uses [in order to] get . . . the most out of the available resources" (Nash, 1977, p. 233). It can be viewed as activity concerned with money and prices (a narrow view), or it can be seen as the science of choice (a broad view). But in all of these cases, economic activity is thought of as having to do with the production, distribution, and consumption of material goods. In these processes, people make choices between alternate uses of resources. Thus, for our working definition, we will consider *economic activity* to be the choices people make in determining how available resources are to be used in producing, distributing, and consuming material goods, and the services associated with them.

Two important points need to be made before we continue. One is that it is extremely difficult to isolate economic activities from other activities in most non-Western societies. As Nash puts it, "we have economic activities *and* activities that have an economic aspect. When a temple dancer in Bali dances, that is not economic, but when she gets a gift or payment for the act of dancing, the dancer has an economic aspect" (1977, p. 233). This kind of relationship can be seen in Western societies, too. Consider the artist or writer who seeks self-fulfillment in his or her work, but who also may be paid for painting or writ-

The cultivation being done by these Masai girls in Kenya represents a conscious choice of economic activity. The Masai are traditionally a nomadic tribe who only recently, as part of a community development project, have begun to engage in horticulture. (Marc and Evelyne Bernheim, Woodfin Camp)

ing. Rarely is an activity purely economic, however.

The other point is that economic choices can be both conscious and unconscious. It sometimes has been argued that members of peasant and primitive societies do not make "rational" or "calculated" economic choices; they supposedly have little foresight or sense of value. But even if this were so, it does not mean that their choices are irrational. If those choices "work"—if they achieve the desired results—then they are the proper choices for those people in that society. The !Kung Bushmen, for example, are food-gatherers, and Westerners have assumed that their lives were a constant struggle to find enough food to stay alive. But as anthropologists who lived with them discovered, they spend only between 12 and 19 hours per week hunting and gathering food, and their diet consists of many more calories than nutritionists have estab-

lished as the necessary minimum. Their "decision" to become gatherers rather than cultivators was not likely a conscious one. The question of whether they should turn to what some might consider the higher standard of living of their horticultural neighbors seems to be answered by the fact that they have what they need without the time and effort that horticulture demands. As one of the Bushmen put it, "Why should we plant when there are so many nuts in the world?" (cited in Mair, 1972, p. 163). And in a severe drought in 1965, many of their horticultural neighbors, whose crops had failed, joined the Bushmen in foraging. Even unintentional and unplanned results can be beneficial.

These two points can be illustrated by the *potlatch* ceremony of the Northwest Coast Indians. In this seemingly irrational event (by Western standards), a man would give away or destroy his most valuable possessions. This was an economic activity because it resulted in a redistribution of material goods within the society. It was also a social event in which the person who gave away the most property achieved the highest status. It was "rational" and "calculated" because the redistribution of wealth contributed to the general well-being of all the members of the community, in addition to conferring status on the individual sponsor.

Production

Production is defined as the various modes used by the members of a society to procure their material means of existence. The concept of production encompasses a vast array of activities ranging from food gathering, hunting, horticulture, and craft work to highly organized industrial operations. Productive operations represent a combination of these following primary factors that depend very heavily on one another: the raw materials available, technology and division of labor. Every production process is made up of an ordered series of activities that develop in accordance with the resources of the environment and the social realities of the particular society.

Production is organized on the basis of the relative scarcity of three *factors of production:* land, labor, and capital. Both land and labor are necessary for subsistence. Water (which could be included with land) is also essential. Clearly, one will not find a settled agricultural economy in areas where fertile land is very limited or large herds of livestock where water holes are scarce. Labor may be "scarce" while a family's children are still very young, so that, for example, a herdsman may have to keep his herd with his father's even though the animals are legally his. As for *capital*—the equipment and supplies used in production—there is some debate on the question of what, if anything, can be labeled capital in a subsistence

economy. In modern, industrial economies, capital is the means of production. A system of capitalism is characterized by the relationship—the separation—between those who own the means of production in a society and those who actually do the work of production. The problem in identifying capital in subsistence or other non-capitalist economies is, then, what *is* capital in the absence of the separation of productive roles? In discussing subsistence economies, we shall have to use a definition of capital that does not separate owners of capital from workers, because there is no such separation in these economies. Broadly defined, then, capital in noncapitalist economies is any goods or services—be they livestock, gardens, cultivation tools, factory equipment, or muscle power—used to produce more goods.

A convenient way of viewing small-scale economic systems has been provided by Nash (1977), who divides the topic into four major themes: (1) technology and division of labor, (2) structure of productive units, (3) systems and media of exchange, and (4) the control of wealth and capital. We will give an overview of these four themes here, and then discuss the first two in the remainder of this chapter. The remaining two will be treated in the following chapter.

Technology and Division of Labor. We define *technology* as the tools and processes by means of which material goods can be produced in greater quantity and with less physical effort. The type of technology available to a society plays an important role in its mode of production. Obviously, industrial economies have much more highly developed technologies than subsistence economies.

Tribal and peasant societies are relatively simple in that they have few tools for making tools; they do not have a wide variety of different productive tasks, and do not use or create much energy. The Bemba of Rhodesia, for example, use a mode of cultivation that involves climbing tall trees, cutting a few branches, burning them, and using the ashes for fertilizer. This method requires few tools, few different types of activity, and only human energy. In industrial economies, on the other hand, tractors are used to plow fields, as contrasted with the hand-held hoes used in subsistence economies. Obviously, tractors enable fewer people to cultivate more space than do hoes, thus freeing more people to do work other than food production.

As we have seen, the division of labor in primitive societies is based primarily on sex, age, and sometimes rank. Workers are largely interchangeable. One individual's skill is about as good as that of any other. People in tribal and peasant societies learn socially appropriate skills in the course of growing up, and within age and sex groups, any worker can readily replace any other worker. Children begin to learn farm and household work almost as soon as they can walk. Since men are considered to have greater strength than women and because they are not hampered by carrying children around on their backs, they often do the heavy work, while women take care of the household. The relative simplicity of technology, with little use of machinery, means the lack of a high degree of specialization.

Structure of Productive Units. In small-scale societies, there are no organizations whose only task is production, such as guilds or factories. Nor is any lasting social unit based solely on productive activities. Often family groups are the major productive units, but their reasons for existence and their activities go far beyond economic considerations. Economic life depends on other kinds of social relationships—kinship bonds, political bonds, territorial bonds, and so on.

In subsistence economies, there is little specialization. Each household provides its own food, clothing, and shelter. Along with more advanced technology comes greater *specialization,* or division of labor. Fewer and fewer people are needed to produce food, while the remainder exchange for food the reward they get for whatever other work they do (for example, teaching children, repairing machinery, etc.). In industrial economies, specialization is extreme—rarely does a household produce its own food, clothing, or shelter, though it may produce some small part of each of these.

Stanley H. Udy (1970) divides *production organizations*—groups that are engaged in the production of some type of material goods—in preindustrial societies into four types: familial, custodial, contractual, and voluntary. A *familial* production organization is based on a kinship group, although not necessarily the nuclear family. Production in the pottery-making community of Amatenango in southeastern Mexico, described later, is based on familial relationships. A *custodial* production organization is based on the obligation to participate. Workers are drawn from groups that have political rather than familial ties. There is an institutionalized authority that can compel others, by force if necessary, to participate in production. Plantations worked by slaves, in the pre-Civil War southern United States, are examples of custodial work organizations. A *contractual* production organization is, as the term implies, based on a voluntary contract between two or more parties. No one is forced to enter into such an agreement in the first place, but once a contract has been agreed to, participation is compulsory. Failure to live up to the agreement brings any number of sanctions, depending on the particular group. This is the type of organization that is most familiar to members of Western societies. Finally, a *voluntary* production organization is based on the self-interest of members—anyone who can do the work and is in the vicinity may join, but there are no sanctions for nonparticipation. Contractual and voluntary organizations are closest to the requirements of industrial economies.

Systems and Media of Exchange. Another feature of tribal and peasant economies is that people are seldom obligated to calculate the costs of doing one thing rather than another. Calculating costs is often impossible or unnecessary, since the uses of time, resources, and people occur as a result of the social structure and are not calculated in terms of increasing productivity. For example, in a society where the women are responsible for tending the fields and the men do the hunting, men would not help the women in the fields even if it might enable them to harvest bigger crops, because the division of labor prohibits it. However, under outside pressures, these divisions can break down or be transformed.

An exchange system can be quite complex. For example, among the Tiv of Nigeria, food can be exchanged for food or for brass rods; brass rods can be exchanged for highly valued goods, women, and slaves; but food cannot be exchanged for highly valued goods. We will examine such systems of exchange in some detail in the next chapter.

Control of Wealth and Capital. In small-scale societies, investment takes the form of using resources to expand existing social systems rather than to transform the society. Hence, many such societies have *leveling mechanisms* whereby people are forced to spend accumulated capital in ways (such as loans to relatives, large feasts, and the like) that are not necessarily productive but are conducive to the perpetuation of social traditions. These are ways of "scrambling" wealth so that social relations will remain unchanged. The *potlatch* described earlier is an example of a leveling mechanism.

Amatenango Economics. The pottery industry of the Mexican village Amatenango, as described by Nash (1961), nicely illustrates the themes just presented. The Indians of Amatenango are a horticultural people, but horticulture alone is not enough to enable them to maintain the standard of living they prefer. The making and selling of pottery, a specialty of the community, helps them to achieve the level of living they expect. Of the 280 households in the town center of Amatenango, only two or three are not involved in producing pottery for sale. Girls in Amatenango are taught from childhood how to make pots, and all the women who are born and grow up there are engaged in pottery making. In a neighboring community that has almost the same natural resources as Amatenango, there is not even a single pot produced.

Since the technology of pottery making is simple and inexpensive, even the poorest families in the community have access to it. The skills are passed on from generation to generation, and the materials needed are readily available. The pottery making is done completely by hand. No wheel, no molds, no ovens are used; just a steel blade for scraping, a smooth board for resting pot bases, a burlap bag or skirt under the potter's knees and nets and bags for carrying the finished pots are needed. The total cost of these items is under $3.00—a price that every household can afford.

The quantity of pottery produced is not geared to the prices brought in the market but to the cycle of celebrations, both religious and secular. At festival times, households need cash; at those times there is a high demand for pots so they are made then and sold quickly, which eliminates storage problems.

The units of production in Amatenango are households, which are kinship groups in which membership comes only by being born or marrying into the unit. The household unit limits the number of workers available for pottery making, in that no one hires out to make pottery for wages, and pottery making itself is part of a woman's job as a member of a household. Since pottery making is only one of many things each household engages in, other activities compete with it for the time and energy of the same group of people.

Certain features of assembly-line production are used in the making of pottery in Amatenango. Each woman works on a different part of a pot—base, body, neck, handle—at the same time. As a woman completes a particular operation, the finished parts are partially dried. The division of labor is most efficient if there are four women in the household, because each one can then be working on a different section at the same time, which results in greater efficiency. If there are more than four women, however, efficiency does not increase very much.

The pricing of pottery is a constant topic of conversation in the community. People are highly aware of relative costs and are very sensitive to economic gain, but not for personal aggrandizement. Economically, they operate on a rational level in the sense of bringing means and ends together; but the value system of the community requires that all households remain fairly equivalent in wealth.

Leveling mechanisms are responsible for maintaining this equality. First, Amatenango's low level of technology and its limited land area impose severe restrictions on the amount of wealth that can be attained by the society as a whole. Second, bilateral inheritance requires that all offspring receive an equal share of the parents' estate, which tends to fracture whatever estates may be accumulated. Third, there are a series of communal offices in which men from each household are expected to serve and to contribute financially, which is a drain on both work time and resources. Fourth, forced expenditure in certain ritual festivals is an obligation of the wealthier households. Amatenango is a society in which wealth is not easily turned to technical and economic uses but is drained by social and religious obligations. Several forces acting together combine to keep the fortunes of the various households nearly equivalent and to maintain the shift of family wealth over time.

Thus, Amatenango is a small-scale economy in which the technology and division of labor are relatively simple. The domestic unit,

or household, is the center of production; the costs and benefits of production are not calculated separately from those of other activities; and the accumulation of wealth is prevented by various leveling mechanisms. In the remainder of this chapter, we will be concerned with the technology and productive units of small-scale societies. We will deal with systems of exchange and control of wealth in greater detail in the next chapter.

Modes of Food Production

A wide variety of productive systems are known to exist in human societies, and they deal in very different ways with the problem of determining how resources are utilized. These systems may be divided into two major categories: subsistence economies and industrial economies. We will look first at subsistence economies, which make up the vast majority of the societies studied by anthropologists.

Subsistence Economies

In a *subsistence economy,* people use what they themselves produce in order to meet their own needs. Although a degree of trade may be transacted, they do not trade their products for other goods through the medium of money. There are three main types of subsistence economy: those based on hunting (and fishing) and gathering wild fruits and roots; those based on herding domestic animals; and those based on raising crops (often in conjunction with a certain amount of animal husbandry). These three modes of food production were once viewed as successive stages of economic development. Today, however, the mode followed by a given society is generally thought to be determined by the resources available and the level of technical knowledge of the people engaged in it. Let us take a closer look at the three main types of subsistence economies.

Hunting and Gathering. Peoples who forage for food by hunting and killing animals, by fishing, and by gathering wild fruit, vegetables, and nuts are known as hunters and gatherers. They raise little if any of the food they eat. Hunters and gatherers live in small groups and must move often to find food. Although each hunting-and-gathering group stays within a particular geographic area, it is not a closed social system. There is social communication among groups in the form of visiting, gift-giving, and intermarriage. Thus, hunting-and-gathering societies consist of a set of local *bands*—small groups of families, numbering perhaps 25 to 100 persons, with simple political organization. Hunting-and-gathering bands are part of a larger community whose members speak the same language and enter into various relationships with one another, including marriage.

The organization of food production in such a society has five important features that result directly from the small size and mobility of the hunting-and-gathering band (Lee & DeVore, 1968):

1. Because they move around to get food, hunters and gatherers have little personal property. Since mobility prevents them from acquiring a great many possessions, wealth differences between individuals are kept to a minimum, which, in turn, leads to a generally egalitarian social system. Individuals and families usually own no more than the basic necessities of life, because they cannot transport much more than that when it comes time to move again.
2. The band is kept small by the nature of the food supply, which, because of limited resources, would be quickly exhausted by a large group. Actually, the size of a band tends to change often as people move from one band to another.
3. No single band has exclusive rights to a particular set of resources. Bands have reciprocal access to food supplies. Moreover, visiting patterns create obligations among groups, so that last year's guests become this year's hosts and must share their food supply.
4. Food surpluses are usually small. Everyone knows where the food is and where other bands are. In effect, food is "stored" in the environment, and people work continually to transfer the food from this storehouse to their stomachs.
5. No band becomes permanently attached to any single area, because the livelihood of its people does not depend on a particular area. Frequent visiting of different resource areas also prevents any one band from becoming attached to a particular area. And, because of the limited amount of personal and collective property, bands can change residence without giving up any interests in land or goods.

Hunters and gatherers such as the !Kung Bushmen of South West Africa must move from place to place in search of food. Thus, they live in small bands and have few personal possessions. (Marvin Newman, Woodfin Camp)

The hunting-and-gathering group, in short, exploits nature directly. This pattern is in sharp contrast to other economic systems, which transform nature for purposes of production.

Economic Implications of Mobility. Marshall Sahlins (1972) notes that mobility is the key to understanding hunters and gatherers. He points out that their economic system is governed by the imminence of diminishing returns. That is, a band will soon use up most of the food resources within a convenient distance from camp. To stay in the same camp is to experience diminishing returns in terms of a reduced supply or a supply of increasingly inferior foods. Anthropologists have also found that when a band does not, for whatever reason, move its encampment, it does so at the cost of searching for food at greater and greater distances from camp. The obvious solution to each of these problems is simply to move to another area.

But the need to move also involves diminishing returns. Tools, clothing, ornaments, and the like become a burden when they have to be moved. The building of large, elaborate houses is out of the question if they will soon have to be abandoned. Thus, small, light objects are better than big objects; one of something usually is better than two of something. Individuals in our society who backpack appreciate the wisdom of such customs.

The fact of diminishing returns, both in productivity and in portability, has social consequences as well. Among these are infanticide and senilicide—the killing of infants and of old people—because they cannot transport themselves. Hunters and gatherers also tend to refrain from sexual relations during the nursing period of an infant (which may be two years or longer) in order to avoid closely spaced births and to control population. Such practices can be seen as resulting from the need to handle people and goods in similarly efficient ways.

Hunting-and-gathering societies have usu-ally been viewed as underproductive and poor. But Sahlins shows that their economic system is actually a creative adaptation to their environment, a way of matching ends and means. Mobility and moderation put hunters and gatherers' ends within range of their technical means. Hunters and gatherers spend an estimated 3 to 5 hours per adult worker per day on food acquisition—a figure many modern workers would envy. In fact, it appears that horticultural economies, which usually have been considered more advanced, actually require more work than the hunting and gathering system. According to Sahlins, the amount of work per capita *increases* with the development of culture, while the amount of leisure *decreases,* since cultivation requires people to work longer and harder in order to produce enough food to survive.

The !Kung Bushmen. Today, societies that depend exclusively upon hunting and gathering are few, but they represent a condition that once characterized all of humanity. In 1966, the population of those who depended exclusively on hunting and gathering was estimated at 30,000—about "enough to fill a medium-sized football stadium," according to Pfeiffer (1972, p. 350), although many more supplement their diets by hunting and gathering. Those few exclusive hunters and gatherers that remain today show great diversity. They are found in every type of region from African deserts, to equatorial forests of Southeast Asia, to Alaskan tundra. These tend to be environments where cultivation would be extremely difficult. Modern hunters and gatherers combine hunting, gathering, and fishing in a variety of ways to obtain sufficient food. Because they are affected by local resources, there is a tendency for particular groups to "specialize" in particular resources, such as caribou or bison, yams or pine nuts, fish or sea mammals.

The !Kung Bushmen of southwest Africa are a classic example of a hunting-and-gathering society (Forde, 1934; Marshall,

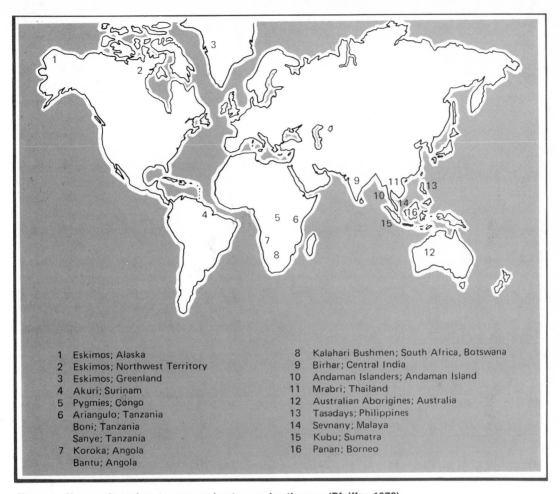

Figure 1   Known sites of contemporary hunters and gatherers. (Pfeiffer, 1972)

1	Eskimos; Alaska	8	Kalahari Bushmen; South Africa, Botswana
2	Eskimos; Northwest Territory	9	Birhar; Central India
3	Eskimos; Greenland	10	Andaman Islanders; Andaman Island
4	Akuri; Surinam	11	Mrabri; Thailand
5	Pygmies; Congo	12	Australian Aborigines; Australia
6	Ariangulo; Tanzania	13	Tasadays; Philippines
	Boni; Tanzania	14	Sevnany; Malaya
	Sanye; Tanzania	15	Kubu; Sumatra
7	Koroka; Angola	16	Panan; Borneo
	Bantu; Angola		

1960). The !Kung are organized into two basic social groups—the family and the band. The family is the primary and most cohesive social unit. At its simplest, a !Kung family is made up of a man and his wife, which may then be augmented by children, dependents such as parents or grandparents, and the daughters' young husbands, who come to give bride-service. !Kung society requires that all men go to live with the family of their brides and give them bride-service, which consists of hunting and providing meat for the bride's family. If the bride's parents are dead, the husband serves whatever relatives she is living with. In a first marriage, bride-service usually lasts until three children are born to the couple. Once his obligations are fulfilled, a man has the right to return to his own family and band, taking his wife and children with him. He may also choose to remain with his wife's family. Since men often marry outside of their bands, the bride-service provides a constant exchange of people among different bands. When the head of an extended family dies, this extended family breaks up, and the nuclear families of the married sons and daughters begin to operate independently of each other. When their offspring marry, these nuclear families become extended families, as the domestic cycle comes full circle.

The band is organized around rights to grassland areas *(veldkos)* and water holes. Individuals have access to water and land only through their band affiliations. Each band has a headman who is the "owner" of the *veldkos* and water and who administers the consumption of these resources by the members of the band. A band is composed of people who are related by birth and by marriage, including the families of parents and their offspring, siblings, aunts, and uncles and cousins. The Bushman band moves several times a year, whenever the food supply becomes scarce. Within the band, each family produces its own food. The women collect roots, berries, and the like, as well as firewood and water. The men go out to hunt almost daily, providing small game such as lizards or rabbits for their immediate families. If any large game is brought into the camp, however, it is usually shared.

The !Kung Bushmen show how closely intertwined economic and social arrangements can be. Bride-service not only provides a framework for deciding who is going to live where and with whom but also ensures that there is a young male hunter in each family. It also acts as a leveling mechanism, since each man has many dependents to support. The primary leveling mechanism, of course, is the fact that a person must be able to carry all of his or her possessions.

Although the different groups of hunters and gatherers that remain today concentrate on different particular resources of the natural environment, their way of life has certain basic characteristics in common: they are highly mobile, constantly moving from place to place; they amass very few personal possessions; they live in small groups, because of the nature of the food supply; food surpluses are usually small; no single group has exclusive rights to a particular set of resources; they have a fantastic knowledge of their natural environment; and no group becomes attached to any single area. All evidence indicates that there is no reason to believe that these fundamental patterns of life observed among present-day hunters and gatherers are substantially different from those followed by past groups.

Pastoralism. *Pastoralism*—raising and herding animals for meat, hides, milk, and the products that can be derived from them—highlights the transition from hunting and gathering to the transformation of nature by cultivation. Pastoralists are found from the equator to the Arctic Circle. Pastoralism, however, has developed as a dominant

Pastoralists may be found from the equator to the Arctic Circle and make their living by raising and herding various sorts of animals. These Finnish Laplanders, for example, raise reindeer. (Dan Budnick, Woodfin Camp)

economy only in the Old World. In the New World, pastoral groups include the Navajo of the North American Southwest and herders in the highlands of South America.

Pastoralists raise a wide variety of animals (camels, donkeys, sheep, horses, cattle, reindeer, llamas, alpacas) and use them for many different purposes. The regions in which they are found include tundra, grassland, desert, and tropical savanna. Pastoralists are not found in forested areas, because their animals usually are not suited to such conditions. Nor are they generally found in well-watered areas—the rewards of cultivation in such areas are higher than the rewards of herding.

There are ways in which pastoralism and cultivation can be combined. One of these is *transhumance,* in which the group winters in permanent villages around lowland pastures, where it engages in some cultivation. It then migrates to the mountains in the summer, taking its livestock along.

Pastoral societies often continue to exist despite the fact that their members are aware of the advantages of cultivation. This may be due in part to a belief on the part of the pastoralists, reinforced by religious sanctions and taboos, that their way of life is superior. The Masai of highland Kenya, for example, have sought to maintain the purity of their particular economy, even using force to drive out cultivators from land that is suited to horticulture. In some places, the pastoralists have subjugated the cultivators and established themselves as an aristocracy. In others, pastoralism is part of a hybrid culture in which the men do the herding and the women do the cultivating. In general, such arrangements are not highly successful.

Pastoralists, like hunters and gatherers, are mobile or "nomadic," but their mobility differs in character from that of hunters and gatherers. Each group has a fairly well-defined territory, and it stays within this area and defends it against invaders (in contrast to the visiting and intermarriage of hunting-and-gathering societies). Within that area are specific sites that are occupied for long periods each year. The life of pastoralists is much less settled than that of cultivators, though; cultivators cannot move quickly—if at all—nor can they take all their food supply with them.

Many, but not all, pastoral societies are characterized by an authoritarian system in which the male head of a household has almost total power over wives, children, and slaves—a pattern that is familiar from Biblical descriptions of the Israelites. It is also common, but not universal, for women to have lower status than men in such societies (but this is often true of horticultural societies as well).

The Ruwala Bedouin. The Ruwala Bedouin are tent-dwelling camel breeders who live in northern Arabia (Forde, 1934). For 9 to 10 months of the year, they occupy well-defined tracts of coarse grassland, rarely entering the sandy desert or rocky country nearby. For part of each year, they must return to settled lands, since the vegetation in their pastures withers during the very hot season.

The Ruwala follow a roughly circular migration pattern. In September, they leave the villages to the west of their territory. They spend the winter moving slowly in scattered groups over the northern pastures. In the spring, they move southward toward the fringes of the desert. Then they follow the pastures and water holes west and north, reaching the villages before the drought strikes. These movements vary in their details from one year to the next, depending on the timing and amount of the rains, though their general form remains the same.

The organization of a Bedouin group is based on the requirements of its animals. The tribal *sheikh* may control a large number of tents, but the tribe does not live as a group. A number of small segments of 50 to 100 people scatter over the pastures seeking grass for their own animals. The camel is the measure

For the Ruwala Bedouin, the camel is the measure of wealth, supplying food and being used as a medium of exchange for other products. (Klaus D. Francke, Peter Arnold Photo Archives)

of wealth. It supplies food and other raw materials, and can be sold to traders or peasants in exchange for weapons, clothing, and grain. A man's wealth depends on the size of his herds, though it may be displayed in the form of slaves, horses, or tent trappings, as well.

Unlike hunters and gatherers, such as the !Kung Bushmen, the Ruwala must store much of their food supply. A well-to-do man starts out from the village with a camel load (about 300 pounds) of grain for each member of his household and an extra load to be used in en-

tertaining guests. The remaining food is obtained from the camel (milk only) or from a few hunters attached to the camp. There is also some gathering of wild foods.

Bedouin tribesmen are related through the male blood line; kin are all descended from the same paternal ancestor and usually remain together. A collection of such groups recognizes the head of the dominant group as its *sheikh*. When families become very large, however, they often must segment into smaller groups, and the ties between them weaken over time. In fact, between different camping groups there may be constant rivalry, as the competition for land and water, in the form of wells, is ongoing. Between different tribes rivalry is intensified, tension is high, and in some cases, a state of war exists between them. Indeed, as Forde (1934) has pointed out, "The life of a [Bedouin] camp is not one of peaceful migration from pasture to pasture. It is punctuated by raiding expeditions small and large against enemy tribes and their herds" (p. 323). This is particularly true during years of severe drought, when pastorage is meager and water is scarce. To the danger of raiding is added that of blood feuds: murder must be either avenged by the kin of the victim by killing the murderer or a relative of the murderer, or a large quantity of wealth must be transferred from the group of the murderer to the group of the person murdered. And yet individual travelers are in little danger. Travelers are welcomed and, by tribal law, given safe conduct through the tribe's territory.

Horticulture and Agriculture. The third main type of subsistence economy is one of plant cultivation. Anthropologists divide cultivation into two types. The first is *horticulture*—plant cultivation using simple tools such as hoes and, mostly, human muscle power. Horticulture is usually done by women on small plots of land. The second type of cultivation is *agriculture*—intensive plant cultivation using plows and other machinery. Agriculture is most often done by men over large tracts of land. Pastoralists and *cultivators*—people who practice some method of raising crops—are often viewed as hostile to one another by nature, and it is true that there have often been conflicts between these groups. Yet it is not pastoralism and horticulture as such that are in opposition but a mobile, relatively unaccumulative life style and a settled, relatively wealthy one. The most prominent characteristics of most cultivating societies is that their members can produce surplus food and thus free others for more specialized tasks.

As mentioned earlier, cultivation can sometimes coexist with hunting and fishing or with herding within a given society, but plough cultivation tends to absorb such a high portion of the community's energy that there is less opportunity or need for other means of food production. Plough cultivators keep animals, but they use them as draught animals, not (usually) for food.

Cultivators vary widely in their economic and social organization as well as in the nature of the crops they grow and the technology they use. Horticulturalists, the most primitive cultivators, use digging sticks with which they make holes for seeds and cuttings and sometimes wooden blades for chopping down weeds. To prepare their gardens, they may use the *slash-and-burn* technique. This involves slashing trees and underbrush, burning off the refuse, and planting in the area thus cleared. This practice is widespread in the Amazon region and has proved to be an effective way of utilizing resources over time, because soil nutrients are replaced by the decaying plant life that covers the earth. New gardens have to be prepared within a few years, since repeated plantings in the same field eventually lead to low yields.

The use of ploughs is characteristic of agriculturalists. In addition to the plough, these cultivators use irrigation devices and fertilizers, as well as techniques such as crop rotation and the planting of crops such as beans that restore the nitrogen content of the soil. There are, however, some advanced cultivating economies that do not depend on the plough. Where rice fields are built in terraces on steep hillsides, as is done by the Ifugao in the Philippines, for example, the plough has no use at all and cultivation is done almost entirely by hand.

The communities of hand cultivators may be smaller and less complex than those of some food gatherers. But, in general, the larger and more stable food supply of cultivators allows them to develop new types of social and political institutions—to organize

The slash-and-burn method of cultivation often involves a considerable amount of work. Notice the scaffold-like structure that was built around the large tree this Yąnomamö man is cutting down as part of the slash-and-burn technique necessary to clear an area for cultivation. (Karl Werdmann, National Audubon Society, Photo Researchers)

in large communities and even into states with formal political institutions. Landholding systems among cultivators range from systems similar to those of hunter-gathers, in which land is held in common, through feudal systems, in which tenants occupy and cultivate plots of land owned by large landowners, as in medieval Europe or in parts of contemporary third-world nations, to private property, as in Western societies today.

Crafts such as weaving, pottery, and metalworking develop further in economies using plough cultivation than in other types of subsistence economies. The reason for this is that, with proper techniques, good land can be used indefinitely and can feed more people than are needed to cultivate it. Thus specialists in other activities can be maintained.

In Western nations, cultivation is closer to an industrial economic system than to a subsistence economy. In fact, it is sometimes called "agribusiness." One farmer, with the help of modern technology and equipment, can manage vast areas and produce huge surpluses of crops.

Although long since out of date, Forde's (1934) description of two cultivating systems illustrates well the types of production systems under consideration here. The Boro and the Cochin systems have subsequently changed, but production systems of this nature are still found in comparable areas.

The Boro of the Western Amazon Forest. The Boro were a group of over 10,000 South American Indians living in about 50 separate settlements in the Western Amazon. They lived in the dense equatorial forest that grows on the rich soil of the region. Their problem was not one of making things grow, but, rather, of clearing the forest in order to plant. To create room for a settlement, they burned down the trees in a relatively open area to make a clearing and then built a single large house 60 to 70 feet long on each side and at least 30 feet high. Each nuclear family had its own fireplace, which is against one of the walls of this house.

Despite all the effort that went into making the clearings and building the communal house, these sites were not occupied for more than a few years. When the gardens lost their fertility and hostile groups learned where the settlement was located, the site was abandoned and a new one found.

The Boro did some hunting but depended mainly on horticulture. The plot owned by the chief of the settlement was usually located in the main clearing. Those of other members of the community were scattered throughout the surrounding jungle, generally within about a mile of the house. To prepare a plot for cultivation, the larger trees were burned down and the smaller growth hacked away with stone axes. At the end of the rainy season, the undergrowth was burned out with a number of small fires. The ground was roughly broken by the men with heavy wooden stakes, and then the women used digging sticks to plant the crops. The men did the heavy work of forest clearing and digging the rough ground and then returned to hunting wild game. The women did the rest of the horticultural work and prepared the food. A plot was exhausted after two or three harvests.

Rice Cultivation in Cochin. Along the Malabar coast of India in the native state of Cochin, an ancient system of plough cultivation was used. Rice was cultivated intensively on thousands of acres of carefully prepared plots. More than half of the population was engaged in rice cultivation and over one-third in various crafts and small-scale industry.

The settlements of Cochin were not compact villages but loose clusters of houses on higher ground that was unsuitable for rice cultivation. The houses of landowners had gardens and groves of fruit trees; those of laborers were scattered among the fields and on the outskirts of the settlements.

Almost all the low-lying land was devoted to rice cultivation. Before the monsoon rains, the plots were tilled with a simple wooden plough pulled by water buffaloes. Women followed the plough and broke up the sods with sticks. Dung and manure were scattered over the plots; after the plots had been soaked by the rains, they were ploughed again. Clods of earth were crushed with a heavy wooden plank, and then a log was dragged over the ground to level it. When the ground had been soaked, the seeds were scattered. Between planting and harvesting, much of the work consisted of maintaining the banks around the fields which controlled the amount of water in them. A second crop of millet, pulses, or oil seeds was grown after the rice had been harvested in order to restore nitrogen to the soil.

Before the British influence became dominant, the political and social organization of Cochin was based mainly on the feudal hereditary rights of landowners and on the Hindu caste system. The royal house was the greatest landowner in the state; large tracts were also controlled by hereditary district chiefs. Some of the land was sublet to tenant farmers, but much of it was worked by agricultural serfs. Subsequently, most of the land was owned by wealthy families and either sublet or worked by laborers.

Industrial Economies

A productive unit in an American automobile plant could consist of a group of machinists who make or assemble specific parts. Consider, for example, the group of workers who make pushrods for the cylinders of an engine. Their activities are limited to producing pushrods and only pushrods. In an industrial economy, interaction among workers is often job specific; that is, it occurs only while they are on the job. The workers have no other rights and obligations to each other. In hunting-and-gathering bands, on the other hand, an extended family not only cooperates in hunting and gathering, but its members also interact socially during the distribution and consumption of the foods collected. They also, of course, share kinship and ritual obligations. Clearly there are important differences between the economy of pushrod makers and the traditional economy of hunters and gatherers. What are those differences?

The Development of Specialization. To begin with, the pushrod makers are engaged in a very small part of the total productive effort. The technology of an industrial economy is highly specialized and job specific, so the work is divided among large numbers of people who specialize in a small part of the total operation. This is not the case among hunters and gatherers, where the only significant division of labor is between the men, who hunt, and the women, who gather. In small-scale societies, the economy is not differentiated from other fields of activity and other domains of thought. It is embedded in a broad web of social relations that serve multiple and diverse functions. How, then, does the extreme specialization characteristic of industrial economies come about?

In small-scale societies, labor is divided on the basis of age and sex. Heavy work is not done by children or old people, but children contribute some work to the household from an early age. Work that has to be done at some distance from the home is usually done by men; men also do work that requires agility, such as climbing trees for fruit. Women cook, gather, and plant, as well as bear children. Some anthropologists have argued that the demands of child rearing, in particular, tend to keep women close to home. Even in subsistence economies, however, there is some specialization. Some members of the society develop skill in weaving, pottery making, or some other craft. But these activities are still centered on the household, and often the items produced are used, exchanged, or given away, not sold.

Greater specialization is stimulated by trade relations with other regions as well as by respect for the skills of the specialist.

Craft specialists do exist even in small-scale, subsistence economies, as exemplified by this weaver in Nepal. (Eugene Gordon, Taurus Photos)

Craftspeople may become organized into guilds, whose members may live close together in a particular village or, as in medieval Europe, a particular quarter of a town or city. The guild is not a kin group but a skill group (although a son may be expected to take up his father's trade).

A specialist may also contribute his or her skills to a cooperative undertaking in which materials and labor are supplied by others. This is a natural outcome of organizing the work through a team—the group that is formed to do a job that requires more labor than can be supplied by a single household (such as harvesting). The "payment" for work of this kind is the right to receive the same kind of help at a later date. In the case of the specialist (for example, the expert who does the carving on a new canoe), the "payment" takes the form of food or some other material good, but the work is done for reasons other than strictly economic ones (for instance, as a political strategy or simply out of neighborliness).

The next step is "entrepreneurship." In the Trobriand Islands, for example, the construction of a sea-going canoe may be organized by a chief who has large quantities of surplus food at his disposal and who sets others to work to enable him to transport the food to another island. But such entrepreneurs do not constitute a class of employers, as they do in an industrial society. It is not until separate classes of employers and employed develop, and the relationship between them is entirely "economic"—that is, one pays the other for labor provided—that the division of labor typical of industrial societies develops.

Other Differences between Industrial and Nonindustrial Societies. Udy (1970) has noted other differences between industrial and subsistence economies, which include the following:

1. The goals of an industrial enterprise are limited to production; they are *specific.* The goals of a subsistence economy are *diffuse;* its activities have other purposes than production.
2. In an industrial economy, rewards for work depend on the amount of work done; thus, achievement is emphasized. In a subsistence economy, rewards are distributed with little regard for the amount of work done.
3. Recruitment of workers is *territorial* in industrial economies and *social* in subsistence economies, in that participation in

production processes depends on prior membership in some other social group.

Udy believes that for an industrial economy to develop, a centralized government is essential. But social scientists have found that the centralization of government tends to encourage custodial rather than contractual forms of production organization. It consolidates control over resources and permits an exercise of power indirectly supported by governmental sanction. And since custodial forms involve social recruitment, reward by ascription, and diffuseness of goals, they hamper industrial development, which is better served by contractual forms of production organization. This may be one reason why industrialization is hard to achieve in many developing nations.

The Colonial Impact. Many of the differences between industrial and nonindustrial economies played a role in the destructive effect of colonialism on the economies of colonized countries. In Africa, for example, where economic and social processes were highly interdependent, European modes of production were meaningless because they required work that was completely separate from social obligations to family, friends, or chiefs. To the Africans, the purpose of work was not only to gain income but also to express and strengthen social relationships. When they were forced to enter the colonial economy as laborers, producers of cash crops, or commercial traders, Africans had to give up many activities that were essential to their traditional social relationships. As a result, the relationships often disintegrated (Dalton, 1967, pp. 76–77).

Many developing nations are organizing themselves in ways that create new and distinctive blends of social and economic institutions—producers' and consumers' cooperatives, for example. This often involves strong central control and "welfare state" policies, in contrast to the relatively uncontrolled market system of the West.

Labor and Leisure

Patterns of Labor

"Primitive" peoples have often been misrepresented by Westerners as lazy. Generally living in climates where nature provides for most of their needs, they supposedly did not have to exert themselves very much—nor did they *want* to work hard enough—to obtain the extra benefits of life. This is a gross misconception. Even the people of the bountiful South Sea islands work hard when hard work is required of them.

Although primitive people may work hard at times and relax whenever they can, this does not mean, as is often implied, that they lack concentration and discipline. The fact is that, like everyone else, they do whatever they need to do to make a living, plus as much more as is necessary to achieve any additional goals that they may have, and that are possible. Primitive people are realists, only their realities differ from ours.

Not only do individuals in small-scale societies perform different amounts of work, but whole families, too, may differ in the amount of work they do. One of the most striking aspects of labor patterns in such societies is the amount of cooperative work performed by groups larger than the conjugal family but smaller than the community—that is, work done through "the voluntary association of a group of men or women whose objective is the completion of a specific, definitely limited task, with which they are simultaneously concerned" (Herskovits, 1965, p. 100). A good example of this type of widespread working group is the *combite* of Haiti.

Essentially, the *combite* is the basis upon which Haitians are able to finish the heavy work of clearing their fields soon enough to get their planting done. When a man needs a field cleared, he puts out the word that he wants a *combite,* or working party, to do the work. As the workers gather, the host prepares food for a feast, either lavish or simple, depending on what he can afford. The work is supervised by a man who makes sure that it progresses quickly enough to finish the work in the available time. The workers, each carrying a hoe, form a line and clear the field to the beat of at least one and sometimes two or three drums, depending on the size of the *combite.* In this way, a field of several acres can be completely cleared in a single afternoon by about 65 workers.

The feast at the end of the day is supervised by the man who supervised the work. He distributes the food, making sure that the best goes to the men who came earliest and worked hardest. Those men who gain the reputation of being shirkers find that when they need help in clearing their own fields, their request is greeted with little enthusiasm.

Thus, it should not be concluded that individual initiative and self-interest are lacking in small-scale societies. It is clear that a person who participates in cooperative work may expect to benefit from the labor of a similar work group in the future. Reciprocity is expressed in diverse fields of activity, including production of goods. Moreover, there is something to be gained—prestige—from being the best worker in the group, and this generates competition that is not always friendly.

Leisure

Anthropologists tend to write very little about leisure, even though it is an important topic. We have noted that people in simple societies work as hard as people in more advanced societies, but we have also mentioned the short working hours of hunters and gatherers. While it appears that they have more leisure than we do, leisure is often seen as a characteristic of more advanced societies.

Every other form of subsistence economy requires more work than hunting and gathering. It is only in the most advanced societies that the invention of "labor-saving" devices becomes necessary. Food gatherers simply refrain from modes of production that require more labor.

The term *leisure preference* has recently been coined by economists to refer to the desire of people in industrial economies to work shorter hours rather than earn more money. But leisure preference may be found in any society anywhere in the world. It prevents some food gatherers from taking up cultivation, and it prevents some cultivators from working to grow more crops. This is not a result of laziness but a purposeful allocation of time to different activities.

"Not By Bread Alone"

It is important to note that "production" in any economic system, even the most simple, is not concerned only with filling nutritional needs. Workers "must produce more than calories if calories are to be produced" (Cook, 1973, p. 850). To produce food, one must first have produced the technology, however simple it might be, that goes into its production. The production of tools and equipment enables humans to provide for their nutritional needs more efficiently. Even hunters and gatherers have weapons, cooking implements, and so on, to make food production easier. And, as was noted earlier, the Bushmen work at food acquisition only a few hours a day, spending the rest of their time otherwise. Many anthropologists have held that humans became "human" when they began making tools and cooperating with one another in food production.

Summary

1. Economic anthropology is concerned with describing the variety of economic systems developed by humankind, classifying them, and relating them to social and cultural arrangements. It takes a holistic approach to economic systems.

2. Economic activity consists of the choices people make in determining how available resources are to be used in producing, distributing, and consuming material goods and services. These activities usually cannot be separated from other activities, and the choices may be either conscious or unconscious.

3. Small-scale economic systems are characterized by simple technology and little division of labor; productive units that serve other functions in addition to economic ones; and the use of leveling mechanisms to prevent the accumulation of wealth.

4. Different modes of production combine with factors of production—land, labor, and capital—in different ways. They also differ in their degree of technological sophistication and division of labor. The nature of the productive unit—familial, custodial, contractual, or voluntary—also varies from one economic system to another.

5. In a subsistence economy, people use what they produce to meet their own needs. Subsistence economies may be divided into three types: hunting and gathering; pastoralism; and horticulture/agriculture.

6. *Hunters and gatherers* live in small groups and move often. They have little personal property, do not produce surpluses, and are not attached to a particular area. Their way of life is not difficult in terms of energy spent, though their standard of living is low, when considered in terms of our own cultural values.

7. *Pastoralism* represents a transition between food collecting and cultivation. Pas-

toralists are nomadic, but somewhat less so than hunters and gatherers. Often they maintain a pastoral way of life even though they are aware of the advantages of cultivation.

8. Horticultural and agricultural societies are settled rather than mobile. Their technologies range from the slash-and-burn technique to plough cultivation. They tend to develop further in social and political terms than societies with other kinds of subsistence economies.

9. The most salient differences between industrial economies and subsistence economies is the extreme specialization characteristic of the former. Others include specific vs. diffuse goals, achievement orientation vs. ascription, and territorial vs. social recruitment.

10. "Primitive" people work as hard as people in industrial societies, but they differ in their leisure preferences. The concept of leisure is culture-bound. Different cultures have different attitudes toward work and time; the attitudes of groups within a given culture may also differ.

23

Distribution and Exchange

IN the preceding chapter, we identified four major features of small-scale economic systems: (1) technology and the division of labor, (2) the organization of productive units, (3) the forms and media of exchange, and (4) the control of wealth and capital. The first two themes served as a framework for our discussion of systems of production; the last two will guide us in this chapter as we study systems of distribution and exchange. *Distribution* refers to the manner in which goods are divided among members of a society. *Exchange* is the process whereby those receiving goods are, in turn, obligated to reciprocate by giving goods in return. What is reciprocated may be other goods or something of equal value, such as money. Although we have separated the four features that characterize small-scale economic systems for easier presentation and discussion, the organization of production in any society is by no means independent of its systems of distribution and exchange.

Any exchange of material goods is just one aspect of an ongoing social relationship—a relationship that shapes and limits the nature of the material transaction. Accordingly, we will focus on the social relationships surrounding the distribution and exchange of goods and services, as well as on the transactions themselves. Not only does the exchange of goods follow the normal patterns of social interaction in a society, but material transactions may underlie or initiate social relationships—"if friends make gifts, gifts make friends."

Systems and Media of Exchange

Systems of exchange of goods and services are necessary to all forms of organized society.

497

Such systems can be divided into three types: reciprocity, redistribution, and market exchange. This classification system, originally proposed by Karl Polyani (Polyani et al., 1957), is used by most anthropologists in their treatments of the economies of various societies. It is important to note that although every society is organized around at least one of these systems, most are organized around two, and many (both Western and non-Western) around all three.

Reciprocity

Reciprocity is an exchange transaction that involves direct movement of goods or services between two parties: *A* gives something to *B,* and *B* in turn gives something to *A.* This type of transaction is illustrated by the diagram in Figure 1. Reciprocity is sometimes viewed as simply a process of balancing values—a one-for-one exchange. This view, however, is misleading. Various kinds of exchange are included in the term reciprocity. Marshall Sahlins (1972) has pointed out that these can be arranged on a continuum according to the degree of balance involved. At one end of the continuum is *generalized reciprocity*—goods, services, or assistance freely given to kin, friends, and neighbors without any explicit

Figure 1   Reciprocity

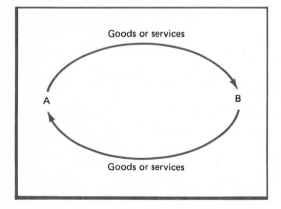

statement that anything is expected in return. In the middle of the continuum is *balanced reciprocity*—the expectation of goods or services of roughly equal value in return for what one gives. At the other extreme is *negative reciprocity,* in which goods or services are obtained through force or deception. The intervals between the points on the continuum are not only intervals between degrees of balance but also intervals of degrees of social distance, which is important in exchange transactions. The intervals also represent intervals of time within which reciprocal exchange takes place (at some distant time, if ever; at about the same time; never). Sahlins emphasizes that these categories have "moral" as well as "mechanical" implications, as will become clear as we study each in turn.

Generalized Reciprocity. Sahlins labels as generalized reciprocity any transaction that at least appears to be altruistic, such as help, sharing, and hospitality. The obligation to reciprocate, if it exists at all, is vague. In transactions of this type, the material aspects of exchange are much less significant than the social aspects. An extreme example is parents' care of their children—children are not expected to reciprocate in direct ways (though in later years children may wince at the oft-repeated phrase, "After all we've done for you. . ."). In most cases of "free giving," it is understood that the recipient should, at some undefined future time, reciprocate if possible. The value or quantity of the return to the donor is also undefined. Finally, despite the vague obligation to reciprocate, failure to do so does not usually stop the giver from giving again.

Balanced Reciprocity. Balanced reciprocity is direct exchange—one thing is exchanged for another of equal value, without delay. *Perfectly* balanced reciprocity, in which the same types of goods in the same amounts are exchanged, sometimes occurs. You may borrow a cup of sugar or an egg from your neigh-

A direct exchange in which values of goods are calculated fairly precisely takes place in this marketplace in Tego, Lomé. (Bernard Pierre Wolff, Photo Researchers)

bor, which you return in kind. But the term usually applies to transactions in which a return of equal value is made within a definite time, such as buying, selling, trade, and payment. These are known as *generally* balanced transactions.

The social relationship underlying balanced transactions is less personal and more economic than that underlying generalized reciprocity. The two sides in balanced transactions are economically and socially distinct. The material aspects of the transaction are at least as important as its social aspects; and the values of the goods and services are calculated fairly precisely. One-way flows of goods or services are not tolerated.

Negative Reciprocity. Negative reciprocity involves trying to get something for nothing. It includes gambling, theft, and the like. This is the most impersonal form of exchange and

the most "economic" in that the material aspects of the transaction are all-important. The two sides are entirely opposed, and there is not necessarily any interaction between them. The flow of goods is in one direction, but the act is one of taking, not giving.

Factors Influencing Reciprocity. Kinship, as might be expected, has a significant effect on the nature of transactions between individuals. Kin ties tend to create generalized reciprocity. This is related to the multiplex nature of the relationship, that is, the overlapping of multiple and diverse interests. Generalized reciprocity therefore occurs frequently in simple, small-scale societies, in which a large percentage of social life is based on kinship. Among the Bemba, for instance, food is normally shared by close kin; during scarcities it is shared more widely. But there are exceptions, as Richards (1939) reports.

I have often seen women take a pot of beer and conceal it in a friend's granary on the reported arrival of some elderly relative. To refuse hospitality with a pot of beer sitting on the hearth would be an impossible insult, but a bland assertion that "Alas, . . . We have nothing to eat here" is sometimes necessary. This would not be done in the case of a near relative, but only with a more distant kinsman . . . or . . . well-known "cadgers." (p. 202)

Other factors that may affect reciprocal transactions are social rank or prestige; relative wealth; and the type of goods involved. The effect of rank difference is roughly opposite to that of kinship. The reciprocity between the person of high rank and the person of low rank tends to be generalized. Polynesian chiefs, for example, have immense obligations to their people. For a Tikopia chief, generosity is a prerogative of office; he is *expected* to give away the food and other things that he accumulates. If a commoner accumulates goods and then disperses them in chiefly fashion, he is likely to incur severe penalties. In short, "to be noble is to be generous."

Since to be "noble" is often also to be wealthy, differences in economic status influence reciprocity in the same way that differences in social status or rank influence it. In societies in which no clear-cut differences are apparent, such as those of hunters and gatherers, anyone who has food is expected to give to anyone who has none—to such an extent that Eskimo hunters have been known to give all their food to others and have none left for their families (Spencer, 1959).

All of these factors—kinship, rank, and wealth—sometimes influence an exchange transaction. Any one factor cannot be separated from the others, in such cases, except for purposes of discussion.

Functions of Balanced Reciprocity. Balanced reciprocity implies willingness to give in exchange for what is received. It means giving up self-interest or hostility for the sake of mutual benefit. Hence, it serves as a vehicle for many types of social "contracts." This is not to say that the exchange itself is not mutually beneficial; rather, we mean to say that the basic purpose of such transactions is to generate a friendly feeling, a degree of sociability, regardless of the material values involved.

Sahlins (1972) outlines some of the types of contracts that often involve balanced reciprocity, including the following:

1. Formal friendship or kinship—pledges of brotherhood and the like, which may be sealed by an exchange of goods.
2. Group alliances—feasts and similar events in which different clans or villages may affirm their friendship by exchanging goods or entertainment.
3. Peacemaking—exchanges that are part of a settlement bringing an end to a hostile situation (including such exchanges as compensation for adultery or homocide, as well as those that terminate warfare).
4. Marriage transactions—the classic form of social/material exchange. The social effects of exchanging cattle or some other material goods at marriage are comparable to those of the exchanges just listed.

It is important to note that while the basis of reciprocity is the exchange of gifts, any gift carries with it an obligation of return, either expressed or implied. This fact is of primary economic importance, for it stimulates the circulation of goods. Consider the following intertribal relationships, which existed in India before the arrival of Europeans:

[The Kota] were musicians and artists for the three neighboring folk of their area, the pastoral Toda, the jungle-dwelling Kurumba, and the agricultural Badaga. Each tribe had clearly defined and ritually regulated obligations and prerogatives with respect to all the others. The Toda provided the Kota with ghee [liquid butter made from cow's milk] for certain ceremonies and with buffaloes for sacrifices at their funerals. The Kota furnished the Toda with the pots and knives they needed in their everyday life and made the music essential to Toda ceremonies.

Figure 2 Balanced reciprocity

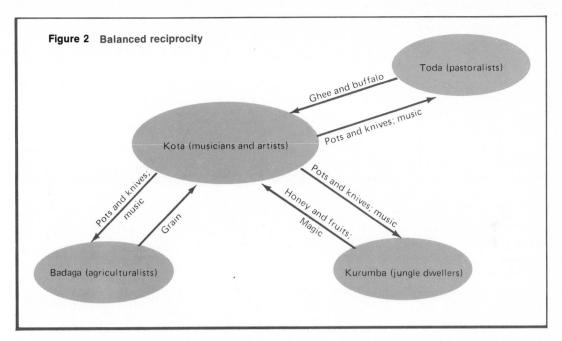

The Kota provided the Badaga with similar goods and services, receiving grain in return. They stood in the same exchange relationship with the forest Kurumba, but these latter, who could only provide meagre material compensation—honey, canes, and occasionally fruits—were able to afford the Kota supernatural protection, since the Kurumba were dreaded sorcerers, so feared that every Kota family must have their own Kurumba protector against the magic which others of this tribe might work against them. (Herskovits, 1965, p. 157)

These relationships were basically social, involving funerals, feasts, and the like, but they influenced and shaped the economic transactions of the four tribes.

The Kula System. Malinowski's (1920) description of *kula,* the circulating exchange of valuables in eastern New Guinea, is a classic example of reciprocity. The *kula* is a special system of trade, separate from the exchange of items such as pottery, dried fish, or canoes. It consists of the circulation of two items that have high value but no practical usefulness: shell armbands *(mwali)* and shell-disk necklaces *(soulava).* They are intended as ornaments but are rarely used for this purpose. The *kula* system covers an immense area that includes the islands to the east of New Guinea, Woodlark Island, the Trobriand Archipelago, and several other islands and archipelagos (see Figure 3). As the map indicates, actual trade of material goods takes place in addition to the *kula* trade.

Kula is carried on according to definite and complex rules. First, viewing the geographic area covered by the system as a circle, the *soulava* travel only clockwise and the *mwali* travel only counterclockwise. Second, neither item remains for very long in the possession of any individual; both are continually being exchanged. Third, *kula* trade is only one form of interaction between individuals living in different communities who have established a specific, life-long relationship with each other. Chiefs have more such relationships than commoners; older men have more than younger men.

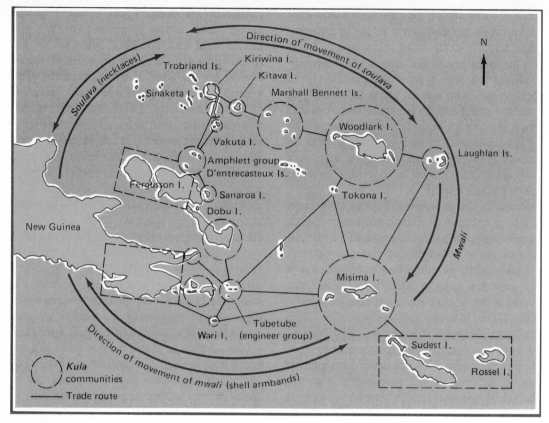

Figure 3 The *kula* system. The dotted circles indicate the *kula* communities; the dotted rectangles indicate the areas indirectly affected by the *kula*. (Malinowski, 1920)

Malinowski described the exchange as follows:

Let us suppose that I, a Sinaketa man, am in possession of a pair of big armshells. An overseas expedition from Dobu in the d'Entrecasteux Archipelago arrives at my village. Blowing a conch shell, I take my armshell pair and I offer it to my overseas partner, with some such words, "This is a *vaga* (initial gift)—in due time, thou returnest to me a big *soulava* (necklace) for it!" Next year, when I visit my partner's village, he either is in possession of an *equivalent* necklace, and this he gives to me as *yotile* (restoration gift), or he has not a necklace good enough to repay my last gift. In this case he will give me a smaller necklace—avowedly not equivalent to my gift—and will give it to me as *basi* (intermediary gift).

This means that the main gift has to be repaid on a future occasion and the *basi* is given in token of good faith—but it, in turn, must be repaid by me in the meantime by a gift of small armshells. The final gift, which will be given to me to clinch the whole transaction, would then be called *kudu* (equivalent gift) in contrast to *basi*. (Malinowski, 1920; in Dalton, 1967, pp. 173–174)

The system is actually more complicated than this. For example, the finest *soulava* and *mwali* have names and histories and are therefore much desired. Those who are especially eager to obtain one of these articles may give its current owner offerings and solicitory gifts. In short, *kula* is an elaborate system of relationships in which both social and economic relationships are governed by the rules of exchange. It is distinctly different from common barter, *gimwali,* since it involves a higher level of trust. The *kula* expresses the value placed on generosity and honor, because the equivalence of the gifts and countergifts cannot be enforced. The temporary possession of a *kula* article brings its owner prestige; but so does the way in which he gives it away.

To put *kula* into perspective, it should be noted that most members of the "ring" are also involved in other forms of material exchange in addition to this form of reciprocity. However, the *kula* transactions form the basis for other kinds of transaction, including trade of consumer products.

Redistribution

Redistribution is a pooling transaction in which goods are collected from the members of a group by a central authority and then divided up among the members of the group. Figure 4 illustrates the process of redistribution. An example of this type of exchange is the Old Testament story in which Joseph interpreted Pharaoh's dream of 7 years of plenty to be followed by 7 years of famine, and Joseph himself was put in charge of collecting and storing food during the years of plenty in

order to redistribute it during the years of famine. One difference between reciprocity and redistribution is implicit in this story, and that is that the social organization of these two types of exchange is quite different. Redistribution is the collective action among several parties, whereas reciprocity is the action and reaction of two parties. Reciprocity requires only two sides; redistribution requires a social center. For this reason, redistribution is associated with groups headed by a central authority, such as a chief. Interestingly, some archaeologists have hypothesized that the building of the pyramids and other monumental architecture in ancient Egypt was also a part of the larger system of redistribution in which both goods and services were "pooled," so that such works were constructed during periods of economic stagnation. Thus, they see them as a kind of huge welfare system.

Redistribution may be a matter of custom, law, or special decision. Sometimes there is actual collection, storage, and redistribution of goods. At other times, the "collection" is not physical but consists of assignment of the right to use the goods in a particular area (that is, group A may have the food grown in this section of field, group B may have the yield from that section). The reason for redistribution can vary too. For example, it may stem

Figure 4   Redistribution

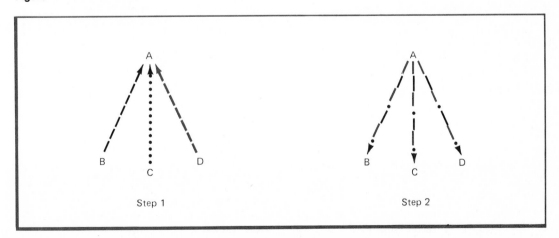

Step 1   Step 2

Sometimes redistribution involves actually collecting, storing, and distributing goods; it can only occur in a social system with a central authority capable of overseeing such activities.
(Jason Lauré, Woodfin Camp)

from the fact that different regions of a large country produce things that other regions cannot produce, or that the time at which food is needed and harvest time may be several months apart. Finally, redistribution may apply not only to whole societies but to smaller groups as well. Such was the case in the medieval manor, where a number of serfs

worked for the lord of the manor who then redistributed the goods among them.

The presence of redistribution implies the existence of a hierarchy. That is, redistribution is impossible unless someone is given the authority to carry out the redistribution; hence, the frequent association of redistribution with chieftainship. Indeed, this relation may create the leadership role itself. In most hunting-and-gathering societies, the central authority needed to redistribute goods is lacking, and reciprocity is more likely to occur there. In addition, redistribution is possible only if there is a large enough surplus to make it worthwhile. As a result, redistributive exchange is found in production systems that are somewhat more advanced than that of simple hunting and gathering.

The Potlatch. The word *potlatch* means simply "giving" in Chinook jargon, a widely used trade language of the north Pacific coast. The *potlatch* of the northwest Pacific coast Indians was a ceremony at which one chief and his group gave away goods—usually trade blankets or copper plaques—to another chief or chiefs and their groups. The gifts were distributed according to the ranks of the recipients. Drucker explains the ceremony of the *potlatch* as follows:

The first step after plans and preparations was the dispatching of an invitation party to the village of the guests. This party was ceremoniously treated, and was given a feast where they could deliver the invitation orally to the assembled group, setting the date on which the guests would be expected. . . .

Among many groups, guests of high rank were called in order of precedence, each in turn being escorted by ushers to a place of honor corresponding to his rank. When more than one group of guests had been invited, an elaborate protocol had to be worked out, the chief of the highest-ranking group being seated first, and the chief of the second-highest group next, then that of the third group, and so on. Then those of second rank were seated. . . .

Women from British Columbia with wares to be given away at a *potlatch*.
(American Museum of Natural History)

Men of lower rank and commoners were seated as a group. . . . When large amounts of riches were to be distributed, more guests were individually seated than at small-scale distributions. Speeches of welcome were made and replied to, supplementing those made on the formal arrival. . . .

The next step was usually the display of crests and performance of dances and songs, not just for entertainment but because these referred to the privileges about to be bestowed. . . . The gifts were distributed, the quantity or nature of each gift was announced by the speaker, and the tallymen busily counted bundles of . . . sticks to keep accounts of the presents and the recipients. . . . Thanks were given by the recipient of each gift, and at the conclusion of the distribution the ranking guest or his speaker made a speech of thanks. . . . (Drucker, 1965, pp. 57–58)

While the effect of a *potlatch* was to redistribute goods, it served important social functions as well. It was a declaration by the host himself of his status. Also, it strengthened the bond between the individual and the group on the one hand, as well as the ties between the host group and the guest group on the other. The latter relationship was reciprocal: the guests were expected to "return" the gifts by having *potlatches* to which the hosts would be invited (much as dinner invitations are "returned" in our society).

A variant was the rivalry *potlatch,* in which large quantities of goods were given away in order to shame a rival. These events resulted from competition between two men for a specific status. The first would hold a *potlatch* to announce his claims; the second would offer a rival *potlatch* (to which the same participants or others were invited) at which he denied his rival's claims and emphasized his own. This kind of competition could go on until one of the contestants went bankrupt and lost his bid to status by default (Drucker, 1965).

The potlatch has sometimes been described as irrational behavior because it differs from the acquisitive behavior that Americans consider normal. But it is just as rational as any other way of procuring honor and power, such as committing oneself to heavy mortgage or auto loan payments for the sake of the status that comes with owning a prestigious house or a luxurious car.

The *potlatch* was the fundamental means whereby political influence and social position were established and maintained among the Indians of the Northwest Coast, where social rank was extremely important. The assumption of any new status was validated by a *potlatch* to which the important people in the society were invited. The distribution of food and other material valuables served as an important mechanism for the distribution of goods. But the primary purpose of the *potlatch* was to proclaim and confirm a particular status, which was frequently accompanied by an honorific title. To assume the title was to assert certain rights. These rights had to be reaffirmed at subsequent *potlatches* when the title or rank came into question. The *potlatch* is a significant example of exchange because it is based on the principle of reciprocity which is fundamental to all systems of exchange. In this case, however, the reciprocal obligation is perhaps more apparent than it is in other systems.

Market Exchange

Market exchange is a price-setting mechanism and is characterized by bargaining behavior. Each party to the exchange wants to arrive at a price that is as favorable to him or her as possible. The important point is that prices can fluctuate; they are not set or predetermined. And since each party is trying to gain an advantage at the expense of the other, the nature of the social relationship involved is basically antagonistic.

The concept of market exchange is inevitably tied to the concept of money. Economists generally define money as a medium of exchange that has no other use and that is taken in exchange for goods and services. The coins, bills, and checks that we use in Western society are, of course, considered money. They are an impersonal, commercial commodity. To people from small-scale societies, however, money may have social, moral, or even emotional connotations. Some anthropologists have included as money the cowrie shells that peoples of Oceania use as mediums of exchange. Others have argued that the shells are not money because their exchange value is limited to obtaining only certain goods or products. The problem of definition stems from using Western money as a model and trying to see whether cowrie shells, cattle, dog teeth, and the like fit the model, rather than trying to find out how the similarities and differences between various types of moneys relate to similarities and differences between various types of economic systems.

The question is, then, what is money? Money may be used for three basic purposes:

1. As a medium of exchange—money enables people to exchange things they want less for things they want more without having to find someone in the opposite situation. Without money, if one needs a specific item, such as a piece of cloth, and has something that he or she is willing to give up, such as an extra chicken, the person may be obliged to hunt high and low before finding someone who wants a chicken and is willing to give a piece of cloth in exchange for it. With money, both individuals can go to a market and buy the cloth and the chicken.

2. As a standard of value—money enables people to compare chickens and cloths, so to speak. Every item that can be exchanged is given a monetary value, and this facilitates its exchange.

3. As a means of payment—money enables people to obtain their choice of a wide variety of products and services. It is unlikely that the bookstore where you bought this book would have appreciated being paid in chickens or pieces of cloth, because it would be difficult for the bookstore manager then to pay bills and salaries with such goods.

In Western societies, money performs all three of these functions. In other societies, however, this is not always the case. Anthropologists therefore distinguish between two types of money—*general-purpose* money and *special-purpose* money (Dalton, 1965).

General-Purpose Money. In a true market economy such as our own, money serves a *general* purpose. It makes it possible to place a value on all goods and services regardless of their type so that they may be readily purchased. It also serves as a general standard of value and is universally used in making pay-

ments. Everything from natural resources to finished goods can be bought in the appropriate market, as can services of all kinds, as well as ceremonial and religious goods. Taxes are paid with money, as are fines. Gifts are bought with money and then given, or the gift itself may take the form of money. In a market economy, even redistribution (taxation) and reciprocity (gift-giving) are transacted by means of money.

Special-Purpose Money. On the other hand, in small-scale economies money may exist, but its purpose is often limited. Such money is termed *special-purpose money*. Different objects may be used in and limited to different types of transactions. Moreover, the objects used may not be "full-time" money, in that they may have other uses as well. Such objects may perform one or two of the functions listed earlier—as a medium of exchange, a standard of value, or a means of payment—but not all three. Special-purpose moneys tend to be used in noncommercial transactions. When tools are exchanged for a bride, the transaction is reciprocal. The tools cannot necessarily be used in other types of transactions but are required for the bridewealth transaction. Similarly, cows, shell armbands, and so forth serve some of the functions that Western moneys serve, but in noncommercial situations. In each case, they are used only for specific transactions. In New Britain, for example, a Tolai man collects strings of shell money to be given out at his funeral; no other form of "money" may be used for this purpose (Matt, 1972, p. 196). In the southwestern part of Zaire, the Lele use raffia aprons as the "price" of initiation into an age set, entry into a cult association, compensation for offenses, and the like. These aprons are rarely used for any other purpose (Douglas, 1958).

Many small-scale societies do not have a single type of money for everything they exchange. Some commodities are used in some kinds of exchange and others in other kinds. That is, various spheres of exchange are separated from one another and use various types of special-purpose money.

An example of a society with multiple and diverse spheres of exchange is the Siane of highland New Guinea. The first sphere consists of the necessities of life—vegetables, small livestock, household utensils—which the Siane call "nothing things." These are exchanged by kinspeople for "help" (loans or informal gifts). The second sphere consists of precious, but not utilitarian, objects that are exchanged on ceremonial occasions such as forming an alliance; these objects are called "things." The third sphere is made up of "small things" (nuts, oil, tobacco, salt) that are not necessities. They are exchanged for one another and cannot be exchanged for either food or ceremonial objects (Salisbury, 1965). An economy of this sort, using various media of exchange, may be termed *multicentric*. This is in contrast to a *unicentric* economy, which uses general-purpose money.

An old man from Yap explaining stone money to his young listeners. (Jack Fields, Photo Researchers)

The Impact of Money on the Tiv. When general-purpose money is introduced to a multicentric economy, the effect is to transform it to a unicentric economy. This transformation does not occur all at once, however; the Tiv of central Nigeria had a multicentric economy before the advent of European traders (Bohannan, 1959). There were three spheres of exchange: (1) a subsistence sphere consisting of foodstuffs, household utensils, and raw materials, which were exchanged by barter; (2) a "prestige" sphere consisting of slaves, cattle, large white cloths, and brass rods, which could be exchanged for one another at certain ceremonies (brass rods served as a standard of value within this sphere); and (3) rights in women and children, which could be exchanged only for similar rights, though brass rods could be used to acquire some—but not all—of those rights. On some occasions "conversions," or exchanges between two different spheres, might occur.

Brass rods could not serve as a general-purpose money because they were not divisible (making "change" was impossible) and were worth far more than most subsistence goods. Within the prestige sphere, they served all three functions of general purpose money. Outside of that sphere, they served only as a means of payment for marriage rights, and then only to a limited extent.

When Europeans introduced general-purpose money, the Tiv used it as a standard of value in the subsistence sphere, while continuing to barter goods within this sphere. They also used general-purpose money as a means of payment in the marriage sphere. It also served as a means of exchange within the subsistence and prestige spheres. Thus, the economy of the Tiv gradually became unicentric even though for a long time most Tiv continued to see it as multicentric.

The introduction of money has had a variety of effects on the Tiv, social as well as economic. Trade has increased immensely, not only within the society but with the outside world as well. In fact, so much produce is traded with outside groups that there is occasionally an artificially created internal shortage of some commodities. The degree of differentiation between individuals in terms of wealth has also increased. Finally, the possibility of using money to "buy" marriage rights has led to a form of indebtedness that did not exist before. In the past, "debt" was in the form of similar rights that could be repaid through marriage in the next generation, rather than in the form of money. With the introduction of general-purpose money, differentiation of individuals on the basis of wealth has increased and probably will continue to do so.

Integration of Economic Systems

We have pointed out several times that the economic aspects of a society cannot be separated from its legal, political, and other aspects. This can be illustrated by the role of the marketplace in West Africa. Economic exchanges are not the only ones that occur in the marketplace. Information is also exchanged: announcements are made there, and news and gossip are passed along. The people who gather in the marketplace provide an audience for dancers and entertainers as well as for political leaders. The marketplace serves as a center for legal activities and sometimes for religious activities as well. In short, the marketplace is a meeting place.

The point of this example is that the various aspects of a society are integrated into a cultural system. Moreover, the nature of that integration varies from one society to another. Thus, when an outside influence is brought to bear on a society such as that of the Tiv—and very few societies are so isolated that they are not influenced by the money and goods of Western nations—the way in which that influence is integrated into the culture depends on the *integrating mechanisms* at work in that particular society. In some societies, these may depend largely on religious activities; in

others, on ritual occasions of various sorts, or on political processes. The integrating mechanisms are the means whereby a given society incorporates new elements into its cultural system.

> # Controlled Wealth and Capital

The task of the anthropologist studying any economic system is to discover not only how goods are produced but also who has access to both resources and goods, who is responsible for their distribution, and finally, how access to goods is legitimated and maintained. In other words, how are production and distribution controlled?

In this section, we will be dealing with two important economic concepts: *capital* and *wealth*. The concept of capital is central to Western economies and can be applied to non-Western societies as well. As for the concept of wealth, at first glance it appears to be a simple one but, as we will see, it is not always easily applied to a particular economic system.

Wealth, Capital, and Interest

If we use the dictionary to define *wealth* as abundance of material possessions or resources that have exchange value, then it is clear that the concept of wealth is foreign to many subsistence economies. In Argentina, a Toba family head who is exceptionally successful in providing for the material well-being of his immediate kin is considered not wealthy but lucky, or perhaps blessed with magical powers. If he is too successful, however, he will be suspected of witchcraft, and he will have to find a way of dispelling those suspicions. This is usually done by means of generosity, which takes the form of a quick distribution of excess goods (usually food or animals). Often this choice is not up to the family head alone; since word travels quickly that a person is well provided for, "relatives" from faraway places who are not as well off may turn up to consume their share. Guests are considered an honor; they are not discouraged from visiting and are not expected to leave until all the goods have been used up and balance has been restored—an effective leveling mechanism. In terms of reciprocity, it is understood that the visiting relatives will reciprocate at some future time, though this does not always happen. If a family does not reciprocate, it may eventually develop a bad reputation and will lack visitors until it can find a means of providing goods that will attract friends and relatives.

The introduction of money and wages to the Toba has had the effect of alienating from the rest of the society a few families that have learned to manage money well and to accumulate wealth. The few Toba who have adopted the notion of wealth have come to identify with the broader Argentine society. The more traditional families still maintain the sharing motif, which contrasts with the concept of wealth. Money management involves controlling equipment, resources, and supplies, and therefore, not distributing excess goods among relatives. Traditional members of the community have responded to this unfamiliar behavior with distrust and suspicion.

Identifying Capital. There is some question as to whether *capital*—equipment and supplies used for purposes of production—exists in nonmonetary economies. Various answers to this question have been proposed. Some anthropologists believe that the capital of such economies consists of crops and livestock. Others suggest that the term capital be applied to resources used in production, such as nets, canoes, adzes, and digging sticks.

According to Richard Salisbury, the capital of nonmonetary economies is "a stock of

goods, present before a productive act is performed, used in production and 'immobilized' from direct consumption while the act is in progress" (1962, p. 122). As Mair (1972) points out, this definition includes natural resources such as trees and gardens, manufactured items such as axes and digging sticks, as well as knowledge or skill. These are all goods that are withheld from immediate consumption for the sake of income—an increase in the amount of goods available for future consumption.

In many cases, capital goods are saved in order to be used on some future occasion. This is considered by some to be a form of capital investment. Mair (1972) writes that "when a Tikopia chief lays a taboo on the consumption of particular foodstuffs in order that they shall be plentiful when the time comes for an important ceremony, he is using the unharvested yams or the unpicked coconuts as capital. The same might be said of the stock of blankets that the Kwakiutl chief must accumulate before a *potlatch*" (p. 202). It is true that the activity for which the goods are saved is not primarily economic in nature—it may be a religious ceremony or a social event. There is no direct "return" on the investment of food or goods, but there *are* noneconomic dividends that are of great concern to the participants.

It is somewhat easier to think of livestock as capital, as Mair points out. When a Japanese peasant buys a buffalo with surplus cash in order to sell it later when cash is short, or when a herder sells butter, hides, and wool for cash that can be used to buy land on which to grow grain that would otherwise have to be bought for cash—these examples may be viewed as capital investment.

Lending in Small-Scale Societies. In Orissa, a state in East India, wealthy landowners finance small traders who buy unhusked rice, husk it, and sell it. Loans are made to individuals who have to pay for a funeral or replace a buffalo.

The lender expects return of the loan, with interest. At the same time, the same people may engage in "friendly loans" that will not pay interest—such as the loan of some rice between harvests, or of a tool or a household utensil. Loans of both kinds are common in small-scale societies (Bailey, 1957).

The person who makes such loans may be thought of as making an investment, but they are not true capital investments because they do not increase production. In fact, they may not even be "economic" transactions if the debtor and creditor live in the same village, in which case the repayment of the debt may be governed by social considerations (such as loss of prestige) rather than by economic ones. Here, again, the notion of investment must be expanded to include noneconomic transactions as well.

It is when loans are made by outsiders that purely economic considerations enter the picture. This is a matter of social distance: the more impersonal the transaction, the more "economic" its nature. Borrowing money from a bank where one is unknown, for example, is a transaction based more on one's assets and ability to repay the loan than is borrowing money—even in large amounts—from relatives or friends. Yet the nature of even purely economic transactions is two-sided. Banks *want* to lend money for the interest it brings and thus advertise their lending service. Another example is that of a Chinese shopkeeper in Mauritius who extends credit to his Indian customers. The Indians make small purchases on credit and pay at the end of the month. If the amount outstanding is not paid in full, the shopkeeper might refuse further credit—but at the possible cost of losing the customer. Thus, what happens is that customers never pay all that they owe; a certain amount is left over, an amount that is tacitly agreed upon by both shopkeeper and customer. This transaction has been described as "a kind of capital investment which the shopkeeper makes in his customer," in return for which he keeps the customer's business (B. Benedict, 1964).

As we have seen, the exchange transactions that anthropologists study in societies that depend primarily on money as a medium of exchange as well as in those that do not are diverse and sometimes complicated. In most instances, however, members of the societies concerned can be counted on to make rational choices in order to attain advantages, both material and nonmaterial. They decide to exchange, by whatever method, something they want less for something they want more. Even where material resources are difficult to obtain and are at a premium, the choices available generally are clear to the individual members of a society, and they choose according to what they consider to be their best interest.

Industrialization and Modernization

It remains to explore what happens to a small-scale society as its economy progresses from subsistence modes of production to industrial modes of production, and concepts such as money, wealth, and capital enter the picture. First, however, it is necessary to stress that we are not talking about a one-way process in which non-Western societies become increasingly industrialized and Westernized; this is not always the case. The development of industrialization in the West was a unique process that depended on the presence of certain noneconomic as well as economic factors. We cannot expect that industrialization in Latin America, Africa, and Asia will progress along the same lines and have the same effects as it did in Western nations. Thus, it is impossible to generalize about "industrialization," "modernization," or "West-

This sisal plant in Tanzania illustrates that industrialization in developing countries reflects the individual needs and characteristics of the local communities. (George Gerster, Rapho/Photo Researchers)

ernization," which are actually rather ethnocentric concepts. Instead, we will discuss the process of change or development in non-Western societies within the framework suggested by Neil Smelser (1963).

Smelser lists the types of changes that occur in developing nations as follows:

1. The change from simple, traditional techniques *toward* the application of scientific knowledge to those techniques (the use of improved seeds, for instance, that will result in more disease-resistant crops);
2. The shift from subsistence farming *toward* commercial agriculture (crops that will be sold for cash, and agricultural labor that is paid wages);
3. The transition from the use of human and animal power *toward* industrialization (people operating machines for money wages, which are used to buy the products made with those machines);
4. Population movement from rural areas *toward* urban areas.

These four types of changes often, but not always, occur together. In many countries, for example, agriculture is being commercialized,

but industrialization proper is not occurring. However, these four changes tend to affect the social structure in similar ways. Smelser terms these effects *structural differentiation, integration,* and *social disturbances.*

Structural Differentiation

Structural differentiation entails the establishment of specialized, autonomous social units in the place of multifunctional ones. For example, when factory industry replaces home-centered industry, the economic functions of the family are transferred to the firm. Instead of gaining a livelihood among family members, one leaves them to work in a different setting. Obligations to fellow workers become simply that, with no real obligations outside the work setting. Likewise, family obligations become devoid of their work aspect. Similarly, the educational role of the family is transferred to the school. What is happening is that one social organization—the family—is changing into two or more organizations that are distinct from, though related to, each other.

Other kinds of differentiation may occur as well. The introduction of cash crops usually leads to a differentiation between the contexts in which production and consumption take place. Market exchange may replace reciprocity and redistribution as a determinant of how goods are distributed. At the same time, the family may "specialize" in emotional gratification and socialization. Even value systems can become differentiated: In a new nation, strong feelings of nationalism may motivate people to work hard and make sacrifices; later, values of wealth, power, or prestige may supplant nationalism as guiding principles.

Integration

As differentiation continues, a new social order replaces the old one as the newly established units become integrated with one another. As mentioned earlier, every society has its own integrating mechanisms. In a developing nation, according to Smelser, there is a continual interplay between differentiation (which divides a society) and integration (which unites it on a new basis). We have mentioned that differentiation separates the social setting in which production occurs from that in which consumption occurs. This creates problems of integration—for instance, how will the interests of employers be integrated with those of employees? These problems give rise to a whole new set of organizations: employment agencies, labor unions, welfare arrangements, and the like. While formerly those concerns were handled in the context of kinship or the local community, they are now assigned to union meetings or social agencies of various sorts. Sometimes religious sects arise which provide a basis for mutual interaction and emotional release.

On a larger scale, industrialization not only separates work from the family but may separate the family from its ancestral community. Urbanization gives rise to another set of integrating organizations: churches, schools, and voluntary associations of various sorts. But this process is by no means steady and smooth, and it is here, in the adjustment to new social and cultural settings, that disturbances occur.

Differentiation requires new activities, norms, rewards, and sanctions that may conflict with traditional ones. The notion of working for wages, for instance, may conflict with traditional norms under which work is a kinship obligation. Until integration takes place, threats to traditionally held values may create emotional and social disturbances. For example, when the Toba of Argentina began to work for wages in the cotton fields, both men and women earned money that could be exchanged for consumer goods. Traditional division of labor, in which males provided the protein in the diet and women provided the fiber (vegetables and fruits), was broken down. Furthermore, some individuals considered money a commodity to be shared like food, whereas others did not consider it "soul-linked" and sharable. Thus, internal conflict was introduced where it did not exist before. Moreover, these changes often occur at an uneven rate, so that economic and educational institutions may differentiate rapidly while political institutions remain more conservative. This usually creates disharmony between actual life experiences and social norms.

Responses to the problems of conflict and disequilibrium may take the form of anxiety, hostility, or fantasy. If enough people respond in the same way, the result may be mass hysteria, outbreaks of violence, religious and political movements, and the like. There is some evidence that social movements have their greatest appeal to people whose social ties have been weakened by differentiation but who have not yet been integrated into a new social order (Smelser, 1963).

It is important to realize that "modernization" may not lead to "modernity"—that a people like the Toba or the Tiv may not be markedly different in the future than they are now. Changes in social structure will vary according to the preindustrial characteristics of the society; the conditions that stimulated development in the first place; the path of development followed by that particular society; and the timing of certain events such as wars and migrations. Economic anthropology can play a crucial role in explaining the process of modernization as it occurs in newly-developing areas and point out possible alternatives to the industrial life that is so familiar to us.

Summary

1. Any exchange of goods is part of an ongoing social relationship that shapes and limits the nature of an exchange transaction. The basic types of economic transaction are reciprocity, redistribution, and market exchange. *Reciprocity* involves direct movement of goods between two parties. It may be divided into three types: *generalized, balanced,* and *negative.* Reciprocity is affected by kinship, rank, and relative wealth. Close kinship creates generalized reciprocity, as do large gaps in rank or wealth. Balanced reciprocity serves as a vehicle for a variety of social "contracts" such as peacemaking and marriage. Its economic importance stems from the fact that it stimulates the circulation of goods.

2. *Redistribution* involves pooling goods at a central location and then dividing them up among the members of the group through the work of a central administrator. Redistribution cannot take place unless there is a central authority with the power to redistribute goods; it thus implies a hierarchy.

3. *Market exchange* involves a medium, such as money, on the basis of which goods are assessed at value and exchanged. In a situation of market exchange, each party wants to arrive at the price that is most favorable to himself or herself. The price therefore fluctuates—it is not predetermined.

4. Money may serve as a medium of exchange, a standard of value, and a means of payment. General-purpose money performs all three of these functions; special-purpose money may serve only one or two.

5. Small-scale societies are multicentric —they have several spheres of exchange and use special-purpose moneys. Unicentric economies use general-purpose money.

6. In many societies, wealth—an abundance of material possessions that have exchange value—is an alien concept. In fact, some societies do not allow their members to accumulate wealth.

7. There is some question as to whether capital exists in nonmonetary economies. Occasionally goods and services are withheld from immediate consumption for the sake of an increase in the goods available for later consumption; this may be viewed as capital. Livestock also can be considered capital in this way.

8. Lending at interest takes place in small-scale societies, but such loans do not increase production.

9. *Industrialization, modernization,* and *Westernization* are ethnocentric terms that refer to economic changes occurring in non-Western societies. These changes involve replacing traditional techniques with more modern technology, shifting from subsistence farming to commercial agriculture, replacing human and animal power with machines, and the movement of people from rural to urban areas.

10. The social effects of these changes may involve structural differentiation (which tends to divide a society), integration (which unites it on a new basis), as well as social disturbances (which result from the lag between differentiation and integration).

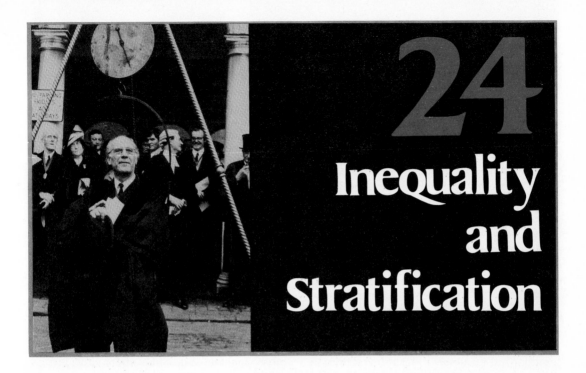

24
Inequality and Stratification

INEQUALITIES are found in all human societies, from simple hunting-and-gathering bands to modern industrial states. In societies such as those of hunters and gatherers, social and economic roles are relatively undifferentiated. Adult males tend to have one type of occupation, and adult females another. In such societies, inequalities are often judgments about individual prowess or the result of some type of supernatural power. As Fallers (1977) points out, every society has its criteria for moral evaluation, an image of the "admirable man." Inequalities exist as a result of comparing how close various individuals come to this ideal.

In complex modern industrial societies, social groups form also on the basis of occupational specialization. Each of these groups possesses a status that is shared by its members. Thus, in complex societies, inequalities often are the result of judgments about rankings of one social group versus another. The arrangement of status within a society into a hierarchy of socially superior and inferior ranks is known as *social stratification* (Hunter & Whitten, 1976, p. 359). Stratification is determined by the value system of a particular society and can be based on political, economic, or ceremonial differences. To identify the characteristics of stratification in a society, one must analyze how inequality is institutionalized within the society (Smith, 1966, pp. 147–148).

In this chapter, we will look at egalitarian societies—those that come closest to granting equality for all their members—and at rank societies—those characterized by a hierarchy of socially graduated ranks. We also will examine three major stratification systems—caste, class, and slavery. Finally, we will consider the effects of stratification on modernization in developing societies.

515

Equality and Inequality in Human Societies

The individual as a participant member of any social group occupies different positions throughout his or her lifetime. As we noted earlier, changes in statuses—social positions—are frequently marked by ritual occasions commonly known as rites of passage. These statuses are not evaluated equally by society; in fact, they are frequently ranked in hierarchical fashion so that individuals in certain ranks or grades have more authority, power, or prestige than individuals in other grades.

Status and Hierarchy

Some anthropological theories seek to account for the existence of status hierarchies in all human societies by referring to the "pecking order" of birds or dominance studies of primates. Although thought-provoking, animal research should not dictate a theory of humankind's "natural" tendency toward hierarchization. Much of the dominance data of primate studies may be invalid because of the conditions under which experiments occurred (laboratory versus natural environment), and due to unprovable assumptions on the part of human observers about what is taking place in the animals' behavior. Thus, the establishment of overall dominance ratings among primates may tell us little about its occurrence in human societies.

In theory, at least, one must allow for the possibility of a human society where all statuses are equal. However, in actuality, all societies assign status, implying hierarchy of one sort or another. Status is based on the relative merit of an individual in comparison to others in a group. Some individuals are judged more highly, and some more lowly than others. A fundamental aspect of human

In unstratified societies, prestige and status result from individual effort and achievement, rather than from judgments made about the ranking of one group over another. (Minoru Aoki, Rapho/Photo Researchers)

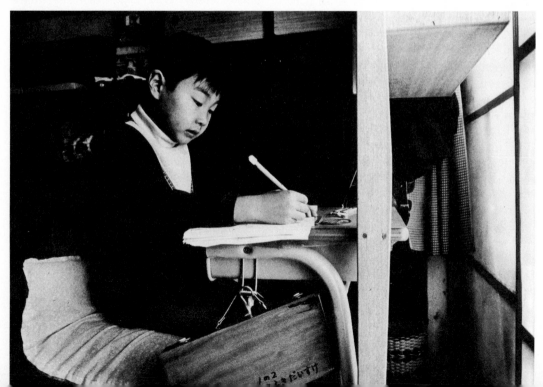

psychology, it seems, is the desire to be highly regarded by one's social group. Status is accompanied by prestige—the power to command admiration. In egalitarian societies, status results from one's individual efforts or "gifts"—for example, one's success as a hunter or one's magical or healing powers. In such instances, status is rewarded in terms of prestige and respect (sometimes associated with fear). In stratified societies, status is rewarded with social advantage as well as prestige.

It is important to note that ranking occurs in all societies, whereas stratification occurs only in some (Fried, 1967, p. 110). Egalitarian societies are not stratified in any real sense because no one group of individuals receives social advantage at the expense of another. Rank societies are stratified in the sense that the ranking is highly formalized and based on factors out of one's control, such as heredity. Labor and economic divisions in rank societies are based primarily on age and sex, as in egalitarian societies. Therefore, even though the rank system differentiates, it does so between individuals, not between groups. It awards advantage solely in terms of prestige symbolically represented, as by a title or rank. Both egalitarian and rank societies can be considered basically unstratified.

Egalitarian Society

True egalitarian societies, where all statuses are equal, exist only in theory. Aside from universal differentiation in terms of age, sex, and kinship roles, there are also differences in the degree of excellence with which one performs a role. However, societies in which occupational alternatives are few are referred to as *egalitarian.* If all adult males hunt and fish for a livelihood, for example, there are no occupational choices open to adult males. (There will, of course, be differences in the excellence with which a person carries out the hunting-and-gathering tasks.)

The lack of occupational options obviously has economic and political implications. If there are no occupational options, there are not likely to be economic or political options since there are few resources to control. Furthermore, despite the different status accorded age or kinship roles, each person can expect to go through the same pattern of age and kinship roles as he or she grows older (Fallers, 1977, p. 259). Equality, in these regards, is achieved over a period of time.

All societies require leadership of some sort. The limited occupational options in an egalitarian society may include that of leader, but most often the leader serves only in times of crisis. For the most part, he receives no special privileges. The role of shaman, or medicine man, is another role these societies may provide. The shaman's supernatural power gives him individual advantage over others. But the society may still be considered egalitarian in that political or religious inequality is limited in nature and controlled. In the case of the !Kung Bushmen, the position of shaman is open to anyone who will take it: equal access ensures the society's egalitarianism.

The !Kung Bushmen have only two specialized roles—that of shaman and headman. The headman receives no rewards except first choice of fireplace and campsite after the site for the band has been chosen. He carries his own load. Although he is of higher status than the other tribe members, his role is voluntarily practiced *and* voluntarily recognized (Smith, 1966, p. 152).

In the society of the Argentine Toba, the positions of political leader and shaman traditionally have been combined. Since everyone does the same work, leadership involves additional burdens of responsibility, rather than relief from subsistence tasks.

The Argentine Toba represent a good example of an egalitarian society. Traditionally, they were a hunting, gathering, and fishing group dependent upon undomesticated nature for subsistence. The society consisted of separate social units comprising extended family bands. The bands varied in size in recent years from several dozen to several hundred. The total population in the Toba area of 150 square miles was about 15,000 members. Each band had a name and roamed a recognized territory, using the resources found there. In each band, the adult males hunted and fished; the adult females gathered and prepared food.

Certain family heads became known as shamans because of their ability to contact supernatural powers in order to heal the sick. Though their status as leaders set some individuals off from others in the band, they hunted and fished along with other adult males. They were called upon to lead only in times of crisis. Furthermore, because of their assumed contact with "companion spirits" and their superior knowledge of the environment, shamans were expected to be more successful in hunting and fishing than other adult males.

The position of shamans differentiated them from others in power and responsibility. Thus, they were called upon occasionally to hear arguments and mediate settlements when disputes arose in the group. In this as well as in the role of leading warriors into battle, their leadership was based upon the ability to interpret general consensus, not to act independently. Leadership in Toba society, as in most other egalitarian societies, constituted a position of responsibility rather than one of privilege. Leaders in such societies generally are expected to work harder than the rest of the group members and to share generously with the needy in order to maintain their higher status.

Since no one *class* of individuals in egalitarian societies is awarded exclusive privileges over others, such societies are considered unstratified. The lack of occupational options ensures that all members of the same sex share the same economic status, except where individual achievement varies. Such achieve-

ment is rewarded with prestige, which is transitory and does not enter any other sphere of existence. The best hunter may lead the hunt, but he does not have any more economic or political power than anyone else. As for different statuses applied to different age groups, the transfer of status to different groups at certain intervals—as occurs in rites of passage—ensures that such inequalities are shared by members of the society over time (Smith, 1966, p. 150). Egalitarian societies tend to be found in environments that can support only limited populations with a simple technology. They tend, therefore, to be small.

Societies with Rank and Titles

A *rank society,* as opposed to an egalitarian one, is characterized by its formalized system of graduated social statuses determined by such factors as heredity. An example of a rank society is that of the Northwest Coast Indians who inherited specific names that signified one's distinct rank (Drucker, 1939, p. 63). Among the African Zulus, kinship ties were important traditionally to social status; the closer a prince was to the reigning king, the higher his social status. Likewise, one's rank was higher the closer one was genealogically to an important ancestor (Smith, 1966, p. 153). In small-scale rank societies, rarely do two individuals share the same rank. The results of sharing a rank can be confusing or disastrous as was shown when two separate Northwest Coast rank societies once joined for the winter. The custom of *potlatch,* in which the order of giving gifts is signified by rank, was thrown off by the presence of two individuals for every rank. Feelings rose quite high, until the visiting chief resolved the dispute by deciding that the host should give first (Drucker, 1939, pp. 57–58).

The *potlatch* shows the ceremonial aspect of rank. In addition to its festive nature, it is a necessary part of the procedure by which one assumes rank position. Names in the Northwest coast groups are ranked individually from higher to lower and are inherited. In order to take one's name, one must have a right to it through heredity. In addition, the naming ceremony has to be done publically and formally with the distribution of gifts— that is, a *potlatch*. Not only was one's name considered a form of wealth, but one had to be wealthy in material goods as well to take on the name (Drucker, 1939, pp. 62–63).

Rank societies probably developed out of egalitarian ones with the transition from dependence on nature to domestication of nature. Such domestication, in creating additional food supply, enabled societies to become larger and to amass surplus goods. They also tended to become more permanently settled, as cultivation of plants dictates.

As societies become larger and more permanent and a new redistributive economy develops, a formalized kinship network tends to develop from an egalitarian one in which mythological genealogies serve as the basis for band membership. When a clearly stated descent principle emerges, genealogical proximity to a particular ancestor becomes significant, especially in developing a kin hierarchy. Ranking is the result (Fried, 1967, p. 116).

With a newly concentrated and more certain food supply, an economic process by which surplus food can be divided comes into existence. In egalitarian bands, food is consumed on the spot or reciprocally exchanged. With the existence of a significant surplus, redistribution becomes a viable procedure and goods begin to be pooled for periodic distribution.

The role of redistributor in a rank hierarchy usually falls to the highest ranking member. Such a role carries with it prestige as well as supported political status. In some societies, it is acquired through personal achievement, often evaluated in terms of generalized reciprocity or extreme generosity (Fried, 1967, pp. 117–118).

Another characteristic of the redistributive economy found in rank societies is the supposed ownership of resources by one member, usually the chief, while in fact such resources are owned by the group. In such cases, the chief's role is more of administrator than owner. Although his permission must be requested to use a strip of land, for example, it is not in his power to refuse a member of the group (Drucker, 1939, p. 59). In rank societies in Polynesia, the association of high rank and high religious standing that comes from the ceremonial advantage that rank bestows enables the chief to use "divine" standing to make some areas taboo. In this case, we can see how rank, at one time purely ceremonial, begins to acquire religious and political significance as well (Sahlins, 1958).

In the earlier stages of development from rank societies to egalitarian ones, the two types of societies have certain aspects in common. The division of labor is much the same in that individuals engage in tasks typical for their age and sex. High rank does not generally relieve one of the necessity of performing an occupational role. But, as the rank system becomes more formalized, high-ranking members begin to abstain from menial tasks. In emerging rank societies, the chief is often the hardest working member. His status depends upon his generosity. With the emergence of the redistributive economy, the goods given away belong to the group, not to him alone. He acts as a sort of tribal banker. If he is no longer engaged in the primary occupation, he becomes dependent for his share of the goods upon the generosity of lower ranking members. Often, he will use feasts as a means to bind such members to him (Sahlins, 1958).

In rank societies, authority gradually emerges as a regular force extending into other aspects of social life. In an egalitarian society, leadership occurs as needed; in a rank society, the role of redistributive agent exists at all times. A different feeling, expressed through ritual, begins to surround leadership and, by extension, rank (Fried, 1967, p. 134). In the transition from egalitarian to rank societies, the hierarchical ordering of status positions and prestige becomes more rigid. Ranks, at first of just ceremonial significance, begin to be associated with social advantage (Fried, 1967, p. 183). Yet rank societies are considered unstratified in that differences in status pertain still to individuals. Stratification occurs when social advantage is awarded to one *group* of people over another.

Stratification Systems

In stratification systems, members of various groups, even though they may be of the same age or sex, have unequal access to basic resources. Different socioeconomic classes, with distinct standards of living, emerge as a result (Fried, 1967, p. 225). One theory of how stratification evolves is that occupations become specialized and ranked in terms of prestige and rewards. Kin groups, for instance, often tend to work together at the same tasks, passing skills on from father to son so that an identification between "role occupant" and "occupational role" is made. This is the supposed genesis of the stratified caste system of India. Other stratification systems, such as class, may be achievement-oriented.

In an unstratified society, even a rank society, access to basic resources is not denied even the lowest ranking member. But in a stratified society, access to resources is limited. Different life chances exist for those who own resources than for those who must pay to gain access to them or to acquire products grown on them. In order to maintain such an order of stratification in which some individuals are denied basic resources necessary to sustain life, powerful sanctions become

necessary. The state emerges to control the internal pressures that accompany stratifications; its agents maintain socioeconomic divisions by enforcing law and order (Fried, 1967, p. 225).

There are many types of stratification systems. The three we will discuss here are caste, class, and slavery. In reality, there is some overlapping of these systems. Controversy often arises, for instance, over whether a particular system is characterized by class or caste. The systems will be presented as ideal types; as such, they may not coincide exactly with reality in any one society.

Caste

A *caste* is a socially distinct group whose membership is determined by birth. Such a group is assigned a particular position in the social hierarchy. Differentiation in terms of access to prestige and resources exists between castes. Boundaries between castes are clearly maintained, principally by the practice of endogamy. One cannot belong to more than one caste, nor can one change castes. Though interaction between castes is rigidly controlled and enforced by custom and/or law, all are mutually interdependent within a society (Berreman, 1968, pp. 333–335).

Two basic types of caste systems exist. The first is the multiple caste system, which is characterized by the existence of intermediate groups between the uppermost and lowermost castes. Each intermediate group is in a position of both relative inferiority and superiority. This type of caste system is best exemplified by the elaborate system found in India, but it exists throughout Asia and Africa as well. The second type is the dual caste system, in which only two castes exist. Each is greatly separated from the other by the fact that no other castes exist between the two extremes. The lower one is viewed as a pariah caste and, as such, is stigmatized and excluded (Berreman, 1968, p. 337). In the Hindu mul-

In the Indian caste system, one's place in the social hierarchy is determined by one's birth—by the caste of one's family. (Paolo Koch, Rapho/Photo Researchers)

tiple caste system, the pariah caste is the group known as Untouchables; such a caste designation also is found throughout Asia and Africa.

Much of our understanding of the multiple caste system comes from the unique type found in India, so much so that arguments have been made for this being the only true caste system. The Hindu caste society consists of four basic divisions called *varnas,* found across India. The society is divided into hierarchically arranged categories of (1) *Brahmans* (priests); (2) warrior-rulers; (3) merchants; and (4) servants. The individuals outside of these categories comprise the group known as Untouchables, the pariah caste. *Varnas* are not organized groups, but are more like general categories. Membership in a *varna* allows people easily to assess each other's status in their local communities. In addition to these basic divisions, some regions are further divided into permanent caste groups, called *jatis,* which are separated by restrictions on marriage, physical contact, and food. Again, they are hierarchically arranged and occupationally specialized. Hereditary occupations, such as those of potters, barbers, and tanners, are associated with particular *jatis*. These groups tend to be local groups.

The notion of relative purity forms the basis of the caste hierarchy. Members of the top caste are considered the purest. The notion of purity is the reason for the separation between castes and for occupational specialization. Contact with a member of a lower caste is believed to be polluting; restrictions are placed on the higher, purer castes in regard to handling polluting items, usually anything associated with blood, death, and dirt.

The caste system in India is part of a pervasive religious system in which people of all ranks strive for removal of impurities as a necessary step toward personal salvation. The caste system is based on an accepted premise of inequality in the social sphere. In contrast, the social system of the United States is supposedly based on presumed equality of all people and tends to be achievement-oriented; it focuses on an individual's capabilities. The Indian caste system is based on ascription; one's place is fairly firmly predetermined by one's birth. Individual social mobility is allowed for only in the belief in reincarnation. By adhering to one's caste rules and living the caste's definition of a good life, an individual hopes that in the next life, he or she will be placed in a higher caste. Otherwise, one's caste cannot be changed; only rarely can the caste of one's offspring be altered. However, collective social mobility is a possibility. The status of one's entire *jati* may change, and with it will come a change in the status of everyone in the *jati*. But individual social mobility, based on one's personal achievement, is not characteristic of the Hindu caste system (Smelser & Lipset, 1966, p. 12).

Stratification by caste also occurs in parts of Africa. There, caste stratification is often based on conquest and subordination of rival tribes rather than on hereditary ascription. In such a system, the separateness of tribes is preserved, even though they are incorporated into and interact with the larger society. An example is the three-caste system that existed in Rwanda. Each caste there was physically different from the others, and these differences were perpetuated by the practice of endogamy. The groups were hierarchically arranged, with political power held by the king and the Tutsi caste, an aristocracy of pastoralists that comprised about 10 percent of the population. The Hutu, who were agriculturalists, comprised the majority of the society. The lowest ranking caste was the Twa, a small minority who functioned as jesters, potters, and hunters. As in the Hindu system, the caste hierarchy was validated by religion; the three castes were united by their belief in the cult of Ryangombe. Members of the Tutsi, Hutu, and Twa castes were all utilized in this cult but in ways that expressed their distinctions from one another. The caste differentiations were maintained by political hierarchy, but the ritual integration of the society was also firmly maintained (Southall, 1970, p. 242).

Boundaries between groups in a caste system, whether the system is in India or in Africa, are clearly defined and maintained. The idea of distinction is preserved even between two castes with minimal differences and maximal interaction (Berreman, 1968, p. 335). As we have seen, differences are maintained by religious, social, and political regulations and customs. Caste is primarily, however, a hierarchy of prestige. The political and economic aspects implied by caste are secondary. A hierarchy based primarily on political and economic power, and only secondarily on prestige, characterizes class stratification. This is the system most familiar in Western societies.

Class

A *class* is a group that shares the same social or economic status. The fundamental requirement is a sharing of traits by group members that distinguishes them as a separate entity within the society. The common trait or traits also identifies them as a group by the rest of society (Drucker, 1939, p. 55). Since such traits are defined largely in subjective terms, the concept of class is more amorphous and open to debate than that of class.

Class stratification may occur on the basis of some measure of privileges received by a group or simply on the basis of whether those people in similar roles think of themselves and act as a group (Smelser & Lipset, 1966, p. 6). In the latter sense, a class *system* did not exist in Western society until the Industrial Revolution. Although the aristocracy in Europe was a ruling class, the majority of people were unclassed. They were separated from each other by the practice of working in kin groups in the home. With industrialization, work was taken out of such groups and brought to factories. A class consciousness then emerged, due no doubt to many factors —easier communication among members of the working class; the general rise of literacy; increased geographic mobility because of one's labor skills; separation from land ties; deprivation at the hands of owners; and the desire for protective legislation for workers. All of these factors served to aid the workers in acting collectively and thinking of themselves as a class (Bendix, 1970, p. 321).

Once work was removed from the sphere of kinship groups, it was no longer ascription-based. Individuals no longer necessarily performed the jobs their parents had done. Occupation began to be determined by the quality of one's performance. And a job's status became based on the economic rewards and social mobility that the job offered. With individuals freer to choose their own occupations and objectives, an achievement-oriented, competitive class system evolved. It became possible, thereby, to determine an individual's ranking within society by evaluating economic as well as social criteria (Gould, 1971, p. 14).

The criteria for judging class usually in-

In Great Britain, characteristics such as accent, manners, and habits tend to reflect one's class background, which traditionally has been based on family connections. Here, the mayor of High Wycombe is weighed in an annual ceremony.
(Homer Sykes, Woodfin Camp)

clude income, occupation, level of achievement within one's occupation, standard of living relative to the rest of the society, kinship connections, education, and relationship to institutions of power such as church, army, or government. The importance of these criteria for defining class varies from society to society. For example, kinship ties may be more important in Great Britain than in the United

States; ethnic characteristics appear to be more important in the United States than in France; education may have greater significance in Germany or Sweden than in the United States; and occupation seems less class-oriented in the United States than in Germany. In the United States, economic factors generally take precedence over all others to a much greater degree than they do anywhere else. Since the criteria are relative, the concept of class cannot by systematized on a cross-cultural basis.

Thus, there is some controversy regarding to what kinds of societies the concept of class can be applied. Some anthropologists insist that class can only be found in market-dominated societies and that it is unique to Western history and culture (Gould, 1970, p. 1; Balandier, p. 91). Although it is true that the manner in which the class system evolved in Western Europe was unique, nontheless class stratification appears to be emerging in other parts of the world, especially in Africa. Occupational prestige, power, income, and education are criteria currently being applied in African societies to produce divisions into class (Southall, 1970, p. 265).

As we have seen, the possibility of social mobility distinguishes class from caste. As the criteria for occupational stratification become achievement oriented, and economic rewards are accompanied by social mobility, a class system of social differentiation may evolve. Class systems are based on the premise that every individual is equal to compete with all others and that the "best" individual will come out the winner in whatever the sphere of competition. However, such a premise describes an ideal state of affairs. In reality, not everyone starts from the same position. Social mobility thereby becomes limited, and inequality tends to gel and become a permanent part of the social system. The stratification system of the United States ideally enables a person to move away from ascribed positions based on hereditary, regional, or ethnic origins. However, ascribed characteristics—especially racial ones combined with prejudices—tend to hinder the ideal operation of the class system (Smelser & Lipset, 1966, p. 9). The same is true in Great Britain, where ascribed characteristics such as accent, habits, and manners reflect one's background and prevent individual mobility from operating ideally. There, social mobility tends to be collective, involving a family's change of status over a period of some generations (Smelser & Lipset, 1966, p. 10).

Slavery

The term *slave* brings to mind a person without rights who is subject to inhumane treatment and experiences a total loss of freedom. This image comes from what we know of slavery as it was instituted in the Western hemisphere, but this was a unique case. A broader definition of a slave is an individual who has lost control over his or her own labor. Anthropologists define *slavery* as a hierarchical system in which one group of people owns the labor and the products of the labor of another group of people. As such, slavery is found all over the world, even in otherwise egalitarian societies. The highest rate of slavery was found in sub-Saharan Africa (Bourguignon & Greenbaum, 1973, p. 42).

Slaves in Africa were not primarily labor units, as they were in the United States, so much as social and political units. People in African societies were viewed as that society's wealth. They not only belonged *in* a society, they belonged *to* it and could be sold in times of need. Therefore, the more dependents within a society, the wealthier the society. The more "acquired outsiders," the more powerful the chief. The ways to acquire a dependent were to marry, beget, adopt, capture, or buy one (Miers & Kopytoff, 1977, p. 65). In the West, slavery was often characterized by the method in which a person was acquired. Rights-in-a-person were commonly sold in African societies by an individual's family or community during marriage and adoption transactions. To the Westerner, this constituted slavery. To the African, such transactions involving purchasing of rights-in-a-person were indicative of marriage, adoption, *or* slavery (Miers & Kopytoff, 1977, p. 5).

The opposite of slavery to most Westerners was freedom; in an African context, the opposite of slavery was *belonging*. That is, slaves were taken, peacefully or by force, from their communities where they had certain bonds, rights, and a social identity. They were put into a strange environment where they were looked upon as nonpersons. Being a slave, in this context, meant establishing new bonds and beginning to acquire a social identity by having a clear status with formal rights and duties. This was the first step toward integration within the new society. The slave was an acquired outsider on the road to being less of a slave with each tie binding him or her to the new society. Although total integration never occurred for the acquired individual whose background was different from that of others in the society, a slave-to-kinship continuum did exist in most African societies. Slave status was not strictly hereditary, nor was the next generation necessarily free. But one's marginal status was reduced by being born in the community. Thus, offspring could be considered half-slave, and the following generation might be considered free. Initially, the slave might be considered a nonperson but, as marginality was reduced, the continuum led in the direction of quasikinship and finally resulted in kinship (Miers & Kopytoff, 1977, p. 4). This is fundamentally different from the West's conception of slaves as a class apart, never integrated into the society as a whole.

The process of incorporating the slave into the new society began with the acquisition of a master. Having a master indicated formal status, mobility from being mere property to being a person with rights. Emotional ties that developed between slave and his or her new family brought no change in formal status but

assured the slave that he or she would not be sold despite the legal possibility of such a sale. Mobility in terms of worldly success also existed for the African slave. A slave could acquire wealth and political power although the legal status would still not be changed. The slave's master still owned him or her, regardless of the power the slave acquired (Miers & Kopytoff, 1977, p. 19).

The use of slaves in Africa as political and social units rather than as labor units is evident in the preference for young women and children to men. Children were easier to integrate into their new society because they were young; women could be married into the society. Men were more difficult to incorporate into the society and were likely to be more difficult to control, especially if they had been taken by force. With the integration of white slave dealers into the African trade, male slaves became of higher value as labor units and greatly changed the structure of traditional African slavery.

Because of this gradual integration of the slave into the new society, it is difficult to determine where slave populations existed. In the West, slave populations made up separate reproductive units whose increase could be easily assessed. But in Africa, the physical reproductive rate diverged widely from the social rate. On the whole, though, the proportion of slaves to free persons was lower in small, relatively undifferentiated societies (Miers & Kopytoff, 1977, p. 60).

In the Northwest Pacific Coast area, slaves were also viewed not so much as labor units but as a measure of status. Therefore, the slave population consisted largely of women and children. An early observer of slavery in this area noted: "As concerns his labor, the slave was no great asset and the principal reason for the "existence of the institution of slavery was that the possession of captives reflected honor and dignity upon their owners" (Curtis, 1913, p. 74)."

According to Drucker, the principal significance of slaves on the Northwest Coast was to "serve as foils for the high and mighty" (1939, p. 56). For this purpose, slaves were sometimes sacrificed ceremonially or killed at the whim of their master, perhaps to show his anger (Fried, 1967, p. 222). Slaves did the same work as everybody else—fishing and paddling canoes. Furthermore, intermarriage between slaves and the free existed. Marriages between free men and slave women were not infrequent. More significantly, slave men and daughters of free men, even daughters of chiefs, married as well. A slave might also become an influential member of society, although his low status as a slave was always remembered and could be used against him (Fried, 1967, p. 223).

Even though slavery is a low-status condition wherever it occurs, nowhere were slaves deprived access to basic resources except in the West. And only in the West was control over one's destiny and the destiny of one's offspring totally lost, to the extent that it continues to temper social relations between blacks and whites today.

Stratification and Modernization

Because modernization first occurred in Western Europe, there is a tendency to assume that the process takes the same form the world over. The process that Europe underwent was peculiar to that area's position as the first to industrialize and assume world power status (Bendix, 1970, p. 327). Nations currently undergoing modernization are in a different position. As "followers," they are able to benefit from Europe's example of what not to do and what to do sooner. But these na-

tions also have feelings of inferiority and domination. Such feelings make it difficult for nationalism to take hold and, in turn, for modernization to develop in the European manner.

The continuity of social change allows for modernization to occur utilizing existing social structure. Eisenstadt (1967) points out that traditional structures in a society shape its modernization process. The example he cites is the initial modernization of India in which the caste system adapted to the new economic and political frameworks. According to Eisenstadt, the fact that modernization was not completed in India had to do with the inability of the new political center to develop common symbols by which to combine the new society with the old traditions, thereby creating a collective identity (1967, pp. 454–456). Eisenstadt's theory of how modernization occurs calls for the existence of independent social, cultural, and political institutions as well as a centralized institutional framework. The centralized institution of government affects traditional structures by redefining individual and group rights and duties as well as maintaining them.

Plural societies consist of people of diverse social, racial, and cultural origin who, during the process of modernization, became more fully incorporated into one social system (Smith, 1970, p. 43). The concept applies to Caribbean, African, Asian, Oceanic, and Latin American nations as well as to the United States. In Polynesia and the Caribbean, pluralism occurred with the intrusion of white settlers who came to trade, proselytize, plant, and administrate (Glick, 1970, p. 95). After this initial intrusion, other immigrant populations followed, either on their own or at the beckoning of planters who needed additional laborers. On the Polynesian island of Vila, for example, after the white immigration came Asians looking for employment, first as laborers, then as shopkeepers and artisans. The next group to come was made up of distant islanders. These groups tended to associate only among themselves, since language was a barrier to interaction between groups and because cultural ties bound group members together. In addition, they often lived separately because of restrictions imposed on housing by the politically dominant white group.

In Africa, plural societies came about again with the intrusion of the white "discoverer." Frontiers between nations were imposed where none had existed before. Within these frontiers were diverse tribes who found themselves amalgamated into one political system without regard to the differences between them (Southall, 1970, p. 257).

These societies, having relatively autonomous social, cultural, and political institutions as well as a centralized government, fill Eisenstadt's modernization requirements. They currently have the task of extending the influence of the centralized institution while also developing a collective identity to incorporate their diverse groups. Jamaica's national slogan, "Out of Many, One People," demonstrates this approach (Smith, 1970, p. 43).

The centralized political institution necessary for modernization also has the effect of giving "official" expression to large-scale stratification. It creates its own hierarchy while imposing the order necessary for modernization. But stratification results from unequal relations. This is true in all societies, from those with minimal government to large-scale, centralized nations (Balandier, 1970, p. 78). It is important to realize that political power and social stratification are linked, so that stratification determines who has power at the same time that those with power influence the social stratification. This is not to say that change will not occur in the system. The aristocracy continued to rule in England during modernization by taking up the middle-class cause. They thereby aided the change in the stratification system to the point where family status and office were separated. It is here that we see the significance of the continuity of social change and the effect of extrinsic factors such as government on existing stratification structure in the cause of the "growth of citizenship" (Bendix, 1970, p. 327).

Hawaii, more than any other state in the United States, represents the incorporation of people of diverse social, racial, and cultural origins into one plural society. (Monroe Pinckard, Rapho/Photo Researchers)

Summary

1. Inequalities exist in all human societies. In egalitarian societies, although lack of job differential ensures that social and economic differences are minimal, inequalities exist on the basis of divisions of labor by age and sex, individual abilities, and the existence of a headman and/or shaman.

2. The division of labor in rank and egalitarian societies is basically the same. However, in rank societies, a formalized system of individual graduated statuses exist, usually for ceremonial purposes. In addition, a redistributive economy develops, which keeps wealth from becoming concentrated in any one family. Societies become larger and more permanent, and a formalized kinship network develops.

3. Egalitarian and rank societies are considered unstratified; neither denies any group basic resources that sustain life.

4. As societies grow more complex, work becomes specialized, and access to basic resources is impaired. True stratification emerges. There are many different types of stratification systems that determine which groups are privileged and which groups are denied privileges.

5. One type of stratification system is the caste system. It is composed of socially distinct groups, hierarchically arranged, whose membership is birth-ascribed and considered unchangeable. Interaction between castes is controlled and endogamy is generally the rule. Two types of caste systems exist—a multiple caste system in which most people are in positions of both relative superiority and inferiority and a dual caste system in which only two groups occur: an elite group and a pariah group.

6. Another type of stratification system is the class system, considered more "open" because social mobility can occur. However, while this is the case ideally, in practice, mobility does not occur with the frequency commonly believed. The notion of class is less clearly defined as it relies on highly subjective criteria for its differentiation.

7. Another type of stratification system is slavery. A *slave* is a person who has lost control over his or her own labor. In Africa, a slavery-to-kinship continuum existed by which the slave was incorporated into the new society over generations. In the Northwest Coast area, slaves could be integrated into the society, often through marriage. Only in the Western hemisphere was slavery a permanent and hereditary classification.

8. The process of modernization is accompanied by three themes, according to Bendix: (1) a continuity of social change, (2) extrinsic factors affecting existing social structures, and (3) a redefinition of individual and group rights and duties.

9. Modernization is furthermore associated with fundamental structural changes determined by traditional social structures, according to Eisenstadt. Autonomous cultural, social, and political spheres as well as a centralized institutional framework are necessary components of a society seeking to modernize. However, their existence does not ensure that modernization will occur but only that the necessary adaptability exists.

10. Many societies currently undergoing modernization are plural societies in which socially and culturally distinct groups are incorporated within a larger societal frame. For modernization to occur, political power must be centralized. Such power is linked with social stratification. Stratification contributes to political power, and political power influences social stratification.

25

Politics and Leadership

OLITICS and leadership are closely linked with the concepts of status and hierarchy because status differences and ranking tend to involve domination and control. And, as we will see shortly, politics is also intimately related to domination and control—in a word, to *power*. A society's leaders exercise power, and they also enjoy high status. Of course, political leaders are not the only people who have power and status, but the connection between the two is most evident in the political arena.

Although political relations are probably as old as human society, political anthropology as a distinct field of study is relatively new. Before the 1940s, anthropologists did not explicitly study the political activities of the members of any given society as a separate field of inquiry, though they did describe political structures and classify political systems according to type. During the past 20 or 30 years, however, there has been increasing emphasis on the competitive aspects of politics—on political factions, the politics of decision making, and political change. Anthropologists now distinguish between the administration of a political system and the struggle for control of that system. Even so, the subject matter of political anthropology is not as clearly defined as that of other branches of the discipline. The study of kinship, for example, is a clearly delimited field of inquiry with a vocabulary of its own. This is not yet true of political anthropology.

In this chapter, we will approach political activities in a manner that is consistent with the view of cultural and social phenomena expressed throughout this book. That is, we will study politics in the context of the total social system, and native ideas about leadership and decision making will be considered in the context of models designed to interpret them. Among the ideas we will consider are the nature of political activity; various types of political systems; the relationship between kinship and politics; conquest and force; and leadership.

The Nature of Political Activity

Political anthropology has been described as "the study of the *processes* involved in determining and implementing public goals and in the differential achievement and use of power by the members of the group concerned with those goals" (Swartz et al., 1966, p. 7).

According to Swartz et al., politics is characterized by three essential qualities:

1. It is *public* rather than private in nature.
2. It always concerns goals or benefits for which there is *competition*.
3. It involves differences in *power*—that is, control—among the members of the group.

The concept of power is at the center of any treatment of politics. Attempts to define power and distinguish it from authority make up a major portion of the study of political anthropology.

Political anthropologists today focus on political *processes*. This emphasis calls attention to the fact that politics is concerned with the arena of political *action* rather than with typologies of political systems. One implication of such an approach is that it entails the study of conflict itself as well as the resolution of conflict. Moreover, it leads us to a focus on the political *activities* of groups ranging from small factions to entire societies, rather than merely on the *structure* of those groups. To use a familiar example: the political system of the United States can be viewed in terms of the three branches of government—executive, legislative, and judicial—and the functions of each. Such a view focuses on structure. The U.S. political system can also be viewed as a continuing struggle among various interest groups for the benefits distributed by the federal government (such as highway funds, tax exemptions, and welfare payments) and the control of valuable resources. This view emphasizes the activities involved in politics.

Power and Authority

The terms *power* and *authority* are often used interchangeably, but to the student of politics they are very different. *Power* is the capacity to take independent action in the face of resistance from persons, groups, or rules (Smith, 1968, p. 193). Thus, power has to do with resistance and confrontation. It is not institutionalized, and it is not always effective. *Authority,* by contrast, is institutionalized and involves the right to take certain actions, including decisions to issue commands. It represents the "set of rules, procedures, traditions, and norms that are regarded as binding when they are applied within a given social unit" (Smith, 1968, p. 193). The leader of a military coup may have power but little authority, whereas an elected official has authority and may often have considerable power as well.

Legitimacy

Political systems combine authority and power; both are needed in the regulation of public affairs. Without power, authority can accomplish little; without authority, power is not institutionalized and thus may lose its effectiveness in the long run. Accordingly, political systems have been defined as being concerned with the maintenance of social order through the use of force. But societies exist in which authority is not backed up by force. Moreover, as Swartz and his associates point out, "force is a crude and expensive technique for the implementation of decisions" (1966, pp. 9–10). Something besides coercion is needed to make a political system work. This additional ingredient is *legitimacy*.

The legitimacy of a political system derives from the values of the members of a society who influence and are affected by the decisions made within that society. Legitimacy is based on the expectation that those who make the decisions will meet certain obligations. Thus, it is not simply a matter of who makes the decisions but also a matter of the content of those decisions. A legitimate court, for example, is expected to arrive at a just verdict.

Compliance with the decisions made in a legitimate system results mainly from the belief that those decisions support the shared values of the members of the society. The degree of compliance within the society will vary, however. For those persons who do not comply with the decisions made by the leaders of a society, coercion may become necessary. This is the link between power and legitimacy: Power is one way of gaining compliance with the decisions made by those who are in positions of authority.

Political Systems and Governments

Anthropologists generally assume that every society has a political system, but those systems are classified in different ways. Some scholars would argue that the term *political system* should be reserved for societies that have governments. Others distinguish between societies that have centralized administrative and judicial institutions—that is, a government—and societies that lack such institutions. In any case, a political system is more than government. It includes both *politics*—the contest to gain power within an authoritative political system—and *administration*—the conducting of public affairs by those who have gained that power. In the following section, we will examine various modes of political organization, emphasizing the way power is achieved and authoritative decisions are made within each one.

Modes of Political Organization

Stateless Systems: Bands and Tribes

Some societies look to a single head, such as a military dictator or a prime minister, as a source of authority; other societies do not. The latter societies are called *acephalous* or "headless." They usually fall somewhere between very small communities (in which a single head is in direct contact with all the members) and very large ones (which can be held together only by a system of authority with a single center). There are some fairly large acephalous communities, however.

An example of an acephalous political system is the Nuer society of the southern Sudan in the early twentieth century. In this society, each kin group was autonomous, and the rights of each individual were enforced by that individual and his or her kin. Homicide, for example, was an injury to the kin group and might be revenged by killing the person who had committed the initial homicide or killing one of the kin. This method of revenge often led to blood feuds, but such a feud could be ended by means of a payment of cattle and a formal reconciliation. Thus, there was a political system of sorts, but no single person was responsible for coordinating the public activities of the tribe.

The Role of the Segmentary Lineage System. As the preceding example suggests, membership in kin groups has a great deal to do with political relations in acephalous societies. Indeed, in such societies, political relations are embedded in kinship relations. This is obvious in societies with segmentary lineage systems.

You will recall from earlier chapters that a segmentary lineage system involves both relations of association and relations of opposition—groups that are associated at one level are in opposition at the next-lower level. In a "segmentary" society such as that of the Nuer, political relations are based on a unilineal system of genealogical relations. The local community is thought of as consisting of a single lineage, but the genealogical system extends beyond the local community.

Relations between local groups—joint or extended families containing three or four generations—are essentially relations between lineages and thus do not change significantly over time, though the groups themselves may vary in size and locality over time. These relations may be competitive, as when rights over land or livestock are in question, but when an outside group threatens these local groups they will merge into a larger group or cluster to oppose the external threat. Thus, the segmentary lineage system serves "the decisive function of unifying 'within' for the purpose of standing 'against' " (Sahlins, 1961, p. 97). It should be noted that the larger entity does not exist under ordinary circumstances. It is called into being when needed and by reference to genealogy; that is, it is genealogically equivalent to groups that merge.

This is, of course, a very general description of how segmentary lineage systems work. There are actually many differences between such systems—in the degree of interdependence among the local groups, for example, and in the degree to which shared religious and social values control relations among them. If the groups are highly independent or very heterogeneous in cultural terms, however, it is unlikely that a true segmentary

lineage system exists. Neighboring Dinka tribes, for example, are divided into a number of subtribes with a tendency to fragment into entities that are absolutely independent of one another. But this segmenting tendency is not matched by any tendency toward fusion into temporary larger groupings. The Dinka thus have no way of withstanding external attacks as do the Nuer.

The Tiv of northern Nigeria illustrate the political role of the segmentary lineage system. The Tiv have been expanding their territory in several directions at the expense of other tribes, a movement that Sahlins (1961) describes as "predatory encroachment." Their success appears to be due to the fact that they can put mass pressure on their borders, whereas their opponents cannot call upon large numbers of people to resist the pressure.

Tiv expansion takes two forms. In one, nicknamed "leapfrog migration," a group from within Tivland crosses the border into a new area and is later joined by related groups. In the second form, "steamroller expansion," a border group may be forced by other groups to move into the territory of a neighboring tribe—"the lineage is simply crowded out as the Tiv side of its land is consumed by the appetites of other Tiv" (Sahlins, 1961, p. 111).

To sum up, the segmentary lineage system is "a social means of temporary consolidation of [a] fragmented tribal polity for concerted external action" (Sahlins, 1961, p. 117). It thus substitutes for a permanent political structure, which does not exist in a tribal society. It occurs only in the presence of intertribal competition, since without opposition there is no need to unite.

Decisions in Acephalous Political Systems. In bands and tribes, as in any social grouping, various decisions must be made. These decisions may be divided into three types: (1) reinforcement, or the prevention of deviation from acceptable forms of behavior; (2) administration, or directing the concerted ac-

Among Australian aboriginal tribes, the "old men" of the tribes are the ruling elders and also perform ceremonial and teaching functions. (Monkmeyer)

Yąnomamö men parading during a feast; shows of violence and aggression in rituals carry over into the life style of this people. (Napoleon Chagnon, Anthro-Photo)

tions of the group; and (3) adjudication, or resolving conflict between people or groups (Service, 1966).

Reinforcement is largely a matter of custom in acephalous societies. If an individual deviates from the society's norms, sanctions such as gossip, ridicule, and withdrawal may be directed at that person. These sanctions do not result from a decision of a person in a position of authority but are based on the general consensus of the members of the group (though the elder males tend to have more authority than other members). In extreme cases, a band may decide to kill a person who consistently harms others. The person chosen to perform the act is a relative of the wrongdoer (in order to prevent a blood feud).

In *administration* areas—decisions that have to do with such matters as moving camp, hunting, and skirmishing with enemies—some leadership is required, but in acephalous systems leadership is not formal. The decision-making authority shifts from one person to another, depending on the type of decision involved. For example, a man who has a great store of ritual knowledge will plan a ceremony, while the most skillful hunter will lead a hunting party. There is no permanently chosen chief or headman. In fact, the word *authority* may be too strong for such situations. *Influence* might be a better word, since the leader is in that position only temporarily, as long as his experience and skill are needed.

Adjudication has to do with how quarrels, feuds, and sometimes wars are settled. This would appear to be a very difficult question in the absence of a formal system for settling disputes. But the fact is that acephalous societies are capable of handling conflict fairly well. When a quarrel occurs, a person—often someone who is related to both parties—will step in to stop the dispute from getting out of hand, as in the following example:

A small crowd had gathered, and, as usual, the family quarrel became a public affair. Several people helped Tu out of the fire, found her barely scorched, but her cousin seized Toma and began to shake him. This enraged Toma so much that he caught the cousin around the waist and threw him into the onlooking crowd. The people said: "We must stop Toma because if he is so angry he may kill someone," and with that they led the cousin out of Toma's sight.

Toma shouted after: "If you do that again, we will get our arrows and fight to the death. Stop here. I am very angry. Do not make me more angry."

One of the men who had helped Tu said to the cousin: "I took his wife from the fire. You, her cousin, almost got killed for the way you went at Toma. If you want to help people, don't get angry with them. Keep calm. Don't increase anger as you did with Toma." With these sage words the incident was over. (Thomas, 1970, p. 308)

If this mediation approach is ineffective, techniques such as the Eskimo song duel or the spear-throwing duel of the Australian aborigines may be used. These contests are decided by public opinion; the loser is considered to have been in the wrong.

Quarrels between people who are members of different bands are more difficult to resolve. One method, mentioned earlier in connection with the Nuer, is retribution. But retribution does not usually restore the original balance between the parties, and feuding may continue for long periods unless some sort of reconciliation takes place.

The Eskimo. The Eskimo provide an example of simple government in bands. They have been described by Lawrence Krader (1968) as follows:

The Eskimos, who live in Alaska in bands of usually no more than 50, have neither chiefs nor advisory councils, nor deliberative assemblies—although they do practice a form of individual economic leadership; in whale hunting, the boat owner has dominance over the crew, and primary right over the catch. Nevertheless, they have no formal government and explicit organs whereby they are ruled; they are without specialized administrators, judges, courts, and written law.

Rather, they have informal means of controlling aggression among people, and righting wrongs. Their primitive legal mechanisms include [for example] the song-duel.

The Eskimos countenance several socially acceptable modes of doing away with people: suicide, senilicide [killing of the old], infanticide, and invalidicide. Homicide is sometimes redressed by blood revenge. . . . The Public or society at large is not involved; it is a private wrong. . . . However, *repeated* murder among the Eskimos is in fact considered to be a matter of public interest; it is a public crime of which the band must take cognizance, and is punishable by death at the hands of a chosen agent of the band. The Eskimos have a simple form of governmental regulation of social behavior: their court is not a permanent institution; it is convened as the occasion warrants, and after the judgment the court is disbanded without fixing a time for reassemblage. (Krader, 1968, pp. 30–31)

Thus, while stateless systems may not have formal government in the way we know it, every society provides means for supporting the rights and obligation necessary for that society to exist. Societies that do not look to a single head for authority are capable of regulating fairly large populations by means of the control mechanisms discussed here and in the chapter on social control.

State Systems: Chiefdoms and Monarchies

Characteristics of State Systems. In a state system, a ruler who is recognized by the society as its head holds supreme authority, which may be delegated to various territorial agents. This is a common form of political system among the societies studied by anthropologists. The state's functions are maintenance of internal peace, defense against external aggression, organization of public works and rituals, and collection of tribute (taxes). Although small societies are sometimes organized in this way, it is more usual among relatively large populations. Naturally, the details of state systems vary greatly. One of the distinguishing features of state systems, though, is that they are run by officials who are free to specialize in the administration of the state. That is, they are not engaged primarily in economic production. This includes both the ruler and subordinate officials.

Subordinates, or agents, are chosen by the ruler or leader. Sometimes the subordinates are kin of the person in authority; sometimes they are nonkin rewarded for loyal service. The subordinate has much to gain from such an appointment—for example, free labor for home and fields and a certain amount of the produce of the community. The duties of the subordinate are to decide disputes, collect tribute, and organize labor for public works. Thus, the positions of both ruler and agent are privileged ones.

It is in the selection of subordinates that politics comes into play. If a central source of authority—that is, a leader—is firmly established, intriguing for one's own or a friend's appointment to an official position consists mainly of pleasing those who are already in positions of authority. If the central authority is weak, political competition may take the form of efforts to gain followers or *clients.* In return for protection, the clients offer service, which can include violent actions such as plundering the possessions of a rival. Those with many followers are more likely to achieve positions of authority in the society. From the client's point of view, the protection involved in the relationship can be highly significant. Mair (1962) describes one such instance of the client relationship:

The client made . . . a token gift—a pot of beer or of the fermented honey which was much prized in Ruanda. . . . The client had the duty of personal service to his lord. He followed him on journeys, to court, or to war. . . . A client who fulfilled his obligations expected to be able to count on his lord's protection in most kinds of trouble. (Mair, 1962, pp. 168–169)

The competition for positions of authority can also extend to competition between princes for succession to a throne. Even when there are specific rules of succession, there is room for such competition. For example, the Zulu rule of succession was that the next chief must be the eldest son of the woman whom his father had married after he himself became chief. But if the heir was a child, a regent would be chosen, perhaps a younger brother of the dead chief. When the heir came of age, the regent, perhaps unwilling to step down, might have built up enough power to prevent the heir from succeeding to the throne. In an effort to avoid problems of this kind, many states have "kingmakers," officials with the authority to choose the successor. Even then, however, competition is not necessarily eliminated. The kingmaker's choice may be challenged, and fighting can continue until one of the rivals is killed.

How States Are Formed. How does an acephalous political system like that of the Eskimos develop into a state system? Some theorists have argued that the state is formed as a result of conquest—one group subjugates another and uses governmental institutions to maintain its domination. Other anthropologists claim that states develop as a result of the unequal distribution of economic goods; those who control more resources can gain control over the rest of the society. But societies have been identified in which neither conquest nor economic control has led to the formation of a state; the Eskimos and the neighboring Chukchi have conquered one another at various times without developing into states.

Krader (1968) believes that statelike institutions—for example, secret religious societies, military or police associations, high councils—play a role in the formation of states. Such institutions tend to counteract the individual's ties to his or her local community and thus link the relationships of local life into a larger whole. They serve the additional functions of providing a wider outlet for tensions generated within small groups and creating a greater variety of choices and more freedom for individuals.

It appears that the crucial factor in the formation of a state is the degree of centralization of authority. Multiple centers of power and authority compete with one another and prevent a state from forming. Several West African peoples, such as the Kpelle, had a king or high chief but also had institutions such as secret societies that had considerable power. Neither the king nor the secret society could achieve ultimate control, and a state did not develop. Similarly, the Plains Indians had well-developed police and military associations as well as chiefs and councils. However, the general pattern of social control was simple and informal, so that no single individual or group could gain enough power to become the dominant force in the society.

As traditional ties are broken down and territorial boundaries become more precise, a state emerges. Eventually, one person or group assumes the central authority in the society, with a monopoly on the legal use of force.

Legitimacy in State Systems. The ruler and subordinates, as we have seen, have a claim to the resources of the country and the labor of its people. Why do the people accept such a system? For one thing, it is often to their advantage to have a relatively formal method of settling disputes. For another, they receive protection against outside attack. And the ritual performed (or financed) by the ruler guarantees the good will of deities or ancestors, something that is considered indispensable in many such societies. The traditional rituals by which a ruler came into office symbolized these obligations: "A Ganda ruler . . . shot arrows towards all four points of the compass to signify that he would conquer his enemies; at the accession of a king of Bunyoro a trial was enacted to remind him of his duty as the source of justice" (Mair, 1972, p. 127).

Counselors and Councils. Even though a state system has a single ruler, it is not necessarily a dictatorship. Decisions are made with the help of counselors. Among the Bantu, for example,

> it was customary for the ruler to have as his chief adviser a man not of his lineage . . . who was expected to be . . . a mouthpiece of popular dissatisfaction. . . . He was expected to listen to people who thought they had been wronged—particularly by unjust punishments—and to remonstrate privately with the ruler and persuade him to make amends without publicly admitting that he was at fault. (Mair, 1972, p. 128)

In most state systems there is also a council of some sort (comprising all the leading subordinate chiefs, for example). This type of arrangement allows for considerable political maneuvering in the decision-making process as well as in the competition for official positions.

An Emergent State System: Ankole. The small kingdom of Ankole in what is now western Uganda provides an example of an emergent state system. It was formerly ruled by the king of the Bahima tribe, to whom other Bahima were clients, following the king in war and receiving in return whatever cattle were seized. (If the king did not share out the booty, the clients might try to overthrow him.) The king was believed to have supernatural powers and was given the titles of Lion, Bull, Land of Ankole, Drum, and Moon. He was required to be virile; if he became ill or senile he was given a fatal poison. Only he had the right to send out raiding parties and make war or peace. He was the highest judicial authority, with the power to sentence clients to death or exile, to torture and curse, and to confiscate property.

Several subordinates were appointed by the king, including the Enganzi, or favorite chief. The Enganzi had to be from another clan and could not himself become king, but he was kingmaker, "prime minister," and war minister. The king ruled through the Enganzi, border chiefs, magicians, and other members of his personal following. The Bahima district chiefs collected tribute from serfs, keeping part and sending the remainder to the king.

The royal succession passed from father to eldest son, but the successor had to be strong enough to withstand potential rivals—younger brothers with greater strength or more followers. During a war of succession, the border chiefs, who could not become king, stood guard against outside invasion. When one of the rivals for the throne had eliminated all the others, the Enganzi enthroned the new king, who then appointed a new Enganzi (Krader, 1968).

Primitive states frequently need to exercise strong control in order to maintain social order.

Colonial Systems

States such as Ankole were radically changed by European colonization in the nineteenth and early twentieth centuries. The goals of the European governments were to gain advantages for their own citizens (in trade, for example) and also to benefit the colonized peoples by teaching them the values of Western civilization. It fact, they believed that it was their moral duty to impose "good" government on primitive peoples. This meant setting up a new hierarchy of officials linking the native officials with the colonial government.

At the interface between the colonial administration and the native peoples was the district commissioner (or some similar official). He did not decide policy but was supposed to see that the central government's policies were put into effect. Among other things, he chose local people to administer those policies—to collect taxes, for example.

Military troops were often part of the colonial apparatus—in this instance, members of the French Foreign Legion in French Guyana. (Y. Jeanmougin/ Viva, Woodfin Camp)

Where possible, he chose individuals who were already in positions of authority. If no such individuals could be found, he would ask the native people to nominate candidates for such positions. This opened up a new arena of competition between native groups in the society. A whole class of people was created, a group that could be considered clients of the colonial government, since they owed their position—and its rewards—to that government. This naturally changed their relationship with the people under their control. They no longer received tribute from the peasants under their authority; instead, they received salaries, which in some cases were substantial. However, under this arrangement, peasants lost the protection and hospitality of the chiefs, while the chiefs became isolated from the people and began to feel like servants of the colonial government.

Max Gluckman (1968) has analyzed the roles of the district commissioner and the native chief under the Dutch administration of Zululand in the mid-1930s. He points out that both commissioner and chief were subject to conflicting pressures because they occupied positions in which two levels of social relations (colonial and native) met and often clashed. The commissioner was at the lowest level of the colonial hierarchy but had some influence over the native people. On the other hand, the chief was at the head of the tribal hierarchy but was at the same time considered a junior official in the colonial hierarchy. The positions of commissioner and chief had little authority.

Both the administrator and the chief were expected to represent the interests of the government at the local level, and both were expected by the local people to represent their interests. This often led to conflict. For example, "a chief who opposed the building of cattle paddocks was praised by his people, but condemned by technical officers; while a chief who asked for cattle paddocks was praised by technical officials and condemned by his people" (Gluckman, 1968, p. 80).

In Zululand, Gluckman found considerable dedication to the native people among the commissioners. They were concerned about producing better breeds of Zulu cattle, for example, or finding ways of helping the Zulu get higher prices for their cattle, or improving their agricultural technology (Gluckman calls this the "development ethic.") The commissioner became involved in "Zulu hopes and fears, aspirations and objections" (p. 75). Many spoke Zulu and knew a great deal about Zulu history and culture.

In general, the policies of colonial governments often failed to take into account the differences in the economics and political organization of the areas under their jurisdiction. Also, the colonial governments were not considered legitimate at the local level and had to depend quite heavily on coercion, despite the dedication of many of their lower-level officials. However, they did make possible the administration of diverse political units, and in this way paved the way for the emergence of modern nation-states.

Political Systems in New Nations

In the new nation-states of Africa, Asia, and Latin America, many diverse groups have had to be united within a brief period. In another chapter, we discussed this process from the standpoint of law. We saw that a basic problem of new nations is that of getting citizens to identify with the nation as a whole rather than with a particular subgroup. As Clifford Geertz (1968) has pointed out, the desire to preserve one's tribal or religious identity can conflict with the desire to be part of an efficient, modern state.

The Need for Integration. As we saw in connection with both social control and with industrialization, the process of development and modernization involves the integration of diverse elements into a new system. This need for integration is especially acute in the political sphere. Somehow, the attachments of citizens to tribe, religion, language, and so forth must be reconciled with the new order. It is not enough simply to deny these attachments, nor can they be wished out of existence.

Political integration occurs in various ways in different states. One tendency that new states have in common, however, is that of lumping together traditional groups into larger, looser units whose frame of reference is not the locality but the nation. In Malaysia these larger groups tend to be ethnic: Malays, Chinese, and Indians. In Indonesia they are commonly regional: the people of Java and those of the Outer Islands. In Nigeria they are based loosely on kinship; in India they have been based somewhat on language. As members of these larger blocks, individuals who never interacted before are doing so now; and in so doing they gradually identify more and more with total society. At the same time, conflicts between the larger blocs are becoming more sharply defined and causing turmoil in the developing states. Such conflicts generate a tendency toward separatism that can disrupt a new state before it has become fully established.

The "Gap." The machinery of government in new states—elections, political parties, civil service—is new, whereas the social structure and culture in these states are traditional. Moreover, the elites created by state formation are concerned about the need for modernization, while the masses—usually peasant majority—tend to be resistant to changes that appear to conflict with traditional values. These factors create a gap between the society as it would like to be and the society as it actually is.

540

This gap, together with the difficulty of achieving unity in a heterogeneous population, complicates the task of developing the political system of a new state. Traditional beliefs, the existing social structure, and illiteracy tend to hold back modernization. Even when trained people are available to serve in the government, they may feel that they are overqualified for such positions. The public, on the other hand, never having had a voice in political decisions, is likely to be overly submissive. Silence on public matters may cause its members to be either overlooked or ordered around "for their own good."

Government in New States. The task of creating the political system of a new state falls quite naturally on its educated and politically aware members, who constitute its elite. The regime with which these individuals are most familiar is the state's former colonial ruler, often a European nation such as France or England. Thus, the elite tend to favor systems based on a democratic model, but the difficulty of setting up a modern state in an environment in which tradition is more powerful than education often leads to a relatively authoritarian political system.

Still, most new states aim, at least initially, toward *political democracy,* a system in which the central element is an elected legislative body whose laws are carried out by an executive with the help of an organized bureaucracy. Political parties are active and opposition is tolerated; in fact, opposition is necessary in such a system.

For a political democracy to be viable, it must meet certain conditions:

1. It must be recognized as legitimate by most of the society.
2. There must be a corps of political leaders who are reasonably informed, competent, and forthright.
3. The opposition group must be coherent

and responsible (for example, it must not oppose merely for the sake of opposition).
4. There must be a trained, competent civil service (the bureaucracy that administers the laws).
5. There must be respect for the rule of law and a disciplined police force, intelligence system, or military to back up the law.
6. There must be established institutions of public opinion—newspapers, universities, civic associations, and the like—with freedom of expression and association.

It is difficult to meet these conditions even in long-established states. In new states, it is extremely difficult. In many cases, the citizens of the new state are united only by the fact that no other state controls their territory. Not only do the people lack a feeling of solidarity, but the ruling elite itself is often torn by conflict.

When the six conditions just listed do not occur together, a more authoritarian regime is likely to develop. And, indeed, such regimes, called *tutelary democracies,* are commonly found in developing nations. President Sukarno of Indonesia has aptly labeled this form of government "guided democracy." In such a system, the power of the legislature and the political parties is reduced, though these elements are not eliminated, and the press is expected to refrain from criticizing the ruling elite. But although freedom of expression is reduced, the rule of law is retained.

A tutelary democracy requires an elite that is considered legitimate by a significant portion of the population, and that elite must avoid excessive use of coercion. A competent, loyal civil service is also needed, along with an independent judiciary. Of course, such a system presupposes a relatively weak state of public opinion (such as the lack of a communications system that generates creative criticism and enlightened opposition). The citizens must accept the existing regime without much opposition. If they are too apathetic, however—or too rebellious—the regime is likely to become a *modernizing oligarchy.* An oligarchy is a form of government in which ruling power belongs to only a few persons.

The concept of a modernizing oligarchy appeals to members of the elite who are concerned with the rapid achievement of both progress and unity. A more authoritarian regime such as an oligarchy is thought to be the cure for "parochialism, disunity and apathy" (Shils, 1960). It is also encouraged by the presence of a heavy counterweight of traditional beliefs and customs that work against the establishment of a political democracy.

A modernizing oligarchy requires a closed, well-organized elite. If it is a civilian elite, it must have control over the military. No effective legislature is established, and opposition is not tolerated. The will of the rulers is carried out by an elaborate bureaucracy, but there is no independent judiciary. The rule of law gives way to the maintenance of order by the police and the army. Such a regime attempts to reduce local, traditional loyalties to an absolute minimum and to stimulate nationalistic feeling.

Although modernizing oligarchies are not uncommon among new states, none has yet succeeded in winning the support of the entire population. Traditional ties are very resistant to forceful efforts to eliminate them. Thus, while an oligarchical system can make some progress toward modernization in certain areas—such as improved transportation, land reform, and the like, they are less successful in other areas, such as private enterprise.

Politics and Warfare

Throughout this chapter we have mentioned conflict—blood feuds, competition for the throne in a traditional state, intergroup conflict in new states. Frequently, such hostilities lead to minor skirmishes in which few people are killed. Sometimes, however, they build up to the level of warfare.

War is often said to arise out of competition for limited resources. But despite the possibility of economic gain (such as booty, captives, or territory) from warfare, studies of the causes of war have shown that economic motives are much less important than other factors. In fact, any gain that may come from victory is unlikely to make up for the costs of war.

Levels of Violence

Warfare is usually an outgrowth of earlier hostilities rather than a planned undertaking. Among the Yąnomamö of Brazil and Venezuela, for example, two villages that do not have a stable alliance cannot coexist for very long without overt hostility. But the initial conflict will not be a full-scale war. According to Napoleon A. Chagnon (1977), the Yąnomamö have several levels of violence. At the lowest level, accusations of cowardice or malicious gossip may lead to a chest-pounding duel between members of different villages. Such a duel may escalate into a side-slapping contest or, more rarely, a duel with machetes, using the flat side of the blade. The next level is club fights, which may take place either within or between villages and which usually arise out of arguments over women. If such a fight involves many people, it can become quite brutal and may cause a village to split up into two groups.

The next level of violence among the Yąnomamö is the raid, or actual warfare. The goal of a raid is to kill one or more of the enemy without losing any members of the raiding party. If there is a single loss, the raid is considered unsuccessful, no matter how many of the enemy are killed. Such warfare is

542 usually motivated by the desire for revenge and is simply a prolongation of earlier hostilities.

Functions of Warfare

Andrew Vayda (1968) has identified several possible functions of primitive warfare:

1. Regulation of the exercise of authority, that is, limiting abuses of power by those in authority. This function is illustrated by the rebellions that occur when a chief or king fails to divide booty fairly.
2. Regulation of relations with other groups. This applies to fighting for revenge (as in cases of insult, theft, nonpayment of bridewealth, rape, trespass, or wounding) and to whatever fighting is necessary for a group to maintain its integrity and possessions.
3. Regulation of the distribution of goods and resources. Warfare appears to serve certain economic functions. But with the exception of the cattle raids of pastoral peoples, it is not always clear how important warfare is in obtaining material gain. It is often the case that a defeated group is forced to give up its land. Although there are cases in which wars end without displacing a group from its land, over the long run, one group may be weakened to such an extent that it is forced to yield its territory to a stronger group. Most warfare among hunters and gatherers involves disputes over the control of marginal territories and its resources.
4. Regulation of demographic variables. In some instances, the purpose of warfare may be to kill as many of the enemy as possible and thus to reduce the total population. In others, the purpose may be to take captives. It should be noted, however, that wars for the purpose of capturing slaves are rare among hunting-and-gathering groups because food pro-

duction is not developed enough to support a slave class. In a few cases, wars have been conducted for the purpose of capturing women (or, more rarely, men or children) in order to correct a population imbalance.

Alternatives to Warfare: The Potlatch Revisited

People who have a tradition of warfare have sometimes abandoned war in favor of some other activity that fulfills the same functions. An example of a case in which the substitution of another activity for warfare was unsuccessful is the situation in New Guinea, where the colonial administration forced the native people to take their land disputes to court instead of settling them by fighting. The courts soon became overloaded; moreover, the disputants were never satisfied by their verdicts. This factor, together with increased population pressure, led to renewed warfare.

An example in which warfare may have been successfully replaced by another activity was the case of the North American Pacific Coast Kwakiutl Indians. As the Kwakiutl themselves put it, "wars of property"—potlatches—replaced "wars of blood," and fighting was done with wealth instead of weapons. This shift occurred during the mid-1800s, a time when the population was declining (owing to epidemics introduced by Europeans), and trade goods such as blankets and bracelets were becoming available in quantities that would not have been possible using Kwakiutl handicraft techniques. Since the Indians were usually able to produce what they needed for subsistence, their cash earnings (such as from commercial fishing and lumbering) were a surplus that could be spent on trade goods used in the potlatch.

Another reason that potlatching substituted for warfare was that war was not a central element of Kwakiutl life. Warfare had been an expression of rivalry, of competition for social prestige. And, as we have seen, this function was fulfilled very well by *potlatching,* which itself is a form of rivalry, "ridden with the imagery and drama and meaning of Kwakiutl warfare" (Codere, 1950, p. 128).

Conquest and territorial expansion, then, are only one aspect of warfare, and not necessarily the most fundamental one in primitive society. Modern warfare is ostensibly sparked largely by ideological considerations, although the underlying function of political and economic factors is also crucial. Warfare does not solve problems; it merely reorients them and puts off the need to solve them until a later time.

Leadership

The Yąnomamö say that the headman's privilege is "to walk ahead on the path." It is true that societies need leaders in time of war, but this is not the only function of a leader. In any centralized political system, the leader's role is to serve as the source of authority. A classic analysis of leadership is that of Max Weber (1947). After pointing out that all leadership requires a certain amount of voluntary submission on the part of followers, he divided authoritative leadership into three major types:

1. *Legal* (or bureaucratic), in which authority is based on a belief in the legality of a system of rules, and obedience stems from loyalty to the office, not the person, of the leader.
2. *Traditional,* in which authority is based on belief in the sanctity of tradition and obedience is to the person who occupies a traditional position of authority.
3. *Charismatic,* in which a specific individual, through exceptional "gifts" or strength of character, gains the devotion of a group of followers.

These three forms of authority are, in Weber's terms, "ideal types," meaning that they are not usually found in their pure forms. President Kennedy, for example, is remembered as a charismatic leader, but as president his authority was based primarily on his legal position as president.

The Role of Consent

Claude Lévi-Strauss (1944) argued that *consent* is the psychological basis of leadership and that give-and-take, or reciprocity, between a leader and followers is central to leadership. To illustrate this point, he described leadership among the nomadic Nambikuara of Brazil.

According to Lévi-Strauss, the leadership of a Nambikuara band was not a product of the band's needs, but the reverse. That is, the leader was a stable nucleus around which a band took shape. The leadership role was not hereditary; the headman needed the support of the group. Therefore, leadership was based on personal prestige and the ability to inspire confidence. Moreover, the chief had no coercive power, so that his legitimacy was based entirely on consent. If members of the group felt that the leader was doing a poor job, they could join another band that they believed to be better managed. Thus, Nambikuara bands fluctuated greatly in size and membership and were especially subject to political intrigues and conflicts.

To prevent such difficulties, the headman not only had to do an outstanding job of choosing campsites, directing the group's gardening efforts, and so forth, but also had to be exceptionally generous. It was expected that everything that came into his hands would be given away within a short time. Lévi-Strauss described the consequences as follows.

This collective greediness not seldom drives the chief to an almost desperate position; then the refusal to give plays about the same part, in this primitive democracy, as the threat to resign followed by a vote of confidence in a modern parliament. When a chief reaches the point where he must say: "To give away is over! To be generous is over! Let another be generous in my place!", he must, indeed, be sure of his power and prestige, for his rule is undergoing its severest crisis. (Lévi-Strauss, 1944, pp. 54–55)

Although consent is the basis of leadership, it is expressed in a continual give-and-take between leader and followers. The Nambikuara chief had certain powers but was also expected to be generous. In return for the effort he made on behalf of the group, he was entitled to take several wives. This was no small privilege, since it meant that other Nambikuara men were obliged to do without. Lévi-Strauss added, however, that reciprocity was not the only reason that some people became leaders. "There are chiefs," he wrote, "because there are, in any human group, men who, unlike most of their companions, enjoy prestige for its own sake, feel a strong appeal to responsibility, and to whom the burden of public affairs brings its own reward" (p. 61).

Lévi-Strauss could just as well have been describing leadership in Toba society. In fact, in many small-scale societies—among the Nuer of East Africa, for example—ritual experts and prophets provide the crucial leadership. Although both types of leader (priests and prophets) mediate between the real world and the spirit world, they differ greatly from each other. Priests inherit their position and with it their authority (traditional leadership). Prophets derive their authority from their extraordinary behavior, which is thought to indicate possession of (or by) spirits (charismatic leadership). Yet each may seek to enhance authority by means of techniques often used by the other. For example, priests may try to increase their influence through charisma (for example, leadership in raids), while prophets may seek to convert their charismatic power

into more stable authority by winning public affirmation of their status.

The Big Man Versus the Chief

The role of reciprocity, together with Weber's list of "ideal types" of authority, is illustrated in the contrast between the "big men" of Melanesia and the paramount chiefs of Polynesia. The big man is a traditional type; such a leader is expected to exert strong personal control over local groups. The paramount chief, on the other hand, has more authority vested in his office; his duties are more clearly defined. The power of the big man is personal power, whereas that of the chief is primarily the power of office.

The big man *creates* his position and therefore is very dependent on his followers. He has to win their loyalty and cause them to be obligated to him; he has to reinforce this reciprocal relationship continually. If there is discontent among his followers, the big man may find himself out of power.

The Polynesian chief, by contrast, holds an inherited position of authority over a permanent group. Both the position and the group exist independently of the individual who happens to be chief. The leader's authority comes from his office. Yet the relationship is still reciprocal. The chief has many privileges, but he cannot overload the ability of the people to supply the goods and labor required to maintain those privileges. That is, he cannot "eat the power of the government too much" or rebellion may ensue.

Leadership in New States

The creation of new states out of colonial regimes provides opportunities for charismatic leaders to emerge and to appeal to whatever nationalistic sentiments exist among the people, thereby creating a following who may sweep them into office when the new government is set up. This kind of leadership can be

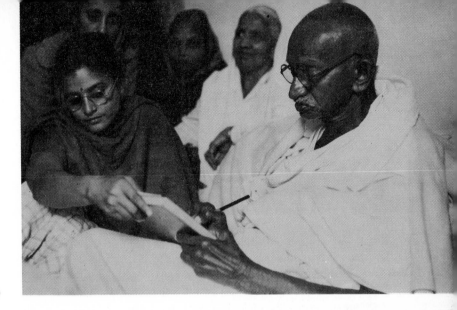

Charismatic leadership in creating new states out of colonial regimes was perhaps best exemplified by Mahatma Gandhi, who led India's move for freedom from British rule.
(Henri Cartier-Bresson, Magnum)

valuable to a new nation. Mahatma Gandhi's role in freeing India from British rule is a prime example. Such larger-than-life individuals may temporarily make up for the lack of political institutions, such as political parties and parliaments, in a new nation. But they do not usually build up such institutions while they are in power. Thus, when they die or are overthrown, the nation may undergo a period of turmoil before a new leader is found or a viable political system is established.

Leadership, then, is clearly associated with political activities and processes. But, in many societies studied by anthropologists, no clear-cut distinction between political and religious leadership is evident. They merge into one, as will be apparent in the following chapter.

Summary

1. Three essential qualities of politics are: (1) It is public rather than private in nature; (2) it concerns goals or benefits for which there is competition; and (3) it involves differences in power among the members of a group.

2. *Power* is the capacity to take independent action in the face of resistance; *authority* is the institutionalized right to take certain actions, including decisions to issue commands.

3. Political systems combine authority and power in regulating public affairs. The members of a political system must believe it is *legitimate* to win compliance with its decisions without undue use of force.

4. Within a political system, a distinction can be made between *politics*—the competition for positions of power—and *administration*—the conducting of public affairs (that is, the carrying out of decisions) by those in power.

5. Stateless or *acephalous* systems—bands and tribes—have no single source of authority. Relations between groups in such societies are sometimes based on a segmentary lineage system.

6. Decisions in stateless systems are largely a matter of custom and public opinion. Tasks that require leadership are coordinated by the person who is most skilled at the task in question.

7. A state system—a chiefdom or mon-

archy—is formed when authority is centralized in a single source that is recognized as legitimate by the society. The state maintains peace, defends against aggression, organizes public works, and collects taxes.

8. In a state system, the ruler chooses subordinates. Individuals compete for these privileged positions by pleasing those in authority or by trying to gain as many clients (followers) as possible.

9. Competition for the throne is not uncommon in state societies, even when there are definite rules of succession.

10. Colonial systems superimposed a second authority structure on the structure already existing in traditional states. This greatly changed political relationships in those societies. Officials that interfaced between the colonial administration and the native peoples were subject to conflicting pressures. They were expected to represent the interests of each group to the other, and those interests often clashed.

11. The main problem facing newly independent states is that of getting citizens to identify with the nation as a whole rather than with a particular subgroup. An intermediate stage in this process is the formation of larger groups that identify more with the total society than with a small part of it.

12. New states are at a tremendous disadvantage in developing their political systems because of conflicting beliefs among disparate members, the lack of an effective communication system, and the absence of enlightened opposition that contributes to the effective implementation of policies.

13. The elite of a new state often tries to set up a *political democracy,* but the difficulty of creating such a system is likely to lead to the establishment of a *tutelary democracy.* Even then, however, the tendency toward authoritarianism may cause the regime to become a *modernizing oligarchy.*

14. Conflict is frequent in political systems of all descriptions. Sometimes these hostilities build up to the level of warfare, which is usually an outgrowth of earlier hostilities rather than a planned undertaking. There may be several levels of violence before full-scale warfare occurs.

15. The functions of warfare are regulation of the exercise of authority, regulation of relations with other groups, regulation of the distribution of goods and resources, and regulation of demographic variables. Sometimes another activity can substitute for warfare, as occurred when the *potlatch* replaced warfare among the Kwakiutl Indians.

16. Weber divides authoritative leadership into three types: *legal,* in which people are loyal to the office, not the person, of the leader; *traditional,* in which obedience is to the person who occupies a traditional position of authority; and *charismatic,* in which an individual gains the devotion of followers through exceptional qualities. These types are rarely found in their pure forms, and more than one type may be found in any given society.

17. Lévi-Strauss points out that the psychological basis of leadership is consent and that it is expressed in a continual give-and-take between leader and followers.

18. Charismatic leaders often emerge in new states and can substitute for political institutions, but they must eventually organize their folllowers and systematize their authority if a viable political system is to emerge.

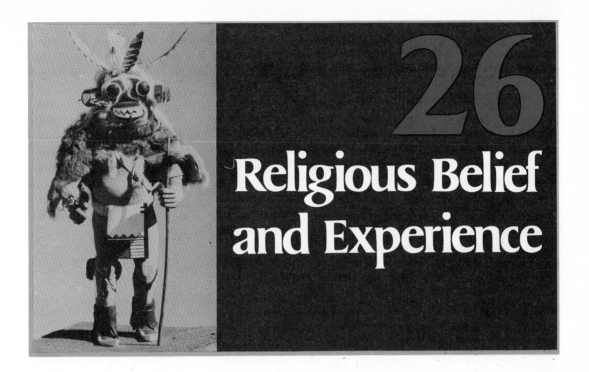

26

Religious Belief and Experience

THE analysis of the crucial concepts of power and authority in the previous chapter is an excellent background against which to begin our discussion of religion. There is a close relationship between politics and religion, between the concepts of *power* and of the *sacred,* as a number of social analysts have remarked. The interrelationship between politics and religion is particularly apparent to anthropologists because the connection is often articulated by members of the societies in which they carry out research. In these societies, as we mentioned in the discussion of kinship, descent groups are involved with ancestors and places of origin, both mythical and real, and with ceremonial and ritual rights and property. The head of the lineage or clan is the link on earth between the living members of the descent group and the sacred ancestral spirits. Among the Lugbara of Uganda, as among many other peoples, patrilineages serve both ritual/

spiritual and genealogical/temporal functions. Those holding power—lineage elders, for example—seek to validate their position by invoking the ancestral spirits and traditions. But those who seek to attain power resort to manipulation by the techniques of witchcraft to mount sometimes effective challenges to the status quo (Middleton, 1960).

A different kind of example is provided by the Toba of Argentina. Among the Toba, religious and secular leadership reside for all practical purposes in the same individual. Practically speaking, one cannot distinguish between shaman and chief. Here the exercise of spiritual power entails political responsibilities; political leadership without the exercise of spiritual power could not be effective.

It would be a mistake, however, to assume that the sacred and the secular are joined only in hunting and gathering or horticultural societies. This association is characteristic of societies at every technological and political level. In fact, our own society, whose founding documents proclaim the doctrine of the separation of church and state and which is considered to be a secularly-oriented society is considered also to be a God-fearing one. High government officials are sworn into office while holding Bibles, and they often make public demonstration of church attendance; legislative sessions are opened with public prayers; and court proceedings involve the taking of oaths invoking the name of God. Religious adherence continues to play a significant role in legitimizing the social order, as well as in challenging that order.

The study of politics, then, is linked to the study of religion by the concept of power. From an anthropological point of view, every society must be analyzed independently to determine the extent to which a distinction between religious and secular power is meaningful or valid in each case. The anthropological perspective on religion—as on other major sociocultural topics—is fundamentally comparative and concerned with the varying roles of religious beliefs and practices in societies throughout the world and throughout human existence.

Defining Religion

Because of the close association between power and the sacred, it is frequently difficult to establish a boundary between the religious and the political spheres. Sometimes, in fact, it is difficult even to distinguish these realms from social interactions in general. Anthropological definitions of religion have, therefore, ranged widely. For the purposes of this text, let us define *religion* as the system of social interactions consisting of those beliefs and activities that order human life by relating humans to spiritual beings and/or powers.

The study of religion in anthropology parallels generally the history of anthropological theory and has, of course, both reflected and contributed to the intellectual climate of each period of thought. There have been, as Geertz (1968b) notes, four basic approaches to the study of religion. The evolutionist approach, represented by Tylor and Frazer, among others, tended to view all human practices, including those of religion, as stages in a historic continuum. In this view, the practices of so-called "primitive" peoples were considered to be survivals of what our earliest ancestors had believed; our own "advanced" civilization was seen as representing the pinnacle of rationality and development.

In the psychological approach, whose primary spokesman was Freud, in his 1913 book *Totem and Taboo,* "primitive" religious practices and beliefs were seen as expressions of neurotic and even psychotic impulses. Freud believed that well-adjusted individuals were able, through "normal" growth processes, to move beyond such fantasy/obsession stages, while neurotics and "savages" continued to act them out. Both of these early approaches —evolutionist and psychological—focused on such "exotic" practices as magic, faith-healing, and belief in many spirits and gods, and examined them more on an individual case than on a cross-cultural basis.

With the advent of the sociological approach most clearly expressed by Emile Durkheim, the focus shifted to a comparative analysis of the role of religion in human life. Religion was seen both as an expression of the cultural whole and its world view on the one hand, and as a mediator in the individual's relationship to his or her society on the other. This orientation is still very much with us and has influenced much of the research and analysis of religion in the twentieth century. In recent years it has been supplemented by the symbolic approach, best exemplified in the theorizing of Lévi-Strauss, on the one hand, and of Geertz on the other. Religion, one of the sets of symbols used in human societies, provides the conceptual model of reality within which the members of society find meaning.

Over the years, each of these four conceptual orientations—evolutionist, psychological, sociological, and symbolic—has given rise to many contributions as well as to numerous studies that combine and synthesize them. Each orientation has its uses even today, but no one provides a total framework within which to discuss the phenomenon of religion. The discussion that follows will not, therefore, adhere exclusively to any one of these viewpoints, but will provide an overview of anthropological approaches to the religious aspect of human existence.

Belief, Ritual, and Religious Experience

Anthropological studies of religion have tended to focus on one or the other of two major components: belief and ritual. Lewis (1971, p. 11) points out that there is a third significant component—spiritual experience—that has been ignored in most studies, probably because it is more an individualized than a communal/social aspect of religion. These three components or, as Lewis calls them, "cornerstones of religion" are the subject of this section.

Belief

The term *belief* refers to statements that are generally held to be true by the members of a given society. Religious beliefs differ from other types of belief in their assertions about supernatural powers or forces. Two different kinds of supernatural forces have been distinguished by anthropologists: *mana* and *animism*. Mana, a Polynesian term, refers to any power that increases one's natural abilities and thereby allows one to perform otherwise impossible tasks and feats. The Dobuans of Eastern New Guinea, for example, believe that *mana* brought on by various charms and incantations may cause crops to grow, enemies to suffer, and evil spells to be averted.

Animism refers to belief in many spirit beings. These spirits have personalities and, like human beings, desires and purposes of their own. They also are thought to have supernatural powers that enable them to accomplish what they want to do. The people of the Zuñi Pueblo recognize well over a hundred male and female spirit beings who exercise dominion over specific aspects of existence—rain, corn, and so on. Certain spirits, or *kachinas,* have identifying characteristics and are represented among the Pueblo by a carved and adorned wooden figurine and, in various ceremonies, by a human wearing an appropriate headdress and costume.

These two types of supernatural powers—mana and animate spirits—are not incompatible. They may even exist together in the belief system of any given group. Perhaps anthropologists have tended to be attracted to the distinction between the two beliefs because of a Western cultural dichotomy between luck, which can be seen as a kind of manalike view of the supernatural, and divine intervention, which, objectively viewed, is a belief in animism. At any rate, both beliefs rely on supernatural intervention for purposes of assisting human beings, and both can be considered religious beliefs as opposed to nonreligious ones.

A secondary distinction between animism and theism—belief in a god or gods—is frequently made also. *Monotheism* refers to religious systems characterized by belief in one god. However, in several monotheistic systems—including Islam, and Catholicism,

This carved wooden figure represents an "ogre" *kachina,* or spirit being of the Hopi Indians. During ceremonies, a man dressed in this costume, mask, and headdress impersonates this *kachina,* one of many in the Hopi pantheon. (Dr. Georg Gerster, Rapho/Photo Researchers)

conceptualized as the supreme being, however. *Polytheism* refers to religious systems characterized by belief in plural, more or less equally powerful gods. Polytheistic systems also include a number of other spirit powers of lesser potency. Although animism also acknowledges the existence of many spirit powers, unlike polytheism, no single one is considered superior to the others in any but a restricted manner. For example, the Toba of Argentina identify powerful spirit beings who are found on the earth, in the heavens, and in the waters deep below the earth. Each of these may be considered powerful for certain purposes, but no one is inherently supreme or superior over the others.

One might think that the belief gap between monotheism and polytheism would be so vast as to be unbridgeable, but this is not the case. Polytheistic systems have little difficulty in adding yet another deity, including a more powerful one, to their well-populated pantheons. This fact has aided the acceptance of Christianity and Islam when they were introduced to native populations by missionaries. Polytheistic deities and animistic practices may persist in such societies on a folk level alongside of the rituals associated with belief in one supreme being.

An issue that has fascinated anthropologists over the years concerns the extent to which primitive beliefs may be comparable with or inherently different from the beliefs of Western, technologically oriented societies. Is belief in a chemical formula for, let us say, fertilizer, significantly different from belief in a formula of words to make yams grow? Is chemotherapy more efficacious than a medicine bundle, or psychoanalysis than a sweat lodge? Westerners generally assume that the one is based on "scientific" knowledge, whereas the other depends on unproven assumptions about nature. However, the differences may not depend so much on knowledge in a factual sense as on the trust of the society's membership in the authority be-

among other Christian groups—spiritual beings in addition to an omnipotent god may be included in the belief system (Mohammed in the former instance, and Jesus, Joseph, Mary, and the saints in the latter). Only one deity is hind each kind of belief. Like all other beliefs and knowledge, religious beliefs depend for their legitimacy and ultimate value upon the social support accorded them:

In June, when rain is needed for the corn . . . the series of [priestly] retreats begins. . . . All Zuñi awaits the granting of rain during these days, and priests blessed with rain are greeted and thanked by everyone upon the street after their retreat is ended. They have blessed their people with more than rain. (Benedict, 1934/1948, pp. 60–61)

Beliefs that would seem strange in one cultural context are perfectly logical and convincing in another. Non-Zuñi Americans cannot accept that a ceremonial withdrawal by a group of men could bring rain. But the Zuñi would be surprised to learn that a present-day cloud-seeding plane could have an effect on precipitation.

Given the enormous variance of human beliefs, early attempts to order them in an evolutionary hierarchy from the most "primitive" forms of animism to the "highest" forms of monotheism have little value for comparative purposes. Beliefs and doubts probably exist in more or less equal amounts in all cultural systems. Whether the object of belief is a supreme being or a forest spirit makes little difference as far as the belief itself and its role in its cultural context are concerned.

Ritual

Because beliefs are highly subjective, there is a tendency for them to be explained differently even by individuals within the same culture. For this reason, it is somewhat difficult to obtain comparable data from one culture to another. Rather than attempt to compare beliefs per se, anthropologists have turned increasingly to the study of ritual.

Ritual is the demonstration of religious belief through performance of specific acts by members of a society. It is possible to describe and analyze the observable activities that con-

stitute rituals. Leach (1968) points out that rituals are aesthetic and communicative acts, conveying messages about a society's value system to its members. In studying rituals, anthropologists are able to compare standardized activities in related contexts from one culture to another, and to analyze in what ways the messages communicated are similar or different.

There is always some question about how the messages of ritual are to be interpreted. Do they "mean what the actors say they mean?" (Leach, 1968, p. 525). Or must the anthropologist interpret the hidden content of the ritual, meanings that the actors may ignore on a conscious level but may act upon unconsciously? This problem was raised early in this book, and it is particularly relevant here. A thorough study of any given ritual would have to take both its stated and latent meanings into consideration. It would weigh the one against the other and judge in what ways the two meanings are complementary and in what ways divergent, as well as determine how both fit, like pieces of a puzzle, into the cultural context.

Leach (1968) argues that it is the status of the actor that is at stake in ritual. The Zuñi priests whose retreat produces rain not only validate the beliefs of their society but secure their own position within it. But if a ritual is not effective—if it does not serve its designated purpose—the person who has performed the ritual is thought to have "lost his touch." He or she is considered for one reason or another to be lacking in power vis-à-vis the spiritual world, and consequently loses prestige and power in the mundane world as well. Ritual performers who have notable success may also use their power to enhance their prestige. In this way, then, ritual also affects the status of the actor. Successful rituals are successful in two ways: they reinforce the society's beliefs, and they raise the status of their performers (Leach, 1968, pp. 525–526). Rituals may occur for the precise purpose of exalting the status of the performer. In some societies, they may be set up to challenge or demean an individual. And sometimes, as in the *potlatch* of the Indians of the Northwest Coast, rituals accomplish both purposes at the same time. In this situation, the giver of the *potlatch* simultaneously raises his status and publicly shames his rivals.

The different types of rituals described and studied by anthropologists will be the subject of a subsequent section of this chapter.

Religious Experience

As we have already observed, anthropological studies have concentrated on belief and ritual, largely ignoring the individual element of religious experience. But in recent years, a few anthropologists have begun to call attention to actual experiences of the supernatural as data in their own right (Lewis, 1971).

On the individual level, there are a number of different kinds of spiritual experiences. At

A voodo celebrant in Haiti, possessed by a *loa* or spirit, has bitten off the head of a live chicken. Ceremonial foods are arranged around a central pit, and a participant *(lower right)* holds an aggregation of ritual objects, including knife, fork, and crucifix, secured to a flask. (Odette Mennesson-Rigaud, Photo Researchers)

one extreme are feelings of peace and of being at one with the universe that may come from such activities as participation in a ritual or meditation. At the other extreme are frenzied manifestations, often interpreted as "possession" by some supernatural force. In between lies a whole range of experiences—dreams, trance, speaking in tongues, auditory and visual hallucinations, and so on. The extent to which spiritual experiences may be induced is highly variable. Such experiences have been found to follow activities such as prolonged solitude, meditation, community participation, different kinds of rhythmic and/or other musical stimulation, hypnosis, fasting, self-mutilation, and drug taking. Some of these manifestations and stimuli were mentioned previously in our discussion of altered states of consciousness. It should be noted that whether such experiences are interpreted as being religious or supernatural manifestations, or as something else entirely (as mental illness, for example), is dependent upon the cultural context in which they occur and the individual involved.

Psychological and Sociological Explanations of Religion

Generally, particular religious beliefs and practices have been studied from the point of view of either psychological or sociological theory, or some combination of the two. Freud and Jung provided the theoretical orientations for the psychological approaches to religion, while Durkheim and Radcliffe-Brown contributed the sociological orientations.

Freud, impressed with the ethnographic material accumulating in his day, held that the religious practices of primitive cultures were symbolic reenactments of unconscious psychological drives. In particular, he articulated the idea that *totemism*—the veneration of an animal or animal spirit alleged to be an original group ancestor—was a symbolic vestige of the oedipal drive to do away with the father. Freud later explained religion as an "illusion" that both gives the individual a feeling of control over the forces of nature, and orders interpersonal relationships within the society, thereby holding the society together. The techniques used to influence or placate supernatural forces are of the same order as those learned by children to avoid offending their parents and thus to guarantee their enduring good graces. What Freud did not realize was that, even at the time of his earliest theorizing on the subject of religion, anthropologists had already moved away from the evolutionist approach on which his interpretations largely depended. Nevertheless, his essential notions that religious practices can be seen as expressions of the unconscious mind, and that rituals and beliefs may be wish-fulfillment elements arising from unconscious or hidden desires have contributed useful interpretive concepts.

Jung, who had originally worked with Freud on some of the ethnographic material that led to *Totem and Taboo,* later returned to the subject (Kardiner & Preble, 1961, pp. 232–233). He believed that there were prototypes or themes which appear in all cultures of the world. He saw widespread phenomena such as fertility rites or flood myths as arising from universal realities impressed on the human mind (Geertz, 1968, p. 401). Jung's explanation has certainly not been the last word on the subject of recurrent cultural phenomena, which continues to interest anthropologists. However, emphasis has shifted from the attempt to generalize universal tendencies, to the effort to identify and compare distinctions.

Durkheim's *The Elementary Forms of the Re-*

ligious Life (1912) was written at about the same time as Freud's work and was influenced by much of the same evolutionist anthropological source material. Durkheim felt that religion provided the essential ingredient that allowed society to cohere. He distinguished between the sacred and the profane, the former constituting the essential aspect of religious assertion, which had always to be separated from the nonreligious human attitudes characterized as profane (Geertz, 1968, p. 402; Kardiner & Preble, 1961, p. 127). Durkheim showed that beliefs transform things or activities that would otherwise be profane into objects or acts that are considered sacred.

Radcliffe-Brown, on the other hand, looked at the functions of religion for society as a whole. He held that what was of practical importance to a society became symbolized in ritual or as sacred objects. He focused on the content of sacred symbols and their role for members of a society. In his view, there would be a neat "fit" between the practical imperatives facing a society and its religious practices.

More recently, anthropologists have turned from strictly psychological and sociological arguments to what Geertz (1968) calls the "semantic" study of religion. There is new interest in the many levels of meaning in religious symbolism and in the variety of expressions given to concepts of the supernatural. In this approach, both primitive and modern religions are viewed as "systems of ideas about the ultimate shape and substance of reality" (Geertz, 1968, p. 406).

Whatever else religion does, it relates a view of the ultimate nature of reality to a set of ideas of how man is well advised, even obligated, to live. Religion tunes human actions to a view of the cosmic order and projects images of cosmic order onto the plane of human existence. (Geertz, 1968, p. 406)

Seen this way, the role of religion is to make a society's designs for living congruent with adaptation to reality. Geertz adds that religion becomes "emotionally convincing" and receives its expression through sacred symbols. It is to this consideration of religion—a system of symbols interpreting reality and making it livable for a society—that we now turn.

Sacred Symbols That Order Human Experience

Two lines that intersect, a six-pointed star, a crescent, a many-armed figure of a dancing woman, a circle bisected by a single wavy line—all are familiar symbols of the world's major religions. But only those symbols that pertain to the particular religion to which we ourselves adhere have the power to move us. As for the symbols of someone else's religion, they are usually no more meaningful to us than are any of the secular symbols—letters, numbers, dollar signs—with which we deal every day. We do, nevertheless, have some comprehension of the significance of many of these religious symbols. We understand that on some level they penetrate the experience of their respective believers; we have, through acquaintance with various works of art and literature from their cultures, gained some inkling of the contexts in which they function. Social anthropologists seek to bring equal comprehension to the less known sacred symbols of the world's cultures—a wooden figure bristling with iron nails from the Congo, a wooden antelope head from West Africa, a carved representation of various animals stacked one atop the other from British Columbia, a charcoal drawing of spears hurling toward huge beasts from a cave in Spain, human sacrifice of the Aztecs, or a many-hued feathered cape from Peru.

It should be clear from intimacy with the

symbols of our own religious traditions that symbols everywhere are embued with meaning. A feathered serpent or a wafer, a sacred circle or a sacred cow all contain many meanings. However such symbols are used—acted out or handled in ceremonies, narrated as myth, reproduced as design—they serve as key integrating elements for the cultures in which they occur. Study of sacred symbols often points the way for our understanding of what makes a given culture cohere. For each culture, then, sacred symbols must be analyzed to identify their character, to learn their meanings for members of the society, and to reveal the deeper messages that give coherence and direction to that culture.

Religion attempts to interpret the inexplicable—dreams, suffering, death, human treachery, natural disasters, and so on. It helps adjust peoples' understanding of the-way-things-are to the-way-we-would-like-things-to-be (Geertz, 1970, p. 325). Sacred symbols such as God and the devil acknowledge the existence of good and evil, and the conflict between them. Most usually, Geertz points out, "the reality of evil is accepted and characterized positively, and an attitude toward it—resignation, active opposition, hedonistic escape, self-recrimination and repentance, or a humble plea for mercy—is enjoined as reasonable and proper" (1970, p. 329). The Judeo-Christian tradition certainly offers examples of all of these responses in the face of adversity.

According to Geertz, religious symbols work by inducing responses in the worshipper (1966, p. 4). These responses take form as moods and as what Geertz called *motivation,* the inclination to perform certain acts and experience certain feelings in particular situations (1966, p. 10). Moods and motivations associated with sacred symbols vary from culture to culture. Motivations induced by religious symbols vary widely, too, and may range from charitable giving to self-mutilation.

However, Geertz has also pointed out that sacred symbols not only provide an integrative role in social life but can also produce conflict and disruption. In his classic study, *The Religion of Java* (1960), Geertz isolated three major "religious variants" (based on animism, Islam, and Hinduism), showing that all three are found in one social system, that each variant generates antagonism between its followers and members who adhere to another variant, and that these conflicts tend to be minimized and even turned to positive social uses in the society concerned. Thus, even in their disruption, sacred symbols can be made to serve positive ends. But the disruptive nature of conflicting religious ideas is not always satisfactorily resolved in a social group. Failure to resolve religious differences can cause tension and stress among the members of a society. History offers numerous examples of conflict due to religious differences.

Religious Specialists

If symbols derive their power from the meanings attached to them, their power commingles with the powers of the religious practitioners who manipulate the symbols. Four categories of religious specialist—shamans, priests, prophets, and sorcerers—are usually distinguished by anthropologists. Distinctions among them are based on such factors as the ways in which they acquire authority; the kinds of rituals they perform; the purposes for which rituals are performed; and the nature of the interactions between the religious leader and other members of the society.

Shamans

Shamans are religious specialists whose primary function is healing the sick and pro-

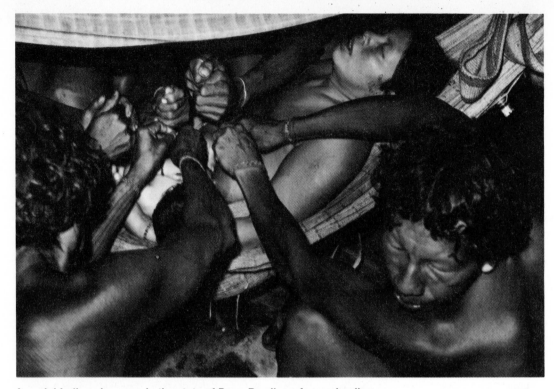

Assurini Indian shamans, in the state of Para, Brazil, perform a healing ceremony over a sick baby cradled in the arms of the mother, who lies in a hammock. A curing ceremony may last for several days and comprise a variety of different rites; shown here is the ritual extraction of the disease-causing substance from the patient's body. (Jacques Jangoux, Peter Arnold Photo Archives)

tecting the community from harm. We class these practitioners as religious because their healing proceeds by supernatural intervention. In our own society at present, the healing function does not usually have supernatural components, except in those religious groups that stress spiritual healing. Shamanism is particularly identified with the circumpolar cultures of Siberia, Alaska, and Canada, but it is a worldwide status, found widely among aboriginal populations in North and South America, in parts of Africa, and in many other locales throughout the world. Societies with a hunting-and-gathering economy are most likely to have shamans as their religious leaders.

Among the Tungus of Siberia, the word *shaman* refers specifically to an individual who has learned healing techniques through direct communication with spirits. In most societies where they are found, shamans generally receive the call to power in dreams and visions, through which they have direct contact with supernatural beings. The skills, perhaps literally the "tricks of the trade," may be revealed in such dreams. But a potential shaman may also be recruited or recognized by an experienced practitioner, often during childhood; the older individual or, on occasion, group of individuals will teach the novice the necessary skills. In Siberia, the call to practice was usually resisted by the individual for as long as possible, and was then heeded only reluctantly. In North America, a vision revealing the gift of healing was usually actively sought, often by solitude and fasting and, in the Plains area, through self-mutilation as well. In Central and South America, such a vision was frequently neither sought after nor avoided, but accepted if it occurred.

Shamans derive power from their ability to communicate directly with the supernatural. Although they may resort to various manipulations and tricks, it is the community's wholehearted belief in and dependence on their spiritual connections that maintain their authority. The rites performed by shamans, while directed toward individual ends, are often public, performed before audiences ranging from a few close relatives and friends of the ill person to an entire village. Shamans conduct ceremonies on an ad hoc basis, whenever someone is ill and requests their services (Lessa & Vogt, 1965, pp. 451–452).

Thus, their work is generally directed toward the satisfaction of individual needs.

Priests

Unlike shamans, *priests* are religious specialists associated with organized churches and are characteristically found in more formally structured societies throughout the world. They receive extensive training, at the conclusion of which they are ordained and legitimated in their offices through formal ceremonies. The members of a priesthood are generally a clearly ranked hierarchy. Priesthood is often hereditary within a family, lineage, or social class. In some cases, however, an individual has a vision or in some other way experiences a "calling" to enter the priesthood. In a number of Catholic communities, a family may select one of its sons at

Novices praying in Bangkok, Thailand. These young boys spend years receiving instruction before becoming Buddhist monks (priests). (Rene Burri, Magnum)

an early age and, in effect, apprentice him to a religious order for his education, with a future career as a priest in view. However recruited, the novice must be taught a substantial body of knowledge concerning traditional beliefs and intricate ceremonials. In religious systems that have a priesthood, these leaders serve as mediators between the people and the supernatural being or beings. Often they are more concerned with the general welfare of the community than with the problems of the individual; in most such societies, there are usually other practitioners of the healing arts who are concerned with the problems of the individual. The other religious leaders discussed in this section characteristically practice as individuals, only rarely participating in group rites and more usually in competition with other practitioners of the same category. Priests, on the other hand, are in constant communication with one another for the good of the community, frequently conducting ceremonies jointly or debating together to resolve difficult issues. The ceremonies presided over by priests frequently take place on a calendric basis, being repeated annually. These ceremonies often reflect the agricultural basis of the society's economy. Our word *ceremony*, in fact, is derived from the name of the ancient Roman goddess of agriculture, Ceres.

Prophets

Like shamans, *prophets* receive visions and communicate directly with supernatural powers on an individual basis. The message contained in the vision is the only preparation required. The Biblical prophetic writings generally, and Isaiah and Jeremiah in particular, are rich in descriptions of prophetic visions. Prophets generally criticize the existing social order and point the way to a better way of life. As prophets gain popularity with their public and develop a following, they sometimes become more priestly than prophetic in function, developing rituals and ceremonies to so-

lidify their authority and to keep followers together in a systematic way. Jesus, for example, was a prophet, not a priest. As the sect based on his teachings expanded, his followers added ceremonial structure to the teachings and eventually founded a priesthood. Especially because the messages of prophets are often conspicuously in opposition to the existing authorities, the tendency to create an alternative power structure becomes quasipolitical in nature. Prophets are therefore prime candidates to lead revitalization movements.

Sorcerers

Sorcerers are religious specialists who can cause harm and kill enemies. Sorcery is often referred to as witchcraft, particularly when evil or harm is the presumed intent or outcome. From the sorcerers' point of view, they also serve community interests since they eliminate the evil that they find therein. They are often required to use their powers against evils brought on by other sorcerers, and are thus in direct competition with one another. Sorcerers are found in societies with varying economic bases. They may receive their calling and skills in a vision; they may also be recognized as powerful individuals by members of their society as a result of a (perhaps inadvertent) demonstration of their power. Lévi-Strauss recounts how one Zuñi found himself both accused and hailed as a sorcerer:

A twelve-year-old girl was stricken with a nervous seizure directly after an adolescent boy had seized her hands. The youth was accused of sorcery [, but although] he denied having any knowledge of occult power [he was not believed. He then] improvised a tale explaining the circumstances by which he had been initiated into sorcery. He said he had received two substances . . . one which drove girls insane and another which cured them. . . . Having been ordered to produce his medicines, he [developed] a complicated ritual [using two roots, simulating] a trance after taking one . . . and after taking the other [pretending] to return to his normal state.

Then he administered the remedy to the sick girl and declared her cured. (Lévi-Strauss, 1963, p. 166)

Despite the girl's apparent recovery, her relatives continued to accuse the lad. In self-defense he created an elaborate story of a family tradition in the magic arts, from which he had inherited the ability to assume the form of a cat and kill his victims. When he claimed that his powers derived from certain magical plumes, he was asked to produce them in evidence. After making up numerous stories about why they could not be located, he finally succeeded in finding an old feather in the plaster of the walls of his home. Then he was required to explain how it was used, which he did with much imaginative invention, concluding his narrative with a lament over the loss of his supernatural powers.

As Lévi-Strauss points out, the significance of this episode lies in the desire of the community to confirm its belief in sorcery as the cause of the girl's illness. The experience itself turned the youth into a sorcerer, at least for the time being. As this episode clearly demonstrates, belief in sorcery is the essential element in the efficacy of sorcery. Belief is, likewise, the key to the effectiveness of all types of religious leaders. Lévi-Strauss distinguishes three areas of belief: the sorcerer's belief in his or her techniques; the victim's belief in the sorcerer's power; the community's belief in the power of sorcery.

The four types of religious leadership just defined are not necessarily vested in separate individuals. These categories are often more descriptive of organization, legitimation, and function than of individuals. There is often an overlap in functions, especially between priests and prophets, priests and shamans, shamans and sorcerers. In a given society, the distinctions between functions may blur so that an individual religious leader may have multiple roles. Among the Toba, for example,

shamans can and frequently do practice sorcery; nor are shamans the only category of healers. These are, then, not so much separate individuals as separate roles or activities that are performed. Religious leaders manipulate key symbols for purposes of gaining advantage, and the control of spiritual power is the essential leadership found in Toba society, however that power may be expressed.

We should note that the manipulation of sacred symbols and of magic can prove dangerous for the practitioner. If harm befalls the community or an individual (as demonstrated in the Zuñi sorcery episode above), the local shaman can be held accountable. If the countermeasures taken do not work, the practitioner may be accused of practicing negative magic on the side, or be thought to have lost power either to supernatural beings or to a more powerful sorcerer.

Some Rituals and Their Uses

Having considered sacred symbols and the practitioners who manipulate them, we turn now to a consideration of the rituals in which those symbols find their uses. The separate acts that, together, comprise a ritual are rites, and so ritual may be considered an aggregation or system of rites. Turner emphasizes that the notion of drama is inherent in ritual: "Both in its plot and its symbolism, a ritual is an epitome of the wider and spontaneous social process in which it is embodied and which ideally it controls" (1968, pp. 273–274).

Most of the anthropological writing about rituals concerns their relation to social structure. We have seen that rituals are, in Leach's view, both aesthetic and communicative acts and that they serve to ratify the values of the society. Vogt (1965), for example, describes the ceremonial meal in Zinacantan in southern Mexico, and shows how it replicates the social structure of the community. Ordinarily, food is served in bowls placed on the floor, but on ritual occasions a special "meal on a table" is served. The table must be a rectangular wooden one oriented on an east-west axis and covered with a pink-and-white striped handwoven cotton cloth. *Posh,* a native alcoholic beverage, is drunk in a particular way three times during the course of the meal. The bottle containing the drink is placed at the east end of the table, at which the highest ranked male sits. The other participants—as few as four or five in a family ritual meal or more than 60 at the annual community-level Fiesta of San Sebastian—are arranged in descending order of rank from the head to the opposite (or west end) of the table. The prescribed foods are tortillas, chicken in broth, coffee, and special bread. A specific ritual sequence of drinking, toasting, eating, and hand-washing activities must be observed.

The settlement pattern of the Zinacantecos, modern-day descendants of the Mayans, spreads outward from the ceremonial center in a densely populated valley to 11 outlying hamlets. Each individual is in turn a member of a patrilocal extended family occupying a house compound; a *sna* consisting of one or more localized patrilineages; a water hole group composed of two or more *snas;* the hamlet; Zinacantan as a whole. Each unit in the social order, from the patrilineages to the hamlet and community center, has prescribed ceremonies. At the household level there are curing and new house dedication ceremonies. There are various calendar-based land right ceremonies at the *sna* and water hole levels. At the hamlet level there are two annual ceremonies, for the New Year and the End of the Year. Finally, there is the annual San Sebastian celebration held in the community center for all of Zinacantan.

The Zinacantecos have a religious hierarchy of 55 ranked positions grouped into a four-level structure. By living for a year in the ceremonial center of the community and engaging in specific rituals at significant personal expense, a man can rise, one step at a time, to the next higher rank. After a year of service, he returns to his hamlet to farm and accumulate enough wealth to attempt the next higher level until, at the end of the process, he attains the uppermost level. An additional religious hierarchy consists of from 100 to 150 shamans, ranked in order of seniority from the time they received their calling.

Vogt's study showed how the rules that apply to one aspect of religion—in this case, a single ritual meal—relate to structural levels in the society, and it opened up new ways of analyzing selected aspects of ritual.

Ancestor Worship

Ancestor worship is a constellation of religious beliefs and rituals found in horticultural and agricultural societies where a kin group controls land rights and usage. Ancestor worship serves as the focus of social relations among the living and reinforces the corporate kin group structure. The kin group is believed to have perpetual existence. Strong generation-to-generation continuity results from the belief that deceased forbears "are regarded as fully functioning members of their kin groups," constantly interacting with their living descendants. (Cohen, 1971, p. 207). The living members of the society are responsible for maintaining continuity with the traditions of the past. The ancestors have the responsibility to oversee their descendants, punishing neglectful behavior and rewarding proper respect for traditions and obligations. Since living relatives such as fathers and uncles are potential ancestors, they must be accorded a high measure of respect in life as well as being venerated after death.

In a study of ancestor worship among the Tallensi of Ghana (formerly the Gold Coast), Fortes has shown how the practice of deifying the spirits of the deceased validates the social order. Despite great fondness between parents and children, there is an avoidance taboo between a father and his eldest son. The son must not wear his father's clothes, use his weapons, nor even look into his granary. As Fortes explains, "breach of the taboos would be an affront to the father's soul and destiny. For a man's soul is in his granary and his vitality is in his garments and weapons because they are covered with the sweat and dirt of his body" (1971, p. 214). When a man dies, rituals provide for the two transitions that must take place. First, the deceased must be officially "transformed from a living person into an ancestor," and secondly, the eldest son must be formally "invested with his father's status." The first-born son is "responsible for his father's mortuary and funeral rites. . . . If he delays . . . the ancestors will take offense and he will suffer" (1971, p. 216). This son offers a libation at all of the ancestor shrines that had been in his father's care, informing them of his death. Next there is a divination session to determine which ancestor had caused the death, and why; death is never considered "natural." Lastly, the son becomes "the main actor in rites which free him to do those things which were forbidden to him in his father's lifetime. . . . No display of grief is permitted in these rites, but strict silence is enjoined on the actors . . . because the dead is deemed to be participating with them and would strike down anyone who broke the ritual silence" (1971, p. 216).

The son, formerly forbidden to share food or drink with his father, in these silent rites now pantomimes doing so, freeing him from the previous taboo. Various offerings are made to the deceased father during the funeral rites. These are accompanied by a chant calling on the deceased by name to accept the offerings "in order that you may reach and join your father and forefathers and let health, peace, childbearing, fertility of fields and livestock now prevail" (1971, p. 216). Thus,

the close relationship between kinship systems and belief systems is most clearly demonstrated in ancestor worship.

Economic Uses of Ritual

Although Fortes emphasized the sociological implications of ancestor worship in maintaining the continuity of the social order, the actors in the rituals are shown to be concerned not only with their places in life as well as in the afterworld but also with the overall economic welfare of the community. Everywhere, the sustenance of the social group is an enormously important issue, and as such is very often the explicit subject of ritual. Rappaport (1971) discusses the role of religious ritual in economic production, noting its practical application as a component of the adaptive strategies of a society for exploiting and regulating the environment. The Tsembaga Mareng of New Guinea are an egalitarian horticultural people, with no centralized political structure. Their predominantly vegetarian diet comes largely from gardens tended by women, who also care for and feed growing herds of pigs. Pigs keep residential areas clean and, allowed to root about in abandoned gardens, eat shoots and seedlings and keep the soil workable for second plantings. But domestic pigs are slaughtered only on ritual occasions—during warfare, illness, or in cases of injury or death, and during the pig festival—when they are distributed to specific individuals according to the occasion, and are consumed in specified quantities. Consequently, the pig population grows, slowly but steadily, until the care and feeding of the animals becomes a major burden on the Tsembaga women, and pigs invading other people's gardens becomes a major source of friction within the group.

The Tsembaga ritual cycle is noncalendric. A description of the ritual cycle could well start with the outbreak of hostilities between two groups from adjacent territories, an event that can be initiated by any man who puts together an alliance of kin:

Each side performs certain rituals which place the opposing side in the formal category of "enemy." A number of [food] taboos prevail while hostilities continue. . . . Fighting could continue sporadically for weeks. Occasionally it terminated in the rout of one of the antagonistic groups. . . . [With the termination of hostilities a group which has not been driven off its territory performs a ritual called "planting the *rumbim,* a special tree. During this ceremony the ancestors are addressed:] We thank you for helping us. . . . We will kill pigs for you now, but they are few. In the future, when we have many pigs, we shall again give you pork and uproot the *rumbim* and stage a *kaiko* (pig festival). (Rappaport, 1971, pp. 231–232)

At the first postwar ritual, many pigs are slaughtered, cooked, and offered to the ancestors. Most of these pigs are distributed to allies who assisted in the fight, although some are eaten by the local group. Some taboos are removed, but because debts to allies and ancestors still remain, certain taboos persist during the period from the planting to the uprooting of the *rumbim,* a ritual plant, including a useful prohibition against becoming involved in another war. The *rumbim* can be uprooted only when there are enough pigs to hold a pig festival. At the start of the festival, a fifth or more of the total pig herd is slaughtered, much of the meat being distributed to former allies. Periodic dances and food distributions continue for about a year, culminating in a massive pig sacrifice:

The pork yielded by the Tsembaga slaughter was estimated to weigh between 7,000 and 8,500 pounds, of which between 4,500 to 6,000 pounds were distributed to members of other local groups in 163 separate presentations. An estimated 2,000 to 3,000 people in 17 local groups were the beneficiaries of the redistribution. (Rappaport, 1971, p. 234)

When the pig festival is finally over, the pig population has been reduced to only very young individuals and numbers about a third of its previous size. All taboos are removed, and the cycle can begin again. As the Tsembaga move through this ritual cycle, the regulation of meat production and distribution is intertwined with kinship obligations and relationships, including the contracting of both sexual liaisons and marriage arrangements (Cohen, 1971, pp. 226–227). Thus, the functions of ritual are not limited to ideological considerations but also serve an economic purpose, as is mostly clearly evident in this example from New Guinea.

Divination and Rituals of Affliction

Divination, the manipulation of the supernatural to discover concealed information, is a particular category of ritual that functions to maintain the social order. In various cultures, divination techniques may be practiced by sorcerers, shamans, or other individuals. The ultimate goal of the procedures, which vary in their details, is always to discover and remove the cause of an existing social disorder. Divination is often required in cases of individual affliction such as illness, death, and other life crises. It may also be required for "the corroboration of a marriage-choice and in individual or collective moves involving some change in social alignments or, perhaps, economic condition; and in situations of loss, calamity, or unresolved conflict, whether on a personal or a much larger scale" (Park, 1967, p. 234). Wherever divination is resorted to, members of the society know the appropriate occasions of its use. Among the Yoruba, for example, divination is required for the selection of a site for a new house. This method gives community sanction to the decision, which otherwise might be held to reflect the particular interest of one individual in locating closer to or further away from others (Park, 1967).

Park points out that the omission of divina-

Divination is a widespread practice that takes many forms. This pregnant woman in the Usambara Mountains of Tanzania has asked the *magama* whether she will have a girl or a boy. The *magama* examines a hen, which the woman held in her left hand and tapped with her right. He finds a notch in the feathers under the left wing, but not under the right; his client will have a **girl.** (Tom Pix, Peter Arnold)

tion in a situation that clearly calls for it might well result in difficulties for the person or group who acted without it. Divination gives legitimacy to acts performed following the divination, and relieves anxiety by pinpointing a cause and prescribing counteractive measures. But it is more than a primitive form of group therapy. It is analogous also to our judicial process, in that its outcome may be a determination of guilt and provision for redress to the satisfaction of the injured party. Turner (1968) points out that "divination and redressive ritual are stages in a single process that is peculiarly sensitive to changes, and especially breakages, in the network of existing social relations" (p. 26).

Several distinct stages are involved in divination: the recognition of a problem; the decision to appeal to divination; the divination ritual itself; perhaps an additional ritual to confirm the verdict; and the appropriate redressive ritual. Among the Ndembu of Northern Rhodesia, where social unity is highly

prized, members of a corporate kin group are reluctant to call on a diviner because this would publicly expose the frictions that are a frequent and inevitable consequence of strong social emphasis on male-dominated hunting activities in a matrilineal, matrilocal society. As social pressures build until one individual becomes literally ill, it becomes more important to cure the person than to persist in ignoring or denying friction within the family. At the point where we might call on the psychotherapist or the lawyer (depending on the manifestation), the Ndembu call in the diviner:

Once this first step is taken with full knowledge of what it may entail, Ndembu feel strongly induced to overcome their divisions and reaffirm their unity [despite] the risk, during this ritual sequence, of quarrels so violent that they may not be restrained. . . . Thus, the typical development of a ritual sequence is from the expression of a wish to cure a patient and redress breaches in the social structure, through exposure of hidden animosities, to the renewal of social bonds in the course of a protracted ritual full of symbolism. . . . Diviners give public utterance to what just could not be said under ordinary circumstances. (Turner, 1968, p. 272)

The result of Ndembu divination is the performance of a ritual of affliction to pacify or to remove the ancestor spirits that are believed to have brought the misfortune or illness (Turner, 1962, p. 251). The victim is, of course, the living kin of those ancestor spirits. A particular curative rite is prescribed for each distinctive manifestation of ancestral anger. Once cured, an individual may become a member of the healing cult for that ailment. Thus, the rituals of affliction serve the additional social purpose of providing a means by which individuals can compete for status. The example of Ndembu divination, then, provides an excellent summary for this section, since the ritual sequence involves restoration of the social fabric and ancestral involvement with living descendants, as well as having points of contact with the productive system.

Myth: The Search for Synthesis

Myth is the verbal rationale for religion, differing from other kinds of verbal material in having, in Kluckhohn's words, "the connotation of the sacred" (1942, p. 145). The relationship of myth to belief is clear: beliefs—those meanings held by the society to be true—are expressed through myth. As Turner (1968) explains, "myths relate how one state of affairs became another: how an unpeopled world became populated; how chaos became cosmos; how immortals became mortal; how the seasons came to replace a climate without seasons; how the original unity of mankind became a plurality of tribes or nations. . . ." (p. 576).

But the relationship between ritual and myth is more problematic, and has given rise to a chicken-or-egg type of discussion. Does ritual arise as a dramatization of myth? Or does ritual exist and myth arise, as Boas suggested, "from the desire to account for it?" (quoted in Kluckhohn, 1942). Evidence exists for both positions. Kluckhohn offers the Mohave and the Bushmen as examples of peoples with "many myths and very little ritual," whereas the Central Eskimo and other groups illustrate every aspect of myth through various rites. In some cultures, some myths are never enacted ritually; some rituals illustrate nonmythic content; some myths have real mythic referents, yet others have only vague mythological connections.

Among the Navaho, who had myths without associated rituals, both legends and rituals were alleged to have originated in dreams or visions, and "all ceremonial practice [was] justified by an accompanying myth" (Kluckhohn, 1942). The characteristic ceremony of the Navaho is devoted to healing. It is performed by a chanter who sings a ritual narrative, illustrating it in a drawing made by trickling colored sands through his fingers onto the prepared floor of a hogan. Each practitioner has his own chant or chants, usually learned through apprenticeship and validated through previous cures. The chants are not handed down in letter-perfect form, however. Navaho belief is extremely wary of exactitude and perfection, and every design, every narrative, must be left with an imperfection or gap, however minimal, to serve as a "spirit outlet" (Kluckhohn & Leighton, 1946).

Myth serves the important role of giving coherence and synthesis to a society's world view. The emphasis is not on myth as opposed to empirical truth but rather on myth as idealized construction that gives security in the face of the ambiguities and incongruities of life. As a Navaho informant told Clyde

Sand painting, an essential component of Navaho healing ceremonies, is restaged in significantly modified form for the photographer. In practice, the healing ceremony is performed inside of a hogan, and lasts for several days. Friends and relatives of the sick person may be present, but outside observers are unwelcome. The painting is created as the healer sings the appropriate chant and is destroyed before the ceremony is over. (Josef Muench Pictorial Photography)

Kluckhohn, "knowing a good story will protect your home and children and property. A myth is just like a big stone foundation—it lasts a long time" (1942).

Myth exists in all societies, serving the essential function of easing social interactions by supporting the world view that makes life tolerable. It should come as no surprise that the integration of ritual and social order described above for the people of Zinacantan is also paralleled by a supporting mythology. Inside a nearby extinct volcano, according to the Zinacantecos,

are a series of corrals, one full of jaguars, another full of coyotes, another full of ocelots, and still another full of smaller animals. . . . The total number [of animals] adds up to 7,600, the same as the population, for each Zinacanteco has . . . an animal spirit companion—a kind of wild animal alter ego, so to speak. . . . The ancestral gods [are believed] to live in their houses inside the mountain and take good care of the [animal spirits]. (Vogt, 1965, p. 608)

But if a Zinacanteco does something wrong, then the ancestral gods stop caring for his or her animal spirit. The unprotected animal alter ego may even get out of the corral and wander about in the forest, where it is likely to be injured. No matter what happens to the animal spirit, it is believed that its human counterpart will suffer the same fate.

Lessa (1965) has shown that myth does not always serve as an explanation of social life, since it can lose its synthesizing capability under the impact of culture contact and change. For example, the people of Ulithi occupy several islets in the Carolinian archipelago of Micronesia. A series of traditionally overlapping myths concerning origins of their world and people, and relationships between the islands of the region, supported a long ritual presentation of all turtles found in the atoll to the local king on the isle of Mogmog in a ceremony with both political and religious content. The turtles are clubbed by the king, and then butchered, roasted, eaten, and distributed, with members of certain lineages performing specific rites, and portions being given to certain lineages and people of non-Ulithi islands according to long-standing custom. For many years, however, the turtle ritual was not performed. A king who had taken office without complete ceremonial had "felt unauthorized to partake in the ritual killing of turtles." His successor, who had become nominally Christian, also feared displeasing ancestral gods and was concerned because of the lack of a traditional investiture. Upon his death, two individuals succeeded jointly to the kingship, one assuming the political and the other the ceremonial aspects of the position, and there was popular pressure for the revival of the turtle ritual. Although the myths supporting the ritual had long since lost their force, because Christianity had made significant inroads in Ulithi, the ritual, with some changes, was revived. Lessa concludes that "influences from Christianity have [removed] the fear of punishment should the turtle ritual be performed contrary to traditional religious procedures—specifically, where the man who wields the club has not been invested as king according to pagan custom. The ritual has had and still retains some political significance reflecting Mogmog's authority" (Lessa, 1965, p. 185). Yet without its myth-derived sanctions, Lessa predicts that the turtle ritual is likely to "disappear under the impact of foreign political administration and changing political ideologies. Myth alone has not and cannot maintain a system in operation unless it is in turn energized by more basic institutions and beliefs" (p. 185). In this instance, then, we see how the original intricate link between ritual, myth, and politics became untangled as a result of changes in a social system due to external causes. Belief and myth went first, and ritual, somewhat changed, remains.

Supernatural Agents of Malevolence

Sorcery and witchcraft are the dark, malevolent side of belief. They do not constitute a religious system; although widespread, they are not found everywhere. But they fall into the study of religion in that their work is accomplished by paranormal, supernatural means. Countermeasures to sorcery and witchcraft, where possible, also involve resort to the supernatural.

Evans-Pritchard's classic study of witchcraft among the Azande of the Congo (1976) is an excellent explanation of supernatural malevolence:

In Zandeland sometimes an old granary collapses. There is nothing remarkable in this. Every Zande knows that termites eat the supports in the course of time and that even the hardest woods decay after years of service. Now a granary is the summerhouse of a Zande homestead and people sit beneath it in the heat of the day. . . . Consequently it may happen that there are people sitting beneath the granary when it collapses and they are injured. . . . Now why should these particular people have been sitting under this particular granary at the particular moment when it collapsed? (1976, p. 22)

The answer in our own society would be simply accident, but apparently there are no accidents among the Azande. There are always reasons why things happen as they do, and the role of witchcraft is to explain the inexplicable; otherwise there would be chaos.

If there had been no witchcraft, people would have been sitting under the granary and it would not have fallen on them, or it would have collapsed but the people would not have been sheltering under it at the time. Witchcraft explains the coincidence of these two happenings. (Evans-Pritchard, 1976, p. 23)

Similarly, among the Argentine Toba unfortunate events are sometimes said to be caused by sorcery. It was claimed, for example, that a certain woman had accidentally killed her son by sorcery. She had intended to kill her brother-in-law, but her son became ill instead and on his deathbed identified his own mother as the source of his illness. When the mother recognized her mistake, it was too late to correct it. She had performed the proper ritual and so death was inevitable, despite the mistaken identity of the intended victim and despite the actual intent of the sorcerer. She did not deny her son's accusation, but no action was taken against her by the immediate family since it was obviously a case of human error. The woman had, in fact, shown hostility toward her brother-in-law, and the accusation that she had killed her son by mistake was comprehensible to all in view of the family conflicts that were known to exist.

Sorcery or witchcraft, if they are to be counteracted at all, usually require using equally strong measures against the original agent. The victim may attempt to return the damage in some way to its initiator. In many cases, this requires divination or some other means to determine the source of the misfortunes.

Sorcery and witchcraft serve to control forces that are potentially disruptive and destructive to social order. In his study of witchcraft in Amatenango, in southern Mexico, Nash (1961b) shows the social process involved. A person or a person's family who has suffered severe illness, death, or other misfortune may suspect witchcraft. If resort to the usual curers does not ameliorate the situation, the person's suspicions may be confirmed. He or she will inquire of a curer to determine who might wish him harm; he might observe his neighbors to determine who might be a suspect. If the person finds a likely candidate and the misfortunes do not abate, he or she determines to kill the suspected witch. The community must then decide whether the killing was justified. This decision depends on whether the community believes the dead person to have been a witch, or whether the killer is believed to have indulged a personal grievance against an innocent member of the community.

The defense of the accused consists, first, of demonstrating that he or she had many misfortunes, undoubtedly the result of witchcraft. He attempts to show that the deceased was a "violator of norms, having acted in various socially inappropriate ways." Finally, the accused tries to convince the community that he is a respected, upstanding individual. The accused, having proved his case, is acquitted by community consensus. Accusations of witchcraft or sorcery that were unacceptable to community moral standards would undoubtedly cause further social disruption, setting off feuds and resulting in deaths held to be unjustifiable. It is more than likely that the alleged witch was someone against whom other members of the community also bore grudges, someone who had given a number of people cause to suspect his or her motives because of antisocial behavior. But lest one imagine that, encouraged by success, the acquitted killer would resort to such action on subsequent occasions, there are social sanctions against such liberties. In a community in which members interact daily, it is difficult to pretend to virtues or status that one does not, in fact, have (Nash, 1961b).

The question is often asked if supernatural malevolence actually occurs or if it is only imagined to occur. The answer seems to be that both may be true, and it is not always possible to determine whether supernaturally caused evils and cures are real or imagined. Belief is the key factor, whether in the efficacy of the sorcerer's malevolence or in the efficacy of the shaman's healing. Lévi-Strauss (1963) identified the combination of three elements, which he called the "shamanistic complex," that apply to shamanistic healing as well as to sorcery. As mentioned earlier, Lévi-Strauss believes that shamanistic healing depends first on the belief of the shaman himself in his calling and his powers. The second element is the belief of the afflicted person. The third source of belief is the community. Kluckhohn showed how these three beliefs interact and are reinforced in the case of a Navaho chanter:

If a Navaho gets a bad case of snow blindness and recovers after being sung over, his disposition to go to a singer in the event of a recurrence will be strongly reinforced. . . . Likewise, the reinforcement will be reciprocal—the singer's confidence in his powers will also be reinforced. Finally there will be some reinforcement for spectators and for all who hear of the recovery. (1942, p. 154)

The cycle of reinforcement among practitioners, patient (or victim), and community constitutes the evidence for the efficacy of the system. Suppose one individual bears ill will toward another and decides to vent unspoken hostilities in some tangible form—sticking pins into a doll representing the victim, or muttering curses while placing twigs on the path that must be taken by the enemy. And suppose, then, that misfortune strikes the intended victim. What evidence does the would-be sorcerer have that the measures taken were not in fact the cause? Is the germ theory of disease any more credible to one who has never peered into a microscope than the notion that a cold is caused by being out in the rain?

Religious Revitalization Movements

The role of a religious conversion experience in changing individual behaviors has been well documented. Our concern here is with the mechanisms by which the conversion experience of an individual becomes the focal point around which a new religion takes shape. Sometimes a cultural system reaches a stage in which its traditional symbols are no longer meaningful and powerful, either because of internal contradiction or through external pressure of some sort (culture contact or natural disaster, for example), or both. At that point, a prophet is likely to come forth. This charismatic individual will lead the group in a movement either to reform an old order or to establish an entirely new one.

Such movements have been known by a variety of terms, including nativistic, messianic, and millennium. Anthony Wallace (1961) proposes that the term *revitalization movements* be used to refer to "conscious, organized efforts by members of a society to construct a more satisfying culture" (1970, p. 372). He argues that religion plays a key role in the revitalization process. According to him, the spiritual experience of conversion is one kind of human response to social and cultural stress. In such situations, there is a perceived need for new codes of behavior and action to deal with the altered situation, since the previous code no longer works. According to Wallace, "new religions are, above all else, movements toward the revitalization of men and society. Periodically, new religions reverse the course of decline and supply the energy and the direction for the upswing toward a new, and often higher, climax of development" (1970, p. 372).

Wallace shows how these elements were involved in the revitalization movement brought by the Seneca Indian chief Handsome Lake to the Iroquois of New York in 1799. The Iroquois had been allied with the British during the American Revolution, in the course of which their warriors were discredited and their villages destroyed. Their traditional land holdings had been confiscated and their people resettled on a scattering of reservations separated from one another by growing communities of white Americans. There they idled, given to drinking and quarreling among themselves.

They faced a moral crisis: they wanted still to be men and women of dignity, but they knew only the old ways, which no longer led to honor but only to poverty and despair; to abandon these old ways meant undertaking customs strange, in some matters repugnant, and in any case uncertain of success. . . .

Into this moral chaos, Handsome Lake's revelations of the word of God sped like a golden arrow, dispelling darkness and gloom. Heavenly messengers, he said, had told him that unless he and his fellows became new men, they [would] be destroyed in an apocalyptic world destruction. They must cease drinking, and quarreling, and making witchcraft, and turn to lead pure and upright lives. He went on, in detailed vision after vision, to describe the sins which afflicted the Iroquois . . . and to prescribe the new way of life. (1970, pp. 373–374)

Only part of Handsome Lake's teaching had specifically religious content; for the most part he dealt with social and economic issues presented by the new situation. He exhorted the Iroquois to accept the agricultural practices of the European settlers, in which men as well as women worked in the fields. He urged that some of them learn to read and write English. And he told them to turn from their emphasis on matrilineal kin group organization and to organize their households around the conjugal family instead. Most of these teachings represented an adaptation to the customs of white Americans of that day, and would have been repugnant to the Iroquois had they not met a clearly felt need in a desperate situation; not been couched in terms of a supernatural vision which was traditionally acceptable; and not been transmitted by a leader with charisma and high credibility among his people.

Another analyst of revitalization movements is Worsley (1957), who offers a somewhat different approach to social and religious movements of this sort. Basing his analysis on studies of such cults as they appeared in Melanesia, he suggests the term *millenarian movements,* which he defines in terms of an expectation of a radical change about to occur in the social order, which leads to activity in preparation for this event on the part of the movements' adherents. These people expect the coming of the millennium—a period of great prosperity, happiness, and peace—and go about preparing for its arrival.

Worsley describes the stages or characteristics of a millenarian movement as found in Melanesia:

A prophet announces the imminence of the millennium. A complete upheaval of the social order is expected: liberators, who may be the spirits of the dead ancestors, American soldiers, or, in one case, the Communist Party of France, will appear, bringing all the material goods the people desire so strongly. Hence the name "Cargo Cult.". . .

In order to prepare for the Day, organizations are set up; new insignia, forms of dress, etc., are adopted; and new codes of morality and of law are drawn up. Often airstrips are cleared in the bush, and huts and stores are built to house the expected goods. (1967, p. 338)

But Worsley further distinguishes between two different types or stages of these movements. In the first, the ideology of the millenarian movement is closely related to the traditional beliefs; there is little attempt to prepare for radical change; preparation activities consist of magical practices intended to secure well-being in daily life. At the other extreme are movements that have clearly political goals and that focus on the construction of a new economic framework; millenarian emphasis in such movements is minimal. Sometimes the political-type movement develops out of the traditional type, but it may also, so to speak, spring fullgrown from the brow of the prophet.

Like Wallace, Worsley sees these movements as heralding a new social order, but he also stresses their political nature in bringing together previously disparate groups. This is where the charismatic leader comes in. In order to become a unifying force, the leader must rise above allegiance to one segment of the community. Worsley points out that this can be most effectively done by projecting his message to the supernatural plane, through a message from a deity or one's ancestors. Appeals to join the movement then rest on allegiance to a common religion that can unite them all.

Both Wallace and Worsley note that there have been many studies of revitalization movements in the Americas, Africa, Asia, and Oceania. All movements seem to share many structural characteristics: a prophet sees a new way; as his followers increase, the message changes to adapt to the new situation. Both Worsley and Wallace agree that these movements represent reorderings of secular and religious life arising out of the emotional atmosphere that accompanies situations of social crisis (Worsley, 1957).

Millenarian doctrines often seem fantastic and illogical to many Westerners. Yet, people who believe in the reality of such cults are unaware of the actual processes by which goods in Western technological society are produced. They are convinced that the Westerners with whom they have contact are concealing from them essential magic techniques that control such goods. The new religious techniques of the cult fill this gap. The Iroquois were fortunate that Handsome Lake's code so accurately responded to the realities of the situation; peoples in Melanesia have been less fortunate in the visions of their millenarian prophets. Worsley shows that these movements tend either to move toward more direct political action or to disappear. If, after a reasonable period of waiting, the ancestors fail to come with the cargo, the cult followers are bound to be disappointed, and will ultimately need a new source of revitalization.

Missionizing Religions

Missionizing religions are those making claims to exclusive insight into "ultimate reality," seeking to spread their beliefs and gain converts by sending representatives to other cultures and peoples. The most expansionist religion is, of course, Christianity. Christian zeal was a major factor in the European explorations and conquests of the sixteenth through the nineteenth centuries. Christian missionaries have circled the globe, frequently arriving at isolated and remote villages before anthropologists. Consequently, the missionary and the anthropologist have had extensive contact with each other, and over the years have developed an ambivalent relationship.

Anthropologists often depend on missionaries for travel facilities, food, and/or lodging until they are able to manage on their own. In turn, missionaries have come to rely on the field knowledge and techniques developed by anthropologists to make contact with native peoples. Morgan inquired of missionaries, among others, for information when he began to study kinship terminology. Numerous other ethnographers have likewise depended on reports prepared by those who were first on the scene. Mutual hostility has sometimes developed over the details of mundane interactions, and even more frequently and basically over the different points of view held by each about the purposes of the other. Many anthropologists charge that missionaries have often made it impossible to

Animal skins and skulls—the wares of the traditional Yoruba "pharmacist"—are symbols that retain their power even as modern medical practice, here exemplified by the physician *(left)*, becomes available. (World Health Organization, Monkmeyer)

study a culture in its "pristine," pre-Christian state. They complain also that natives are coerced into adopting new beliefs before missionaries try to understand the value system and world view with which they are interfering. Missionaries, on the other hand, are suspicious of anthropologists who take advantage of their hospitality and knowledge of the language and culture, and then end up criticizing them.

It has been argued that the major impact of Christian missionizing has been secular rather than religious (Miller, 1970). The world view expressed in the day-to-day activities of Christian missionaries is a rational, cause-and-effect response to experience. Missionary attitudes toward and teachings about disease, accidents, natural catastrophes, the learning experience, and even the physical structure of the universe largely reflect naturalistic rather than supernaturalistic beliefs. Events and experiences that were traditionally explained in the context of a supernaturalistic universe are removed from their customary setting. Thus, missionaries often undermine the traditional sacred symbols that provide coherence and meaning to all life, even while attempting to instill new symbols. This process is often concurrent with rapid social, technological, and political changes introduced by nonreligious agents; but missionaries, in effect, support these external pressures.

The acceptance of new symbols is a complex issue, only partially understood. Societies are most likely to adopt those beliefs and practices that make the most sense both in terms of traditional understandings and in their comprehension of the new situation with which they are confronted. The integration of a new symbol or other component is not arbitrary; rather, the utility of the concept for the culture must be demonstrated. For this reason, an external meaning system cannot be imposed on any culture by a single individual. Therefore, anthropologists' concerns about a

culture being "ruined" or destroyed by a missionary are largely unfounded.

Christianity is not the only missionizing religion, of course. Islam, although less active today than centuries ago, once spread rapidly throughout the Middle and Near East. Buddhism was exported from its birthplace in India to all corners of Asia (and in our own day is having a significant impact on some members of Western civilization as well). But Christianity has certainly been the most active and persuasive—and at times aggressive—in pursuit of converts. It must be acknowledged that part of the appeal of Christianity and the reason for its success is its close tie to Western ideology and technology. The dominant role played by Western Europe and the United States in world affairs has contributed to missionary success. But because of the relationship between Western political power and Christianity, many third world countries have become suspicious of and inhospitable to all missionaries. Anthropologists too have become unwelcome and for similar reasons, since they are also identified with a social and cultural system that is no longer welcomed by many peoples of the world.

Finally—and especially where the study of religion is concerned—anthropologists unintentionally bring to their research an inevitable taint of culture bias. Most researchers are from Western Europe or North America and are themselves participant members of a Christian culture. Kluckhohn (1942) has stated, for example, that probably because of the emphasis placed by Christianity on belief, which is rare from a cross-cultural perspective, a "cultural screen" existed between anthropologists and their data. Only relatively recently has an objective eye been cast on the function of religion among social subsystems in a given cultural context. The task of the anthropologist is to acknowledge this screen and attempt to arrive at the understandings that lie behind it.

Summary

1. There is a close relationship between politics and religion, between power and the sacred: the leader with authority in the religious arena is often a political leader as well. Even where political and religious authority are separate, however, the trappings of political leadership often become strongly tinged with the aura of the religious.

2. Religion may be defined as the system of social interactions consisting of those beliefs and activities that order human life by relating human beings to spiritual beings and/or powers. Belief, ritual, and individual experience are everywhere components of religious systems.

3. The term *belief* refers to statements that are generally held to be true by the members of a given society. Religious beliefs differ from other types of beliefs in that they make assertions about supernatural powers or forces. *Mana,* the belief that supernatural forces are inherent in animate and inanimate objects alike, and *animism,* a belief in the existence of spirit beings, have been distinguished by anthropologists as two widely held kinds of belief.

4. *Ritual* is the demonstration of religious belief through performance of specific acts. Rituals are communicative and aesthetic acts that reinforce a society's value system by dramatizing and symbolizing its beliefs.

5. Individual experiences in religion may vary from a feeling of "peace with the world" to "possession" by a supernatural force, and include a range of states in between. Some states of supernatural experience may be induced by solitude, fasting, drugs, or even self-mutilation.

6. In all religions, sacred symbols have the power to move the believer. They also serve as key integrating factors in a culture by articulating the "ultimate concerns" experienced by its members.

7. Most societies have one or more kinds of religious leader, whether *priest, shaman, prophet,* or *sorcerer.* The differences between each of these categories depend largely on how the religious specialists are called and trained and how they practice. These terms represent different categories of action rather than individual actors, so that one individual could conceivably practice more than one specialty at the same time. Shamans, prophets, and sorcerers practice as individuals and are most likely to have visions and direct contact with the supernatural. Priests must serve some kind of apprenticeship and learn a large body of belief and ceremonial material. Priests and prophets are largely concerned with the overall welfare of the community. Shamans are predominantly concerned with healing, while sorcerers may cause harm and attempt to ferret out evil influences by destroying the culprits. They may use *divination,* a ritual technique often relied upon to determine the source of misfortune or to solve social problems.

8. *Myth* is the verbal rationale of religion; it is symbolic narrative that has a sacred or supernatural component. Ritual may illustrate myth, but either may exist without reference to the other. Myth provides coherence and synthesis regarding the questions of deeper significance expressed in a culture. It often offers resolutions concerning the ambiguities and contradictions of life.

9. Sorcery or witchcraft reflects the malevolent side of the supernatural. These are explanations of the otherwise inexplicable, resorted to when life and misfortunes become intolerable.

10. Religions change through time—often dramatically, due to the appearance of a charismatic leader who has had a revelation. The appearance of radically new religious

574 movements at a time of social and economic disintegration has often been observed, and the terms *revitalization* and *millenarian movements* have been given to this phenomenon. The degree of acceptance and persistence of such movements is variable, and depends on individual as well as social factors. Most likely a key determinant is the effectiveness of a movement's teachings in coping with difficult present realities.

11. Missionizing religions make exclusive claims about their grasp of reality. They seek adherents and actively organize their followers in systematic ways. Missionaries and anthropologists often find themselves in conflict, yet depend on one another in various ways.

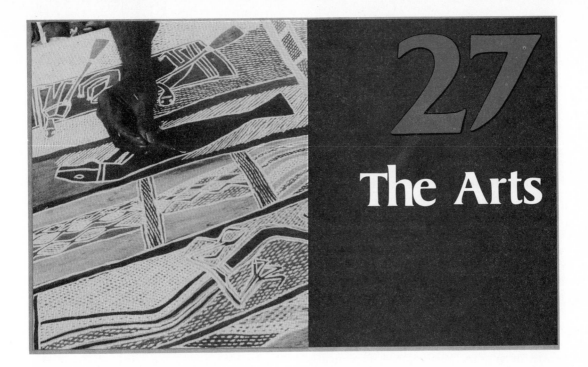

27

The Arts

THE subject of art is one of the most elusive in anthropology. There is, first, the age-old problem of how to define art. The problem is not merely one of definition, but rather that art is considered something to be enjoyed and appreciated on an emotional-response level as well as something to be analyzed. Western cultural attitudes toward art and those who create it, notions of what is and is not art, and the uses to which art should be put all get in the way of the anthropological study of art. Because no adequate social theory of art has been advanced, anthropologists tend to interpret art from the societies they study in terms of the attitudes associated with art in their own society. As pointed out earlier, culture bias is a major problem for anthropology in general, but it is perhaps even more true with art than with other topics. The antiestablishment stance of the artist, an aesthetic based on relationships of forms, art as status symbol and

object, and the mystique of the creative impulse are only a few of the preconceptions that most Westerners hold that prevent their meeting non-Western arts with open-minded as well as wide-eyed interest.

Toward an Anthropology of Art

The Relationship of Art and Culture

The primary issue facing anthropologists concerns, of course, the nature of the relationship between art and culture. Do all cultures have art? To what extent is art involved in the lifestyles of a given culture? How does the role played by art differ from one culture to another? How is it similar? In order to respond to these questions, anthropologists must arrive at some understanding about what is included in the topic "art."

Even a superficial acquaintance with cultures other than our own demonstrates the enormous variability in the place accorded to art and artists, and the role of the appreciators or audience, in different human societies. Geertz (1976) has pointed out that "the capacity, variable among peoples as it is among individuals, to perceive meaning in pictures [or poems, melodies, buildings, pots, dramas, statues] is, like all other fully human capacities, a product of collective experience." He explains further that "participation in the particular we call art" can develop only "out of participation in the general system of symbolic forms we call culture" (p. 1488). Thus, our cultural conditioning determines the sensibility we bring, as appreciators, to our experiences of any art. Furthermore, a particular view of culture obviously influences the direction from which the study of art will be undertaken. However, in order to determine what is considered art in any given society, it is essential to analyze the cultural system from a broader perspective.

Art is, then, inseparable from culture. But paradoxically, the outcome of artistic activity is often an object that can be (and most often has been) removed from and studied without reference to its cultural context (Merriam, 1964, p. 97). Art, existing in some form at a given time, is by its very nature concrete. But the aesthetic appreciation of art is highly individual and subjective. Precisely because art can be separated from its cultural context, it is attractive as a subject for anthropological study.

One difficulty in discussing art is that it is necessary to translate experiences expressed in visual (or auditory) form into language, using words that are not always compatible with the original expression. Goldwater (1973) sees the arts as being "primary documents" rather than secondary expressions of more fundamental ideas. In other words, art, as an essential part of culture, reflects the cultural whole and is not merely a support for some aspect of it.

The problem of meaning, of course, is central to any discussion of culture and art. All humans are the product of their time and place of creation. The anthropologist must, although this is most difficult, guard against interpreting unfamiliar arts in the terms made familiar by art historians in Western culture (Forge, 1973). We must always pause to realize that our use of categories such as sculpture, masks, and paintings, derives from the history and role of the arts in our own society. Although these are useful categorizations for us, they do remove us from the cultural context at which we are ultimately trying to get. At the same time, we must also recognize that art in other cultures may fall into categories, such as body painting or cuisine, that we have never acknowledged in quite that light. Further, as Forge points out, "some cultures devoid of art in the sculpture and painting sense possess rich visual systems of great aesthetic powers," which focus on other, perhaps natural "art" products.

But there is no question that Westerners have over the years been drawn to the creative products of foreign cultures. Marveled at when displayed by returning explorers in the sixteenth and seventeenth centuries, later collected as curiosities, the so-called "primitive arts" have long appealed to the Western appetite for the exotic. Possession of "primitive" art objects has been a status symbol of sorts for centuries. Displayed by the wealthy, these objects were, along with curiosities of biology and geology, the foundations of collections that would become great museums in the eighteenth and nineteenth centuries. Certainly, in that time, the appreciation accorded such works depended more on their exotic value than their aesthetic worth. But at the end of the nineteenth century and the beginning of the twentieth, painters and sculptors in France became aware of the visual impact

Wood carvings from Africa, such as this head for a reliquary *(left)* **used by the Fang of Gabon excited European collectors and artists.** (Charles Uht, Courtesty of the Museum of Primitive Art). **Amedeo Modigliani was one Parisian artist whose paintings were influenced by African sculpture. Note the similarities between this** *(right)* **and the Fang mask** *(left)* **in overall facial contours, the curvature of the sides of the nose, and the high forehead and arch of the eyebrows.** (The Metropolitan Museum of Art, gift of Charles F. Ikle, 1960)

of masks especially and carved figures from Africa.

But no matter how great the visual power of such objects, no matter how deep our aesthetic appreciation of them, the symbolic content of individual design elements contained within the object is not comprehensible by us in the same terms as those in which they are comprehended by a member of their culture of origin. Beyond the universality of "the human body, its parts, and its functions [as] a source of many powerful symbols in ritual as well as art in most human societies," Forge has noted, "there seems little evidence of genuine universal symbols in the plastic arts or indeed in any other medium of communication" (1973, p. xiv). Even where the same design

element appears in the products of vastly different cultures, vastly different meanings are attached to it. The swastika, for example, is a design element whose use is widespread—it was one of the body marks of Buddha in India, it was used in Crete and ancient Rome, it has been an American Indian design to indicate the four directions, it appeared in China as a symbol of benevolence, and of course it was the notorious symbol of the Nazis in Germany. Its use in each context obviously evoked different emotions and held different connotations.

This brings us back to the object itself or, as d'Azevedo puts it, a created "product or effect of a particular kind" (1973, p. 7). Merriam points out that objects or effects that can be

578 considered art are produced in all cultures, although there are many cultures that do not have a concept of art as a distinct category of endeavor (1964). The study of so-called primitive art has increasingly attracted art historians, but dance, music, folklore, drama, painting, and a vast variety of other possible media for artistic activity have attracted the interest of few modern anthropologists or other social scientists. However, such fields as ethnomusicology, ethnodance, and folklore studies are beginning to fill the gap, and art historians are becoming aware of the extraordinarily rich resources to be found in the non-Western arts. In relatively recent years, too, the created works of nonprimitive, non-Western societies have been subjected to cross-cultural analysis and interpretation. This field is potentially an enormously rich one, and must include such outstanding products as the poetry of Islamic cultures; the dance and sculpture of India; graphic, dramatic, literary, culinary, and textile arts of China and Japan; the verbal and occult heritage of Judaism; and architecture as a category in itself.

The Problem of Aesthetics

Aesthetics refers to the study of beauty and of psychological responses to it. The problem of aesthetics is really twofold. First, as we have mentioned in passing in the preceding pages, there is the problem of setting *our* aesthetic standards to one side when confronting the art works produced in an unfamiliar cultural context. Second, there is the question of determining the aesthetic principles on which art of another culture is based. This last point further subdivides into analysis of the problem of aesthetics from the two points of view of creator and appreciator. In some cultures, the same word is used to mean "good" and to describe an aesthetically attractive object. Thus, "good" and "beautiful" become one concept, but the vocabulary for aesthetic appreciation is not further defined, although the

These four sculptures, from different times, different lands, and different cultures share many aesthetic qualities, such as clarity of line and form, a fine surface, erectness, serenity, and balance. *Above left*—an *ibeji* (twin figure) made by the Yoruba of Nigeria (Eliot Elisofon, Museum of African Art, Eliot Elisofon Archives); *above right*—marble caryatids (draped female figures supporting an entablature) from the Erechtheum (porch of the Maidens) on the Acropolis in Athens, fifth century, B.C. (George Holton, Photo Researchers, Inc.); *bottom left*—bronze statuette of a young ballet dancer by Degas (The Metropolitan Museum of Art, bequest of Mrs. H. O. Havemeyer, 1929, the H. O. Havemeyer Collection); *bottom right*—gilded wooden sculpture of Buddha (The Metropolitan Museum of Art, Rogers Fund, 1943)

elements that make one object "good/ beautiful" and another not may be explained in detail. An observer in Igala, Nigeria, reports Sieber (1971), had only two words of critique for a mask shown to him: "one identified the mask type, the other indicated that it was well done" (p. 130). But, as Thompson (1971) reports, among the Yoruba, also of Nigeria, several thoroughly understood critical standards are regularly applied to their human figures sculptured in wood. These standards include concepts of clarity of line and form, high polish of the surface, symmetry, appropriate position of various elements, erectness, technical skill, and a term Thompson translates to refer approximately to a suitable balance between representation and abstraction. Most of these qualities can be found also in a Degas bronze figure of a dancer; a marble column in the form of a female figure upholding a pillar of the Parthenon; or a gilded representation of the Buddha. With what words, one wonders, did viewers of turn-of-the-century France, Golden Age Greece, or eleventh-century China appraise these works?

The existence of similarities in the formal qualities of these four objects does not result in similarity of form. Yet all have the power to move us, and they likely held that power in their time and place of creation as well. Is

there, then, a universal aesthetic response? Although no one has actually demonstrated the existence of a universal aesthetic response some hold that there is one. Goldwater, for example, claims that "the aesthetic is concerned with power, with the heightened impact of a perfect object whether it be beautiful, ugly, or frightening" (Forge, 1973, p. xxi).

Stout (1971) emphasizes that understanding of aesthetics from an anthropological perspective will only be achieved through collecting statements from primitive artists about their work and that of their colleagues and through actually studying and being apprenticed to native craftsmen. He suggests, too, the necessity of conducting cross-cultural experiments in which objects from one society are presented to members of another for their aesthetic judgments. This was precisely the

BaKwele mask. (The Metropolitan Museum of Art, The Michael C. Rockefeller Memorial Collection of Primitive Art)

approach taken in an experiment a few years ago in which 39 photographs of BaKwele masks were shown to both a number of art students at Yale University and to BaKwele mask carvers and users themselves. There was a surprising amount of agreement on the order in which the masks were ranked. However, there was also strong evidence that the BaKwele were evaluating in terms of standards different from those of the Yale students. Child and Siroto (1965) suggest that these objects can be appreciated by anyone who enjoys visual art, and that both sets of judges could be sensitive to variations in excellence, despite differences in stated evaluative criteria.

On this evidence one might tentatively conclude that, although aesthetic principles are highly variable from one culture to another, there does exist some widespread human capacity to transcend cultural boundaries in the appreciation of some types of art products. But much more attention to this topic will have to be paid by anthropologists before we can approach any degree of understanding about the universals and the particulars of human aesthetic sensibilities.

Some Conceptual Approaches

Interest in primitive art developed largely in terms of the sculptural arts, these being the most readily separated from their cultural contexts and brought into Western collections. While anthropologists were emphasizing fieldwork as a way to get at cultural meanings, the study of the arts came to be considered an area of interest for museums. Museums set up their own departments of ethnology, and university departments of anthropology established their own museums, as at the University of Pennsylvania, UCLA, and elsewhere. For years, emphasis was placed on "collecting," as opposed to studying the art objects *in situ* (in their original place). Expeditions went into the field to gather as many objects as possible, often at the same time as ethnographers, but with different goals. The long period of collecting, and the consequent study of objects as objects, out of their cultural context, has had several implications. There was, first, a focus on the portable graphic or sculptural arts, and to a lesser extent on the oral traditions; there was comparative neglect of music, dance, drama, body decoration, architecture, and other less collectible products of the creative enterprise. Second, the spotlighted, isolated objects were interpreted in terms of accepted approaches of art analysis—forms, isolated motifs, and comparisons from one object to the next. With this frame of reference, art historians entered the picture as analysts of primitive art, spurred by the discovery of these works by prominent artists. Picasso, Modigliani, and Lipchitz, for example, all incorporated design elements from African sculpture in their work. Third, and as a consequence of the first two considerations, comparisons focused on similarities and differences in the works, and led naturally to speculations about presumed diffusion of elements from one culture to another in the past. Such studies implied that lack of change was inherent in the creative products of non-Western peoples, although familiarity with the history of the products of their own civilization should have informed scholars otherwise.

The study of art in anthropology generally follows the course of the conceptual views of culture outlined in the chapter The Culture Concept. Those committed to an evolutionary view attempt to locate the evolution of art forms; those interested in diffusion (principally Boas himself) attempt to trace the spread of artistic elements from one culture to another as a means of investigating the diffusion of culture. Diffusion is only one kind of interaction in which elements of design or other separable components of the arts move

The similarities of form and design between these two pottery vessels cannot be accounted for by diffusion or culture contact. The polychrome *olla* (bowl) *(above)* was made in Acoma Pueblo, New Mexico around 1900. (Photograph courtesy of the Museum of the American Indian, Heye Foundation). **The large jar *(below)* was made in Iran around 3700 B.C.** (The Metropolitan Museum of Art, Joseph Pulitzer Bequest, 1959)

across cultural boundaries. Mutual borrowing of elements, trading of objects between neighboring cultures, and the commissioning of works by artists of other tribal backgrounds are some other ways that art elements cross cultural boundaries. Beyond these factors, there is the simple fact that artists everywhere can use only the materials at their disposal. We mentioned in an earlier chapter the relationship between the materials available for art and the ecological niche within which a society is located. The available natural materials are similar thoughout a wide region, and so the peoples of that region have similar media at hand. Thus, the peoples of Africa below the Sahara work largely in wood; in desert areas and north of the Sahara, however, sun-baked mud is the more readily available material. American Indians throughout the eastern woodlands laboriously prepared porcupine quills and tinted them with natural dyes to make designs and add color to articles made of deerskin. When more colorful European glass beads were introduced, they were eagerly accepted as an art material, being much easier to work with and capable of producing a more dramatic effect. Eventually, entire new art products were developed, based on new ways of using the new material.

The combination of intercultural diffusion of art ideas and the regional availability of art materials means that art products within a culture area are readily identifiable. Within each culture area, such as West Africa or the American Plains, the distinctive cultural or tribal differences of style stand out. Thus, one cannot talk of African art but must distinguish its different areas and subareas; and then move further to distinguish between Yoruba, Ibo, Ibibio, Ekoi, and dozens more within even such a geographically limited area as present-day Nigeria.

Those anthropologists strongly influenced by the functionalist school tend to emphasize the manner in which art serves to integrate and bolster other aspects of culture. We have discussed above the complex interrelationships between arts and cultures, interrelationships that will become increasingly apparent in the latter part of this chapter as we look at different categories of the arts.

Art as Communication

Without communication, the artist has failed. Picasso's comment on the communicative function of art is well known: "Art is a lie," he said, "that makes us see the truth." Art communicates in the realms of politics and religion, economics and social life—indeed, in every aspect of human existence.

The intention to communicate need not be clearly stated or even intended to accomplish this end. An art product communicates not only what the artist intends but also what the spectator reads into it. Where there is a shared cultural frame of reference, the two kinds of content may merge and become a total or nearly total whole. But where the cross-cultural gap yawns wide, there may be a chasm of meaning. Yale art students and BaKwele mask users may have shared some standards of visual appreciation for masks, but the *meanings* conveyed to members of the two groups were very different indeed. The Americans tended to respond to such qualities as symmetry, idealization of form, and technical skill; they may have envisioned the masks on walls in galleries or homes as objects to be appreciated. They could not have looked at them in terms of how well certain ritual or spiritual functions would be enhanced through their use. Nor could they have envisioned the masks as part of a kinetic experience, as when the masks are worn by costumed individuals moving against the natural backdrop of BaKwele dwellings and scenery to a musical accompaniment. And the Americans could not have imagined the cultural familiarity or the accumulation of experience with such objects that went into the BaKwele appreciation.

Even where directly representational elements appear in art, they carry symbolic content, meanings beyond the forms immediately depicted. The form may itself be a symbol, a unit in a kind of "cultural code" (Munn, 1971, p. 336). Munn shows how, for example, among the Walbiri of central Australia, a simple circle can represent a circular path, a water hole, certain fruits, the base of a tree, or fire. Designs based on the circle, such as concentric circles or spirals, can be totem centers, a totemic animal or plant, buttocks, female genitals, or breasts (Munn, 1973, pp. 194ff), among others. Similar catalogues could be made of meanings attached to other design elements—the oval, arc, straight line. Munn (1971) concludes that, for "any system of culturally standardized representations . . . where one can identify discrete, recurrent units through which visual contrasts are made," it should be possible to define the meanings attached to each symbol (p. 336).

Where Walbiri designs may have secular or religious content according to their context, the design elements of the Tiv of Nigeria have no particular religious symbolism but are instead representations of natural elements such as lizards, swallows, and drinking gourds (Bohannon, 1971, p. 179). In such cases, meanings can be readily determined; according to Bohannon, there is no point in looking further for deeper meaning. At the other extreme, art elements can be intentional representations designed to convey a specific message. The arrangement of purple and white beads in a string of wampum or the design woven into a wampum belt had immediate or historic content for its Iroquois audience; meetings of the chiefs opened with someone literally "reading" the wampum.

The meanings of art can be even more specific than this. It is not necessary to delve into symbolic content of specific design elements to understand the meanings of art objects in terms of the situations that call for their use. A mask worn by a tribal judge in Liberia clearly conveys the power of the judgments rendered by its wearer. When the "mask" speaks, the Dan or Guere people are certain to heed the decision. Similarly, when a Crow warrior carries a painted buffalo-hide shield covered with attached objects, everyone knows that the supernatural spirits have favored him. Art appears at initiation ceremonies as ratification of a belief system, part of the trappings that enhance the prestige of royalty. Art may be purely secular as well, adorning everyday utility objects—a design painted on a jar; animal or human figures carved on the wooden door of a granary; colorful stripes woven into cloth strips; or beaded flowers appliquéd onto moccasins.

Graburn (1976) has shown that one of the most important communications of art is to identify members of an in-group within a society and to distinguish one society from another: "All people surround themselves with material objects that express their individual identity and their identity within a social category" (pp. 23–24). This is as true of our complex civilization as it is of small societies. Thorstein Veblen, the American economist, called attention to the trappings of conspicuous consumption that delineated the nouveau riche from the bourgeoisie out of which they arose; the "old rich" had no difficulty in distinguishing their own set of privileges from those "put on" by upstarts. Similarly, Graburn notes that "threatened identities often lead to a revival of archaic traditions" (p. 25). He cites a number of American Indian examples, such as the renaissance of Hopi kachina figures to counter missionizing attempts of the Catholic Church. More recently we have seen "the new ethnicity" emphasizing traditional national costumes, songs, and so forth. As black Americans find cultural roots in resurrecting aspects

These two examples of utilitarian objects enriched by art are from North America. The baby carrier *(left),* made and used by the Kiowa of Oklahoma, is decorated with colorful bead embroidery and trim. The steel knife *(right)* has a bone handle carved to represent the head of a raven; pieces of shell are inlaid for eyes. It was made and used by the Tlingit of British Columbia. (Photographs courtesy of the Museum of the American Indian, Heye Foundation)

Among the Ashanti of Ghana, men are weavers of kente cloth strips, which are sewn together to form wide lengths of fabric worn as robes *(left).* The carved wooden figure *(right)* is a heddle pulley, made and used by the Baule of the Ivory Coast; it is part of weaving equipment, used to separate warp threads. Two heddle pulleys can be seen in use in the loom pictured at *left.* The Ashanti and the Baule are culturally-related peoples. (Photographs by Eliot Elisofon, Museum of African Art, Eliot Elisofon Archives)

of their distant African heritage (discovering the verbal and sculptural arts of the lands of their forebears in the process), a new Afro-American identity and art are being created.

The Artist and Society

If there are, cross-culturally speaking, few valid generalizations that can be made about art objects, there are even fewer generalizations applicable to artists. In some societies, artists are specialists, individuals known far and wide for their skill (or whose products are known far and wide for their efficacy). The Kilenge of western New Britain, Melanesia,

distinguish between artists and master artists, certain of whom are recognized as possessing particular competence (Dark, 1967, p. 142). The artist, who is an individualist par excellence in our own society, is not always in a similar position in preindustrial societies. Among the Basongye of the Congo, for example, the role of musician—but not that of composer—is one of the few permissible routes to individual accomplishment. Because of the cultural opposition to individualization, musicians deny also being composers and attribute their musical innovations to other nearby cultures (Merriam, 1964, p. 78). The Tiv of central Nigeria are interested more in the art than in the artist and are more concerned with the ideas conveyed by a piece of art than with the way it was created (Bohannon, 1971, p. 175). Among the Tiv, carving

An Eskimo prepares the ivory tusk of a bull walrus before carving. (Georg Gerster, Rapho/Photo Researchers, Inc.)

may even be a communal enterprise, with someone picking up and working on a piece that another has put down. However, carvings of figures, as opposed to utilitarian objects such as bowls, are usually the work of a single individual. Yet the only acclaim such a master carver receives is to have it said that his work always (as opposed to sometimes) comes out well.

Unlike the Tiv, the Eskimos are more interested in the artistic process than in its product: "When you feel a song within you, you sing it; when you sense a form emerging from ivory, you release it" (Carpenter, 1971, p. 165). Carpenter vividly shows us the Eskimo artist at work:

As the carver holds the unworked ivory lightly in his hand, turning it this way and that, he whispers, "Who are you? Who hides there?" And then: "Ah, Seal!" He rarely sets out, at least consciously, to carve, say, a seal, but picks up the ivory, examines it to find its hidden form and, if that is not immediately apparent, carves aimlessly until he sees it, humming or chanting as he works. (Carpenter, 1971, p. 163)

Sometimes artists are self-taught; sometimes they must serve an apprenticeship or pay a fee for instruction and admission to a guild; sometimes they inherit the artistic function in their families. In Japan, a particularly promising apprentice may be adopted into a family of artists to continue a dynasty of creativity. This is especially so in dance and the dramatic arts but also holds true in traditional crafts and graphic arts. Himmelheber (1967) describes the casts of wood carvers and brass casters of the Senufo of West Africa:

These craftsmen do not cultivate fields. They live from what the farmer caste brings them in exchange for their work. They then practice their craft from morning till night, producing an enormous number of woodworks, both artistic and of everyday use (mortars, pestles, handles for axes). They form separate quarters in the villages, even entire villages of their own. Visiting such a quarter one finds a great number of carvers in each compound, sometimes 30 or 40, busily at work. (pp. 195–196)

At the opposite end of the spectrum, there are some societies in which every member is expected to produce works of art. Among the Tiwi of Oceania, all males have a number of opportunities to carve funeral poles, as well as to practice singing, dancing, body painting, ceremonial basket making, and the carving and painting of ceremonial spears (Goodale & Koss, 1971, p. 198). Artistic proficiency brings prestige. Thus, the inexperienced welcome the call to be in the group that will carve funeral poles, which gives them the opportunity to observe more experienced master carvers at close hand.

Much of the recent attention in the anthropological study of art has focused on the artist. In fact, d'Azevedo, who titled his 1973 book *The Traditional Artist in African Society*, considers the role and function of the artist the most important area of research. As he says, the problem is not one of biography but rather of identifying the kind of individual behavior and social action that coincide with artistry. We must not lose sight of the fact that artists are members of their social systems who are influenced by the response to their products as much as by their own creativity. The aspiring Tiwi carver receives a great deal of feedback from his audience:

The workers are commissioned as a group and . . . are given general directions as to how many poles should be cut and how big they should be, directions which indicate the employer's [the family of the dead] wishes and abilities to pay for the work done. . . . Finally . . . the employers judge each pole individually and lay out their payment (in goods) according to their evaluation. (Goodale & Koss, 1971, pp. 188–189)

Meanwhile, there has been much discussion of all the poles by members of the community. Works accorded high payment will be remembered by those who have seen them

Arts intersect each other in many ways. This painting on the bark of the sago palm decorates the front of a spirit house in New Guinea. (George Holton, Photo Researchers, Inc.)

when it is their turn to carve, and those carvers whose works were evaluated highly will be encouraged to continue along the same lines. Thus criticism has a very practical impact.

By itself, studying an individual artist cannot explain art in any type of society. The study can, however, enlarge our understanding and appreciation of the created product. It is to those products that we now turn our attention.

Visual Arts

Under the heading of visual arts are included the best-known categories of the so-called primitive arts—the graphic and

sculptural expressions created in numerous cultures of our own day, the recent past, and also of the previous vast period known to us through archaeology. The visual arts also include many less familiar categories: textile (weaving) and other fiber arts, including basketry; body decorating, including makeup, "jewelry," and costume; and architecture.

The term *graphic art* generally refers to such two-dimensional products as paintings and drawings on canvas, cave walls, stones, fabric, bark, and so on. The *sculptural* or *plastic arts* are three-dimensional products, including sculpture and utilitarian items such as furniture, tools, and containers. There is an area in which the graphic and plastic arts overlap, since many three-dimensional objects are adorned with two-dimensional designs applied over or incised into the surface. This is true, for example, of body painting, of the painted funerary carved poles of the Tiwi, and of pottery. It also applies to the *molas* of the Cuna of San Blas Island off the coast of Panama, made by a "negative appliqué" technique in which strips of cloth are cut out to let an underlayer of fabric show through.

As a three-dimensional constructed form, architecture, too, is considered among the plastic arts, although it surely deserves to be in a category by itself. Paradoxically, although dwellings and other structure types are carefully described and their construction detailed in ethnographic reports, the cross-cultural analysis of building styles and materials, and

This Yirrhala (Australia) man is applying a white earth paint to bark cloth. (Georg Gerster, Rapho/ Photo Researchers, Inc.)

their influence on people's lives, has been virtually nonexistent. Potentially fascinating questions for exploration include the relationship of house size and style to social organization, child-rearing practices and socialization of the young, marital and intrafamily relations, cooperation, and division of labor.

Within any one category of the visual arts there are numerous variations. The fiber arts include braiding, knotting, and twining, techniques that produce hammocks, carrying bags, baskets, and ropes. They also include weaving. Even the simplest of looms, such as the plain frame loom of the Navaho, can be used to produce elaborate objects. A backstrap type of loom is found in many parts of South America and Africa. The Senufo and Baule peoples of West Africa carve weaving accessories with as much care as they use for their ritual masks. Fibers and cloth are colored with brilliantly hued earth dyes. The Navaho produce their own wool and dye it. In many African cultures, dried corn kernels or pebbles are tied with string or sewn in a design onto a large stretch of cloth that is then dyed. The wax-resistant batik dying of Indonesia is well known. Other fabric-decorating techniques of note include the block printing of India and the mud painting (using dark clays or mineral powders) of West Africa.

The category of body decorating comprises simple painting with colored earths; scarification; jewelry inserted into openings made in nose, ears, lips, or permanently secured about the neck; other kinds of jewelry; dress, costume, or ornamentation; hairdressing and hair styling. The "mudheads" of New Guinea literally build masks onto their own heads, then paint the masks and the exposed portions of their faces and bodies with light-colored clay for certain ritual occasions. Studies of body decoration identify styles and symbolic content of specific decorative elements. Scarification may indicate the rank of an individual's family, for example, and a hairdo may distinguish married from unmarried women. Such studies also investigate the occasions calling for special dress or appearances, as well as those for which special costume is not required. It would be interesting to analyze, for example, the reasons why a society pays a great deal or no particular attention to clothing and body decoration on such occasions as weddings, funerals, and agricultural or puberty ceremonies.

The technical abilities and skills called for are often outstanding. The ikat dyers and weavers of India and Indonesia, for example, are able to dye fibers so that the design will appear in the weaving. The large bronze heads and plaques of Benin, and the small brass figures of animals and humans of the Ashanti, are created by a process used in our society by jewelry designers and sculptors.

Intimate knowledge of materials and technology is essential. Clay must be selected, processed to remove impurities, tempered with sand or with finely ground pottery so it will fire evenly, shaped with walls of even thinness for even firing, and dried carefully before firing. A small damp patch can cause an explosion in the kiln and ruin a week's output. Fires must be built and tended, paints and other kinds of finishes must be prepared, and perhaps supernaturals must be called on for assistance to ensure the quality of the results.

Today's artists and artisans in our society can buy most of their supplies ready for use, or nearly so. In all other times and places, preparation of equipment has been an essential and time-consuming preliminary to the main event of creating. Cro-Magnon artists, for example, made brushes from animal hair or the ends of twigs, fraying them either by chewing or pounding them with a stone. Paint was daubed on rock walls with pads of animal fur or with the flat side of bones or stone. Powdered pigment could be blown onto a wall through a hollow bone. Flat stones with dried patches of color on them—Ice Age palettes—have been found in caves. And shells stained with pigment—the equivalent

of paint jars—have also been found. There have even been flat stones covered with superimposed scratchings—a version of sketchpads (Rensberger, 1978, p. 40). Some of these same materials are used by non-Western artists today. The pigments used in cave painting were made by pulverizing colored minerals and mixing them with binders made from animal fat, egg white, blood, vegetable juices, and fish glue (a gelatinlike substance made by cooking fish scraps in water). Apparently, different binders were used for different types of rock, the selection being made on the basis of a variety of technical problems, such as the texture and porosity of the rock and whether the surface was damp or dry. Because Ice Age artists used such techniques, many of their frescoes have withstood the ravages of time better than have some of the masterpieces of the Renaissance (Rensberger, 1978).

In dealing with prehistoric arts such as cave paintings and some other most expressive three-dimensional products as well, we are truly faced with the concept of art as primary document. Few artifacts of any culture are more expressive than the dramatic and sensitive forms traced in soft-colored earths on the walls and ceilings of Altamira in Spain, Lascaux in France, and numerous other Cro-Magnon cave sites.

The distinction is often made between artist and craftsperson, as though the former produces a finer, more rarified product intended for aesthetic appreciation only, whereas the latter produces only utilitarian objects. This distinction, however, is barely valid for the products of our own culture, and not at all valid for those of most non-Western societies.

In any culture, an artisan/craftsperson may also be an artist, whereas many artists, alas, are found on close acquaintance to be artisans instead. The product—and its impact on its audience—is what counts. All arts, from the anthropological point of view, are practical, in

Arts meet in costume for dances that are part of ritual. *Above*—basket spirit masks are worn by Asmat witch doctors in a ceremony in West Irian, **West New Guinea** (George Holton, Photo Researchers, Inc.); *below*—carved wooden **headdress masks are part of the costume worn by the Sande women's society of the Mende of Liberia. The mask represents one of the spirits from which the society derives its authority and function—training girls for adulthood** (Clardun, Monkmeyer)

the sense that they serve a cultural function. An easel painting has as specific a role to play in Pennsylvania as does a sheet of bark cloth in Polynesia.

D'Azevedo reminds us that the word *art* carries with it some of its earlier connotations of a special skill or technique (1973, p. 7). Non-Western societies may concentrate their creative impulses on objects of utilitarian value. But if the conception and the technique are of that high quality meant by the word *art,* then the product—basket or box, silver teapot or clay water jar—is indeed a work of art.

Dance

All human societies appear to have members who dance, although the occasions for dancing and the forms it takes vary enormously from one culture to another. Although dance is widespread as a cultural phenomenon, not all individuals participate. In numerous societies, dance is an activity for males only. Sometimes, as in parts of the Middle East, dance is performed by males for an all-male audience. More frequent perhaps is the situation in which dance is performed by women for an all-male audience (also found in the Middle East, and elsewhere). The European pattern of exclusively mixed dancing is comparatively unusual.

A culture usually has more than one kind of dance activity or, rather, dances on several different kinds of occasions. Dance most frequently appears as a component in ritual, "during religious ceremonials and community festivals of birth, maturation, courtship, marriage, harvest, death" (Lomax, 1968, p. 224). Dance is, as a repetitive series or sequence of body movements, a kind of ritualized behavior in and of itself, and even secular occasions for dance take on a ceremonial significance as a result.

Dance may be a cultural universal, but it is not an exclusively human activity, at least in the broadest sense. Mating "dances" have been described for various animal species, especially among insects and birds. As a consequence, the question may be raised as to whether the rhythmic, repetitive body movements in space that we call dance have some natural base. Perhaps dance is behavior that continues to be based on a biological drive even while its form and meaning are shaped by culture.

The approaches of anthropology to dance have followed the same sequence previously described. The evolutionist approach, responsible for some of the earliest ethnographic descriptions and influenced by Victorian morality, regarded dance as a primitive form of behavior that would be abandoned as peoples became "civilized." The personality and culture approach saw dance as a psychological safety valve for the individual within a controlling social environment. American ethnologists concentrated on cultural context, and described dance societies, dancers and their paraphernalia, and the role of dance within the culture, to the exclusion of actual choreography. European studies, more interested in folklore than in cultural context, emphasized dance forms (Royce, 1977, p. 213). Most recently, the focus has been both functionalist and structuralist, the former concerned with dance in relation to the cultural whole, the latter with dance as a communicative system, its symbolic content, and means of transmission.

A particularly ambitious study was undertaken by Lomax and several associates, who attempted to correlate dance style movements and other aspects of social life, particularly those movements utilized in work activities. His analysis of dance movements— *choreometrics*—in 43 cultures represents a cross-cultural comparison similar in order to that of the Human Relations Area Files studies. An example of the categories of dance movements the Lomax team analyzed was whether the torso is held "as a solid, block-like structure" in "one-unit" movement, or whether movement is of "two-unit" type, with "clearcut twists at the waist or undulating movements spreading from the center of the torso into other segments of the body" (Lomax, 1968, p. 237).

By comparing dance forms as seen in ethnographic films, the Lomax team noted such factors as the carry-over of posture from work stance into dancing stance. These observations led to their hypothesis that "movement style in dance is a crystallization of the most frequent and crucial patterns of everyday activity" (p. 226). They also identified seven dance-style regions that correlated closely to song-style regions previously identified. Previous analysis had shown that song performance styles were culturally related to subsistence activity. For example, "the social structures of the song teams of a society seem to resemble those of its work teams" (Lomax, 1968, p. 224). Thus, similar results in several respects were obtained for both dance and song.

It is not sufficient for *us* to define dance; we must also consider definitions from the cultures studied. Such definitions may combine music with dance, or may exclude certain categories of dance, or distinguish between ritual and secular dance (Royce, 1977, p. 10). Royce suggests that it may be more useful to consider dance events, such as weddings and festivals, than to restrict our observations to dances and dancing. A dance event may, as she shows for a Zapotec wedding, consist of a particular combination or sequence of different dances (p. 11).

The most useful studies still seem to be those that investigate dance within a particular culture with a view to the messages that are communicated. Dance may mean different things to those who create it, those who per-

An elaborately costumed and made-up dancer from Kerala, South India. The dancer will perform the *Kaliyattam,* a sacred dance originating from Shakti worship and performed to appease the gods and goddesses. (Van Bucher, Photo Researchers, Inc.)

form it, and those who view it. Dance communicates through its kinesthetic quality, unique in the arts, which evokes a sympathetic kinesthetic response in the audience (Royce, 1977). But dance communicates through other channels as well. There is the visual component—what is seen, under conditions of lighting or shadow, and by whom in what company. There are sounds, both of accompaniment and of physical exertion, such as feet against ground or stage, and there are also channels of touch and smell.

Dance may communicate by miming spirit beings or animals, as in the deer dance of the Mexican Yaqui or the kangaroo dance of indigenous Australians, or by miming activities such as war and harvesting. Dance may be metaphorical, as in the rain dance in which the Sioux circle about a container of water four times, drop to the earth, and then drink from the container. And dance may be abstract, with body movements themselves being the center of attention. The hand-movement dances of India, in which each movement represents an action or a portion of a narrative tale, and foot movement is relatively minimal, can be a combination of all three possibilities. Most cultures have dances of all three types, so that these are ways of interpreting dances but not of categorizing cultures in regard to dance.

Bateson (1972) points out that the messages communicated in dance may not always be fully conscious or clearly intended. In fact, he seems to suggest that the reason one communicates through dance rather than verbally is that there is an attempt to convey a "partly unconscious message" or perhaps "a message about the interface between conscious and unconscious" (p. 138). Thus, the meanings of dance are to be found on many levels. It is precisely this multimessage aspect of dance that gives it a unique quality and makes it attractive for study.

Music

Music, too, is found everywhere. The cross-cultural approach to this art has been undertaken by the interdisciplinary field of *ethnomusicology*—the study of music in culture (Merriam, 1968, p. 351). Within the study of music in culture, there are two distinct emphases. The first is musicological, concerned with such matters as construction, rhythm, scale, melody, instrumentation, vocalization styles, and so on. The second is more strictly anthropological, focusing on the uses and meanings of music, the performer and the audience, and the cultural context.

The role of music, as of other arts, varies from one culture to another. Music has accompanied virtually every kind of human activity in some time or place. Many cultures, such as our own, have numerous kinds of and occasions for music. The Flathead Indians have 14 distinct categories of situations calling for music, each with a number of subcategories. In the camps of African Bushmen and Pygmies, there seems always to be some

music activity going on. In a Basongye village, on the other hand, many days may elapse without any kind of music being heard; indeed, the only event that requires musical accompaniment is the periodic new moon ceremonial (Merriam, 1964).

Everywhere, the human life cycle provides countless occasions for song: lullabies and puberty ceremony songs, courting and marriage songs, family and funeral songs. There are work songs, songs for war and for peace. A variety of musical expressions are associated with religious occasions everywhere; texts of prayers and myths are set to music, and there are songs for cults and for curing, for divination and for meditation. Music is often inseparable from dance as well as from drama. In our own diverse and complex society, musical preference is often a group identification symbol, which varies according to age, class, and occupational and educational status.

Among the cattle-herding Tutsi of Ruanda, there are songs for boasting, war, and greeting; songs for young women who meet to gossip; children's songs; religious songs; songs of flattery, courtship, and marriage. There is also a substantial catalogue of songs relating to cattle: songs in which two men sing competitively in praise of a particular cow or of one cow over another; songs to accompany evening cowherding; songs to sing while drawing water for cattle; songs to sing with other herders in the evening; songs in praise of the royal cattle; songs for showing cattle off to visitors, special flute songs to foil nighttime cattle thieves; and songs recounting events in which cattle figured (Merriam, 1959a, p. 50).

Music can be made in many ways; human vocalization is only one of them. Naturally occurring materials such as hollow rods or animal bones, hollow logs and reeds or grasses provided the models for numerous native instruments. But new instruments are created as new materials become available: the development of the steel drum, now the characteristic music sound of the Caribbean, dates back only

A number of different percussion instruments are represented in this group of Mangbetu musicians who are accompanying the *nebembo* **(circle dance) in Zaire.** (Photograph by Eliot Elisofon, Museum of African Art, Eliot Elisofon Archives)

Graphic art, music, and dance come together in this painted dance drum of the Montana Crow. (Photograph courtesy of the Museum of the American Indian, Heye Foundation)

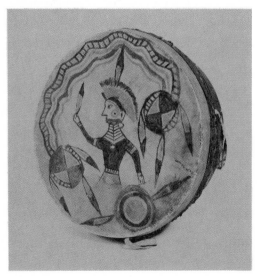

to World War II. Empty oil drums left in Trinidad were found to have, with minimal shaping by humans, a most appealing tonal quality.

The world's inventory of instruments is vast. Many instruments are essentially rhythm-producing, with limited variation, if any, in pitch. Frisbie (1971) lists five kinds of rattles, sticks beaten on the ground, and a water drum for the Bushmen; seven kinds of clappers, hand bells, foot stomping and hand clapping, rattles, and hollow log drums for the Pygmies. Both of these groups have an even greater variety of pitched instruments, both wind and string varieties. Common throughout Africa is the sansa, kalimba, or thumb piano, which is both percussive and pitched. It consists of narrow metal strips of varying lengths attached to a board, played by pressing on the unattached ends of the metal strips

(Frisbie, 1971). A simple wind instrument consisting of a hollow reed or narrow piece of wood or root, with holes to be stopped by the fingers for different pitch levels, is found in some version in every part of the world.

As with his studies of dance, Lomax (1962) and colleagues (1968) has identified some correlations of musical styles with other aspects of social organization and social structure, such as work. Thus, choral music is found in conjunction with cooperative labor, whereas yodeling is characteristic of the lone herder. His conclusions have been questioned, and his particular methodology challenged, but his music studies constitute one of the most ambitious cross-cultural musicological attempts. It is interesting to note that Frisbie (1971), utilizing different techniques, arrived at conclusions similar to those of Lomax in her studies of Pygmy and Bushman music and social life. She seems to support Lomax, giving additional authority to his results. Such comparative studies are only in the formative stages, but they indicate the kinds of interrelationship which might be investigated.

The communicative power of music is well known but, contrary to romanticized popular notions, music is not a universal language. In fact, the available evidence indicates that between different music styles lie substantial barriers to communication (Merriam, 1964). In an experiment reminiscent of that of Child and Siroto with the BaKwele masks above, Morey (1950) chose selections "from Schubert, Davies, Handel, and Wagner which expressed fear, reverence, rage, and love respectively, as well as a control selection from Beethoven (which) did not express a generally acknowledged emotion" (Merriam, 1964, p. 111). Students and teachers at a mission school in Liberia for whom these selections were played did not respond. The same pieces, when played for members of a remote village, caused large portions of the audience, especially women, to get up and leave. Morey concluded that music does not convey emotion to listeners whose cultural experience of music is different from that of the composer of the music (Morey, 1940, p. 354). This may seem surprising, since we respond to a wide range of music types, but then our contemporary musical upbringing has exposed us to greater variety than any people in history have experienced.

Changes in music styles and uses accompany culture change. Among the Toba of Argentina, music was primarily performed by individuals; recently, however, Pentecostal-type religious practices were introduced, and group singing during services became widely adopted. Traditionally, shamans sang to cure their patients, to control stormy weather, to appease the spirits when approaching a graveyard, and on other occasions of danger which required intervention from supernatural powers. Singing in churches in Toba communities today plays much the same role and serves to induce the ecstatic trance that is a component of the religious service.

Verbal Arts and Folklore

As speech is universal and characteristically human, so is the possession of a tradition of verbal arts. The verbal arts are a major component of folklore, which comprises also the nonverbal traditions of sports and games as well as folk dancing. All cultures have verbal art forms; among some peoples, many different forms are found. However, not every category of verbal arts is found everywhere. For example, there are many peoples, among them the Toba, who have no tradition of drama. On the other hand, drama is extremely important in many parts of the Far East—Indonesia, China, and Japan in particular—and many types of dramatic productions occur in those societies.

Dundes points out that among nonliterate peoples the verbal arts "correspond in part to the written literature of literate societies" (1968, p. 117). Dundes asserts further that oral literature should be analyzed in the same ways as are customarily applied to written literary products, in terms of structure, style, aesthetics, social and psychological content, and so on. However, this has too rarely been the case, for reasons that have to do with the ways in which oral literature has usually been collected and perceived.

Systematic collection began in early nineteenth-century Germany with the Grimm brothers, who were to a large extent motivated by a romantic view of the oral folk tradition as a link to an idealized past. As ethnology developed later in that century, quantities of folk tales, song lyrics, proverbs, jokes, and so on were transcribed. A major portion of field data has always concerned folklore, but anthropologists have not always known what to do with such materials. Usually they have been attached to anthropologists' ethnographies in the form of one or more appendices, occasionally annotated as to the identity of the singer or storyteller. Seldom was the total cultural context included; as a result, there have been far too few studies comparing the roles of particular aspects of the verbal arts among cultures.

The most useful studies of folklore describe the context in which tales are recounted or verses sung; the roles of the individual telling the tales or singing the song; the purposes they serve (entertainment, social cohesion, etc.); and the audience. Among the Toba, for example, certain tales are told only by elderly women, others only by shamans, others by any adult male. In our own culture, much of our verbal literature is told only by adults to children; another segment only by men to each other; and there is always a body of oral material told by children to one another. Elsewhere, certain songs or stories may be told only by those who have had a vision,

reached a certain age (elderly men, adolescent girls), or are members of a particular secret society. Jokes of certain kinds may be exchanged only between age mates, or only between a woman and her son-in-law, or between a young man and his uncle. Thus, who tells the stories, the content of the stories, in what context they are told, and for what purpose—all are important aspects of folklore that have seldom been adequately explored.

An additional problem crops up in the very act of translating the oral tradition into print. As Dundes shows, most published materials "have been edited to conform with the canons of written tradition and consequently the printed tale bears only a slight resemblance to the oral original" (168, p. 122). Current recording technology is of some assistance here, since it allows for preservation of the oral production, and videotaping permits the context to be preserved as well. However, the equipment itself may intrude on the spontaneity and unself-consciousness of a performance.

Folk tales probably have been told since the beginnings of culture, long before writing was developed, and they continue to be told today. Dundes (1968) distinguishes three major categories of oral folk narrative. *Myth* is a sacred narrative, set in a time span at least in part prior to creation and concerned with essential relationships of earth, humans, and the supernatural. *Folk tales* are usually set in the postcreation past ("once-upon-a-time") and deal with the adventures of an individual pursuing a personal goal. *Legends* are set in historic time and the real world, and may tell of supernaturals or provide explanations for origins of names or customs.

Products of the verbal arts—like those of dance and music but unlike those of most visual arts—are ultimately a collective effort rather than an individual one. Transmitted in oral-aural fashion ("from mouth to ear") over long periods of time, the insertion of changes becomes inevitable. Some cultures are less tolerant of variation than others: Eskimo narrators are corrected by members of their audiences if alterations are made in a tale. But because there is constant interaction between creator and appreciator while oral literature is in production, a recitation may vary in response to audience feedback or even to the composition of the audience, the particular occasion, or more personal factors. Verbal art forms must be considered always as work in progress: a tale "is *never* completed," according to Dundes (1968, p. 120). But if it does change, then the different versions may provide indications of where the culture has been and where it is going. Too often ethnologists have neglected to record variant texts and their contexts.

James L. Peacock, in a classic study (1968) of drama in Indonesia, has shown how audience response can alter the content of dramatic folklore from one community to another. These plays utilize fantasy and mockery to confront crucial aspects of social existence. Peacock's study shows how analysis of the content of folklore and the changes in its content—in this case, in a dramatic production—can identify key symbols and issues in a changing society.

Precisely because it is verbal, oral literature is readily accessible for study. It is valuable as an indication of a people's world view, of their understandings of reality, and for clues to culture contact in the far distant past. Dundes, for instance, believes that relationships between peoples, as between Asian peoples and American Indians, is attested to by numerous parallels in the folk tales in those cultures.

A number of recent studies have compared the oral traditions of African peoples with those of American blacks. Cycles of stories that in Africa featured spider or rabbit trickster characters appear widespread throughout black-settled areas of the New World. A particularly interesting black American verbal art form is "the Dozens," a verbal competition in which two or more contestants vie in hurling insulting spontaneous rhymed couplets at each other (boxer Mohammed Ali is a master of the form). Some have asserted that this game originated in the United States as an outlet for emotion in response to the cultural suppression and oppression of blacks. But Chimezie (1976) has recently pointed out significant similarities of the American game and several African versions, and sees the American form as having developed out of an African heritage. This study also interprets the content of many of the verbal exchanges, both in the African and American forms of the game, in terms of similarities between the mother-centered family units of most Africans and those of Afro-Americans.

Games and Sports

Games and sports are included in this chapter for several reasons. First, they are forms of folklore, transmitted within a culture from one generation to the next. Second, as is true for some of the verbal and dramatic acts, they provide recreation or entertainment for participants and observers. Similarly, they may be used as accompaniment to other cultural activities. Finally, they express cultural meanings and values.

Games of one sort or another are found in all cultures. Some game categories, too, are virtually universal. Many are played with materials widely available; earth or sand, beans, seeds, shells, and pebbles are to be found everywhere. As a result, counter games, such as Go, checkers, and African chess (*kala*) are widespread. Archaeologists have discovered that games and sports such as ball games appear to have been commonplace throughout the New World long before the arrival of Europeans. Thus, games are very old in human history.

Ashanti men playing *wari* (elsewhere in Africa known as *kalah* or *mankala*) in Ghana.
(Photograph by Eliot Elisofon, Museum of African Art, Eliot Elisofon Archives)

Clearly, games are not played by children alone. In fact, children's games constitute a special subcategory; they often serve to teach adult roles and skills as well as cultural values. Games are important in reinforcing social precepts on every level. It was no accident that one of our most popular games ever invented—Monopoly, which gave practical training in the mechanics of the capitalistic society's money dealings (mortgages, manipulating interest, taxes, etc.)—caught on like wildfire during the Depression, for games also serve psychological wish-fulfillment functions.

As a human cultural universal with clear

ties to animal behavior, play has biological and psychological connotations. Our concern here, however, is with what Huizinga (1950) calls "play as a function of culture proper" (p. 5). He notes, first, that play is itself a social construction. It is everywhere separated from "ordinary" or "real" life or "serious" activity, and is voluntary.

Burridge (1968) provides a good illustration of an anthropological study of a game that serves as a model for social behavior among the Tangu of Oceania. The game is called *taketak,* the word for the spines of coconut palm fronds planted in the ground in two massed groups; opposing teams spin tops made from a dried hemisphere-shaped fruit rind with a spindle inserted into the palm fronds. The game is competitive, but not in a way familiar to us. The goal is to demonstrate the equivalence of both teams; in other words, *not* to come out ahead. Burridge describes two versions of the game. In the form played in a more acculturated area, one team may actually win. "Yet no team that loses is content to leave it at that. A return match is arranged in which every effort is made by *both* sides to come out equivalent in the series" (p. 317). In the older version, skill is required to hit the palm fronds with the top when necessary and also to miss them if it is expedient. Not outdoing the opposing team is the important thing. Similarly, in Tangu culture, "food exchanges and the rivalries that go with them can also be ended by mutual consent" at a point at which two individuals or groups are even. Thus, the values of the culture are replicated in the game.

Games and sports are cultural elements subject to borrowing and diffusion, much as are music, dance, and designs. The same form adopted in a new cultural setting may be given altogether different meaning by new participants. Toba games were not highly competitive traditionally, but they have learned to play soccer exceedingly well, and Toba teams now compete with neighboring teams. Games and sports can also be adopted because they are associated with the higher status of the group originally possessing them. Thus, rugby, cricket, polo, squash, and tennis have been widely adopted in British colonial outposts. In Barbados, for example, race tracks and cricket fields are shown with pride as "places of interest."

As with other topics discussed in this chapter, the anthropological analysis of material relating to games and sports has barely begun. Aside from the availability of certain natural materials, such as rubber for balls or wicker for baskets, why should certain types of sports develop in one cultural context and not in another? What are the differences between games traditionally played by women and those played by men? What do we know of games built around subsistence activities (fishing, planting, and the like), games that provide psychological release, games for children, games for old people? Where are sports participants an honored group? Where and under what circumstances are all members of a society expected to participate actively? The available ethnological data have seldom been

Music, dance, acrobatics, costume, and myth enhance each other, as shown in this water color, *The Delight Makers,* painted by Fred Kabotie, a twentieth century Hopi Pueblo artist. (Photograph courtesy of the Museum of the American Indian, Heye Foundation)

analyzed for their game and play materials. Only when such material has been carefully looked at and studies have been designed to investigate these problems, will we begin to fully understand the roles, now very much obscured, played by play in human cultures.

This chapter has been able to touch on only a small number of the many aspects of the arts in human societies that are (or should be) under investigation by cultural anthropologists. A point mentioned only in passing remains to be emphasized here, and that is the multidimensional nature of the artistic enterprise. Art forms are frequently used to enhance each other, creating a heightened impact that is greater than the sum of the parts. Japan provides two examples, Noh drama and the tea ceremony. Noh drama is a distinct form requiring costumes, music, dance, oral literature, makeup, architecture, and carved and painted masks. The tea ceremony involves a specified relationship between crafted objects, an interior architectural setting and furnishings; it must be fully responded to by all the senses of the performer and participants.

Similar examples can be cited for numerous other cultures. The Kwakiutl *potlatch*, at the furthest possible remove from the serenity of the tea ceremony, is equally a multisensory, multidimensional experience for participants, involving dance, music, oral narrative, carved and painted masks, costumes, food, competitions, and more. And on a miniature scale, Ashanti proverbs are frequently illustrated in tiny sculptures of animal or human figures formerly used as weights for gold dust.

It is with a feeling of awe that we observe many outstanding works of art produced in our own and other cultures. But knowledge of the varieties of artistic productions found throughout the world should instill in us an even greater awe for the vast human capacity for creativity and appreciation. It should also make us humble to realize how limited are our individual capacities, as members of one cultural tradition. Can we stretch our sensory perceptions and intellectual equipment to confront the range of human creativity with adequate comprehension of cultural relationships and appreciation of aesthetic values? The cross-cultural contribution of anthropology is a first and essential step in that direction.

Summary

1. Art is universal. It exists, and has existed, everywhere, in every culture, at every time. Anthropologists are concerned with art in relationship to culture. Art involves behavior on the part of the audience as well as of the artist. Of all aspects of culture we have examined thus far, the arts are unique in that they result in a product separable from its cultural context.

2. The separable art objects of non-European cultures were first collected as curiosities. In the nineteenth century, the primitive arts, including music and oral literature, were discovered by Europeans and Americans and hailed as representing an idealized, natural, preindustrial, uncorrupted world. By the turn of the century, these works, and especially the carved wood sculptures of Africa, were discovered by the avant garde, particularly the French artists and writers. Such works influenced the development of modern art at the same time as they were being discovered by early anthropologists. Boas and his students saw evidence of cultural contact and diffusion, especially in the visual art products of nonliterate societies.

3. Art is important as communication; but we must understand it within its cultural context in order to comprehend the full meaning of its message.

4. No category of art is overlooked by

non-Western cultures. The visual arts comprise not only graphic and sculptural productions but also production of utilitarian crafts and architecture. Many visual art objects are produced to accompany religious rituals. Some objects are status symbols, but the greatest number are the everyday items that people make for their own use.

5. Dance is found everywhere. In most cultures, there are multiple kinds of dances and occasions for dance. Anthropologists are concerned not only with how and on what occasions people dance, but also with who does the dancing and who is in the audience. There is some evidence linking dance movements to movements used in subsistence activities. Ethnomusicology investigates both such technical considerations as construction, melody, and instrumentation on the one hand, and focuses on the performers and the audience, on meanings and the functions of music within the society, on the other.

6. Oral literature, a branch of folklore, consists of tales such as myths and legends, which may be accompaniments to ritual, pure entertainment, or serve still other functions. Games and sports, also a branch of folklore, are the "play" element in cultures everywhere. Games are as old as human culture, but the spirit in which one culture plays may be very different from that of the next.

7. Not only are arts universally found, but they are also often multidimensional, with one art form being used as an accompaniment to heighten the impact of another. Everywhere, human sensory perceptions interact with the products created by talented individuals, following cultural aesthetic precepts.

PART FIVE

Anthropology in the Modern World

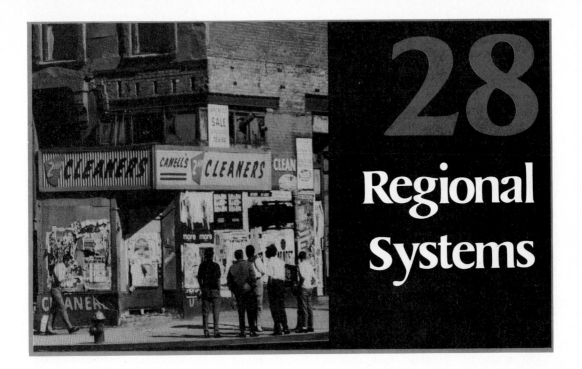

28

Regional Systems

OST anthropological field studies, as our examples throughout this text have shown, consist of intensive investigations of local communities. The field methods and techniques described in an earlier chapter were designed to interpret data about activities and beliefs collected by participant-observers in close, day-to-day contact with their subjects. The anthropological perspective that has developed over the years is the cumulative result of generalizations from a large number of such individual local studies.

We have also seen, from the time of World War II, that there have been scattered attempts to deal with some categories of data on a national or regional scale. The national character studies of the 1940s and 1950s, mentioned earlier, were a notable exception to the otherwise pervasive local approach. However, such broad-scale investigations failed at the time to gain a permanent place in

anthropological research, primarily because the conclusions often seemed simplistic and superficial.

But even earlier, soon after the turn of the century, it was becoming apparent that an alternative to the local community approach was needed—an approach that would explore the interactions of local communities and the larger regional units or systems to which they belong.

The development of the culture-area concept in the early years of this century marked the growing recognition that cultural relationships do not begin and end within the boundary of the local group. It became obvious that when there are ties of language and sharing of artifacts, diffusion of ceremonies and songs, there had to have been substantial interactions among people, both as individuals and as groups. The cultural ecology studies of the 1950s and 1960s also went beyond the locality in their focus on interactions within regions, importance of a larger, regional perspective in anthropological study. Redfield's influence was, if anything, enhanced by the fact that his work coincided with the cultural transitions going on throughout the world in the so-called "developing societies," a fact that gave considerable impetus to support investigations of this sort.

Redfield's model has a number of limitations, however, the major one being his definition of folk and urban societies as structural opposites. In focusing on differences and describing each type in polarized terminology, structural similarities were ignored, and the interrelationships and balances between the two were overlooked. Furthermore, it was taken for granted that change was unidirectional through time, that societies were inevitably becoming more urban, and that this was an irreversible trend. Thus, what began as an analysis of the interconnections between different kinds of communities ended as an analysis of the changes that take place when folk societies become urbanized.

Edmund Leach also utilized a broader perspective in his study of the *Political Systems of Highland Burma* (1954). By lifting his sights beyond any one local community, Leach saw that two apparently contradictory ideologies —hierarchical and egalitarian—formed a framework within which he could relate the activities of all local groups at a single point in time. As Leach saw it, social groups in the Kachin Hills Area characterized by one ideology were under various social pressures to take actions that would move them towards the other ideology. These pressures worked against the establishment of complete dominance of either type in any one community. Indeed, Leach found that the local community could not be isolated. While the people of the region "may speak different languages, wear different kinds of clothes, live in different kinds of houses," they were interrelated in significant ways: "They understand one another's ritual. Ritual acts are ways of 'saying

things' about social status, and the 'language' in which these things are said is common to the whole Kachin Hills Area" (p. 279). Leach also recognized that most societies are not in a state of stability but are, rather, always in a process of change and that clear lines between local groups usually cannot be drawn: "Many . . . tribes are, in a sense, ethnographic fictions" (p. 291). Other ethnographers, in dealing with a limited area and what they perceived as a single culture, imposed unity on their material by making distinctions and choices between the "ideal" culture of which the people spoke and the actual culture in which they lived. But Leach, by focusing on the larger regional system, was able to interpret data, not as a reflection of a gap between the ideal and the real, but as part of the larger whole in which two cultural extremes were continually exerting a push-pull effect upon each other.

While we are discussing the development of a regional focus in studying societies we should mention the influence of international events. After World War II, government concern over the administration of occupied nations and territories initiated some research and led to the development of area studies, particularly in the Far East and Pacific. Such studies were later expanded to other parts of the world.

The attention paid in the late 1960s to the role of ecological factors in the formation and arrangement of social and cultural systems also prompted a regional focus in anthropology. The research of Fredrik Barth (1956, 1969) called attention to the manner in which different ethnic groups exploit distinct resources of a given environment to the extent that these groups become interdependent. In a study in Swat, North Pakistan (1956), for example, Barth showed that "different ethnic groups will establish themselves in stable co-residence in an area if they exploit different ecological niches, and especially if they can thus establish symbiotic economic relations"

(p. 1088). By focusing on the social boundaries of these groups (1969), he was able to show the degree to which one local group forms a part of the larger system made up of additional groups. According to Barth, the resulting interactions give each ethnic group its unique cultural character. As he argues, attention to one ethnic group, and not to its interactions with other groups, would lead to serious distortions.

Rappaport's analysis (1967) of the "pig culture" of the Tsembaga of Highland New Guinea, referred to previously, is another contribution in cultural ecology that utilized a regional focus. In this culture, ritual and warfare between a number of individual local groups combine to maintain ecological balance throughout a region.

While all such approaches have been useful in expanding the horizon of field research, Smith (1976) has recently argued that none of them really establishes a clear conceptual framework or a methodology for truly *regional studies.* She proposes to do this through a *level-specific regional analysis,* distinguishing the local, regional, and national as three distinct levels for research. Her own work is at the regional level, which she views as being halfway between the local and national (pp. 4–5).

Level-Specific Regional Analysis

According to Smith's model, local and regional systems are both *nodal forms of organization,* because they consist of territories peripheral to or clustering around a *node* or *central place.* The periphery may be completely rural or may comprise several smaller nodes or centers along with their peripheral territories.

One may define a nodal region at any level, to include larger or smaller areas of interdependence. Local systems are those in which both material and nonmaterial exchanges are organized around at least one higher-level node, [while] regional systems . . . include a number

of levels of hierarchically organized communities . . . having a truly "urban" central place, complex linkages between communities and higher-level centers, and an organized pattern of nested local systems within them. (1976, p. 9)

The concepts of region, center, and periphery, borrowed from geography, serve to illuminate the spatial distribution of social and cultural systems. Smith argues that the view of "complex societies as nested regional systems, discrete in some aspects and overlapping in others at each level," (1976, p. 4) provides a framework that accommodates previous work so that new studies can add significantly to insights already gained.

Perhaps the best illustration of this approach is Smith's own analysis of exchange systems in agrarian societies. By concentrating on the "spatial organization of distribution" (1976, p. 314) she discerned the relationship between the distribution of goods and the organization of elites, which allowed her to demonstrate the crucial role of control over the means of exchange. She was able, on the regional level, to see that social and economic power was wielded by those who were in control of a "critical resource," which might be "a means of production, such as land, . . . a means of destruction, such as fire power, . . . a simple means of subsistence, such as salt, that cannot be locally procured or produced" (p. 311), or a means of distribution, such as transport animals or marketplaces. By stressing control over the means of exchange, rather than mere control over the means of production, Smith also was able to show the relationship between different types of stratification systems. Had she focused more narrowly, at the local community level, Smith would not have been able to see beyond the production system to the region-based distribution and stratification systems.

At about the same time, Beck utilized the same concepts of center and periphery in her analysis of the caste system of a region in southern India (1976). And Appleby used a but these studies were usually devoted primarily to economic considerations, not to the social relationships that might be associated with them.

When anthropologists began to turn their attention to the study of complex contemporary societies, they at first attempted to conduct research using what were called *community studies,* which were similar to the kind of fieldwork they had used to collect data on small-scale societies. In nearly every case the study of social relationships would stop at the edge of the village, much as it had stopped at the edge of the tribal camp. In this way, physi-

Regional systems consist of related communities; villages interact with each other and with a larger urban center. Here, roads lead in all directions from Lier (Lierre), Belgium, connecting the urban center with surrounding farm communities in a panoramic view from 1595.

cal or arbitrary political boundaries were confused with social and economic ones.

Research in village communities was displaced to some extent in the 1960s by the beginning of what has come to be called *urban anthropology*. But in most cases only the site of research had shifted. Believing that cities were the centers of activity, anthropologists continued to situate themselves in one place and study a street gang, a neighborhood, or even a whole city—as a unit in and of itself.

Again, by the 1950s it was apparent to many anthropologists that some of the assumptions inherent in the participant-observer, local community type study were due for reconsideration. The most basic of these assumptions is that intensive study of a single group or community, however small or large, will reveal all the significant dimensions of the culture as a whole. As Smith would later point out, "the standard anthropological monograph on a small community suffers theoretical limitations because of its narrow parochialism, and . . . studies of large-scale, national systems do little to illuminate the lives of people who live in small rural communities—the majority of mankind" (1976, p. 4). Thus, it was realized that in complex societies, study of contexts broader than the local community is crucial. To comprehend all of the dimensions of a *complex society* anthropologists must deal with all levels of interaction, from small-scale communities to the progressively larger units of which they are a part. The ultimate, all-encompassing level, of course, would be the entire international community, consisting of all the societies in the world. However, regional systems, consisting of related communities and their many areas of interaction, are more feasible and realistic. Here we shall discuss the development of the regional approach, which is assuming greater significance, and the application of the anthropological perspective to issues of contemporary urban society.

Toward a Regional Perspective

One of the earliest and most influential attempts to go beyond the local community was Robert Redfield's study of *The Folk Culture of Yucatán* (1941), mentioned in an earlier chapter, in which he posited the connections between what he described as rural, folk culture of a village and the urban, industrial center of which the village was a satellite. As we have pointed out, Redfield contrasted these two different social and cultural settings: He saw the *folk society* as socially satisfying; integrated and stable; and homogeneous and isolated, while he viewed the urban society as disintegrated and constantly changing; heterogeneous; and a part of a larger, even more complex social system.

In later studies Redfield posited the existence of communities halfway between these, those in which the folk society underwent "transformation" to urbanization. In *primary urbanization* the precivilized folk society becomes a peasant society attached to an urban center; the peasant and urban communities that result, however, both "share a common culture." In *secondary urbanization,* external cultural influences alter the folk, peasant, or partly urbanized society, resulting in the creation of "not only a new form of urban life in some part in conflict with local folk cultures but also new social types in both city and country" (Redfield & Singer, 1971, pp. 344–345).

Redfield's model of these different categories of communities and their interconnections—which has come to be known as the *folk-urban continuum* (1960)—stimulated much research on societies in the process of transition from one type to the other. In so doing, his model also called attention to the similar regional approach in his study of an economy based on the export of a single commodity—wool—in the Puno region of southern Peru (1976). These and other analyses demonstrate Smith's point that "the *flows* of goods, services, information, and people through [a] network of centers . . . structure and maintain internodal relations" on a regional basis (1976, p. 8).

Case Studies from a Regional Perspective

In a study of regional cults, Werbner argues that Smith's "level-specific approach ignores activities overriding and not congruent with the boundaries and subdivisions of a nation. Similarly neglected are the phenomena which define international or non-national regions. Theoretically, the approach introduces a bias towards nesting relations and it does not allow for cultural variability, i.e., the variable importance of different conceptions held by the people studied themselves of their fields of relations" (1977, p. xi). Werbner goes on to propose a regional approach "without the three tiered model or its level-specific assumptions." By focusing on religious ideology and change, Werbner and his colleagues demonstrated how a religious cult can be modified by local beliefs and actions, yet integrated with divergent groups on the basis of common premises. Werbner illustrates his approach with a study of the High God cult of Mwali, or Mwari, of southern Africa. Congregations of the cult are found in spatially distinct regions scattered through Zimbabwe, Botswana, Mozambique, and the Transvaal. Each region is not continuous but rather "a set of many separated pieces" (p. 180), and each "extends over thousands of square miles across ethnic, district, and even international boundaries" (pp. 179–180). Werbner demonstrates that when faced with such material, one has no choice but to examine both the narrow range of the cult and its more in-

clusive context. In his words, "The more a cult spreads across major ethnic and political boundaries, the more its organization may have to be variable and its ritual and symbolism transcultural" (p. 179). Therefore it must be studied on multiple levels at the same time.

The value of seeing the region as a system also is shown by English (1966) in his research on settlement and economy in the Kirman basin in southeastern Iran. He points out that social scientists usually have divided society in the Middle East into three sectors: the city, the village, and the tribe.

Invariably, such authors preface their discussions by warning readers that one must *not* view these segments as discrete economic realms and cite examples to illustrate the mutual interdependence of each sphere: city dwellers depend on village-grown crops; villagers receive basic commodities . . . from the city; tribesmen supply wool and milk products to marketplaces in return for grain. Having delivered this warning, these writers proceed to discuss each segment as a self-contained system: cities are viewed as islands in a barren land, linked by networks of roads and caravan trails, and occupied by traders and processors who share in "urban" as opposed to "folk" culture; villages are isolated, self-sufficient, inward-looking peasant communities with few external relations; tribes are ethnic and/or political groups who migrate periodically in prescribed patterns. (p. xvii)

Rejecting this view, English concentrates instead on "the distribution and diversity of settlements and their functional integration in a complex regional organization" (p. xviii). As a result, he is able to make the following points:

1. The existence of Kirman City, the administrative, economic, and social capital of the region, depends on the coordination and exploitation of resources in the surrounding areas and not (as traditionally viewed) on its position on a trade route.

2. The villages in the Kirman basin, like those

in most areas of the Middle East, are not isolated, homogeneous units with bare subsistence economies, as many writers have portrayed them. They differ from each other in size, complexity, and economic basis, and some even have occupational organization structures as complex as that of Kirman City itself.

3. The economic and social arrangements made between landlord and peasant, carpet manager and weaver, and wool merchant and herder are very similar to each other and thus reflect the patterning of the regional system.

4. Modernization throughout the region has impacted more on social patterns than on economic organization.

This is an important study, as it integrates economic and social data from a regional perspective. Similarly, Cohen and Middleton (1970) focused on the political arena from a regional perspective. In our discussion of the politics of new nations in an earlier chapter, we examined the processes by which small groups are sometimes incorporated into nation-states. We see here that analysis of economic, political, religious, as well as more purely social transactions, benefits from the use of a regional perspective. Attention to the environment and ecological niches of different populations also contributes to this perspective. Thus, it is essential to include a regional aspect when analyzing local systems.

Geertz has attempted to put the regional approach into theoretical perspective. He points out that what anthropologists do best is "microsociology" (1972, p. 461), the intensive study of small-scale social systems, and urges that more attention be paid to the transition "from comprehensive ethnography in simple societies . . . to specialized microsociology in complex ones," especially in understanding the kinds of generalizations that can be made on the basis of such studies. As he puts it, anthropologists study

the same sorts of processes in micro that others study in macro. One can study metabolism at the level of the cell, the organism, or in ecology, the community of organisms. And though one gets different sorts of insights from each approach, one doesn't try to argue that a tropical forest is just a huge cell, or a cell a miniature tropical forest. Rather, one tries to make the diverse findings complementary, to shed light on one another in such a way that the general processes of metabolism are better understood. It is no different here: what one learns in Sidi Walu of a hundred souls and what one learns in the Casablanca of several hundred thousand is neither more nor less general than the other. It is just that some things can be learned about a certain problem—here politics and social change—in one place that are difficult or impossible to learn in the other, and vice versa. (1972, p. 462)

Too often anthropologists have assumed that the locality itself, and not what takes place within it, is of primary concern. Thus, the boundaries of the community have all too often become the boundaries of research.

Geertz calls also for (1) the "disaggregation" of "megaconcepts," (pp. 462–464) such as landlord-tenant and urban-rural; (2) abandonment of the tendency to validate hypotheses, often originating in other disciplines; and (3) concentration instead on deriving new conceptualizations. Geertz himself has been making useful contributions to regional studies for many years, and his early study of form and variation in a Balinese village is a classic example (1959).

All of the approaches we have been discussing represent attempts to transcend the local community in order to gain perspective and insight into the patterns and processes of more complex levels of social organization. Ultimately, however, anthropologists must return to a local community to study the influence of the regional system on its beliefs and practices. One does not solve the problem of overemphasizing the locality by overemphasizing the region, the nation, or any other organizational level. The relationships among the various levels are important and must be discerned, but the whole is more than simply the sum of its parts. In other words, while anthropologists use the regional perspective to good advantage, they cannot afford to neglect the local communities in which human beings demonstrate the real events that make up their lives.

Societies in Transition

Throughout this text, culture has been shown to be dynamic. People's designs for living change continually, and so the study of a given cultural phenomenon at one time and place does not necessarily characterize that phenomenon for all times and places. Similarly, societies are in a continual process of transition: external factors such as environmental change, culture contact, and immigration, together with internal factors such as invention, human interaction, and birth- and deathrates, continually alter the nature of any social group. But most studies have not taken the fact of continual culture change into account. However, the one key area in which such alterations have been taken for granted and have been built into every research design is peasant studies. This is because peasant societies have been considered by definition to be in a transitional state of development, somewhere between so-called folk societies and so-called urban societies. The central concept in peasant studies is that of change, frequently broadened to include the regional nature of change. For this reason, it is useful to consider such studies as examples of the kinds of contributions anthropologists have made to understanding the dynamic nature of societies, especially from the perspective of regional considerations.

Peasant Studies

The subsistence basis of *peasant society* is, of course, agriculture, which can readily be distinguished from the horticulture of tribal

In the Andes mountains of Ecuador, the trade network functions through markets held in a different village every day. Here, a bus brings vendors from the previous day's village to the marketplace of Zumbagua, where they will join people from the surrounding district in selling produce, handcrafts, and factory-produced goods. (Bob Kelly, Photo Researchers, Inc.)

societies in its greater productivity, due to more effective techniques for exploiting the environment. But in some ways peasants are not unlike many so-called "primitive" cultivators, since they, too, grow crops mostly for their own consumption. In both, too, predictable food surpluses may allow some members of the community to be non-food producing and become artisans or develop other skills, while receiving food from others in return for their services or products. Despite their often considerable productivity, peasant agriculturists cannot be considered farmers or business-minded. Their concerns are those of householders, not entrepreneurs (Wolf, 1966a, p. 2).

Some anthropologists have distinguished between the two categories, claiming, for example, that peasants constitute "part-societies with part-cultures" (Kroeber 1948, p. 284). Such a statement recognizes the fact that peasant societies form parts of larger, more complex social systems but ignores the fact that a similar case can be made for most, if not all, "primitive" cultivating societies, since very few of these are completely isolated and self-sufficient. Most participate in elaborate and long-established networks of trade and, as we have pointed out in previous chapters, many also interact with neighboring groups in such diverse fields of endeavor as warfare, marriage, and ceremony (Wolf, 1969, pp. 2–3).

How, then, do peasant societies differ from tribal societies? One key difference, it is argued, is in the kinds of interactions with outside groups and their implications for the local community. In tribal societies, as Sahlins (1960, p. 408) points out, because *"de facto* control of the means of production is decentralized, local, and familiar . . . economic relations of coercion and exploitation and the corresponding social relations of dependence and mastery" do not arise. Any surpluses are transferred directly, usually to fulfill kinship or similar intergroup obligations.

In peasant society, on the other hand, *de facto* control of some *critical resource* (as Smith put it) is in the hands of a dominant group. Peasants must transfer their surpluses to the elite in exchange for access to the critical resource, and the ruling group can then use "the surpluses both to underwrite its own standard of living and to distribute the remainder to groups in society that do not farm but must be fed for their specific goods and services in turn" (Wolf, 1966a, pp. 3–4).

Wolf shows that, contrary to widespread notions, the development of cities is not the crucial factor in altering tribal sociopolitical organization, but rather

> the crystallization of executive power. . . . Not the city but the state is the decisive criterion of civilization and it is the appearance of the state which marks the threshold of transition between food cultivators in general and peasants. Thus, it is only when a cultivator is integrated into a society with a state—that is, when the cultivator becomes subject to the demands and sanctions of power-holders outside his social stratum—that we can appropriately speak of peasantry. (p. 11)

However, because of the dynamic nature of social systems, there is no one type of peasantry. As Wolf explains, "our world contain[s] both primitives on the verge of peasantry and full-fledged peasants . . . societies in which the peasant is the chief producer of the store of social wealth and those in which he has been relegated to a secondary position" (p. 12).

Wolf's extensive study, which details both the kinds of relationships that various peasantries have with outside groups and their ways of coping with the resulting pressures, represents a significant contribution to this field. Wolf sees the interaction with outside groups as posing a crucial dilemma for peasants that ultimately is responsible for the constantly changing character of peasant societies. This dilemma is the need to synchronize the demands of the external elite with the requirements of the individual household. In the face of such vicissitudes of life as periodic changes in quantity of production (due to weather, illness, etc.) and greater demands from landlords or priests, peasants have two apparently opposite strategies for coping: increase production or curtail consumption.

An increase in production enables peasants to compete in a market; however, achieving a marketable surplus is difficult because the only real capital of peasants is the physical labor of the household, and they usually hold land under obligation to landlords. Being in an essentially subsistence economy, they also accumulate little cash or other negotiable property. However, as Wolf shows, this can be done when the economic and/or religious power structure that keeps the peasant economically encumbered is weakened, as occurred in sixteenth century England, in China, and in prerevolutionary Russia, accounting for the rise of a wealthy peasantry in those (and other) places.

By means of the alternate strategy, retrenching toward total reliance on the production of the household for all goods and services, peasants can reduce and virtually eliminate their interaction with the outside world, and thus be less subject to the pressures for change imposed from without. Wolf sees this as the explanation for the well-known conservatism of peasantry: "they fear the new as they would fear temptation: Any new novelty may undermine their precarious balance" (p. 16).

Yet even in a retrenchment situation, peasants tend to retain social and ceremonial ties within their own communities. "As long as these can be upheld, a peasant community can ward off the further penetration of outside demands and pressures, while at the same time forcing its more fortunate members to share some of their labor and goods with their less fortunate members" (pp. 16–17).

Wolf shows further that these two strategies, though apparently opposites, are not mutually exclusive. "Periods in which the first strategy is strongly favored may be followed by others when the peasant retrenches and renews his social fabric within a narrower orbit. Similarly, at any given time, there will be some individuals who will risk . . . testing the limits of traditional social ties, while others prefer the security [of] following the norm. . . . A peasantry is always in a dynamic state, moving continuously between two poles in the search for a solution to its basic dilemma" (p. 17).

Through its strategies and, as Wolf argues, supported by its ideological values, peasants interact on regional levels with other similar peasant communities and with various kinds of what Smith referred to as "central places" for religious, marketing, political, or other interactions.

Diaz and Potter similarly stress the relationships with people outside of their immediate communities as the characteristic or defining feature of peasantry. They describe peasant social institutions as "Janus-faced—looking both toward the requirements imposed by the larger political and economic order and toward the customary expectations of the peasant community" (1967, p. 154). They also point out the interrelationships between peasant communities: "People from other villages may be sources of spouses, or they may provide the aid and protection villagers need when they travel away from home," describing the different networks which serve as the axes of peasant life. The economic network, which may be "spread intricately across the countryside, spaced with markets of varied sizes and organization" is comprised "of persons to whom peasants sell their surplus handicrafts and produce, and from whom they purchase the goods that they themselves do not produce" (p. 165). There are also religious networks, such as an area served by a particular shrine or temple, or a pilgrimage route. There are marriage networks that structure kinship patterns; these may intersect the economic or religious networks, as when a marketing area provides the boundaries within which spouses must be selected, or when a ceremonial occasion provides the opportunity for courtship. Or the marriage network may set up special relationships between communities, as in the case of exogamous intermarrying villages. There may be other kinds of networks, such as mutual protection associations or irrigation societies. But above all stands the state-established administrative unit, which creates "political relationships that cut across village boundaries," such as the *municipio* of Mexico or the *mura* of Japan. Potter and Diaz conclude that:

The peasant village is thus clearly not an isolated whole; it has both vertical and horizontal ties extending from the village to the larger society and civilization. . . . it is impossible to understand the social life of any peasant community without taking state policy and its history into account. (p. 167)

Potter also has stressed the transitional nature of peasantry in his analysis of the urban, industrial impact on peasant communities (1967b). His study of rural Communist China (1967a) details the impact of a centralized administration and its revolutionary policies on a quintessentially traditional (and vast) peasantry.

Cultural Brokers

A considerable amount of attention has been paid in anthropological studies of peasantry to *cultural brokers,* the mediators who serve as bridges between the local peasant community and the outside world. This concept was originally put forth by Wolf (1956), who saw cultural brokers as those who "mediate between community-oriented groups in communities and nation-oriented groups which operate primarily through national institutions." Again, cultural brokers "stand guard over the crucial junctures or synapses of relationships which connect the local system to the larger whole." In Mexico, as he shows, historically there have been several categories of individuals who served this function—leaders of Indian communities, owners of haciendas, or political leaders in more recent times. From our own society the local political leader or ward chief in the cities certainly served in such a capacity, mediating between the immigrant ethnic groups (which had been, it must be emphasized, uprooted from peasant communities) and the new urban system of which they had become a part. Similar examples could be cited from numerous societies; however, it is important to recognize that the specific functions served by culture brokers vary with the cultures involved and the specific problems being coped with at a given time.

Silverman, for example, describes what she calls the community-nation mediator in traditional central Italy, where she found that "the concept of the mediator proved to be most pertinent for understanding the relationship of the community to the larger society during a particular period" (1967, p. 280). In the community she studied, the patrons were those individuals who had ties extending beyond the locality, and who, as the only literate members of the community, translated the national culture at the local level and in various ways served as "economic, political, social, and ideological link[s] to the larger society" (p. 289). Because of changes in "the groups which perform[ed] mediation functions" as well as structural changes in the "links between community and nation" following World War II, however, Silverman, concludes that "the mediator represents a general form of community-nation relationship which characterizes an early phase in developing nation-states, and which regularly gives way as integration of the total society advances" (p. 292).

It is not hard to understand why such a role is needed. Peasants attempt to develop relationships with individuals of superior wealth and power to gain economic and political security. In many peasant societies, particularly in Latin America and the Mediterranean, individuals involved enter into *patron-client relationships*. Patrons gain prestige and power and can call on the support due them from their clients in the event of political need. (The discussion of ritual kinship in an earlier chapter illustrated some of these relationships.) As Diaz and Potter (1967, p. 164) point out, cultural brokers "often assume leadership among peasants, exercising power and authority on the levels of society beneath the state administration." And in doing so, according to Diaz and Potter, this group also acts as a buffer, representing the interests of peasant community and state to one another, so that their brokerage is also political in nature.

Léons (1977) has described the rise of one such patron, Juan Mendoza, to a position of provincial political leadership in Bolivia. As a storekeeper, he had built up a network of creditors who became his political followers at a time of revolution and land reform. All followed his lead in voting, giving him the power to determine who would occupy local office. He became the source through which government programs, including land distribution, were delivered to the community and its people, who of course enhanced his power further as he was able to be generous to those who supported him and withhold benefits from his detractors. With a solid mass of voters behind him, Mendoza has been able to negotiate with whatever government came to national power. Léons focuses on the economic networks that made possible Mendoza's rise to power in the first place and those that he developed as his resources accumulated along with his political power. Her analyses of one individual's dealings, within as well as beyond the local community, illustrate how political and economic factors are interwoven and how a cultural—or in this case political—broker functions to relate the community to the region and the nation.

Wolf (1966a), with whom the cultural broker concept originated, applied it further in a discussion of the character of interpersonal relationships—kinship, family, friendship, and patron-client—that span a region. One of his conclusions was the possibility "that complex societies in the modern world differ less in the formal organization of their economic or legal or political systems than in the character of their supplementary interpersonal sets" and that it is these supplementary sets that make possible the functioning of the great institutions" (p. 19).

This approach points the way, for example, to a new way of viewing the family in contemporary society; instead of lamenting the passing of the traditional family, our attention should turn to understanding the ways in which new interpersonal relationships, both within and outside the family, serve to integrate individuals with the institutions of modern society.

Abandoning the "Peasant" Concept

Peasant studies have contributed significantly to the anthropological literature and have served to lift the sights of anthropologists to larger regional issues and interactions. But the question must be asked: Is "peasantry" a category like, for example, hunter-gatherers? The answer must be no. If it were, then all of the societies described as such, from Indonesia to Bolivia, and contemporary China to medieval England, would be much more similar in many more ways than they demonstrably are. These and other societies are indeed complex, in the sense that they are parts of larger economic, political, and cultural systems; but they have very few specific characteristics in common. The typologies to which peasant communities have been assigned by Wolf (1966b) and others imply that they have in common cultural form and/or content in addition to certain economic/subsistence patterns and that these differ significantly from those of other types of societies. These implications, however, are not substantiated by ethnographic evidence (Miller, 1976). For example, family farming is found in many other societies than those considered in peasant studies, including so-called folk societies, as well as both modern capitalist and communist states. Then again, the relationships of the various so-called peasant communities to regional markets, national economies, or regional or national cults and religions, have been very different in different times and places. In fact, the variability of "peasant" societies may be due as much to historical considerations as to ecological and cultural factors. Comparisons based on a limited number of similarities in economic structures may well be useful, but typologies formed on this basis are probably misleading.

In fact, many of these studies seem to show an actual bias against their subjects in applying to them such patronizing terms as *limited good, little tradition,* or *patron-client.* This would seem to represent an example of *ethnocentrism* in the very discipline that coined the term to combat such attitudes. It is almost as though the analysts are rejecting the cultural patterns they observe, perhaps reflecting the contemporary bias against people who appear to allow themselves to be exploited. If they are seeing their subjects as representatives of an earlier, less developed stage in our own civilization, it is a curious holdover of the kind of ethnocentrism that produced the evolutionary models of a century ago.

But the strongest reason for abandoning the concept of peasantry is that it is a construct that anthropologists have imposed on their data. Definitions of peasants are impossible precisely because they are arbitrarily imposed from without and not based on true similarities. Finally, the identification of peasants as part-society, part-culture can only inhibit an open-minded approach to study of the communities concerned (Miller, 1976, p. 21). No society is ever part-anything; every society is a coherent whole to those participating in it. And since all societies are in dynamic process, there is no point in singling out so-called peasant communities as prime examples of transition.

This is not to suggest that the studies cited here have failed to contribute significantly to anthropological understanding. They certainly have contributed, as our discussion has clearly indicated. But let us call them what they truly are—studies of family-farm-based communities within regional systems. Without the imposition of arbitrary constructs, the data should speak for themselves. It is more important to understand differences, and the reasons for and implications of their existence, than it is to force data into artificial typologies.

Urban Anthropology

As anthropologists followed their objects of study from rural hinterlands into cities, and as they began to train their sights on their own culture (and on the communities surrounding their universities), there developed a subdiscipline that came by the late 1960s to be known as urban anthropology. Peasant studies played a key role in this development, since they inevitably led to studies of what Geertz calls the "post-peasant problem" (1962, p. 5). Here anthropology entered a whole new arena, the study of modernization, the coming together of old societies to form new states, and the kinds of human interactions that take place in today's ultra-complex urban communities.

However, it has never been quite clear whether the proper study of this subdiscipline should be the urbanization process itself, the comparison of different kinds of cities around the world, or the application of anthropological insight and perspective to urban problems, particularly in American culture.

Even before the peasant studies ushered in by Redfield's work, anthropological methodology was being applied to selected communities within modern, industrial nations. These community studies, as they came to be called, often crossed the boundary between anthropology and sociology, as in Warner's *Yankee City* (1963, based on work begun in 1930) or the Lynds' studies of Muncie, Indiana (1959, 1963). Later studies using similar techniques were those done in a city neighborhood by sociologists Whyte (1955) and Gans (1962), while anthropologists Vidich and Bensman (1958) applied the same methodology to a community in New York State, examining its ties to the wider regional and national scene. Community-study methods were subsequently applied to urban centers in developing nations, which continue to be an important area of investigation.

Archaeological studies of early civilizations and the earliest urban settlements, which seek to establish the relationship between the development of cities and economic and sociopolitical processes have contributed also to the anthropological understanding of urbanism.

Rethinking Urban Anthropology

A basic problem in defining the purview of urban anthropology has been, as Eames and Goode observe, "the Western ethnocentrism of many concepts dealing with the urban." As a consequence of this bias, no "universal, culture-free definition of urban centers" has been offered, and studies often suffer from an underlying anti-urbanism (1977, p. 53). (This is, of course, not peculiar to anthropologists; anti-urbanism appears to be a paradoxical, permeating, and persistent American characteristic.)

The archaeological perspective is essential to remind us that for most of pre-history and history, the city has been non- or pre-industrial. London in Shakespeare's time and Edo under the shogunate in Japan are only two cities that existed for many centuries prior to their present-day high degree of industrialization (Edo is now Tokyo). Many examples of nonindustrial cities can also be cited: Benin in Africa, "Old" Delhi in India, ancient Rome, Ur in Sumer, Tikal of the Mayans.

Sjoberg has conceived the ancient city as primarily a locus of governmental and religious functions and only secondarily as a center of economic function (1960). Traditional cities still exist, of course, in many parts of the world, and they have been and are being fruitfully studied. But Sjoberg's description of the pre-industrial city is an idealization that suffers from the same kind of problems as those noted before for peasant typologies. For most of the defining characteristics he cites, exceptions can also be cited (Keesing, 1976). Even in its pre-industrial forms, the city is too complex for simple typologies.

Cities as Subjects or Settings?

Anthropologists who use the city as their center of investigation have many different concerns. For some, cities are themselves subjects to be studied. But for others, as Keesing states, "cities [are] *settings;* one studies a neighborhood, a housing project, a street corner, as before one had studied a village or a band—as a microcosm, a social world in miniature." The city as a *setting* and understanding "how cities create new modes of human experience" (1976, p. 506) are precisely what most urban anthropology is all about.

Eames and Goode note three different types of urban studies in anthropology: the migration of peasants to cities, urban problems, and ethnographies of selected urban settings or groups—in all of which the city is used as a setting. But mention should also be made of studies in which the city itself is the

Long before the industrial urban complexes of modern times, the pre-industrial city was a sprawling, densely-populated center serving many functions, as this view of London and Westminster in 1584 demonstrates. (The Bettman Archive)

subject, such as Fox's *Urban Anthropology* (1977). The most representative example of migration-to-cities studies is that of William Mangin (1970), which contains articles on the movements of rural villagers to urban centers in the major continents of the world, with particular emphasis on Latin America. These migrations are frequently to slum areas of the city, and the life in these areas is depicted and described, along with the articulation of slums with larger urban environments.

Migration studies thus lead directly to problem-oriented research in cities. A notable example is the work of Oscar Lewis, who went from studying *Life in a Mexican Village* (1963) to studying the urban poor. Lewis conceptualized a "culture of poverty" based on his studies of Mexican and Puerto Rican families, which he held was characteristic of urban poor in many parts of the world. As a scheme for viewing similarities that cross-cut cultural boundaries, Lewis's concept has been useful, but it has also been controversial with respect to both topic and method. Valentine, for example, criticizes both Lewis's notions that urban poverty is inevitably self-perpetuating and the idea that there is a distinct poverty culture that transcends national/cultural boundaries. In *Culture and Poverty* (1968) Valentine provides alternative ways of viewing poverty and the poor.

Undoubtedly, many of today's urban problems, not only in the United States but throughout the world, are a direct result of

Among the concerns of urban anthropology are population subgroups of the city. The world of unemployed black men who spend their days "hanging out" on street corners, such as in this scene, is explored in *Tally's Corner,* **a classic ethnography.** (Jim Cron, Monkmeyer)

rural-to-urban migration. Uprooted from the relatively homogeneous societies with simpler social and economic structure and thrust into urban settings, individuals discover that familiar rules and relationships no longer apply. With traditional networks disrupted, new support systems must be devised. The language barrier is only one of many cultural hurdles that must be crossed by most such migrants. Their accustomed techniques for manipulating available resources are no longer workable. (They were often no longer workable in the traditional setting either; an extensive period of economic malfunctioning—due to population pressures, weather conditions, or other factors—is the customary prelude to rural-to-urban migration.)

The third type of urban study identified by Eames and Goode, ethnography applied to a selected urban subgroup, is well illustrated by Elliot Liebow's work among unemployed black men in Washington, D.C., *Tally's Corner* (1967). Another classic urban ethnography is that of James Spradley, who studied alcoholics, primarily in Seattle. His work, entitled *You Owe Yourself a Drunk* (1970), attracted a lot of attention not only in anthropology but in other disciplines as well. Both of these studies were based on *intensive interviewing* and on extensive participant-observation. Both attempted to grasp the participants' point of view (the "native" point of view as we describe it in traditional anthropological studies), and both succeeded to

the extent that order and rationality became apparent where disorder and irrationality had appeared before to an outside observer. Both studies also identified the structures of interaction between the populations concerned and particular elements of the broader society of which these participants formed a part. And both call for a new perception of the world as lived by the people they studied, identifying the external constraints that give life among these natives its distinctive character.

Urban anthropology is itself developing subfields. Two that are assuming particular importance at present are ethnic studies and the related development of medical anthropology. Urban ethnic studies developed from studies of migrations to cities, since the ethnic subgroups clustered in urban settings originated as transplanted "peasant" or "folk" groups. A key example of how traditional anthropological subject matter became a subject for urban anthropology is the case of Ameri-

The anthropological perspective can enhance our understanding of the components of urban problems and assist in devising solutions. Providing preventive medical care for all segments of a diverse population is one such problem. Here, residents of a New York City neighborhood wait for free medical tests given in a mobile van. (Irene Bayer, Monkmeyer)

can Indians. And so-called ethnic studies have been spurred by government policies of funding programs for minority groups and by minority competition for this attention. The anthropological perspective has made a great contribution to understanding in this area.

Medical anthropology is concerned with provision of modern medical care to the various ethnic groups comprising contemporary (although not necessarily urban) society, and it is thus problem oriented. But studies of the perception of illness, reactions to medical intervention, the expression of pain, and how illness is managed in the native cultural setting must be drawn from traditional ethnographic materials or investigated directly using ethnographic techniques (Grossman, 1976).

Similarly problem-oriented is the exploration of food habits and nutrition from an anthropological perspective. In part this, too, is an outgrowth of ethnic studies, but it has important application to problems of world nutrition and food supply. The relationship of food habits to a variety of ecological and social factors has been touched on earlier in this text.

Current issues, rather than social problems as such, are also leading to new areas for urban anthropological investigation. The theorizing and publications that have come out of the women's movement have led to the realization that in every society women are enculturated differently from men, and that cultures in effect consist of subcultures in respect to the two sexes. Lakoff's study of women's language in our society (1973) is a case in point. Women anthropologists today are bringing a new perspective to traditional topics and are, for example, engaged in such projects as comparison of women's roles in traditional societies. An early woman-centered study was Laura Bohannan's (1949) analysis of Dahomeyan marriages, which focused on rights to women and the status of women (and their children) as a consequence of different marital situations. Even earlier, of course,

were Mead's studies of child-rearing and adolescence, which gave full emphasis to female development and women's roles (1928, 1930).

Similarly, the development of interest in gerontology in recent years has led to ethnographic studies of the elderly, such as that of Myerhoff and Tufte in a community center for Jewish senior citizens in Venice, California (1975). An early antecedent was the extensive cross-cultural compilation and analysis of Simmons (1970) on *The Role of the Aged in Primitive Society*.

From Urban to Global Perspective

Studies in and of the city inevitably have multidisciplinary implications; sociology, psychology, and economics are brought to bear along with anthropology. Anthropology in its urban focus can serve as a synthesizing agent, marshaling the whole range of social science approaches without restriction. There is no particular virtue in maintaining distinctions between disciplines. As Eames and Goode state, "There will be an overlap in those segments of all social science disciplines focused on the city. The mature development of anthropology as well as urban anthropology demands that we not waste so much energy on concern over our domain or turf" (1977, p. 17).

The important point is that, no matter what the subject of study, the anthropological perspective is crucial. The recent emergence of urban anthropology may seem to be a variety of things, with no clearly defined area of study, but it can lead to fruitful insights. As Keesing says, "An anthropology that studies urban life in comparative perspective can perhaps fulfill in this new realm the historical role of anthropology in the social sciences: sorting the culture-bound from the universal, and hence pushing toward a genuinely comparative understanding of human ways" (1976, p. 506).

But it is becoming increasingly obvious that in shifting the focus from local, rural communities to large urban centers, anthropologists can repeat the same mistake of myopia. Rather than make cities themselves the center of study, human populations of cities, along with their ties to rural homelands or foreign countries, should constitute the field of study. Extension of study to fill a regional framework would be valid whether the site of the study is the United States, Latin America, Europe, Africa, Asia, or Oceania.

The regional and world perspective proposed here would locate any study in a larger framework incorporating all the factors that play a role in the lives of the people concerned. It is not the focus of study that should necessarily be changed, but rather the scope of interpretation. The methodology would continue to be what Geertz calls *microsociology,* carried out with participant-observer techniques, but the data elicited would be interpeted in broader terms than is generally now being done. As Redfield said in 1956: "I

Toward a global perspective . . . (Marylin Yee, *The New York Times*)

624 think we shall come to study regional systems. We shall study such systems, not, as we now tend to do, from the viewpoint of some one small local community looking outward, but from the viewpoint of an observer who looks down upon the whole larger regional system" (cited in Smith, 1976, p. 3). It is time that this prophetic vision of the potentialities of anthropological research in today's world be realized.

Summary

1. In recent years anthropological studies have moved beyond their traditional focus on a local community to the larger region with which the community is integrated.

2. Redfield's *The Folk Culture of Yucatán,* an early study emphasizing links between a village and its region, contrasted the homogeneous, stable folk culture of the village with the heterogeneous, disintegrated urban culture of the city that served as its political, religious, and commercial center. Redfield's concept of a folk-urban continuum held that there was a definite tendency toward urbanization, and that peasant societies were in an intermediate stage of transition from one to the other. This model inspired a number of so-called "peasant studies," which detailed the networks by which peasant communities in different parts of the world are tied to the regions in which they are situated.

3. Level-specific regional analysis has been proposed by Smith as a methodological approach, the levels being local, regional, and national. This approach views communities in terms of their spatial arrangement vis-à-vis a "central place" that serves as hub to a number of interconnected satellite localities. Regional studies of various kinds have been applied productively to analyses of religious cults, economic systems, political organization, and social stratification.

4. Peasant societies have been studied as agricultural, family-farm-based, and held in a dependent relationship to an external dominant group that has control over a critical resource such as land or access to markets. Peasants have been described as "Janus-faced," looking both to the impositions by the outside forces and to the requirements of their own community.

5. The interactions of peasants and the dominant elite has been described as a client-patron relationship. Cultural brokers are individuals who mediate between the peasant community and the outside world, usually in such areas as commerce and politics.

6. However, in all other respects, so-called peasant communities are quite varied in different places and at different times in the human past, and thus there is really no one socio/political/economic system that can be singled out as "peasantry." So-called peasant societies coexist within modern industrial states, both capitalist and communist, as well as in developing nations. Because much of the terminology applied to peasant societies seems to reflect an ethnocentric bias on the part of researchers, and because categories are artificial constructs imposed from without, the concept of *peasantry* as an economic/social cultural unit should be abandoned.

7. The subdiscipline of urban anthropology developed out of community studies, as anthropologists followed the migrations of their traditional subjects of study from rural hinterlands into cities and as they turned their attention to the societies of which they themselves are a part. New perspectives and areas of investigation are still in the process of development.

Epilogue

IN an earlier chapter we discussed the two crises for anthropology identified by Claude Lévi-Strauss in 1967. The first stems from a drastic change in the anthropologist's laboratory. Since World War II, small isolated groups of primitive people, once favorite objects of study, have nearly disappeared. Some of these primitive groups were reduced by maltreatment on the part of colonial powers or by infectious diseases introduced from the outside world. But even the survivors among these peoples have not emerged unaltered from their encounters with representatives of more technologically developed societies. As Lévi-Strauss notes, the result of Western contact with primitive groups has been a transformation in these once isolated cultures. In effect, all humans now seem close to becoming members of one civilization based on Western technology.

The second crisis facing anthropologists today is the increasing hostility shown them by third and fourth world peoples. This crisis is a product of anthropology's history. In the past, anthropologists came to be identified with colonial powers, even as they sought to avoid this identification. Furthermore, they sometimes treated the people they had come to study as "scientific objects" rather than as independent human beings with sensitive feelings. Viewed in this light, one can readily understand how resentment toward anthropological fieldwork developed.

Both of these crises have affected anthropologists' ability to gather data for analysis. But there also exists a crisis in anthropology at a more theoretical level; that is, at the level of analysis. The approaches of holism (seeing an overall picture), fieldwork, and comparison, once the distinct characteristics of anthropology, have now been adopted by such other disciplines as economics, sociology, and psychology. As researchers in the social sciences came to recognize the interrelationship of economic, social, and political processes, the idea of anthropology as a separate, well-defined field has been called into question (Kaplan & Manners, 1972). In fact, many studies published by anthropologists today include strong doses of related fields, from economics to political science, in their analyses (Needham, 1970).

With primitive societies practically vanished, many anthropologists have changed the focus of their studies in recent years. Some have begun to investigate small units within large industrial societies, such as urban neighborhoods or workers in a factory or hospital. Others have attempted to analyze larger units, even whole nations or regions, while continuing to use the same holistic approach once employed to study small communities. And still other researchers have focused on important or powerful groups within a complex society, hoping in this way to understand many of the hidden factors controlling large-scale systems (Kaplan & Manners, 1972).

Thus, anthropologists have shifted the directions of their studies both as a result of changes in field conditions and in response to changes in their adoption of theory from other social sciences. They have also altered their research techniques in response to the resentment shown to them by new nations. In general, anthropologists have become more concerned with the way in which their fieldwork may disrupt or harm the cultures they are investigating.

One of the most important ethical difficulties anthropologists have faced in recent years is related to the question of work undertaken for government agencies. On occasion, governments have used the results of anthropological fieldwork as a source of intelligence information. Once gathered, this information has been kept secret and used to direct political and military operations in foreign countries. In 1971, the American Anthropological Association responded to this problem by adopting the Principles of Professional Responsibility, insisting that all research results obtained by anthropologists be available to the public (American Anthropological Association, 1973, p. 1). This position taken against secrecy may demonstrate to the developing world that anthropologists today do not intend to be used as representatives of colonial powers.

Besides recognizing the rights and independence of nations in the process of modernization, the 1971 statement of principles also emphasizes the rights of individuals under investigation. According to the guidelines of the statement, anthropologists have a duty to explain the purpose of their studies to subjects and to respect their privacy. Of course, such guidelines are not always easy to apply in fieldwork, as a recent book on the ethical dilemmas of anthropology (Rykiewich & Spradley, 1976) demonstrates. For example, one researcher found many difficulties in studying marriage and family behavior in a small elite group in Western Africa. The topic she was interested in was itself very sensitive and required keeping information confidential. When writing a report on her fieldwork, she realized that many of her subjects would eventually read the results, and so she felt obligated to not only disguise identities but also tone down her findings (Harrell-Bond, 1976).

Another ethical problem in anthropological fieldwork arises when the researcher takes a political or moral position on the events he or she is in the process of recording. For example, an anthropologist studying the inhabitants of the Marshall Islands in the Pacific found himself increasingly drawn into disputes about whether the islands should seek independent status or permit the development of large American military installations. Although, as a professional researcher, he felt it would be best to remain neutral, he did develop strong opinions against the American military presence. Later, he felt that he could have helped the Marshallese make a wise decision by discussing politics more openly with them (Rynkiewich, 1976). Thus, while it is possible to state as a general principle that anthropologists should not interfere in the internal affairs of the societies they study (Beals, 1969), in practice, neutrality is not always easy to maintain.

Working under government contract, maintaining the confidentiality of sources, and dealing with one's own political opinions in the field—these are day-to-day ethical problems for an anthropologist. On a more theoretical level, the ethical problems posed by the practice of anthropology and the other social sciences have recently come under discussion. As noted by Lévi-Strauss, anthropologists have often tended to treat the people they study as "scientific objects," and not as human beings involved in a struggle for existence. As one remedy for this prejudiced outlook, he recommended that third world anthropologists come to study Western cultures. Certainly such a program would reverse the traditional situation of Westerners as observers and third world people as objects studied. Similarly, one sociologist recently stated that researchers in his field need to stop considering humans as two different and unequal breeds: those who investigate and those who are the objects of the investigations. He adds that every study in the social sciences involves the interaction between the researcher and those who are studied. Thus, the results of a research project in the social sciences can reveal as much about the culture and the values of the investigator as about the culture and values of those under examination (Gouldner, 1970).

Furthermore, if all research results are influenced by the values of the investigator, then it should be the investigator's responsibility to understand exactly how his or her views affect what is seen. This idea of social sciences committed to values is of course sharply different from traditional notions about the possibility and desirability of a completely value-free or objective approach (Gouldner, 1970).

In some respects, the recognition that their findings are often colored by their own views may make anthropologists less convinced that they can offer the right answers to political or social problems that involve conflicting values. On the other hand, there is no reason why this recognition of a commitment to values should prevent anthropologists from contributing to the discussion of public policy. In fact, the principles adopted by the American Anthropological Association in 1971 affirm that anthropologists have a duty to help develop an "adequate definition of reality" on which public policy can be based. (When offering advice, of course, anthropologists need to be honest about the limitations in their knowledge and in the methodology of their discipline.)

One of the ways in which anthropologists have undertaken to help formulate policies is through the analysis of future trends. Naturally, there are difficulties involved in attempting to describe the future on the basis of anthropological insights gained through research. A student of the future must be able to focus on those present trends that will have the most importance for later events, and these are not easy to recognize. A second type of difficulty arises when anthropologists or other social scientists are asked to help formulate plans to improve social conditions, such as poverty, unemployment, or white-collar crime. Such planning often involves the adoption of a specific value system. In effect, anthropologists may be asked to set cultural goals for societies whose members hold a wide variety of beliefs. Of course, the ability and the right of any one person or group of persons to define such goals is frequently questioned (Kaplan & Manners, 1972).

On the other hand, it seems likely that people will always spend a significant amount of time and energy planning for the future, and there is no reason why anthropologists should not play an important role in this endeavor. In fact, as Margaret Mead has pointed out, anthropological knowledge has some special contributions to make to *futuristics*, the science of the future. Anthropologists, she writes, have studied humankind over very long periods of time and thus have gained insight into the way innovation has changed pace. The rapid population growth following the development of agriculture and the accelerating rate of technological change since the beginning of the Industrial Revolution two centuries ago are both familiar phenomena to the anthropologist. By a process of comparison or analogy, anthropologists may be able to develop a similar understanding of the rapidly accelerating changes that may occur in the future. Second, the ability of anthropologists to deal with an entire culture at once, considering all its aspects, may make them particularly suited to analyze the global problems of the future (Mead, 1971).

The publication of Alvin Toffler's *Future Shock* in 1970 marked the beginning of a widespread awareness of the special qualifications of social scientists for the analysis of the future. Yet, at the same time, there are researchers who dispute the idea that futuristics can merely borrow methods from such existing disciplines as anthropology. According to this view, future rates of change *cannot* be studied simply on the basis of the past, as proposed by Margaret Mead. Margoroh Maruyama, for example, argues that it is the unprecedented event that determines the future. Thus, researchers in futuristics must be occasionally capable of abandoning all assumptions in order to imagine completely different rates and types of development. Nevertheless, this capacity for imagination cannot become just a tendency toward fantasy. The imaginative predictions and solutions to future problems need to be grounded in a scientist's and experimentalist's ability to develop realistic accounts of events. It is perhaps not surprising then that most early studies of the future have dealt with technological and economic trends. It is only recently that topics with less technical content and greater value orientation, such as cultural aspects of future society, have been investigated (Maruyama, 1971).

Confronting the ethical problems of fieldwork and focusing their analytical skills on future trends and problems are two important responses on the part of anthropologists to the crises in their discipline. But it may be safely predicted that while anthropology will continue to change its focus and its techniques, its basic aims will not be discarded. As Lévi-Strauss wrote in 1967, anthropology has always helped to expand our comprehension of humanity. There will no doubt continue to be a need for anthropologists to aid in the processes of communication and interpretation.

Glossary

abiotic features the nonliving parts of the environment, including temperature, precipitation, humidity, soil types, and solar radiation.

acclimatization the ability of an individual's phenotype to change in response to environmental forces.

Acheulean tradition a toolmaking tradition that first appeared about 1.2 million years B.P. in the Olduvai beds and persisted until about 100,000—70,000 B.P., when it was replaced by the Mousterian tradition. It is characterized by the hand ax and the soft-hammer technique.

adapids Eocene primates, probably ancestral to modern lemurs.

adaptation the ability of a living organism to maintain or regain stability under conditions of environmental change.

adaptive radiation rapid speciation, which often occurs as organisms adapt to environments where there are many potential but unoccupied niches.

administration the conducting of public affairs by those who have gained that power.

Aegyptopithecus an arboreal Oligocene primate with both primitive and advanced traits that

suggest it is on or near the line leading from the omomyids to modern apes and humans.

aesthetics the study of beauty and of psychological responses to it.

affinal kin individuals who are legally related through marriage.

affinity relationship by marriage.

age grade a category of persons arranged according to age only.

age set a group of members of a given age grade who pass together through various life stages.

agnatic descent *see* patrilineal descent.

agriculture intensive plant cultivation using technological means such as plows.

allele any of the genes controlling alternative forms of the same trait, as the genes for green and yellow pea color in pea plants. Alleles are found at the same locus on homologous chromosomes.

Allen's rule the principle that short-limbed animals are more likely to be found in cold climates, while animals with long limbs are more commonly found in warm climates. Trait distribution studies have given support to Allen's rule.

allopatric speciation speciation that occurs

629

when part of an expanding population moves to a new area, thereby creating geographic separation between the new and the old groups.

ambilocal residence a pattern in which a newly married couple is expected to live for a period of time with or near the bride's parents and for another period of time with or near the groom's parents.

amino acids simple acids that form the basic structural units of proteins.

anagenic evolution the persistence of a population as a single evolutionary unit through time.

anaptomorphids a varied mixture of Eocene primates that ate both insects and fruit.

ancestor-focused group descent group that traces descent to a common ancestor.

angiosperms flowering plants, shrubs, and trees.

Anthropoidea a suborder of the order *Primates* whose members include monkeys, apes, and humans.

anthropological spatial theory a spatial theory based on the premise that spatial patterns are the result of culturally established beliefs about how a society should organize itself.

anthropology the organized study of human beings.

anthropometry the study of the measurements of the human body.

anvil a rock against which a stone being flaked is struck.

arboreal tree-living.

archaeological culture a grouping of artifacts that reappears consistently in a number of similar dwellings or sites.

archaeology the study of the history, lifestyles, and processes of change in prehistoric human cultures.

archaeomagnetic dating a method for dating the age of cultural artifacts involving an analysis of changes in the earth's magnetic field as reflected in the orientation of minerals in pottery samples.

archaic tradition one of two major traditions of the Mesolithic Age in North America. The archaic tradition began about 9,000 years B.P. in the Eastern woodlands of North America and lasted until about 4,000—3,000 years B.P.

artifact an article made or used by humans.

assemblage a group of subassemblages that show the influence of cultural patterns in an entire community.

attribute a significant trait of an object made by humans.

attribute analysis a method for organizing the remains of an archaeological culture involving the analysis of the significant traits of each artifact, which are regarded as clues to culturally patterned behaviors.

Aurignacian tradition an Upper Paleolithic toolmaking tradition of unknown origin that lasted from about 33,000 to 25,000 years B.P.

Australopithecus africanus The earliest of the African gracile hominids, found in South Africa and probably in East Africa as well.

Australopithecus boisei a later East African robust hominid.

Australopithecus habilis The gracile East African hominid. Holders of the two-lineage hypothesis place it in the same genus as *A. africanus*.

Australopithecus robustus An African robust hominid found at Swartkrans and in East Africa as well. Thought by some to have been an ancestor of *Australopithecus boisei*.

autecology the study of growth and aging of the individual and its interactions with the environment.

authority the institutionalized right to take control and to take certain actions; it represents rules, procedures, and accepted actions considered binding when applied within a given society.

avunculocal residence the pattern of residence in which the newly married couple lives with or near the groom's mother's brother.

baboon any of a largely terrestrial group of Old World monkeys found throughout Africa and on the Arabian peninsula.

backed blade a specialized Upper Paleolithic blade tool with one dulled and one sharpened edge, useful in general cutting and scraping.

balanced polymorphism the stabilization of the frequency of contrasting alleles that occurs when a heterozygote is advantageous to the population.

balanced reciprocity an exchange transaction in which one expects goods or services of roughly equal value in return for what one gives.

band the basic unit of human society that existed before about 12,000 years B.P. The only subunit of these egalitarian groups was the family or groups of related families held together by kinship and marriage bonds. Leadership was not institutionalized. Or, more simply, a small group of families, numbering 50 to 100 persons, with simple political organization.

basic personality structure the cluster of tendencies common to the personalities of individuals who shared early experiences as a result of being brought up in the same culture.

behavior system a set of activities that have a

functional relationship to one another. Examples are feeding and communication.

belief   statements that are generally held to be true by the members of a given society.

Bergmann's rule   the principle that large animals are better adjusted to cold climates than small animals. Trait distribution studies have tended to confirm Bergmann's rule.

Beringia   the continental shelf beneath the Bering Strait that was temporarily exposed as expanding glaciers trapped normally circulating water as ice and caused sea levels to drop. Upper Paleolithic groups apparently migrated across Beringia from Siberia to Alaska.

bilateral descent   the rule of descent, used in our society, in which the individual traces his or her ancestry through lineal relatives of both sexes.

biolocal residence   the pattern of residence in which the newly married couple has a choice of living with or near the parents or kin group of either the bride or groom.

biomass   the total mass of living tissue at a given trophic level.

biospecies   a reproductively isolated population of living organisms capable of breeding successfully with one another.

biotic diversity   the number of different kinds of life forms in an area.

biotic features   the living parts of the environment.

bipedalism   use of only the two back limbs in locomotion.

bipolar working   a method of removing flakes by striking a stone held against an anvil, producing percussion effects at both ends of the flake.

blade   long, thin flake with parallel sides characteristic of the Upper Paleolithic toolmaking tradition.

borer   a sharp-pointed Upper Paleolithic blade tool probably used to drill holes in wood, bone, shells, or skins.

B.P.   an abbreviation for the phrase "before present." Anthropologists have established the year 1950 as the "present," or base, year for their calculations.

brachiation   arboreal locomotory type in which the animal swings from branch to branch, using only its hands and arms for support.

breccia   a matrix of fossilized bone and limestone. Many of the South African hominid fossils have been found in this material, which makes them hard to date.

bridewealth   goods and/or valuables given to the bride's kin group by the groom or his kin group.

Bronze Age   the prehistoric period immediately following the Neolithic Age. It was characterized by the use of bronze as the chief metal in the art of metallurgy, which developed during that time.

burin   tool characteristic of the Upper Paleolithic, used to cut and shape wood and bone.

buttress   a thickening of the bone as an adaptation to greater strength. The human lower jaw, for example, is buttressed with the structure forming the chin.

canines   cone-shaped teeth between the incisors and the premolars, used to grip food during mastication and for threatening displays.

capital   equipment and supplies used to produce more goods.

carbon 14 dating   a method used for dating the age of an archaeological site. It involves measuring how much of the heavy carbon isotope C^{14} is present in an archaeological sample.

carnivore   a flesh-eating animal.

Carpolestidae   a late Paleocene family of the superfamily *Plesiadapoidea*.

caste   a culturally and socially distinct group whose membership is determined by birth and that is assigned a particular position in the social hierarchy.

Catarrhini   one of two infraorders in the suborder *Anthropoidea*, consisting of the Old World primates: Old World monkeys, apes, and humans.

catastrophism   Georges Cuvier's nineteen-century theory that periodic castrophes killed all existing species, preserving their remains as fossils, and allowing the earth to be populated again by new divine creations.

centralization   part of Flannery's explanation of state formation. Centralization refers to the degree to which the various subsystems of the society are linked to the highest controlling bodies.

central place subtheory   a subtheory of the economic spatial theory based on the premise that in economically sophisticated urban communities, least-cost distribution of goods and services will dictate the development of a network of smaller sites spaced in a hexagonal pattern around a large central site.

Cercopithecoidea   a superfamily in the suborder *Anthropoidea*, consisting of the Old World monkeys.

cerebellum   the center of muscular coordination, which lies at the base of the brain.

cerebral cortex   the heavily convoluted outer layer that overlies the rest of the human brain. It is the center of motor control, speech, memory, association of new experiences with old, and the integration of sensory information.

ceremonial center typically a cluster of temples and related buildings that seem to have been designed for religious purposes rather than as dwelling places for a large number of people. Ceremonial centers were a feature of Mesoamerican civilizations.

chiefdom a form of prestate social organization that first appeared in the Near East around 7,500 years B.P. Chiefdoms are often theocracies with a ruler or member of his family serving as a high religious official. The leader's power is a function of his position rather than his personality. Social stratification is present, as is part-time economic specialization.

childhood determinism the notion that childhood training shapes adult personality.

chimpanzee largely arboreal ape found in western and central Africa.

chopper a heavy, primitive pebble tool having one or two edges used for chopping.

chopper-tool culture one of two different cultural traditions that emerged from the Oldowan tradition.

chromosomes the long threadlike structures in the cell nucleus that contain the genetic material in the form of DNA.

chronometric dating dating that measures a deposit's distance in time from the present. Also called *absolute dating.*

circumscription theory Robert Carneiro's explanation of the evolution of complex societies. When growing populations that are geographically circumscribed (set off by geographical barriers that severely limit the population's access to other lands) or socially circumscribed (prevented from moving by the surrounding populations) fight one another for scarce resources, defeated populations become part of a larger state.

city a central place that performs economic and political functions for the surrounding area.

civilization a society characterized by the presence of cities or large towns that are inhabited by people who are citizens of some kind of legal commonwealth. Civilization has also been more vaguely defined as a society with sophisticated artistic, architectural, philosophical, economic, and political features.

cladogenic evolution evolution in which the original population splits into two or more distinct biological units.

clan a unilineal descent group in which relationships between members cannot be demonstrated and are simply assumed; clans often trace their descent to an ancestor in the distant past.

class a group that shares the same social or economic status.

classic Neandertals one of two groups of late archaics referred to in the pre-Neandertal theory. According to the theory, classic Neandertals were isolated by glacial advances in Western Europe and developed into a specialized form that could survive in the harsh climate.

cleaver a variation on the Acheulean hand ax. The cleaver has three cutting edges and may have been used in chopping, hacking, and prying apart carcasses.

cline a gradual shift in gene frequencies over a stretch of territory.

Clovis tradition the earliest tradition of points in the New World. Also called the Llano tradition.

coercion model of social order model based on the belief that order is a product of force and constraint of conflicting elements in society.

coevolution an evolutionary association between two populations so close that a change in one niche immediately redefines the other.

cognitive anthropology *see* ethnoscience.

cognitive dissonance inconsistency between an individual's outlook or self-image and new experiences or situations.

collateral relatives kin who are not related in a direct biological line, such as father's brother or mother's sister.

community a group of interrelated populations that exist in a definable area.

comparative anatomy the systematic comparison of the bodily structures of organisms. The discipline is useful to physical anthropologists in reconstructing fossils, inferring structure-function relationships, and ascertaining phylogenetic relationships among species.

complementary filiation kin relationships through the parent who does not determine descent.

complex genetic trait a phenotype controlled by a large number of alleles at many loci.

composite tools tools having several parts. Such tools were first used during the Mousterian Era.

conjugal family family arrangement consisting of two mates of opposite sex and their offspring.

consanguineal kin individuals who are biologically related by "blood."

consensus model of social order model based on the belief that order results from the general agreement of the members of society on a set of values that are more important to them than any differences of opinion among them.

consumer an organism that gets its energy from

complex compounds. Primary consumers get these compounds by eating plants; secondary consumers eat primary consumers.

continental drift the gradual movement of land masses on plates of the earth's crust, beginning approximately 200 million years ago.

controlled comparison a comparative method of study that considers together only groups that show strong social or cultural similarities.

convergence evolutionary trend that occurs when two unrelated species or groups of species independently evolve similar biological and behavioral characteristics because of the similarity of their niche structure.

craniometry the descriptive analysis of skulls.

Cretaceous Period the period in the earth's history extending from about 145—65 million years B.P. and dominated by dinosaurs.

cross cousins children of the opposite-sex siblings of one's parents—the children of one's mother's brothers and one's father's sisters.

cross-cultural comparison a study that compares features of one culture with those of another to see if there are regularities in the ways humans approach various facets of social life.

cultivators people who practice some method of raising crops.

cultural brokers mediators who serve as bridges between the local peasant community and the outside world.

cultural ecology the study of the relationship of specific cultural features to a group's adaptation to its total habitat.

cultural relativism the attempt to understand and evaluate each cultural system in terms of its own internally consistent logic.

culture something shared by everyone in a particular society, learned from one another and from past generations, that influences the way we think and act; that which is learned and shared rather than genetically transmitted.

culture and personality school *see* psychological anthropology.

culture core according to Steward, the economic and subsistence activities that seem most directly involved with enabling people to survive in their particular environment.

culture shock a psychological response to an unfamiliar culture; characterized by disorientation, anxiety, and sometimes mental breakdown, depression, or even suicide.

cusps points or premolars and molars that aid in grinding and shearing.

customary control *see* informal control.

decomposer an organism such as a bacterium that breaks down the remains of organisms, recycling organic and inorganic compounds.

deep structure in transformational grammar, the underlying meaning of a sentence.

dendrochronology a method of dating archaeological sites based on a sequence of tree rings established for the area.

dental arcade the arch formed by the rows of the teeth.

dental comb structure found in many prosimians, formed by projecting incisors and canines and used for grooming the fur.

denticulate Mousterian tradition one of five distinct general toolmaking traditions in Mousterian France. Tool assemblages found during this period are characterized by fine-toothed tools. Hand axes, points, and scrapers are either missing from this period or of poor quality.

descent the principle that links one generation to another in a systematized manner.

descent group a group of kin related by common descent—by certain specified rights and obligations across generations.

desert tradition one of two major traditions of the Mesolithic Age in North America. The desert tradition began about 9,000 years B.P. in the arid western regions of North America and lasted until European contact.

developmental acclimatization adjustments to the environment that occur during the growth period of the individual.

diffusion the spread of culture traits from one culture to another by historical contacts.

directional selection a form of selection that favors a trait held by a minority of the population at one end of the distribution curve.

disruptive selection a form of selection that favors the forms of a trait found at extreme ends of the trait distribution curve. The form presently most common is now at a disadvantage.

distinctive features the differences in sound that speakers recognize unconsciously in minimally different words.

diurnal active during the day.

divination the manipulation of the supernatural to discover concealed information.

divorce the lawful dissolution of the legal ties established at marriage.

DNA deoxyribonucleic acid. A large double-stranded molecule that controls the making of proteins in the cell. It is the main component of the chromosomes.

dominant gene gene that masks the effect of recessive alleles, so that the trait it controls becomes the phenotype.

double descent the rule of unilineal descent that traces ancestry through *both* father's and mother's lines.

dowry goods given to the bride or the newly married couple by the bride's kin group.

Dryopithecus a genus of Miocene apes, believed by many to have been ancestral to both modern apes and humans.

early archaic *Homo sapiens* the earliest form of *Homo sapiens,* which dates from about 275,000 to 75,000 years B.P. Important physical characteristics include a mouth area that is noticeably larger than that of late erectines.

early *Homo erectus* the form of *Homo erectus* that existed before 500,000 B.P. Early *Homo erectus* fossils have been found in Africa and tropical and subtropical parts of Java, China, and Europe. These hominids had a more erect posture, lighter jaws, smaller molars, and bigger brains than the early African hominids.

early modern humans hominids having a nearly modern anatomy that appeared during the latter part of the Würm glaciation. By 30,000 to 25,000 B.P., early modern humans were found in all areas now inhabited by humans. Their features—including reduced tooth and jaw sizes, flatter faces, and generally less robust bone structures—resemble those of contemporary humans.

East African gracile any of a group of small, omnivorous, bipedal hominids thought to have evolved into *Homo erectus.* It has been classed as *Australopithecus habilis* and as *Homo habilis.*

East African robust Any of a lineage of human-sized, bipedal, vegetarian hominids, the earliest of which have been classed as *Australopithecus robustus,* and the evolved forms of which are named *Australopithecus boisei.*

ecology the study of the relationships between organisms and their environments.

econiche sum of all the interactions occurring between a population and its biotic and abiotic environments. Also called *niche.*

economic activity the choices people make in determining how available resources are to be used in producing, distributing, and consuming material goods and services.

economic spatial theory a spatial theory based on the premise that, in the long run, societies tend to develop spatial patterns that minimize their costs and maximize their profits.

ecosystem the interaction of a biotic community and the physical environment of an area.

egalitarian society a society in which occupational alternatives are few.

ego-focused group descent group that consists of people closely related to oneself (Ego) rather than to an ancestor.

electrophoresis a method for determining rates for recessive mutations.

enculturation the process whereby members of a society acquire the characteristics of a given culture, learning its language and generally acquiring competence in the culture.

endocranial cast mold made of the inside of the skull in order to approximate the shape of the brain.

endogamy the expectation that a marriage partner will be chosen from within the social group of which one is a member.

end scraper a specialized Upper Paleolithic blade tool characterized by sharpened surfaces on both ends. End scrapers were probably used in hollowing out bone and wood or in removing bark, as well as in scraping skins.

environmental determinism the belief that the reason for the presence of a specific cultural feature could be traced to the habitat in which it occurred; also called environmentalism.

environmentalism *see* environmental determinism.

environmental possibilism the belief that environmental factors limit the adaptive possibilities for a given culture but do not determine which adaptions or choices a society/culture makes.

Eocene Epoch the second epoch of the Cenozoic Era, 58—36 million years B.P.; prosimians proliferated and diversified during this time.

epoch the major subdivision of a period.

era major geological division of the history of the earth.

ethnic group a population that is biologically self-perpetuating; shares fundamental cultural values expressed in unified forms; is characterized by internal communication and interaction; and considers itself to have particular identity.

enthnocentrism the tendency to judge other cultures by the standards of one's own culture.

ethnographic analogy the process of making inferences about prehistoric cultures based on observations of living groups whose cultures are presumed to be similar in some way.

ethnography a detailed and noninterpretive description of the social life, values, and thought of a given social group.

ethnology a study of culture that compares

different cultures, often on a theoretical basis.

ethnomusicology the study of music in culture.

ethnoscience an approach to studying other cultures that claims that use of native language categories enables one to identify native points of view; also called cognitive anthropology.

ethology the scientific study of animal behavior.

evolution continuous biological change in frequencies of genetically determined traits in a population over generations.

exogamy the expectation that the choice of a marriage partner will be from a social group of which one is not a member.

extended family family arrangement consisting of the oldest male and his wife, the married sons and their wives, all the unmarried daughters, and the young dependent children of all the married pairs.

extrasomatic adaptation nonbiological forms of change that characterize culture change.

family taxonomic category ranking above genus and below order.

faunal succession the principle that animal species change with time, without regression to earlier forms. This assumption helps paleontologists date strata in relative terms on the basis of index fossils.

first-order behavior the mechanical actions of an organism's body that make up functional complexes such as feeding and locomotion.

fission the permanent division of a clan or lineage into two or more segments.

fission-track dating a method of chronometric dating based on measurement of the short tracks made in rock by particles of radioactive uranium atoms as they decay.

Flannery's process model an attempt to explain the transition from chiefdoms to states that centers on the processes by which a society becomes more complex.

folk-urban continuum Redfield's model of certain specific categories of communities and their interconnections.

Folsom tradition tradition of the southwestern and western United States, dating from about 11,000 to about 9,000 years B.P.

foramen magnum the opening in the base of the skull through which the spinal cord passes.

formal control social control characterized by a systematized set of rules and procedures for managing disputes.

fossil the preserved remains of an organism that lived in the past.

founder effect a special case of genetic drift that occurs when a small part of a larger population founds a new population. The founders do not have the genetic variety of the original group. Thus the genetic makeup of the founder group and its descendants may differ from that of the original population.

fraternal polyandry the marriage of a woman to two or more brothers at the same time.

frontal lobes in humans, the seat of initiative and concentration.

fusion the recombination, usually temporary and in response to a specific need, of segmented lineages.

gametes the reproductive cells that join in fertilization to produce a zygote. In humans, the male gametes are sperm and the female gametes are eggs.

gene the basic unit of inheritance, located on the chromosomes.

gene flow the movement of genes from one population to another through interbreeding.

generalized characteristics primitive traits inherited early in the evolution of a lineage and modified by later specialized adaptations for particular niches. Primate dental and limb structures are generalized characteristics of the order.

generalized Neandertals one of two groups of late archaics referred to in the pre-Neandertal theory. According to the theory, generalized, or early, Neandertals evolved from the preglacial, early archaic form that spread throughout Europe, the Middle East, and North Africa. Holders of the theory believed that this group evolved into modern humans.

generalized other according to G. H. Mead, a person's mental representation of the expectations of society; an abstract entity that enables a person to see things from the perspective of his or her entire group.

generalized reciprocity an exchange transaction in which goods, services, or assistance are freely given to kin, friends, and neighbors without any open statement that anything is expected is return.

genetic drift a random change in gene frequencies from one generation to the next. Drift is most likely to occur in small populations.

genotype the genetic composition of an organism.

genus biological grouping that ranks below the family and that may include one or more related species.

geographical circumscription a condition in which a population in an area isolated by geographical barriers is severely limited in its access to other lands.

gibbon mostly arboreal, Southeast Asian ape, whose long and powerful arms and shoulders make it the most skilled brachiator.

gift exchange exchange of gifts or payments by each of the two kin groups being linked to each other by a marriage.

Gigantopithecus large, ground-living pongid descendant of *Dryopithecus* that became extinct in the Pleistocene Epoch.

glume any of the tough, inedible husks found on wild grains that hold kernels tightly, despite vigorous threshing.

Gondwana the southernmost of the two supercontinents formed as Pangaea broke apart.

gorilla large terrestrial ape, inhabiting tropical rain forests of central Africa.

grammar linguistic rules dealing with the ways language is structured into larger units of meaning.

grammatical transformations a set of "rewrite rules" that breaks units of the deep structure of a sentence into noun and verb phrases and transforms them into the surface structure of the sentence.

group marriage the marriage of two or more women to two or more men at a time.

guenon any group of arboreal Old World monkeys (genus *Cercopithecus*).

hammerstone a rock used to strike flakes from another rock to produce an edge.

hand ax the tool most characteristic of the Acheulean tradition. It has two chopping edges that meet to form a point and a broad base for easy gripping. *Homo erectus* may have used the hand ax for such functions as skinning, butchering, and digging.

herbivore a plant eater.

heterozygous having different alleles at the same locus on homologous chromosomes.

holism the attempt in anthropology to incorporate various fields of knowledge into a meaningful understanding of humanity.

home range the area within which an adult organism normally moves.

hominid member of the family Hominidae, which includes humans and their extinct direct ancestors.

Hominoidea superfamily containing the gibbons, the apes, and humans.

Homo erectus an early hominid ("erect man") that lived during most of the early and middle Pleistocene. Fossils have been found with Oldowan and Acheulean tools.

Homo habilis. the East African gracile hominid thought by holders of multiple-lineage theories

to have been the earliest fossil hominid in the genus *Homo*.

homologous chromosomes the members of a chromosome pair made up of the contribution of the female and male parent and containing the same gene loci.

Homo sapiens "intelligent man," the species of modern humans that first appeared in the late middle Pleistocene.

homozygous having the same allele at the same locus on homologous chromosomes.

horticulture plant cultivation using simple tools and, mostly, human muscle power.

hunters-and-gatherers peoples who forage for food by hunting animals, by fishing, and by gathering wild fruits, vegetables, and nuts.

ilium the large bone forming the top part of the human pelvis.

inbreeding a phenomenon closely related to genetic drift, resulting from the mating of biological relatives. Inbreeding limits the amount of genetic variation in a population and increases the probability homozygous pairs will occur.

incest taboo the prohibition of sexual access to certain categories of kin.

incisors teeth in the front of the jaw that are generally used to seize and cut food.

index fossil a fossil common to a broad geographical area and used to compare the age of remains at different sites.

informal control social control that consists of traditional or customary rules, beliefs, and procedures that are not arranged systematically; also called customary control.

infraorder taxonomic category ranking above suborder and below superfamily.

integration the modification of borrowed culture traits to fit local cultural, social, or environmental factors.

intrusion the presence of younger remains in the same geological layer as older ones, due to a process such as burial or an earthquake.

Iron Age the prehistoric period that was characterized by the use of iron as the chief metal in the art of metallurgy. Toward the end of the Iron Age, written records, which ended the prehistoric period, began to appear.

joint family *see* extended family.

kindred any group of close consanguineal relatives, without reference to either maternal or paternal line of descent.

kinesics the study of body movement and gesture as means of communication.

kinship the relationships between individuals based on descent and marriage.

kula **system**   a special system of trade in New Guinea that consists of the circulation of shell armbands and shell necklaces for ceremonial purposes.

langur   any of a group of slender, long-tailed, Asiatic monkeys in the subfamily Colobinae.

late archaic *Homo sapiens*   the second earliest group of *Homo sapiens,* which dates from 75,000 to 40,000 years B.P. Fossils of this age found in Europe have traditionally been referred to as "Neandertal" and are associated with the Mousterian culture.

late *Homo erectus*   the form of *Homo erectus* that is dated between 500,000 and 275,000 years B.P. These hominids were characterized by expanded brain centers and reduced chewing apparatus.

Laurasia   the northern continental land mass, consisting of what would become North America, Europe, and Asia, according to the principle of continental drift. It became distinct about 180 million years B.P.

law of independent assortment   Mendel's principle that the inheritance of one trait is not affected by the inheritance of others. In fact, linkage causes genes on the same chromosome to be inherited together.

law of particulate inheritance.   Mendel's principle that genes exist in the cells as separate particles.

law of segregation   Mendel's principle that the alleles of a pair separate to become part of gametes, which contain one allele or the other.

learning   the acquisition of experience in the course of growth. The results of learning are stored in the brain, not in the genes.

legal pluralism   the existence within a society of more than one legal system at the same time, some of which may actually be in conflict with one another.

leisure preference   the desire of people in industrial economies to work shorter hours rather than earn more money.

Lemuriformes   infraorder of the suborder *Prosimii,* whose members include indrises, aye-ayes, and lemurs.

Levallois technique   Mousterian toolmaking technique that involved the careful preparation of a core so that flakes could be struck in precise, preshaped forms. This method produced longer, sharper cutting edges than previous methods.

level-specific regional analysis   method of research that distinguishes the local, regional, and national as three distinct levels.

levirate   the practice requiring or permitting a man to marry the wife of his deceased brother.

limbic system   part of the brain, located below the cortex; translates sensory stimuli into states of arousal or emotion.

lineage   a unilineal descent group in which relationships among members are known and demonstrable; members of lineages often trace their descent to a common ancestor of several generations back.

lineal relatives   kin related in a direct biological line.

linearization   part of Flannery's explanation of state formation. Linearization refers to the process by which lower-order controls are bypassed by higher-order controls.

linguistic universals   *see* universal grammar.

Llano tradition   toolmaking tradition of the United States, associated with the hunting of large and small game and the Clovis point.

locus   the position of a gene on the chromosome.

long-term acclimatization   gradual change that occurs during years of exposure to a particular stress and produces a phenotype more compatible with the environment.

Lorisiformes   infraorder of the suborder *Prosimii,* whose members include lorises and galagos.

Lower Paleolithic   the first of the three periods of the Paleolithic Age. It was the time of the Oldowan, Acheulean, and chopper-tool traditions.

Lung-shan culture   a state in Chinese civilization (4,600—3,850 years B.P.) characterized by rapidly increasing productivity, increased population density, larger, more permanent settlements, the beginnings of social stratification and role specialization, more frequent warfare, and the spread of farming villages into new areas.

macaque   largely terrestrial Old World monkey similar to baboons, but found in a range from India to Japan.

macroevolution   refers to physical change that has occurred over millions of years. The study of macroevolution tends to be more descriptive than the study of microevolution and less able to produce data needed to understand the action of all evolutionary processes.

Magdalenian tradition   an Upper Paleolithic toolmaking tradition that appeared about 16,000 years B.P. and replaced the Solutrean tradition. It lasted about 6,000 years.

mandible   the lower jaw.

mangabey   any of several species of Old World monkeys (genus *Cercocebus*) native to the tropical rain forests of Africa.

market exchange   an exchange transaction in

which the parties to the exchange bargain to reach a price that is acceptable to both.

marriage a socially recognized and stable union providing sexual access, legitimating offspring, and establishing other rights and obligations between the marriage partners and other units of society.

masseters a set of facial muscles that attach to the zygomatic arch and move the lower jaw.

matrilateral belonging to one's mother's side.

matrilineal descent the rule of unilineal descent that traces ancestry through the female line; also called uterine descent.

matrilocal residence the pattern of residence in which the groom goes to live with the bride in the household headed by her mother.

meddling One of Flannery's mechanisms destructive of complex societies. It is the unnecessary, unproductive bypassing of lower-order controls.

meiosis the division of sex cells to form gametes, each with half of the number of chromosomes contained in a body cell.

Mesoamerica region that now encompasses central and southern Mexico and Central America.

Mesolithic Age a term whose literal meaning is the "Middle Stone Age." It refers to a very short transitional period between the last Upper Paleolithic cultures and the Neolithic period and represents a time just before the emergence of agriculture.

metacommunication a message that tells the receiver how another message is to be interpreted.

Metal Age a prehistoric period made up of the Bronze Age and the Iron Age.

Micoquian tradition one of five distinct general toolmaking traditions in Mousterian France. Tool assemblages found during this period are characterized by lance-shaped hand axes often with concave edges and thick bases.

microenvironment environment that has been modified by means of culture.

microevolution refers to short-term biological change. The study of microevolution can include an examination of how and why evolutionary changes occur.

microlith any of a variety of small blades that appeared during the European Mesolithic Age. Microliths (usually less than an inch long) were used alone, as tips for arrows, and as part of a number of other tools. Such tools were often well suited to the hunting of small game.

midden an accumulation of refuse around a dwelling.

Middle Paleolithic the second of the three periods of the Paleolithic Age.

minimal pairs pairs of words that differ in only one sound such as *pat* and *bat* in English.

Miocene Epoch the fourth epoch of the Cenozoic Era. The earliest hominid probably appeared during this epoch, which ranges from 22—6 million years B.P.

mitosis the process of cell division in which the genetic material of body cells is duplicated and distributed equally to the two daughter cells.

modal personality proposed by Du Bois, the characteristics of tendencies shared by *most* members of a given culture.

model a system of relations that is thought to be parallel to, or a simulation of, a set of relations under study.

modernizing oligarchy a form of government in which ruling power belongs to only a few.

moieties the two groups into which a society may divide, in order to exchange women through marriage; each moiety consists of a number of either clans or phratries.

molars large rear teeth equipped with cusps and shearing ridges for grinding and shearing food before swallowing.

monogamy the marriage of one man to one woman at a time.

morph the smallest unit of meaning in a given language.

morphology the study of the ways in which morps in a given language combine into words.

Mousterian of Acheulean tradition One of five distinct toolmaking traditions in Mousterian France. Tool assemblages of this tradition have two forms: Type A includes numerous varied hand axes and flake tools including scrapers. Type B includes many denticulates and knives but few hand axes or scrapers.

Mousterian tradition a tool tradition that lasted from about 100,000 years B.P. to about 40,000 years B.P. and is marked by the presence of hand axes, flakes, points, and burins.

mutation spontaneous alteration of the genetic material. Genetic mutations affect a single nucleotide sequence on a chromosome, while chromosomal mutations involve rearrangements of long sequences on whole chromosomes.

myth the verbal rationale for religion, differing from other kinds of verbal material in having the connotation of the sacred.

natives indigenous people; those belonging to a region.

natolocal residence a pattern of residence in which an individual resides in the house in which he or she was born.

Natufian culture a Near Eastern culture that took the place of the Kebaran culture about

12,000 years B.P. The Natufians lived in the coastal foothills that were part of the Levant. There is some evidence of herding, harvesting of wild grains, and growing sedentism.

natural selection the process by which nature acts on the variation within a population so that the better-adapted contribute their genes to the next generation more successfully than the poorly adapted. This mechanism of evolution allows a population to adapt to a changing environment.

Neandertal traditional label for late archaic *Homo sapiens* fossils found in Europe. The label comes from skeletal fragments discovered in 1856 in a grotto in Neander Valley, Germany.

negative reciprocity an exchange transaction in which goods or services are obtained through force or deception.

Neolithic Age a term whose literal meaning is the "New Stone Age." It refers to the prehistoric period beginning with the invention of agriculture and ending with the invention of metal working.

Neolithic revolution a term used to describe the change from a hunting-and-gathering economy and a flaked-stone-tool technology to an economy based on farming and a technology that included polished stone tools, pottery, and weaving.

neolocal residence the pattern of residence in which the newly married couple establishes its residence without regard to the residence of either partner's family of origin.

new archaeology the modern form of archaeology, characterized by the pursuit of three goals: (1) the reconstruction of cultural history, (2) the detailed description of the way of life of earlier cultures, and (3) the analysis of the reasons for cultural change.

New World monkey any member of the extremely varied infraorder *Platyrrhini,* including the marmosets and the cebid monkeys.

niche see *econiche.*

nocturnal active at night.

nome any of the local districts scattered along the Nile Valley in Egypt that appeared around 6,000 years B.P.

normal distribution a distribution that, graphically represented, takes the form of a bell-shaped curve.

notched blade a specialized Upper Paleolithic blade tool, perhaps used to shave wood in fashioning the shafts of arrows or spears.

nuclear family *see* conjugal family.

nuclear zone theory Braidwood's theory of the origins of agriculture. According to him, human culture at the end of the Mesolithic was ready to begin food production. In certain Near Eastern zones, the presence of animals and plants that could be domesticated provided the needed stimulus.

nucleotide the basic unit of DNA, consisting of a sugar, a phosphate, and an organic base.

oasis model theory proposed by V. Gordon Childe to explain the origins of food production. Childe thought domestication became a necessity in oases in which humans, plants, and animals were concentrated during a post-Pleistocene drying trend.

obsidian a glasslike black or banded igneous rock often used by prehistoric people in the manufacture of tools.

obsidian hydration a method for dating the age of obsidian tools, based on the measurement of the depth of the water-absorbing layer in obsidian.

occipital lobe the posterior lobe of the cerebral cortex in which the visual cortex is located. Analysis of visual images takes place here.

Oldowan tradition a name for the earliest stone tools, which were made by striking one pebble against another to form a single crude edge. Tools of this type were first uncovered in the lower beds at Olduvai Gorge in East Africa.

Old World monkey any member of the superfamily *Cercopithecoidea,* including colobus monkeys, langurs, guenons, mangabeys, baboons, and macaques.

olfactory lobe the part at the forward end of each cerebral hemisphere responsible for the reception of sensory inputs from the nose.

Oligocene Epoch the third epoch of the Cenozoic Era, 36—22 million years B.P., in which primitive monkeys and apes first appeared.

Oligopithecus an early generalized Oligocene primate, possibly ancestral to the Miocene pongids.

Omomyidae a tarsier-like member of the anaptomorphid subfamily. May have been a direct ancestor of the catarrhines and therefore of the hominids.

opposability the ability to move the thumb opposite the other fingers, allowing manipulation of objects.

orangutan an arboreal ape found in Borneo and Sumatra.

order taxonomic category ranking above family and below class.

osteology the study of bones. Physical anthropologists apply it to the study of variation among prehistoric human populations.

ostracism the rejection or exclusion of an individual by the general consent of the group of which he or she is a member.

paleoanthropology the study of fossils and their environment as they bear on the evolution of hominids.

Paleocene Epoch the earliest epoch of the Cenozoic Era, 65–58 million years B.P. Primates probably first became a clearly distinct order during this epoch.

Paleo-Indians the original human inhabitants of the New World.

Paleolithic Age a term whose literal meaning is the "Old Stone Age." It initially referred to the culture stage in which humans made chipped stone tools. Currently, the term stands for the period of cultural development during the glacial advances and retreats of the Pleistocene Epoch. The Paleolithic Age is often divided into three parts: the Lower, Middle, and Upper Paleolithic.

paleomagnetic dating a method of chronometric dating based on the history of the reversal of the earth's magnetic field. The orientation of the field at a given time is indicated by the pattern of metallic particles in the rock.

paleospecies anatomically similar extinct animals.

palynology the analysis of pollen as a method of relative dating or as a means of reconstructing prehistoric environments.

parallel cousins children of the same-sex siblings of one's parents—the children of one's mother's sisters and father's brothers.

parallel descent the rule of unilineal descent in which males trace ancestry through males and females through females.

parallelism an evolutionary trend that occurs when two closely related species or groups of species begin to exploit similar but geographically separate ecosystems in similar ways.

Parapithecus a small Oligocene primate presumed to be an early Old World monkey.

parietal lobes areas of the cerebral cortex that receive and integrate auditory, somatic, and visual information from other parts of the brain.

Paromomyidae a family of the superfamily *Plesiadapoidea*. Members include *Purgatorius*, Paleocene, and Eocene representatives.

participant observation a method of fieldwork in which the anthropologist lives for a period of time among the subjects of his or her study.

pastoralism raising and herding animals for meat, milk, and the products that can be derived from them.

patrilateral belonging to one's father's side.

patrilineal descent the rule of unilineal descent that traces ancestry through the male line; also called agnatic descent.

patrilocal residence the pattern of residence in which the bride goes to live with the groom in the household headed by his father.

pedigree an analysis of the genotypes of related persons, based on a study of their phenotypes.

Peking Man original name for the *Homo erectus* fossils found near Chou-kou-tien, China.

pentadactyl five-finger, five-toe pattern.

percussion flaking method of using one stone to strike off flakes from one or both sides of another. The hammerstone and anvil were used in percussion flaking to produce Oldowan tools.

Perigordian tradition an Upper Paleolithic toolmaking tradition that existed about 35,000 — 18,000 years B.P. It probably evolved from the Mousterian of Acheulean tradition.

period major subdivision of an era.

personality the collective response patterns within every human being that determine the behaviors, thoughts, and feelings of the individual.

phase a period in the history of a culture that is named on the basis of one kind of artifact typical of it.

phenotype the physical and physiological traits of an organism. The phenotype is the result of genetic composition and environmental forces.

phonemes the distinctive but meaningless sounds heard by native speakers of a language.

phonemics the study of the manner in which sounds are used to communicate meaningfully in a given language.

phonetics the study of speech sounds from a physiological point of view.

phonology the study of human speech sounds.

phratry the several clans that claim common descent from the original common ancestor.

phylogeny a history of the evolution of a group of genetically related organisms.

phylum taxonomic category more general than class and less general than kingdom.

Plano tradition the Paleo-Indian cultural tradition of the New World, which succeeded the Clovis and Folsom traditions and was found throughout North America.

plate tectonics the study of the motion of the continental plates of the earth's crust.

Platyrrhini one of two infraorders in the suborder *Anthropoidea*, consisting of the New World monkeys.

Pleistocene Epoch a geological epoch extending from about 1.9 million years B.P. to about 10,000 years B.P., marked by a cool climate and periodic glaciation.

Plesiadapidae a family of the Paleocene superfamily *Plesiadapoidea.* Many of its traits foreshadow those of later primates.

Plesiadapoidea the superfamily whose members include early primates of the Paleocene Epoch.

Pliocene Epoch a geological epoch extending from about 6 to 1.9 million years B.P., during which the first undisputed hominids evolved.

political democracy a system in which the central element is an elected legislative body whose laws are carried out by an executive with the help of an organized bureaucracy; political parties are accepted and active.

political system a system that applies to societies that have governments, politics, and administration.

politics the contest to gain power within an authoritative political system.

polyandry the marriage of one woman to two or more men at a time.

polygamy plural marriage; polygyny, polyandry, and group marriage are forms of polygamy.

polygyny the marriage of one man to two or more women at a time.

polypeptide chain a chain of amino acids bonded one to the next.

Pongidae the one of three families in the superfamily *Hominoidea,* whose living members include chimpanzees, gorillas, and orangutans.

population an interbreeding group of relatively similar individuals who share the same environment; the level at which evolutionary processes work.

population ecology the study of the interactions of populations with other populations and with the abiotic features of the environment.

population genetics a branch of genetics that studies evolutionary processes in populations by testing statistical models of change in gene frequency.

potassium-argon dating method of chronometric dating based on the decay of unstable potassium isotopes into inert argon.

potlatch a ceremonial feast of the northwest Pacific coast Indians at which a chief gave away goods to another chief in order to gain prestige.

power the capacity to take independent action in the face of resistance from persons, groups, or rules.

power grip a grasp in which the fingers and thumb clamp an object tightly against the palm.

precision grip a grasp in which the index finger is placed against the thumb, allowing fine manipulation of objects; characteristic of monkeys, apes, and humans.

precocial strategy reproductive pattern in which fairly mature young are born in small litters after a long gestation period. Primates follow this strategy.

prehensility the ability to grasp.

premolars teeth found behind the canines, used for grinding and shearing.

pre-Neandertal theory one of three major theories explaining the presence of variation in late archaic human fossils. This theory holds that two groups of late archaics—the generalized, or early Neandertals and the classic Neandertals—evolved from the preglacial, early archaic form. Many experts believe that the generalized Neandertals evolved into modern humans.

prepottery neolithic A and B a 2,000-year period in the Near East (between about 10,000 and 8,000 years B.P.) in which wild plants and animals were domesticated but pottery had not yet appeared.

presapiens theory one of three major theories explaining the presence of variation in late archaic human fossils. This theory, which is generally discounted by modern anthropologists, holds that the European Neandertals branched off from *Homo erectus* stock as long ago as 250,000 years B.P. and became extinct at the end of the Würm glaciation, while another group of hominids developed modern human anatomical traits.

prescriptive marriage rules obligations that require individuals to marry certain relatives.

priests religious specialists associated with organized churches and characteristically found in more formally structured societies.

primary follicles one of two kinds of hair follicles found on sheep and goats. Primary follicles produce the straight hairs of the visible coat.

primary institutions according to Kardiner, those institutions that shape basic personality structure, including family and kinship arrangements, subsistence patterns, and institutionalized activities associated with feeding, weaning, and sex training.

primary urbanization stage during which precivilized folk society becomes a peasant society attached to an urban center.

primate a member of the order *Primates,* which includes prosimians, monkeys, apes, and humans.

Primates mammalian order that includes prosimians, monkeys, apes, and humans.

primatology the study of the biology and the behavior of nonhuman primates.

prime-mover theory an attempt to explain the

transition from chiefdoms to states in terms of a single initial cause.

producer an organism (such as a green plant) that produces its own organic compounds from inorganic materials. Many producers are food sources for other organisms.

production the various modes used by members of society to procure their material means of existence.

production organizations groups engaged in the production of some type of material goods.

projectile point rock or pebble altered for use as the tip of a spear or arrow.

promotion part of Flannery's explanation of state formation. Promotion refers to the elevation of a preexisting institution to a higher level or the elevation of one role of an existing institution to the status of a new institution.

prophets religious specialists who receive visions and communicate directly with supernatural powers on an individual basis; they are generally called upon to criticize the existing social order and to point the way to a better way of life.

Prosimii one of the two primate suborders; it includes the *Tarsiiformes, Lorisiformes,* and *Lemuriformes.*

proteins large, complex molecules that are made up of amino acids and that serve as enzymes and basic components of cell structure.

proxemics the study of the ways in which various societies use physical space in human interaction.

psychological anthropology an area of study in anthropology that analyzes culture as expressed in the behaviors, thoughts, and feelings (or personality) of its individual members; also known as "culture and personality school."

Purgatorius the earliest known primate, dated to the late Cretaceous Period.

quadrupedalism use of all four limbs in running or walking.

Quina-Ferrassie tradition one of five distinct general toolmaking traditions in Mousterian France. Tool assemblages are dominated by scrapers, some of which were designed for extremely specialized functions.

rachis the fiber that connects the seed to the stem of the plant. The rachis found on wild wheat and barley is brittle, making harvesting very difficult.

radiocarbon dating a method of absolute dating frequently used to date items up to 50,000 years old. It is based on the decay of the radioactive carbon isotope C^{14}.

radiometric dating dating techniques based on the rate of decay of radioactive isotopes in the rocks surrounding fossil finds.

Ramapithecus a Miocene primate more evolved than dryopithecine apes, but of questionable hominid status.

random culture change change brought about because of children's imperfect repetition of their parent's behavior. Some random differences between the generations gradually show up as changes in the way most people in a group behave.

rank society a society characterized by a formalized system of graduated social statuses.

recessive gene gene whose effect is masked by a dominant allele, and whose phenotype is expressed only in the homozygous condition.

reciprocity an exchange transaction that involves direct movement of goods or services between two parties.

redistribution an exchange transaction in which goods are collected from the members of a group by a central authority and then divided up among the group.

reference group a group with which individuals identify themselves as members or aspire to be identified.

relative dating dating that determines whether one deposit is older or younger than another. Methods include stratigraphy and analysis of the fluorine, nitrogen, or uranium content of remains.

releaser stimulus that serves as a trigger of instinctual behavior.

reliability the degree to which the results of an experiment or a set of scientific observations can be obtained on another trial.

religion the system of social interactions consisting of those beliefs and activities that order human life by relating humans to spiritual beings and/or powers.

reproductive isolation the absence of interbreeding between two populations.

ribosomes small bodies that are found in the cytoplasm and are the site of protein synthesis.

ritual the demonstration of religious belief through performance of specific acts by the members of a society.

ritual kinship the formalized relationship modeled on kin relations that one may have with a nonkin individual.

RNA ribonucleic acid. A nuclear acid active in transferring genetic information from DNA to the ribosomes for use in protein synthesis. Messenger RNA and transfer RNA are active in this process.

role models members of society already engaged in a role that an individual can later expect to assume.

role theory the theory that individuals learn from observing those around them.

sagittal crest bony ridge along the top of the skull in some nonhuman primates.

salvage archaeology the study and removal of material from an area that is about to be destroyed or disturbed.

sanctions means of dealing with or controlling deviant or socially unacceptable behavior.

Sapir-Whorf hypothesis the theory that language reflects the way in which speakers of the language perceive and think about the world.

Scala Naturae an arrangement of nature in scale of perfection, from the divine (most perfect) to humans, apes, simpler animals, plants, and inorganic matter. Also called the Great Chain of Being.

secondary follicles one of two kinds of hair follicles found on sheep and goats. Secondary follicles produce hairs found on the woolly undercoat.

secondary institutions according to Kardiner, those institutions through which basic personality structure is expressed, including taboo systems, religion and rituals, folktales, and art.

secondary urbanization stage in which external cultural influences alter the folk, peasant, or partly urbanized society.

second-order behavior interaction between individuals and between populations. Social behavior and communication are examples.

sedentism the process of settling in permanent villages inhabited year round.

sedimentary rock rock formed of bits of other rock transported from their source and deposited in water.

segmentation the subdivision of a clan or lineage into subgroups.

segregation part of Flannery's explanation of state formation. Segregation refers to the extent to which various administrative tasks are split up among separate units of the bureaucracy.

semantics the study of meaning.

serial monogamy a form of monogamy that consists of a series of monogamous marriages, one after another.

seriation a method of relative dating based on arrangement of samples of a kind of artifact (such as a vase or coin) in a chronological sequence.

sexual dimorphism the presence of a difference in form between the males and females of a species.

shamans religious specialists whose primary function is healing the sick and protecting the community from harm; their healing proceeds by supernatural intervention.

Shang Dynasty the earliest Chinese state (3,850—3,050 years B.P.) for which there is archaeological evidence. The Shang Dynasty comprised the communities of the lower and middle Huang Ho River and was characterized by networks of building clusters, increased population density, and more sophisticated communications techniques.

shouldered point an Upper Paleolithic tool probably affixed to spears or arrows for fighting or hunting.

sickle cell anemia disease resulting from the homozygous occurrence of the gene Hb^s, which causes the red blood cells to take an abnormal "sickle" shape.

significant others according to G. H. Mead, those individuals in one's life with whom one deals most intensively—parents, siblings, teachers, peers—and from whom one learns social roles.

simian shelf bony structure behind the front teeth in the front part of the lower jaw of apes.

simple genetic trait a phenotype controlled by a few alleles at a single locus.

single population study a method for studying the process of selection in human populations. Anthropologists work with one population and try to establish the advantages offered by particular genes possessed by that group.

site a space of ground containing evidence of human occupation that archaeologists select for their dig.

Sivapithecus a late Miocene primate, thought to have descended from dryopithecine apes, and a possible hominid ancestor.

slash-and-burn technique of cultivation that involves slashing trees and underbrush, burning off the refuse, and planting in the cleared area.

slavery a hierarchical system in which one group of people owns the labor and the products of the labor of another group of people.

social circumscription condition in which a population is prevented from moving by surrounding hostile populations.

social group a group of individuals who come together for the purpose of achieving certain common goals and who interact in predictable ways that serve the interests of the group over a period of time.

socialization the process whereby an individual new to a society learns to function as a member of that society, including the learning of social roles.

social stratification the arrangement of status within a society into a hierarchy of socially superior and inferior ranks.

sociobiology the scientific study of the genetic basis of behavior and its evolution.

sociolinguistics the study of language use within a speech community.

soft-hammer technique a technique, part of the Acheulean toolmaking tradition, in which a bone or a stick was used to flake away edges of a stone. This technique became popular when people discovered that they could use it to control the size and shape of the flake better than with the hammerstone, used to make Oldowan tools.

Solutrean tradition an Upper Paleolithic toolmaking tradition that replaced the Perigordian and Aurignacian traditions about 18,000 years B.P. This tradition lasted only about 2,000 years and was known for its fine flintwork, especially in laurel-leaf blades.

sorcerers religious specialists who can cause harm and kill enemies.

sororal polygyny the marriage of a man to two or more sisters at the same time.

sororate the practice requiring or permitting a man to marry the sister of his deceased wife.

South African gracile an early bipedal, omnivorous Plio-Pleistocene hominid generally classified as *A. africanus*.

South African robust a specialized hominid, mainly bipedal and probably a vegetarian, that was about twice as heavy as the South African gracile. Often classified as *A. robustus*.

spatial model a reconstruction of the economic, social, and environmental systems as revealed in the spacing of archaeological sites.

specialized characteristics adaptations not shared by all members of a lineage.

speciation the splitting of a population into one or more new biological species.

species a group of organisms whose shared biological background permits individuals to mate with one another and to produce fertile offspring.

stabilizing selection a form of selection that favors a trait with the highest frequency in a population.

state an independent political unit that includes many communities in its territory, with a centralized government that has the power to collect taxes, draft citizens for work and for war, and enact and enforce laws. Social stratification is present.

steppe any of the vast, level, treeless plains of southeastern Europe or Asia.

stereoscopic vision vision in which images from each eye overlap to allow perception in three dimensions.

stratification the layering of sedimentary deposits.

stratigraphy the study of layers of sedimentary deposit and their sequence.

structural-functionalism an approach to the study of culture that assumes that every relationship and institution has a function and is understood as a part of a larger whole, called society.

subassemblage a group of artifacts reflecting a particular behavior of a subgroup of a community. Studying the knives, points, and scrapers, for instance, can tell us something about how the hunters of a culture hunted.

subsistence economy an economic system in which people use what they themselves produce in order to meet their own needs.

suitor service a period during which a groom lives with and works for the kin group of the bride.

superfamily taxonomic classification ranking above family and below infraorder.

superposition the principle that a given sedimentary layer is younger than the layer beneath it.

surface structure in transformational grammar, the outward appearance of a sentence; the sounds we hear.

sympatric speciation speciation that occurs when parts of an original population no longer interbreed, though they coexist in the same area.

syntax the study of the rules for combining words into larger units of meaning, such as phrases or sentences.

synthetic theory of evolution the currently accepted theory of evolution, which combines theories of natural selection, Mendelian genetics, mutation, and population genetics.

taiga a subarctic forest region dominated by spruce and fir that begins where the tundra ends.

tarsiids small Eocene primates ancestral to today's tarsiers.

Tarsiiformes infraorder in the suborder *Prosimii,* whose only remaining member is the tarsier.

taxonomy the science of classifying extinct and living organisms according to biological similarity and evolutionary relationship. Also, the classification system itself.

technology the tools and processes by means of which material goods can be produced in greater quantity and with less physical effort.

temporal muscles facial muscles that attach to the top of the skull and move the lower jaw.

terrestrial ground-living

thermoluminescence a method used for dating artifacts. It involves the measurement of the amount of light released by pottery when heated.

thick description understanding the meaning of social patterns to those who take part in them.

torus a bony swelling such as that at the back of the head of early *Homo erectus.* Powerful neck muscles were attached to the torus.

totem a plant or animal considered sacred and claimed as a symbol or emblem by a clan.

traditional archaeology archaeology as it was practiced from the early nineteenth century until the 1950s. It concentrated largely on finding and cataloguing things and using these things to reconstruct cultural history. Even though the artifacts uncovered by traditional archaeologists revealed a variety of cultural traits, this method obscured the nature of prehistoric human behavior.

trait distribution study a method for studying the process of selection in human populations. In trait distribution studies, anthropologists work with data from many populations to chart the frequency of a single gene and find correlations between its frequency and various environmental features.

transect a single strip of land crossing an area possibly containing an archaeological site. Archaeologists may search a transect rather than survey the whole area.

transformational grammar a grammar, introduced by Chomsky, that explains the *surface structure* of a sentence as the result of transformational operations on the *deep structure* of the sentence.

transhumance seasonal movement of livestock and people between two regions.

tribe a form of social organization that existed by about 9,000 years B.P. Larger than a band, a tribe is made up of groups of families related by common descent or by membership in a variety of kinship-based groups such as clans or lineages. There is little or no social stratification, and central leadership is often weak.

triplet a group of three nucleotides that together control the synthesis of a specific amino acid.

trophic hierarchy a series of categories, each of which is broadly defined in terms of how the organisms that belong to it get their energy.

tundra large, level, treeless plain characteristic of cold climates.

tutelary democracy a system in which the power of the legislature and the political parties and freedom of expression is reduced.

type the basic unit of the traditional organizational system for classifying artifacts.

typical Mousterian tradition one of five distinct general toolmaking traditions in Mousterian

France. Hand axes are rarely present, but scrapers are common.

uniformitarianism the theory that existing processes, acting as they do today, were responsible for all change in the past.

unilineal descent the most common rule of descent, which traces relations through one line of parentage.

universal grammar according to Chomsky, a substructure of rules or principles common to all languages.

Upper Paleolithic the last of three periods of the Paleolithic Age, characterized by pressure flaking and cave art.

uranium-lead dating a method of chronometric dating based on analysis of the decay into lead of certain unstable isotopes of uranium.

urbanism the process by which cities are formed.

usurpation One of Flannery's mechanisms destructive of complex societies.

uterine descent *see* matrilineal descent.

uxorilocal residence the pattern of residence in which the groom goes to live with the bride in the vicinity of her kin group or family of origin.

validity the degree to which scientific observations record the facts and values they claim to record.

varve analysis a method of relative dating in which varves (layers of silt deposited by glacial runoff annually in lakes) are placed in sequence.

vertical clinging and leaping method of locomotion employed by some prosimians; consists of leaping from tree to tree and clinging to the vertical trunks between leaps.

virilocal residence a pattern of residence in which a married couple lives with or near the husband's family.

voluntary association any group that one joins by choice to accomplish a common purpose.

Wittfogel's hydraulic theory an attempt to explain the transition from chiefdom to states in terms of the need for large-scale irrigation in dry areas. Village farmers, dependent on an adequate water supply, joined in a larger political unit that could build and operate irrigation canals.

Yang-shao culture a culture of about 6,000 years ago that existed along the Huang Ho River in the Chung-yuan region of north-central China. The earliest Chinese farming occurred during this cultural period.

zygomatic arch a bony extension of the cheekbone in the human skull, running along the side of the face.

zygote the cell created by the union of the male and female gametes in fertilization.

Bibliography

ABERLE, D. F., BRONFENBRENNER, U., HESS, E. H., MILLER, D. R., SCHNEIDER, D. M., & SPUHLER, J. N. The incest taboo and the mating behavior of animals. *American Anthropologist,* 1963, 65, 253–264.

ADAMS, R. E. W., & CULBERT, T. P. The origins of civilization in the Maya lowlands. In R. E. W. Adams (Ed.), *The origins of Maya civilization.* Albuquerque: University of New Mexico Press, 1977.

ADAMS, R. McC. *The evolution of urban society.* Chicago: Aldine, 1966.

ADAMS, R. McC. Developmental stages in ancient Mesopotamia. In S. Struever (Ed.), *Prehistoric agriculture.* Garden City, N.Y.: Natural History Press, 1971.

ADAMS, R. McC. Patterns of urbanization in early southern Mesopotamia. In P. J. Ucko, R. Tringham, & G. W. Dimbleby (Eds.), *Man, settlement and urbanism.* London: Duckworth, 1972, pp. 735–749.

ALDRED, C. *Egypt to the end of the Old Kingdom.* New York: McGraw-Hill, 1965.

ALEXANDER, B. K., & BOWERS, J. M. The social structure of the Oregon troop of Japanese macaques. *Primates,* 1967, 8, 333–340.

APPLEBY, B. Export monoculture and regional social structure in Puno, Peru. In C. A. Smith (Ed.), *Regional analysis. Vol. II: Social systems.* New York: Academic Press, 1976.

AMERICAN ANTHROPOLOGICAL ASSOCIATION. *Professional ethics: Statements and procedures of the American Anthropological Association.* Washington, D.C., 1973.

ARMELAGOS, G. J., & DEWEY, J. R. Evolutionary response to human infectious diseases. *Bioscience,* 1970, 157, 638–644.

AUSTIN, D. *Heat stress and heat tolerance in two African populations.* Unpublished doctoral dissertation, Pennsylvania State University, 1974.

BAILEY, F. G. *Caste and the economic frontier.* Manchester: Manchester University Press, 1957.

BAKER, P. T. Human biological diversity as an adaptive response to the environment. In R. H. Osborn (Ed.), *The biological and social meaning of race.* San Francisco: W. H. Freeman, 1971.

BALANDIER, G. *Political anthropology* (A. M. S. Smith, Trans.). London: Penguin, 1970.

BALIKCI, A. Shamanistic behavior among the Netsilik Eskimos. *The Southwestern Journal of Anthropology,* 1963, 19(4), 380–396.

BAMBERGER, J. *Kayapó age grades: A case of political*

development in central Brazil? Paper presented at the 75th Annual Meeting of the American Anthropological Association, Washington, D.C., 1976.

BANTON, M. Voluntary associations: Anthropological aspects. In D. Sills (Ed.), *International encyclopedia of the social sciences* (Vol. 2). New York: Macmillan, 1968.

BARNOUW, V. *Culture and personality* (Rev. ed.). Homewood, Ill.: Dorsey, 1973.

BARTH, F. Ecological relationships of ethnic groups in Swat, North Pakistan. *American Anthropologist,* 1956, *58,* 1079–1089.

BARTH, F. (Ed.) *Ethnic groups and boundaries: The social organization of culture difference.* Boston: Little, Brown, 1969.

BASSO, K. H. Ice and travel among the Fort Norman Slave: Folk taxonomies and cultural rules. *Language in Society, 1,* 31–49.

BATESON, G. *Naven.* Stanford: Stanford University Press, 1936.

BATESON, G. Morale and national character. In G. Watson (Ed.), *Civilian morale.* Boston: Society for the Psychological Study of Social Issues, Second Yearbook, 1942.

BATESON, G. The message "This is play." In J. B. Schaffner (Ed.), *Group processes.* New York: Josiah Macy Foundation, 1956.

BATESON, B. *Steps to an ecology of mind.* New York: Ballantine, 1972.

BEALS, R. L. *Politics of social research: An inquiry into the ethics and responsibilities of social scientists.* Chicago: Aldine, 1969.

BECK, B. E. F. Centers and boundaries of regional caste systems: Toward a general model. In C. A. Smith (Ed.), *Regional analysis. Vol. II.: Social systems.* New York: Academic Press, 1976.

BEHRENSMEYER, A. K. Taphonomy and paleoecology in the hominid fossil record. *Yearbook of Physical Anthropology, 1975, 19,* 36–50.

BENDER, D. R. Agnatic or cognatic? A reevaluation of Ondo descent. *Man,* 1970, *5* (1), 71–87.

BENDIX, R. Tradition and modernity reconsidered. In L. Plotnicov & A. Tuden (Eds.), *Essays in comparative social stratification.* Pittsburgh: University of Pittsburgh Press, 1970.

BENEDICT, B. Capital, saving and credit among Mauritian Indians. In R. W. Firth & B. S. Yamey (Eds.), *Capital, saving and credit in peasant societies.* Chicago: Aldine, 1964.

BENEDICT, R. *Patterns of culture.* New York: Houghton Mifflin, 1934. (New American Library Mentor paperback edition, 1948.)

BENEDICT, R. *The chrysanthemum and the sword.* New York: Houghton Mifflin, 1946.

BENEDICT, L. W. People who have two souls. 1916. In M. Mead & N. Calas (Eds.), *Primitive heritage.* New York: Random House, 1953.

BERREMAN, G. D. The concept of caste. In D. Sills (Ed.), *International encyclopedia of the social sciences* (Vol. 2). New York: Macmillan, 1968.

BILSBOROUGH, A. Patterns of evolution in Middle Pleistocene hominids. *Journal of Human Evolution, 1976, 5,* 423–439.

BINFORD, L. R. A consideration of archaeological research design. *American Antiquity,* 1964, 29(4), 425–441.

BINFORD, L. R. Post-Pleistocene adaptations. In S. R. Binford & L. R. Binford (Eds.), *New perspectives in archaeology.* Chicago: Aldine, 1968.

BINFORD, L. R. Archaeological systematics and the study of culture process. In M. P. Leone (Ed.), *Contemporary archaeology: A guide to theory and contributions.* Carbondale: Southern Illinois Press, 1972.

BLACK, F. L. Infectious diseases in primitive societies. *Science,* 1975, *187,* 515–518.

BLACK, R. M. *The elements of paleontology.* New York: Cambridge University Press, 1970.

BOAS, F. *Changes in bodily form of descendants of immigrants.* Partial report on the results of an anthropological investigation of the U.S. Immigration Commission. Washington, D.C.: U.S. Government Printing Office. (Senate Document No. 208, 51st Congress, 2nd Session.)

BOAS, F. *Race, language, and culture.* New York: Free Press, 1940.

BODMER, W. F., & CAVALLI-SFORZA, L. L. *Genetics, evolution and man.* San Francisco: Freeman, 1976.

BOGORAS, W. The Chuckchee. In M. Mead & N. Calas (Eds.), *Primitive heritage.* New York: Random House, 1953. (pp. 425–428.)

BOHANNAN, L. Dahomean marriage: A reevaluation. *Africa,* 1949, 19(4), 273–287.

BOHANNAN, P. The impact of money on an African subsistence economy. *The Journal of Economic History,* 1959, 19(4), 491–503.

BOHANNAN, P. Kinship networks and kinship terminology. In *Social anthropology.* New York: Holt, Rinehart & Winston, 1963.

BOHANNAN, P. Artist and critic in an African society. In C. M. Otten (Ed.), *Anthropology and art.* Garden City, N.Y.: Natural History Press, 1971.

BORDERS, W. At farm in the Great Indian desert, the camel is man's best friend. *The New York Times,* April 23, 1978, p. 15.

BORDES, F. *The old stone age.* New York: McGraw-Hill, 1968.

BOSERUP, E. *The conditions of agricultural growth:*

The economics of agrarian change under population pressure. Chicago: Aldine, 1965.

BOUGHEY, A. S. *Ecology of populations* (2nd ed.). New York: Macmillan, 1973.

BOURGUIGNON, E. Dreams and altered states of consciousness in anthropological research. In F. L. K. Hsu (Ed.), *Psychological anthropology* (Rev. ed.). Cambridge, Mass.: Schenkman, 1972. (pp. 403–430.)

BOURGUIGNON, E. Psychological anthropology. In J. J. Honigman (Ed.), *Handbook of social and cultural anthropology.* Skokie, Ill.: Rand McNally, 1973.

BOURGUIGNON, E., & GREENBAUM, L. S. *Diversity and homogeneity in world societies.* HRAF Press, 1973. (pp. 51–56.)

BOURKE, J. B. Trauma and degenerative disease in ancient Egypt and Nubia. *Journal of Human Evolution,* 1972, *1,* 225–232.

BRACE, C. L. Sexual dimorphism in human evolution. *Yearbook of Physical Anthropology,* 1973, *17,* 252–283.

BRACE, C. L., NELSON, H., & KORN, N., *Atlas of Fossil Man.* New York: Holt, Rinehart & Winston, 1971.

BRAIDWOOD, R. J. *Prehistoric men* (7th ed.). Glenview, Ill.: Scott, Foresman, 1967.

BRAIDWOOD, R. J. et al. *Prehistoric investigations in Iraqi Kurdistan.* Studies in Ancient Oriental Civilization, *31.* Chicago: University of Chicago Press, 1960.

BRAIN, C. K. The Transvaal ape-man-bearing cave deposits. *Transvaal Museum Memoir,* 1958, No. 11.

BRAIN, R. *The last primitive peoples.* New York: Crown, 1976.

BROSE, D. S., & WOLPOFF, M. H. Early Upper Paleolithic man and Late Middle Paleolithic tools. *American Anthropologist,* 1971, *73,* 1156–1194.

BROTHWELL, D. The question of pollution in earlier and less developed societies. In P. R. Cox & J. Peel (Eds.), *Population and pollution.* London: Academic Press, 1972.

BROWN, L. R. Human food production as a process in the biosphere. *Scientific American,* 1970, *223,* 162–163.

BROWN, R. (Ed.) *Psycholinguistics.* New York: Free Press, 1970.

BROWN, R. *Words and things.* Glencoe, Ill.: The Free Press, 1957.

BUETTNER-JANUSCH, J. *Origins of man.* New York, Wiley, 1966.

BUETTNER-JANUSCH, J. *Physical anthropology: A perspective.* New York: Wiley, 1973.

BUETTNER-JANUSCH, J., & HILL, R. L. *Molecules and monkeys.* In H. K. Bleibtreu, *Evolutionary anthropology.* Boston: Allyn & Bacon, 1969.

BULLARD, W. R. Maya settlement pattern in northeastern Petén, Guatemala. *American Antiquity,* 1960, *25,* 355–372.

BUNZEL, R. L. Psychology of the Pueblo potter. 1929. In M. Mead & N. Calas (Eds.), *Primitive heritage.* New York: Random House, 1953. (pp. 270–275.)

BURLING, R. Cognition and componential analysis: God's truth or hocus pocus? *American Anthropologist,* 1964, *66,* 20–28.

BURRIDGE, K. O. L. A. Tangu game. *Man,* 1957, *57,* 88–89.

BUTZER, K. W. *Environment and archaeology.* Chicago: Aldine, 1971.

BYERS, D. S. The region and its people. In D. S. Byers (Ed.), *The prehistory of the Tehuacán Valley* (Vol. 1). Austin: University of Texas Press, 1967.

CAMPBELL, B. G. *Human evolution* (2nd ed.). Chicago: Aldine, 1974.

CARNEIRO, R. L. The theory of the origin of the state. *Science,* 1970, *169,* 733—738.

CARPENTER, E. The Eskimo artist. In C. M. Otten (Ed.), *Anthropology and art.* Garden City, N.Y.: Natural History Press, 1971.

CARTMILL, M. *Primate origins.* Minneapolis: Burgess, 1975.

CHAGNON, N. A., *Proceedings, 111th International Congress of Anthropological and Ethnological Sciences,* 1965, *3,* 251.

CHAGNON, N. A. Tribal social organization and genetic micro-differentiation. In G. A. Harrison & A. J. Boyce (Eds.), *The structure of human populations.* Oxford: Clarendon Press, 1972.

CHAGNON, N. A. *Studying the Yąnomamö.* New York: Holt, Rinehart & Winston, 1974.

CHAGNON, N. A. *Yąnomamö: The fierce people.* New York: Holt, Rinehart & Winston, 1977.

CHAGNON, N. A., NEEL, J. V., WEITKAMP, L., GERSHOWITZ, H., & AYRES, M. The influence of cultural factors on the demography and pattern of gene flow from the Makiritare to the Yąnomamö Indians. In F. Hulse (Ed.), *Man and nature.* New York: Random House, 1975.

CHANG, K. C. *Early Chinese civilization: Anthropological perspectives.* Cambridge, Mass.: Harvard University Press, 1976.

CHILD, I. L., & SIROTO, L. BaKwELE and American aesthetic evaluations compared. In C. F. Jopling (Ed.), *Art and aesthetics in primitive societies.* New York: Dutton, 1971.

CHILDE, G. V. *Man makes himself.* New York: New American Library, 1951.

CHIMEZIE, A. The dozens: An African-heritage

theory. *Journal of Black Studies,* 1976, 6(4), 401–419.

CHOMSKY, N. *Aspects of the theory of syntax.* Cambridge, Mass.: M.I.T. Press, 1965.

CHOMSKY, N. *Language and mind.* New York: Harcourt Brace Jovanovich, 1972.

CHURD, C. H. *Man in prehistory.* New York: McGraw-Hill, 1969.

CLARK, G. *The Stone Age hunters.* New York: McGraw-Hill, 1967.

CLARK, G. *World prehistory.* New York: Cambridge University Press, 1970.

CLARK, J. G. D. *The prehistory of Africa.* New York: Praeger, 1970.

CLARK, J. G. D. Star Carr: A case study in bioarchaeology. *An Addison-Wesley Module in Anthropology,* 1972, 10.

CLARK, W. E. L. *History of the primates.* Chicago: University of Chicago Press, 1965.

CLARKE, A. D. B., & CLARKE, A. M. Some recent advances in the study of early deprivation. *Child Psychology and Psychiatry.* 1960, 1, 26–36.

CLARKE, D. L. Spatial information in archaeology. In *Spatial archaeology.* New York: Academic Press, 1977.

COCKBURN, T. A. *The evolution and eradication of infectious diseases.* Baltimore: Johns Hopkins University Press, 1963.

CODERE, H. Fighting with property. *Monographs of the American Ethnological Society,* 1950, No. 18.

COE, M. D. *Mexico.* New York: Praeger, 1962.

COE, M. D., & FLANNERY, K. V. Microenvironments and Mesoamerican prehistory. In S. Struever (Ed.), *Prehistoric agriculture.* Garden City, N.Y.: Natural History Press, 1971.

COHEN, M. *The food crisis in prehistory.* New Haven, Conn.: Yale University Press, 1977.

COHEN, R. Generalizations in ethnology. In R. Naroll & R. Cohen (Eds.), *A handbook of method in cultural anthropology.* New York: Columbia University Press, 1970. (pp. 31–50.)

COHEN, R., & MIDDLETON, J. (Eds.). *From tribe to nation in Africa: Studies in incorporation processes.* Scranton, Pa.: Chandler, 1970.

COHEN, Y. A. (Ed.). *Man in adaptation: The institutional framework.* Chicago: Aldine, 1971.

COLLINS, D. Culture traditions and environment of early man. *Current Anthropology,* 1969, 10(4), 267–296.

COLUM, P. *Myths of the world.* New York: Grosset & Dunlap, 1930.

COOK, S. Economic anthropology: Problems in theory, method, and analysis. In J. J. Honigmann (Ed.), *Handbook of social and cultural anthropology.* Skokie, Ill.: Rand McNally, 1973.

COMAS, J. *Manual of physical anthropology.* Springfield, Ill.: Charles C. Thomas, 1960.

COON, C. S. *The origin of races.* New York: Knopf, 1962.

CROSBY, A. W. *The Columbian exchange: Biological and cultural consequences of 1492.* Westport, Conn.: Greenwood, 1972.

DAHRENDORF, F. *Class and class conflict in industrial society.* Stanford: Stanford University Press, 1959.

DALTON, G. Primitive money. *American Anthropologist,* 1965, 67, 44–65.

DALTON, G. (Ed.). Traditional production in primitive African economies. In *Tribal and peasant economies: Readings in economic anthropology.* Garden City, N.Y.: Natural History Press, 1967.

d'AZEVADO, W. L. (Ed.). Introduction. In *The traditional artist in African societies.* Bloomington: Indiana University Press, 1973.

DARK, P. J. C. The study of ethno-aesthetics: The visual arts. In J. Helm (Ed.), *Proceedings of the 1966 Annual Spring Meeting of the American Ethnological Society,* 1967. (pp. 131–148.)

DARWIN, C. *The descent of man* (1871). (Facsimile of the first edition.) New York: International Publications, 1962.

DARWIN, C. *On the origin of species by means of natural selection* (1859). (Facsimile of the first edition with an introduction by L. Mayr.) Cambridge, Mass.: Harvard University Press, 1964.

DAY, M. H. Femoral fragment of a robust Australopithecine from Olduvai Gorge, Tanzania. *Nature,* 1969, 221, 230–233.

DEETZ, J. *Invitation to archaeology.* New York: Doubleday, 1967.

DEETZ, J. F. Archaeology as a social science. In M. P. Leone (Ed.), *Contemporary archaeology.* Carbondale: Southern Illinois Press, 1972.

DE VORE, I., & HALL, K. R. L. Baboon ecology. In I. De Vore (Ed.), *Primate behavior.* New York: Holt, Rinehart & Winston, 1965. (pp. 20–52.)

DIAZ, M. N., & POTTER, J. M. Introduction: The social life of peasants. In J. M. Potter, M. N. Diaz, & G. M. Foster (Eds.), *Peasant society: A reader.* Boston: Little, Brown, 1967.

DIETZ, R. S., & HOLDEN, J. D. The breakup of Pangaea. *Scientific American,* 1970, 223, 30–41.

DOBZHANSKY, T. *Mankind evolving.* New Haven, Conn.: Yale University Press, 1962.

DOBZHANSKY, T. Genetic entities in hominid evolution. In S. L. Washburn (Ed.), *Classification and human evolution.* Chicago: Aldine, 1963, pp. 347–362.

DOLHINOW, P. J. (Ed.). *Primate patterns.* New York: Holt, Rinehart & Winston, 1972, pp. 352–382.

DOLHINOW, P. J., & BISHOP, N. The development

of motor skills and social relationships among primates through play. In P. J. Dolhinow (Ed.), *Primate patterns.* New York: Holt, Rinehart & Winston, 1972, pp. 312–337.

DOUGLAS, M. Raffia cloth distribution in the Lele economy. *Africa,* 1958, *28,* 109–122.

DRUCKER, P. Rank, wealth, and kinship in Northwest coast society. *American Anthropologist,* 1939, *41,* 55–65.

DRUCKER, P. *Indians of the Northwest Coast.* Garden City, N. Y.: Natural History Press, 1963.

DRUCKER, P. *Cultures of the North Pacific coast.* San Francisco: Chandler, 1965.

DU BOIS, C. *The people of Alor: A social-psychological study of an East Indian island.* Minneapolis: University of Minnesota Press, 1944.

DUNDES, A. (Ed.). *Every man his way: Readings in cultural anthropology.* Englewood Cliffs, N.J.: Prentice-Hall, 1968a.

DUNDES, A. Oral literature. In J. A. Clifton (Ed.), *Introduction to cultural anthropology: Essays in the scope and methods of the science of man.* Boston: Houghton Mifflin, 1968b.

DUNN, F. L. Epidemiological factors: Health and disease in hunter-gatherers. In R. B. Lee & I. DeVore (Eds.), *Man the hunter.* Chicago: Aldine, 1968.

DYSON-HUDSON, R., & DYSON-HUDSON, N. Subsistence herding in Uganda. *Scientific American,* 1969, *220,* 76–89.

EAMES, E., & GOODE, J. G. *Anthropology of the city: An introduction to urban anthropology.* Englewood Cliffs, N.J.: Prentice-Hall, 1977.

EGGAN, D. Hopi dreams in cultural perspective. In G.E. von Grunebaum & R. Callois (Eds.), *The dream and human societies.* Berkeley: University of California Press, 1966.

EGGAN, F. Social anthropology and the method of controlled comparison. *American Anthropologist,* 1954, *56,* 743–763.

EIBL-EIBESFELDT, I. Ethological perspectives on primate studies. In P. C. Jay (Ed.), *Primates: Studies in adaptability and variability.* New York: Holt, Rinehart & Winston, 1968. (pp. 479–486.)

EIBL-EIBESFELDT, I. Phylogenetic adaptation as determinants of aggressive behavior in man. In J. de Witt & W. W. Hartrup (Eds.), *Determinants and origins of aggressive behavior.* The Hague: Mouton, 1974. (pp. 29–54.)

EIMERL, S., & DE VORE, I. *The primates.* New York: Time-Life, 1965.

EISELEY, L. *Darwin's century.* New York: Doubleday, 1961.

EISENSTADT, S. N. Transformation of social, political, and cultural orders in modernization. In R. Cohen & J. Middleton (Eds.), *Comparative politi-* cal systems: Studies in the politics of pre-industrial societies. Garden City, N.Y.: Natural History Press, 1967.

ELGIN, S. H. *What is linguistics?* Englewood Cliffs, N. J.: Prentice-Hall, 1973.

EMBER, M., & EMBER, C. R. The conditions favoring matrilocal versus patrilocal residence. *American Anthropologist,* 1971, *73,* 571–594.

ENGLISH, P. W. *City and village in Iran: Settlement and economy in the Kirman Basin.* Madison: University of Wisconsin Press, 1966.

ESCH, H. The evolution of bee language. *Scientific American,* 1967, *216,* 97–103.

EVANS-PRITCHARD, E. E. The Nuer of the Southern Sudan. In M. Fortes and E. E. Evans-Pritchard (Eds.), *African political systems.* London: Oxford University Press/African Institute, 1970. (pp. 272–297.)

EVANS-PRITCHARD, E. E. (Ed.). The notion of witchcraft explains unfortunate events. In *Witchcraft, oracles, and magic among the Azande.* Oxford: Clarendon Press, 1976.

EVELETH, P. B. The effects of climate on growth. *Annals of the New York Academy of Science,* 1966, *134* (2), 750.

FAGAN, B. *In the beginning.* Boston: Little, Brown, 1975, p. 149.

FAGAN, B. *People of the earth* (2nd ed.). Boston: Little Brown, 1977.

FALLERS, L. A. Equality and inequality in human societies. In S. Tax & L. G. Freeman (Eds.), *Horizons of anthropology* (2nd ed.). Chicago: Aldine, 1977.

FARB, P. *Man's rise to civilization as shown by the Indians of North America from primeival times to the coming of the industrial state.* New York: Dutton, 1968.

FERNEA, E. *A street in Marrakech.* New York: Doubleday, 1975.

FIRTH, R. *We, the Tikopia: A Sociological study of kinship in primitive Polynesia.* Boston: Beacon Press, 1963.

FISHMAN, J. A. Bilingual attitudes and behavior. *Language sciences,* 1969, *5,* 5–11.

FISHMAN, J. A. *Sociolinguistics: A brief introduction.* Rowley, Mass.: Newbury House, 1970.

FLANNERY, K. V. The ecology of early food production in Mesopotamia. *Science,* 1965, *147,* 1247–1255.

FLANNERY, K. V. The vertebrate fauna and hunting patterns. In D. S. Byers (Ed.), *The prehistory of the Tehuacán Valley* (Vol. 1). Austin: University of Texas Press, 1967.

FLANNERY, K. V. The cultural evolution of civilizations. *The Annual Review of Ecology and Systematics,* 1972, *3,* 399–425.

FLINT, R. F., & SKINNER, B. J. *Physical geology* (2nd ed.). New York: Wiley, 1977.

FORD, C. S., & BEACH, F. A. *Patterns of sexual behavior.* New York: Harper, 1951.

FORDE, C. D. *Habitat, economy and society: A geographical introduction to ethnology.* New York: Dutton, 1934.

FORGE, A. *Primitive art and society.* New York: Oxford University Press, 1973.

FORTES, M. (Ed.). *Marriage in tribal societies.* Cambridge Papers in Social Anthropology, No. 3. Cambridge: Cambridge University Press, 1962.

FORTES, M. Pietas in ancestor worship. In Y. A. Cohen (Ed.), *Man in adaptation: The institutional framework.* Chicago: Aldine, 1971.

FOSTER, B. L. Ethnicity and commerce. *American Ethnologist,* 1974, *1,* 437–448.

FOULKS, E. F. *The Arctic hysterias of the North Alaskan eskimo.* Washington, D.C.: American Anthropological Association, 1972.

FOX, R. *Kinship and marriage.* Harmondsworth, Middlesex, England: Penguin, 1967.

FOX, R. *Urban anthropology: Cities in their cultural setting.* Englewood Cliffs, N.J.: Prentice-Hall, 1977.

FRAKE, C. O. The diagnosis of disease among the Subanun of Mindinao. *American Anthropologist.* 1961, *63,* 113–132.

FRAKE, C. O. Cultural ecology and ethnography. *American Anthropologist,* 1962, *64,* 53–59.

FRAKE, C. O. How to ask for a drink in Subanun. In J. Gumpery & D. Hymes (Eds.), *The ethnography of communication.* American Anthropologist Special Publication, 1964a, *66*(6), part 2.

FRAKE, C. O. A structural description of Subanun "religious behavior." In W. Goodenough (Ed.), *Explorations in cultural anthropology.* New York: McGraw-Hill, 1964b.

FRAYER, D. W. A reappraisal of *Ramapithecus. Yearbook of Physical Anthropology,* 1974, *18,* 19–29.

FRAZER, J. G. *Anthologia anthropologia: The native races of Africa and Madagascar.* London: Lund Humphries, 1938.

FREEMAN, L. C. Conflict and congruence in anthropological theory. In R. Manners & D. Kaplan (Eds.), *Theory in anthropology.* Chicago: Aldine, 1968. (pp. 193–195.)

FREILICH, M. (Ed.). *Marginal natives: Anthropologists at work.* New York: Harper & Row, 1970.

FRIED, M. H. *The evolution of political society: An essay in political anthropology.* New York: Random House, 1967.

FRIED, M. H. *The study of anthropology.* New York: Thomas Y. Crowell, 1972.

FRISBIE, C. J. Anthropological and ethnomusicological implications of a comparative analysis of Bushmen and African Pygmy music. *Ethnology,* 1971, *10,* 265–287.

FRISCH, J. E. Individual behavior and intertroop variability in Japanese macaques. In P. C. Jay (Ed.), *Primates: Studies in adaptation and variability.* New York: Holt, Rinehart & Winston, 1968, pp. 243–252.

FRISCH, R. E. Population, food intake and fertility. *Science,* 1978, *199,* 22–30.

FROMKIN, V., & RODMAN, R. *An introduction to language.* New York: Holt, Rinehart & Winston, 1974.

GAJDUSEK, D. C. Factors governing the genetics of primitive human populations. *Cold Spring Harbor Symposia on Quantitative Biology,* 1964, *29,* 121–127.

GANS, H. *The Levittowners.* New York: Pantheon, 1967.

GARDNER, R. A., & GARDNER, B. T. Teaching sign language to a chimpanzee. *Science,* August 15, 1969, 664–672.

GARN, S. M. *Human races.* Springfield, Ill: Charles C. Thomas, 1965.

GEERTZ, C. Ritual and social change: A Javanese example. *American Anthropologist,* 1957, *59,* 32–54.

GEERTZ, C. Form and variation in Balinese village structure. *American Anthropologist,* 1959, *61* (6).

GEERTZ, C. *The religion of Java.* Glencoe, Ill.: The Free Press, 1960.

GEERTZ, C. Studies in peasant life, community. and society. In B. J. Siegel (Ed.), *Biennial review of anthropology.* Stanford: Stanford University Press, 1962.

GEERTZ, C. (Ed.). The integrative revolution: Primordial sentiments and civil politics in the new states. In *Old societies and new states: The quest for modernity in Asia and Africa.* Glencoe, Ill.: The Free Press, 1963. (pp. 105–145.)

GEERTZ, C. Religion as a cultural system. In Michael Banton (Ed.), *Anthropological approaches to the study of religion.* London: Tavistock, 1966.

GEERTZ, C. (Ed.). The integrative revolution: Primordial sentiments and civil politics in the new states. In *Old societies and new states.* Chicago: University of Chicago Press, 1968a.

GEERTZ, C. Religion. I.: Anthropological study. In D. Sills. (Ed.), *International encyclopedia of the social sciences* (Vol. 13). New York: Macmillan, 1968b.

GEERTZ, C. Ethos, world-view and the analysis of sacred symbols. In E. A. Hammel & W. S. Simmons (Eds.), *Man makes sense: A reader in modern cultural anthropology.* Boston: Little, Brown, 1970.

GEERTZ, C. The wet and the dry: Traditional irrigation in Bali and Morocco. *Human Ecology,* 1972a, *1*(1), 23–39.

GEERTZ, C. Summary comments. In R. Antoun & Iliya Harik (Eds.), *Rural politics and social change in the Middle East.* Bloomington: Indiana University Press, 1972b.

GEERTZ, C. *The interpretation of cultures.* New York: Basic Books, 1973.

GEERTZ, C. On the nature of anthropological understanding. *American Scientist,* 1975, *63,* 47–48.

GEERTZ, C. Art as a culture system. *MLN,* 1976, *91,* 1473–1499.

GIBBS, J. L., Jr. Poro values and courtroom procedures in Kpelle chiefdom. *Southwestern Journal of Anthropology,* 1962, *18*(4), 341–350.

GIBBS, J. L., Jr. Marital instability among the Kpelle: Toward a theory of epainogramy. *American Anthropologist,* 1963, *65,* 552–559.

GIFFORD, E. W. Miwok lineages and the political unit in California. *American Anthropologist,* 1926, *28,* 389–401.

GILMORE, D. Varieties of gossip in a Spanish rural community. *Ethnology,* 1978, *17,* 89–99.

GLICK, P. B. Melanesian mosaic: The plural community of Vila. In L. Plotnicov & A. Tuden (Eds.), *Essays in comparative social stratification.* Pittsburgh: University of Pittsburgh Press, 1970.

GLUCKMAN, M. Kinship and marriage among the Lozi of northern Rhodesia and the Zulu of Natal. In A. R. Radcliffe-Brown & D. Forde (Eds.), *African systems of kinship and marriage.* Oxford: Oxford University Press, 1950.

GLUCKMAN, M. (Ed.). Les rites de passage. In *Essays on the ritual of social relations.* Manchester: Manchester University Press, 1962.

GLUCKMAN, *Order and rebellion in tribal Africa.* London: Cohen and West, 1963.

GLUCKMAN, M. Inter-hierarchical roles: Professional and party ethics in tribal areas in South and Central Africa. In M. J. Swartz (Ed.), *Local-level politics: Social and cultural perspectives.* Chicago: Aldine, 1968.

GOLDSBY, R. A. *Race and races.* New York: Macmillan, 1977.

GOLDSCHMIDT, W. *Sebei law.* Berkeley: University of California Press, 1967. (pp. 245–260.)

GOLDWATER, R. Art history and anthropology: Some comparisons of methodology. In A. Forge (Ed.), *Primitive art and society.* New York: Oxford University Press, 1973.

GOODALE, J. C., & KOSS, J. D. The cultural context of creativity among Tiwi. In C. M. Otten (Ed.), *Anthropology and art.* Garden City, N.Y.: Natural History Press, 1971.

GOODALL, J. Chimpanzees of the Gombe Stream Reserve. In I. DeVore (Ed.), *Primate behavior.* New York: Holt, Rinehart & Winston, 1965. (pp. 458–461.)

GOODENOUGH, W. H. A problem in Malayo-Polynesian social organization. *American Anthropologist,* 1955, *57,* 71–83.

GOODENOUGH, W. H. Residence rules. *Southwestern Journal of Anthropology,* 1956, *12,* 22–37.

GOODENOUGH, W. H. *Description and comparison in cultural anthropology.* Chicago: Aldine, 1970.

GOODY, J. Bridewealth and dowry in Africa and Eurasia. In J. Goody & S. J. Tambiah (Eds.), *Bridewealth and dowry.* Cambridge: Cambridge University Press, 1973.

GORER, G., & RICKMAN, J. *The people of Great Russia: A psychological study.* New York: Chanticleer, 1950.

GOUGH, E. K. The Nayars and the definition of marriage. *Journal of the Royal Anthropological Institute,* 1959, *89,* 23–34.

GOULD, H. A. Castes, outcastes, and the sociology of stratification. *International Journal of Comparative Sociology,* 1960, *1*(2).

GOULD, H. A. *Caste and class: A comparative view.* A McCaleb Module in Anthropology. Addison-Wesley Modular Publications, 1971.

GOULDNER, A. W. *The coming crisis of Western sociology.* New York: Basic Books, 1970.

GRABURN, N. H. H. (Ed.). Introduction: Arts of the Fourth World. In *Ethnic and tourist arts: Cultural expressions from the Fourth World.* Berkeley: University of California Press, 1976.

GRANQVIST, Hilma. *Marriage conditions in a Palestinian village.* Helsingfors: Akademische Buchhandrung, 1931.

GREULICH, W. W. A comparison of the physical growth and development of American-born and native Japanese children. *American Journal of Physical Anthropology,* 1957, *15,* 489–515.

GRINNELL, G. B. *The Cheyenne Indians: Their history and way of life* (Vol. 1). New York: Cooper Square Publishers, 1962.

GROSSMAN, L. Ethnicity and health delivery systems. In P. S. J. Cafferty & L. Chestang (Eds.), *The diverse society: Implications for social policy.* Washington: National Association of Social Workers, 1976.

GULLIVER, P. H. The Jie of Uganda. In J. L. Gibbs, Jr. (Ed.), *Peoples of Africa.* New York: Holt, Rinehart & Winston, 1965.

HALL, E. T. Proxemics. *Current Anthropology.* 1968, *9,* 83–95.

HALL, K. R. L. Social learning in monkeys. In P. C. Jay (Ed.), *Primates: Studies in adaptation and variability.* New York: Holt, Rinehart & Winston, 1968, pp. 383–397.

HAMILTON, T. H. *Process and pattern in evolution.* New York: Macmillan, 1967.

HARDESTY, D. L. *Ecological anthropology.* New York: Wiley, 1977.

HARLOW, H. F. The nature of love. *American Psychologist,* 1958, *13,* 673–685.

HARLOW, H. F., & HARLOW, M. Learning to love. *American Scientist,* 1966, *54,* 244–272.

HARLOW, H. F. et al. From thought to therapy: Lessons from a primate laboratory. *American Scientist,* 1971, *59,* 538–549.

HARNER, M. The ecological basis for Aztec sacrifice. *American Ethnologist,* 1977, *4,* 117–133.

HARRELL-BOND, B. Studying elites: Some special problems. In M. A. Rynkiewich & J. P. Spradley, *Ethics and anthropology: Dilemmas in fieldwork.* New York: Wiley, 1976.

HARRIS, M. *Cows, pigs, wars, and witches.* New York: Vintage/Random House, 1974.

HARRISON, G. A., & WEINER, J. S. Some considerations in the formulation of theories of human phylogeny. In S. L. Washburn (Ed.), *Classification and human evolution.* Chicago: Aldine, 1963. (pp. 75–84.)

HARRISON, S. The challenge to Indian nationalism. *Foreign Affairs,* 1956, *34.*

HARTL, D. L. *Our uncertain heritage.* Philadelphia: Lippincott, 1977.

HAUSER, P. M., & SCHNORE, L. F. (Eds.). *The study of urbanization.* New York: Wiley, 1965.

HELBAEK, H. Domestication of food plants in the Old World, *Science,* 1959, *130,* 365–372.

HERSKOVITS, M. J. *Economic anthropology: The economic life of primitive peoples.* New York: Norton, 1965.

HESTER, T. R., HEIZER, R. F., & GRAHAM, J. A. *Field methods in archaeology.* Palo Alto, Cal.: Mayfield, 1975.

HIMMELHEBER, H. The present status of sculptural art among the tribes of the Ivory Coast. In J. Helm (Ed.), *Proceedings of the 1966 Annual Spring Meeting of the American Ethnological Society,* 1967. (pp. 192–197.)

HOCKETT, C. D. The origin of speech. *Scientific American,* 1960, *203,* 88–96.

HOLE, F. Questions of theory in the explanation of culture change in pre-history. In C. Renfrew (Ed.), *The explanation of culture change.* (Models in prehistory.) London: Duckworth, 1973.

HOLE, F., & HEIZER, R. A. *An introduction in prehistoric archaeology.* New York: Holt, Rinehart & Winston, 1973.

HOLLOWAY, R. L. The casts of fossil hominid brains. *Scientific American,* 1974, *231,* 106–115.

HOOTON, E. A. *Crime and the man.* Cambridge, Mass.: Harvard University Press, 1939.

HOSTETLER, J. A., & HUNTINGTON, G. E. *Children in Amish society: Socialization and community education.* New York: Holt, Rinehart & Winston, 1971.

HOWELLS, W. W. Neanderthal man: Facts and figures. *Yearbook of Physical Anthropology,* 1974, *18,* 7–18.

HRDY, S. B. Infanticide as a primate reproductive strategy. *American Scientist,* 1977, *65,* 40–49.

HUIZINGA, J. *Homo ludens: A study of the play-element in culture.* Boston: Beacon Press, 1955.

HULSE, F. S. Migration and cultural selection in human genetics. *The Anthropologist* (Special Volume), 1968, 1–21.

Human teeth in China dated at 1–7 million years, *The New York Times,* February 6, 1978.

HUNTER, D. E., & WHITTEN, P. *Encyclopedia of anthropology.* New York: Harper & Row, 1976.

HUNTINGFORD, G. W. B. *The Nandi of Kenya: Tribal control in a pastoral society.* London: Routledge & Kegan Paul, 1953.

HYMES, D. Linguistic method in ethnography: Its development in the United States. In P. Garvin (Ed.), *Method and theory in linguistics.* The Hague: Mouton, 1971a.

HYMES, D. Sociolinguistics and the ethnography of speaking. In E. Ardener (Ed.), *Social anthropology and linguistics.* ASA Monographs, 10. London: Tavistock, 1971b.

HYMES, D. *Foundations in Sociolinguistics: An ethnographic approach.* Philadelphia: University of Pennsylvania Press, 1974.

ISAAC, E. On the domestication of cattle. In S. Struever (Ed.), *Prehistoric agriculture.* Garden City, N.Y.: Natural History Press, 1971.

ISAAC, G. L. Early hominids in action: A commentary on the contribution of archeology to understanding the fossil record in East Africa. *Yearbook of Physical Anthropology,* 1975a, *19,* 19–35.

ISAAC, G. L. Stratigraphy and cultural patterns in East Africa during the middle ranges of Pleistocene time. In K. W. Butzer & G. L. Isaac (Eds.), *After the australopithecines.* The Hague: Mouton, 1975b.

ISAAC, G. L. The food-sharing behavior of protohuman hominids. *Scientific American,* April, 1978, 90–108.

654

JACOBS. J. *The economy of cities.* New York: Vintage, 1970.

JAY, P. C. The common langur of north India. In I. De Vore (Ed.), *Primate behavior.* New York: Holt, Rinehart & Winston, 1965.

JENKINS, F. A. *Primate locomotion.* New York: Academic Press, 1974.

JOHANSON, D. C., & BRILL, D. Ethiopia yields first "family" of early man. *National Geographic,* December 1976, 790–811.

JOLLY, A. *The evolution of primate behavior.* New York: Macmillan, 1972.

JOLLY, C. J. The seed-eaters: A new model of hominid differentiation based on a baboon analogy. *Man,* 1970, *5:* 5–26.

JU-KANG, WOO. Mandible of Sinanthropus Lantianensis. *Current Anthropology,* 1964, *5*(2), 98–101.

JU-KANG, WOO. The skull of Lantian man. *Current Anthropology,* 1966, 7(1), 83–86.

KAPLAN, D., & MANNERS, R. A. *Culture theory.* Englewood Cliffs, N. J.: Prentice-Hall, 1972.

KARDINER, A. *The individual and his society.* New York: Columbia University Press, 1939.

KARDINER, A., & PREBLE, E. *They studied man.* New York: Crown, 1961.

KAY, R. F., The functional adaptations of primate molar teeth. *American Journal of Physical Anthropology,* 1975, *43,* 195–216.

KEESING, R. M. Theories of culture. In B. Siegel, A. Beals, & S. Tyler (Eds.), *Annual review of anthropology* (Vol. 3). Palo Alto, Calif.: Annual Reviews, Inc., 1974. (pp. 73–97.)

KEESING, R. M. *Cultural anthropology: A contemporary perspective.* New York: Holt, Rinehart & Winston, 1976.

KEESING, R. M., & KEESING, F. M. *New perspectives in cultural anthropology.* New York: Holt, Rinehart & Winston, 1971.

KENNEDY, K. A. R. *Neanderthal man.* Minneapolis: Burgess, 1975.

KETTLEWELL, H. B. D. The phenomenon of industrial melanism in *Lepidoptera. Annual Review of Entomology,* 1961, 6, 245–262.

KLUCKHOHM, C. Myths and rituals: A general theory. *Harvard Theological Review,* 1942, *35,* 45–79.

KLUCKHOHN, C., & KELLY, W. H. The concept of culture. In R. Linton (Ed.), *The science of man in the world crisis.* New York: Columbia University Press, 1945.

KLUCKHOHN, C., & LEIGHTON, D. C. *The Navaho.* Cambridge, Mass.: Harvard University Press, 1946.

KLUCKHOHN, C., & MURRAY, H. A. (Eds.). *Per-*sonality in nature, society, and culture (2nd ed.). New York: Knopf, 1962.

KOLATA, G. B. !Kung hunter-gatherers: Feminism, diet and birth control. *Science,* 1974, *185,* 932–934.

KOPYKOFF, I., & MIERS, S. African "slavery" as an institution of marginality. In S. Miers & I. Kopykoff (Eds.), *Slavery in Africa.* Madison: University of Wisconsin Press, 1977.

KOTTAK, C. P. Race relations in a Bahian fishing village. *Luso-Brazilian Review,* 1967, *4,* 35–52.

KRADER, L. *Formation of the state.* Englewood Cliffs, N.J.: Prentice-Hall, 1968.

KRETZOI, M., & VÉRTES, L. Upper Biharian (Inter-Mindel) pebble-industry occupation site in Western Hungary. *Current Anthropology,* 1965, 6(1), 74–87.

KROEBER, A. L. Classificatory systems or relationship. *Journal of the Royal Anthropological Institute,* 1909, *39,* 77–84.

KROEBER, A. L. *Anthropology.* New York: Harcourt, 1923.

KROEBER, A. L. *Anthropology* (Rev. ed.). New York: Harcourt, 1948.

KROEBER, A. L., & KLUCKHOHN, C. (Eds.). *Culture, a critical review of concepts and definitions.* New York: Random House, 1952.

KURTEN, B. Continental drift and evolution. *Scientific American,* 1969, *220,* 54–64.

KUMMER, B. K. F. Functional adaptation to posture in the pelvis of man and other primates. In R. H. Tuttle (Ed.), *Primate functional morphology and evolution.* The Hague: Mouton, 1975.

LABARRE, W. Some observations on character structure in the Orient: The Japanese. *Psychiatry,* 1945, *8,* 326–342.

LABARRE, W. *The human animal.* Chicago: University of Chicago Press, 1954.

LABOV, W. *Sociolinguistic patterns.* Philadelphia: University of Pennsylvania Press, 1972.

LAKOFF, R. Language and women's place. *Language in society,* 1973, *3,* 45–80.

LASKER, G. W. Human biological adaptability. *Science,* 1969, *166,* 1480–1486.

LEACH, E. R. *Political systems of highland Burma: A study of Kachin social structure.* Boston: Beacon Press, 1954.

LEACH, E. R. Polyandry, inheritance and the definition of marriage. *Man,* 1955, *54,* 182–186.

LEACH, E. R. Golden bough or gilded twig? *Daedalus,* 1961, *90,* 371–387.

LEACH, E. R. Ritual. In D. Sills (Ed.), *International encyclopedia of the social sciences* (Vol. 13). New York: Macmillan, 1968.

LEACH, M. (Ed.). Swastika. In *Standard dictionary of*

folklore, mythology, and legend. New York: Funk & Wagnalls, 1950.

LEAKEY, M. D. Olduvai Gorge (Vol. 3). Cambridge: The University Press, 1971.

LEAKEY, M. D. Cultural patterns in the Olduvai sequence. In K. W. Butzer & G. L. Isaac (Eds.), After the australopithecines. The Hague: Mouton, 1975.

LEAKEY, M. D., HAY, R. L., CURTIS, G. H., DRAKE, R. E., JACKES, M. K., & WHITE, T. D. Fossil hominids from the Laetolil beds. Nature, 1976, 262, 460–466.

LEAKEY, R. E. F. Evidence for an advanced Plio-Pleistocene hominid from East Rudolf, Kenya. Nature, 1973, 242, 447–450.

LEAKEY, R. E. F. Australopithecus, Homo erectus and the single species hypothesis. Nature, 1976, 261, 572–576.

LEAKEY, R. E. F. Origins. New York: Dutton, 1977.

Leakey's find—tracks of an ancient ancestor. Time, March 6, 1978, 75.

LEE, R. B. !Kung bushman subsistence: An input-output analysis. In A. P. Vayda (Ed.), Environment and cultural behavior. Garden City, N.Y.: Natural History Press, 1969.

LEE, R. B., & DeVORE, I. (Eds.). Problems in the study of hunters and gatherers. In Man the hunter. Chicago: Aldine, 1968.

LeGROS CLARK, W. E. An introduction to the study of fossil man (5th ed.). Chicago: University of Chicago Press, 1965.

LÉONS, M. B. The economic networks of Bolivian political brokers: Revolutionary road to fame and fortune. In R. Halperin & J. Dow (Eds.), Peasant livelihood: Studies in anthropology and cultural ecology. New York: St. Martin's, 1977.

LEOROI-GOURHAN, A. The evolution of Paleolithic art. Scientific American, February, 1968.

LESSA, W. A. The decreasing power of myth on Ulithi. In W. A. Lessa & E. Z. Vogt, Reader in comparative religion: An anthropological approach (2nd ed.). New York: Harper & Row, 1965.

LESSA, W. A., & VOGT, E. Z. Reader in comparative religion: An anthropological approach (2nd ed.). New York: Harper & Row, 1965.

LeVINE, R. A., & LeVINE, B. B. Nyansongo: A Gusii community in Kenya. Six Cultures Series (Vol. 2). New York: Wiley, 1966.

LÉVI-STRAUSS, C. The social and psychological aspects of chieftainship in a primitive tribe: The Nambikuara of northwestern Mato Grosso. Transactions of the New York Academy of Sciences, 1944, 16–32.

LÉVI-STRAUSS, C. Social structure. In A. L. Kroeber (Ed.), Anthropology today. Chicago: University of Chicago Press, 1953.

LÉVI-STRAUSS, C. Structual anthropology. New York: Basic Books, 1963.

LÉVI-STRAUSS, C. Today's crisis in anthropology. In S. Rapport & H. Wright (Eds.), Anthropology. New York: Washington Square Press, 1967.

LÉVI-STRAUSS, C. The concept of primitiveness. In R. Lee & I. De Vore (Eds.), Man the hunter. Chicago: Aldine, 1968. (pp. 349–352.)

LEWIS, I. M. Ecstatic religion. Baltimore: Penguin, 1971.

LEWIS, O. Life in a Mexican village: Tepoztlan restudied. Urbana: University of Illinois Press, 1951.

LIEBERMAN, P. On the evolution of language: A unified view. In R. H. Tuttle, (Ed.), Primate functional morphology and evolution. The Hague: Mouton, 1975. (pp. 203–212.)

LIEBERMAN, P., & CRELIN, E. S. On the speech of neanderthal. Linguistic Inquiry 2, 1971, 203–222.

LIEBOW, E. Tally's corner: A study of Negro street-corner men. Boston: Little, Brown, 1967.

LITTLE, K. L. The role of the secret society in cultural specialization. American Anthropologist, 1949, 51, 199–212.

LITTLE, K. L. Voluntary associations in urban life: A case study of differential adaptation. In M. Freedman (Ed.), Social organization: Essays presented to Raymond Firth. Chicago: Aldine, 1967.

LITTLE, M. A., & BAKER, P. T. Environmental adaptation and perspectives. In P. T. Baker & M. A. Little (Eds.), Man in the Andes. Stroudsburg, Pa.: Dowden, Hutchinson & Ross, 1976.

LITTLE, M. A., & MORREN, G. E. B., Jr. Ecology, energetics, and human variability. Dubuque, Iowa: William C. Brown, 1976.

LLOYD, P. C. Divorce among the Yoruba. American Anthropologist, 1968, 70(1), 67–81.

LOMAX, Song structure and social structure. Ethnology, 1962, 1(4), 425–451.

LOMAX, A. Folk song style and culture. Washington, D.C.: American Association for the Advancement of Science, 1968. (No. 88.)

LOWIE, R. The history of ethnological theory. New York: Rinehart, 1937.

LYND, R. S., & LYND, H. M. Middletown: A study in contemporary American culture. New York: Harcourt, 1959.

LYND, R. S., & LYND, H. M. Middletown in transition. New York: Harcourt, 1963.

MacNEISH, R. S. Ancient mesoamerican civilization. Science, 1964, 143, 531–537.

MacNeish, R. S., Patterson, T. C., & Browman, D. L. *The central Peruvian prehistoric interaction sphere* (Vol. 7). Phillips Academy, Andover, Mass.: Papers of the Robert S. Peabody Foundation for Archaeology, 1975.

Maddi, S. R. *Personality theories: A comparative analysis.* Homewood, Ill.: Dorsey, 1968.

Maglio, V. J., Vertebrate fauna from the Kubi Alfi, Koobi Fora and Ileret areas, east Rudolf, Kenya. *Nature,* 1971, *231.*

Mair, L. *Primitive government.* Baltimore: Penguin, 1962.

Mair, L. *An introduction to social anthropology* (2nd ed.). Oxford: Clarendon, 1972.

Malefijt, A. De Waal. *Images of man: A history of anthropological thought.* New York: Knopf, 1974.

Malinowski, B. Kula; the circulating exchange of valuables in the archipelagoes of eastern New Guinea. *Man,* 1920 (No. 51), 97–105. [In George Dalton (Ed.), *Tribal and peasant economies. Readings in economic anthropology.* Garden City, N.Y. The Natural History Press, 1967.]

Malinowski, B. *Argonauts of the Western Pacific.* London: Routledge & Kegan Paul, 1922.

Malinowski, B. *Coral gardens and their magic.* London: Allen & Unwin, 1935.

Malinowski, B. *A diary in the strict sense of the term.* London: Routledge & Kegan Paul, 1967.

Mandlebaum, D. G. (Ed.). *Selected writings of Edward Sapir in language, culture and personality.* Berkeley: University of California Press, 1949.

Mangelsdorf, P. C., MacNeish, R. S., & Galinat, W. C. Domestication of corn. *Science,* 1964, *143,* 538–545.

Mangin, W. *Peasants in cities: Readings in the anthropology of urbanization.* Boston: Houghton Mifflin, 1970.

Mann, A. *A paleodemography of* Australopithecus. Berkeley: University of California Press, 1968.

Mann, A., & Trinkaus, E. Neandertal and Neandertal-like fossils from the Upper Pleistocene. *Yearbook of Physical Anthropology,* 1973, *17,* 169–193.

Marcus, J. Territorial organization of the lowland classic Mava. *Science,* June 1, 1973, 191–195.

Maretzki, T. W., & Maretzki, H. *Taira: An Okinawan village.* Six Cultures Series. (Vol. 7). New York: Wiley, 1966.

Margalef, R. *Perspectives in ecological theory.* Chicago: University of Chicago Press, 1968.

Marsden, H. M. Antagonistic behavior of young rhesus monkeys after changes induced in social rank of their mother. *Animal Behavior,* 1968, *16*(1), 38–44.

Marshack, A. Some implications of the paleolithic symbolic evidence for the origin of language. *Current Anthropology,* 1976, *17,* 274–282.

Marshall, G. Marriage: Comparative analysis. In D. Sills (Ed.), *International encyclopedia of the social sciences* (Vol. 10). New York: Macmillan, 1968. (pp. 8–19.)

Marshall, L. !Kung bushman bands. *Africa,* 1960, *30*(4), 26–43.

Martin, P. S. The revolution in archaeology. In M. P. Leone (Ed.), *Contemporary archaeology.* Carbondale: Southern Illinois Press, 1972.

Martin, R. O. Strategies of reproduction. *Natural History,* 1975, *84,* 49–57.

Maruyama, M. Toward human futuristics. In M. Maruyama & J. A. Dator (Eds.), *Human futuristics.* Honolulu: Social Science Research Institute, University of Hawaii, 1971.

Mason, W. A. Naturalistic and experimental investigations of the social behavior of monkeys and apes. In P. C. Jay (Ed.), *Primates: Studies in adaptation and variability.* New York: Holt, Rinehart & Winston, 1968. (pp. 398–419.)

Maybury-Lewis, D. *Akwē-Shavante society.* New York: Oxford University Press, 1974.

McDermott, W. C. *The ape in antiquity.* Baltimore: Johns Hopkins University Press, 1938.

McKern, T. W. *The search for man's origins.* An Addison-Wesley Module in Anthropology, Module #53. Reading, Mass.: Addison-Wesley, 1974.

McKusick, V. A., Hostetler, J. A. Egeland, J. A., & Eldridge, R. The distribution of certain genes in the Old Order Amish. *Cold Spring Harbor Symposium on Quantitative Biology,* 1964, *29,* 99–114.

Mead, G. H. *Mind, self, and society.* Chicago: University of Chicago Press, 1934.

Mead, M. *Coming of age in Samoa.* New York: Morrow, 1928.

Mead, M. *Growing up in New Guinea.* New York: Morrow, 1930.

Mead, M. *Sex and temperament in three primitive societies.* New York: Morrow, 1935.

Mead, M. The study of national character. In D. Lerner & H. D. Lasswell (Eds.), *The policy sciences.* Stanford: Stanford University Press, 1951. (pp. 70–85.)

Mead, M. A note on contributions of anthropology to the science of the future. In M. Maruyama & J. A. Dator (Eds.), *Human futuristics.* Honolulu: Social Science Research Institute, University of Hawaii, 1971.

Mead, M., & Metraux, R. (Eds.). *The study of cul-*

ture at a distance. Chicago: University of Chicago Press, 1953.

MELLAART, J. *The Neolithic of the Near East.* New York: Scribner's, 1975.

"Mennonite Dissident Shunned by Church and Wife," *The New York Times,* July 23, 1973.

MERRIAM, A. P. Purposes of ethnomusicology: An anthropological view. *Ethnomusicology,* 1963, *7,* 206–213.

MERRIAM, A. P. *The anthropology of music.* Evanston, Ill.: Northwestern University Press, 1964a.

MERRIAM, A. P. The arts and anthropology. In. S. Tax (Ed.), *Horizons of anthropology.* Chicago: Aldine, 1964b.

MEZZROW, M., & WOLFE, B. *Really the blues.* New York: Random House, 1946. (pp. 71–77).

MICHELS, J. W. *Dating methods in archaeology.* New York: Seminar Press, 1973. (p. 4.)

MIDDLETON, J. *Lugbara religion: Ritual and authority among an East African people.* New York: Oxford University Press, 1960.

MILLER, E. S. The Christian missionary, agent of secularization. *Anthropological Quarterly,* 1970, *43*(1), 14–22.

MILLER, E. S. *Rethinking the concept "peasantry."* Unpublished manuscript prepared for presentation at the Third Annual Meeting of the Working Group in Social Articulation, Quito, Ecuador, December 1976. (Available from author, Department of Anthropology, Temple University.)

MILLER, G. T., Jr. *Living in the environment: Concepts, problems and alternatives.* Belmont, Cal.: Wadsworth, 1975.

MILLON, R. Social relations in ancient Teotihuacán. In E. Wolf (Ed.) *The Valley of Mexico: Studies in prehistoric ecology and society.* Albuquerque: University of New Mexico Press, 1976.

MILNER, R. B., & PROST, J. H. The significance of primate behavior for anthropology. In N. Korn & F. Thompson (Eds.), *Human evolution* (2nd ed.). New York: Holt, Rinehart & Winston, 1967. (pp. 125–136.)

MILTON, J. B. Fertility differentials in modern societies resulting in normalizing selection for height. *Human Biology,* 1975, *47,* 189–200.

MINTZ, S. W., & WOLF, E. R. An analysis of ritual co-parenthood (compadrazgo). *Southwestern Journal of Anthropology,* 1950, *6,* 54.

MITCHELL, J. C. Marriage, matriliny, and social structure among the Yao of southern Nyasaland. *International Journal of Comparative Sociology,* 1962, *3,* 29–32; 35–37; 39–40.

MITCHELL, J. C. On quantification in social anthropology. In A. L. Epstein (Ed.), *The craft of anthropology.* London: Tavistock, 1967. (pp. 17–45.)

MOODY, P. A. *Genetics of man* (2nd ed.). New York: Norton, 1975.

MOONEY, J. An Indian messiah. 1892. In M. Mead & N. Calas (Eds.), *Primitive heritage.* New York: Random House, 1953. (pp. 412–424.)

MORRIS, D., & MORRIS, R. *Men and apes.* London: Hutchinson, 1966.

MORRIS, L. N. *Human populations, genetic variation and evolution.* San Francisco: Chandler, 1971.

MUNN, N. D. Visual categories: An approach to the study of representational systems. In C. F. Jopling (Ed.), *Art and aesthetics in primitive societies.* New York: Dutton, 1971.

MUNN, N. D. The spatial presentation of cosmic order in Walbiri iconography. In A. Forge (Ed.), *Primitive art and society.* New York: Oxford University Press, 1973.

MURAYAMA, M., & NALBANDIAN, R. M. *Sickle cell hemoglobin.* Boston: Little, Brown, 1973.

MURDOCK, G. P. *Our primitive contemporaries.* New York: Macmillan, 1934.

MURDOCK, G. P. Double descent. *American Anthropologist, 42*(4), 1940, 555–561.

MURDOCK, G. P. *Social structure.* New York: Macmillan, 1949.

MYERHOFF, B. G., & TUFTE, V. Life history as integration: An essay on an experimental model. *Gerontologist,* 1975, *15,* 541–543.

NADEL, S. F. Witchcraft in four African societies: An essay in comparison. In S. Ottenberg & P. Ottenberg (Eds.), *Cultures and societies of Africa.* New York: Random House, 1960, (pp. 407–419.)

NAPIER, J. R. Fossil hand bones from Olduvai Gorge. *Nature,* 1962, *196,* 409.

NAPIER, J. R. *Monkeys without tails.* New York: Taplinger, 1976.

NAPIER, J. R., & NAPIER, P. H. *A handbook of the living primates.* London: Academic Press, 1967.

NASH, M. The social context of economic choice in a small society. *Man,* 1961a, *219,* 186–191.

NASH, M. Witchraft as social process in a Tzeltal community. *American Indigena,* 1961b, *20,* 121–126.

NASH, M. *Primitive and peasant economic systems.* San Francisco: Chandler, 1966.

NASH, M. The organization of economic life. In S. Tax & L. G. Freeman (Eds.), *Horizons of anthropology* (2nd ed.). Chicago: Aldine, 1977.

NEEDHAM, R. The future of social anthropology: Disintegration of metamorphosis? In *Anniversary contributions to anthropology: Twelve essays.* Leiden: E. J. Brill, 1970.

658

NEEDHAM, R. *Rethinking kinship and marriage.* London: Tavistock, 1971.

NEETING, R. McC. The ecological approach in cultural study. Addison-Wesley Modular Publications, 1971, (Module 6). (pp. 1–30.)

NELSON, N. C. *Prehistoric archaeology.* In F. Boas, *General anthropology.* Boston: Heath, 1938. (pp. 146–148.)

NEWCOMBE, H. B. In M. Fishbein (Ed.), *Papers and Discussions of the Second International Conference on Congenital Malformations.* New York: International Medical Congress, 1964.

OAKLEY, K. P. *Man the tool-maker.* Chicago: University of Chicago Press, 1959.

OLIVER, O. O. In M. Herskovits, *Economic anthropology: The economic life of primitive peoples.* New York: Norton, 1965.

OTTENBERG, S., & OTTENBERG, P. (Eds.) *Cultures and societies of Africa.* New York: Random House, 1960.

PARK, G. K. Divination and its social contexts. In J. Middleton (Ed.), *Magic, witchcraft, and curing.* Garden City, N.Y.: Natural History Press, 1967.

PARSONS, J. R. Settlement and population history of the basin of Mexico. In E. Wolf (Ed.), *The Valley of Mexico: Studies in prehistoric ecology and society.* Albuquerque: University of New Mexico Press, 1976.

PATAI, R. *Sex and family in the Bible.* New York: Doubleday, 1959.

PATTERSON, T. C. *America's past: A New World archaeology.* Glenview, Ill.: Scott, Foresman, 1973.

PEACOCK, J. L. *Rites of modernization.* Chicago: University of Chicago Press, 1968.

PELTO, P. J. *Anthropological research: The structure of inquiry.* New York: Harper & Row, 1970.

PELTO, P. J., & PELTO, G. H. Ethnography: The fieldwork enterprise. In J. J. Honigman *(Ed.), Handbook of social and cultural anthropology.* Skokie, Ill.: Rand McNally, 1973. (pp. 241–281.)

PERKINS, D., & DALY, P. The beginning of food production in the Near East. In R. Stigler, R. Holloway, R. Solecki, D. Perkins, & P. Daly (Eds.), *The Old World: Early man to the development of agriculture.* New York: St. Martin's, 1974.

PETERS, E. L. Some structural aspects of the feud among the Bedouin of Cyrenaica. In J. G. Peristiany (Ed.), *Contributions to Mediterranean Sociology.* The Hague: Mouton, 1963a.

PETERS, E. L. The tied and the free. In J. G. Peristiany (Ed.), *Contributions to Mediterranean sociology.* The Hague: Mouton, 1963b. (pp. 167–188.)

PFEIFFER, J. E. *The emergence of man* (2nd ed.). New York: Harper & Row, 1972.

PIANKA, E. R. *Evolutionary biology.* New York: Harper & Row, 1974.

PILBEAM, D. R. *The evolution of man.* London: Thames & Hudson, 1970.

PILBEAM, D. *The ascent of man.* New York: Macmillan, 1972.

PILBEAM, D. Adaptive response of hominids to their environment as ascertained by fossil evidence. *Social Biology,* 1972, *19,* 115–127.

PILBEAM, D., MEYER, G. E., BADGLEY, C., ROSE, M. D., PICKFORD, M. H. L., BEHRENSMEYER, A. K., & SHAH, S. M. I. New hominoid primates from the Siwaliks of Pakistan and their bearing on hominoid evolution. *Nature,* 1977, *270,* 689–695.

PITT-RIVERS, J. The kith and the kin. In J. Goody (Ed.), *The character of kinship.* Cambridge: Cambridge University Press, 1973, (pp. 89–105.)

POLYANI, K. et al. (Eds.). The economy as institutional process. In *Trade and market in the early empires.* New York: The Free Press, 1957.

POTTER, J. M. From peasants to rural proletarians: Social and economic change in rural Communist China. In J. M. Potter, M. N. Diaz, & G. M. Foster (Eds.), *Peasant society: A reader.* Boston: Little, Brown, 1967a.

POTTER, J. M. Introduction: Peasants in the modern world. In J. M. Potter, M. N. Diaz, & G. M. Foster (Eds.), *Peasant society: A reader.* Boston: Little, Brown, 1967b.

PREMACK, A. J., & PREMACK, D. Teaching language to an ape. *Scientific American,* 1972, *227*(14), 92–99.

PREMACK, A. J. *Why chimps can read.* New York: Harper and Row, 1976.

PREMACK, D. "Language and Intelligence in Ape and Man." *American Scientist,* 1976, *64,* 674–683.

QUEEN, S. A., & HABENSTEIN, R. W. *The family in various cultures* (4th ed.). Philadelphia: Lippincott, 1974.

RAPPAPORT, R. A. *Pigs for the ancestors: Ritual in the ecology of a New Guinea people.* New Haven, Conn.: Yale University Press, 1967.

RAPPAPORT, R. A. Ritual regulation of environmental relations among a New Guinea people. In Y. A. Cohen (Ed.), *Man in adaptation: The institutional framework.* Chicago: Aldine, 1971.

RATHJE, W. L. Socio-political implications of lowland Maya burials: Methodology and tentative hypotheses. *World Archaeology,* 1970, *1,* 359–374.

RATTRAY, R. S. *Ashanti.* Oxford: Oxford University Press, 1923.

REDFIELD, R. *Tepoztlan—A Mexican village.* Chicago: University of Chicago Press, 1930.

REDFIELD, R. *The folk culture of Yucatán.* Chicago: University of Chicago Press, 1941.

REDFIELD, R. *The little community and peasant society and culture.* Chicago: University of Chicago Press, 1960.

REDFIELD, R., & M. B. SINGER. City and countryside: The cultural independence. In T. Shanin (Ed.), *Peasants and peasant societies: Selected readings.* Baltimore: Penguin Books, 1971.

REID, R. M. Effects of consanguineous marriage and inbreeding on couple fertility and offspring mortality in rural Sri Lanka. In B. A. Kaplan (Ed.), *Anthropological studies of human fertility.* Detroit: Wayne State University Press, 1976. (pp. 139–146.)

RENSBERGER, B. The world's oldest works of art. *The New York Times Magazine,* May 21, 1978, 27–29; 32; 37; 40; 42.

RHEINSTEIN, M. Problems of law in the new nations of Africa. In C. Geertz (Ed.), *Old societies and new states: The quest for modernity in Asia and Africa.* Glencoe, Ill.: The Free Press, 1963. (pp. 220–246.)

RICHARDS, A. I. Land labor and diet in Northern Rhodesia (2nd ed.). London: Oxford University Press, 1961.

RICKETSON, O. G., & RICKETSON, E. B. Uaxaction, Guatemala group—1926–1931. Washington, D.C.: Carnegie Institution of Washington, 1937, publication #477.

RIVIERE, P. G. Marriage: A reassessment. In R. Needham (Ed.), *Rethinking kinship and marriage.* London: Tavistock, 1971.

ROBINSON, J. T. *American Journal of Physical Anthropology,* 1952.

ROBINSON, J. T. *Early hominid posture and locomotion.* Chicago: University of Chicago Press, 1972.

ROE, D. *Prehistory: An introduction.* Berkeley: University of California Press, 1970.

ROSEN, S. I. *Introduction to the primates: Living and fossil.* Englewood Cliffs, N.J.: Prentice-Hall, 1974.

ROYCE, A. P. *The anthropology of dance.* Bloomington: Indiana University Press, 1977.

RYNKIEWICH, M. A. The underdevelopment of anthropological ethics. In M. A. Rynkiewich & J. P. Spradley (Eds.), *Ethics and anthropology: Dilemmas in fieldwork.* New York: Wiley, 1976.

RYNKIEWICH, M. A., & SPRADLEY, J. P. *Ethics and anthropology: Dilemmas in fieldwork.* New York: Wiley, 1976.

SAFER, J. Parallel descent and mother/daughter marriage among the Saha. Paper presented at the Annual Meeting of the American Anthropological Association, Mexico City, November 1974.

SAFER, J. Parallel descent: Does it exist? Paper presented at the Annual Meeting of the American Anthropological Association, San Francisco, December 1975.

SAHLINS, M. D. *Social stratification in Polynesia.* Seattle: University of Washington Press, 1958.

SAHLINS, M. D. Political power and the economy in primitive society. In G. E. Dole & R. L. Carneiro (Eds.), *Essays in the science of culture in honor of Leslie A. White.* New York: Crowell, 1960.

SAHLINS, M. D. The segmentary lineage: An organization of predatory expansion. *American Anthropologist,* 1961, *63*(2), 332–345.

SAHLINS, M. D. Culture and environment: The study of cultural ecology. In S. Tax (Ed.), *Horizons of anthropology.* Chicago: Aldine, 1964. (pp. 132–147.)

SAHLINS, M. D. *Stone age economics.* London: Tavistock, 1972.

SALTHE, S. N. *Evolutionary biology.* New York: Holt, Rinehart & Winston, 1972.

SANDERS, W. T., & PRICE, B. T. *Mesoamerica: The evolution of a civilization.* New York: Random House, 1968.

SANDERS, W. T., PARSONS, J. R., & LOGAN, M. H. Summary and conclusions. In E. Wolf (Eds.), *The valley of Mexico: Studies in prehistoric ecology and society.* Albuquerque: University of New Mexico Press, 1976.

SANDISON, A. T. Pathological changes in the skeletons of early populations due to acquired disease, and difficulties in their interpretation. In D. R. Brothwell (Ed.), *The skeletal biology of earlier human populations.* New York: Pergamon Press, 1968.

SAPIR, E. *Language.* New York: Harcourt Brace Jovanovich, 1921.

SAPIR, E. Culture, genuine and spurious. In D. Mandelbaum (Ed.), *Selected writings of Edward Sapir in language, culture and personality.* Berkeley: University of California Press, 1949. (pp. 308–312.)

SARICH, V. M. The origin of the hominids: An immunological approach. In S. L. Washburn & P. C. Jay (Eds.), *Perspectives on human evolution.* New York: Holt, Rinehart & Winston, 1968. (pp. 94–119.)

SAUL, F. P. Disease in the Maya area: The pre-

Columbian evidence. In T. P. Culbert (Ed.), *The classic Maya collapse.* Albuquerque: University of New Mexico Press, 1973.

SAWKINS, F. J., CHASE, C. G., DARBY, D. G., & RAPP, G. *The evolving earth.* New York: Macmillan, 1974, p. 11.

SCHALLER, G. B. The behavior of the mountain gorilla. In I. De Vore (Ed.), *Primate behavior.* New York: Holt, Rinehart & Winston, 1965.

SCHNEIDER, D., & SHARP, L. The dream life of a primitive people: The dreams of the Yir Yoront of Australia. W. H. Goodenough (Ed.). American Anthropology Association. Ann Arbor: University Microfilms, 1969.

SCHOLANDER, P. F., LANGE ANDERSON, K., KROG, J., VOGT LORENTZEN, & STEEN, J. Critical temperature in Lapps. *Journal of Applied Physiology,* 1957, *10*(2), 231–234.

SCHULTZ, A. H. *The life of primates.* New York: Universe Books, 1969.

SCHWAB, W. B. Kinship and lineage among the Yoruba. *Africa,* 1955, *25,* 352–373.

SERVICE, E. R. *The hunters.* Englewood Cliffs, N.J.: Prentice-Hall, 1966.

SERVICE, E. R. *Origins of the state and civilization.* New York: Norton, 1975.

SHEFFLER, H. W. Structuralism in anthropology. In J. Ehrmann (Ed.), *Structuralism.* New York: Anchor Books, 1970. (pp. 56–79.)

SHELDON, W. H. *The varieties of human physique.* New York: Harper, 1940.

SHELDON, W. H. *The varieties of temperament.* New York: Harper, 1942.

SHEPRO, D., BELANARICH, F., & LEVY, C. *Human anatomy and physiology: A cellular approach.* New York: Holt, Rinehart & Winston, 1974.

SHILS, E. Political development in the new states: I, II. *Comparative studies in society and history,* 1960, *2*(4), 266–292; 379–411.

SHIMER, H. W. *An introduction to the study of fossils.* New York: Macmillan, 1924.

SIEBER, R. The aesthetics of traditional African art. In C. F. Jopling (Ed.), *Art and aesthetics in primitive societies.* New York: Dutton, 1971.

SILVERSTEIN, M. Language as a part of culture. In S. Tax & L. G. Freeman (Eds.), *Horizons of anthropology* (2nd ed.). Chicago: Aldine, 1977. (pp. 119–131.)

SILVERMAN, S. F. The community-nation mediator in traditional Central Italy. In J. M. Potter, M. N. Diaz, & G. M. Foster (Eds.), *Peasant society: A reader.* Boston: Little, Brown, 1967.

SIMMONS, L. W. *The role of the aged in primitive society.* Hamden, Conn.: Shoe String Press, 1970.

SIMONS, E. L. The early relatives of man. *Scientific American,* July 1964, 56.

SIMONS, E. L. *Primate evolution: An introduction to man's place in nature.* N.Y.: Macmillan, 1972.

SIMONS, E. L. *Ramapithecus. Scientific American,* 1977, *236,* 28–35.

SINGER, M. A survey of culture and personality theory and research. In B. Kaplan (Ed.), *Studying personality cross-culturally.* New York: Harper & Row, 1961.

SJOBERG, G. *The preindustrial city.* New York: Free Press, 1960.

SMELSER, N. J. Mechanisms of change and adjustment of changes. In W. E. Moore & B. F. Hoselitz (Eds.), *The impact of industry.* Paris: International Social Science Council, 1963.

SMELSER, N. J., & LIPSET, M. Social structure, mobility, and development. In N. J. Smelser & S. M. Lipset (Eds.), *Social structure and mobility in economic development.* Chicago: Aldine, 1966.

SMITH, C. A. (Ed.), *Regional analysis Vol. II: Social systems.* New York: Academic Press, 1976.

SMITH, M. G. Pre-industrial stratification systems. In N. J. Smelser & S. M. Lipset (Eds.), *Social structure and mobility in economic development.* Chicago: Aldine, 1966.

SMITH, M. G. Political organization. In D. Sills (Ed.), *International encyclopedia of the social sciences* (Vol. 12). New York: Macmillan, 1968a.

SMITH, M. G. Secondary marriage in northern Nigeria. In P. Bohannan & J. Middleton (Eds.), *Marriage, family, and residence.* Garden City, N.Y.: The Natural History Press, 1968b. (pp. 298–323.)

SMITH, P. E. *The consequences of food production.* Addison-Wesley Module in Anthropology, Module #31. Reading, Mass.: Addison-Wesley, 1972.

SOUTHALL, A. W. Stratification in Africa. In L. Plotnicov & A. Tuden (Eds.), *Essays in comparative social stratification.* Pittsburgh: University of Pittsburgh Press, 1970.

SPENCER, R. F. The North Alaskan Eskimo: A Study in ecology and society. Smithsonian Institute of American Ethnology. Bull. 171. Washington, D.C.: U.S. Government Printing Office, 1959.

SPRADLEY, J. *You owe yourself a drunk: An ethnography of urban nomads.* Boston: Little, Brown, 1970.

STALLINGS, W., JR. *Dating prehistory ruins by tree rings.* Santa Fe, N.M.: Laboratory of Anthropology, School of American Research, General Series, Bulletin 8, 1939.

STERN, T., & OXNARD, C. E. Primate locomotion: Some links with evolution and morphology. *Primatologie, 4.* Basel: S. Karger, 1973.

STEWARD, J. *Theory of culture change.* Urbana: University of Illinois Press, 1955.

STOCKING, G. W., Jr. (Ed.). *The shaping of American anthropology, 1883–1911: A Franz Boas reader.* New York: Basic Books, 1974.

STOUT, D. B. Aesthetics in "primitive societies." In C. F. Jopling (Ed.), *Art and aesthetics in primitive societies.* New York: Dutton, 1971.

STRAUS, W. L., & CAVE, A. J. E. Pathology and posture of neanderthal man. *Quarterly Review of Biology,* 1951, *32,* 348–363.

SWANSON, G. *The birth of the gods: The origin of primitive beliefs.* Ann Arbor: University of Michigan Press, 1960.

SWARTZ, M. J., TURNER, V. W., & TUDEN, A. (Eds.). *Political anthropology.* Chicago: Aldine, 1966.

SWINDLER, D. R. *Dentition of living primates.* London: Academic Press, 1976.

SZALAY, F. G. Systematics of the Omomyidal. *New York Bulletin of the American Museum of Natural History,* 1976, *156*(3), 420.

SZALAY, F. S. A review of some recent advances in paleoprimatology. *Yearbook of Physical Anthropology,* 1973, *17,* 39–59.

TAMBIAH, S. J. Dowry and bridewealth and the property rights of women in South Asia. In J. Goody & S. J. Tambiah (Eds.), *Bridewealth and dowry.* Cambridge: Cambridge University Press, 1973.

TEMPLE, S. A. Plant-animal mutualism: Coevolution with dodo leads to near extinction of plant. *Science,* 1977, *197*(4306), 885–886.

TERRACE, H. S., & BEVER, T. G. What might be learned from studying language in the chimpanzee? The importance of symbolizing oneself. *Annals of the New York Academy of Sciences,* 1976, *280,* 579–587.

THENIUS, E. *Fossils and the life of the past.* Heidelberg: Springer-Verlag, 1973.

THOMAS, E. M. Leadership in the Bushman band. In P. K. Bock (Ed.), *Culture shock.* New York: Knopf, 1970.

THOMPSON, R. F. Aesthetics in traditional Africa. *Art News,* 1968, *66*(9), 44–45; 63–66.

TOBIAS, P. The Taung skull revisited. *Natural History,* 1974, *88,* 38–43.

TOBIAS, P. V. Brain evolution in the hominoidea. In R. H. Tuttle (Ed.), *Primate functional morphology and evolution.* Paris: Mouton, 1975.

TROTTER, R. J. From endangered to dangerous species. *Science News,* 1976, *109,* 74.

TURNBULL, C. The lesson of the pygmies. *Scientific American,* 1963, *208,* 28–37.

TURNER, V. W. *Schism and continuity in an African society.* Manchester: Manchester University Press, 1957.

TURNER, V. W. *The drums of affliction.* Oxford: Clarendon, 1968.

TYLOR, E. B. *Origins of culture.* (Primitive Culture, Part I.) New York: Harper & Row, 1958.

UDY, S. H. *Work in traditional and modern society.* Englewood Cliffs, N.J.: Prentice-Hall, 1970.

VALENTINE, C. *Culture and poverty.* Chicago: University of Chicago Press, 1968.

VALENTINE, J. W. *Evolutionary paleoecology of the marine biosphere.* Englewood Cliffs, N.J.: Prentice-Hall, 1973.

VAN LAWICK-GOODALL, J. *In the shadow of man.* New York: Dell, 1971.

VAYDA, A. P., & RAPPAPORT, R. A. Ecology, cultural and noncultural. In J. A. Clifton (Ed.), *Introduction to cultural anthropology.* Boston: Houghton Mifflin, 1968. (pp. 477–497.)

VIDICH, A., & BENSMAN, J. *Small town in mass society.* Princeton: Princeton University Press, 1958.

VOGEL, F. "Mutations in man." From *Genetics today, proceedings of the XI International Congress of Genetics.* New York: Pergamon, 1965.

VOGEL, F., & CHAKRAVARTTI, M. R. ABO blood groups in a rural population of West Bengal and Bihar (India). In C. J. Bajema (Ed.), *Natural selection in human populations.* New York: Wiley, 1971.

VOGET, F. W. *A history of ethnology.* New York: Holt, Rinehart & Winston, 1975.

VOGT, E. Z. Structural and conceptual replication in Zinacantan culture. *American Anthropologist,* 1965, *67.*

VOLPE, E. P. *Understanding evolution* (3rd ed.). Dubuque, Iowa: William C. Brown, 1977.

VORZIMMER, P. J. Darwin and Mendel: The historical connection. *Isis,* 1968, *59*(196, Part 1).

WALLACE, A. F. C. *Culture and personality.* New York: Random House, 1961.

WARNER, W. L. *Yankee City.* New Haven, Conn.: Yale University Press, 1963.

WASHBURN, S. L., & LANCASTER, C. S. The evolution of hunting. In R. B. Lee & I. De Vore (Eds.), *Man the hunter.* Chicago: Aldine, 1968.

WATSON, R. A., & WATSON, P. J. *Man and nature: An anthropological essay in human ecology.* New York: Harcourt Brace Jovanovich, 1969.

WEBER, E. *Europe since 1715: A modern history.* New York: Norton, 1972.

WEBER, M. *The theory of social and economic organization* (A. M. Henderson & T. Parsons, Trans.). Glencoe, Ill.; The Free Press, 1947.

WEINER, J. S. *The natural history of man.* New York: Universe Books, 1971.

WERBNER, R. P. *Regional cults.* New York: Academic Press, 1977.

WHITE, L. A. *The science of culture.* New York: Farrar, Straus & Giroux, 1949.

WHITE, L. A. *The evolution of culture.* New York: McGraw-Hill, 1959.

WHITE, T. D., & HARRIS, J. M. Suid evolution and correlation of African hominid localities. *Science,* 1977, *198.*

WHORF, B. L. The relation of habitual thought and behavior to language. In J. B. Carroll (Ed.), *Language, thought and reality; selected writings of Benjamin Lee Whorf.* Cambridge, Mass.: M.I.T. Press, 1956.

WHYTE, W. F. *Street corner society: The social structure of an Italian slum.* Chicago: University of Chicago Press, 1955.

WILCOCKS, C. *Medical advance, public health and evolution.* New York: Pergamon Press, 1965.

WILLEY, G. R. *An introduction to American archaeology* (Vol. 1). Englewood Cliffs, N.J.: Prentice-Hall, 1966.

WILLEY, G. R. The rise of Maya civilization: A summary view. In R. W. Adams (Ed.), *Origins of Maya civilization.* Albuquerque: University of New Mexico Press, 1977.

WILLEY, G. R., & SHIMKIN, D. B. The Maya collapse: A summary view. In T. P. Culbert (Ed.), *The classic Maya collapse.* Albuquerque: University of New Mexico Press, 1973.

WILSON, E. O. *Sociobiology: The new synthesis.* Cambridge, Mass.: Harvard University Press, 1975.

WITTFOGEL, K. *Oriental despotism: A comparative study of total power.* New Haven, Conn.: Yale University Press, 1957.

WOLF, A. P. Childhood association and sexual attraction: A further test of the Westermarck hypothesis. *American Anthropologist,* 1970, *72,* 503–515.

WOLF, E. R. Aspects of group relations in a complex society: Mexico. *American Anthropologist,* 1956, *58*(6), 1065–1078.

WOLF, E. R. *Peasants.* Englewood Cliffs, N.J: Prentice-Hall, 1966a.

WOLF, E. R. Kinship, friendship, and patron-client relations in complex societies. In M. Banton (Ed.), *The social anthropology of complex societies,* New York: Tavistock, 1966b.

WOLFENSTEIN, M. French parents take their children to the park. In M. Mead & M. Wolfenstein (Eds.), *Childhood in contemporary cultures.* Chicago: University of Chicago Press, 1955. (pp. 114–115.)

WOLPOFF, M. H. Sexual dimorphism in the Australopithecines. In R. H. Tuttle (Ed.), *Paleoanthropology: Morphology and paleoecology.* Paris: Mouton, 1975.

WOLPOFF, M. H. Some aspects of human mandibular evolution. In J. A. MacNamara, Jr. (Ed.), *Determinants of mandibular form and growth.* Ann Arbor, Mich.: Center for Human Growth and Development, 1975.

WOOLF, C., & DUKEPOO, F. Z. Hopi Indians, inbreeding, and albinism. *Science,* 1959, *164,* 30–37.

WORSLEY, P. M. Millenarian movements in Melanesia. In J. Middleton (Ed.), *Gods and rituals: Readings in religion, beliefs and practices.* Garden City, N.Y.: Natural History Press, 1967.

WRESCHNER, E. The red hunters: Further thoughts on the evolution of speech. *Current Anthropology,* 1976, *17,* 717–718.

WRIGHT, G. E. *Biblical archaeology.* Philadelphia: Westminster Press, 1960.

WRIGHT, H. T. Recent research on the origin of the state. *Annual Review of Anthropology,* 1977, 379–397.

YERGIN, D. The Chomskyan revolution. *The New York Times Magazine,* Dec. 3, 1972, 42–43ff.

ZUCKERMAN, S. *The social life of monkeys and apes.* New York: Harcourt, Brace, 1932.

Indexes

Name Index

Italic page numbers refer to those pages on which respective subjects are illustrated.

Subject Index

677

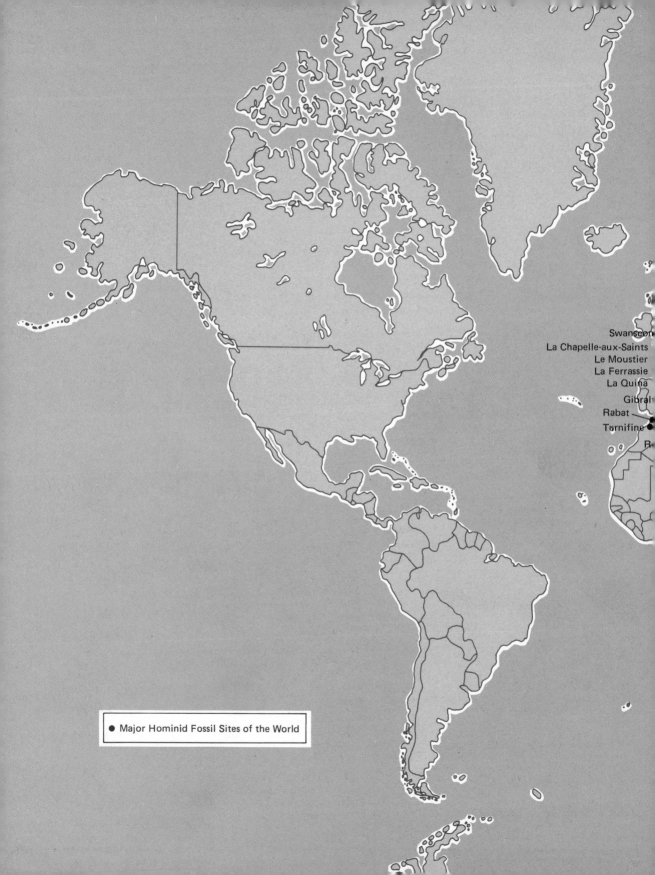

Swansco[n]
La Chapelle-aux-Saints
Le Moustier
La Ferrassie
La Quina
Gibral[tar]
Rabat
Ternifine

B[...]

● Major Hominid Fossil Sites of the World